KU-299-467

# *SMALL GROUPS*

STUDIES IN SOCIAL INTERACTION

# *SMALL GROUPS*

## STUDIES IN SOCIAL INTERACTION

*Edited by*

*A. PAUL HARE*
HARVARD UNIVERSITY

*EDGAR F. BORGATTA*
RUSSELL SAGE FOUNDATION

*ROBERT F. BALES*
HARVARD UNIVERSITY

1962

ALFRED·A·KNOPF *NEW YORK*

L. C. CATALOG CARD NUMBER: 55–6636



THIS IS A BORZOI BOOK,
PUBLISHED BY ALFRED A. KNOPF, INC.



*Published June 1955; second printing, February 1961; third printing, September 1962*

# Preface

THE STUDY of small groups is important not only to those who specialize in social science, but also to those of us who want to understand better our own behavior and the behavior of our fellows. In the study of small groups the events we are interested in relating to each other occur within a limited range of space and time. It becomes possible to make the actual observations required by our theories without encountering many of the difficulties present in examining similar phenomena on a larger scale. As Homans puts it in *The Human Group*, one stands some chance to "get all the way around" a small group, and to relate a diversity of factors to each other.

Small groups are often so called because they have the same advantage for the participant that they do for the scientist studying the group—they are groups that are small enough so that the individual participant can "get all the way around" and fill out his relationship to each other person by some direct interaction with him. One can assemble small groups in the laboratory or observe them in the field, and obtain a large range of information about overt behavior, perception of members, attitudes toward each other, values and consensus on values, degrees of satisfaction, and so on, in a degree of detail not possible when the number of persons involved is too large to be held within the mind of the single participant. The study of social interaction and its related causes and effects in small groups is a microscopic method in more senses, perhaps, than has commonly been recognized. The idea that a small group may bear many general resemblances to larger-scale social systems is fairly common by now. However, the idea that the content analysis of discussion in a small group such as, for example, a therapy group can be a microscopic method of studying culture is not so common. In the study of small groups we are concerned with the microscopic study of sub-cultures, just as we are concerned with the microscopic study of small social systems. Similarly, in the total process which goes on in small groups we are observing the process by which personality elements are developed and elaborated in the individual.

The study of small groups is thus a method for the study of social systems, of culture, and of personality—all three. Its strategic significance in the development of social science generally is that it relates all three of these types of structure to a common base—the social process out of which they arise and through which they change. This field of research does not "belong" to any one of the recognized social sciences alone. It is the common property and concern of all. It has historical roots in each of them, and, as it develops, may be expected to contribute to each of them. Small group research is more than the study of one concrete "compartment" of social phenomena among many others. It is the study of the generic social process on the microscopic level.

Most of the social sciences and a number of applied disciplines are vitally involved in small group research at the present time. Quite a number of *social psychologists* are working in the field, both with a *psychological* and a *sociological* emphasis. From *clinical psychology* there are a number of workers interested in problems of *interviewing*, *counseling*, and *psychotherapy*. A large number of workers of different disciplines who study the roles of *family* members, the *socialization of the child*, and the internal dynamics of the family may be considered students of small groups. Still another historical root may be found in a line of speculation and later research concerned with the process of *group thinking*, *group problem-solving*, and the *operation of seminars*, *boards*, *panels*, and *decision-making committees*. There is a very lively interest among *educational psychologists* in classroom and instructional groups. Still other interest stems from problems of administration in all sorts of settings—*educational*, *recreational*, *religious*, *governmental*, *industrial*, and *military*. The conviction seems to be growing that problems of *administration*, *human relations on the face to face level*, *leadership*, *job training*, and the like are pretty much the same no matter what the concrete job of the organization.

In the social process we may expect to find the seeds, at least, of the organizations of activities that we view on a more general level as personality, society, and culture. And similarly, in various patterned aspects of the social process we may expect to find the concrete referents of many of the higher-order abstractions we use to describe these more fully developed and complicated structures. The study of small groups may perform a clarifying service in showing us how certain of our common concepts in social science, such as status, role, function, motivation, trait, culture pattern, and the like, are really only useful abstractions from the same concrete events—the behavior of individuals in interaction with each other. We often express the desirability of translation from one frame of reference to another, say from a sociological to a psychological to a cultural. The translation can probably best be made, not from one set of abstractions directly to the other, but by relating each of them to the more microscopic level of process which provides the basic reference material with which all are concerned.

The book is divided into four parts. The first part is concerned with the historical and theoretical background of the field. The second contains a collection of studies which view the social process from the perspective of the single individual in a social situation. The third contains studies in which the perspective is more that of an external observer viewing the group as a system of social interaction and describing its characteristics. The final part is a guide to the research literature in the field in the form of an annotated bibliography of about 580 titles.

There is a saying that "it is a wise child that knows its own father." The field of small group research is so new that it has not yet recognized sufficiently even the more important of its ancestors. It is our hope to make a beginning in this direction in Chapters 1 and 2, where we have included some of the early theoretical and empirical classics of the field. In Chapter 3 on current theory we have tried to obtain a more or less representative selection of points of view which are either current and thriving in the field at present, or have been influential in the development of current theory and research. Throughout the book, within each chapter, the articles are arranged so far as possible in order of their dates of publication. We hope that this may be helpful in giving some impression of the developmental history of the field. The impression cannot be exact, however, since in a number of cases the authors worked for some considerable period before publishing the particular selection we have included, and their work was known to other persons working in the field.

The annotated bibliography in Part IV in many ways will give a truer picture. It will be noted that the parent fields of thought represented show a broad range, embracing anthropology, sociology, social psychology of several different traditions, clinical psychology, psychiatry, mental testing, sociometry, and parts of mathematics as well as many applied fields. Small group research is not identified in an exclusive sense with any of the existing disciplines. It is a method of approaching problems which are primary concerns of each of the major fields of the behavioral sciences.

In Parts II and III we have in general tried to include substantial empirical studies which contain source data from which further theorizing may be done. We hope that the studies we have chosen carry enough information so that the creative reader of the book will be able to make generalizations that have not previously been stated, and perhaps even new discoveries. It is our opinion that the facts and empirical generalizations available even now are adequate for a new and powerful synthesis, in mathematical form, of certain basic aspects of the interaction process. Simmel's reluctant apology of fifty years ago that such an attempt "during the foreseeable future . . . would be a wholly fantastic enterprise" stands as a prediction which has been seriously undermined by now.

Although the line of division is not absolutely distinct, there is a difference in perspective that may be recognized between the studies in Part II and those in Part III. When one tries to understand the immediate motives for behavior, it is more or less natural to take the point of view of the acting *subject*, as an individual facing a social situation, being influenced by factors in that situation, and in turn attempting to influence it through his behavior. One can do this for a specific subject, for each of the subjects in the group taken as a series, or try to arrive at some kind of average. This, generally speaking, is the perspective of Part II.

On the other hand, when one tries to understand how the situation gets to be what it is for a given subject at a given time, it is natural to take the perspective of an *observer* who takes into account the reciprocal orientation and behavior of two or more persons who adjust and readjust their relation over the course of time by some series of interactions. From this perspective one sees uniformities in the patterns of relationship and communication as they are developed and maintained between the individuals viewed as an interdependent system. This, in general, is the perspective of Part III.

One should not suppose that either perspective excludes the other. They are both abstracted from the same process. It may be true that persons differ in the perspective which seems most natural to them, but the student of human behavior should be able to take either or both, as required by the problem.

The ease of taking a given perspective is certainly influenced by the research techniques that are available. One of the impressions that emerges strongly from a study of the history of the field is a sense of the intimate connection between the discovery or development of methods of research and the development of new bodies of theory. It is no accident that the problem of "together and apart" was a very early theoretical preoccupation; it rested on perhaps the simplest of all methods of experimental manipulation. The sociometric theory of likes and dislikes rests on a basically simple questionnaire, and the more recent upsurge of interest in social perception rests on an extension—the use of questions in which the subject is asked to predict how others will answer. The experimental manipulation of exposing the same individual to a series of relationships and the ability to reduce large masses of observations to simpler form by statistical methods are essential to the development of substantial theory of the consistency of individuals. Studies featuring these techniques are included in Part II.

The perspective of Part III, which views the group as a system of interaction, is equally dependent upon the development of research methods. A whole area of theory concerning the properties of various types of communication networks hinges around the fact that one can experimentally manipulate the channels of communication between members of a group. A new dimension of theoretical development opens up when one is able to obtain measurements of a set of interdependent variables through a long time series, as one can in the observation of overt interaction or other sorts of content analysis of communication. Indeed, the very concept of a system can have little reality unless a series of measurements through time can be visualized. Similarly, for this order of conceptualization, one must be able to visualize a number of different sorts of variables each measured separately. One cannot go far in the development of theory about how and why the roles of members in a group become differentiated from each other without the prior development of many methods of measurement: personality measures, interaction measures, perception measures, and rating and choice measures.

The problem of leadership appears early and late. Of all the perennials in the field, this one is the hardiest. No matter which perspective one takes, it looms prominently. From the individual perspective it is perhaps the most salient form of influencing and being influenced by others in the social situation. From the perspective of the group as a differentiated system, it is perhaps the most salient form of role differentiation. Theory about leadership ranges from the most simple-minded notions to the most complex and subtle. Hardly any variable is easier to manipulate, by appointment, choice, or instruction, but hardly any is harder to analyze and control. This is true in practical affairs as in the scientific laboratory. But as the problem is difficult, the rewards of solving it are great. It is a safe prediction that leadership will continue to be a focus of much small group research.

The problem of "getting all the way around" the literature is almost as hard to solve as the problem of getting all the way around the group. The annotated bibliography in Part IV has been carefully selected after an extended search of the literature. We hope it will be of aid to student, teacher, researcher, and practitioner alike. Although the desire to promote the scientific development of the field was uppermost in our minds in the selection of these titles, we hope that the annotations can be read with profit, and perhaps even with pleasure, by anyone who wants to obtain a bird's eye view of the literature.

We wish to acknowledge the contributions of many persons who have helped us in the past in guiding our interest in small groups or in the present in the actual preparation of this volume. Of the persons who have influenced one or more of us by their interest and guidance, we especially wish to mention Professors Gordon W. Allport, Joseph B. Gittler, J. L. Moreno, William F. Ogburn, Talcott Parsons, Malcolm G. Preston, Tomatsu Shibutani, Samuel Stouffer, Herbert A. Thelen, W. Lloyd Warner, and Wellman J. Warner.

Since the "Bibliography of Small Group Research" published in *Sociometry* in 1954 served to set limits for the field of "small groups" and provided a source useful to us in our task with this book, we are particularly indebted to Fred L. Strodtbeck, its senior editor, and to the many others who contributed to its development.

Much of the detailed and tedious work involved in checking form and in the preparation of copy for the printer has been done by Joyce E. Goldberg. Also, we are much indebted to Elizabeth Cohen and Barbara Beran who assisted in the process of annotating articles and books which appear in the bibliography. We are grateful to the Harvard Laboratory of Social Relations which allowed us use of its many facilities.

Finally, we are indebted to the authors who have given us permission to include their work in this volume, and to the American Psychological Association, American Sociological Society, *Sociometry*, *Human Relations*, and the other organizations and publishers who have given permission to reprint their materials.

A. PAUL HARE
*Harvard University*

EDGAR F. BORGATTA
*Russell Sage Foundation*

ROBERT F. BALES
*Harvard University*

October 6, 1954

# Contents

## PART I

## HISTORICAL AND THEORETICAL BACKGROUND

CHAPTER 3 : Current Theory



# *PART* II

## THE INDIVIDUAL IN SOCIAL SITUATIONS



CHAPTER 4 : Together and Apart

# PART III
# THE GROUP AS A SYSTEM OF SOCIAL INTERACTION

# *PART* I

# *Historical* AND *Theoretical* *Background*

# *Introduction*

THE HISTORICAL *origins of small group research are diffuse and diverse. Of the many pioneers, we have chosen a few to represent the rest. Most of the writers who have treated the development of social and cultural phenomena, as well as many who have been concerned with the development of the self and the internalization of social norms, have had something to say about small groups. They found that in some way the origins of the phenomena they were seeking could be seen on the small group level, or that the comparison of small with large groups gave them a more generalized perception than could be had by confining their interest to groups of larger size.*

*Simmel, who was writing about groups of two and three persons at the turn of this century, is a particularly good example of a theorist whose urge toward generalized theory led him to a long, clear look at the factor of size itself as a determinant of the form of social relationships. Durkheim, Cooley, and Mead, as well as Simmel, all in their own ways, were deeply concerned with the problem of the social control of behavior and saw the phenomenon of "internalization" as intimately tied up with the interaction of the individual with others in small groups. Indeed, if there is any preoccupation which has been more characteristic of small group theory than the interest in leadership, it is the more general theme of social control—an interest in the social conditions under which the motivation of individuals is most effectively developed, maintained, and changed.*

*Most of the early research in the field is easily associated with this theme. Among the earliest relevant experimental studies are those of Triplett in 1898, concerned with a curious facilitating or "dynamogenic" effect that occurred when people were together and in competition rather than alone. The alone and together theme was given a new impetus in the early twenties by the experiments of F. H. Allport, and is still active today. The study of child development by first hand observation is another important source of small group research which goes back at least to the turn of the century. We have chosen Terman's 1904 study of the "Psychology and Pedagogy of Leadership" among children as an early landmark. Terman's study is classic in its foreshadowing of methods and themes that were to be developed later in the work of Goodenough, Anderson, D. S. Thomas, Pigors, and many others. Piaget's work on children's games is almost in a class by itself as an exemplification of the study of the small group as the creator and carrier of a sub-culture. Here, also, the theme of social control is prominent.*

*The failure of social control in the larger society and its re-establishment with reversed content in the small group has provided the motive for many important studies. We have taken the work of Thrasher on the gang to represent the work in the field of gangs of other pioneers, such as Puffer, Furfey, and Whyte. Riddle's study, in 1925, of aggressive behavior in a small social group is still ahead of much present-day laboratory research in the use of physiological measures, although some research of this type is now being done in hospital settings. Current developments in the theory of games and economic behavior are likely to give rise to small group studies that will look back to Riddle's work as a pioneer effort. Although systematic observations of individual and group behavior in the factory had been made in the early part of the century by F. K. Taylor and other proponents of scientific management, the Western Electric researches, described here in an early article by Turner, are generally regarded as the classic studies in the industrial area of small group research.*

*In Chapter 3 we present a series of selections in current theory representing a number of different points of view. Current theory in the technical sense is still far from unified, in spite of the widespread conviction that it can and will be. Differences in language, imagery, and interpretive thought-models always present a certain amount of difficulty. But the difficulties are, after all, familiar. All the traditional dilemmas and puzzles that have been encountered by the behavioral sciences in their struggle toward an understanding of human behavior are encountered in small group theory. Small group research may well be the setting in which many of the traditional dilemmas will be resolved and the divergent perspectives merged. This hope, as much as the desire to obtain answers to practical problems, is probably a major factor in the widespread appeal of the field. We believe that, in spite of the fact that the pieces have not yet been completely fitted together, the serious reader of Chapter 3 can hardly fail to gain a sense of an emerging congruence, and feel a sense of this hope.*

# CHAPTER 1

# EARLY THEORY

## *Division of Labor*

### EMILE DURKHEIM

*WHILE Durkheim's* Division of Labor *centers on societal problems, the reference frequently is to group organization in a generic sense. His analysis of the division of labor has many modern counterparts in the emphases on concepts such as role differentiation and the problem of equilibrium. Here we have reproduced three very brief sections which summarize major points of relevance for small group (and large group) organizational theory.*

WE KNOW, in effect, that, wherever organic solidarity is found, we come upon an adequately developed regulation determining the mutual relations of functions. For organic solidarity to exist, it is not enough that there be a system of organs necessary to one another, which in a general way feel solidary, but it is also necessary that the way in which they should come together, if not in every kind of meeting, at least in circumstances which most frequently occur, be predetermined. Otherwise, at every moment new conflicts would have to be equilibrated, for the conditions of equilibrium can be discovered only through gropings in the course of which one part treats the other as an adversary as much as an auxiliary. These conflicts would incessantly crop out anew, and, consequently, solidarity would be scarcely more than potential, if

FROM *Division of labor*. Glencoe, Ill.: Free Press, 1947. Reprinted by permission of the publisher.

mutual obligations had to be fought over entirely anew in each particular instance. It will be said that there are contracts. But, first of all, all social relations are not capable of assuming this juridical form. We know, moreover, that a contract is not self-sufficient, but supposes a regulation which is as extensive and complicated as contractual life itself. Besides, the links which have this origin are always of short duration. A contract is only a truce, and very precarious; it suspends hostilities only for a time. Of course, as precise as this regulation may be, it will always leave a place for many disturbances. But it is neither necessary nor even possible for social life to be without conflicts. The role of solidarity is not to suppress competition, but to moderate it.

Moreover, in the normal state, these rules disengage themselves from the division of labor. They are a prolongation of it. Assuredly, if it only brought together individuals who united for some few moments to exchange personal services, it could not give rise to any regulative action. But what it brings face to face are functions, that is to say, ways of definite action, which are identically repeated in given circumstances, since they cling to general, constant conditions of social life. The relations which are formed among these functions cannot fail to partake of the same degree of fixity and regularity. There are certain ways of mutual reaction which, finding themselves very conformable to the nature of things, are repeated very often and become habits. Then these habits, becoming forceful, are transformed into rules of conduct. The past determines the future. In other words, there is a certain sorting of rights and duties which is established by usage and becomes obligatory. The rule does not, then, create the state of mutual dependence in which solidary organs find themselves, but only expresses in clear-cut fashion the result of a given situation. In the same way, the nervous system, far from dominating the evolution of the organism, as we have already said, results from it (2, p. 746). The nerve-cords are probably only the lines of passage which the streams of movements and excitations exchanged between different organs have followed. They are the canals which life has hewed for itself while steadily flowing in the same direction, and the ganglia would only be the place of intersection of several of these lines (3, pp. 438 ff.). Because they misunderstood this aspect of the phenomena, certain moralists have claimed that the division of labor does not produce true solidarity. They have seen in it only particular exchanges, ephemeral combinations, without past or future, in which the individual is thrown on his own resources. They have not perceived the slow work of consolidation, the network of links which little by little have been woven and which makes something permanent of organic solidarity.

We are now in a position to solve the practical problem that we posed for ourselves at the beginning of this work.

If there is one rule of conduct which is incontestable, it is that which orders us to realize in ourselves the essential traits of the collective type. Among lower peoples, this reaches its greatest rigor. There, one's first duty is to resemble everybody else, not to have anything personal about one's beliefs or actions. In more advanced societies, required likenesses are less numerous; the absences of some likenesses, however, is still a sign of moral failure. Of course, crime falls into fewer different categories; but today, as heretofore, if a criminal is the object of reprobation, it is because he is unlike us. Likewise, in lesser degree, acts simply immoral and prohibited as such are those which evince dissemblances less profound but nevertheless considered serious. Is this not the case with the rule which common morality expresses when it orders a man to be a man in every sense of the word, which is to say, to have all the ideas and sentiments which go to make up a human conscience? No doubt, if this formula is taken literally, the man prescribed would be man in general and not one of some particular social species. But, in reality, this human conscience that we must integrally realize is nothing else than the collective conscience of the group of which we are a part. For what can it be composed of, if not the ideas and sentiments to which we are most attached? Where can we find the traits of our model, if not within us and around us? If we believe that this collective ideal is that of all humanity, that is because it has become so abstract and general that it appears fitting for all men indiscriminately. But, really, every people makes for itself some particular conception of this type which pertains to its personal temperament. Each represents it in its own image. Even the moralist who thinks he can, through thought, overcome the influence of transient ideas, cannot do so, for he is impregnated with them, and no matter what he does, he finds these precepts in the body of his deductions. That is why each nation has its own school of moral philosophy conforming to its character.

On the other hand, we have shown that this rule had as its function the prevention of all agitation of the common conscience, and, consequently, of social solidarity, and that it could accomplish this role only by having a moral character. It is impossible for offenses against the most fundamental collective sentiments to be tolerated without the disintegration of society, and it is necessary to combat them with the aid of the particularly energetic reaction which attaches to moral rules.

But the contrary rule, which orders us to specialize, has exactly the same function. It also is necessary for the cohesion of societies, at least at a certain period in their evolution. Of course, its solidarity is different from the preceding, but though it is different, it is no less indispensable. Higher societies can maintain themselves in equilibrium only if labor is divided; the attraction of like for like less and less suffices to produce this result. If, then, the moral character of the first of these rules is necessary to the playing of its role, it is no less necessary to the second. They both correspond to the same social need, but satisfy the need differently, because the conditions of existence in the societies themselves differ. Consequently, without speculating concerning the first principle of ethics, we can induce the moral value of one from the moral value of the other. If, from certain points of view, there is a real antagonism between them, that is not because they serve different ends. On the contrary, it is because they lead to the same end, but through opposed means. Accordingly, there is no necessity for choosing between them once for all nor of condemning one in the name of the other.

But if the division of labor produces solidarity, it is not only because it makes each individual an *exchangist*, as the economists say (1, p. 248); it is because it creates among men an entire system of rights and duties which link them together in a durable way. Just as social similitudes give rise to a law and a morality which protect them, so the division of labor gives rise to rules which assure pacific and regular concourse of divided functions. If economists have believed that it would bring forth an abiding solidarity, in some manner of its own making, and if, accordingly, they have held that human societies could and would resolve themselves into purely economic associations, that is because they believed that it affected only individual, temporary interests. Consequently, to estimate the interests in conflict and the way in which they ought to equilibrate, that is to say, to determine the conditions under which exchange ought to take place, is solely a matter of individual competence; and, since these interests are in a perpetual state of becoming, there is no place for any permanent regulation. But such a conception is, in all ways, inadequate for the facts. The division of labor does not present individuals to one another, but social functions. And society is interested in the play of the latter; in so far as they regularly concur, or do not concur, it will be healthy or ill. Its existence thus depends upon them, and the more they are divided the greater its dependence. That is why it cannot leave them in a state of indetermination. In addition to this, they are determined by themselves. Thus are formed those rules whose number grows as labor is divided, and whose absence makes organic solidarity either impossible or imperfect.

But it is not enough that there be rules; they must be just, and for that it is necessary for the external conditions of competition to be equal. If, moreover, we remember that the collective conscience is becoming more and more a cult of the individual, we shall see that what characterizes the morality of organized societies, compared to that of segmental societies, is that there is something more human, therefore more rational, about them. It does not direct our activities to ends which do not immediately concern us; it does not make us servants of ideal powers of a nature other than our own, which follow their directions without occupying themselves with the interests of men. It only asks that we be thoughtful of our fellows and that we be just, that we fulfill our duty, that we work at the function we can best execute, and receive the just reward for our services. The rules which constitute it do not have a constraining force which snuffs out free thought; but, because they are rather made for us and, in a certain sense, by us, we are free. We wish to understand them; we do not fear to change them. We must, however, guard against finding such an ideal inadequate on the pretext that it is too earthly and too much to our liking. An ideal is not more elevated because more transcendent, but because it leads us to vaster perspectives. What is important is not that it tower high above us, until it becomes a stranger to our lives, but that it open to our activity a large enough field. This is far from being on the verge of realization. We know only too well what a laborious work it is to erect this society where each individual will have the place he merits, will be rewarded as he deserves, where everybody, accordingly, will spontaneously work for the good of all and of each. Indeed, a moral code is not above another because it commands in a drier and more authoritarian manner, or because it is more sheltered from reflection. Of course, it must attach us to something besides ourselves but it is not necessary for it to chain us to it with impregnable bonds.

## REFERENCES

1. de Molinari. *La morale economique.*
2. Perrier. *Colonies animales.*
3. Spencer. *Principles of biology*. Vol. II.

# *The Significance of Numbers for Social Life*

GEORG SIMMEL

THE PRESENT studies begin by examining forms of social life, combinations and interactions among individuals. But they do so in one respect only: the bearing which the mere *number* of sociated individuals has upon these forms of social life. It will immediately be conceded on the basis of everyday experiences, that a group upon reaching a certain size

FROM Kurt H. Wolff, *The sociology of Georg Simmel*. Glencoe, Ill.: Free Press, 1950. Reprinted by permission of the translator and publisher.

must develop forms and organs which serve its maintenance and promotion, but which a smaller group does not need. On the other hand, it will also be admitted that smaller groups have qualities, including types of interaction among their members, which inevitably disappear when the groups grow larger. This quantitative determination of the group, as it may be called, has a twofold function. Negatively speaking, certain developments, which are necessary or at least possible as far as the contents or conditions of life are concerned, can be realized only below or above a particular number of elements. Positively, certain other developments are imposed upon the group by certain purely quantitative modifications. Yet not even these developments emerge automatically, for they also depend on other than numerical characteristics. The decisive point, however, is that they are not the result of these characteristics alone, for they emerge only under certain numerical conditions.

## *The Quantitative Determination of Group Divisions and of Certain Groups*

OBVIOUSLY, the notions "large" and "small" groups are extremely crude scientific designations, indeterminate and vague. They are useful, really, only as a suggestion that the sociological form of the group depends upon its quantitative aspects. But they are quite insufficient to show the real connection between the two in any more precise manner. Yet it is perhaps not always impossible to determine this relation more exactly. To be sure, during the foreseeable future in the development of our knowledge, it would be a wholly fantastic enterprise if we wanted to express the formations and relations so far discussed in exact numerical values. Nevertheless, within modest limits, namely in regard to characteristic sociations among small numbers of persons, certain traits can be indicated even at this stage of our knowledge. As transitions from complete numerical determinateness, I shall discuss some cases in which the quantitative determination of the group is already of some sociological significance but is not yet fixed in every detail.

### NUMERICALLY EQUAL SUBDIVISIONS

The number operates as a classificatory principle within the group. That is, parts of the group which are formed through enumeration function as relative units. At this point, I merely emphasize this general principle; later I shall discuss the significance of particular individual numbers. The division of a unified group, and more especially, its division not only from top to bottom, in terms of ruling and being ruled, but among its coordinated members, is one of the most extraordinary advances made by mankind. It is the anatomical structure which forms the basis of the higher organic and social processes. The classification may derive from ancestry, or from associations based on voluntary pledges, or from identity of occupation, or from grouping by local districts. All these principles of classification are combined with the quantitative principle: the mass of existing men or families is divided by a certain number and thus yields numerically equal subdivisions. To each of them, the whole has approximately the same relation as each subdivision has to its component individuals. This principle is, however, so mechanical that in order to operate it must be combined with a more concrete one: numerical equal subdivisions are composed either of persons who are somehow related—relatives, friends, neighbors—or of equals or unequals who supplement one another. Yet the numerical identity constitutes the formal principle of classification, even though it never decides *alone*. But it always plays its role, which may be very important, or may be almost negligible.

# *The Isolated Individual and the Dyad*

OUR STATEMENTS up to this point concerned social formations which depend on the number of their component elements. But our insight was incapable of formulating this dependence in a way which would have allowed us to derive sociological consequences from certain specific numbers. This is not impossible, however, if we content ourselves with sufficiently simple structures. If we begin with the lower limit of the numerical series, there appear arithmetically definite magnitudes as the unequivocal presuppositions of characteristic sociological formations.

## THE ISOLATED INDIVIDUAL

The numerically simplest structures which can still be designated as social interactions occur between two elements. Nevertheless, there is an externally even simpler phenomenon that belongs among sociological categories, however paradoxical and in fact contradictory this may seem—namely, the isolated individual. As a matter of fact, however, the processes that shape elements in the *dual* are often simpler than those required for the sociological characterization of the *singular*. For this, two phenomena are above all relevant here: isolation and freedom. The mere fact that an individual does not interact with others is, of course, not a sociological fact, but neither does it express the whole idea of isolation. For, isolation, in so far as it is important to the individual, refers by no means only to the absence of society. On the contrary, the idea involves the somehow imagined, but then rejected, existence of society. Isolation attains its unequivocal, positive significance only as society's effect at a distance—whether as lingering-on of past relations, as anticipation of future contacts, as nostalgia, or as an intentional turning away from society. The isolated man does not suggest a being that has been the only inhabitant of the globe from the beginning. For his condition, too, is determined by sociation, even though negatively. The whole joy and the whole bitterness of isolation are only different reactions to socially experienced influences. Isolation is interaction between two parties, one of which leaves, after exerting certain influences. The isolated individual is isolated only in reality, however; for ideally, in the mind of the other party, he continues to live and act.

A well-known psychological fact is very relevant here. The feeling of isolation is rarely as decisive and intense when one actually finds oneself physically alone, as when one is a stranger, without relations, among many physically close persons, at a "party," on a train, or in the traffic of a large city. The question whether a group favors or even permits such loneliness in its midst is an essential trait of the group structure itself. Close and intimate communities often allow no such intercellular vacuums. When we speak of anti-social phenomena like wretched persons, criminals, prostitutes, suicides, etc., we may refer to them as a social deficit that is produced in a certain proportion to social conditions. In a similar way, a given quantity and quality of social life creates a certain number of temporarily or chronically lonely existences, although they cannot as easily be ascertained by statistics as can these others.

## ISOLATION

Isolation thus is a relation which is lodged within an individual but which exists between him and a certain group or group life in general. But it is sociologically significant in still another way: it may also be an interruption or periodic occurrence in a given relationship between two or more persons. As such, it is especially important in those relations whose very nature is the denial of isolation. This applies, above all, to monogamous marriage. The structure of a particular marriage, of course, may not even involve the finest and most intimate nuances of the mates. But where it does, there is an essential difference between the case in which they have preserved the joy of individual isolation in spite of the perfect happiness of their life in common, and the case in which the relation is never interrupted by devotion to solitude. The second case may have various reasons. Habituation to the life in common may have deprived isolation of its attractiveness; or insufficient certainty of love may make interruption by solitude feared as unfaithfulness or, what is worse, as a danger to faithfulness. At any rate, it is clear that isolation is not limited to the individual and is not the mere negation of association. It also has a positive sociological significance. As a conscious feeling on the part of the individual, it represents a very specific relation to society. And furthermore, its occurrence changes the nature of both large and very intimate groups, whereby it may be the cause as well as the effect of this change.

## THE DYAD

We see that such phenomena as isolation and freedom actually exist as forms of sociological relations, although they often do so only by means of complex and indirect connections. In view of this fact, the simplest sociological formation, methodologically speaking, remains that which operates between two elements. It contains the scheme, germ, and material of innumerable more complex forms. Its sociological significance, however, by no means rests on its extensions and multiplications only. It itself is a sociation. Not only are many general forms of sociation realized in it in a very pure and characteristic fashion; what is more, the limitation to two members is a condition under which alone several forms of relationship exist. Their typically sociological nature is suggested by two facts. One is that the greatest variation of individualities and unifying motives does not alter the identity of these forms. The other is that occasionally these forms exist as much between two groups—families, states, and organizations of various kinds—as between two individuals.

Everyday experiences show the specific character that a relationship attains by the fact that only two elements participate in it. A common fate or enterprise, an agreement or secret between two persons, ties each of them in a very different manner than if even only three have a part in it. This is perhaps most characteristic of the secret. General experience seems to indicate that this minimum of two, with which the secret ceases to be the property of the one individual, is at the same time the maximum at which its preservation is relatively secure. A secret religious-political society which was formed in the beginning of the nineteenth century in France and Italy, had different degrees among its members. The real secrets of the society were known only to the higher degrees; but a discussion of these secrets could take place only between any two members of the high degrees. The limit of two was felt to be so decisive that, where it could not be preserved in regard to knowledge, it was kept at least in regard to the verbalization of this knowledge. More generally speaking, the difference between the dyad [1] and larger groups consists in

1 Never Simmel's term, but shorter and more convenient than his, which here, for instance, is "*Zweierverbindung*" (union of two).—Tr.

the fact that the dyad has a different relation to each of its two elements than have larger groups to *their* members. Although, for the outsider, the group consisting of two may function as an autonomous, super-individual unit, it usually does not do so for its participants. Rather, each of the two feels himself confronted only by the other, not by a collectivity above him. The social structure here rests immediately on the one and on the other of the two, and the secession of either would destroy the whole. The dyad, therefore, does not attain that super-personal life which the individual feels to be independent of himself. As soon, however, as there is a sociation of three, a group continues to exist even in case one of the members drops out.

## THE EXPANSION OF THE DYAD: THE TRIAD VS. THE DYAD

This peculiar closeness between two is most clearly revealed if the dyad is contrasted with the triad.[2] For among three elements, each one operates as an intermediary between the other two, exhibiting the twofold function of such an organ, which is to unite and to separate. Where three elements, A, B, C, constitute a group, there is, in addition to the direct relationship between A and B, for instance, their indirect one, which is derived from their common relation to C. The fact that two elements are each connected not only by a straight line—the shortest—but also by a broken line, as it were, is an enrichment from a formal-sociological standpoint. Points that cannot be contacted by the straight line are connected by the third element, which offers a different side to each of the other two, and yet fuses these different sides in the unity of its own personality. Discords between two parties which they themselves cannot remedy, are accommodated by the third or by absorption in a comprehensive whole.

Yet the indirect relation does not only strengthen the direct one. It may also disturb it. No matter how close a triad may be, there is always the occasion on which two of the three members regard the third as an intruder. The reason may be the mere fact that he shares in certain moods which can unfold in all their intensity and tenderness only when two can meet without distraction: the sensitive union of two is always irritated by the spectator. It may also be noted how extraordinarily difficult and rare it is for three people to attain a really uniform mood—when visiting a museum, for instance, or looking at a landscape—and how much more easily such a mood emerges between two. A and B may stress and harmoniously feel their *m*, because the *n* which A does not share with B, and the *x* which B does not share with A, are at once spontaneously conceded to be individual prerogatives located, as it were, on another plane. If, however, C

2 Again not Simmel's term, but again more convenient than "*Verbindung zu dreien*" (association of three) and the like.—Tr.

joins the company, who shares *n* with A and *x* with B, the result is that (even under this scheme, which is the one most favorable to the unity of the whole) harmony of feeling is made completely impossible. Two may actually be *one* party, or may stand entirely beyond any question of party. But it is usual for just such finely tuned combinations of three at once to result in three parties of two persons each, and thus to destroy the unequivocal character of the relations between each two of them.

The sociological structure of the dyad is characterized by two phenomena that are absent from it. One is the intensification of relation by a third element, or by a social framework that transcends both members of the dyad. The other is any disturbance and distraction of pure and immediate reciprocity. In some cases it is precisely this absence which makes the dyadic relationship more intensive and strong. For, many otherwise undeveloped, unifying forces that derive from more remote psychical reservoirs come to life in the feeling of exclusive dependence upon one another and of hopelessness that cohesion might come from anywhere but immediate interaction. Likewise, they carefully avoid many disturbances and dangers into which confidence in a third party and in the triad itself might lead the two. This intimacy, which is the tendency of relations between two persons, is the reason why the dyad constitutes the chief seat of jealousy.

# *Primary Groups*

## CHARLES H. COOLEY

BY PRIMARY groups I mean those characterized by intimate face-to-face association and cooperation. They are primary in several senses, but chiefly in that they are fundamental in forming the social nature and ideals of the individual. The result of intimate association, psychologically, is a certain fusion of individualities in a common whole, so that one's very self, for many purposes at least, is the common life and purpose of the group. Perhaps the simplest way of describing this wholeness is by saying that it is a "we"; it involves the sort of sympathy and mutual identification for which "we" is the natural expression. One lives

FROM *Social organization* by Charles H. Cooley; copyright 1909 by Charles Scribner's Sons, 1937 by Elsie Jones Cooley; used by permission of the publishers.

in the feeling of the whole and finds the chief aims of his will in that feeling.

It is not to be supposed that the unity of the primary group is one of mere harmony and love. It is always a differentiated and usually a competitive unity, admitting of self-assertion and various appropriative passions; but these passions are socialized by sympathy, and come, or tend to come, under the discipline of a common spirit. The individual will be ambitious, but the chief object of his ambition will be some desired place in the thought of the others, and he will feel allegiance to common standards of service and fair play. So the boy will dispute with his fellows a place on the team, but above such disputes will place the common glory of his class and school.

The most important spheres of this intimate association and cooperation—though by no means the only ones—are the family, the play-group of children, and the neighborhood or community group of elders. These are practically universal, belonging to all times and all stages of development; and are accordingly a chief basis of what is universal in human nature and human ideals. The best comparative studies of the family, such as those of Westermarck (7) or Howard (5), show it to us as not only a universal institution, but as more alike the world over than the exaggeration of exceptional customs by an earlier school had led us to suppose. Nor can anyone doubt the general prevalence of play-groups among children or of informal assemblies of various kinds among their elders. Such association is clearly the nursery of human nature in the world about us, and there is no apparent reason to suppose that the case has anywhere or at any time been essentially different.

As regards play, I might, were it not a matter of common observation, multiply illustrations of the universality and spontaneity of the group discussion and cooperation to which it gives rise. The general fact is that children, especially boys after about their twelfth year, live in fellowships in which their sympathy, ambition and honor are engaged even more, often, than they are in the family. Most of us can recall examples of the endurance by boys of injustice and even cruelty, rather than appeal from their fellows to parents or teachers—as, for instance, in the hazing so prevalent at schools, and so difficult, for this very reason, to repress. And how elaborate the discussion, how cogent the public opinion, how hot the ambitions in these fellowships.

Nor is this facility of juvenile association, as is sometimes supposed, a trait peculiar to English and American boys; since experience among our immigrant population seems to show that the offspring of the more restrictive civilizations of the continent of Europe form self-governing play-groups with almost equal readiness. Thus Miss Jane Addams, after pointing out that the "gang" is almost universal, speaks of the interminable discussion which every detail of the gang's activity receives, remarking that "in these social folk-motes, so to speak, the young citizen learns to act upon his own determination." (1, p. 177)

Of the neighborhood group it may be said, in general, that from the time men formed permanent settlements upon the land, down, at least, to the rise of modern industrial cities, it has played a main part in the primary, heart-to-heart life of the people. Among our Teutonic forefathers the village community was apparently the chief sphere of sympathy and mutual aid for the commons all through the "dark" and middle ages, and for many purposes it remains so in rural districts at the present day. In some countries we still find it with all its ancient vitality, notably in Russia, where the mir, or self-governing village group, is the main theatre of life, along with the family, for perhaps fifty millions of peasants.

In our own life the intimacy of the neighborhood has been broken up by the growth of an intricate mesh of wider contacts which leaves us strangers to people who live in the same house. And even in the country the same principle is at work, though less obviously, diminishing our economic and spiritual community with our neighbors. How far this change is a healthy development, and how far a disease, is perhaps still uncertain.

Besides these almost universal kinds of primary association, there are many others whose form depends upon the particular state of civilization; the only essential thing, as I have said, being a certain intimacy and fusion of personalities. In our own society, being little bound by place, people easily form clubs, fraternal societies and the like, based on congeniality, which may give rise to real intimacy. Many such relations are formed at school and college, and among men and women brought together in the first instance by their occupations—as workmen in the same trade, or the like. Where there is a little common interest and activity, kindness grows like weeds by the roadside.

But the fact that the family and neighborhood groups are ascendant in the open and plastic time of childhood makes them even now incomparably more influential than all the rest.

Primary groups are primary in the sense that they give the individual his earliest and completest experience of social unity, and also in the sense that they do not change in the same degree as more elaborate relations, but form a comparatively permanenent source out of which the latter are ever springing. Of course they are not independent of the larger society, but to some extent reflect its spirit; as the German family and the German school bear somewhat distinctly the print of German militarism. But this, after all, is like the tide setting back into creeks, and does not commonly go very far. Among the German, and still more among the Russian, peasantry are found habits of free cooperation and discussion almost uninfluenced by the character of the state; and it is a familiar and well-supported view that the village commune, self-governing as regards local affairs and habituated to discussion, is a very widespread institution in settled communities, and the continuator of a similar autonomy previously existing in the clan. "It is man who makes monarchies and establishes republics, but the commune seems to come directly from the hand of God." (4, ch. 5)

In our own cities the crowded tenements and the general economic and social confusion have sorely wounded the family and the neighborhood, but it is remarkable, in view of these conditions, what vitality they show; and there is nothing upon which the conscience of the time is more determined than upon restoring them to health.

These groups, then, are springs of life, not only for the individual but for social institutions. They are only in part moulded by special traditions, and, in larger degree, express a universal nature. The religion or government of other civilizations may seem alien to us, but the children or the family group wear the common life, and with them we can always make ourselves at home.

By human nature, I suppose, we may understand those sentiments and impulses that are human in being superior to those of lower animals, and also in the sense that they belong to mankind at large, and not to any particular race or time. It means, particularly, sympathy and the innumerable sentiments into which sympathy enters, such as love, resentment, ambition, vanity, hero-worship, and the feeling of social right and wrong.[1]

Human nature in this sense is justly regarded as a comparatively permanent element in society. Always and everywhere men seek honor and dread ridicule, defer to public opinion, cherish their goods and their children, and admire courage, generosity, and success. It is always safe to assume that people are and have been human.

It is true, no doubt, that there are differences of race capacity, so great that a large part of mankind are possibly incapable of any high kind of social organization. But these differences, like those among individuals of the same race, are subtle, depending upon some obscure intellectual deficiency, some want of vigor, or slackness of moral fiber, and do not involve unlikeness in the generic impulses of human nature. In these all races are very much alike. The more insight one gets into the life of savages, even those that are reckoned the lowest, the more human, the more like ourselves, they appear. Take for instance the natives of Central Australia, as described by Spencer and Gillen (6), tribes having no definite government or worship and scarcely able to count to five.[2] They are generous to one another, emulous of virtue as they understand it, kind to their children and to the aged, and by no means harsh to women. Their faces as shown in the photographs are wholly human and many of them attractive.

1 These matters are expounded at some length in Cooley (2).
2 Compare also Darwin's views. (3, ch. 7)

And when we come to a comparison between different stages in the development of the same race, between ourselves, for instance, and the Teutonic tribes of the time of Cæsar, the difference is neither in human nature nor in capacity, but in organization, in the range and complexity of relations, in the diverse expression of powers and passions essentially much the same.

There is no better proof of this generic likeness of human nature than in the ease and joy with which the modern man makes himself at home in literature depicting the most remote and varied phases of life—in Homer, in the Nibelung tales, in the Hebrew Scriptures, in the legends of the American Indians, in stories of frontier life, of soldiers and sailors, of criminals and tramps, and so on. The more penetratingly any phase of human life is studied the more an essential likeness to ourselves is revealed.

To return to primary groups: the view here maintained is that human nature is not something existing separately in the individual, but a *group-nature or primary phase of society*, a relatively simple and general condition of the social mind. It is something more, on the one hand, than the mere instinct that is born in us—though that enters into it—and something less, on the other, than the more elaborate development of ideas and sentiments that makes up institutions. It is the nature which is developed and expressed in those simple, face-to-face groups that are somewhat alike in all societies; groups of the family, the playground, and the neighborhood. In the essential similarity of these is to be found the basis, in experience, for similar ideas and sentiments in the human mind. In these, everywhere, human nature comes into existence. Man does not have it at birth; he cannot acquire it except through fellowship, and it decays in isolation.

If this view does not recommend itself to common sense I do not know that elaboration will be of much avail. It simply means the application at this point of the idea that society and individuals are inseparable phases of a common whole, so that wherever we find an individual fact we may look for a social fact to go with it. If there is a universal nature in persons there must be something universal in association to correspond to it.

What else can human nature be than a trait of primary groups? Surely not an attribute of the separate individual—supposing there were any such thing—since its typical characteristics, such as affection, ambition, vanity, and resentment, are inconceivable apart from society. If it belongs, then, to man in association, what kind or degree of association is required to develop it? Evidently nothing elaborate, because elaborate phases of society are transient and diverse, while human nature is comparatively stable and universal. In short the family and neighborhood life is essential to its genesis and nothing more is.

Here as everywhere in the study of society we must learn to see mankind in psychical wholes, rather than in artificial separation. We must see and feel the communal life of family and local groups as immediate facts, not as combinations of something else. And perhaps we shall do this best by recalling our own experience and extending it through sympathetic observation. What, in our life, is the family and the fellowship; what do we know of the we-feeling? Thought of this kind may help us to get a concrete perception of that primary group-nature of which everything social is the outgrowth.

## REFERENCES

1. Addams, Jane. *Newer ideals of peace.*
2. Cooley, C. H. *Human nature and the social order.*
3. Darwin, C. *Descent of man.*
4. De Tocqueville, A. *Democracy in America.* Vol. 1.
5. Howard. *A history of matrimonial institutions.*
6. Spencer, & Gillen. *The native tribes of Central Australia.*
7. Westermarck. *The history of human marriage.*

# The Social Foundations and Functions of Thought and Communication

GEORGE H. MEAD

MEAD'S *theoretical conceptualization in* Mind, Self and Society *is today one of the landmarks of social psychology. Here we have reproduced a small section on communication and social organization.*

THE PRINCIPLE which I have suggested as basic to human social organization is that of communication involving participation in the other. This requires the appearance of the other in the self, the identification of the other with the self, the reaching of self-consciousness through the other. This participation is made possible through the type of communication which the human animal is able to carry out—a type of communication distinguished from that which takes place among other forms which have not this principle in their societies. I discussed the sentinel, so-called, that may be said to communicate his discovery of the danger to the other members, as the clucking of the hen may be said to communicate to the chick. There are conditions under which the gesture of one form serves to place the other forms in the proper attitude toward external conditions. In one sense we may say the one form communicates with the other, but the difference between that and self-conscious communication is evident. One form does not know that communication is taking place with the other. We get illustrations of that in what we term mob-consciousness, the attitude which an audience will take when under the influence of a great speaker. One is influenced by the attitudes of those about him, which are reflected back into the different members of the audience so that they come to respond as a whole. One feels the general attitude of the whole audience. There is then communication in a real sense, that is, one form communicates to the other an attitude which the other assumes toward a certain part of the environment that is of importance to them both. That level of communication is found in forms of society which are of lower type than the social organization of the human group.

In the human group, on the other hand, there is not only this kind of communication but also that in which the person who uses this gesture and so communicates assumes the attitude of the other individual as well as calling it out in the other. He himself is in the role of the other person whom he is so exciting and influencing. It is through taking this role of the other that he is able to come back on himself and so direct his own process of communication. This taking the role of the other, an expression I have so often used, is not simply of passing importance. It is not something that just happens as an incidental result of the gesture, but it is of importance in the development of cooperative activity. The immediate effect of such role-taking lies in the control which the individual is able to exercise over his own response.[1] The control of the action of the individual

1 From the standpoint of social evolution, it is this bringing of any given social act, or of the total social process in which that act is a constituent, directly and as an organized whole into the experience of each of the individual organisms implicated in that act, with reference to which he may consequently regulate and govern his individual conduct, that constitutes the peculiar value and significance of self-consciousness in these individual organisms.

We have seen that the process or activity of thinking is a conversation carried on by the individual between himself and the generalized other; and that the general form and subject matter of this conversation is given and determined by the appearance in experience of some sort of problem to be solved. Human intelligence, which expresses itself in thought, is recognized to have this character of facing and dealing with any problem of environmental adjustment which confronts an organism possessing it. And thus, as we have also seen, the essential characteristic of intelligent behavior is delayed responses—a halt in behavior while thinking is going on; this delayed response in a cooperative process can take place in the conduct of the individual himself if he can take the role of the other. It is this control of the response of the individual himself through taking the role of the other that leads to the value of this type of communication from the point of view of the organization of the conduct in the group. It carries the process of co-operative activity farther than it can be carried in the herd as such, or in the insect society.

And thus it is that social control, as operating in terms of self-criticism, exerts itself so intimately and extensively over individual behavior or conduct, serving to integrate the individual and his actions with reference to the organized social process of experience and behavior in which he is implicated. The physiological mechanism of the human individual's central nervous system makes it possible for him to take the attitudes of other individuals, and the attitudes of the organized social group of which he and they are members, toward himself, in terms of his integrated social relations to them and to the group as a whole; so that the general social process of experience and behavior which the group is carrying on is directly presented to him in his own experience, and so that he is thereby able to govern and direct his conduct consciously and critically, with reference to his relations both to the social group as a whole and to its other individual members, in terms of this social process. Thus he becomes not only self-conscious but also self-critical; and thus, through self-criticism, social control over individual behavior or conduct operates by virtue of the social origin and basis of such criticism. That is to say, self-criticism is essentially social criticism, and behavior controlled by self-criticism is essentially behavior controlled socially.[2] Hence social control, so far from tending to crush out the human individual or to obliterate his self-conscious individuality, is, on the contrary, actually constitutive of and inextricably associated with that individuality; for the individual is what he is, as a conscious and individual personality, just in as far as he is a member of society, involved in the social process of experience and activity, and thereby socially controlled in his conduct.

The very organization of the self-conscious community is dependent upon individuals taking the attitude of the other individuals. The development of this process, as I have indicated, is dependent upon getting the at-

---

and the thinking for the purposes of which it is delayed (including the final selection, as the result of the thinking, of the best or most expedient among the several responses possible in the given environmental situation) being made possible physiologically through the mechanism of the central nervous system, and socially through the mechanism of language.

2 Freud's conception of the psychological "censor" represents a partial recognition of this operation of social control in terms of self-criticism, a recognition, namely, of its operation with reference to sexual experience and conduct. But this same sort of censorship or criticism of himself by the individual is reflected also in all other aspects of his social experience, behavior, and relations—a fact which follows naturally and inevitably from our social theory of the self.

titude of the group as distinct from that of a separate individual—getting what I have termed a "generalized other." I have illustrated this by the ball game, in which the attitudes of a set of individuals are involved in a cooperative response in which the different roles involve each other. In so far as a man takes the attitude of one individual in the group, he must take it in its relationship to the action of the other members of the group; and if he is fully to adjust himself, he would have to take the attitudes of all involved in the process. The degree, of course, to which he can do that is restrained by his capacity, but still in all intelligent processes we are able sufficiently to take the roles of those involved in the activity to make our own action intelligent. The degree to which the life of the whole community can get into the self-conscious life of the separate individuals varies enormously. History is largely occupied in tracing out the development which could not have been present in the actual experience of the members of the community at the time the historian is writing about. Such an account explains the importance of history. One can look back over that which took place, and bring out changes, forces, and interests which nobody at the time was conscious of. We have to wait for the historian to give the picture because the actual process was one which transcended the experience of the separate individuals.

Occasionally a person arises who is able to take in more than others of an act in process, who can put himself into relation with whole groups in the community whose attitudes have not entered into the lives of the others in the community. He becomes a leader. Classes under a feudal order may be so separate from each other that, while they can act in certain traditional circumstances, they cannot understand each other; and then there may arise an individual who is capable of entering into the attitudes of the other members of the group. Figures of that sort become of enormous importance because they make possible communication between groups otherwise completely separated from each other. The sort of capacity we speak of is in politics the attitude of the statesman who is able to enter into the attitudes of the group and to mediate between them by making his own experience universal, so that others can enter into this form of communication through him.

CHAPTER 2

# EARLY RESEARCH

## *A Preliminary Study of the Psychology and Pedagogy of Leadership*

LEWIS M. TERMAN

*THE section of Terman's study presented below represents one of the earliest systematic experimental and observational researches reported in the literature of this country. The focus on suggestability, deriving directly from the work of Binet, was expanded in this study. Readers will note that the design of experiment and sophistication of interpretation are "modern."*

### LEADERSHIP AMONG CHILDREN

#### *Experimental*

THE FOLLOWING experimental study was made. It is in part a repetition of some work done by Binet (1, p. 330 ff.). It seemed, however, that the study should embrace a much larger number of pupils [1]

ABRIDGED from the article of the same title in *Pedagogical Seminary*, 1904, II, 413-451. Reprinted by permission of the author and publisher.

1 Binet used only 24.

and should also be made more intensive. That is, facts concerning the pupils should be gained from other sources than the tests.

One hundred pupils of the Bloomington, Indiana, public schools acted as subjects. They were distributed as follows:

| | | |
|---|---|---|
| Grade 2, | 12 boys and 12 girls |
| " 4, | 12 " " 12 " |
| " 6, | 8 " " 12 " |
| " 8, | 8 " " 8 " |

In addition, 8 boys and 8 girls, in the colored school, ranging from the 5th to the 8th grade, were tested separately.

The general aim was to discover those pupils who might be termed "leaders" of their fellows, and to ascertain the qualities whereby they held this ascendency. It is evident that without long personal acquaintance with each pupil, and without opportunity for long and careful observations of their actions during work and play, the outcome of the study must be meager enough. The results are not claimed to have a high degree of absolute value.

The tests were as follows: on a heavy cardboard about 16 x 24 inches were fastened pictures and objects, to the number of ten. The pupils were withdrawn, four at a time, to an unoccupied and quiet room. To throw them off their guard they were told that they were to engage in a memory test. It was further explained that the cardboard would be turned so that they could view for ten seconds the objects and pictures pasted on the other side. After the removal of the cardboard from sight they were to answer a number of questions concerning what they had seen. They were given to understand that we would record the reply of each pupil and the order in which it was given. They were therefore urged to reply both quickly and correctly. The answers were given with loud voice. The instructions were always repeated till they were clearly understood.

Binet used only three pupils in each group. On consideration, it seemed best to have more. Groups of five were first tried but the order of the replies being too difficult to get, the number was reluctantly reduced to four. Binet also chose one member of each group to act as chairman of that group, allowing him to read the questions, to record the answers, and at the same time to act as subject himself. To say nothing of the relative disadvantage thus thrown on such pupil, it appeared that even so slight an exhibition of preference on the part of the experimenter would likely affect the group spirit. Accordingly all were allowed to stand on equal footing, either myself or an assistant asking the questions while the other kept the records. The girls and the boys were tested separately. Moreover, except in the colored school, the pupils of any group were chosen from a single grade.

Twenty-three questions were asked concerning the objects and pictures, 11 of which were catch questions; that is, they asked about things which were not on the cardboard. These were intended to serve as a test of the pupils' suggestibility. It was found somewhat difficult to hit upon the right sort of catch questions and to locate them properly in the series. Two extremes were to be avoided. The traps must not be too glaring, else the suspicions of the subject would be aroused. Neither must they be so easily led up to that none would escape them. Usually they were separated by fair questions, and the more obvious ones were placed toward the latter part of the list, since we hoped by that time to have won the confidence of the pupils.

When all the 100 subjects had been thus tested in groups of 4, a second series was begun in an exactly analogous way, with a new set of objects on the cardboard and a new set of 23 questions, 9 of which were catches. Eighty of the former 100 pupils participated. For this series of experiments the former groups were broken up and new ones formed. In the latter, the pupils were intentionally so chosen that each group would contain at least one pupil who had shown himself a leader, and one who had appeared to be an automaton in the previous tests. It could thus be determined whether the rank of a pupil in any group of the first series had wholly a relative, or to some extent an absolute meaning.

In elaborating the results the following points were noted for each pupil:

1. The number of times his reply was first, second, third, or fourth.
2. Originality.
3. The number of times each pupil of a group imitated each of the others.
4. Total number of imitations made by each.
5. Total number of times each pupil was imitated, by all the others.
6. Suggestibility, as measured by the number of times the subject fell into the trap.

The arbitrary use of some of the above terms must be explained. "Originality" means that the answer could not have been influenced by the answer of any other pupil. This does not, however, preclude its being suggested by a trap question. The "originality" can be shown in two ways: First, by answering before all the others; second, by giving an answer which, though not first, differed from the preceding answers in such a way that it could not have been influenced by them. Here, it must be acknowledged, there was often room for doubt, since it was not always possible to calculate just how far contrary suggestion was at work. "Suggestibility" was computed in per cent. If the pupil fell into all the traps his "suggestibility" was reckoned 100%. If into 4 out of a total of 8, 50%, etc. The other items will be made clear by the following illustration: Suppose that in answer to a question the same reply was given by all, A, B, C, and

D, in a group. If A answers first, he is "original." B answers second, and since his answer is the same as A's, he is credited with one "imitation." C answers third and therefore "imitates" A and B once each. D answers fourth and therefore "imitates" A, B, and C once each. That is, A makes no "imitation," B makes one, C makes two, and D makes three. A was "imitated" three times, B twice, and C once.

As expected, certain of the pupils answered first nearly always, while others were generally last and were content to repeat exactly or with slight variation the answer of another. For example, in one group:

| | FIRST | SECOND | THIRD | FOURTH |
|---|---|---|---|---|
| A answered | 1 | 4 | 8 | 10 |
| C " | 9 | 6 | 5 | 2 |

It soon became evident that not always could those who answered first be called "leaders." Fifteen times it occurred that the group rank of pupils in quickness and in number of times "imitated" differed radically, *i.e.*, by as much as two places. Here, we have an unmistakable exhibition of personal preference. Those who have not the initiative for framing an answer of their own, will prefer to repeat the answer of one pupil rather than that of another. The first reply is a stimulus which always tends to result in an activity of the other pupils suggested by it or imitative of it, but in the above fifteen cases the tendency was generally overcome by some inhibition. It likewise happened several times that the quickest were not the most "original." With twelve pupils there was a wide divergence between the group rank in "originality," and that in number of times "imitated." Another, and perhaps more significant result was the fact that low "originality" often accompanied low "suggestibility," and vice versa in fact the average "suggestibility" of the *leaders* was slightly greater than that of the *automatons*, the percentage being 62 and 59 respectively. Their comparative "originality," however, was 13.4 and 5.6, out of a total of 23 questions answered. This fact may have been due to the intense desire of the leaders to answer first, though the subjects were repeatedly reminded that it was as important to answer correctly as to answer quickly.

A greater number than expected, namely, 19 out of 80, obtained in the second series of tests a radically different rank from what they had gained in the first series. Of 22 leaders in the second series, 12 had been leaders in the first series, and five had occupied very low rank. Out of 32 automatons in the second series, 18 had been so in the first series, and 7 had occupied very high rank.

The following table shows the grade and sex differences for "originality." Each number represents the number of original answers out of the total set of 23.

| GRADE | 2 | 4 | 6 | 8 | COLORED | AVERAGE FOR EACH SEX | |
|---|---|---|---|---|---|---|---|
| boys | 8.50 | 8.33 | 9.25 | 10.12 | 9.50 | 9.14 | Series I |
| girls | 7.16 | 6.91 | 8.00 | 10.62 | 9.62 | 8.50 | |
| boys | 9.85 | 7.25 | 8.00 | 10.00 | 7.12 | 8.44 | Series II |
| girls | 6.37 | 5.87 | 8.00 | 9.62 | 8.87 | 7.75 | |
| Average for each grade | 7.97 | 7.09 | 8.31 | 10.09 | 8.78 | 8.45 | |

The following table shows the percentage of "suggestibility."

| GRADE | 2 | 4 | 6 | 8 | COLORED | AVERAGE FOR EACH SEX | |
|---|---|---|---|---|---|---|---|
| boys | 50 | 77 | 77 | 45 | 73 | 64 | Series I |
| girls | 66 | 76 | 77 | 52 | 77 | 69 | |
| boys | 72 | 76 | 91 | 45 | 78 | 72 | Series II |
| girls | 86 | 97 | 90 | 55 | 61 | 78 | |
| Average for each grade | 68.5 | 81.5 | 83.7 | 49.2 | 72.2 | 71 | |

The second part of our task was to get further facts about the pupils that would throw light on the cases of leadership among them. This the teachers were kind enough to furnish by answering 22 questions in regard to each pupil. They are as follows:

1. Age? 2. Size, in relation to grade? 3. Dress? 4. Is dress gaudy? 5. Any physical peculiarity or deformity? 6. Health? 7. Are parents wealthy or otherwise prominent? 8. Is it an only child? 9. Quality of school work? 10. Notable for boldness or daring? 11. A leader in games or pranks? 12. If so, is it by forcing others or by natural attraction? 13. Liked or disliked by other pupils? 14. Why? 15. Fluent of speech in conversation? 16. Any dramatic qualities? 17. Looks? 18. Reads much or little? 19. Timid or forward? 20. High tempered or amiable? 21. Selfish or considerate? 22. Emotional or deliberate in temperament?

Questions like 2, 3, and 9 were graded on a scale of five. To illustrate, 1 = very large, 2 = large, 3 = average, 4 = small, 5 = very small. Questions like 16, 18, 19, and 20 were graded similarly on a scale of three. Some of the most important results are summed up in the following table.

| | GRADE | 2 | 4 | 6 | 8 | COLORED | AVERAGE |
|---|---|---|---|---|---|---|---|
| Age in years | Leaders | 7.67 | 10.43 | 13.20 | 14.75 | 14.00 | 12.01 |
| | Automatons | 7.40 | 10.17 | 12.60 | 14.80 | 14.60 | 11.91 |
| Size, on scale of five | Leaders | 2.16 | 2.62 | 2.33 | 3.20 | 2.00 | 2.46 |
| | Automatons | 3.11 | 3.00 | 2.80 | 3.00 | 3.00 | 2.98 |

| | GRADE | 2 | 4 | 6 | 8 | COL-ORED | AVER-AGE |
|---|---|---|---|---|---|---|---|
| Dress, on scale of five | Leaders | 2.50 | 3.28 | 1.83 | 1.80 | 2.50 | 2.38 |
| | Automatons | 2.70 | 3.25 | 2.40 | 2.00 | 2.60 | 2.59 |
| Quality of work, scale of five | Leaders | 2.40 | 2.14 | 2.50 | 2.20 | 3.00 | 2.41 |
| | Automatons | 2.50 | 3.50 | 2.60 | 3.00 | 2.60 | 2.84 |
| Looks, scale of three | Leaders | 2.25 | 1.62 | 1.50 | 1.20 | 2.00 | 1.72 |
| | Automatons | 2.11 | 2.12 | 2.20 | 1.75 | 2.20 | 2.09 |
| Selfishness, scale of three | Leaders | 2.20 | 1.56 | 2.00 | 1.20 | 2.25 | 1.84 |
| | Automatons | 2.00 | 2.00 | 2.00 | 2.25 | 2.00 | 2.05 |

Several of the questions do not furnish data to show anything clearly. To sum up the chief results, the pupils who were leaders in the tests are larger, better dressed, of more prominent parentage, brighter in their school work, more daring, more fluent of speech, better looking, greater readers, and less selfish than the automatons. It was found that a surprising number of times the leaders were graded on size, dress, and school work either as 5 or 1. To illustrate, in grade 4 the leaders are graded on school work as 1, 1, 5, 1, 1, 5, 1. The automatons of the same grade received the following ranks on the same question: 3, 4, 3, 3, 4, 3, 5, 3. This indicates that possibly there is a tendency for children to be influenced by what is unusual; that they are on the lookout for striking qualities of whatever sort; anything to get clear of tiresome mediocrity.

Finally, the same pupils, excepting those in grade 2, were allowed to answer the following questions:

What one of your schoolmates would you rather be like if you were not yourself? Why? Several other questions were asked calling for ideals, but the answers were so scattered that no well defined tendency could be made out. Above all it was desired to find out how much oftener, if any, those pupils stamped as leaders by the experiments would be chosen consciously as ideals by their mates, than would the automatons. The results show that they were chosen 4½ times as often. The fact is important as indicating the validity of the method of experimentation and the great importance of suggestion and imitation as elements in leadership.

## *Summary of Experimental Results*

1. A large number maintain a well defined rank either as first or last in the groups.

2. The leaders in the tests were twice as often mentioned by the teachers as being leaders, and further were chosen 4½ times as often by their mates as ideals.

3. Suggestibility, as measured by these tests, rises from the second to the fourth grade and then falls rapidly in the succeeding grades. The

naïveté with which the smallest children gave correct answers to the catch questions was remarkable. It reminds one of the old story of the king who thought to appear in procession before his people in a magic garment, visible to all except the wicked, and whose nakedness was denounced only by a little child.

4. The pupils show marked choice in imitating the answers of others. Circumstances favor the quickest, but not always are these the most imitated.

5. The leaders have a high average suggestibility. This may indicate that there is some truth in the assertion, often made, that to be a leader it is more important to lead the way than to be right.

6. The group rank of many pupils in the second series was radically different from what it had been in the first. This does not seem to be due to a wide divergence between the average reaction time or "originality" of the second group as compared to the first. It is the group spirit as mirrored in the consciousness of each pupil. In one group a certain pupil *feels* himself inferior; he follows, therefore, the answers of the others. In another group the same pupil may *feel* himself superior, and be so regarded by the others. This recalls Emerson's words: "Who has more soul than I, masters me, though he should not raise his finger. . . . Who has less, I rule with like facility."

7. The leaders in the tests, according to the testimony of their teachers, are on the average larger, better dressed, of more prominent parentage, brighter, more noted for daring, more fluent of speech, better looking, greater readers, less emotional and less selfish than the automatons.

8. As regards the reasons given by the pupils for choosing certain of their schoolmates for ideals, intelligence increases in importance rapidly from the second to the eighth grade and goodness as rapidly falls.

9. According to the opinion of the teachers, such pupils are preferred most often for the following qualities, given in order of their importance: intelligence, congeniality, liveliness, and goodness.

10. The data were not suited to bring out race differences in the qualities of leadership.

## REFERENCE

1. Binet, A. *La suggestibilité.*

# *The Influence of the Group upon Association and Thought*

FLOYD H. ALLPORT

## INTRODUCTION

IF SOCIAL psychology is to achieve the title of an independent science, it is high time that its many speculative theories and crude generalizations be subjected to experimental methods. The data of this science, it appears to the writer, may be for convenience subsumed under two heads, viz.: (1) the behavior of an individual in direct response to social stimulus, that is in response to some form of behavior in others, and, (2) behavior which is the response to a nonsocial stimulus, *e.g.*, a column of figures to be added, or a meal to be eaten, when such response is modified by the presence and actions of other persons. Responses to direct and incidental social stimuli are, in brief, the two classes of data for social psychology.

The following experiments bear upon certain problems of the second class of data mentioned. The method employed was to compare the mental processes (in this case association and thought) of the individual when alone with his reactions to similar and equivalent stimuli when a member of a "co-working or co-feeling" group. In this manner the part played by incidental or contributory social stimulation was determined.[1]

## GENERAL METHOD

It was considered advisable to eliminate all incentives to rivalry which were not inherent in the very nature of the situation (*i.e.*, individuals working on similar tasks in one another's presence). The subjects were instructed not to regard their work as competitive; overt comparisons be-

FROM *Journal of Experimental Psychology*, 1920, 3, 159–182. Reprinted by permission of the author and the American Psychological Association, Inc.

1 A brief historical account of the study of the influence of the group upon the individual may be found in an article by Burnham (1).

tween individuals were also prohibited. The time given for the tests was constant, hence no one subject finished before the others. In this way rivalry, which is a distinct social problem and which should be studied separately, was reduced to its natural minimum. Each subject, however, was instructed to acquire the attitude of doing his best in both the group and the solitary work.

The subjects were arranged in groups, containing from 3 to 5 subjects each. The groups had no changes of personnel during a whole experiment. The subjects were upper classmen and graduate students in psychology at Harvard and Radcliffe Colleges. They were 26 in number, though not more than 15 were used in any single experiment. There were 24 men and 2 women. In age they ranged from 20 to 40 years, 26 being the average age.

In the group work the subjects were seated one on each side of a table 3 feet by 5 feet in dimensions. In groups of 5 two subjects sat at one of the longer sides. The same seats were retained by subjects throughout the course of an experiment. Care was taken to secure conditions, such as type of table, light, air, seating of the subjects, etc., in the rooms used for solitary work comparable to those conditions in the room where the subjects worked as a group.

The free chain associations which were to be written were started by a stimulus word, for example "building" or "laboratory," written at the top of a sheet of paper given to each subject. The same stimulus words were employed in the two conditions, *T* and *A*.[2] It was also emphasized in group work that the same stimulus word was given to all. It is not believed that the presence of the experimenter in the group work materially affected the results of the social influence.

In all experiments except the first constant intervals of time were given, in the group by spoken signal, and alone by buzzers placed in each room and tuned down to inobtrusive intensity. Control tests were given in the group, using the buzzer for signals in order to determine whether the buzzer itself played a part in the results. No difference was found in the average, between group tests given by the buzzer and those given by verbal signal. The writing materials (pen, pencil, etc.) used by each subject were kept as constant as possible throughout the experiment.

## SUMMARY OF CONCLUSIONS

### A. *The Influence of the Group upon Association*

#### I. QUANTITATIVE ASPECTS

1. The main result of the preceding experiments on association is the conclusion that the *presence of a co-working group is distinctly favorable*

2 *I.e.*, "Together" and "Alone."

*to the speed of the process of free association.* In various tests from 66 per cent to 93 per cent of the subjects show this beneficial influence of the group.

2. The beneficial group influence is *subject to variation according to the nature of the task.* In the more mechanical and motor requirements, such as writing *each word* associated, the group stimulus is more effective than in the more highly mental or more purely associational tasks such as writing only every *third* or *fourth* word.

3. There are *individual differences* in susceptibility to the influence of the group upon association. One type, who are nervous and excitable, may succumb to the distracting elements of the group activity and may show either no effect, or else a social decrement.

4. *In its temporal distribution* the beneficial effect of the group is greatest in the first part of the task and least toward the end of the task.

5. There is a tendency for the *slow individuals to be more favorably affected* in speed by the group co-activity than the more rapid workers. There are, however, certain striking exceptions.

6. *The variability in output* among the individuals varies generally with the social influence. Hence it is usually greatest in the group work. A striking exception to this occurs in the tests where rivalry is correlated with the social increment, and where only every third or fourth word is written. Here the variability is greatest in the solitary work. This result is in agreement with that of earlier investigators working on different processes.

7. There is suggestive but *not conclusive* evidence that the output of associations in a group where all the members are forming associations in the same category is greater than that in groups in which the members are divided in the trend of their associations between opposite or contrasted categories.

### II. QUALITATIVE ASPECTS

8. A greater number of *personal associations* are *produced alone* than in the group.

9. In harmony with this fact is the tendency for subjects to produce *ideas suggested by their immediate surroundings* with *greater frequency in the group* than alone.

10. Less clear cut, but very probable, are the tendencies to produce a *greater number of "free rising" ideas in the group,* and to produce a greater number of words *suggested mainly by the initial stimulus word when working alone.*

### III. FACTORS IN THE SOCIAL INFLUENCE

11. There are two opposing groups of factors in the influence of the social condition upon the association process. They are:

(1) Facilitating Factors:

(*a*) *Facilitation of movement* by perceptions or ideas of movements in others near us.

(*b*) *Rivalry* intrinsic in the bare social setting of a group working together. Rivalry is well correlated with the beneficial influence of the group in tests of a more mental sort (and less mechanical) such as writing every *fourth* word only. It is not so correlated when each word is written.

The beneficial effects of the group in experiments where the rivalry consciousness is closely correlated with this influence is less than in experiments where it is not so correlated, but where other factors—for example, motor facilitation—serve as the stimulus of the group.

(2) Impeding Factors: distraction, over-rivalry, emotions. Of the two groups, the facilitating is by far the more important in the total effect upon the work.

12. Beside the comparisons already indicated, we may note the general agreement of our work with that of earlier students in the *speed* improvement of mental operations, as shown by the quantity of the product, under conditions of working with others.

## B. *The Influence of the Group upon the Thought Process*

13. In the highly controlled association of the thought process, as typified in written argument, more ideas are produced in the group than when working alone. Again we find an increased flow of thought owing to the social stimulus.

14. Among the ideas so produced, those of superior quality, however, are of relatively greater frequency in the solitary than in the group work. Ideas of a lower logical value are relatively more numerous in the group work.

15. More words are used in the arguments produced in the group than in those produced in solitude.

16. From the above facts, and also from the introspection of the subjects, we may conclude that the presence of the group influences the reasoner toward a more conversational and expansive form of expression. The more intense logical thinking of solitude gives way in the group to extensity of treatment.

17. These results appear to be related to the common observation that work requiring imagination or more concentrated and original thought is best performed in seclusion. There is also a connection suggested with the writer's experiments upon the social influence in attention and mental work. In that investigation, as well as in the present, the social influence was found to improve the quantity but not the quality of the mental performance.

REFERENCE

1. Burnham, W. H. The group as a stimulus to mental activity. *Science*, 1910, 31, 761–767.

# *Aggressive Behavior in a Small Social Group*

ETHEL M. RIDDLE

*RIDDLE'S experiment with a group of six poker players is of great historical significance since it heralded the joining of several approaches of research. It was a combination of the group suggestibility experiment with psychometric measurement and introspective reports. We have reprinted the review given the research by Murphy, Murphy, and Newcomb since the original monograph is too long and detailed to be presented here.*

AN ELABORATE experimental approach to a highly competitive situation is Riddle's study of a series of poker games. Six college students participated. Each knew the others well, and within a short time all were accustomed to the situation of having their game in the laboratory. They agreed, furthermore, to various more or less disturbing or boring interruptions and distractions, such as the frequent recording of their feelings and attitudes, and the wearing of rubber stethograph tubes during the course of the experimental periods. They were, to be sure, paid for the time given to the experiment, but none showed any hesitation in betting his own money. The players were allowed to fix their own limits, a 5-cent ante and a 20-cent limit. This was higher than usual for most of them. By the time the experimenter was ready to take records, the players appear to have been able to lose themselves quite naturally in the game. For each draw, each player was required to fill out a "schedule A": "How anxious are you to beat each player?" (ratings from + 100 to − 100 for

FROM G. Murphy, Lois B. Murphy, & T. M. Newcomb, *Experimental social psychology*. New York: Harper & Bros., 1937. Reprinted by permission of the authors and publisher.

each of his antagonists). Schedule B asked, "Did you try to bluff anyone during this game?" and "Did anyone try to bluff you during this draw?"; and presented a scale for the emotional state ranging from + 100 (elated) to – 100 (gloomy). On schedule C was recorded the bodily state, from maximum excitement to maximum physical retardation.

A curious set of intercorrelations appears in which the three variables to be considered are: (1) the player's own hand; (2) the player's desire to win; (3) the player's own bet. The correlation between the first and third is + .62, and that between the first and second is + .53. Since the player's own hand can be only a cause and not a result of these other two factors, whereas the second and third factors may be causally related to each other, it becomes important to partial out the influence of one factor at a time in order to find the causal relations. When this is done, it turns out that the correlation between hand and bet falls to + .44, while that between hand and desire is + .09. The highest correlation of all, however, is between desire and bet, which is + .63. Riddle argues that the bet acts as a stimulus to desire rather than desire as a stimulus to bet.

A further problem in motivation appears in response to one's opponent's hand. By a similar technique Riddle shows that the opponent's bet correlates only + .05 with the player's own bet when the player's desire to win is partialed out. With this and much other statistical material, Riddle reaches the conclusion that the desire to win in this game situation is only to a slight extent aroused by the size of the player's own hand value. It is aroused more fully by the value of the opponent's hand. The influence of one's own hand is, of course, to increase one's own bet, and the effect of the opponent's hand is to inhibit one's bet. When, however, the balance has been struck and the bet made, this bet in turn duly determines the total strength of the desire to win. The method devised here seems entirely practicable in the study of even more complicated competitive situations.

A series of interesting individual differences appear among the six players. One, for example, has about the same desire to win over all of his opponents, whereas another's desire to win varies greatly with the particular opponent he is trying to beat at a given time. This leads to the question whether one player, who greatly stimulates the desire of other players to beat him, has any peculiar characteristics of his own which may explain the trend. He certainly has. A study of the number of times that a player bluffed and the number of times that his opponent knew he was bluffing shows that player A (the one whose bets aroused in other players such a desire to win) bluffed 31 times—far more than the number of times anyone else bluffed. Only seven times did the opponent against whom the bluff was aimed recognize that A was bluffing. Players B and C each tried only once to bluff during the whole experiment, and both were detected. On the other hand, the number of times a player suspected that he was being bluffed varied all the way from one to thirty. The number of times that this suspicion coincided with the actual attempt to bluff him was rather small, and only one of the six players seemed to be able to tell definitely when he was being bluffed.

It turns out that successful and unsuccessful efforts at bluffing are the very heart of the situation, and that precise quantitative analysis throws much light upon the causes of aggressive and defensive responses of the players. Correlations are worked out for size of bets, amount of bluffing, suspicion of being bluffed, amount won, etc., some of which are illuminating. The correlations between the average winning per draw and the tendency to be "bluffed against" is + .97. Whether a player wins or loses has, however, but little effect upon the opponent's judgment as to whether he is bluffing. The player who makes the highest bets, has the largest pile, and whose hands are running high, is, in general, thought by his opponents to bluff frequently. The player who is most successful in the game, who is most likely to win by good hands and a large pile, and who is most aggressive in his betting is the one against whom bluffs are most frequently directed. It turns out that the betters are not, in general, eager to win against those from whom they could most easily win; the weak player is not the one against whom the bluffs are directed. Quite contrary to the hedonistic interpretation, the goal here, even when measured in money terms, is very specific. It is not simply a desire to win money where it can be won most safely or in the largest amount, but rather, where an aggressive attitude and an exhibition of skill afford a direct challenge. On the other hand, the player who attempts to bluff most frequently is unlikely to be the one with the highest average desire to win, but rather the one whose desire varies most from game to game, and from opponent to opponent. The one who is really anxious to win seems to be definitely low in his willingness to risk money. The man "with the least adequate means of defense," whose pile and hands are low, is the one who most frequently thinks he is being bluffed.

# *The Gang*

FREDERIC M. THRASHER

THRASHER's The Gang *was one of the early systematic studies of small group informal organization. From this classic we have selected sections on size of gang, two and three boy gangs, and personality and role differentiation. Case materials, which are copiously presented in the text, are omitted here.*

## *The Size of the Gang*

THE NECESSITIES of maintaining face-to-face relationships set definite limits to the magnitude to which the gang can grow. The size of Itschkie's group was determined by the number of boys readily able to meet together on the street or within the limited space of their hang-out. The gang does not usually grow to such proportions as to be unwieldly in collective enterprises or to make intimate contacts and controls difficult.[1] Ordinarily, if all members are present, what is said by one of the group can be heard by all. Otherwise, common experience becomes more difficult and the group tends to split and form more than one gang. The number of "fringers" and hangers-on upon whom the gang can count for backing, however, may be larger, especially if it has developed a good athletic team.

Greater growth can be accomplished only through modifications of structure, such as those resulting from conventionalization. When a gang becomes conventionalized, assuming, for example, the form of a club, it may possibly grow to large proportions. The original gang, however, probably now becomes an "inner circle," remaining the active nucleus in



1 College fraternity policy, based on long years of experience in attempting to maintain intimate relationships and unity of purpose among its members, illustrates the necessity of controlling numbers. Thirty-five to forty members seems to be the maximum size for such a group if these conditions are to be maintained and communal life is to be carried on in the fraternity homes. If, for financial or other reasons, a fraternity grows to larger proportions, it is the custom to refer to its house satirically as a "hotel."

such cases. The additional members may develop their own cliques within the larger whole or maintain merely a more or less formal relationship to the organization. In many cases such a club is the result of the combination of two or more gangs.

Table 1 does not include the major portion of the gang clubs; these vary in number of members ordinarily from 20 or 25 to 75 or 100; only a few of the more prosperous clubs exceed 100 members. It will be seen

TABLE 1

*Approximate Numbers of Members in 895 Gangs*

| NO. OF MEMBERS | NO. OF GANGS | PERCENTAGE OF TOTAL |
|---|---|---|
| From 3 to 5 (inclusive) | 37 | 4.1 |
| From 6 to 10 | 198 | 22.1 |
| From 11 to 15 | 191 | 21.5 |
| From 16 to 20 | 149 | 16.7 |
| From 21 to 25 | 79 | 8.8 |
| From 26 to 30 | 46 | 5.1 |
| From 31 to 40 | 55 | 6.1 |
| From 41 to 50 | 51 | 5.7 |
| From 51 to 75 | 26 | 2.9 |
| From 76 to 100 | 25 | 2.8 |
| From 101 to 200 | 25 | 2.8 |
| From 201 to 500 | 11 | 1.2 |
| From 501 to 2,000 | 2 | .2 |
| Total gangs | 895 | 100.0 |

that 806 of these gangs have memberships of 50 or under; these are largely of the non-conventionalized type. Most of the remaining 89 have memberships ranging from 51 to 2,000, though not all of them have been conventionalized.

## *The Two- and Three-Boy Relationship*

What has been defined as a "two-boy gang" or an "intimacy" must not be overlooked in discussing the inner organization of the gang. In this type of relationship there is generally a subordination of one boy to the other. In one instance other members of the group expressed it in this way, "Jerry is running Alfred now." Hero-worship, open or tacit, plays an important part in such cases. Sometimes the abilities of one boy supplement those of the other.

In many of these cases one boy tends to become utterly enthralled by the other; and there grows up a devotion hardly to be excelled even in the cases of the most ardent lovers of opposite sexes.[2] While these in-

2 The intimacy in the gang provides a satisfaction for the boy's wish for response. One boy may fascinate another and the two be completely wrapped up in one another. While attachments such as these would probably be regarded as homosexual by the Freudians, they exist in most cases without definite sex impulses and are to be regarded as entirely normal and practically universal among boys.

timacies usually develop in pairs (the introduction of a third person many times making for complications and friction), yet it sometimes happens that the relationship may include three boys who cooperate in perfect congeniality.

It is relations of this sort, existing before the gang develops, that serve as primary structures when the group is first formed and that shape the growth of its future organization. The intimacy partly explains why many of the exploits of gang boys are carried out in pairs and trios. The boys often prefer to have a favored pal or two associated in an enterprise rather than bring in the whole gang.

The two- and three-boy relationship is often much more important to the individual boy than his relationship to the gang. In such cases a boy would doubtless forego the gang before he would give up his special pal or pair of pals. A series of such palships, one or two of which may be more highly prized than others, are characteristic of boys of the non-gang areas of the city and also of gangland boys who are not in gangs. In other words, under different conditions, the two- and three-boy relationship becomes a completely satisfactory substitute for the gang and the wish for recognition from a larger circle, if imperative, is gratified through membership in the family, the school, the club, and other groups and institutions to which the boy has access.

### *The "Organism" as a Whole*

Each gang as a whole, and other types of social groups as well, may be conceived of as possessing an action pattern. Every person in the group performs his characteristic function with reference to others, or to put it another way, fills the individual niche that previous experience in the gang has determined for him. Lacking the group, personality in the sense here used would not exist. The action pattern of a group tends to become fixed and automatic in the habits of its members; it may persist long after the formal organization of the group has changed.

Yet the action pattern which characterizes each group can hardly be thought of as rigid and static; for it must be constantly changing to accommodate losses and additions of personnel, changes in its members due to growth and increasing experience, and other changes within and without the gang.

## PERSONALITY AND THE ACTION PATTERN OF THE GANG

Every member of a gang tends to have a definite status within the group. Common enterprises require a division of labor. Successful conflict necessitates a certain amount of leadership, unreflective though it may be, and a consequent subordination and discipline of members. As the gang develops complex activities, the positions of individuals within the group are defined and social roles become more sharply differentiated. As a result of this process there arises a more or less efficient and harmonious organization of persons [3] to make possible a satisfactory execution of collective enterprises and to further the interests of the group as a whole. This is the action pattern of the gang.

The conflicts of the gang with outsiders and the execution of its other enterprises and activities result in a sort of social stratification in its membership. There are usually three, more or less well-defined, classes of members: the "inner circle," which includes the leader and his lieutenants; the rank and file, who constitute members of the gang in good standing; and the "fringers," who are more or less hangers-on and are not considered regular members.

The inner circle is usually composed of a constellation of especially intimate pals formed about the leader. The rank and file—the less enterprising and less capable—are subordinated to the inner circle, just as it, in turn, tends to be subordinated to the leader. Most gangs are not closed corporations, however, but have a certain group of hangers-on or associates—the fringers, who may be "kid followers" or admirers. They constitute a sort of nebulous ring, not to be counted on to go the full length in any exploit and likely to disappear entirely in case of trouble. Yet the gang usually tolerates them for their applause and their occasional usefulness. A gang in embryo sometimes forms in this fringe.

## *The Struggle for Status*

Internally the gang may be viewed as a struggle for recognition.[4] It offers the underprivileged boy probably his best opportunity to acquire status and hence it plays an essential part in the development of his personality.

This struggle in the gang takes the form of both conflict and competition, which operate to locate each individual with reference to the others. As a result the gang becomes a constellation of personal interrelationships with the leader playing the central and guiding role. It may be considered as a "unity of interacting personalities"; but it may also be regarded as an accommodation of conflicting individualities more or less definitely subordinated and superordinated with reference to each other and the leader.

It is in these very roles, subordinate though they may be, that personality is developed. Any standing in the group is better than none, and there is always the possibility of improving one's status. Participation in gang

3 Like the family, the gang may be conceived of as a "unity of interacting personalities." See Burgess (1).

4 See Thomas (2, pp. 31–32).

activities means everything to the boy. It not only defines for him his position in the only society he is greatly concerned with, but it becomes the basis for his conception of himself. The gang boy might well say "I would rather be a fringer in the hang-out of the gang than to dwell in the swell joints of the dukes forever."

For this reason the gang boy's conception of his role is more vivid with reference to his gang than to other social groups. Since he lives largely in the present, he conceives of the part he is playing in life as being in the gang; his status in other groups is unimportant to him, for the gang is his social world. In striving to realize the role he hopes to take he may assume a tough pose, commit feats of daring or of vandalism, or become a criminal. Thus, his conception of his essential role as being in the gang helps to explain why the larger community finds difficulty in controlling him. If acquiring a court record, or being "put away" in an institution, gives him prestige in the gang, society is simply promoting his rise to power, rather than punishing or "reforming" him. Agencies which would attempt to redirect the boy delinquent must reach him through his vital social groups where an appeal can be made to his essential conception of himself.

## *The Process of Selection*

There is a process of selection in the gang, as a result of the struggle for status, whereby the ultimate position of each individual is determined. The result of this process depends largely upon the individual differences—both native and acquired—which characterize the members of the group. Other things being equal, a big strong boy has a better chance than a "shrimp." Natural differences in physique are important and physical defects play a part. Natural and acquired aptitudes give certain individuals advantages. Traits of character, as well as physical differences, are significant; these include beliefs, sentiments, habits, special skills, and so on. If all members of the gang were exactly alike, status and personality could only be determined by chance differences in opportunity arising in the process of gang activity. In reality, both factors play a part.

That physical differences are important in determining status is indicated by the fact that the biggest boy or the strongest is often leader by virtue of that fact alone, for bulk usually means an advantage in fighting. Mere size, too, may enable a bully to gain control of the gang; his tenure as leader, however, is always uncertain.

Physical disabilities often help to determine status in the gang, as elsewhere, through the mechanism of compensation. The defect in such cases serves as a drive to some type of behavior whose excellence will make up for the lowered status which the boy feels himself likely to possess on account of his disability. Compensation arises, therefore, because of the discrepancy between his possible role and his conception of the role he feels he ought to play.

If a boy can compensate in some effective manner for a disability, it may not serve as an insurmountable barrier to leadership.

Fighting is one of the chief means of determining status in the gang; each member is usually rated on the basis of his fistic ability. In a fight to determine which of two contenders is the better, the gang usually guarantees fair play, equalizing the conditions as nearly as possible. In some gangs the best fighter is considered the leader; he can defend his title against all comers.

In addition to fighting, excelling in any other activity in which the gang engages is a method of gaining recognition. For most gangs this applies particularly in the field of athletic prowess, but it may apply equally to some form of daring or predatory activity. "Hardness" is frequently a means of getting prestige; usually the boy who has been arrested, has a court record, or has been put away to serve a sentence is looked upon with admiration.

## *Special Roles in the Gang*

Besides leadership there are other social functions in the gang. Like leadership, these are also determined by individual qualities in the process of struggle and activity. They evolve as a result of group experience; they are determined by interaction in all of its complexities. The principal roles in the gang are sometimes distinguished from each other as being different types of leadership.[5]

If the imaginative boy does not have the qualities of geniality and physical force to give him pre-eminence, he may become the brains of the gang.

Like the jester of old, the "funny boy" is tolerated in spite of behavior that might otherwise be insulting. His irresponsibility is generally excused because of its humorous possibilities. This type of behavior is sometimes the result of an attempt to compensate for some trait—such as a high-pitched voice—which gives undesirable status in the gang.

A very undesirable status in the gang is that of a "sissy," a rating which may arise through effeminate traits, unwillingness to fight, or too much interest in books or other cultivated pursuits. It usually carries with it a girl's nickname. Ordinarily boys will go to any length to avoid such a role.

Another personality type which often emerges in the gang is the "show-off." He is the egotist, the braggart, the boaster, the bluffer, the "loud-mouth" of the group; and the other members usually discount him accordingly. He may resort to "loudness" to gain attention not otherwise

5 See Woods (3, pp. 115–116).

forthcoming, or, in his naïve conception of his role in the gang, he may simply be overestimating himself. His resulting status is certainly unforeseen by him and even unsuspected in certain cases.

Every gang usually has its "goat." He is a boy who is considered uncommonly "dumb"; he may be subnormal, as measured by psychological tests; and he can usually be depended upon to get caught if anybody does. Boys of this type are sometimes known as "goofy guys," if they combine some special peculiarity with their dumbness. Inexperienced boys are often used as "cats'-paws" in the exploits of the gang.

The nature, number, and variety of specialized roles, which in their interrelationships constitute the action pattern of the gang, must depend to a large extent upon the nature and complexity of the activities and enterprises undertaken. If the gang maintains a team, individual aptitudes play an important part in assigning places. Special abilities are useful in carrying out certain types of activities. The gang itself may become highly specialized (a functional type), as in the case of the development of some particular line of athletic sport or criminal pursuit. The more specialized the gang, the more highly differentiated is usually the division of labor among its members.

## REFERENCES

1. Burgess, E. W. The family as a unity of interacting personalities. *Family*, 1926, 3–9.
2. Thomas, W. I. *The unadjusted girl.*
3. Woods. *The city wilderness.*

# *Test Room Studies in Employee Effectiveness*

C. E. TURNER

THROUGH the courtesy of the Western Electric Company, a report is presented here upon the public health aspects of certain studies in the conduct of which the writer served as consultant. The investigations have been too extensive to be encompassed adequately in this

FROM *American Journal of Public Health*, 1933, 23, 577–584. Reprinted by permission of the author and publisher.

brief paper which will be limited to a description of this new type of industrial research and some of the major outcomes of the study.

The establishment of the test room study was the result of a 3-year investigation conducted by the company in cooperation with the National Research Council upon the relationship between illumination and the productivity of employees. A literal interpretation of the results would have suggested that poor illumination is desirable, for a comparison of two comparable groups of workers showed that those working with gradually reduced illumination had a higher output than those with ideal illumination. Such a conclusion would be obviously absurd.

What the investigation really showed was that the type of laboratory investigation which is possible in the exact sciences, where all but one factor can be controlled, is not possible in the study of human beings, and that other factors had entered the experiment which were more important than illumination. This suggested to G. A. Pennock, now Assistant Works Manager, the desirability of undertaking a study of employee effectiveness under test room conditions in which all of the factors affecting the physical and mental status of the worker could be observed with the greatest possible completeness. The company sought to learn those conditions under which people work best. We wished to study the human energy flowing into the product in order that we might deal with it more intelligently.

In April, 1927, 6 experienced female operators, chosen at random, were removed from the department in which they were working to a small test room in the corner of a regular shop. Their work was the assembly of telephone relays and involved putting together a coil, an armature, contact springs and insulators in a fixture, and securing the parts in position by means of four machine screws. The girls were invited to the office of the Superintendent in charge where the plan and objectives of the study were explained to them. Although shy at this first meeting, they readily consented to take part in the study. They were expressly cautioned to work at a comfortable pace and not to make a race out of the test.

The working equipment in the test room was like that in the regular department except that there was a hole in the bench at the right of each girl's position into which completed relays were dropped. The relay falls through a chute actuating a flapper gate. The opening of the gate closes an electrical circuit which controls a perforating device which in turn records the completion of the relay by punching a hole in a moving tape. This tape moves at the rate of $\frac{1}{4}''$ per minute and has space for a separate row of holes for each operator. The punched tape furnishes a complete output record for each girl for each instant of the day. The tape mechanism also carries a bank of 5 message registers giving a numerical record of the total number of relays completed by each operator.

As we began the test, our objectives were stated in the form of 6 questions:

1. Do employees actually get tired out?
2. Are rest pauses desirable?
3. Is a shorter working day desirable?
4. What is the attitude of employees toward their work and toward the company?
5. What is the effect of changing the type of working equipment?
6. Why does production fall off in the afternoon?

Fairly good answers have been secured to all of these questions except No. 5. New questions have constantly arisen and some of them have been satisfactorily answered.

Some description may well be given of the test room method as a means of research in industrial health and employee effectiveness. It is the observational method dealing simultaneously with many variables. Some factors can be controlled and made constant. One condition is changed at a time; but there are certain conditions which are not subject to experimental control. These must be watched carefully and interrelationships established. Too often scientists have been guilty of the *post hoc, ergo propter hoc* fallacy. They have changed one condition and regarded it as the cause of all subsequent events. Such factors as the physical or mental health or the attitude of the employee cannot, of course, be accurately measured quantitatively. Over long periods of time, however, many factors can be satisfactorily evaluated by means of proper statistical procedures.

Disregarding the problems of placement and working equipment, it has been our assumption that the effectiveness of an individual will vary with (a) his bodily status or physiological efficiency (health, skill, endurance); (b) his mental state (contentment and freedom from worry, fear, anger, hate, shame, or other morbid preoccupations); (c) his zest for work (determined by the enjoyment in performing the work, the feeling of justice in his treatment, and the desire for securing reward).

Certain specific changes having to do with the length of the working day or week, with the introduction of rest periods and with the sitting position of the operators have been made. These are described in Table 1.

At the beginning of the study, output records were kept for each girl in her regular department for 2 weeks without her knowledge. The girls were then moved to the test room where they worked for 5 weeks before any changes in working conditions were introduced. The intentional changes subsequently introduced have not by any means been the only ones studied. The following statement presents other differences which we have recognized between test room and shop conditions.

In the test room, the group piecework basis of payment paid each girl more nearly in proportion to her individual effort, since she was paid with a group of 6 instead of 100 or more. The girls in the test room assembled fewer different types of relays. The operators could read their exact output at any time from the recorder. The test room was not quieter; if anything, it was somewhat noisier than the regular department. New conditions of work provided an element of novelty. The girls realized that the experiment was receiving the attention of company officials, which meant that they were being noticed as individuals.

TABLE I

| PERIOD NUMBER | PERIOD NAME | DURATION |
|---|---|---|
| 1. | In Regular Department | 2 weeks |
| 2. | Introduction to Test Room | 5 " |
| 3. | Special Group Rate | 8 " |
| 4. | Two 5 Minute Rests | 5 " |
| 5. | Two 10 Minute Rests | 4 " |
| 6. | Six 5 Minute Rests | 4 " |
| 7. | 15 Minute a.m. Lunch 10 Minute p.m. Rest | 11 " |
| 8. | Same as No. 7, but 4:30 stop | 7 " |
| 9. | Same as No. 7, but 4:00 stop | 4 " |
| 10. | Same as No. 7, (Check) | 12 " |
| 11. | Same as No. 7, but Sat. a.m. off | 9 " |
| 12. | Same as No. 3, (No Lunch or Rests) | 12 " |
| 13. | Same as No. 7, but operators furnish own lunch. Company furnishes beverage | 31 " |
| 14. | Same as No. 11 | 9 " |
| 15. | Same as No. 13 | 31 " |
| 16. | Same as No. 13, except operators change position | 4 " |
| 17. | Same as No. 16, except 4:15 stop and Sat. a.m. off | 25 " |
| 18. | Same as No. 17, except Friday p.m. off | 15 " |

Beginning with Period 7, rest periods have begun at 9:30 in the morning and 2:30 in the afternoon.

There has been a fundamental change in supervision. There was no group chief in the test room, but instead a "friendly observer" of the experiment. Discipline was secured through leadership and understanding. The girls were allowed to talk and to leave the bench whenever they liked; they were not compelled to pick up parts from the floor at the time they were dropped. An *esprit de corps* grew up within the group.

The girls were given physical examinations every 6 weeks. They objected to this at first but later each trip to the hospital became a "party."

Three types of records are kept in the test room in order that changes may be determined in (1) output, (2) the individual, (3) conditions of work.

1. *Changes in production* may be accurately measured and constitute one evidence of the effectiveness of the worker. By means of a conversion factor, all output data were expressed in terms of a single type of relay. From the

output records previously mentioned, we have determined for each operator (1) the daily output; (2) the average hourly output at different times of day, for different days of the week and for different periods of the study; (3) average weekly output; (4) the number of defective relays; (5) the amount of repair work done. During the first few periods of the study, 15-minute output records were computed in order to study variability or uniformity of performance.

2. Data concerning *changes in the health, the habits, or the attitudes* of the operators have been secured from (1) physical examinations, (2) the comments of operators, (3) attendance irregularities, (4) occasional series for blood pressure and pulse rate records, (5) vascular skin reaction readings, (6) records of the hours of sleep, (7) social case records, (8) intelligence and dexterity tests, (9) questionnaires to reflect attitude toward working conditions, (10) diet records over certain periods.

3. *Changes in condition of work* have been indicated above. Records have also been kept of the types of relays assembled, the temperature and humidity of the room and any differences in the quality or methods of handling raw materials.

## FINDINGS

The first specific problem which the test room sought to study was the effect of rest pauses which were introduced in Period 4. We did learn much concerning rest pauses but soon found that there was a continually rising output in the test room which was in large measure at least independent of rest pauses. At the end of 4 years, the individual operators had increased their output from 40 to 62 per cent. The relationship of this increase to rest pauses is shown in Chart 1. It will be seen that output rose appreciably in Period 3 before rest periods were introduced. In Period 12, rest periods were entirely eliminated and during 12 weeks, output reached a new height. This continued and the unexpected increase in production which was independent of hours of work showed the absurdity of any experiment in which rest periods are introduced and changes in output ascribed to this cause without checking to see whether other factors may have been responsible. With the reintroduction of rest pauses in Period 13, total output rose still further.

We inevitably became more and more concerned with the task of finding the explanations for the remarkably increased output. Was it because of better health or at the expense of health of the worker? Was it due to lessened fatigue? Was it due to changed pay incentive? Was it due to an improved mental state on the part of the worker, to the elimination of unhappy preoccupations, or a greater zest for work?

These studies gave us new knowledge of two types: (1) more information concerning the relative importance of fatigue, working conditions and mental attitudes as factors in the increased output; (2) specific information concerning the effect upon employee efficiency of certain specific factors like sleep, rest pauses, and sitting position.

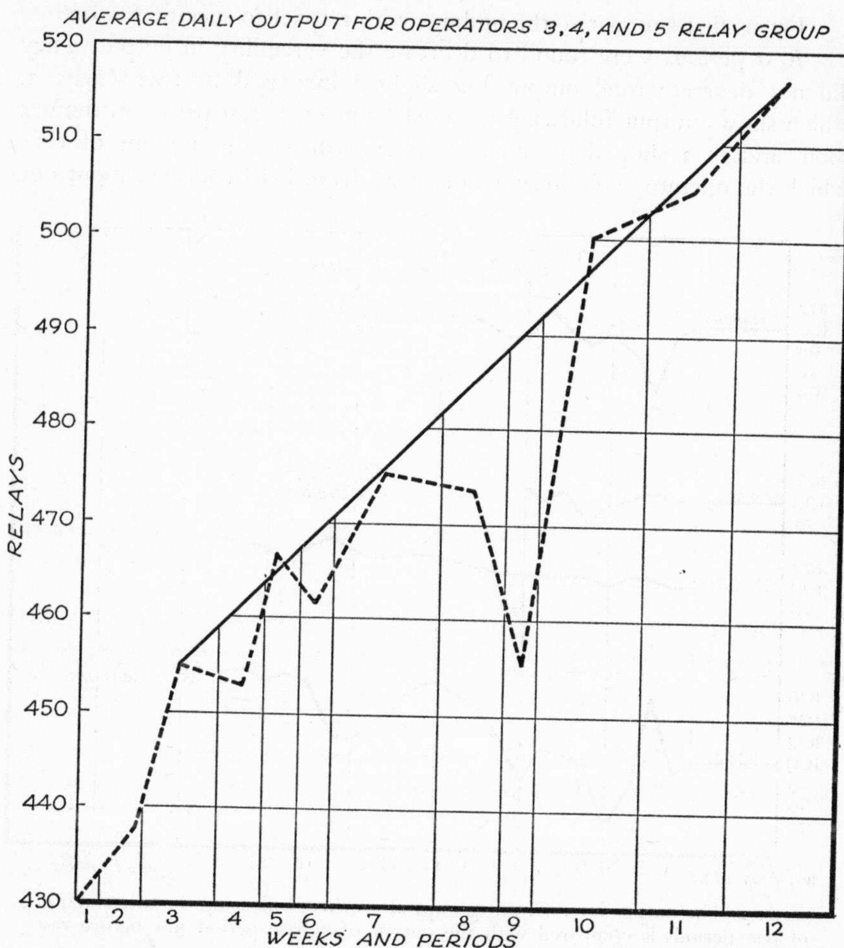


CHART 1. Solid line shows daily output increase from one full-day period to the next full-day period. Dotted line shows the actual average daily output. The work periods indicated at the bottom of the chart are as follows: (1) regular department (2 weeks), (2) test room (5 weeks), (3) special gang rate (8 weeks), (4) two 5-minute rests (5 weeks), (5) two 10-minute rests (4 weeks), (6) six 5-minute rests (4 weeks), (7) lunch rest (11 weeks), (8) lunch rest and 4:30 stop (7 weeks), (9) lunch rest and 4:00 stop (4 weeks), (10) same as period 7 (12 weeks), (11) lunch rest and Sat a.m. off (9 weeks), (12) same as No. 3 (12 weeks).

It is impossible to present here the detailed statistical evidence upon which conclusions are based. These data may be found in the Progress Reports issued by the company and it is probable that many of them will be included in a summarizing volume which is in preparation. We give a brief statement of the more important findings and ask the reader to check the statistical evidence from the Progress Reports if he wishes to do so.

Let us first summarize the findings with respect to specific factors:

*Rest periods* were found to decrease the variability in output. They did not decrease total output but slightly increased it. (See Chart 2, which shows output following the establishment of rest pauses in the test room and in 3 shop departments.) They reduced the amount of time which the operator voluntarily took away from her bench by about one

CHART 2. The output for different groups of workers following the introduction of rest periods is compared with the output of a base period just before rest pauses were put into effect.

half. Single 10- or 15-minute rest periods in the middle of the half day were preferred to more frequent shorter rest pauses.

The physical examinations showed that the increased output was not at the expense of the *health* of the worker. The health of the girls remained constant or improved slightly.

The question naturally arose as to whether the increased output was due to muscular *fatigue*. The study of the weekly output curve indicates that appreciable cumulative muscular fatigue does not exist. Vascular skin tests and pulse product readings were both taken to detect differences. They did not show cumulative fatigue and the latter test indicated less fatigue in this group than among workers in other occupations who had been tested elsewhere.

It seemed likely that the more satisfactory *basis of payment* may have been a factor in increasing output. We sought to check this by setting up 2 other test groups. One group of relay assemblers was left in the regular department but paid as a small group. A group of mica splitters who had always been paid on a straight piecework basis were put in a test room. With Group I, we administratively changed only the pay incentive, al-

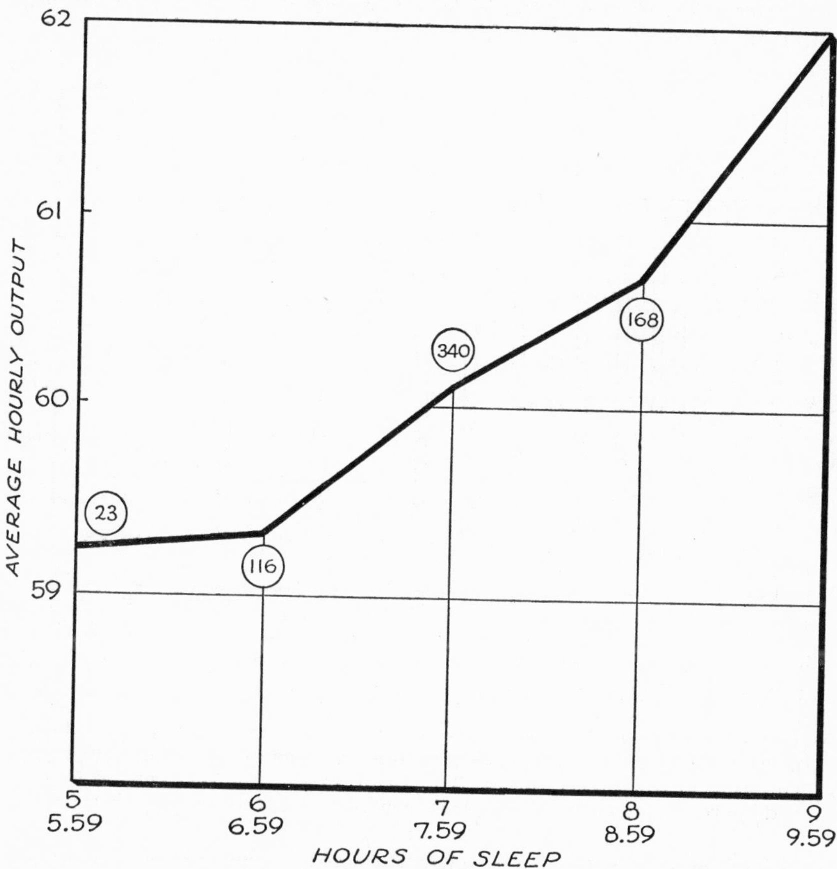


CHART 3. Comparison of output with hours of sleep showing an average of averages for 5 operators of the first relay assembly group. Figures in circles indicate the number of observations for each point.

though changes in attitude may also have taken place. With Group II, we provided test room conditions but did not change the pay incentive. The output in both groups went up over 10 per cent in a few months. We are inclined to believe that changed pay incentive may have been one factor in increasing output but it certainly was not the only factor.

An analysis of output on days following various amounts of *sleep* showed that sleep has a definite, though not a dominant effect on output. Chart 3.

A comparison of the output for the first hour after the operators changed from one type of relay to another with the average output for the first full day following such a change showed that there is not a decrease in output immediately after so slight a *change in the nature of the work*.

*Shortening the working week* did not show an increase in hourly output but shortening the working day did show such an increase. Chart

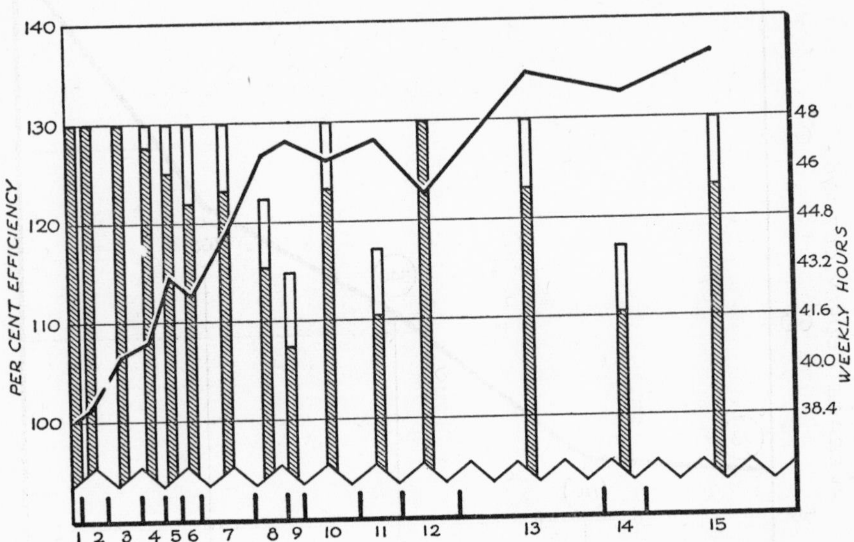


CHART 4. Percentage of efficiency in relationship to the length of the working week for operators 3 and 4 of the relay group. The types of working week in the different periods were as follows: (1) regular departments, (2) test room, (3) special gang rate, (4) two 5-minute rests, (5) two 10-minute rests, (6) six 5-minute rests, (7) a 15-minute morning rest with lunch and 10-minute afternoon rest, (8) same as No. 7 with 4:30 stop, (9) same as No. 7 with 4:00 stop, (10) same as No. 7, (11) same as No. 7 with Sat a.m. off, (12) same as No. 3 with no rests, (13) same as No. 7, (14) same as No. 11, (15) same as No. 13.

4 shows increases in efficiency when the week became shorter by reducing the length of the working day, but no increases when Saturday work was omitted. (Periods 11 and 14.)

The girls engaged in this type of work did not show a change in output during *menstrual periods*.

Changes in *sitting position* showed that the output of an operator is influenced by the workers sitting beside her.

Complete individual social case records were kept for test room employees. There is a definite relationship between output and satisfactory or unsatisfactory *home conditions and social relationships*.

We at first thought that the *novelty* of test room conditions might be partly responsible for increased output but the continuing increase in production over a 4-year period suggests that it was not of great importance. In the judgment of the girls themselves, certain elements of the test room situation were listed in the following order of importance: (1) the small group, (2) the type of supervision, (3) earnings, (4) novelty, (5) interest of the girls in the experiment, (6) the attention given in the test room by officials and investigators.

In order to test the effect which the test room observer himself might have upon the group, the one who had been in the test room since its beginning was removed and his assistant placed in charge. The supervision in the test room remained approximately the same; there seemed to be no measurable effect which could be assigned to the change in personalities.

# CHAPTER 3
# CURRENT THEORY

## *The Equilibrium of Groups*

ELIOT D. CHAPPLE and CARLETON S. COON

A STATE of equilibrium may be defined as follows: if a small force is impressed upon a system, a change or adjustment takes place within the system, and once this force is removed, the system returns to approximately its previous state.

States of equilibrium are characteristic not only of individuals, but also of groups of individuals. In other words, the individuals of whom a group is composed adjust their interaction rates to each other; as they separately attain equilibrium, the group attains it likewise. Therefore a disturbance which upsets the equilibrium of one member will affect the others also.

If one of the members of a family becomes sick, we can observe how the relations of the group change in response to the new situation. This change is particularly evident if the sick person is one who works in an office and is habitually away from home most of the day. The daily visits of the doctor introduce a new person into the system of relations which we are studying, a person, furthermore, to whom all members of the family have to adjust. Secondly, the constant requirements of the patient greatly increase the frequency of interaction between him (or her) and the members of the family who live at home. In the third place, the normal

FROM *Principles of anthropology*. New York: Henry Holt & Co., 1942. Reprinted by permission of the authors and publisher.

interaction rates between the members of the family living at home are disturbed. As the patient's health improves, these disturbances of the family equilibrium decrease; when the patient returns to work, the quantitative character of the relations within the family becomes approximately what it was before the illness started.

At this point, it may be profitable to remind the reader that the equilibrium of the internal environment, the equilibrium of the individual in relation to others, and the equilibrium of the group are similar and related phenomena. We have pointed out that disturbances in the external environment produce consequent disturbances in the internal environment, and vice versa. The actions of others stimulate the autonomic nervous system, and a change in the internal environment, as for example a severe illness accompanied by a rise in temperature, produces marked changes in the interaction rate between the affected individual and his group.

Since the equilibrium of an individual depends upon the differences between the interaction rates of the persons with whom he interacts, one of the commonest phenomena which can disturb his equilibrium is a change in the personnel of his group. Changes of this type include the loss of a member, the substitution of one member for another, and the addition of a new individual to the already existing personnel.

If one wishes to discover whether or not a given group of individuals (for example, five persons) has attained a state of equilibrium, he may do so by applying two tests. The first of these is to observe whether or not the rates of interaction between the individuals in the group are constant within clearly defined limits; that is, whether or not significant increases or decreases are taking place in the frequency of events, in the origin-response ratio, in the interaction rate within the event, and in the degree of synchronization. If the rates are constant and no such changes are taking place, equilibrium has been attained.

The second test is to see whether or not, after a disturbance takes place, the rates return to their previous values. They will do this if the group is in a state of equilibrium. When the personnel of such a group is changed, however, the previous state of equilibrium cannot be restored, unless the new member has exactly the same interaction rate as the person whom he has replaced, which rarely happens.

When one member of our group of five individuals dies, changes in the relations of all members must take place before the group can attain a new state of equilibrium. In the development of this new equilibrium, each individual must adjust his own rates in some way. Let us suppose that one of the members, A, has been interacting daily for about an hour a day at a given rate with B, the deceased member. If A is to maintain his state of equilibrium, or at least return to a state somewhat similar to his old one, he must find some outlet for the interaction to which he was accustomed. This means that, in order to make up for what he has lost, he will have to increase his interaction with one or more persons, either within the circle of the surviving members of the group, or outside it. His interaction rate, and the rates of the persons to whom he makes his new adjustment, must be synchronized if his previous equilibrium is to be restored. If this cannot be done, he will try to attain a new state of equilibrium at a different level of interaction.

Similar readjustments take place when a new individual is substituted for the deceased member. In this case, the new person will almost certainly have an interaction rate different from that of his predecessor, and he will consequently produce a different state of equilibrium in each of the other members. The amount of interaction which he contributes may be greater or smaller than that provided by the previous member; the new man may also have a much higher origin rate, or again, he may have a slow and phlegmatic rate of interaction. In any case, the other members of the group will be obliged to adjust to him, as he will to them. This process of mutual adjustment takes place slowly; the original members must be conditioned to the newcomer, and the reverse.

Let us consider a third situation, in which a new individual is added to the group without the loss of an original member. In this case, two results usually occur; the older members of the group adjust themselves to the newcomer, and the increase in the number of individuals concerned often causes a decrease in the individual interactions that take place. The resulting interaction rates represent a new distribution of the separate rates of the constituent individuals.

The process of adjustment which takes place within a group as the aftermath of a disturbance is marked by cyclical fluctuations; by days on which the members of the group fail to adjust, interrupt each other, become angry, and are unable to work together—days on which the regular routine, to which the members have been conditioned, is upset. As the group gradually regains its equilibrium, the range of these fluctuations decreases and the rhythm of the routine interactions becomes more constant.

As we can readily understand through our knowledge of the conditioning process, the degree to which a state of equilibrium becomes stable depends upon the length of time that the interaction rates, of which the equilibrium is composed, remain constant. This is equally true in respect to individuals and to groups. The longer, therefore, the individual or the group maintains his, or its, equilibrium, the more fixed and automatic will the conditioning of the individual, or individuals, concerned become.

The degree of stablity has an important bearing on the ability of the individual or group to withstand disturbances of equilibrium; as a rule, the greater the stability, the stronger and, at the same time, less elastic is the state of equilibrium. For example, a group with a high interaction rate and a long history of continued stability will maintain its equilibrium under the impact of powerful external forces, but an internal change, such as the loss of a member, will produce serious effects, and its adjustment to a new equilibrium after the loss will be a slow and difficult process, if such an adjustment can be made at all.

There is, therefore, a great difference between groups, as well as between the individuals of whom they are composed, in their ability to withstand major changes of environment; and this ability depends in part, as we have seen above, on the relative stability of the states of equilibrium concerned.

# *The Analysis of Situational Fields in Social Psychology*

LEONARD S. COTTRELL, JR.

IN COMMON with many others operating in the vague and complex field of social psychology, I find it impossible at this juncture to produce a logically rigorous system of assumptions and concepts with which to analyze and interpret human social interaction. Notwithstanding the rickety condition of the present formulation, I deem it worthwhile to expose it for critical examination by fellow workers in the hope of gaining new perspectives on it myself.[1]

There are no essentially new terms in this formulation. I am particularly aware of the influence on my own thinking of the work of Charles H. Cooley, George H. Mead, Ellsworth Faris, Sigmund Freud, and Kurt Lewin. Those familiar with recent developments in social psychology will also see that the present statement is in line with a general current which is also manifest in the work of H. S. Sullivan, R. D. Lasswell, J. L. Moreno, Karen Horney, Erich Fromm, W. L. Warner, and many others.

In what follows, I shall be taking the position, familiar to most sociologists, (1) that any item of social behavior is understood only as it is

FROM *American Sociological Review*, 1942, 7, 370-382. Reprinted by permission of the author and publisher.

1 I wish to express my appreciation for the many helpful suggestions I have received from Ruth Gallagher Goodenough, Ward H. Goodenough, and Ralph White with whom I have frequently discussed the ideas in this paper.

seen as a functional part of a situation composed of interacting selves; (2) that in functioning in an interactive system, the organism not only develops the response patterns representing its part in such an interact but actually incorporates the response patterns of the other(s) in its reactive system; and (3) that when one elaborates the two foregoing assumptions into a working system of social psychology, he finds it necessary to modify radically the atomistic methods of traditional psychology which treat of reflexes, traits, motives, and various other behavioral syndromes which are referred to the individual with a minimum of attention to precise specification of the interactive context.[2]

## I. ILLUSTRATIVE MATERIAL

I shall begin this discussion by introducing some very simple concrete materials to which it may be convenient to refer later. These materials will also serve to indicate a few of the problems of interpretation for which I believe the situational approach offers a possible solution.

*First Illustration.* *B* (aged 14 months) was as curious about his environment as most children of his age. The knobs on the gas cook stove were particularly fascinating. The mother, though usually rather patient and indulgent toward his explorations, met these particular manipulative efforts with very firm "No! No's!," pulling him away and starting him off in other directions. After this interact had been repeated several times, *B* found the field clear for another try. He pulled up to the knobs and as he started to take hold he suddenly let loose a torrent of "No! No! No's!" with vigorous shaking of his head; whereupon he backed off to survey the situation. He seemed a little surprised at hearing the parental admonition when no parent was present but he took another look and repeated the whole act again. He finally crashed through this rudimentary conscience and twisted the forbidden knobs, at which point adult intervention ended the scene.

This performance is interpreted here as a simple instance in which the child manifested an incorporated (introjected) act of the other and responded to his own action with the action of the other. At a later stage in his career, he may refer to certain of such "other" parts of self-other patterns as his conscience.

*Second Illustration.* At a later age (26 months), the child mentioned above put on more complicated performances which may be regarded as manifestations of his introjection of more complex "other" activity. A fairly typical instance may be cited.

One late afternoon near the dinner hour, *B* knotted his face into something of a scowl and pitched his normally low voice into something approaching an infant growl.

2 This type of treatment has its uses and is entirely suitable for many purposes but not for analysis of social interactional phenomena.

"I want some meat for my supper," he said to his mother. Then added, "I'm daddy and I've come home from work." The mother took the cue and addressed him as daddy, asked how his little boy *B* was, etc., etc.

At the table, he insisted on taking his father's place at the head of the table, assigning the displaced parent to the high chair. He wished to serve but had to submit (after some protest) to being assisted in this part of his role. He admonished "*B*" not to spill his "brown milk" referring to the father's coffee. He referred to his milk as "white coffee," saying only big people could drink white coffee. After the meal, *B* continued to act in his capacity as daddy and "read" a story to his "son" and finally undertook to put him to bed. The father finally balked at being put in the crib, giving as his reason that the crib might break down. The two then agreed to "pretend" to put the father in the crib.

It is interesting to note that if the father acted out of character, *B* prompted him with very definite direction as to how "*B*" should act. Moreover if the mother or the maid did not treat *B* himself as father and the father as *B*, they were peremptorily put back into the proper relationship by *B*.

*Third Illustration.* *Y*, a woman aged 35, was the second of three children. The oldest child was a boy and the youngest, a girl. The father was a very adequate person and a benevolent patriarch. All the family seemed devoted to him, but *Y* was his favorite child from the time of her birth. When the younger daughter was born, *Y*, at that time about four, became very ill and the father gave her all of his attention. From that time on, *Y* was practically an invalid. She consistently regarded herself as weak, helpless, and dependent. She expected and received the appropriate solicitous behavior from family and friends. She was suspected of tuberculosis, anemia, etc. No positive findings were made and no treatment was effective. Meanwhile, the father gave most of his time and interest to his sick daughter. If the daughter improved a little and essayed a trip, she would become ill and her father would have to go for her and bring her home. There grew up between father and daughter a very intimate bond of communication and understanding. This "conditioning" of *Y* went on until she was nearly 30 years of age. At that time, her father died suddenly after a brief illness.

The day after his death, *Y*, who for nearly 30 years could hardly climb the stairs, got up, took the dazed family in hand, directed arrangements for the funeral, supervised the settling of the estate, and went off to take a short business course in order to prepare herself for a job. She already knew much about her father's business and, with her special preparation, she brushed her older brother aside and took over the supervision of the father's business and made a success of it. She has become the "father" of the family, and is now locally famous for her advocacy of vigorous living. Her father had been quite a water sportsman; she became an even better one. In many ways, she manifested her vigorous responsibility-assuming attitudes in her relations with others.

Apparently her illness was functional rather than organic. But leaving aside this and other interesting problems in the case, we are interested here in interpreting the shift in personality as a manifestation of a rather complete incorporation of the father's role. With this interpretation, *Y's* behavior becomes intelligible. For example, she does not expect her brother and the other members of her family to become independent. She expects them to be dependent upon her for leadership and aid. With the suggested interpretation, we are not surprised at this attitude toward the other members of her family. Nor shall we be surprised if she should show a reversion to her former dependent, cared-for self if she ever falls in love with an adequate, solicitous older man. On the other hand, she may well marry or otherwise take unto herself a very dependent to-be-cared-for person to fuss over.

*Fourth Illustration.* The following experiment was tried in a class in social psychology.

A case study was broken up into descriptions of behavior of the person in different areas of his life activity. Each separate description was read to the class and the students were asked to rate the subject on a few traits on the basis of the single description. The raters were told that each description was of a different person. This may be illustrated by giving two condensed descriptions and the resulting median ratings from one case.

Description of *A*, aged 10: "The parents complain that *A*, their oldest child, is a very difficult child at home. He is moody, sulks a lot, refuses to cooperate, does his work under protest, fights and bullies the younger children, and is frequently very cruel to them. He is always causing a quarrel or a fight and is stubborn and defiant in his attitude toward the parents . . . , etc."

Description of *B*, aged 10: "When the teachers referred *B* to the clinic, he was described as a very isolated and shy child. He did what he was required to do in class work but was very timid and diffident about participating in discussions or volunteering to do anything. He was always on the sidelines in anything the class or play groups did. He was frequently bullied by children smaller and younger than himself, and never seemed to stand up for himself with his equals or superiors. He cried easily and seemed to have a general feeling of inferiority. He frequently daydreamed in class . . . , etc."

The group of raters was then told that the excerpts represented rating on the same personality. The group was then asked to rate the person on the basis of their knowledge of him in all of the different situations from which the various descriptions of him were derived. This assignment was found to be very difficult and no one was satisfied with his ratings. The ratings showed more scatter than did the ratings on separate situations. When questioned as to how they decided on a general rating some were found to have struck some kind of informal average; others rated the person on what was probably his most frequently manifested behavior; still others rated the person on what they decided was his "truest" self.

If time permitted us to present an analysis of this case, it could be shown that the different behavior patterns of the child in question were functionally related to the particular roles or positions he had in the different situations. The adjustive work which was intensive and resulted in considerable success was chiefly a matter of establishing the child in a different relationship to the situations in which he was having difficulty, partly by situational changes and partly by helping him to redefine his situations.

*Fifth Illustration.* A university personnel office referred a secretary for consultation. The difficulty seemed to be that although a very skillful worker, she couldn't or wouldn't hold a position very long. The interviews revealed that no matter what the job situation appeared to be when she started it, she would very shortly establish a relationship with the other members of the staff in which she perceived herself to be the object of antagonism and injustice. The interpretation drawn from her history rested chiefly on the rigid conception of a self-other pattern in which she expected rejection and hostility and reacted by retaliative behavior. This frame of relationships she projected on every new situation.

## II. SOME PROPOSITIONS CONCERNING INTERPERSONAL BEHAVIOR

The foregoing concrete instances suggest certain ideas which may be stated in the form of propositions. The general point of view may be tested by determining the truth or falsity of these propositions. They are presented not as proved principles but as propositions to be tested.

The following propositions refer to interpersonal activity. Later we shall indicate the way this frame of reference may be applied to interaction of groups.

I. When human organisms respond to each other over a period of time, the activity of each becomes the stimulus pattern for a more or less stabilized response pattern in the other(s), assuming that the motivational components remain essentially unchanged.

*Definition 1.* A series of conditioned acts comprising the reciprocal responses of all members of a social situation is referred to as an interact pattern.

*Definition 2.* An internally consistent series of conditioned responses by one member of a social situation which represents the stimulus pattern for the similarly internally consistent series of conditioned responses of the other(s) in that situation is called a role.

II. The impact upon one human organism, *A*, of the activities of another, *B*, not only stimulates and conditions a response pattern of *A* to *B* but also conditions in *A* the response pattern of *B* to *A as A has perceived that action*, and vice versa. The latter pattern is not necessarily manifested overtly but must be assumed to exist at least in incipient or attitudinal form.

(This process of responding by reproducing the acts of the other(s) has been referred to by various writers as taking the role of the other, identification, introjection, sympathy, empathy, imitation.)

*Definition 3.* This process of "double conditioning" is referred to as the incorporation or internalization of an interact pattern.

*Definition 4.* An internalized interact is referred to as a self-other pattern.

III. It follows from II that each member of an interpersonal relationship is not only conditioned to respond to the acts of the other(s) with his own act series but is conditioned to respond to his own response series as a stimulus series with actions he incorporates from the other(s).

Hence, after the interactive experience has been repeated enough times, it is possible for each member to carry out the entire interact alone, at least in incipient form.

Propositions I–III may be crudely represented schematically in the following diagrams.

1. Assume two unconditioned organisms *A* and *B* with motives $S_A^D$ and $S_B^D$ respectively. Assume further that the activities of each become a stimulus series for the other. This condition can be represented thus:

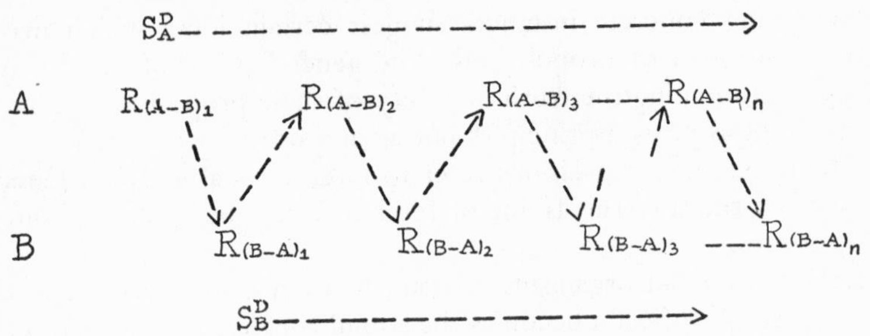


where $S^D$ is the motivational component and $R_{(A-B)}$ and $R_{(B-A)}$ are the responses of *A* to *B* and *B* to *A* respectively.

2. Let the conditions in 1 be repeated a number of times and by proposition II, we have:

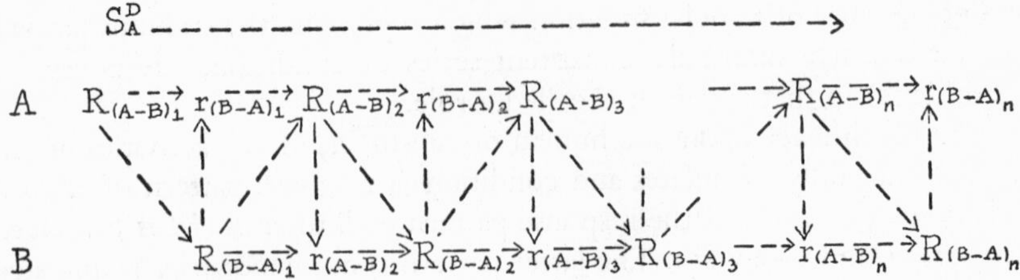


where *r* represents the incorporated response of the other.

The responses of each have now been incorporated by the other as expected "other" responses to the own-self responses.

3. When responses represented in 2 have been established, it is then possible for each member of the pair to carry out the interact in incipient form, thus:

$$S_A^D \dashrightarrow$$

$$(A \leftarrow\!-\!\rightarrow B') \quad r_{(\bar{A}-\bar{B})_1} \dashrightarrow r_{(\bar{B}-\bar{A})_1} \dashrightarrow r_{(\bar{A}-\bar{B})_2} \dashrightarrow r_{(\bar{A}-\bar{B})_n} \dashrightarrow r_{(B-A)_n}$$

and $(B \leftrightarrow A')$ can be similarly represented. Where $B'$ and $A'$ represent the incorporated response series of $B$ into $A$ and $A$ into $B$ respectively.

The instances cited above in First and Second Illustrations will serve as very simple illustrations of the processes considered in Propositions I–III.

If these propositions can be proved, then in analyzing or treating personalities, it becomes necessary to assume that the reactive system includes not only those response patterns the person has manifested but also the response patterns of the others of his life situations. Thus, from this point of view the rebellious child is also in part the authoritarian parent; the saint is part sinner; the communist is part capitalist; the Southern White is part Negro psychologically.

IV. The self-other patterns of each member of an interact system are frequently not congruent. The more intimate the contact through time, the greater will be the tendency for the patterns to coincide. (Exceptions to this latter statement will be found in cases where personality structures are extremely rigid such as those found among neurotics.)

V. A self-other pattern once established tends to persist either as a dynamic tendency (if motivational components remain integrated with it) or as a latent pattern which can be reproduced, given appropriate situational and motivational conditions. (See Third and Fourth Illustrations above.)

VI. A self-other pattern once established tends to be projected on new interact situations unless the components and structure of the field are very unlike that in which the pattern was developed. Projection means here, that if through interaction, $A$ has developed a self-other pattern of $(A \leftrightarrow B')$, then if *A's* contact with $C$ is not too unlike that with $B$, $A$ will expect $B'$ behavior from $C$ and will behave toward $C$ in terms of those expectations. If $C$ does not fit the pattern, an exploratory period will yield a self-other pattern in $A$ of $(A \leftrightarrow C')$.

Under certain conditions, the personality is rendered so insecure by having to develop new relational patterns that it clings rigidly to those it has even where they are maladaptive to the objective situation as seen by an observer. (See Fifth Illustration above.)

VII. Self-other patterns established early in the life of the organism are more likely to be persistent and pervasive than are those acquired later.

1. The earlier patterns are projected on a wider variety of new, later, situations. By reacting to anticipated "other" responses, the person is more likely to receive the responses he expects. This process reinforces the previous self-other pattern.

2. Feelings of anxiety arising from having to function in an unknown pattern of interaction will tend to reinforce those patterns which have already been established even though they may appear to an observer to result in frustrations.

VIII. From I, II, and III it follows that every interact series that becomes established as an incorporated self-other pattern provides the organism with two or more (depending on the number of roles in the pattern) response systems or roles. The interact ($A \leftrightarrow B$) produces a self-other pattern in $A$ of $A$ and $B'$ and in $B$ of $A'$ and $B$. Under certain conditions, $A$ will act overtly in the role $B'$ rather than as $A$.

This fact is of considerable importance in accounting for or predicting major changes in personality. (See Second and Third Illustrations.)

IX. The human organism will incorporate a limited number of self-other patterns with which it functions in the series of situational fields in which it exists.

*Definition 5.* Personality is the population of self-other patterns and their intra-personal organization. (See Fourth Illustration.)

X. The personality system includes self-other patterns developed by other persons and acquired through the process of identification.

Propositions concerning the factors which govern the selection of identification patterns cannot be presented now. Motivational factors, personality structure and situational pressures all operate in determining the selection.

XI. The self-other patterns composing a personality are not all given direct overt expression with equal frequency or completeness. Certain patterns will dominate the system while others remain latent or gain indirect expression.

Propositions covering the determinants of dominance cannot be presented here. The three general factors mentioned in connection with Proposition X are the important ones.

XII. All personality systems are subject to internal stress due to the activity of contradictory roles. The greater the number of incompatible roles and the more overlapping the situations are which evoke them, the greater the amount of conflict in the personality.

XIII. Persons seek to minimize conflict by: (1) living within a restricted and simply structured field; (2) keeping separated those situations requiring incompatible roles; (3) remaining "unconscious" of contradictory roles by such mechanisms as projection, reaction formation, conversion, etc.; (4) developing a master definition of the situation such as a philosophy of history, a theology, or a philosophy of life which gives consistency, meaning, and integration to their various patterns.

XIV. The person responds in a social situation according to his own definition of the situation.

This definition will usually deviate from that of an observer, unless or until the latter is closely identified with the former. (See Proposition II.)

*Definition 6.* By the social situation is meant the system of self-other patterns comprising a given interact. (The terms social situation and social interact as used here are equivalent and may be used interchangeably.)

*Definition 7.* By definition of the situation is meant the system of expected "other" responses aroused in a given personality by a given situation.

From Definitions 6 and 7 it is evident that a social situation as seen by an observer may not coincide with a given participant's definition of it. Moreover, the various participants will necessarily have differing definitions of the situation. This raises the interesting questions of how consensus is achieved, how communication takes place, and how we understand another person. These are subjects which call for the formulation and testing of additional propositions.

XV. It follows from the foregoing propositions that understanding the behavior of a personality requires an observer to comprehend its several definitions of the situation. This calls for a partial identification with the subject.

XVI. It follows further that items of behavior such as attitudes, traits, etc., studied apart from the context provided by the actor's definition of the situation, yield meaningless results.

If these propositions are valid, they call for a radical shift in much of our methodology in social psychology. (See Fourth Illustration above.)

## III. APPLICATION TO ANALYSIS OF COLLECTIVE BEHAVIOR

The foregoing propositions have been aimed at the analysis of interpersonal relations. If space permitted, we could show that with slight modifications, the same general propositions would hold when applied to behavior in and between groups. To discuss group interaction, we do not need to desert the vocabulary we have found useful in describing individual personality phenomena. Groups of individuals occupy functional positions in relation to other groups, and the overt behavior characteristics, ideologies, and frames of reference which individual members show are functionally related to these positions.

This approach to group interaction focuses attention upon the way an individual actually participates in intergroup relations, upon the meaning of these relations to the individuals involved. Symbols have meaning when they arouse an incorporated structure of acts. Group interaction is mediated by symbolic tags, which serve to identify self and "other" roles for groups. These tags, or symbols of identification, refer to an act and counteract structure in which the "I" or self role is actually a "we" role, and the role of the other is the behavior expected from any member of a group of others, or a "they" role.

The average individual in our society is able to act in the name of many such symbolized groups. His role for some of them is laid down in very early interaction, for instance his role as a member of a particular family in the community, or the roles appropriate to sex or class positions. Other worlds of secondary symbolic participation open up to him as he matures, so that he comes to have as many symbolized selves as there are groups which claim his allegiance. Which of these selves gains overt expression at a given time depends upon the way in which self-other relations of a particular moment are perceived by the actor. In times of international crisis, the individual's attention is directed consistently toward the stage on which national symbols represent the acting roles. He interprets the acts of other national groups from his position as an American or as a Briton or as a German. He feels insecure when a hostile national group increases its armed strength, or he feels righteous and belligerent when his personal surrogate is able to wave the Big Stick. Similarly his attention is drawn to a field dominated by the symbols "capital" and "labor," when he becomes aware of his interests involved on that front. His identification with one or the other of these groups provides him with a role position from which to perceive and interpret events and actions in this particular field.

Group interaction of this sort can be arrested at almost any degree of inclusiveness, simply by defining a dominant "we-they" relationship. A skillful employer can block attempts to organize his workers if he can keep racial, national, or religious antagonisms alive. Indeed, the formula "divide and rule," expressed in situational terms, means to prevent effective opposition by defining the field for interaction about irrelevant or less inclusive symbols. The Ministry of Propaganda of the German Reich uses this technique to disable the nations it opposes, while at the same time it subordinates every other symbol of identification within Germany to establish the supremacy of the national symbol.

Propaganda, from this point of view, is simply a technique for defining fields of group interaction and for keeping the focus of attention on these fields. Groups that play for high stakes of power and prestige must develop refined propaganda methods, first of all to hold group interaction in desired areas of "we-they" relationships, and then to control the specific expectancy patterns of those relationships.

Space does not allow for further elaboration of the application of situational analyses to collective behavior. Enough has been said to indicate the general line along which such applications might proceed.

## IV. THE SOCIAL ACT

The discussion thus far has been centered on the patterning of a series of reciprocally related responses of two or more social selves. Motivational components of these acts have been indicated but the integration of a theory of motivation and the present theory has not been made explicit. The limits of this paper permit of only a bare indication of the way this problem may be approached.

An adequate conception of the social act and the ways it may be analyzed seems to me to furnish an excellent lead to the desired integration. A social act is conceived of here as a series of reciprocally related acts by units called selves, which series forms a dynamic perceptual unit. The general form consists of a beginning or precipitating condition, the definition of goals or end relations toward which the interacting units conceive themselves to be moving, a series of relevant intermediate activities, and finally some kind of end-state of relationship of the implicated selves.[3] This end-state varies in its degree of permanence. A social act is usually not perceived in the same way by actors and observers of the social act. Thus, a social act which one may describe as a parent disciplining his child may be perceived by the child as an unwarranted aggression by a stupid but powerful bully, by the parent as an unpleasant part of the task of fitting the child for participation in larger social acts of the family and community life, and by an observer as an overt expression of jealousy which the parent holds toward the child and rationalizes as parental duty. The social act of a strike or a war is too obviously a differently defined experience by participants to need elaboration here. To understand the behavior of a participant, it is therefore necessary to perceive the social act as he does—his notion of how it started, the goals he perceives for himself and the other selves implicated and the functional relevance he assigns to the intermediate activity.

This conception of the social act calls for two supplementary modes of analysis which, used separately, yield incomplete knowledge but together provide a relatively complete frame of reference which will make intelligible most if not all behavior with which the social psychologist is concerned.

1. Human social activity may be analyzed as motivated or goal-directed actions. The analytical problem is to determine the motives and goals.

3 It should be noted that a social act may take place intrapersonally among the selves composing a part or all of a single personality.

2. Goal-seeking activity which concerns the social psychologist always implicates more than one self. Hence, the motivational analysis must be supplemented by an analysis of the self-other patterns which emerge out of and function in the interaction of motivated organisms. Two organisms may both need affection but the self-other pattern into which this motive has been integrated may differ widely.

It may be well to add the caution that motive-goal analysis when used alone tends to reify such terms as affection, security, etc., as entities the organism wants. It must always be kept in mind that satisfactions or goal responses classed as affection, security, etc., involve a set of responses that must be made to the self's acts. Hence, the goal is not a "thing" but a reciprocal system of activity. Barriers which block the organism are not static elements of a maze he must learn but are responses which other interacting selves make to his acts. These barriers may be overt responses from others objectively present or introjected patterns within the personality system.

From this discussion it will be seen that the boundaries of a social act are determined with respect (1) to goals, and (2) to the interacting self-other patterns implicated in the activity. On the goal-directed axis, we may say a social act begins when a terminal or goal response is defined. The end point in the act lies between two points on the continuum. The first is that point at which, if the action is stopped, the symptoms of frustration would be at a maximum. The second is that point at which, if the action is stopped, the symptoms of frustration would be minimal.

On the interact axis, the social act is limited by what we have called the person's definition of the situation. (See Definition 7.)

A great many important implications for social psychological analysis emerge from this view of the social act but discussion of them must be omitted.

## V. SOME IMPLICATIONS

The theoretical orientation suggested in this paper implies a good many changes in research method as well as in practical techniques in therapeutic procedures, in education for social living, as well as in the way people approach the actual problems of living together in the family, the community, and the world.

*Research Method.* The theoretical position outlined here does not require one to question the value for many purposes of much experimental work and measurement of abstracted trait attributes which may justifiably be called atomistic and which have passed for social psychological research. However, it makes it necessary to insist that such work be deliberately and self-consciously oriented to a situational frame of reference. Attitudes, motives, traits, emotions, opinions, and national, and racial group characteristics can no longer be studied in abstraction or with vague references to "the general social situation" if results are to have any meaning. The behavior indicated by such terms must be tied to a specifically defined social interact frame. Predictions of behavior must be made in terms of probable behavior in a specified situational context as perceived by the actor. This of course requires a vocabulary adapted to situational description. It also requires an enormous amount of research to establish major types of social situational patterns in which the persons must function.

Perhaps the most important methodological implication is the one calling for skills by which an investigator can assimilate himself to the acting perspective of his subject, individual or group. Such skills are sometimes referred to as intuition, sympathetic or empathetic introspection, identification-projection, role taking, etc. Whatever the name and whatever the actual process, the proposed orientation requires that the processes involved be made as explicit as possible and as subject to testing, verification, and operational formulation as possible. The way this method is made more explicit and subject to testing may not, to be sure, be the same way in which other methodological devices are handled, but that does not essentially alter the requirement.

*Therapeutic Method*. The marked shifts in phrasing the therapeutic problem and in therapy itself may be appreciated by a review of the recent work of Fromm (1), Horney (2, 3), Moreno (4, 5), and Sullivan (6). Instead of seeking for the traumatic cyst in the psyche, the complex, or the strayed libido, the focus is on the self-other patterns and their genesis, distortions, projection, etc., as seen in actual operation in the interview, on the clinical stage, and as reported from extraclinical experiences. Problem behavior is not given a clinical name and treated as a disease entity but is regarded as a function of the situational fields and the positions in them which the subject represents. The various innovators in psychiatric therapeutic work state their orientation and therapeutic procedures differently, but it is not hard to see that they all point in the direction of a situational orientation.

*Education*. There are obviously many implications for formal as well as informal education relevant to the development of a healthy basic self-other orientation. I wish to suggest what this view of human behavior implies for education for citizenship. One of the deepest problems of modern society is to deal with the profound and dangerous cleavages that threaten the basic consensus on which the society rests. Totalitarianism is one answer to the intransigent oppositions generated in western cultures. A democratic solution of the problem requires that the citizens interacting in their roles as members of opposing groups become increasingly able to take the roles of their opponents. It is only through this ability that integrative solution of conflict rather than armed truces can be arrived at. Education for citizenship must develop content and techniques in social studies that will enable the child and youth readily to see the community and the world through the eyes of persons occupying many different functional positions in his society. This is important not only in education for living with and solving problems with different race, class, and national groups, but in education for marriage and family living as well.

I suspect that a major shift must take place from teaching mere abstract knowledge about society to greater emphasis on the presentation of life experiences of many different persons with whom the student may become identified and thus experience the world and its problems as others of his society experience it.

*Social Adjustments.* The opportunity to observe persons operating in marriage, parent-child, and local community relations has left me with a very definite opinion that facility for seeing situational relations and a wide range of genuine (not merely verbal) role taking ability greatly increases the probabilities that conflicts and maladjustments will be dealt with integratively and constructively rather than in repressive destructive ways. Attribute thinking about and diagnoses of social problems leads to witch-hunting and futile efforts to exterminate the bad. Situational thinking and role taking skill open up broad possibilities for creative inventions of techniques and social arrangements for treating and preventing disintegrative and destructive processes.

## REFERENCES


1. Fromm, E. Die psychoanalytische Characterologie und ihre Bedeutung für die Socialpsychologie. Z. *f. Soc. Forsch.*, 1932, 1, 252–277.
2. Horney, Karen. Conceptions and misconceptions of the analytical method. *J. nerv. ment. Dis.*, 1935, 81, 399–410.
3. Horney, Karen. *New ways in psychoanalysis*. New York, 1939.
4. Moreno, J. L. Interpersonal therapy and the psychopathology of inter-personal relations. *Sociometry*, 1937, 1, 9–76.
5. Moreno, J. L. Psychodramatic treatment of marriage problems. *Sociometry*, 1939, 3, 1–23.
6. Sullivan, H. S. Conceptions of modern psychiatry. *Psychiatry*, 1940, 3, 1–117.

# *Group Emotion and Leadership*

FRITZ REDL

FREUD'S article on *Group Psychology and the Analysis of the Ego* has influenced psychoanalytic literature since 1921, mainly in two directions. A series of valuable attempts have been made to expand psychoanalytic explorations through the application of sociological, anthropological, and socio-economic theory. Then, in the field of education some of the later publications in the *Zeitschrift für Psychoanalytische Pädagogik* clearly recognize the growing importance of group psychology, especially for educational practice. Strictly speaking, however, Freud's article has not found supplementation on the same level on which the author started his investigation of the problem.

This is all the more surprising, because people during the last decade have been more interested in these problems. They clearly understand how futile it is to attempt to interpret events in the world at large without more thorough group psychological consideration. In addition, there is no doubt that Freud's article is incomplete, and that it does invite more supplementation than any of his other writings. The methodological equipment used and the material to which it is being applied chiefly characterizes his paper.

The *methodological equipment* is markedly different from the one he would have used had he written the article after his concepts and fundamental theories had undergone their later changes. This would be especially true if it were applied to the following points:

His concept of the *ego-ideal*—frequently called *ideal-ego*—is not yet differentiated into the two components which he later distinguished as elements derived through an incorporation of parental threats—conscience—and the residues of a narcissistic cathexis of personality traits—*ego-ideal*—in the later meaning of the term. He used the term *ego-ideal* in a way which comprised both functions indiscriminately.

ABRIDGED from *Psychiatry*, 1942, 5, 573–596.  The reprinted portion represents approximately the first half of the article as it appears in *Psychiatry*.

In his use of the term *identification* Freud changed his meaning several times during the course of the article. In some places, he distinguished between the "establishment of an object in the ego-ideal" on the one hand, and the "identification of the group members 'in their ego' " on the other hand. Elsewhere, he used the term in its later meaning.

Freud's article appeared shortly before he developed his theory of the differentiation of love-drives and aggressive drives. There is no doubt that the application of these concepts would make considerable difference. It seems especially promising to apply this differentiation to the chapter on group psychological explanations of the army.

The *material* Freud used for his discussion is also responsible for some of the peculiarities of his publication. He applied the insight gained out of rich experience in handling individual patients and used these to draw analogies with situations in "the church," "the army," and other group psychological phenomena. The generality of some of his formulations is clearly due to the fact that he did not compare concrete personality experience with equally direct group psychological experience. This is why his formula reads: "Such a (primary) mass is a number of individuals, who have put one and the same individual in the place of their ego-ideal and have, through doing so, identified with each other in their ego."

In general, there can be little doubt of the validity of this formula, but there is serious doubt of its adequacy for every group formation found in practice. Of course, Freud purposely excluded from his investigation those group formations which occur without the influence of a "leader." Even if one follows him in this limitation of the problem, it seems highly probable that this formula needs modification and supplementation. It must, perhaps, be partly replaced by other formulæ, if it is to cover the rich field of practical group formations around a *central* person of some kind.

This investigation tries to supplement Freud's study in the points just mentioned. It attempts to utilize the methodological equipment developed after 1921; it applies this equipment on such group psychological observations which could be gained from practical work with groups of children and adolescents, in school and camp situations. Nevertheless, the fundamental object of investigation remains strictly the same: an attempt to examine the intra-psychical emotional and instinctual events in the members of groups, especially those which happen "round" some *central* person, and are constituent factors in group formative processes.

## PSYCHOANALYTIC EXPLORATION AND SOCIOLOGY

The final word about the relationship between the two fields has not been written—nor should this study be weighted with such an attempt. However, methodological considerations of this sort are sufficiently vital that a clear statement as to the author's position might well help to avoid a number of possible misunderstandings. This can easily be done.

A psychoanalytic study of *group emotion* is not identical with a psychoanalytic study of *the group* or *groups*. It is only the first which is being attempted. To try the second seems nonsensical. "Groups" are phenomena containing so many different ingredients that the attempt to bring them to any one formula by the technique of psychoanalytic exploration must remain futile. Indeed, an attempt to do so seems analogous to the idea that any one person could be understood by psychoanalytic methods exclusively, eliminating all the data about this person's organic structure, for example. The importance of understanding the manifold factors constituting group life—psychological, socio-economic, and all others—is, therefore, fully recognized, but this paper does not attempt to deal with all of them. It purposely singles out only one of the aspects of group life, the emotional and instinctual relationships between persons who constitute a group. This is, therefore, an attempt to supplement, not to substitute, work with other or wider aspects of the problem.

Neither is this an attempt to mix psychoanalytic with "sociological" viewpoints. Such mixtures are frequently offered as an advanced development. Attempts at keeping the psychoanalytic technique in its *pure form* are threatened with the stigma of narrow-mindedness and lack of "sociological sensitivity." Yet, this study obviously confines its scope to the merely psychoanalytic sphere for the following reasons.

It is hoped that some blend between psychoanalytic and sociological insights may eventually be created. However, it is definitely felt that the time is not yet ripe. One cannot mix two things before one has them. Today, there is a *Sociology of the Group* on the one hand and a *Psychoanalytical Psychology of the Person* on the other. These two do not blend. The product of such mixing is either a sociology with a certain number of friendly complements to the contribution of psychoanalytic thought, or a psychoanalytic study with more or less eager recognition of the importance of sociological research. The desirable blend would first require a *Psychoanalytic Psychology of the Group*. To develop this, following the steps made in that direction by Freud's article, seems to be the first task. Only after exhaustive studies will there be some meaningful integration between sociology and psychoanalysis.

## DEFINITIONS AND BASIC ASSUMPTIONS

### *Group Emotion*

The term *emotion* is used here with the same wide meaning that is implied in phrases like "the emotional development of children," for example. In all these cases emotion "proper" is not alone intended, drives as well are included. Since the word *drive* does not have an adequate adjective, a further complication has been introduced into these formulations. The term *instinctual* will be used as adjective for drive. The summarizing of emotions and drives under the same phrase is a deplorable shortcoming, but it corresponds to a widespread scientific habit based on terminological tradition and convenience.

When "group emotions" are discussed, it is realized that they do not occur in a vacuum, but they are events that take place within and among the persons who constitute a group. In all probability they are composed of the same ingredients found in any "emotion," although they occasionally seem to obey their own special laws. The term *group* does not seem to designate some special quality, but rather, the "conditions for their arousal." *Thus, by "group emotions," reference shall be made to instinctual and emotional events taking place within persons under the pressure of group formative processes.*

From this definition it is obvious that further distinctions should be made. Not all of the emotion people have while they are in a group is really "group" emotion. Thus, for example, a pair of lovers holding hands in a political propaganda meeting might justly refuse to have the love emotion in which they participated considered under the category of group-emotion. Where it seems necessary this difference can be taken care of by calling emotions which are not the result or cause of the group formative process going on concurrently, just "*individual*" *emotions*—although it is realized that this term is misleading insofar as any emotion is, basically, a process happening within a personal situation. Furthermore, not all group emotions are equally *basic* to the process of group formation. Some, for example, are the source of group formation. The adoration one hundred people have for one and the same person may make this person their leader. It is basic for the formation of the group. On the other hand, on the basis of this group formation, a number of other emotional relationships may develop between these persons which might not otherwise have been experienced. These emotions are the result of, rather than the cause for, group formative processes. Thus, for example, *A* may begin to distrust *B*, without any highly "personal" hate against him, merely on the basis of a general group aversion which has developed through the role *B* has played within his group. In that case *A's* feeling toward *B* is the product of a special group emotional constellation. The following distinction will therefore be made:

*Constituent group emotions* are instinctual and emotional events in the potential members of a group which are basic to the group formative processes; *secondary group emotions* are such instinctual and emotional procedures within and among the members of a group as have developed on the basis of some group formative processes.

Of course, any emotion may be constituent in one situation and secondary in another. The diagnosis as to the one or the other situation is not always easy, although vital for the judgment and influence of group formative processes.

## *The Central Person*

Freud called the person around whom the group formative process crystallizes the "leader," following a well rooted linguistic habit. However, since 1921, quite a few things have happened which make all more sensitive to the tremendous differences of meaning which this word assumes under certain circumstances. This investigation, especially, led to the discovery of a number of types of group formation, which do occur "around a central person," but for the designation of which the word "leader" simply does not lend itself. It is therefore necessary to begin with a terminological correction, reserving the word "leader" for only one type of role of the person central for group formation and relationships with members, giving different names to the other forms.

By *central person* is meant person "around whom" group formative processes take place, the "crystallization point" of the whole affair. The word "central" is simply willful and should not be taken literally. "Focal" might be better for logical reasons, but for linguistic purposes, it is unsatisfactory.

The term *central person* designates the one through emotional relationship to whom the group formative processes are evoked in the potential group members.

Ten types of "leadership"—ten different roles which this *central person* may play in group formation—can easily be distinguished.

The object of this investigation must be recognized as the study of drive-relationships and emotional procedures within each member of a group, on the basis of which group formative processes are evoked.

Freud's limitation of the topic to those types of group formation which occur "around some person," is followed, excluding other mass psychological investigations from this study.

The weight of the study is on the constituent group emotions, the secondary consequences of group formation on the emotional relationships between the members are only alluded to occasionally for the purpose of illustration. The interpersonal relations should provide the basis for another study, equally important for the purpose of education.[1]

1 Studies made by Kurt Lewin of the University of Iowa, and Ronald Lippitt of New York, furnish data on this topic.

### *Basic Assumptions*

The methodological equipment developed by Freud is used in this study. During this work two further assumptions are suggested, both of a metapsychological character. They are the assumption of the *guilt-and-fear-assuaging effect of the initiatory act*, and the assumption of the infectiousness of the unconflicted on the conflicted personality constellation, or of the *spatial repetition compulsion*. These two assumptions will be explained in detail; a partial attempt at their justification will be made in this study.

## TEN TYPES OF GROUP FORMATION

All the *Ten Types* presented deal with group formation "around" a central person. The difference between the ten types lies in the different role of the central person for the basic processes of group formation. The method which has been used to present these ten types is somewhat involved. Its peculiarity for the whole problem will become a topic of discussion later. Let it suffice at this point to say that an attempt has been made to present each type by describing one or more "illustrative examples." The explanation and formula which is thought to differentiate the type from others is then given. This summarizes the nature of the constituent group formative processes at work.

The "examples" are not necessarily identical with clinical material, nor are they to be used as "proof" for the formula which follows them. The examples are intended as illustrations for the purpose of introduction and explanation of each type. In condensing many observations into a composite picture, a host of practically irrelevant items were discarded in order to isolate one process. These illustrative examples will be best understood if they are taken as graphic slides. They all claim to be based on concrete reality experiences, but none of them pretends to be a photograph. Problems of frequency and actuality—for example—will be taken up in "discussion" of the ten types immediately following their presentation.

### *Type 1: "The Patriarchal Sovereign"*

*Illustrative Example:* This group is composed of approximately ten-year-old children, most of whom are just at that point in their development where they most fully represent the end states of "childhood" immediately before the outbreak of preadolescent symptoms. In charge of them is a teacher who fits the following description: "He is an elderly gentleman of stern but not unfriendly exterior, decided but fundamentally mild in his manner. He stands for 'order and discipline' but they are values so deeply ingrained in him that he hardly thinks of them explicitly, nor does it occur to anyone to doubt them in his presence. He believes in good and thorough work, knows very clearly what he expects and leaves no doubt about it in the minds of his students." The atmosphere of the classroom may be easily described. The children accept his values without question. Their emotions about him are a mixture of love and adoration, with an element of anxiety in all those instances in which they are not quite sure of his approval. As long as they behave according to his code they feel happily secure—sheltered. Thoughts and imaginations which do not comply with his code are suppressed in his presence. The jokes he makes, or acknowledges, are funny. If one youngster is not quite so ready as the others to concentrate his filial adoration upon this type of a teacher, makes unfitting remarks, unruly gestures, or shows lack of submission, the others will experience a deep feeling of moral indignation—even though they may have enjoyed this youngster's jokes a few minutes previously during the recreation period. They all love their teacher and trust him infinitely, but certain thoughts must never enter their minds in his presence. When questioned or doubted by this teacher, tears come more easily than words; behind the happy security felt in his presence there is a nagging fear of its loss which streams into awareness every once in a while without apparent cause.

*Explanation:* These youngsters love their teacher, but that is not all that occurs. Their love is of a type which leads to "identification." It would be absurd to say that they want to be like their teacher, but they want to behave so that their teacher will approve of them.

*Formula:* These children become a group because they incorporate the "super-ego"—conscience—of the central person, into their own. On the basis of this similarity between them, they develop group emotions toward each other.

## *Type 2: "The Leader"*

*Illustrative Example:* This group of boys are between fifteen and seventeen years of age. Most of them are far beyond their preadolescence—at the verge of transition from earlier adolescence into later adolescence. The teacher in charge of them is, or has the appearance of being, very young. He has an attractive exterior. He is somewhat juvenile but not too unpleasantly so in his views and behavior. He also stands for "work and discipline," and gets his youngsters to comply without much outward pressure. However, the basis on which he gets them to accept his authority is a little different. He differs from the patriarch mainly in that he strongly sympathizes with the drives of the children. They are clearly aware of it. He plays a dual role in his teaching. In his own super-ego, he is identified with the order and the demands of the school which he represents; but he is keenly aware of the instinctual demands of the youngsters. In order to combine both he has to display considerable technical skill. If he succeeds, he makes his class feel secure and happy; if he fails, they are frightened either of him or of their own drives. The children adore him, but they also accept what he stands for without much question. The boy who misbehaves is not the greatest danger to the emotional equilibrium of the group. He elicits moral pity rather than indignation from the others. The danger is the boy who tries to get a more intensive emotional counter response from the teacher than the others, while less ready to pay for it by conscientious output of work. He is hated and despised by them. A single youngster in that group, feeling negatively viewed by the teacher, is unhappy rather than frightened. Undesirable thoughts and actions still remain confessable. To be "understood"–accepted–is the minimum requirement of group happiness in this class.

*Explanation:* A central person of this kind appeals to the love emotions as well as to the narcissistic tendencies in the children. However, it would be difficult to say that they put the teacher in the place of their "conscience." Rather they place him in the other part of their super-ego, in what is usually called their "ego-ideal," which means that they start wishing to become the type of person he is.

*Formula:* The children become a group because they incorporate the teacher's personality into their ego-ideal. On the basis of this similarity they develop group emotions toward each other. This formula coincides most closely with that of Freud in *Group Phychology and the Analysis of the Ego.*

## *Type 3: "The Tyrant"*

*Illustrative Example:* This is a class of children approximately ten years old, near the verge of preadolescence. In charge of them is an elderly, or middle-aged teacher, among whose motives for teaching were one or both of the following: He is compulsively bound to repeat a certain pattern of "discipline" against the children because this is the only way he can prove late obedience to some of the demands of his own parents; or, his most intensive drive satisfactions lie in the direction of sadism, and he has to use the children as objects for that purpose. This teacher will not "stand for" anything, but has to "impose" some kind of capricious "order" or "discipline" all the time. Nor will he be satisfied to do so quietly. He will require a noisy machinery of special tricks, rules, and revenge techniques. His concept of discipline, too, will be of the most compulsive, unrealistic sort; the way he works it out is as "unchild-minded" as possible. In short, there is a "regular tyrant" in charge of this class. Everyday psychology might tempt one to expect children to hate the teacher and fight him as much as they dared. Indeed, this does happen in a few examples, which I will describe later. The entirely different reaction from the youngsters is surprising. These children submit easily. They rebel against the silly pedantry of this tyrant less vehemently than other groups do against the reasonable demands of their beloved leader. Nor do they submit only temporarily. What they show is genuine "identification." How strong is this identification? This is illustrated by the youngster who does dare to rebel in such a class. He has a difficult time. He has everyone against him, the teacher, the other youngsters, and himself. The others show intensive signs of moral indignation, eventually becoming afraid of the child.

However, one difference seems obvious. The emotional relations these youngsters develop among themselves seem less intensive than in the other illustrations. Children of such classes develop little "comradeship"—unlike those who just hate their teacher without identifying with him—and they seem to be afraid of each other, and distrustful. They seem to fear that too much intimacy might endanger the successful repression of their hostility and might force them to realize what cowards they are.

*Explanation:* Doubtless, the identification of these children with their tyrant is genuine. He is the central person for that group. Unlike the two previous illustrations, this identification occurs from a different motive. It is not love which causes them to identify, but fear. Of course, not all fear leads into identification, but it does in the type just described.

*Formula:* These children incorporate the super-ego of the central person into their own by way of identification, the outgrowth of fear of the aggressor, and on this basis establish group emotions between each other.

## *Type 4: The Central Person as Love Object*

Freud mentioned an example of group formation which he exempted from the leadership type. It fits into the pattern according to the broadened concept of the *central person* I have introduced.

Imagine a number of women who are in love with a singer or pianist and crowd around him after his performance. Certainly each of them would prefer to be jealous of all the others. However, considering their large number and how impossible it is for them to reach the aim of their infatuation, they resign and instead of pulling each other's hair, they act like a uniform group. They bring ovations to their idol in common actions and would be glad to divide his locks among themselves (2).

The life in the school class furnishes two similar examples for illustration.

*Illustrative Example, 1:* There is a group of sixteen-year-old girls in a class of a girls' high school. In charge of them is a male teacher—young, attractive, but narcissistic enough so that they are not too greatly frightened sexually from the outset. It is known that in some such cases "the whole class falls in love with him." From that moment on, they will act like a group in many ways along the line of Freud's example. Despite their infatuation for him, it would not be surprising if the teacher complained that he had trouble with discipline—that these girls did not obey him or follow his wishes without pressure. It seems that this kind of "being in love" with the central person does not make for "identification" described in *Type 2.*

*Illustrative Example, 2:* In a coeducational class of approximately sixteen-year-old children, there is one especially pretty girl, rather narcissistic. In similar situations one frequently finds a whole cluster of boys loving and adoring her in various ways, but equally unsuccessful insofar as their wish for exclusive possession goes. The girl is equipped with special skill for keeping them all equidistant and yet equally near. Symptoms of dense group formation may sometimes be observed among these boys. They seem very close to each other, and yet their relationship is not genuine friendship. It is on a group emotional basis. This becomes evident when the girl ultimately decides in favor of one of her suitors. The other boys then begin to hate him as their rival, with the exception perhaps of the one or two who may move even closer to the successful colleague and, thus, enjoy some of the satisfactions denied to them *via* the mechanism of *altruistic concession* (1).

*Explanation:* There is no doubt that the group emotional symptoms are genuine and that the teacher in *Example 1* and the girl in *Example 2* are playing the role of the central person without whose presence this type of group formative process would not have been evoked. However, it is also evident that these central persons could not be called "leaders" by any interpretation of the term—that the other children do not "identify" with them. Nor do they incorporate their central person's standards. The central person remains "outside" but does call out a display of group emotional symptoms in these children.

*Formula:* The children choose one and the same person as an object of their love, and on the basis of this similarity they develop group emotions between each other.

## *Type 5: The Central Person as Object of Aggressive Drives*

*Illustrative Example, 1:* A type of teacher similar to the one described under the heading of "tyrant" is less intensive in his sadism, less superior in the rest of his personality traits. He is in charge of a group of rather problematic adolescents in a school setup which is so well regimented through an established system of suppressive rules that no one dares to rebel, because it would be too futile. These children obey their teacher under the constant application of pressure. They behave sufficiently well to keep out of trouble, but they do so grudgingly. They neither identify with the teacher nor with what he represents. Their relationship toward him—with the possible exception of a "sissy" in the class—is one of intensive hatred, of piled-up aggression which is kept from exploding only by their reality-insight. And yet, although they do not identify with the teacher, the emotions they develop toward each other will be truly positive and strong. The amount of "comradeship" these children display is enormous—greater than in any of the other groups. He who dares to identify with the hated oppressor is an outcast—arouses a lynching attitude in the rest of the class. Their feeling toward him is one of moral indignation, but its content it different from the other examples. It is moral indignation "from beneath," to use one of Nietzsche's terms.

*Illustrative Example, 2:* Here is a group of children who have developed no special group structure. There is no person in charge of them with a sufficiently outspoken personality to encourage any of the previously mentioned types of group formation. A new youngster suddenly enters the class who differs from them in that he is a very outspoken type. This new youngster is especially narcissistic, defiant, lofty, and unskilled in handling other people's weaknesses. If he is intellectually superior, he need not even be of a different ethnic group. Everyone's aggression is immediately turned against him. At the same time one may observe that his entrance into the class has indirectly influenced group formative processes. They move closer together; their common aggression against him seems to "bind" them, and they become more of a "group" than they were before.

*Explanation:* This new youngster cannot be called a "leader." The others neither like him nor "identify" with him. They do quite the contrary; and yet, he does apparently become the focal point of their group formative procedures, much as the teacher did in *Example 1*.

*Formula:* The children choose one and the same person as an object of their aggressive drives and through this similarity develop group emotions about each other.

## *Type 6: The Organizer*

*Illustrative Example:* In a class of approximately thirteen-year-old boys there are five who find clandestine enjoyment of the cigarette as a symbol of adulthood. And yet, all five are of the type who have decided worries about how they can obtain cigarettes. They have neither the money to buy them, the courage to do so, nor the impudence to steal them from their fathers. Preadolescent revolt against adult concepts of what a good child should be has not progressed far enough. A new boy, for whom smoking is no great problem, enters the class. He neither invites, instigates nor encourages the others in this enterprise. They all know that he can get the desired cigarettes for them if they but ask. I have seen cases where hardly any other factor was involved. The boys neither loved nor admired this youngster; on the contrary, he was rather looked down upon as socially inferior. They did not fear him nor did he use any direct or indirect pressure upon them. Yet, by the mere fact of getting them the cigarettes, they suddenly eventuated into a regular "group," held together on the basis of their participation in the same forbidden pleasure.

*Explanation:* Perhaps this example seems more complicated—less credible—than the others, being unaccustomed to finding this function of the organizer isolated. Usually, it is coupled with other roles which the central person assumes for the potential group members. Although there are not many clear examples of this type, they cannot be reduced to any of the other types because neither love, hatred, nor identification is involved.

*Formula:* The central person renders an important service to the ego of the potential group members. He does so by providing the means for the satisfaction of common undesirable drives and thus prevents guilt feelings, anxieties, and conflicts which otherwise would be involved in that process for them. On the basis of this service, the latent undesirable drives of these youngsters can manifest openly. Through this common conflict-solution, group emotions develop in the interpersonal situation.

## *Type 7: The Seducer*

*Illustrative Example, 1:* In a group of thirteen-year-old boys, six, involved in "group masturbation," are apprehended. The first superficial examination by school authorities reveals apparent, unequal participation. Some were onlookers, none were mutually active; all agreed that one of them was the "leader" of the gang. After thorough investigation the following situation was revealed. The obvious "culprit" was most "actively" engaged in masturbation. He was the "first to start it." However, he was not at all active in encouraging the others to join or to perform likewise. He was a little more developed than any of them; he masturbated freely at home without special guilt feelings. Masturbation meant something entirely different for him than for them, nor did he need the group from the standpoint of sex satisfaction. He gained nothing from the group situation, except prestige. He was not homosexual in the usual sense of the term; more surprising, perhaps, is the fact that the others neither especially loved nor feared him. They were more infantile than he. They had sufficiently conquered their anxieties about sex curiosity to take the first step in active experimentation on a highly pregenital level. However, they might not have done so alone, since that would have made them feel guilty about it. Actually, they used this boy for the purpose of "seduction." They needed him and the group situation allowed them to overcome their restrictions. Only after he was the "first one to do it" were they ready and able to join.

*Illustrative Example, 2:* A class of fifteen-year-old children, in high spirits toward the end of their morning sessions, wait for their teacher to arrive. He is somewhat late. He is the "leader" type, with a slight patriarchal tendency. Recently, at an examination period, a considerable amount of tension and dissatisfaction was extant. The relationship between them and their teacher was rather strained. He now enters the room. They stand at attention as was expected. Suddenly, one youngster, neither much liked, respected, nor feared by the others, starts yelling aggressively in a much more rebellious manner than anyone would have expected, especially toward this teacher. There is a moment of surprise. Before the teacher can react manifestly, they all join in. The whole class is in an uproar, more intensively so than any of them can afterwards "understand."

*Explanation:* Both examples beyond doubt represent group formation through the existence of a central person. In both cases the potential group members had much in common before the group formative processes began. It is also evident that they did not start before the central person committed the "first act." Apparently what evoked the group emotional reactions was the fact that these central persons committed an "initiatory" act. Through this act, the satisfaction of undesirable drives became possible in others, who would otherwise not have openly expressed them.

This concept of the "initiatory act" is not an invention but the description of a procedure observed so frequently in school and adult life that it does not require proof. It needs, however, to be explained. Thus far, I do not attempt to show why the "first act" may have such magical power over other people's suppressed drives. I simply allude to the fact here and keep its explanation for a later presentation.

What occurred in these children is here described. There is a strong increase in the intensity of undesirable drives—sex, in *Example 1*, aggressions, in *Example 2*. The personal super-ego of these children remains strong enough to suppress any possibility of the drives becoming overt. The ego of these children is in a predicament. Pressed with equal strength from oppressed drives and super-ego demands, it knows not what to do. Anxiety and uneasiness are the usual emotional accompaniments of such disturbances to balance. It is on the basis of such a situation that the effect of an "initiatory act" seems to take place.

*Formula:* The central person renders a service to the ego of the potential group members. He does this by committing the "initiatory act" and thus prevents guilt feelings, anxieties, and conflicts. On the basis of this service, the latent drives of these children manifest openly. Through this common conflict-solution, they develop group emotions.

## *Type 8: The Hero*

*Illustrative Example:* This is the same tyrant-group described under *Type 3*—where all the children were fully identified with their oppressor—at a later interval. These children have developed further into preadolescent rebelliousness. Their reality insight begins to fade in important issues: yet sufficiently frightened, they keep their defensive identification against rebellious wishes. The tyrant now begins to make deplorable mistakes. He chooses, for example, one child as the preferable object of his sadism and persecutes him more and more persistently. The others almost pity the child, but pity would imply criticism of their tyrant, and that would tend to revive their own dangerously rebellious feelings against him. So, they hold as tightly to their protective identification with the oppressor as they can. However, one of them has more courage. Something in his history makes him less able to endure this—or, perhaps, his insight into the real dangers implied by rebellion dwindles more rapidly. In any event, he is one day unable to tolerate the teacher's attack upon his victim. This boy defends his colleague and is considered "fresh" and reckless. The whole class gasps with surprise. They expect something fearful to happen. Surely the teacher will kill that child, or lightning will strike out of the clear sky. But no avenging stroke of lightning descends to quell the rebellion. The teacher is evidently too surprised or frightened momentarily to know what to do. When he demonstrates his fury, it is too late. The "hero" has worked his miracle. All the youngsters have altered their sentiments, at least secretly. Now they adore him and even start identifying with him. He takes his punishment, but remains victorious.

*Explanation:* The situation is similar to the one previously described, but events now move in the opposite direction. These youngsters suffer similarly from a number of suppressed tendencies—such as just rebellion in favor of a suffering colleague—however, they are too fearful of the realistic consequences of such feelings. Their personal cowardice hinders them from doing what they feel is right, but what would have awful consequences for them. Again the hero commits the "initiatory act." Through his demonstration of courage the others suddenly discard anxieties and dare—if not to act, then, at least—to feel what their own standard of justice has long wanted them to experience.

*Formula:* The central person renders a service to the ego of the potential group members. He does so by committing the "initiatory act" and thus saves them anxieties and conflicts. The "initiatory act," however, leads in the direction of moral values *versus* cowardly self-protection this time. On the basis of this service the undesirable tendencies toward cowardly submission in these children are conquered. Through this common conflict-solution group psychological emotions are evoked.

## *Type 9: The "Bad Influence"*

There are children in many classes who are constantly being accused of being "undesirable elements" by all teachers, parents, and by the other children, too. And yet, they can scarcely be accused of "having an evil" influence. Usually what they are accused of is unclear but it is assumed that their mere presence in the classroom affects the others badly—"brings out the worst in them." And yet it would be embarrassing to say how they do this. Accusations made against them often have to be withdrawn, because no definite basis exists in fact. Nothing can be proved. Sometimes, admittedly, these children are not so difficult to manage; they are better than the influence they are accused of having on the others. Fundamentally, this is an accusation of seduction through magic. Apparently belief in the infectiousness of something within these children seems absurd, and yet, it is not. The background upon which the accusations are made is usually true. These children do affect the others, not overtly—quite in contrast to the "seducer type"—but, by their presence in the same room, something happens to these youngsters which makes them unruly, full of "dirty" ideas, or just difficult to manage. What supports this?

*Illustrative Example:* In a botany class of eleven-year-old children, a word is mentioned which reminds those who "know" of a sex situation. About a dozen are preoccupied with associations of this sort. When the word is mentioned, they all look at one boy, then at each other. They grin. He grins back. The whole room, at this moment, is divided in two. The threads of this little clique are spread like a net over it. Next day a nearly identical situation recurs. However, that boy happens to be absent from class. Nothing happens. The children fail to make the same association as the day before. Their little "gang" remains submerged in the group without interruption.

*Explanation:* This type again is very similar to that of the "seducer"; the difference, however, rests in the technique used for "seduction." Nothing like the "initiatory act" is implied here. The explanation has to be reduced to a more descriptive statement to show how the "bad influence" works. The dynamic explanation must be considered later.

With the inner constellation of the potential group members similar to that described in the seduction type, it can apparently be said that they possess a number of undesirable drives which seek expression; their super-ego is in command of the situation, so that satisfaction of these undesirable drives is impossible without the penalty of remorse and anxiety; and, the ego of these children is in a "bad jam," squeezed between the urges of their drives and the demands of a strong super-ego.

The inner constellation of the "bad influence" type of a central person is different from that of the group members. In him there is no conflict. His drives in the same direction do not set loose conflicts and problems for him. He faces them and does not care. Alertness, on the part of the others to this event seems sufficient encouragement for the expression of what they had just been trying to suppress. This really means the assumption of a definite process which might best be described by saying that the "unconflicted" personality constellation has an infectious influence on the conflicted whenever they meet. This again is the description of an easily observable fact, which by itself provides no understanding of the process. However, it is enough to explain the group formative processes in these cases. It is important to realize that these examples of so-called "bad influence" are usually group psychological procedures.

*Formula:* The central person renders a service to the ego of the potential group members. He does so by virtue of the "infectiousness of the unconflicted personality constellation upon the conflicted one." Through this, he saves them the expense of guilt feelings, anxieties, and conflicts. On the basis of this service, the latent undesirable drives of these children can manifest openly. Through this common conflict solution, these children develop group emotions in relationship with each other.

## *Type 10: The "Good Example"*

*Illustrative Example:* The same class as the one mentioned in the previous example contains another group of boys who "gang up" with each other even more intensively than do the undesirable ones. Nevertheless, the teacher would hesitate to call them a "gang" or even a group. They are just a bunch of very good friends, he would say. However, one of them is the obvious center, and he "has a marvelous influence" upon the others. They are much nicer when he is around. If pressed, the teacher could hardly explain how that boy manages to influence them for he obviously does nothing. In looking at this group more closely, the following situation is discovered. These children are not "friends" in the personal meaning of this term. All are at that stage where they are full of new curiosities of which they are afraid, because they would feel guilty in satisfying them. This one boy, however, is far removed from any undesirable thought or act.

*Explanation:* The inner constellation in the potential group members shows a number of undesirable drives seeking expression, the super-ego is decidedly against this but scarcely able to maintain its position for long, and the ego is in a "bad jam" about how to maintain balance in such a situation. The inner constellation of the central boy in this situation contains no conflict of this kind. The mere idea of expressing undesirable thoughts in his presence is impossible. So, the group moves closer to him; in his presence they feel secure. What they fear is their own drives; what they look for is some support for their endangered super-ego. The situation is the exact reverse of the "Bad Influence" example.

*Formula:* The central person renders a service to the ego of the potential group members. He does so by virtue of the "infectiousness of the unconflicted personality constellation upon the conflicted one." Through this, he saves them the necessity to face their own drives of which they are afraid, and conflicts resulting from this. This time, however, the solution leads in the direction of moral values instead of undesirable drives. On the basis of this service, the children can suppress their undesirable drives according to the command of their own super-ego. Through this common conflict solution they develop group emotions in the relationship with each other.

## SUMMARY

For the purpose of rapid summary, these ten types can be grouped into three main categories and tabulated.

### *The Role of the Central Person for the Group Formative Process*

| | |
|---|---|
| *The Central Person as an Object of Identification* | |
| On the basis of love | |
| Incorporation into conscience | Type 1 |
| Incorporation into the "ego ideal" | Type 2 |
| On the basis of fear | |
| Identification with the aggressor | Type 3 |
| *The Central Person as an Object of Drives* | |
| As an object of love drives | Type 4 |
| As an object of aggressive drives | Type 5 |
| *The Central Person as an Ego Support* | |
| Providing means for drive satisfaction | Type 6 |
| Dissolving conflict situations through guilt-anxiety assuagement | |
| Through the technique of the initiatory act in the service of drive satisfaction | Type 7 |

and in the service of drive defense — Type 8

Through the "infectiousness of the unconflicted personality constellation over the conflicted one" in the service of drive satisfaction — Type 9

and in the service of drive defense — Type 10

## REFERENCES


1. Freud, Anna. *The ego and the mechanisms of defense.* London: Hogarth, 1922.
2. Freud, S. *Group psychology and the analysis of the ego.* London: Hogarth, 1922.


# *The Principles and Traits of Leadership*

CECIL A. GIBB

## INTRODUCTION

THE PROBLEM of leadership as a psychological phenomenon is closely related with considerations of the nature of personality and achieves some clarity if the relation between the two concepts is briefly considered. Psychologists have defined personality generally in one of two ways: (*a*) as the effect the individual has on other people or (*b*) as the total pattern of habits of cognition, affection, and conation. The latter use is that more frequently chosen. Personality in this sense is an abstraction from observed behavior and the apparent relations of this behavior to the individual's needs and to the environment. As Burt has recently pointed out (2),

> [the individual is never an isolated unit and] what the psychologist has to study are the interactions between a "personality" and an "environment"—the behavior of a dynamic mind in a dynamic field of which it forms a part.

ABRIDGED from *Journal of Abnormal and Social Psychology*, 1947, 42, 267–284. Reprinted by permission of the author and the American Psychological Association, Inc.

The writer is indebted to Emeritus Professor H. T. Lovell and to Professor W. M. O'Neil for a critical reading of a draft of this paper.

"Leadership" is a concept applied to the personality-environment relation to describe the situation when one, or at most a very few, personalities are so placed in the environment that his, or their, "will, feeling, and insight direct and control others in the pursuit of a cause" (9).

Leadership has usually been thought of as a specific attribute of personality, a personality trait, that some persons possess and others do not, or at least that some achieve in high degree and others scarcely at all. The search for leaders has often been directed toward finding those persons who have this trait well developed. The truth would seem, however, to be quite different. In fact, viewed in relation to the individual, leadership is not an attribute of the personality but a quality of his role within a particular and specified social system.[1] Viewed in relation to the group, leadership is a quality of its structure. And, depending upon the definition of "group," this particular quality may become a "*sine qua non.*" Without leadership, there is no focus about which a number of individuals may cluster to form a group. A group is here defined as two or more people in a state of social interaction. Group activity means that individuals are acting together in some fashion; that there is some order of the different lines of individual action. There is a division of labor within a group that is accepted by all members of the group. In a discussion group, for example, the speaker performs a task different from that of other members. Both he and the members act in expected ways, and yet their behavior may be collective. The coherence occurs because of the common understandings or cultural traditions as to how they should behave. Similarly, the concept of leadership as a cultural norm plays a considerable part in the emergence of a leader. And this would seem to be the significance of Warren's parenthetic statement that "leadership depends on attitudes and habits of dominance in certain individuals and submissive behavior in others" (11). It is not implied that these are instincts variously strong in some individuals and weak in others, but that these are accepted ways of behaving within the cultural framework and that therefore they tend to determine the field forces acting in a group situation.

## LEADERSHIP THEORY

This dynamic conception of groups composed of dynamic entities or personalities interacting will accord well with Lewin's notion (7) that the individual's characteristics and actions change under the varying influence of "the social field." It does not seem unreasonable to claim that groups have

1 "The place in a particular system which a certain individual occupies at a particular time will be referred to as his *status* with respect to that system" (8, p. 76). "In so far as it represents overt behavior, a *role* is the dynamic aspect of a status: what the individual has to do in order to validate his occupation of the status" (8, p. 77).

a capacity to propel to leadership one or more of their number; and, what is more, the choice of a specific individual for the leadership role will be more dependent upon the nature of the group and of its purpose than upon the personality of the individual; but it will be most dependent upon the relation between the personality and the group at any particular moment. That is to say, in Linton's terms, that the group choice of a leader will be determined by the status of individual members. This claim does not lose sight of the nature of the individuals who constitute the group, and it does not assert that any member may be propelled to leadership nor does it suggest that the social situation alone makes the leader. Leadership is both a function of the social situation and a function of personality, but it is a function of these two in interaction; no additive concept is adequate to explain the phenomenon. There is no justification for saying that personality qualities which make for leadership exist in a latent form when not being exercised in a social situation. Any qualities of personality common to leaders in varying situations may also exist in persons who never achieve leadership status. What might be called the attributes of leaders are abstracts from a total interactional situation and are qualities of a particular social role. In the absence of this kind of social situation the latent existence of the same pattern of qualities cannot be inferred. Again, this does not mean that there can be no potential leaders, but it does mean that the potentiality cannot be directly known any more than capacity can be known except as a back-inference from expressed ability.

Leadership is not usually an enduring role unless an organization is built up which enables an individual to retain the role after he ceases to be qualified for it. In this case leadership becomes domination or mere headship. In the absence of such an artificial restriction, the interaction within the group is very fluid and the momentary group leader is that person who is able to contribute most to progress toward the common goal. Ten men previously unknown to each other are set a common problem, such as transporting heavy radio equipment to the top of a steep cliff. In the initial stages they are ten individuals thinking of possible solutions. One may find a solution which he communicates to the others. Usually this establishes interaction. The ten now become one group and the group focus is the man, A, who offered the solution. He is the leader at the moment. He is in the position of influencing their behavior more than they influence his. He is in the role of initiator of group action, which at this point consists of discussion. If now his plan is accepted, the group goal changes. It has been the choice of a plan and for that phase A occupied the leadership role. The goal now, however, is the execution of the plan. Two things may happen. A, by virtue of a prestige he has acquired, may continue in the role of leader or he may find another individual, B, naturally taking over. The group problem is now more practical, and B may, by virtue of his different innate capacities or previous experiences, be better able to contribute to the group project. Leadership then passes naturally to B, and, if difficulties are met and a third man, C, offers a solution, the role may pass to him. On the other hand, it is possible that all of these individuals, A, B, and C, may find their retention of the leadership role very short lived and even momentary only because another member of the group, D, rises to a more permanent occupancy of the role by virtue of his ability to translate suggestions into working orders, and by virtue of his greater social effectiveness.

Observation of group behavior in this way strongly supports the contention that leadership is not an attribute of personality or of character. It is a social role, the successful adoption of which depends upon a complex of abilities and traits. But even more, the adoption of a leadership role is dependent upon the specific situation. The same individual in the same group may alternate between the role of leader and follower as the group goal changes. Most frequently the individual is propelled into a position of leadership by virtue of his capacity for interpersonal contribution in the specific situation. There is, however, a generic aspect to leadership as Du Vall (3) has pointed out. This is indicated by the fact that the person of all-round superiority is more frequently in situations in which he is able to make a contribution.

The first main point to be made, then, in leadership theory is that leadership is relative always to the situation. Men may come together and yet not constitute a group. Until the individuals of the aggregation are given a common object or goal, there will be no social interaction and consequently no group formation. Each may face an individual problem and achieve an individual solution. But when many face a common problem and one or more of the individual solutions is communicated to others then there is interaction, and, if that interaction is focused upon one or two individuals in the group, then he or they are leaders for the time being. Clearly, in order that such a situation may develop, it is necessary that there should be a problem, and that it should be such a problem as to afford an opportunity for the play of individual differences in its solution. The circumstances must be such as to require a choice. As Schneider (10) has pointed out, it is the social circumstances which make particular attributes of personality attributes of leadership. While the social circumstances are such as to demand the original formulation of a plan, inventing ability will be an attribute of personality determining the adoption of a leadership role. But, the plan having been formulated, the social circumstances then demand not invention but social effectiveness as an attribute of personality essential for the leadership role. And, unless the same individual possesses both attributes, the leadership passes from one to another. The situation determines which of many attributes of personality will be attributes of leadership at any given moment. That is why Pigors (9) observes that, "whenever an obstacle physical or mental prevents the flow of action, the group welcomes any manifestation of individual difference that tends to resolve this uncertainty or to facilitate group action."

Leadership, then, is always relative to the situation (*a*) to the extent that a certain kind of situation is required before the leadership relation will appear at all, and (*b*) in the sense that the particular set of social circumstances existing at the moment determines which attributes of personality will confer leadership status and consequently determines which members of a group will assume the leadership role, and which qualities of personality function to maintain the individual in that role. This was one of the things indicated by Thrasher's study of juvenile gangs in Chicago. Leadership seemed to be a quality that came out as the group moved about together—it was the result of the social situation. This is, in fact, the second principle of leadership theory. It is that individual accession to the leadership role is dependent upon the group goal and upon the capacity of the individual to contribute to the achievement of the goal. Pigors says:

> It is nonsense to talk of leadership in the abstract since no one can just lead without having a goal. Leadership is always *in* some sphere of interest, and *toward* some objective goal seen by leader and follower (9).

Only in so far as the individual can contribute to group progress in the required direction has he any claim to a hearing, and, unless he can establish himself with his fellow members, he will not receive recognition as their leader. This is, of course, to raise the question whether the leader can exercise a creative influence upon the group's goals and activities or whether he can do no more than express and exemplify already accepted ideals and contribute to progress in the direction of an accepted goal perhaps by pin pointing and clarifying a previously vague conception. Klineberg (5) suggests that a compromise is indicated in that "the leader has great influence but only on certain groups under certain conditions. Change these or change him," he says, "and the resulting behavior is markedly altered." Schneider (10), on the other hand, claims that the "new" history as written by Marx, Turner, Beard, and others, "sees leaders as a product of the times and leadership as a function of the circumstances of the moment." The problem seems to be indeterminate because there is no denying that the "great men" of history have been responsible for changes in the social situation of which they were a part but there is no way of telling to what extent these changes would have occurred anyway or under the leadership of another group-chosen personality.

The third characteristic of the leadership process to which attention may be drawn is that its basic psychology is that of social interaction. There can be no leadership in isolation, it is distinctly a quality of a group situation. There can be no leader without followers. An individual's intellectual quality may be very superior and his individual solution of a group problem may be excellent but he is not a leader until his solution is communicated, and then not until other people are associated with him in giving expression to his ideas. Leader and follower must be united by common goals and aspirations and by a will to lead, on one side, and a will to follow, on the other, i.e., by a common acceptance of one another. From this it follows that the individual must have membership character in the group which makes him its leader, because leaders and followers are interdependent. This is the first of Brown's (1) "field dynamical laws of leadership," and the first of Du Vall's (3) criteria of the leadership process. The leader must be a member of the group; he must share the group objectives and aspirations. Stated in other words, this principle of mutual interaction between the leader and the group implies that the individual chosen leader must have certain qualities of personality which, derived as they are from his group-membership-character, confer upon him a certain social effectiveness and determine his acceptability.

Having group-membership-character, it is upon individual differences that one depends for election to leadership status. It is because there are individual differences of capacity and skill that one, and usually only one, of a group emerges having a pattern of qualifications superior to others for meeting present group needs. But these "superior" persons must not be too different. Followers subordinate themselves not to an individual who is utterly different but to a member of their group who has superiority at this time and who is fundamentally the same as they are, and who at other times is prepared to be a follower just as they are.

For Jennings (4):

> Leadership is definable by a manner of interacting with others. . . . Both isolation and leadership were found to be products of interpersonal interaction and not of attributes residing within the persons. . . . No simple variable such as the length of time the individual had been in the community or his chronological age relative to other members, or his intelligence or even his greater opportunity for contacting others, appears to account for the particular choice-status accorded him. Instead the reciprocal interplay maintaining between the individual and those in the same field and constituting the individual's personality as the latter view him appears to be the underlying basic explanation of isolation and leadership.

The determination of the role to be played by the individual is the group reaction to his interpersonal contribution. The close relation between leader and followers is therefore apparent.

The leader inevitably embodies many of the qualities of the followers. Any individual's personality at a given point in time reflects the field forces with which it is interacting. The personality which most adequately reflects those forces is the one most likely to be propelled to leadership. Thus it is that La Piere and Farnsworth (6) are led to make the point that because there is such close interaction between the leader and the led it is often difficult to determine just who affects whom and to what extent. For this reason it is possible for leadership to be nominal only. This possibility is emphasized by a carry-over of prestige from one point in time to another. The fact that individual A in our earlier example was intellectually quickest with a suggested solution of the group problem established him as a focus of attention in the minds of the others. Momentarily, at any rate, he became their leader and they became followers. A definite interactional pattern was established. A social-cultural evaluation was made of him by the others. That is precisely what is meant by prestige. Prestige is a distinction attaching to a person in the minds of others. It depends, as we have now seen, on the qualities ascribed to the individual by other members of the group. As Young points out, prestige is a special case of the point

> that a man's personality reflects others' image and recognition of him. A leader's prestige rests upon the apperceptive background of the followers. The leader takes on the qualities which his adherents project on him (12).

This, too, is Brown's (1) second "field dynamical law of leadership," that the "leader must represent a region of high potential in the social field," i.e., that he must have prestige and this he acquires by symbolizing the ideals of all members of the group. In some instances it may be said that prestige within a group is acquired by virtue of an external appointment or by virtue of a certain status in an institution which embraces that group, as in the case of a parish priest. In such a case the assumption of a leadership role is made easier, but it is still true that it will be retained only while the individual so appointed is able to symbolize the ideals of the group members. In other words, the personality thus "made" leader must so reflect the field forces within the group with which it is interacting as to have had potential leadership status if membership without leadership could have been granted by the appointment.

Reviewing leadership theory one may say, then, that its three most important principles are, first, that leadership is always relative to the situation–relative, that is, in two senses: (*a*) that leadership flourishes only in a problem situation and (*b*) that the nature of the leadership role is determined by the goal of the group; and this is, in fact, the second principle of leadership, that it is always toward some objective goal. The third principle is that leadership is a process of mutual stimulation–a social interactional phenomenon in which the attitudes, ideals, and aspirations of the followers play as important a determining role as do the individuality and personality of the leader.

These principles lead us to accept Pigors' (9) definition of leadership as a "process of mutual stimulation which, by the successful interplay of relevant individual differences controls human energy in the pursuit of a common cause." And any person may be called a leader "during the time when and in so far as, his will, feeling, and insight direct and control others in the pursuit of a cause which he presents."

As Jennings says:

> the "why" of leadership appears not to reside in any personality trait considered singly, nor even in a constellation of related traits, but in the interpersonal contribution of which the individual becomes capable in a specific setting eliciting such contribution from him (4).

provided that the individual superiority is not so great as to preclude solidarity of purpose.

Such a theory of the leadership process excludes such group situations as those organized for professional tuition, expert advice, management, and the like, and excludes the concept of headship. When once the group activity has become dominated by an established and accepted organization, leadership tends to disappear. Even if this organization originally served the leadership role, any continuance of the organization as such, after the causal set of circumstances has ceased to exist, represents a transition to a process of domination or headship, where headship is regarded, as Warren (11) defined it, as "a form of authority determined by caste, class or other factors than popular selection and acceptance," and where domination is defined by Pigors (9) as

> a process of social control in which accepted superiors assume a position of command and demand obedience from those who acknowledge themselves as inferiors in the social scale; and in which by the forcible assumption of authority and the accumulation of prestige a person (through a hierarchy of functionaries) regulates the activities of others for purposes of his own choosing.

The characteristics of this process of domination as distinct from that of leadership are that: (*a*) the position of headship is maintained through an organized system and not by the spontaneous recognition of the individual contribution to the group goal; (*b*) the group goal is arbitrarily chosen by the autocratic head in his own self-interest and is not internally determined; (*c*) there is not really *a group* at all, since there is no sense of shared feeling or joint action; and (*d*) there is in this process a wide social gap between the group members and the head, who strives to maintain this social distance as an aid to his coercion of the group through fear.

This concept of domination and headship is important because it is so different from that of leadership and because so much so-called leadership in industry, education, and in other social spheres is not leadership at all, but is simply domination. It is not, however, necessary that headship should preclude leadership.

## REFERENCES

1. Brown, J. F. *Psychology and the social order.* New York: McGraw-Hill, 1936.
2. Burt, C. The assessment of personality. *Brit. J. educ. Psychol.*, 1945, 15, 107–121.
3. Du Vall, E. W. *Personality and social group work.* New York: Association Press, 1943.
4. Jennings, Helen H. *Leadership and isolation.* London: Longmans Green, 1943.
5. Klineberg, O. *Social psychology.* New York: Holt, 1940.
6. La Piere and Farnsworth. *Social psychology.* (2nd Ed.) New York: McGraw-Hill, 1942.
7. Lewin, K. *A dynamic theory of personality.* New York: McGraw-Hill, 1935.
8. Linton, R. *The cultural background of personality.* New York: Appleton-Century, 1945.
9. Pigors, P. *Leadership or domination.* Boston: Houghton-Mifflin, 1935.
10. Schneider, J. Social class, historical circumstances and fame. *Amer. J. Sociol.*, 1937, 43, 37–56.
11. Warren, H. C. *Dictionary of psychology.* Boston: Houghton Mifflin, 1934.
12. Young, Kimball. *Social psychology.* (2nd Ed.) New York: Crofts, 1945.

# *"Subjective" and "Objective" Elements in the Social Field. The Three Step Procedure*

KURT LEWIN

ONE last point concerning conceptualization and general methodology may be mentioned. To predict the course of a marriage, for instance, a psychologist might proceed in the following way. He might start by analyzing the life space of the husband H. This analysis would involve the relevant physical and social facts in the husband's surroundings, including the expectations and character of his wife W, all represented in the way the husband, H, perceives them. Let us assume that this analysis is sufficiently complete to permit the derivation of the resultant forces on

FROM Kurt Lewin, Frontiers in group dynamics: Concept, method and reality in social science; social equilibria and social change. *Human Relations*, 1947, 1, 5–41. Reprinted by permission of Mrs. Gertrude W. Lewin and the publisher.

the husband (Fig. 1a). This would be equivalent to a prediction of what the husband actually will do as his next step. The data about the life space of the husband might be sufficiently elaborate to determine the resultant force on the wife W, as he sees her (Fig. 1a). This resultant force, however, would not indicate what the wife will actually do but merely what the husband expects his wife to do.

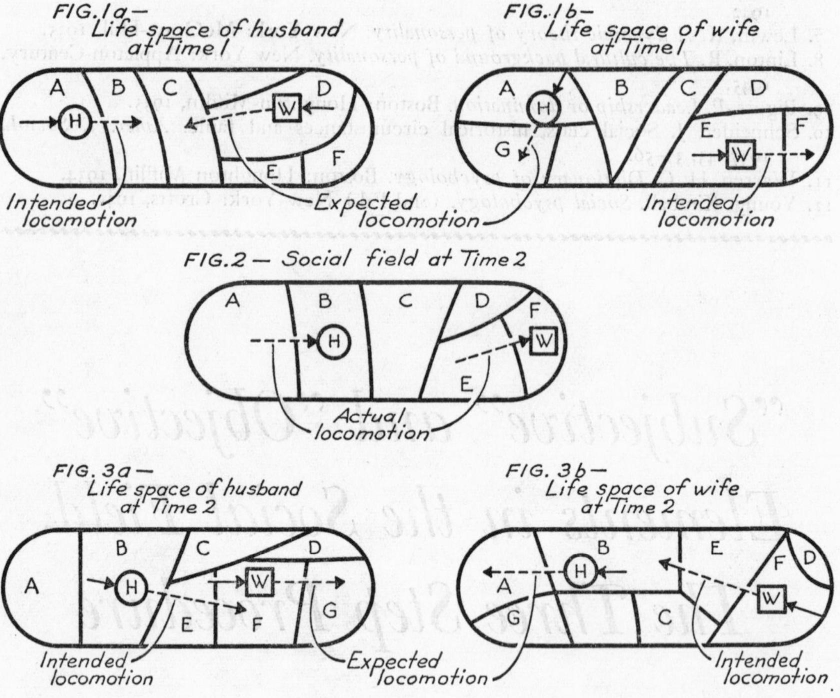


To derive the next conduct of the wife, her life space would have to be analyzed (Fig. 1b). Usually the wife will see the situation, including herself, W, and her husband, H, somewhat differently from her husband. Let us assume she sees her husband located in an area corresponding to his own perception of himself; that she perceives her own position, however, as being in region e rather than d; and that the cognitive structure of the intermediate regions b and c are for her, too, somewhat different from what they are for her husband. Corresponding to this difference between the life spaces of the husband and wife, the resultant force on the wife, W, may point to the region f rather than to c. This means that the wife will actually move forward f rather than toward c as her husband expected.

The considerations thus far give the basis for predicting the next moves of husband and wife to the region b and f respectively (Fig. 2):

analyzing the two psychological ("subjective") fields gives the basis for predicting the actual ("objective") next step of behavior.

But how do we proceed from here if we are to answer the social problem of the fate of the marriage? Neither husband nor wife had expected their partner to behave as he or she actually did. Obviously, the next step will depend largely on how each will react to this surprise, how each will interpret the conduct of the other, or, more generally speaking, how each will "perceive" the new situation.

The husband who has expected his wife to move from d to c and now sees her moving in the opposite direction, to f, may interpret this to mean that his wife has "changed her mind." In this case he may expect her next move to proceed in the same direction, namely toward g (Fig. 3a). Furthermore, the behavior of his wife is likely to change for him the "meaning" of c, that is, the cognitive structure of the situation. The wife who sees her husband move to b rather than g may perceive this to be an excursion to an activity which would be completed in a certain time after which he would return to a (Fig. 3b). She therefore decides to join her husband in b (Fig. 3b), whereas her husband, having a different perception of the situation (Fig. 3a), intends to move on to f, which he perceives as being closer to his wife.

Obviously, husband and wife will soon be in trouble if they do not "talk things over," that is, if they do not communicate to each other the structure of their life spaces with the object of equalizing them.

This analysis of the history of a marriage has proceeded in a series of three steps: first, a separate analysis of the psychological situation of the husband and that of the wife, at time 1 with the purpose of deriving the next behavior of each. Second, representing the resultant sociological ("objective") situation at time 2. Third, deriving with the help of the laws of perception the resultant psychological situation for husband and wife at time 2. This would give the basis for the next sequence of three steps, starting with the analysis of the psychological situation of the persons involved predict their actual next step.

Such a procedure looks involved, particularly if we consider groups composed of many members. Is it possible to eliminate the "objective," or the "subjective," aspect of this analysis? Actually, social science faces here two types of question; one concerning the size of units, the other concerning the role of perception in group life. It would be prohibitive if the analysis of group life always had to include analysis of the life space of each individual member.

Analysis of group life, can proceed rather far on the basis of relatively larger units. In the end, of course, the theory of small and large units has to be viewed in social science as well as in physical science, as one theoretical system. But this stage can be reached only after an attack on both the larger and the smaller units.

Unfortunately, treating groups as units does not eliminate the dilemma between "subjective" and "objective" aspects of social fields. It seems to be impossible to predict group behavior without taking into account group goals, group standards, group values, and the way a group "sees" its own situation and that of other groups. Group conflicts would have quite different solutions if the various groups concerned did not perceive differently the situation existing at a given time. To predict or to understand the steps leading to war between two nations A and B it seems to be essential to refer to the group life space of A and to the different group life space of B. This means that the analysis of group interaction has again to follow a three-step procedure, moving from the separate analysis of the life space of each group to the group conduct in the total social field and from there back again to the effect on the group life space.

This procedure of analysis which swings from an analysis of "perception" to that of "action," from the "subjective" to the "objective," and back again is not an arbitrary demand of scientific methodology, nor is it limited to the interaction between groups or between individuals. The procedure mirrors one of the basic properties of group life. Any kind of group action or individual action, even including that of the insane, is regulated by circular causal processes of the following type: individual perception or "fact-finding"—for instance, an act of accounting—is linked with individual action or group action in such a way that the content of the perception or fact-finding depends upon the way in which the situation is changed by action. The result of the fact-finding in turn influences or steers action.

Certain schools in psychology, sociology, and economics have had the tendency to eliminate the problems of perception. The analysis of all social sciences, however, will have to take into account both sections of this circular process.

# *Contributions of Sociometry to Research Methodology in Sociology*

J. L. MORENO

TWO THESES spearheaded my original program of research in social science, (*1*) "The whole of human society develops in accord with definite laws" (6, p. 4), (*2*) "A truly therapeutic procedure cannot have less an objective than the whole of mankind" (6, p. 3). From the point of view of "system" the two theses led logically to the differentiation between Sociometry and Sociatry.[1]

According to Sociometry, society systems are preference or attraction-repulsion systems. This is claimed to be true not only of human, but also of non-human societies. It also claimed that human preferential systems cannot be examined adequately by the old methods of fact-finding objectivity as statistical methods and observational methods, but that the methods themselves and the instruments derived from them have to undergo a process of *subjectification* in order to return to the researcher endowed with a more profound objectivity, having gained a grasp of the social processes on the depth level. This new *sociometric objectivity* can well be contrasted with the old *positivistic* objectivity of Comte.

It is due to this striving of sociometric method towards a superior and more complete objectivity that we gave systematic emphasis:

FROM *American Sociological Review*, 1947, 12, 287–292. Reprinted by permission of the author and publisher.

---

1 "The imbalances within the social atom and their reflection upon the development of psychological currents and networks give social psychiatry a nosological basis and differentiate it as a discipline from psychiatry proper. Psychiatric concepts as neurosis and psychosis are not applicable to socioatomic processes. A group of individuals may become *sociotic* and the syndrome producing this condition can be called a *sociosis*" (6, p. 192). See also Moreno (8).

(a) To the study of social structures in statu nascendi (concept of the moment).

(b) To the shift from the gross examination of social aggregates to minute atomistic events, from the macroscopic to the microscopic method (6, pp. 134–164, ch. 9) of investigation.

(c) To the development of situational sociology (situation and role analysis).

(d) To operational and measurement procedures, and above all,

(e) To a revolution of the relationship between the investigator and his subjects.

They themselves were thus motivated to be and turned into researchers of each other. A community of a thousand people for instance, became animated by sociometric devices to account for their social feelings and possibly to correct them. Sociometry became then, paraphrasing the famous saying of Lincoln: *the sociology of the people, by the people, and for the people*. The operation of sociological research became itself socio (mass) centered instead of individual centered.

It is due to this reorientation in research methodology that new instruments of a great variety have been invented and their number is still rapidly growing. They have been differentiated in accord with their particular focus, in (*1*) sociometric tests, (*2*) action tests, (*3*) situation tests, (*4*) role tests, (*5*) spontaneity tests, (*6*) psycho-dramatic tests, (7) sociodramatic tests. The new and provocative material required original forms of presentation. The chief innovations have been (a) the sociogram (1931), (b) the sociomatrix, and (c) the "action matrix" (1923).

We have contrasted the macrosociologies of Comte, Marx, Sumner, etc., with the "micro-sociologies" among which sociometry is the most conscious representative. By sociomicroscopic configurations we do not mean only the informal small groups, but the dynamic social units of which they are comprised, the pattern variants of social atoms, the clustering of social atoms into larger associations invisible to the eye of the human observer (social molecules), psychosocial networks, the clustering of numerous such networks into more comprehensive formations; finally the study of dyads, triangles, quadrangles, pentagons, and chains of persons. We assumed that the study of these primary atomic structures of human relations is the preliminary and indispensable groundwork to most macrosociological investigations.

Sociology owes to Sociometry a few genuine generalizations among which are most prominent (a) the law of social gravitation or mobility,[2] (b) the sociogenetic law,[3] (c) the sociodynamic law,[4] (d) the reality test

2 Stated by Moreno (6) and furthered by Deutschberger, along sociometric lines (3), approached from a different angle by Stouffer (14), Stewart (12, 13), Thorndike (15), and Bassett (1). See also Moreno (6, ch. 20, pp. 342–345).

3 Stated by Moreno (6), furthered by Jennings (5) and Criswell (2).

4 The idea of a sociodynamic law has been formulated by Moreno (6, 7, 8).

of social configurations (11), (e) the law of the social atom,[5] and (f) the tele phenomenon.[6]

## (A) THE LAW OF SOCIAL GRAVITATION OR MOBILITY

My first formulation of a law of social gravity was: "Mankind is a social and organic unity.—Tendencies must emerge between the different parts of this unity drawing them at one time apart and drawing them another time together.—These attractions and repulsions or their derivatives may have a near or distant effect not only upon the immediate participants in the relation but also upon all other parts of that unity which we call mankind.—Its organization develops and distributes itself in space apparently according to a law of social gravity which seems to be valid for every kind of grouping irrespective of the membership (6, p. 3).

This was thirteen years ago. Since then a number of studies have been advanced in which the idea of such a law was postulated. It may be worthwhile to compare the methods brought forth by non-sociometric [2] sociologists, Stouffer (1940), Stewart (1941), Thorndike (1942), with the methods proposed by sociometrists from Moreno (1934) to Deutschberger (1946). According to my formulation the movements of populations are propelled by two processes. One process draws the groups apart; the other process draws the groups together. The sociometric formula of social gravitation states:

People 1 (P1) and People (P2) move towards each other—between a locality X and a locality Y—in direct proportion to the amount of attraction given (a1) or received (a2), in inverse proportion to the amount of repulsion given (r1) or received (r2), the physical distance (d) between the two localities being constant, the facilities of communication between X and Y being equal.

The formulas of Stouffer and Stewart, based on statistical analysis of number and distance, even if correct in themselves, are unsatisfactory because of their symbolic character, leaving the people out, the dynamics of inter-personal and inter-group relations. Stewart's finding can be easily integrated into the sociometric formula which then would read as follows:

People 1 (P1) and People (P2) move towards each other in direct proportion to the amount of attraction given (a1) or received (a2), in inverse proportion to the amount of repulsion given (r1) or received (r2) and in inverse proportion to the physical distance (d) between locality X and locality Y, the residences of P1 and P2 respectively, the facilities of communication between X and Y being constant.

I applied the sociometric findings in a small community to the macrosociological phenomenon of inter-state migration.[4] Comparing the census

5 Stated by Moreno (6). See also Jennings (4).
6 Stated by Moreno (6).

figures of spontaneous migration of people from one state to the other, from east to west, from the south to the north, within a given period, with the sociometrically explored migrations in a small community, I suggested that the same law which determines the migratory movements in a small community dominates the spontaneous migration of people throughout the territory of the United States. Sociometric evidence further indicated that the desire for migration (the number of potential and frustrated attempts) is many times larger than the migration which becomes manifest. It indicates, too, that the parts of the country towards which these potential unfulfilled migrations tend, are important phenomena in the analysis of social gravitation. Census reports provide us only with the end results. They do not register the full process, the invisible processes of migration, from the statu nascendi of an embryonic striving on, all the intermediary stages of a plan up to the act of migration itself. A full understanding of migratory movements cannot be attained without their recognition.[7]

## (B) THE SOCIOGENETIC LAW

Another important generalization introduced by sociometry (6, pp. 65–66) is usually called the sociogenetic law. It states that the highest forms of group organization have evolved from simple ones: between the simplest patterns of groups formed by infants and the most complex formed by adults there are numerous intermediary stages. Parallel with this process of social differentiation a characteristic differentiation and growth of socio-sexual structure takes place within the group. The course of differentiation may differ from one culture to another, from a pre-literate to a modern society, but a common basic core of evolutionary patterns and a parallel trend should be found in all of them. From a sociatric point of view, the sociogenetic law is a challenge to the therapist. It is probable that a comparative study of cultures will show a great degree of variety in the evolutionary trend taken by their infant groups moving up to their adult groups, but it is doubtful that the trend itself can be abolished. The sociogenetic and social gravity laws both are merely symptoms of societies which are basically preference systems. Abolishing the laws entirely would mean that these systems of preference themselves have vanished and that human nature and human society have turned into forms which must be considered as unreal to our comprehension.

## (C) THE SOCIODYNAMIC LAW

The sociodynamic law is divided into a first and a second part. The first part (6, p. 74) states that the income of emotional choices per capita is

7 Deutschberger furthered the study of social gravitation in terms defined by mathematical procedures by directly submitting U.S. census tracts to sociometric tests and comparing the patterns of attracting in changing neighborhoods.

unevenly divided among the members of the group regardless of its size or kind; comparatively few get a lion's share of the total output of emotional choices, out of proportion with their needs and their ability to consummate them; the largest form an average income of choice group within their means to consummate them and a considerable number remain unchosen or neglected. The scores when plotted form a J curve, about two-thirds of the population receiving scores below chance and a relatively few obtaining high scores. Though an equal number would have been expected on the basis of chance the proportion of isolates was generally greater than the proportion of stars.

The second part states that if the opportunities of being chosen are increased by increasing the size of the group and the number of choices per capita, the volume of choices continue to go to those at the top end of the range (the "stars") in direct proportion to the size of the group and to the number of choices permitted per capita, furthering the gap between the small star group, the average group, and the neglected group. The excess "profit" gained by the already overchosen members must be ascribed to a chain and network effect which operates in cases of non-acquaintance (with the chosen individual) in addition to the score based on acquaintance (with the chosen individual). The direct factor is proximity choice, the indirect factor, a symbolic choice. An individual, A, may score high in his face to face group, but because of his "role" (he may be a baseball player, an actor, or a senator) his ultimate score may turn out to be a multiple of the initial score (role corresponds here to what is usually meant by status; status is too much of an abstraction, but role implies a living and concrete function).

The sociodynamic law affects all human relations, it operates, (a) on the inter-personal level and (b) on the inter-group level. It is found in some degree in all social aggregates whatever their kind, whether the criterion is search for mates, search for employment, or in socio-cultural relations. Its effect may change in degree but it is universally present, appearing like a halo effect, *inherent in every* social structure. A particularly significant effect takes place on the level of economic relations. The "surplus" choice becomes analogous to the surplus value observed by Marx in the process of accumulation and production of capital. The distorted profit picture in economic relations is a reflection of the distorted choice picture on the inter-personal and inter-group level. The social revolution on the class struggle is therefore a displacement from the microscopic to the macroscopic level. Social revolution on the macrosociological level is only *part* of the struggle. Marx was operating on the gross, macrosociological level of events. He often used intuitively near-sociometric ideas—a "macro" sociometrist. He was therefore rarely altogether wrong, but also rarely altogether right. Being unaware of the social microscopy of modern sociometry, he committed many grave errors (9) of insight. It would be interesting to envision what effect this knowledge would have had upon his theory and method of social revolution. It appears at least that the place of revolutionary action should have been reoriented towards the smallest units of human relations, the social atoms, the primary receptacles of "preferentiation," in order to become truly and permanently effective. The sociodynamic effect does not cease to be effective in a socialistic system of society. It assumes only different forms. The sociodynamic law offers, from a sociatric point of view, a most serious challenge to the therapist. It can be argued that it is not a law of nature but a manifestation of our present cultural values. The fact that there are very few extremely high scores may be due to the cultural factor of the value we place on competition and skill. But according to sociometric tenets, laws of nature are not absolute but themselves products of nature and vulnerable to change. It considers the spontaneity or plasticity of the universe, physical and social, as preliminary to all laws of nature. The chances are that the sociodynamic effect can be *reduced* by therapeutic devices, like sociometric group reconstruction and spontaneity training applied on a world wide scale.

## (D) THE REALITY TEST OF SOCIAL CONFIGURATIONS

A further contribution has been made by sociometry towards foundations of an objective sociology by formulating in terms defined by mathematical procedures a measure of social configurations. Based on their varying deviation from chance the degree of social significance of social configurations can be calculated. The generalizations resulting from this test should become a fruitful field for all sociological investigations dealing with the integration and disintegration of groups.

## (E) THE LAW OF THE SOCIAL ATOM

The old sociological term socius, metaphorically and vaguely used in presociometric literature, has regained in my discovery of the social atom a precise definition and has opened the way for fruitful hypotheses and practical research. The hypothesis states that as the individual projects his emotions into the groups around him and as the members of these groups in turn project their emotions toward him, a pattern of attractions and repulsions, as projected from both sides, can be discerned on the threshold between individual and group. This pattern is called his "social atom." "Every individual's social atom retains a significant *consistency* in its ratio of positive reciprocation and its interchoice ratio between two time points. The incidence of patterns at one time and at a later time in the same community is a relatively constant factor in the structure of attractions and in the structure of rejections which characterize it. There are found, in a given community, specific choice and rejection patterns and they show an orderly distribution within it. Yet, while the incidence of certain patterns may be relatively constant, the findings further show that the individuals occupying particular patterns at one time may or may not be the same individuals who occupy them at the later time."

## (F) THE TELE PHENOMENON

I defined Tele as *the socio-gravitational factor responsible for the degree of reality of a social configuration above chance.* It operates between individuals, drawing them to form *more* positive or negative pair-relations, triangles, quadrangles, polygons, etc., than by chance. The factor responsible for the degree of irreality of social configurations *near or below* chance, can be called transference. Tele and transference (the pathological distortion of tele) became thus amenable to a sociometric type of quantification. Sociometrists differentiate therefore three types of relationships: reality produced relations (often described as coexistential, co-operational, two way or objectified relations), delusional relations, and esthetic relations. The reality produced relations are tele phenomena; it is upon them that the solidity and permanency of social relations depend. The delusional relations are transference phenomena and play a role in psychopathology. The esthetic relations are empathy phenomena, empathy being the one-way "Einfuehlung" into objects. It is harmful to stretch the meaning of transference to cover all human relationships beyond the definition given to it by its coiner. It is particularly meaningless because if we make transference an over-all term we would have to differentiate three types of transference, reality bound transference, delusional transference, and esthetic transference. This gives lip service to the "word" transference but it does not change the facts. It is preferable therefore, to have for every operation a specific term expressing it. In this manner the three phenomena, tele, transference, empathy, which were dormant and inherent in Mesmer's animal fluid, have been identified by sociometrists as independent functions and again brought together and shown in combined operation. Studies of the warming up process of individuals towards each other have revealed that the importance which psychoanalysis has given to transference is exaggerated. The tele phenomenon is operating already in the first meeting of two individuals. The longer a relationship lasts the more it becomes dominated by tele and not by transference. Even if the transference portion was large to begin with, it vanishes often as the relationship goes on. This is found to be true of all inter-individual relations, even of the relation between physician and patient. As the relationship endures the projectional aspects recede and the real attributes of the physician are perceived. In other words, true transference, in the psychoanalytic sense, diminishes in quantity and intensity as individuals mature and as groups gain in cohesion and integration. The effect of social catharsis is to increase tele production and to decrease transference production between members of groups. Tele, therefore, can be defined as the group binder, transference as the group *disintegrator*. That the factor tele operates between persons has been demonstrated by sociometric methods (11). It operates, (a) between persons like A B, who are mere acquaintances, (b) between persons like A B, who are not only mere acquaintances but who are attracting or rejecting one another in reference to one or more specific criteria, (c) between persons like A B, who are *unacquainted* persons but related to each other via a criterion; like A B, who are unacquainted *and* unrelated to each other by a criterion.

## (G) SOCIOMETRIC TEST OF INTERGROUP RELATIONS

The most promising new development is the application of sociometric methods to intergroup relations. The one method now widely used is the *sociodrama* (10), stemming from psychodrama which studies interpersonal relations. Sociodrama studies intergroup relations by means of action methods. Psychodrama and sociodrama tests explore two different areas found interwoven in every group.

Another method suggested by the writer is a new sociometric test modified for the measurement of intergroup relations. The new sociometric test of inter-group relations differs from its twin test of interpersonal relations by the *systematic and gradual reduction of the choice area* permitted. Whereas for instance, in the interpersonal test the tendency was to extend for the individual the area of choice to a maximum, a maximum of self-expression, in order to gain insight into the endo-social thresholds, the tendency of the inter-group test is gradually to limit the choice area and focus his attention upon the restricted area. A sociometrist of a neighborhood may direct the inhabitants to choose their associates *only* among the Negroes, the Spanish, and the refugees and leave themselves, the American born out of being chosen. The expression of preference is then limited to the three minority groups. Or he may direct the inhabitants to choose their associates only among representatives of certain vocations, physicians, teachers, and lawyers, for instance, leaving all other vocations out. Through the data received, role (intergroup) preference instead of only individual preference comes to expression. Without losing the specificity of individual choice, the more varied and reduced the areas are, the more the results will gain a group categorical character. In proportion to the degree to which choice areas are reduced, there will result a scale ranging from a maximum degree of individual choice expression, to a maximum of group characterizations of its choice.

The *rapprochement* between sociometry and the social sciences is rapidly increasing. These are signposts indicating the trend, but there are many more. It means an advance of the combat forces against the threat of sociometric cultism, to an extent indispensable with any pioneering endeavor. This development, however, is in itself a case illustration of the law of gravity operating between sociometry and the social sciences. The progressive factors are increasing, the retarding factors are shrinking.

## REFERENCES

1. Bassett, R. E. *Sociometry*, 1946, 9.
2. Criswell, Joan H. A sociometric study of race cleavage in the classroom. *Arch. Psychol.*, 1939, No. 235.
3. Deutschberger, P. Patterns of attraction in changing neighborhoods. *Sociometry*, 1946, 9, No. 4.
4. Jennings, Helen H. Experimental evidence of the social atom. *Sociometry*, 1942, 5, 135–145.
5. Jennings, Helen H. *Leadership and isolation.* London: Longmans, Green, 1943.
6. Moreno, J. L. *Who shall survive?* 1934.
7. Moreno, J. L. *Statistics of social configurations*, 1937–8.
8. Moreno, J. L. Sociometry and the cultural order. *Sociometry*, 1943, 6, 299–344.
9. Moreno, J. L. Marxism, Comtism and sociometry. *Sociometry*, 8, No. 2.
10. Moreno, J. L. Sociodrama. *Psychodrama Monogr.*, No. 1. Beacon House, N.Y.
11. Moreno, J. L., & Jennings, Helen H. Sociometric statistics of social configurations. *Sociometry*, 1938, 1, 342–374.
12. Stewart, J. Q. The gravitation or geographical drawing power of a college, 1941.
13. Stewart, J. Q. Influence of a population at a distance. *Sociometry*, 1942.
14. Stouffer, S. A. Intervening opportunities. *Amer. sociol. Rev.*, 1940.
15. Thorndike, E. L. The causes of inter-state migration. *Sociometry*, 1942.

# *Concepts and Methods in the Measurement of Group Syntality*

RAYMOND B. CATTELL

## I. FIRST THINGS FIRST IN SOCIAL PSYCHOLOGY

NOW THAT social psychology has recognized its major concern to be the psychology of groups—in relation to one another and to individuals—the time is ripe to discuss research methods and concepts for arriving at *the description of group behavior.*

FROM *Psychological Review*, 1948, 55, 48–63. Reprinted by permission of the author and the American Psychological Association, Inc.

It is to be hoped that history will not repeat itself by recapitulating in social psychology the unnecessarily wayward and wasteful course of individual psychology. The development of an exact science of prediction in relation to individual personality required, as in other biological sciences, the prior provision of accurate description, measurement, and classification of phenomena. Actually amateur speculation and incontinent "explanation," remote from actualities of measurement or observation, ran riot and sadly delayed progress by deflecting the attention of researchers, until recent years, from the basic and unescapable discipline of a true science of personality measurement.

This contribution to social psychology begins, therefore, with the challenge that the solution of the vital practical and theoretical social problems now clamoring for attention requires scientific workers to restrain themselves from superficial "research" until a correct foundation for the meaningful description and measurement of groups has been achieved. It then proceeds to propound concepts, methods, and experiments for this foundation. It asserts, as a logical premise, that to arrive at laws governing the development and interaction of groups, we must first have some accurate means of defining a group at a given moment.

We have, in short, to establish a branch of psychology concerned with the "personality" of groups. "Establish" is used advisedly; for at present—in spite of much talk about "culture patterns"—methods and concepts simply do not exist. The sociologists, recognizing that a group cannot be defined in merely political or economic terms, have turned to the psychologist for a science of the living group entity, but, for reasons evident in the following section, they have yet done so in vain. Mannheim (24), typical of sociologists disappointed in constructive synthesis by the psychologists' impotence, well says "The main reason for our failure in this branch of human studies is that up till now we have had no historical or sociological psychology."

## II. THE DIMENSIONS OF SYNTALITY

By "personality," in the individual, we mean "that which will predict his behavior in any given, defined situation" (8). Mathematically we take a pattern of indices which defines the personality and another set defining the situation, arriving therefrom at an estimate of the ensuing behavior. Psychologically we speak of the former—the personality indices—as a structure of traits—a set of more or less permanent "readinesses," which function behaviorally under the impact of a stimulus situation.

For the corresponding structure in the group an unambiguous term is needed. Examination of many possible verbal roots indicates *syntality* as best indicating the "togetherness" of the group, while having sufficient suggestive parallelism to "personality" and "totality." Further, we may perhaps speak appropriately of the syntality of a group as inferred from the "synaction" of its members—the group action as defined below. Syntality covers dynamic, temperamental, and ability traits of the group.[1]

The measurement of syntality can profit greatly from the technical advances gained in the measurement of personality. The early failures of personality study mentioned above came not only from an attempt to abort the descriptive phase of psychology, but from an inability, once the necessity of description was admitted, to find any better foundation for measurement than the numberless shifting sands of arbitrary "traits" in poorly designed *ad hoc* "tests." All that has been altered, by the original work of Spearman, Burt (5), Thurstone (35) and many others, which made the concept of the unitary trait meaningful. Although this work has yet scarcely affected applied psychology it has, in the last fifteen years, delivered psychology already from a confused impasse. It first enlightened the measuring of abilities, and later, by the work of Guilford, Mosier, Reyburn, and others on questionnaire response and the present writer's analyses of surface and source traits, was carried to those unitary traits of temperamental and dynamic nature which could complete the description of personality.

It is easy to see now that if factorial methods had been applied from the beginning to the description and measurement of personality, using R-technique for common traits and P-technique (8) for unique traits, a true perspective of the important dimensions would have been obtained much earlier than by the hit-or-miss methods of clinical "intuition." The measurement of abilities, for example, would have been saved many a discouraging, profitless circuit of "philosophical" debate as to the nature of various abilities, as well as many acrimonious, ineffectual arguments as to the criteria against which measures should be validated. The disillusionment of students with overburdened lists of personality "types"—each peculiar to the university at which he happened to be studying—would also have been avoided.

Social psychology now stands where the study of individual personality then stood. In effect psychologists have accumulated a few fragmentary aspects of group syntality from various isolated studies. They have chanced upon "morale" (although the label probably covers such different variables as group persistence against difficulties and mean level of individual idealism), aggressiveness, authoritarian-democratic stucture, isolationism, degree of freedom from internal dissension, etc. Mostly these "dimensions" of group behavior have been seized upon in response to the

1 Apparently the only other use of syntality, a specialized and remote one, is in C. Morris's *Signs, language and behavior*, New York: Prentice Hall, 1946. The derived term, synergy, employed below, has been used (apart from its physiological use) in sociology by Lester Ward (37) but again in a far wider and less technical, defined sense than here. These contexts are so remote that no danger of confusion arises.

suggestion of some immediate practical problem, without regard to any over-all theory or to long-term scientific needs in social psychology. The slightest consideration of the whole natural history of groups would probably suggest more important variables than these for describing their total behavior.

An embarrassing harvest of muddle, moreover, is likely to be reaped if the application of large terms for small variables continues very long with respect to the labeling of group traits. Is it fitting, for example, to describe experimental groups as Totalitarian or Democratic (in science as distinct from journalism) when no proof is offered that these are unitary patterns or when the variables actually measured are perhaps the least important for defining that total pattern, if it exists as a single pattern?

It would seem better to stick to modest, less interpretive, more contingent labels for more completely definable experimental variables, until the true patterns emerge and are confirmed.

Social psychology, therefore, now awaits its foundation of accurately described syntalities, alike at the level of culture patterns, of institutional groups, and of small committees. That foundation can be achieved *by factor analysis of a "population" of groups, on a suitably chosen collection of group behavior variables.* Our purpose here is not to present particular results but to examine the promise and the limitations of this novel application of factorization and discuss the conditions under which it is valid. Nevertheless, the discussion will be guided at least by certain rough and qualitative observations already possible on the first two studies now proceeding in the field, and to be reported elsewhere (11, 12). The first is a study of 60 nations, factorizing 40 variables by R-technique, checked by two small sample studies employing Q- and P-techniques (8, 11). The second (12) factorizes a rich variety of group performances from 25 groups of six people each, i.e., of "committee size." For effective exploration with the new method requires that it be brought to bear on widely different group sizes and forms.

A general requirement of the method is that the variables shall be chosen with the utmost catholicity to cover all aspects of group behavior. The application of this principle to individual personality in the "personality sphere" concept (8) has already rewarded us with factors which not only clarify long familiar, previously foggy, clinical syndromes, but also reveal important dimensions which were never conceptualized. By attention to this principle in the realm of social psychology we can expect similarly to discover those factors which will describe most of the differences of groups in terms of relatively few unitary traits or meaningful dimensions. They may turn out to be familiar dimensions such as morale, democratic organization, industrialization, etc. or may open our eyes to functionally new "wholes" or dimensions of groups. Thereafter, by assigning measurements on these primary dimensions to any given culture pattern we can accurately define its syntality, as the necessary basis for developmental and causal studies.

## III. THE FACTORIZABLE CHARACTERISTICS OF GROUPS: LOGICAL ANALYSIS

As we concentrate on the choice of variables we run into certain problems of assortment which can perhaps be solved to a certain degree by armchair reflection. This and the following section constitute attempts thus to achieve the maximum clarity of experimental design and problem formulation, with the adoption of definite hypotheses.

Out of deference to majority opinion we ought perhaps to ask at the outset the supposedly devastating question whether such a thing as a group mentality exists at all. It is of historical if not of scientific importance that McDougall's penetrating pioneer analysis (25) of "the group mind" was badly received by a certain section of American psychologists. In the descendants of this sectional opposition the allergic reaction to his expression is still so strong as to paralyze thought, and writers who pander [2] to irrationality have for years operated with McDougall's concept by circumlocutions. The rejection was not due to opposition to Hegelianism, for McDougall's able philosophical preamble explicitly refuted Hegelian mysticism and accepted Hobhouse's searching anti-idealist criticisms. The probably correct, but more trivial explanation was that this contribution to social psychology was launched at an unfortunate moment. For a large number of callow students in psychology were unable at that time to recognize any manifestation of mind unless formally, or often actually, reduced to the twitching of a dog's hind leg. From the drouth of this sterile atomism they presently rushed, with undiminished lack of judgment, down a steep place into the sea of ineffable, unmeasurable—but far from inaudible—Gestalt.

Fortunately a steady nucleus of naturalistic observation and methodological constructiveness survived and developed, despite those local setbacks, and despite the disturbances from the clamorous medieval tournaments among the pseudo-philosophical "isms" of psychology. Meanwhile the idea was further developed by Gurwitch (18) in sociology, and, in more vague terms, by Whitehead and by Roethlisberger in industrial psychology. Finally, the main line of development in pure psychology has given us better technical methods, notably factor analysis and its variants, for investigating behavioral wholes and dynamic patterns.

It could be argued that any study of total organisms, such as McDougall proposed, should have been postponed until new methods had been

2 To the objection that many psychologists misconceive the term one must reply as Freud did to Max Eastman's similar objection to the precisely defined notion of the Unconscious, "Cannot they correct their misconceptions?"

invented, but this is quite different from asserting (a) that reflexology is capable of explaining the behavior of organisms as such, or (b) that wholes do not exist. Of the difficulties of the social psychologist at that juncture McDougall wrote (25, p. x), ". . . to the obscure question of fact with which he deals, it is in the nature of things impossible to return answers supported by indisputable experimental proofs. In this field the evidence of an author's approximation towards truth can consist only in his success in gradually persuading competent opinion of the value of his views." His optimism about the existence of a large reservoir of competent opinion proved unjustified. But the vigor of prejudice has one virtue: that it forces the development of precision methods from the conclusions of which the prejudiced cannot escape.

McDougall himself, unfortunately, failed to develop the method here described, but many of his conclusions about group behavior are likely to prove correct, and his basic contention that it is rewarding to deal with groups as single entities remains the springboard whence we take off into new research fields. His arguments for treating the group as an organism or mind which have never been refuted, are set out below [3] together with

3 The behavior of a group has more formal resemblance to the behavior of an individual organism than to any other natural entity, principally in the following respects:

(1) A group preserves characteristic behavior habits and structure despite the continual replacement of actual individuals.

(2) It shows memory for group experiences and learning.

(3) It is capable if responding as a whole to stimuli directed to its parts, i.e., it tends to solve problems of individuals and sub-groups by group action.

(4) It possesses drives which become more or less integrated in executive functions of nutrition, acquisition, aggression, defense, etc. Groups vary in dynamic integration analogously to the variation of individuals in character.

(5) It experiences "moods" of expansiveness, depression, pugnacity, etc. which modify characteristic behavior and energy output as do emotional states in the individual.

(6) It shows collective deliberation, a process highly analogous to the trial-and-error thinking of the individual, when held up in a course of action. Similarly the act of collective volition, through legislatures and executives, is closely analogous to the resolution of conflicting dynamic demands in the individual.

A group also tends to exercise some choice on admission or rejection of those who aggregate towards it. This, like some few other basic characteristics of groups, has no analogy in the individual mind, except the remote one of selective learning and attention.

Against these it can be urged (a) that the grey matter or total nervous system is more dispersed than that associated with the single biological organism, and (b) that there is no group consciousness corresponding to individual consciousness. Both of these are doubtful objections, but in any case they are outside the realm of psychological observation. They *may* account for the systematic differences research will undoubtedly find between the "group mind" and the individual mind; they do not jeopardize the aim of using the group as a behavioral unity and reference point in psychological research. A less bald outline of the theoretical arguments over the group mind has been set out by the present writer elsewhere (7). Extremely few "experimental" (as distinct from historical) treatments of groups as unitary organisms yet exist to demonstrate the practicability of the hypothesis; but Thorndike's treatment of cities (34), showing them to have persistent characteristic traits, already offers some pragmatic proof. Characteristic (c) above—that all parts react adjustively (perhaps homeo-

certain new observations on the question. That some psychologists should ever have congratulated themselves on their "realism" (rather than on mere concrete thinking and failure of abstraction) in rejecting the group as an organic entity, is still more surprising when one observes that hard-headed lawyers, politicians, and statesmen deal operationally with groups *as* groups every day.

As to the behavior from which the group mentality is to be inferred, however, there runs alike through McDougall's and other psychologists' writings what we consider a rather serious confusion of characteristics. On grounds of logical analysis we suggest that there are *three* aspects or "panels" to be taken into account in defining a group.

(*1*) *Syntality Traits* (Behavior of the group as a group). The group behavior recorded here concerns any effect the group has as a totality, upon other groups or its physical environment. Just as the individual may show more willed (conscious), and less organized (neurotic symptom, temperament) behavior, so the group behavior will range from action by (a) whatever organized will and executive agencies the group processes, to (b) less organized, uncontrolled elements and so to (c) unorganized mass action, expressing largely the average individual as under (*3*) below. For example, the sheer amount of food the group eats would be largely a function of this last kind.

A catalogue of syntality traits, analogous to the personality sphere, as advocated above, is not easy to obtain, since there is no dictionary as of personality traits. We have proceeded by (a) making an exhaustive study of the many incisive writings on group characteristics, e.g., Benedict (1), Brogan (3), Cole (13), Keyserling (23), Mead (26), Siegfried (32), and Münsterberg (29), and of the characterizations found in history and (b) by using the *personality sphere* (8) as a guide to possibly important areas of behavior in syntality.

Most of these traits will be inferred from external behavior of the group, but the executive will of the group can manifest its properties also in *internal action*, e.g., in deliberately changing internal organization, suppressing internal revolt. Examples of syntality traits are: aggressiveness against groups (e.g., acts of declaration of war), efficiency in exploitation of natural resources, isolationism, energy in trading, reliability in commitments, proneness to trade cycles or to revolutions.

(*2*) *Characteristics of Internal Structure.* These concern the *relationships among the members of the group.* The character of unification and of government is primary, and this may vary from a practically unstructured crowd through horde leadership and the incipient democratic leadership in Moreno's (27) vague "tele or the movement of feeling to-

statically) to stimuli affecting limited segments—will be taken as the primary definition of the group.

ward leader individuals" to a highly organized legislature and executive. Internal structure characters issue in syntality traits but they are not themselves the behavior of the group.

Examples of structural characters are: all sorts of indices expressing degree of heterogeneity in various characteristics, indices of class structure, pattern of institutions and organs such as church, army, family, modes of government, and communication.

(3) *Population Traits.* These are mere aggregate values—definitions of the personality of the *average* (or typical, modal) member of the group. It is noticeable that in the literature of group characteristics the bulk of observations actually concern the typical member of the population rather than the group syntality.

Examples of population characteristics are: average intelligence, crime incidence, attitudes on moral and religious questions, and all that is usually gathered by population polls.

The probable relationship among these three [4] panels is that if we knew all the laws of social psychology we could predict the first from the second and third. Alternatively, if we knew the third and the environment of the group we could predict the second, i.e., the type of group structure which would emerge, and therefore, ultimately, the first, i.e., the group behavior. This is no denial of the principle that the mind of the group is fashioned by individuals and in turn fashions the individual mind. In the extreme instance of the second where we are dealing with a practically unstructured crowd, the first and third become practically identical.

From the interim observations available in our experiments we can already generalize the hypothesis that the changes in syntality traits produced by changes in population traits will be qualitatively as well as quantitatively different from the latter. For example, an increment in average intelligence may change character-like qualities in the group, while a difference between groups in average emotional stability of the population may appear as a difference in the ability of the group *per se* to solve cognitive complexities. This we shall call the *theory of emergents* (or syntal emergents).

## IV. SEVEN THEOREMS ON THE DYNAMICS OF SYNTALITY

The implicit conception of group which most people unconsciously adopt in such discussions as the above is of an aggregate composed of a number of individuals whose *whole existence* is bound up with the group. Real

4 It may be objected that we overlook a fourth ingredient in the definition of the group—namely the group tradition. It is true that this "momentum" of the group is as important as its material existence and that groups of any maturity are composed of the dead as much as of the living. These traditions, however, exist in the minds of the living—the constitution of the United States, for example, would be ineffective if no one knew about it—and are adequately included in all three panels above.

groups are rarely of this kind and for the most profitable application of the new method to general group investigation it behooves us first to analyze as far as possible what the situation is with regard to varieties of groups and the modifications of method required to cope with them. This analysis turns principally on the dynamic relations within and between groups, for temperamental and ability characters do not differ in any systematic way, as far as we can see, from those known in individuals.

Sociologists have written a good deal about group classification and, more tangentially, about dynamics, and we must first glance at the evolution of opinion among outstanding representatives. Gumplowicz in his classical treatment (16) outdistanced most of the psychologists of a generation later by conceiving that laws can be formed about the behavior of groups ("The behavior of collective entities is determined by natural laws") but failed to agree with the present integrative psychological position by maintaining somewhat unnecessarily that this behavior had no relation to "the motives and natural qualities of (constituent) individuals." Ross (30) proceeded to carry the study of groups into a classificatory system which included "Fortuitous groups" (crowds), "Natural groups" (families, clans), "Interest groups" (states, confederacies, guilds), and also, but less happily, "Likeness groups" (professions, classes) in which presumably nothing dynamic but only a logical bond might hold the members together. Gillin and Gillin (15) adopt a somewhat similar classification, but descriptively and without implying fundamental psychological differences. To the psychologist a merely logical classification is untenable. *Every* group is an interest group—in the sense that its existence arises from a dynamic need—or else it is not, in any psychological sense, a group. Sorokin and Zimmerman's (33) distinction between "systems" and "congeries" seems to be a statement of this issue in other terms.[5]

Even when sociologists, however, have recognized that a group exists only because and so long as it satisfies psychological needs, they have failed to appreciate the nature of the ergic (10) and the metanergic needs that are involved in its support. Hayes (20), Hart (19), Von Wiese (36), and others stress or dwell wholly upon security, as if small groups form, and then aggregate into larger groups, only under threat. This may be a common motive—indeed fear and gregariousness may account for practically all association in the lower animals. But in man, with his power of learning ways of long-circuited satisfaction, the whole gamut of primary ergs—hunger, escape, self assertion, curiosity, sex, gregariousness, etc.—may participate in group formation. The sheer fact of groups needing to have adequate dynamic basis, obvious though it may now be, needs em-

5 The satisfaction of a need through the physical existence of the group is the basic definition of existence of a psychological group. The definition that a group exists when there is "internal interaction" of individuals seems less fundamental to the present writer, and indeed derivative from the above primary condition.

phasis at this juncture in social psychology because the extension of group experiment of the present kind brings the risk that, in the artificial situation of experiments, groups will be employed which are not created by a real purpose of the participants.

Beyond this fundamental character the psychologist has next to recognize the fact of *dynamic specialization*, a phenomenon tied up with the almost universal occurrence of overlapping groups. For the simplification of a first experimental approach we have chosen, as described above, self-contained groups: nations, which have relatively shadowy loyalties beyond themselves, and committee groups in a control "vacuum" situation in which no other loyalties of the members are brought into action or conflict. But the great majority of existing social groups, other than nations, are overlapping, in the sense that individuals belong simultaneously to several groups. This situation exists because, as Cole succinctly puts it (13), "an association (group) can always be made specific in function, while man can never be made so."

From this arise some intricate but important relations among groups and between group structure and the dynamic structure of the individual. For brevity and precision we shall formulate these relations in *seven theorems concerning the psychodynamics of groups*, the first of which will simply state the conclusion of the above few paragraphs' discussion.

*Theorem 1. The Dynamic Origin of Groups: Definition of Synergy.* Groups are devised for achieving individual satisfaction and exist only when they provide a means to the ends of individual ergic goals.

The interest, "ergic investment," or "need satisfaction" tied up with the existence of the group must be clearly conceived as having three parts or modifications: (*1*) First there is the total individual energy going into the group—absorbed by its activities—which we have called the group *synergy*. (*2*) As Rousseau (31) pointed out, however, "the general will" is not the same as "the will of all." In Bosanquet's (2) phrase, the individual wills "cancel one another" resulting in "sovereignty." In our vectorial theory of dynamic traits certain components nullify one another, as shown by the difference between the resultant expressing the dynamic interest of the group and the non-vectorial sum of the individual interests. The unified attitude which emerges as the dynamic intention of the group *per se* we shall call the *effective synergy* or effective investment. It is the energy expressed in gaining the outside goals for which the group has come together (*3*). The difference between the total synergy and the effective synergy is absorbed in internal friction and in maintaining cohesion of the group. This we may call the *intrinsic* or *group maintenance synergy*. It is a loss by internal friction and absorption. Without more space than can be given here it is not possible to analyze the rather complex transformations in group maintenance. This synergy absorbs not only selfish, anti-social and aggressive motivations, which "cancel out," but also the self-submissive and self assertive satisfactions of leader-follower activity and the needs of the gregarious drive. The latter is usually satisfied wholly in the group and does not pass on into effective synergy, though, like some other intrinsic synergy expenditures, it does "effective" work in the sense of preserving group cohesion.

Though the magnitude of the intrinsic synergy normally has to be inferred from the difference of (*1*) and (*2*), it manifests itself directly as an active resistance when attempts are made to dissolve the group. Intrinsic synergy is *relatively* (not absolutely) great, in comparison with effective synergy, in a recreational club interested in sociability; effective synergy is relatively great in a political party, a scientific institute, or a religious missionary society. However, in the special situation of an attempt to dissolve the group *all* the energy may be thrown back into cohesive activities, so that the last statement will no longer be true.

*Theorem 2. The Vectorial Measurement of Group Synergy.* To measure the total vectorial intrinsic and effective investment in a given group, i.e., the total group *synergy*, we have to take account of (*1*) the number of people interested; (*2*) the intensity or strength of the satisfaction each gains; (*3*) the ergic quality (vector direction (10)) of the satisfactions, and (*4*) the subsidiation relations of these satisfactions with respect to other groups and other purposes of the individuals concerned.

The number of people interested in a group will depend partly on the demostatic level or percolation range (6) of the idea involved, from the point of view of intelligence level, and partly on the dynamic needs it sets out to satisfy. For the present we can set aside this mere number, as a multiplier of whatever other measurements we make.

The measurement of dynamic quantity and quality has been treated systematically elsewhere (10). An attitude is a vector quantity defined as to direction (quality) by: $(aF_1)$ $(bF_2)$ $(cF_3)$ . . . etc., where $F_1$, $F_2$, etc. are coordinates corresponding to basic drives (ergs) or to general sentiment structures (and therefore common social institutions) and a, b, etc. are coefficients for the particular attitude, expressing the extent of its subsidiation to each of these common and basic goals. The strength of the attitude is expressed by

$$S = aF_1 + bF_2 + cF_3 \ldots \text{etc.},$$

where a, b, and c are as above, and $F_1$, $F_2$, etc. have satisfaction values specific for that group.

The synergy of the group is the vectorial resultant of the attitudes toward the group of all its members. Individual attitudes will vary slightly in direction and some of this deviation will be cancelled in the vectorial sum—in other words, it will be lost in the internal friction of the group.

The rest will appear either as intrinsic investment, constituting the basic strength of cohesion of the group, or as effective investment, constituting the interest of the group as such.

The effective synergy of the group can finally be expressed as a vector quantity on the same coordinates as for individual attitudes.

*Theorem 3. Syntal Subsidiation and the Dynamic Lattices of Groups.* The effective synergy of any group goes out to purposes which are outside the group and consequently sets up habits of reacting which are subsidiary (10), with respect to some ultimate goal of the group's activity. The formation or partial support of other (mostly ancillary) groups is generally part of the subsidiation chain. For example, a nation sets up an army as a means to its goal of security or aggression, and a country club may set up a committee to engineer a swimming pool as part of its synergy purpose of providing recreation. The use of group B as a tool by group A is not incompatible with the use of A by B, and, as in personal subsidiation (10), paths will form a complex, *dynamic lattice* with transflux and retroaction.

Some typical syntal subsidiations in the group and individual habits which form institutions are illustrated in the dotted lines in the following diagram. The nation supports universities because they are on its subsidiation chain to the goal of an educated democracy. It favors the family as maintaining population stability, while cities contribute to its desire for revenue and prestige. Both the family and the city, as groups, in turn have need of the nation, which satisfies their need for protection, etc. The army, in pursuit of its purposes, founds an Army Air Force and this in turn sets up a psychological Personnel Section. Although these latter accord with the will of the nation they are not directly in the subsidiary chain of the nation's purpose of self defence, but draw their origin from separate successive synergies of Army and Army Air Force. The nation, as it were, delegates synergy to the army and, as a group, has no sense of these further purposes.

*Syntal dynamic lattices are quite different and distinct from the dynamic lattice patterns of individuals*, even of the particular individuals who happen to constitute chief executives of groups. (Compare dotted with continuous lines in the diagram.) This happens increasingly with the growth of specialized labor and of general currency. Nevertheless the two sets of dynamic lattices necessarily add up to the same activities and the same energy total—save for the loss between intrinsic and effective synergy.

Problems of relationship of syntal lattices and personal lattices will be different for overlapping and non-overlapping groups. Some groups, e.g., nations, demand a sovereignty which will not permit members to belong to other, generally similar, groups, or to experience subjection to the purposes of other groups. Most groups, however, have overlapping personnel, and this creates dynamic problems in connection with syntal subsidiation more complex than for non-overlapping groups.

Syntal subsidiation chains will not normally end in ergic goals, as do those of individuals. The basic goals of the group concern the preservation

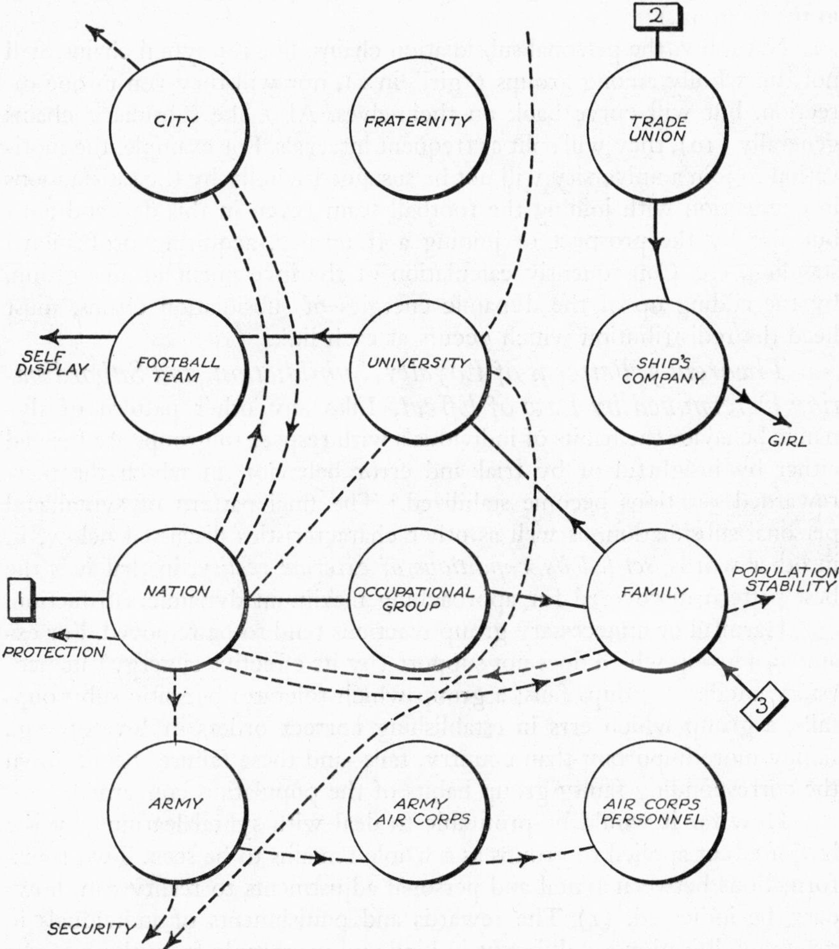


and expansion of the group. They can be resolved into ergic goals, by analysis, but they are not individual biological goals in themselves.

*Theorem 4. Personal Subsidiation of Groups in the Individual Dynamic Lattice*. The subsidiation chains occurring in the dynamic lattice of the individual (10) often include groups as "links." For example, an *émigré* doctor may acquire citizenship (Group 1) in order that he may belong to his professional group (Group 2) in order that he may maintain his family (Group 3). (Chain 1 in the diagram.) Or a man may belong to a trade union (Group 2), in order to be able to join a ship's company (Group 2) in order to travel to see his girl. (Chain 2 in the diagram.) Or, to illustrate a different direction, a young man half in mind to leave the parental roof may maintain his belonging to the family in order to be sent to a university in order to get onto the university football team. (Chain 3 in the diagram.)

Naturally, the personal subsidiation chains, like the syntal chains, will not run wholly among groups ("girl" in 2), nor will they run in one direction, but will curve back on themselves. Also like subsidiary chains generally (10), they will split at frequent intervals. For example, the motivation to join a university will not be sustained wholly by the satisfactions in connection with joining the football team (even in this day and age) but also by the prospect of joining a fraternity, acquiring professional standing, etc. Consequently calculation of the investment in any group, by the adding up of the dynamic energies of subsidiation chains, must heed the redistribution which occurs at each link.

*Theorem 5. Patterns of Loyalty, Subsidiation, and Subordination Determined by Law of Effect.* Like any other pattern of dynamic behavior the habits of individuals with respect to groups are formed either by insightful or by trial and error behavior, in which the most rewarded reactions become stabilized.[6] The final pattern of syntal and personal subsidiation, as well as other characteristics discussed below, is, in other words, *settled by conditions of external reality*, in that it is the best pattern discovered for approaching maximum dynamic satisfaction.

Harmful or unnecessary group reactions tend to be removed. For example, a group which does not support (by its effective synergy) its necessary ancillary groups fails; a group which tolerates parasitic subgroups fails; a group which errs in establishing correct orders of loyalty, e.g., family more important than country, fails--and these failures break down the corresponding faulty group habits of the population concerned.

How far it would be profitable to deal with syntal learning by the law of effect applied to groups as a whole remains to be seen. Two transformations between syntal and personal adjustments to reality can, however, be indicated. (*1*) The rewards and punishments of individuals in group modification are different in kind and magnitude from those of the group. For example, the defeat of a nation may mean death to some, economic loss to others, loss of self regard for all. The "death" of a nation—its total disintegration—may mean no more than the necessity for the individual to acquire new language and other habits. (*2*) Not only are individual rewards different, but they are also often delayed, indirect and harder to associate, insightfully, with their group causes. Since group learning eventually takes place through this "secondary" learning of indi-

6 If any proof of this is needed, it is offered, for example, by Mowrer's neat experiments on the social behavior of the rat (28).

viduals it is not surprising that the acquisition of intelligently adapted and integrated group behavior is a slower and more painful process than similar learning with respect to the purposes of individuals.

In referring to the group behavior that has to get adapted to reality we have spoken of a hierarchy of loyalty, as well as of the previously described personal subsidiation lattice and syntal subsidiation (or "subordination") lattice. The relation of these to one another is tentatively discussed in the next section.

That personal, individual behavior shall fit in with the requirements of syntal subsidiation and integration is assured mainly by (a) the creation of forces in the individual super ego which augment personal subsidiation trends usually of a more purely ergic level, and (b) the shifting of rewards to "artificial" points by money and other tokens exchangeable for dynamic satisfaction. Thus when many desire the defense of a country but few volunteer for the army an army of mercenaries may be made "loyal" to the country by rewards transferred from the money representing and created by the dynamic attachments of others to their country. Money is thus one way, the principal way, of transferring dynamic energy from one point to another. This needs to be taken into account in any attempt at dynamic calculus and offers one of the bridges from psychology to economics.

*Theorem 6. Synergic Constancy in a Closed System (Fixed Population) with Overlapping Groups.* By reason of the principle of constancy of individual mental energy (on which we proceed in such matters of individual dynamics as learning or neurosis) certain relations follow in the synergies of overlapping groups.

Chief among these deduced relations is that of *constancy of total synergy in overlapping groups*, providing certain conditions are maintained. Not all of the individual's energy goes into groups, so condition (*1*) is that the non-group investment remain constant. Condition (*2*) is that the group activities remain on the same level with regard to long circuiting (or goal distance). This is necessary for two reasons. First, the individual's energy becomes expressed more readily if he is permitted less long circuited satisfaction. Since some groups occasion less suppression and internal conflict in individuals than others, releasing more of the individual's total energy for external expression, this condition is not easily satisfied. Secondly, new groups can be linked on to a personal subsidiation chain of groups without calling on fresh energy, provided the population has not reached its toleration limit for long circuiting. For example, if a man has interest in a golf club he may be induced to join a society for the preservation of the golf course, without drawing on any new springs of interest. But this long circuiting may strike him as a bore. There are probably further conditions related to his interest in golf which will only become evident when the principle of constancy of individual mental energy is more accurately worked out. For example, we are arguing on the condition of constancy of what psychoanalysts would call "object libido investment," not of total energy, and certain social changes might alter the ratio of object libido to the total energy.

A corollary on this theorem is that the liquidation of any group structure will then automatically create—for psychological rcasons alone and without regard for social needs and real conditions—a readjustment among the synergies of the remaining overlapping groups. They must alter their patterns to give new qualities of satisfaction—or else the residue must be taken up by some new group, equivalent in synergy, if not in intellectual content, to the lost group. For example, the dissolution of football teams might result in the activities of political parties taking on the characteristics of street fighting. A calculus of group readjustment could thus be founded on the ergic mensuration of vectors of synergy.

*Theorem 7. Isomorphism of Syntality Change and Personality Change.* Although the structures and functions of groups, overlapping or non-overlapping, are always ultimately shaped by the conditions of reality (as in Theorem 5 above), their form at any moment depends also on the readiness of individual minds to learn quickly or to depart quickly from that structure which is, realistically, optimum.

There will thus be a close parallelism (modified by the nature of the intrinsic relations within the groups) between syntality traits and personality traits of the population, especially those concerned with learning and dynamic stability. For example, the immediate cause of stability of group structures is the stability of the corresponding attitudes and sentiments in the individual mind. Nothing prevents an army marching to the capital and taking charge of a nation except the higher loyalty of the patriotic sentiment, in relation to the army sentiment, in the minds of the individual soldiers. (In fact Roman legionaries abroad sometimes experienced such a growth of the sentiment toward their army fellows that unscrupulous generals could use them to overpower the Republic.) The "realistic" checks ultimately make this unrewarding (to the army and to the nation), but the immediate check is only the inherent stability (disposition rigidity) of sentiments in the individual mind.

Among the chief parallel characteristics that may be suggested are syntal conservatism (resistance to gradual change) and personal, individual *disposition rigidity;* syntal integration and personal intelligence level; syntal freedom from fashions and boom-depression cycles and individual emotional maturity; syntal democratic political conflict and personal tolerance for internal mental conflict (since group conflict in overlapping groups brings parallel personal mental conflict), and so on. Some evidence that the first of these relations can be demonstrated in data already available has been set out by the present writer elsewhere (9). In so far as this theorem operates, the advance of social psychology as an exact science is limited by the advance of personality measurement.

## V. SYNTALITY MEASUREMENT AND THE DYNAMIC RELATIONS OF GROUPS

The implications of the above theorems for the design of experiments directed to determining the dimensions of syntality are numerous and we have space to emphasize only a few.

In the first place, the dynamic makeup (synergy) of groups will vary far more than that of individuals, both in strength and quality. Consequently it may be profitable to sort groups into classes of more comparable kinds before starting experiments. Sorokin, Zimmerman, and Galpin (33) have already proceeded with group classification essentially on this basis, into "elementary groups" which satisfy a single need and "cumulative groups" which hold their members by many ties. The dynamic vectorial methods suggested here simply carry this to greater quantitative meaning and exactness.

Secondly, group syntality will usually be far more narrow in dynamic content than the dynamic expression of individuals. Groups can fight, ally, acquire, fear, protect, submit, assert themselves, seek food, etc., but sexually directed behavior, for example, is rare (the rape of the Sabines, and matrimonial agencies, apart). The choice of dynamic variables for factorization therefore needs to aim at more dense representation in narrow ergic directions.

Theorem 2 above, that synergy can be expressed with regard to the ergic coordinates used for individuals leaves open the possibility that factorization may show synergy to be conveniently expressible also in terms of some relatively basic goals of groups *per se*. For example, the interests of an insurance company or a library may be as intelligible, if not as apt for dynamic calculus, when expressed in terms of service to a few basic social institutions as of basic human ergs.

This remains to be clarified by our initial experiments, as also does the question whether any laws systematically relate syntal and personal dynamic lattices and the hierarchy of typical individual loyalty to groups discussed in Theorem 5. There are concepts here which can only be tentatively defined and interrelated. Is "loyalty" to a group determined by "duty" (super ego investment) or by total synergy? Is the order of loyalty the same as the order of "social distance" (17) among people in the various groups, or, more likely, the same as the syntal subsidiation order? Can the correct order of syntal subsidiation be determined by asking "Could this group exist at all without that?" or must a situation always be arranged in which some conflict between the groups, from the standpoint of individual loyalties, exists? Is it possible that groups can only conflict in so far as their subsidiation paths are different? These questions will be dealt with elsewhere. Thirdly, because of the sensitive interdependence of groups, in regard to synergic quantity and quality, the synergy of most groups and especially the smaller, subordinate ones, will be much more liable to gross fluctuations than the total dynamic traits of the individual. So great a "function fluctuation" makes factorization more difficult but no less worth while. It requires "snapshot" measurement by R-technique, or the special use of P-technique. Measurement of the changing synergies of groups offers the true basis for discovery of the laws governing syntal subsidiation and other group interrelationships.

The measurement of syntalities with respect to their dynamic make-up and subsidiation relationships offers the prospect not only of putting the description of group behavior on an altogether higher level of exactness, but of making possible a new branch of study employing a kind of "dynamic bookkeeping" with respect to overlapping groups and the energy investments of individuals. From this "bookkeeping" the data for a whole field of new laws regarding the psychodynamics of groups emerge. For example, many overlapping groups are approximately isomorphous (in the sense of mathematical group theory) so that their synergies would behave as approximately complementary.

Pursuit of measurable relationships in the dynamics of personalities and syntalities opens up also two extremely important developments of psychology—ethics and economics. A good deal of the morality of individual behavior is admittedly weighed in terms of the effects of the latter on the welfare of groups (whether or not we accept the whole theoretical basis of Mill and Bentham). Indeed, the calculations of discrepancy between constituent individual attitudes and group synergies become in effect an estimation of individual morality—if the general position of Mill and Evolutionary Ethics (7) is accepted.

Similarly the key to the whole relationship of psychology and economics lies in these calculations. For groups to achieve their objects it is necessary to transmit interest energy from place to place. Transmission along a subsidiation chain takes place for groups and for individuals principally by tokens (money) but the process is perhaps clearer for groups. As frequently mentioned in sociology the most consistent characteristics of existing primary groups (other than behaving as a totality) are (*1*) order and (*2*) taxation. Synergy expresses itself most frequently through the latter. Members of a group tax themselves, proportionally to the strength of their interest in the existence of the group. This money is at once a measure of the strength of their individual attitudes and of the group synergy; for, generally it is not by work on the part of the members themselves that the group synergy expresses itself, but by the work of others paid for by the taxation of the group. That cost could be used as a measure of desire, thus uniting economic and psychodynamic measures, is not a new idea but an old one which was found wanting (8, 10). Only when it is considered in the total setting of group dynamics, apparently, can it be made workable.

These theoretical vistas in group dynamics can be glanced along but not followed, here. For the dynamic traits of groups are only one aspect of the total syntality and have been examined more analytically only because it appears that syntality differs from personality more in dynamic structure than in ability or temperament traits. However, the upshot of our examination is that dynamic characteristics, especially if they are sampled with proper regard to the nature of group synergies, can profitably be included in the same factorization with measures of group temperament and group abilities.

## VI. SUMMARY

(*1*) Social psychological research can advantageously be centered on the behavior of groups as organic, functionally integrated entities. Group syntality has more resemblances than differences with regard to individual personality, suggesting profitable transfer of research methods from one to the other.

(*2*) Effective research on the development, abnormalities, and interrelations of groups can proceed only on a foundation of syntality measurement. The dimensions of syntality can be found by factor analysis.

(*3*) Factor analysis must rest on an even sampling of a wide range of group characteristics. The characteristics of groups have to be sought at three levels: (1) Syntality—the behavior of the group; (2) Structure—the relations of individuals in the group; (3) Population personality traits—the individual characteristics averaged.

(*4*) Groups differ from individuals most radically in their dynamic make-up or synergy, especially because of the structural possibilities of overlapping groups. This does not invalidate the factorization of group characteristics but it introduces complications requiring special attention to the design of investigation.

(*5*) The dynamic relationships which have to be heeded in the design of experiments to investigate group syntalities, and which require investigation in their own right as prime determiners of the behavior of groups, have been expressed in seven theorems. These theorems may be briefly labelled: (1) Dynamic origin of groups; (2) Vectorial measurement of synergy; (3) Subsidiation in the syntal lattice; (4) Subsidiation in the personal lattice; (5) Hierarchies of loyalty from the law of effect; (6) Synergic constancy in a system of overlapping groups; and (7) Isomorphism of syntality change and personality change.

## REFERENCES

1. Benedict, R. *Patterns of culture.* New York: Houghton Mifflin, 1934.
2. Bosanquet, B. *The philosophical theory of the state.* London: Macmillan, 1910.
3. Brogan, D. W. *The American character.* New York: Knopf, 1945.
4. Buell, R. L. *International relations.* New York: Holt, 1929.
5. Burt, C. *Factors of the mind.* London: Univer. of London Press, 1940.
6. Cattell, R. B. Some changes in social life in a community with a falling intelligence quotient. *Brit. J. Psychol.*, 1938, 28, 430–450.
7. Cattell, R. B. *Psychology and the religious quest.* New York: Nelson, 1938.
8. Cattell, R. B. *The description and measurement of personality.* New York: World Book Co., 1946.
9. Cattell, R. B. The riddle of perseveration. II. Solution in terms of personality structure. *J. Person.*, 1946, 14, 239–268.
10. Cattell, R. B. The ergic theory of attitude and sentiment measurement. *Educ. Psychol. Measmt.*, 1947, 7, 221–246.
11. Cattell, R. B. The syntality of national culture patterns: I. R-technique on 63 nations. (Publication to be announced.)
12. Cattell, R. B. & Wispe, L. The dimensions of syntality in structured groups of six persons. (Publication to be announced.)
13. Cole, G. D. H., & Cole, M. *A Guide to modern politics.* London: Gollancz, 1934.
14. Cole, G. D. H. *Social theory.* New York: Frederick Stokes, 1920.
15. Gillin, J. L., & Gillin, J. P. *Introduction to sociology.* New York: Macmillan, 1946.
16. Gumplowicz, L. *Outlines of sociology* (trans. by F. H. Moore). Philadelphia: American Academy of Political and Social Science, 1899.
17. Gurnee, H., & Baker, E. The social distances of some common social relationships. *J. abnorm. soc. Psychol.*, 1938, 33, 265–269.
18. Gurwitch, A. *The sociology of law.* New York: Philosophical Library, 1942.
19. Hart, H. N. *Science of social relations.* New York: Holt, 1931.
20. Hayes, E. C. *Principles of sociology.* New York: Appleton, 1923.
21. Hobhouse, L. T. *The metaphysical theory of the state.* New York: Macmillan, 1918.
22. Jennings, H. Structure of leadership–development and sphere of interest. *Sociometry*, 1938, 1, 99–143.
23. Keyserling, H. *Das Spektrum Europas.* Berlin: Deutsche Verlags-Anstalt, 1928.
24. Mannheim, K. *Man and society.* New York: Harcourt, Brace, 1940.
25. McDougall, W. *The group mind.* New York: Putnam, 1920.
26. Mead, M. *And keep your powder dry.* New York: Morrow, 1943.
27. Moreno, J. L., & Jennings, Helen H. Statistics of social configurations. *Sociometry*, 1938, 1, 342–374.
28. Mowrer, O. H. *An experimentally produced "social problem."* (Film, obtainable Harvard Educ. Dept.), 1939.
29. Münsterberg, H. *The Americqus.* Garden City: Doubleday, 1914.
30. Ross, E. A. *Foundations of sociology.* New York: Macmillan, 1905.
31. Rousseau, J. J. *Du contrat social.* Amsterdam: Rey, 1762.
32. Siegfried, A. *France, a study in nationality.* London: H. Milford, Oxford Univer. Press, 1930.
33. Sorokin, R. A., Zimmerman, C. C., & Galpin, C. J. *A systematic source book in rural sociology.* Minneapolis: Univer. of Minnesota Press, 1930.
34. Thorndike, E. L. *Your city.* New York: Harcourt, Brace, 1939.
35. Thurstone, L. L. *The vectors of the mind.* Chicago: Univer. of Chicago Press, 1935.
36. Von Wiese, L. *Systematic sociology* (trans. by H. Becker). New York: John Wiley, 1932.
37. Ward, L. F. *Pure sociology.* New York: Macmillan, 1903.

# *Adaptive and Integrative Changes as Sources of Strain in Social Systems*

ROBERT F. BALES

THE STUDY of complete societies suggests a number of tentative generalizations which may be useful to the student of small groups. In order to take advantage of what is known, however, one needs first to abstract from complete societies those aspects of structure which are also found in small groups. Second, one needs to infer from the kinds of structural variation found in societies, both historically and cross culturally, what the mechanisms underlying changes from one state of structure to another may be, so that useful hypotheses about changes in the structure of a single group, within a small time span, can be deduced.

Looking at large scale systems in a very abstract way, one can form an idea of two "chains of events" or "series of strains" starting from opposite poles and proceeding in opposite directions, tending to cancel each other out, and each in its terminal effects tending to set off the opposite chain of events. One chain of events has its starting point in the necessities of adaptation to the outer situation and proceeds in its series of strains through changes in the division of labor, changes in the distribution of property, authority, and status and has its malintegrative terminal effects in the disturbance of the existing state of solidarity. The other chain of events has its starting point in the necessities of integration or reintegration of the social system itself and proceeds in its series of strains through a reactive (or perhaps aboriginal) emphasis on solidarity which exerts a dissolving, undermining, equalizing, or curbing effect on the differential distribution of status, on differences in authority, differences in distribu-

FROM R. F. Bales, *Interaction process analysis: A method for the study of small groups.* Cambridge: Addison-Wesley, 1949. Reprinted by permission of the author and publisher.

tion of property, and differences in functional roles in the division of labor, with an ultimate terminal effect that may be maladaptive. The social system in its organization, we postulate, tends to swing or falter indeterminately back and forth between these two theoretical poles: optimum adaptation to the outer situation at the cost of internal malintegration, or optimum internal integration at the cost of maladaptation to the outer situation.

The series of hypotheses below is an attempt to state our conception of these interconnections in the most general way possible, for all sorts of small groups:

As particular functional problems (instrumental, adaptive, integrative, or expressive) become more acute, pressing, or continuous, more demanding in time and effort, strains are created toward the definition of specific social roles, differentiated in terms of particular persons, who are given the implicit or explicit responsibility of meeting and solving the specific functional problems as they arise in the group. Furthermore:

As the felt importance of the specific function performed by a particular person increases, strains are created toward an increase in his generalized social status. Conversely, as the felt importance of the particular function decreases, strains are created toward a decrease in his generalized social status.

As the functional social roles in a group become more specific, differentiated, and formal, more demanding in time and effort of the particular individuals performing the roles, strains are created toward a more individualistic and inequalitarian distribution of access to resources and rewards, both in terms of access to the instrumentalities involved in the performance of the function and in terms of some reward or compensation for the loss of time and effort and the value rendered to the group. Furthermore:

As the felt advantage of a particular person in the distribution of access to resources increases, strains are created toward an increase in his generalized social status. Conversely, as the advantage of the particular person decreases, strains are created toward a decrease in his generalized social status.

As the functional social roles in a group become more specific, differentiated, and formal, strains are created toward a more differentiated and centralized exercise of directive control in order to coordinate and regulate these special functions. Furthermore:

As the directive control of a given person increases, strains are created toward an increase in his generalized social status. Conversely, as his directive control decreases, strains are created toward a decrease in his generalized social status.

Moreover, to point up the significance of the foregoing tendencies, as status differences between persons increase, strains are created toward a less solid (more neutral, indifferent, or antagonistic) relation between them. Thus, to conclude, as the functional roles performed by persons in a group become more specific, differentiated, and formal, strains are created toward a less solidary relation between them.

This is a conception of a series of changes in social relationships "set off" by changes in the functional problems which the group faces in its problem solving process. It is a somewhat more abstract statement of the kinds of relationships we tend to find in larger social systems between the occupational system and the institutions of property, authority, social stratification, and solidarity, each of which finds its more abstract statement in the series of hypotheses above.

The phenomena in one way or another associated with this series of changes in the larger social system are extremely varied and interesting. This is not the place to attempt to present a convincing analysis, but they would include, as we view it, the institutionalization of a certain "indifference," "impersonality," "impartiality," or "emotional neutrality" as an explicit obligation in the performance of certain roles, such as those of the judge, the doctor, the administrator, the foreman, etc.; compulsive tendencies toward absenteeism, migration, isolation, refusal to communicate; the formation of sects, schisms, minority sub-groups, etc. In another direction they may include the practice of black magic, witchcraft, and sorcery; compulsive striving for and retention of symbols of achievement, wealth, power, authority, and prestige; compulsive striving for symbols of love, acceptance, solidarity; ritual and symbolic attempts to increase the solidarity of the whole group; fantasy about and romanticization of desired symbols of security, such as symbols of achievement, wealth, power, authority, prestige, love, acceptance, solidarity; etc. In still another direction, the phenomena may include active attacks on or modifications of the existing division of labor, and the existing system of property and authority; compulsive competitiveness and rebelliousness; passive resistance and non-cooperation; the designation of specific targets for aggression, such as scapegoats within or outside the group; the permission of aggressive displays in certain contexts, such as in drinking, warfare, or punishment of transgressors; the prohibition and inhibition of aggressive tendencies such as complaining, agitating, "conniving," and meeting in secret; the establishment of certain modes of self-aggression, such as mutilation, flagellation, asceticism; etc.

The series of hypotheses above have to do with certain changes which are "set off," as it were, by changes in the division of labor which, in turn, is closely related to the task demands facing the group. There is a complementary or contrary series of changes, we hypothesize, which are "set off" by changes in the state of solidarity of the group. The general terminal effect of the first chain of events is to produce strains toward a lesser solidarity. One of the possible reactions to this strain is a reactive, compulsive attempt to secure and retain symbols of love, acceptance, solidarity, and the initiation of rituals and fantasies on this theme, as mentioned above. However, this reaction may go so far as to create difficulties in its own right. From the point of view of the overall functioning of social systems in terms of the various kinds of flexibilities they need to have, *either* marked uncontrolled antagonism or marked uncontrolled solidarity has its "dangers." In general, both tend to be regulated and controlled as to when, toward whom, and to what degree they may be expressed in action or institutionalized in a social relationship. A very strong relationship of solidarity (as well as a marked antagonism) between persons or within sub-groups or even of the group as a whole, may interfere with the adaptation and integration of the whole group by the following "chain of events":

As solidarity between persons of different status increases, strains are created toward a merging, or equalization of their status, both as they view the relation and as others view the relation. In general, members of solidary groups tend to be classed together in the scale of stratification, and individual mobility in the scale of stratification involves some loosening or breaking of former ties of solidarity. Solidarity and status differences are in certain respects incompatible. However:

The adaptation of the social system to its outer situation requires a certain degree of neutrality, mobility, and recognition of status differences in certain social relationships since:

As solidarity between persons performing specific, differentiated, and formal roles increases, strains are created toward a more diffuse, less differentiated, and less formalized performance of functional social roles, which in turn may be accompanied by a loss of efficiency and responsibility, a loss of the inducement of increased status, a perversion of function from group ends to the individual ends of the persons immediately involved, and so may threaten the adaptation and integration of the group as a whole. (Nepotism, favoritism, particularism, etc.)

Similarly:

As solidarity between persons having different advantages in the distribution of property rights increases, strains are created toward a more "communal," "equalitarian" distribution of property rights, which may tend to interfere with the adaptation and integration of the whole group by the dissociation of reward from functionally specific tasks, and consequent reduction of motivation to the efficient performance of explicit functions on behalf of the group.

Similarly:

As solidarity increases between those in authority and those subjected to control, strains are created toward a more diffuse, less differentiated, and less formal exercise of authority, which in turn may interfere with the adaptation and integration of the whole group by making it difficult or impossible for the persons in authority to require or demand that which is necessary but unpleasant, difficult, or dangerous.

Thus, to sum up, as sub-group or interpersonal solidarity increases in the contexts mentioned above (i.e., in functionally specific, differentiated, and formal contexts), strains are created toward insecurity through the threat of a less effective adaptation of the system as a whole to the outer situation, and various reactive attempts to remove or express this insecurity may be expected. In larger social systems there are various interesting phenomena which are apparently associated with this series of strains. Again, simply to give some examples, we would include: limitation of contact, by avoidance or physical segregation; institutionalization of "impersonality" or "impartiality," as mentioned above; prohibition (in functionally specific contexts where they might be disruptive) of certain activities which symbolize or tend to create solidarity, such as sexual approach (note incest taboos), performance of personal favors, eating together (note food taboos), drinking together, marrying, loaning of money or other articles, similarity in dress, speech, etc. In another direction, the damaging effects of over-strong sub-solidarities may be counteracted to some extent by communal rituals directed toward the maintenance and creation of sentiments which will (1) secure the allegiance and obligations of individuals and sub-groups to the group as a whole, (2) make for a conscientious performance of specialized function, and (3) justify the existing differentiation of property, authority, and status, in terms of a more general overarching system of major values and hierarchical sub-values. In still another direction, the damaging effects of malintegrative sub-solidarities may be combatted by creating an emphasis on some threat to the group as a whole and by making an aggressive attack on personal or impersonal aspects of the outer situation in such a way as to increase the overall solidarity at the expense of sub-group solidarities.

# A Formal Theory of Interaction in Social Groups

HERBERT A. SIMON[1]

TO A PERSON addicted to applied mathematics, any statement in a non-mathematical work that contains words like "increase," "greater than," "tends to," constitutes a challenge. For such terms betray the linguistic disguise and reveal that underneath the words lie mathematical objects—quantities, orderings, sets—and hence the possibility of a restatement of the proposition in mathematical language. But what purpose, other than an aesthetic one, does such a restatement serve? In this paper I shall attempt to show, by means of a concrete example, how mathematization of a body of theory can help in the clarification of concepts, in the examination of the independence or non-independence of postulates, and in the derivation of new propositions that suggest additional ways of subjecting the theory to empirical testing.

The example we shall use is a set of propositions that constitutes a part of the theoretical system employed by Professor George C. Homans, in *The Human Group* (2), to explain some of the phenomena that have been observed of group behavior. This particular example was selected for a number of reasons: first, although non-mathematical, it shows great sophistication in the handling of systems of interdependent variables; second, Professor Homans takes care with the operational definition of his

FROM *American Sociological Review*, 1952, 17, 202–211. Reprinted by permission of the author and publisher.

---

1 I am indebted, for stimulation, assistance, and suggestions in the formulation of this theory, to my colleagues in a research project on administrative centralization and decentralization sponsored at Carnegie Institute of Technology by the Controllership Foundation, and particularly to Professor Harold Guetzkow, who has worked closely with me at every stage of the theory formulation. Valuable help has also been received from Professor George C. Homans of Harvard University, and from seminars at Columbia University and the University of Chicago, and a session at the 1951 annual meetings of the American Sociological Society, where various portions of the paper were read and discussed.

concepts, and these concepts appear to be largely of a kind that can be measured in terms of cardinal and ordinal numbers; third, Professor Homans' model systematizes a substantial number of the important empirical relationships that have been observed in the behavior of human groups. Whether his theory, in whole or part, turns out to be correct or incorrect (and this is a question we shall not raise in the present paper), it will certainly receive careful attention in subsequent research on the human group.

## THE SYSTEM: CONCEPTS AND POSTULATES

The system will be described in my own language. After I have defined the variables and set forth the postulates, I will discuss what I believe to be the relationship between the system and the language that Homans employs in his book.

### *The Variables*

We consider a social group (a group of persons) whose behavior can be characterized by four variables, all functions of time:

I(t)—the intensity of *interaction* among the members;
F(t)—the level of *friendliness* among the members;
A(t)—the amount of *activity* carried on by members within the group;
E(t)—the amount of activity imposed on the group by the external environment (the "*external system*")

This particular set of variables includes most of those employed by Homans in the first part of his book (he adds others in his later chapters), and the italicized terms are the ones he uses. In this paper we will assume that operational definitions (Homans' or others) have been assigned to the variables, such that the behavior of a group at any moment in time can be measured in terms of the four real numbers, I, F, A, and E. For our purposes, we need to make only two points clear about these operational definitions.

First, since the units in which such variables can be measured are somewhat arbitrary, we shall try to make use only of the ordinal properties of the measuring scales—the relations of greater or less—and, perhaps, of certain "natural" zero points.

Second, since the variables refer to the behavior of a plurality of human beings, they clearly represent averages or aggregates. For the interaction variable, I, let $I_{ij}$ represent the number of interactions per day (or the time, per day, spent in interaction), of the $i^{th}$ member of the group with the $j^{th}$ member. Then we could define I as the average rate of interaction per member—i.e., as $1/n$ times the sum of $I_{ij}$ over the whole group, where n is the number of members. Similarly, we could define F as the average friendliness between pairs of members; and A might be defined as the average amount of time spent per member per day in activity within the group.[2] Finally, E might be defined as the average amount of time that would be spent per member per day in activity within the group if group members were motivated only by external pressures.[3]

## *The Postulates*

We postulate three sets of dynamic relations among the variables, treating I(t), F(t), and A(t) as endogenous (dependent) variables whose values are determined within the system: while E(t) is an exogenous (independent) variable.

(*1*) The intensity of interaction depends upon, and increases with, the level of friendliness and the amount of activity carried on within the group. Stated otherwise, we postulate that interaction is produced, on the one hand, by friendliness, on the other, by the requirements of the activity pattern; and that these two causes of communication are additive in their effect. We will postulate, further, that the level of interaction adjusts itself rapidly—almost instantaneously—to the two variables on which it depends.

(*2*) The level of group friendliness will increase if the actual level of interaction is higher than that "appropriate" to the existing level of friendliness. That is, if a group of persons with little friendliness are induced to interact a great deal, the friendliness will grow; while, if a group with a great deal of friendliness interact seldom, the friendliness will weaken. We will postulate that the adjustment of friendliness to the level of interaction requires time to be consummated.

(*3*) The amount of activity carried on by the group will tend to increase if the actual level of friendliness is higher than that "appropriate" to the existing amount of activity, and if the amount of activity imposed externally on the group is higher than the existing amount of activity. We will postulate that the adjustment of the activity level to the "imposed" activity level and to the actual level of friendliness both require time for their consummation.

2 The concept of "activity within the group" might require rather sophisticated treatment. For example, time spent by a worker in daydreaming about his family or outside social relations might, ideally, be excluded from his activity within the group. For some purposes, we might wish to regard as "activity within the group" *uniformities* of behavior among group members—that is, the degree to which activity lies within the group might be measured by similarity of behavior. On this point, see Homans (2, pp. 119–121).

3 This formulation reveals that the direct measurement of E might pose greater problems than the direct measurement of the other variables. In most cases, we would attempt to measure E indirectly in terms of the magnitude of the force producing E—in somewhat the same manner as the force of the magnetic field is sometimes measured by the strength of the current producing it. The problem is by no means insoluble, but we do not wish to deal with it in detail here.

These three relations can be represented by the following equations, where $\frac{dx}{dt}$ represents the derivative of x with respect to time.

$$(1.1) \quad I(t) = a_1F(t) + a_2A(t)$$

$$(1.2) \quad \frac{dF(t)}{dt} = b[I(t) - \beta F(t)]$$

$$(1.3) \quad \frac{dA(t)}{dt} = c_1[F(t) + \gamma A(t)] + c_2[E(t) - A(t)]$$

All constants in these equations are assumed to be positive.

If we look at equation (1.2), we see that $\beta F$ may be regarded as the amount of interaction "appropriate" to the level, F, of friendliness. For if $I = \beta F$, then F will have no tendency either to increase or decrease. The reciprocal of the coefficient $\beta$, that is, $1/\beta$, might be called the "congeniality coefficient" since it measures the amount of friendliness that will be generated per unit of interaction.

Similarly, from equation (1.1) we see that $a_1F$ may be regarded as the amount of interaction generated by the level, F, of friendliness in the absence of any group activity. That is, if $A=0$, then $I=a_1F$. Further, the coefficient $a_2$ measures the amount of interaction generated per unit of group activity in the absence of friendliness. Hence, $a_1$ and $a_2$ might be called "coefficients of interdependence."

Finally, from equation (1.3) we see that the reciprocal of the coefficient $\gamma$ measures the amount of activity that is generated per unit of friendliness, in the absence of external pressure. We may call $1/\gamma$ a coefficient of "spontaneity." The remaining coefficients, b, $c_1$, and $c_2$, determine how rapidly the system will adjust itself if it starts out from a position of disequilibrium.

## *Relation to Homans' System*

These equations, and their verbal interpretations, appear to represent with reasonable accuracy the larger part of the generalizations about the interrelations of these four variables which Professor Homans sets forth in Chapters 4 and 5 of his book.[4]

The next section of this paper will be devoted to an analysis of the system represented by equations 1–3. It should be emphasized again that this system is only a partial representation of the complete system of

4 See especially the italicized statements in Homans (2, pp. 102, 111, 112, 118, 120). The reader can perhaps best test the translation himself by reference to Professor Homans' text. In doing so, he should take due note of footnotes 2 and 3 above. Professor Homans has been kind enough to go over the equations (1.1)–(1.3) with me. He concludes that the mathematical treatment does not do violence to the meanings of his verbal statements, but that the equations do not capture all of the interrelations he postulates—that they tell the truth, but not the whole truth. With this later qualification I would concur.

hypotheses proposed by Homans, and, of course, an even sketchier representation of reality. Furthermore, the assumption of linear relations in the equations is a serious oversimplification, which will be remedied in a later section of the paper. Nevertheless, the system incorporates several of the important relationships that might be hypothesized as holding among the four variables and which Homans found did, in fact, hold in the situations he investigated.

## THE SYSTEM: DERIVATIONS FROM THE POSTULATES

A number of well-known techniques may be applied to derive consequences from the system of postulates that could be tested by comparison with empirical data.

(*1*) The equations might be solved explicitly to give the time path the system would follow from any particular initial position. This presents no mathematical difficulties, since systems of linear differential equations with constant coefficients can be solved completely and explicitly. On the other hand, the solutions would be useful for prediction only if the constants of the equations were known or could be estimated. For this reason, the explicit solutions would seem to be of interest at a later stage in the development of measurement instruments and testing of the theory, and we will not dwell on them here.

(*2*) The equilibrium positions, if any, of the system might be obtained, and their properties examined. This would permit us to make certain predictions about the behavior of the system when it was in or near equilibrium.

(*3*) The conditions for stability of the equilibrium might be examined. Since a system that is in equilibrium will not generally remain there unless the equilibrium is stable, we will ordinarily be justified in using the conditions of stability in predicting the behavior of any system that is observed to remain in or near equilibrium.

(*4*) Starting with the assumptions of equilibrium and stability, we may be interested in predicting what will happen if the independent variables or the constants of the system are altered in magnitude—that is, what will be the new equilibrium position to which the system will move. This method, the method of "comparative statics," is one of the most powerful for deriving properties of a gross qualitative character that might be testable even with relatively crude data.

Our method, therefore, will be to derive first the conditions of equilibrium, next the conditions of stability, and finally the relations that can be obtained by applying the method of comparative statics.

## *Equilibrium*

An equilibrium position is one in which the variables remain stationary. Hence the conditions of equilibrium can be found by setting dF/dt and dA/dt equal to zero in equations (1.2) and (1.3), respectively, and solving the three equations for I, F, and A in terms of E. Designating by $I_o$, $F_o$, and $A_o$ the equilibrium values corresponding to $E_o$, we find:

$$(1.4)\quad I_o = a_1F_o + a_2A_o$$
$$(1.5)\quad 0 = b(I_o - \beta F_o)$$
$$(1.6)\quad 0 = c_1(F_o - \gamma A_o) + c_2(E_o - A_o)$$

Eliminating $I_o$ from (1.5) by using (1.4), we get:

$$(1.7)\quad F_o = \frac{a_2}{\beta - a_1} A_o$$

Substituting this value of $F_o$ in (1.6) and solving for $A_o$, we get:

$$(1.8)\quad A_o = \left[\frac{c_2(\beta - a_1)}{(c_1\gamma + c_2)(\beta - a_1) - (c_1a_2)}\right] E_o = \left[\frac{c_2(\beta - a_1)}{c_2(\beta - a_1) + c_1\{\gamma(\beta - a_1) - a_2\}}\right] E_o$$

whence:

$$(1.9)\quad F_o = \left[\frac{c_2a_2}{(c_1\gamma + c_2)(\beta - a_1) - (c_1a_2)}\right] E_o$$

## *Stability of Equilibrium*

To determine whether the equilibrium is stable, we consider the so-called "characteristic equation" associated with equations (1.2) and (1.3) after I has been eliminated by substitution from (1.1):[5]

$$(1.10)\quad \begin{vmatrix} -b(\beta - a_1) - \lambda & ba_2 \\ c_1 & -(c_1\gamma + c_2) - \lambda \end{vmatrix} = 0$$

When expanded, this becomes:

$$(1.11)\quad \lambda^2 + \{c_1\gamma + c_2 + b(\beta - a_1)\}\lambda + b\{(\beta - a_1)(c_1\gamma + c_2) - a_2c_1\} = 0$$

It is a well-known property of such dynamical systems that for stability the real parts of the roots of $\lambda$ must be negative, and conversely, that if the real parts of the roots are negative, the system will be stable. By solving (1.11) for $\lambda$, this can be shown to imply:

$$(1.12)\quad c_1\gamma + c_2 + b(\beta - a_1) > 0, \quad \text{and}$$
$$(1.13)\quad (\beta - a_1)(c_1\gamma + c_2) - a_2c_1 > 0.$$

Since all constants are assumed positive, we obtain from (1.13) the requirement that:

$$(1.14)\quad \beta > a_1$$

5 The mathematical theory involved here is discussed in Samuelson (4, p. 271).

If (1.14) holds, (1.12) will, in turn, be automatically satisfied.

Hence (1.13) and (1.14) together give us necessary and sufficient conditions for stability. We proceed now to an interpretation of these conditions.

Stability condition (1.14) may be written:

$$(1.15)\quad \beta F_o > a_1 F_o$$

That is, we require for stability that the amount of interacton ($\beta F_o$) *required to generate* the equilibrium level of friendliness be greater than the amount of communication ($a_1F_o$) that would be *generated* by the equilibrium level of friendliness in the absence of any group activity. For if this were not so (i.e., if $a_1 > \beta$), an initial level of friendliness, $F_1$ would produce interaction, $I_1 = a_1F_1$, which would further increase the friendliness to $F_2 = I_1/\beta = \frac{a_1F_1}{\beta} > F_1$, and we would get an ascending spiral such that the amount of friendliness and the amount of interaction would increase without limit:

$$F_1 < F_2 < F_3 < \cdots < F_n, \quad \text{and}$$
$$I_1 < I_2 < I_3 < \cdots < I_n$$

We can show that the other stability condition, (1.13), is required to prevent a similar ascending spiral between A and F.

## *Behavior of the System: Comparative Statics*

The equalities and inequalities we have derived as conditions for equilibrium and stability of equilibrium enable us to deduce certain propositions about how the system will behave when its equilibrium is disturbed, assuming the equilibrium to be stable.

Equilibrium may be disturbed by a change in E, the task imposed on the group, or by changes in one or more of the coefficients of the system (e.g., an increase or decrease in $a_2$). We wish to predict how the variables of the system will respond to such a shift.

The change in the equilibrium value of A with a change of E can be determined from (1.8). Stability requires (by (1.14)) that the numerator of the right-hand side of (1.8) be positive, and (by (1.13)) that the denominator be positive. Hence:

$$(1.16)\quad \frac{dA_o}{dE_o} > 0$$

From (1.7), remembering (1.14), we get similarly:

$$(1.17)\quad \frac{dF_o}{dA_o} > 0, \text{ hence } \frac{dF_o}{dE_o} > 0$$

Finally, from (1.4), we get:

$$(1.18)\quad \frac{dI_o}{dE_o}=a_1\frac{dF_o}{dE_o}+a_2\frac{dA_o}{dE_o}>0$$

We conclude that an increase in the activities required of the group by the external environment will increase (when equilibrium has been re-established) the amount of group activity, the amount of friendliness, and the amount of interaction. As E decreases toward zero, A, F, and I will decrease toward zero. But this is precisely the hypothesis that Homans employs to explain social disintegration in Hilltown (2, pp. 356–362), and to explain the difference in extension between the primitive and modern family (2, pp. 263–265).

We ask next how large $A_o$ will be in relation to $E_o$. From (1.8), in its second form, we see that the numerator on the right-hand side will be larger than the denominator if and only if:

$$(1.19)\quad \gamma(\beta-a_1)<a_2$$

If (1.19) holds, then, we will have $A_o>E_o$, otherwise $A_o \leq E_o$. We will refer to a group satisfying condition (1.19) as one having *positive morale*. If the condition is not satisfied, we will say the group has *negative morale*.

What relations among the coefficients are conducive to positive morale? From (1.19), we see that $a_2$ should be large, relative to the product of $\gamma$ and $(\beta-a_1)$. But large $a_2$ means high interdependence, i.e., the group tasks are highly interrelated. From our previous interpretation of $\gamma$ (i.e., that $1/\gamma$ measures spontaneity), we see that a high degree of spontaneity is conducive to positive morale—with large $1/\gamma$, or small $\gamma$, friendliness will tend to produce a relatively large amount of activity in addition to that required by the external environment.

As mentioned above, another condition conducive to positive morale is that $(\beta-a_1)$ be small: that there be a strong feedback from friendliness to more interaction to more friendliness. But we have seen that an approach to zero of $(\beta-a_1)$ means an approach to an unstable condition of the system (see equation (1.13)).

Now, from the stability condition (1.13), we know that a large value of $(\gamma c_1+c_2)$ aids stability, but if we want $\gamma$ small relative to $a_2$ for positive morale, we must depend on the ratio $c_2/c_1$ for stability. That is, under conditions of positive morale we require that the activity level, A, be more strongly influenced by the external demands than by the level of friendliness.

While we must be careful not to expect too much from a theory as highly simplified as this one, it may be interesting to note that the phenomenon of negative morale appears to be not unrelated to Durkheim's concept of *anomie*. In particular, a division of labor within a group that would result in little interrelationship of tasks ($a_2$ small) would, in our theory, be conducive to negative morale. This is a prediction that has received a considerable amount of substantiation from the Hawthorne studies and other empirical observations in industrial sociology.

We may inquire finally as to the time path whereby the system readjusts itself when it is disturbed from an initial equilibrium by a change in $E_0$. It can be shown that the roots of $\lambda$ in (1.11) are real. This implies that the system will not oscillate, but will start out toward the new equilibrium at a rapid rate, approaching it asymptotically.

## GENERALIZATION TO A NON-LINEAR SYSTEM

It is time now to relax the assumption of equations (1.1)–(1.3) that the relations among the variables of the system are linear. The reason for dwelling at length on the linear equations is that they can be regarded as an approximation to the more general equations of the non-linear system in the neighborhood of points of equilibrium.

Since we really do not have much empirical data as to the exact forms of the functions relating our variables, we shall strive in our treatment of the non-linear system to make as few assumptions as possible about these functions. The price we shall have to pay is to restrict ourselves largely to a graphical treatment and to the derivation of gross qualitative results. Nevertheless, in view of the roughness of the empirical observations we might hope to make, this restriction cannot be regarded as unduly serious at the present stage of development of the theory.

We will now assume our equations to be:

$$(2.1) \quad I = f(A,F)$$

$$(2.2) \quad \frac{dF}{dt} = g(I,F)$$

$$(2.3) \quad \frac{dA}{dt} = \psi(A,F;E)$$

where f, g, $\psi$ are functions whose properties remain to be specified. If we replace I in (2.2) by its value as given by (2.1) we obtain, in place of (2.1)–(2.2) a new equation:

$$(2.4) \quad \frac{dF}{dt} = g(f(A,F), F) = \phi(A,F)$$

where $\phi$ is again a function of unspecified form. Henceforth, we will work with the system comprised of equations (2.3)–(2.4)–two differential equations for the determination of F and A.

Our method will be graphical, based on the "phase diagram" of F and A.[6] Let us regard E, for the present, as a constant–a given parameter.

6 On the method employed, see Lotka (3, pp. 77–97, 143–151).

Equation (2.3) gives us the time rate of change of A, and (2.4) the time rate of change of F, both as functions of F and A. Dividing the second by the first we get

$$dF/dA=\frac{dF/dt}{dA/dt}=\phi(A,F)/\psi(A,F;E)$$

the rate of change of F relative to A for each pair of values of F and A. Now consider a graph (Figure 1) whose x-axis measures A, and whose y-axis measures F. Through any point $(A_1, F_1)$, draw a short line segment with slope $\phi/\psi=dF/dA$. Then this segment points along the path on which our system would begin to move if started from $(A_1, F_1)$.

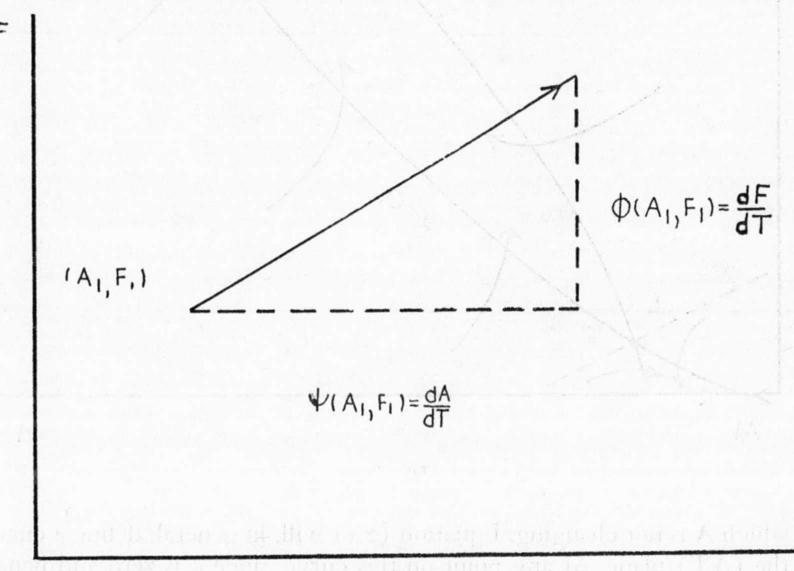


FIG. 1

By drawing such a line segment for each point of the (A,F)-plane, and connecting these into continuous curves, we find the paths the system will follow from any initial positions to the subsequent position (and possibly to equilibrium). The collection of all such paths is commonly called the "direction field" of the system (see Figure 2).[7]

Now consider the set of points

$$(2.5) \quad \frac{dA}{dt}=\psi(A,F;E)=0$$

7 For a more detailed explanation of the construction of the direction field, see Ford (1, pp. 9–11). The direction field corresponding to the linear system of this paper is discussed and illustrated by Ford (1, pp. 48–52). His Fig. 14, p. 51, corresponds to the case of stable equilibrium.

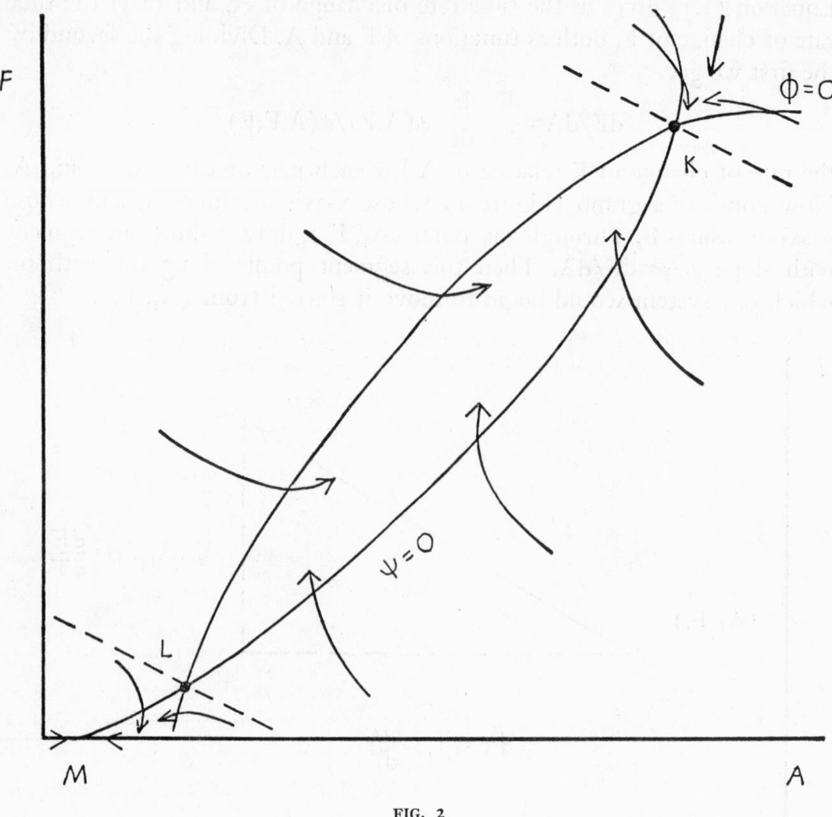


FIG. 2

at which A is not changing. Equation (2.5) will, in general, define a curve in the (A,F)-plane. At any point on this curve, since $\psi$ is zero and hence A is constant, but not F, the path of the system will be vertical (either upward or downward as $\phi>0$ or $\phi<0$, respectively).

Consider next the sets of points

$$(2.6)\quad \frac{dF}{dt}=\phi(A,F)=0$$

at which F is not changing. At all points on this curve, since $\phi$ is zero, the path of the system will be horizontal (either to right or left as $\psi>0$ or $\psi<0$, respectively).

At the point, or points, where (2.5) and (2.6) hold simultaneously—that is, where the two curves intersect—the system will be in stable or unstable equilibrium. The equilibrium will be stable if any path very close to the point of equilibrium leads toward it and unstable if any path very close to it leads away from it. (This definition of stability can be shown to be equivalent to a suitable generalization of the analytic definition we employed in the linear case.) Figure 2 illustrates the direction field and the curves $\psi=0$ and $\phi=0$. There are two points of equilibrium, K and L. Equilibrium at K is stable, at L unstable.

It should be remarked that if the system starts off at any point *above* the lower of the two broken lines in the figure, it will, in time, approach the point of stable equilibrium, K; while if the system starts off below this broken line, F and A will ultimately decline and approach the point M—the group will, in fact, dissolve.

Now the paths taken by the system from various initial points will depend on the locations of the curves $\psi=0$ and $\phi=0$, and their points of intersection. The particular shapes and positions of the curves, as drawn in Figure 2, represent empirical assumptions as to the shapes of the functions $\psi$ and $\phi$. What can we legitimately assume about these functions? To answer this question we must ascertain the empirical significance of the two curves $\psi=0$ and $\phi=0$.

Equation (3.3) says, in effect, that for a given amount of external pressure (a given value of E) the amount of activity undertaken by the group (A) will tend to adjust itself to the level of friendliness (F). Our empirical assumption is that, given E, greater friendliness will tend to produce greater activity. If this is so, then the equilibrium value of A must increase as F increases; that is, the curve $\psi=0$ must have a positive slope. We now make the second empirical assumption: that there is a saturation phenomenon—that as F continues to increase, A will increase only at a diminishing rate. If this is so, the curve $\psi=0$ must be concave upward as we have drawn it. In the particular case illustrated in Figure 2, it is assumed that E is sufficiently great so that there will be some activity even in the absence of friendliness. This is represented by the fact that the curve cuts the x-axis to the right of the origin. Later, we will consider the case also where this condition does not hold.

Equation (2.4) says that the amount of friendliness in the group (F) will tend to adjust itself to the amount of group activity (A). Again we assume that greater activity will tend to produce greater friendliness; hence that the curve $\phi=0$ must have a positive slope. If we now assume that this mechanism is also subject to saturation, the curve must be concave downward. Finally, we assume that unless the activity is above a certain minimum value there is no tendency at all for friendliness to develop ($\phi=0$ cuts the x-axis to the right of the origin).

In the particular case shown, $\phi=0$ cuts the x-axis to the right of $\psi=0$. If this were not so, the point L would disappear and the system would move toward the stable equilibrium, K, from *any* initial point, including the origin. We will consider this case later. In the particular case shown, $\psi=0$ is sufficiently far to the right that it intersects $\phi=0$. If this were not so, the system would move toward the origin from *any* initial point. This case also will be considered later.

Finally, it should be mentioned that the particular assumptions we have made about the curves do not depend in any essential way upon the precise indexes used to measure F and A. For any given scale used to measure F or A, we can substitute another scale, provided only that the second scale has the same zero point as the first and does not reverse the *direction* of change (i.e., that we do not have $F_1 > F_2$ on the first scale but $F'_1 < F'_2$ for corresponding situations measured on the second). To be more precise, our concavity properties may be altered but not the order or character of the equilibrium points or the presence or absence of the region below the lower broken line. Since the conclusions we shall draw depend only on these properties of the graph, a change in the index employed cannot affect our results.

Suppose now that we begin with the system in equilibrium at K, and progressively reduce E, the external pressure to activity. A reduction in E may be assumed empirically to reduce (through the mechanism of equation (2.3)) the equilibrium value of A associated with each value of F—i.e., to move the curve $\psi=0$ to the left. In the simplest case (in first approximation) we may assume that the shape of the curve is unchanged. Then, as $\psi=0$ moves to the left, its intersection, K, with $\phi=0$ will move downward and to the left along $\phi=0$. We have shown:

### *Proposition 2.1*

As E is decreased the equilibrium levels of A and F will be decreased.

This proposition also held in our linear system.

As $\psi=0$ continues to move to the left (continued reduction in E) the two curves will eventually intersect at a single point of tangency. Let us call the value of E corresponding to this position of tangency $E_T$. As E is reduced below $E_T$, the two curves will no longer intersect and all paths of the direction field will lead to the x-axis and, if $\psi=0$ now intersects with the y-axis, the system will come to rest at the origin. We have shown:

### *Proposition 2.2*

As E is decreased below some critical value, $E_T$, F will go to zero; and for some sufficiently small value of E (equal to or less than $E_T$ depending on the location of the intersection of $\psi(A,F;E_T)$ with the x-axis) A will go to zero.

Here we find, in the non-linear case, a new phenomenon—a dissolution of the group. It might be supposed that if a group has been dissolved by reducing E below $E_T$ it can be restored by again increasing E to $E_T$. This does not follow. For if the system is initially at the origin, its path will lead toward K only if $\psi=0$ intersects the x-axis to the right of $\phi=0$.

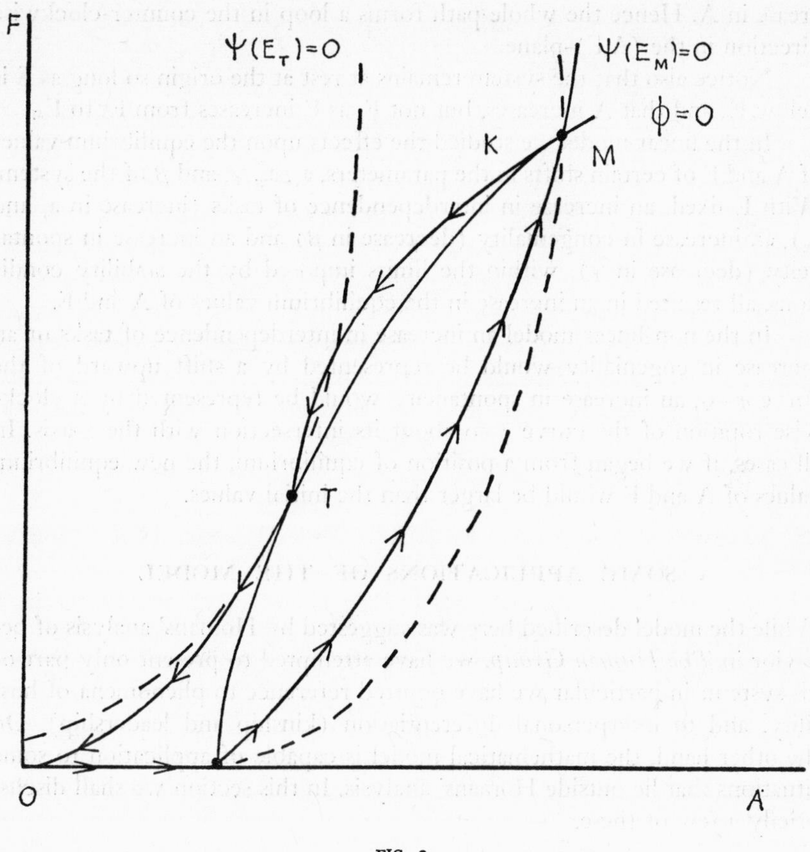


FIG. 3

But the smallest value of E for which this condition holds is obviously greater than $E_T$. From this follows:

*Proposition 2.3*

The level of E required to bring a group into existence is greater than the minimum value, $E_T$, required to prevent the group, once formed, from dissolution.

To illustrate Proposition 2.3 we show, in Figure 3, the path that will be followed by F and A when E is (*1*) reduced from some initial value, $E_K$, to $E_T$, (*2*) then to some lower value, $E_L$, (*3*) then increased to $E_{\circ}$, where $\psi$=o intersects the origin, (*4*) finally increased to $E_M$ where $\psi$=o intersects the x-axis just to the right of $\phi$=o. In the descending portion of the path, the decrease in F lags behind the decrease in A; while in the ascending portion of the path the increase in F again lags behind the increase in A. Hence the whole path forms a loop in the counter-clockwise direction in the (A,F)-plane.

Notice also that the system remains at rest at the origin so long as E is below $E_0$ and that A increases, but not F, as E increases from $E_0$ to $E_M$.

In the linear model we studied the effects upon the equilibrium values of A and F of certain shifts in the parameters, $a_1$, $a_2$, $\gamma$, and $\beta$ of the system. With E fixed, an increase in interdependence of tasks (increase in $a_1$ and $a_2$), an increase in congeniality (decrease in $\beta$) and an increase in spontaneity (decrease in $\gamma$), within the limits imposed by the stability conditions, all resulted in an increase in the equilibrium values of A and F.

In the non-linear model an increase in interdependence of tasks or an increase in cogeniality would be represented by a shift upward of the curve $\phi=0$; an increase in spontaneity would be represented by a clockwise rotation of the curve $\psi=0$ about its intersection with the x-axis. In all cases, if we began from a position of equilibrium, the new equilibrium values of A and F would be larger than the initial values.

## SOME APPLICATIONS OF THE MODEL

While the model described here was suggested by Homans' analysis of behavior in *The Human Group*, we have attempted to present only part of his system: in particular we have omitted reference to phenomena of hostility, and to interpersonal differentiation (kinship and leadership). On the other hand, the mathematical model is capable of application to some situations that lie outside Homans' analysis. In this section we shall discuss briefly a few of these.

### (*1*) *Formation of Cliques*

Define variables $I_1$, $A_1$, $F_1$, and $E_1$ to refer to behavior in a specified group, $G_I$; and $I_2$, $A_2$, $F_2$, and $E_2$ to refer to behavior in a group, $G_{II}$, which is a subgroup ("clique") within $G_I$. Then we might postulate equations of the form:

$$(3.1)\quad \frac{dA_1}{dt}=\psi_1(A_1,\ F_1,\ A_2;\ E_1)$$

$$(3.2)\quad dF_1/dt=\Phi_1(A_1,\ F_1)$$

$$(3.3)\quad dA_2/dt=\psi_2(A_2,\ F_2,\ A_1;\ E_2)$$

$$(3.4)\quad dF_2/dt=\Phi_2(A_2,\ F_2)$$

These equations are similar in form to (2.3) and (2.4) except for the presence of the "coupling" variables: $A_2$ in (3.1) and $A_1$ in (3.3). The meaning of this coupling is that activity within the clique ($A_2$) is assumed to interfere with and depress activity in the larger group ($A_1$) and activity within the larger group ($A_1$) is assumed to interfere with clique activity

$(A_2)$. We might also have further complicated the model by adding coupling terms to (3.2) and (3.4) ("conflict of loyalties").

The behavior of the system (3.1) to (3.4) can be studied as follows. We take $E_1$ and $E_2$ as fixed. Then for any given value of $A_2$, we can set (3.1) and (3.2) equal to zero and find the corresponding equilibrium value, $A^*_1$, of $A_1$. This value, $A^*_1$, will depend on $A_2$, and, under our assumptions will decrease as $A_2$ increases. Similarly, from (3.3) and (3.4) we can find the equilibrium value, $A^*_2$ of $A_2$ for each value of $A_1$. A position of equilibrium of the whole system will be found at the intersection of the two curves $A^*_1 = A^*_1(A_2)$ and $A^*_2 = A^*_2(A_1)$ in the plane whose x-axis represents $A_1$ and whose y-axis represents $A_2$. If the two curves do not intersect, then the clique and the group cannot coexist in equilibrium. Even if the curves intersect, the equilibrium may be unstable, but we cannot here go into the exact conditions of stability.

### (2) *Competition of Groups*

Instead of a clique within a group we might have two groups competing for the membership of a single individual. In this case, the variables $A_1$, $F_1$, $I_1$, $E_1$ would refer to the intensity of his activity in the first group; $A_2$, $F_2$, $I_2$, $E_2$ to the intensity of his activity in the second group. We can then proceed exactly as in the first case.

### (3) *Activity of an Individual*

The variables in equations (2.3) and (2.4) need not be interpreted as group activity. Instead, A might be interpreted as the amount of time per day an individual devotes to *any* particular activity, F as the amount of satisfaction he obtains from the activity, E as the pressure on him to engage in the activity. In this case we might want to make different assumptions as to the shapes of the curves, $\phi=0$ and $\psi=0$, in the phase diagram than in the previous cases, but the general approach is the same. Similarly the model of equations (3.1)–(3.4) might be interpreted to refer to an individual's distribution of attention between two activities.

### (4) *Regulatory Enforcement*

Still another application of models of this general class would be to the phenomena associated with the enforcement of a governmental regulation (e.g., gasoline rationing). Here A would be interpreted as the actual degree of conformity to the regulation, F as the social pressure to conform, E as the effect of formal enforcement activity. The reader may find it of some interest to translate the theorems we have previously derived into this new interpretation.

## CONCLUSION

In this paper we have constructed a mathematical model that appears to translate with tolerable accuracy certain propositions asserted by Homans to hold for behavior in human groups. We have examined at some length what assumptions the model requires and what further propositions can be deduced from it. In particular, we have seen that it offers an explanation for some of the commonly observed phenomena relating to the stability and dissolution of groups. In the last section we have shown that models of this general class can be applied to a rather wide range of behavioral phenomena beyond those originally examined. We do not imply from this that the psychological mechanisms involved in all these situations are identical. The underlying similarity appears to be of a rather different character. In all of these situations there are present: (a) an external (positive or negative) motivational force toward some activity, and (b) a secondary "internal" motivational force induced by the activity itself. It is the combined effect of two such motivational forces that produces in each case phenomena of the sort we have observed. And especially when the relations are not linear (and the non-linear must be supposed to be the general case), "persistent" and "gregarious" patterns of behavior can result.

## REFERENCES

1. Ford, L. R. *Differential equations.* New York: McGraw-Hill, 1933.
2. Homans, G. C. *The human group.* New York: Harcourt, Brace, 1950.
3. Lotka, A. J. *Elements of physical biology.* Baltimore: Williams & Wilkins, 1925.
4. Samuelson, P. A. *Foundations of economic analysis.* Cambridge, Mass.: Harvard Univer. Press, 1947.

# An Approach to the Study of Communicative Acts

THEODORE M. NEWCOMB

THIS paper points toward the possibility that many of those phenomena of social behavior which have been somewhat loosely assembled under the label of "interaction" can be more adequately studied as communicative acts. It further points to the possibility that, just as the observable forms of certain solids are macroscopic outcomes of molecular structure, so certain observable group properties are predetermined by the conditions and consequences of communicative acts.

The initial assumption is that communication among humans performs the essential function of enabling two or more individuals to maintain simultaneous orientation toward one another as communicators *and* toward objects of communication. After presenting a rationale for this assumption, we shall attempt to show that a set of propositions derived from or consistent with it seems to be supported by empirical findings.

## CO-ORIENTATION AND THE A–B–X SYSTEM

Every communicative act is viewed as a transmission of information, consisting of discriminative stimuli, from a source to a recipient.[1] For present purposes it is assumed that the discriminative stimuli have a discriminable object as referent. Thus in the simplest possible communicative act one person, A, transmits information to another person, B, about something, X. Such an act is symbolized here as AtoBreX.

The term "orientation" is used as equivalent to "attitude" in its more

FROM *Psychological Review*, 1953, 60, 393–404. Reprinted by permission of the author and the American Psychological Association, Inc.

1 This statement is adapted from G. A. Miller's definition: " 'information' is used to refer to *the occurrence of one out of a set of alternative discriminative stimuli.* A discriminative stimulus is a stimulus that is arbitrarily, symbolically, associated with something (or state, or event, or property) and that enables the stimulated organism to discriminate this thing from others" (9, p. 41).

inclusive sense of referring to both cathectic and cognitive tendencies. The phrase "simultaneous orientation" (hereinafter abbreviated to "co-orientation") itself represents an assumption; namely, that A's orientation toward B and toward X are interdependent. A–B–X is therefore regarded as constituting a system. That is, certain definable relationships between A and B, between A and X, and between B and X are all viewed as interdependent. For some purposes the system may be regarded as a phenomenal one within the life space of A or B, for other purposes as an "objective" system including all of the possible relationships as inferred from observation of A's and B's behavior. It is presumed that a given state of the system exists when a given instance of AtoBreX occurs, and that as a result of this occurrence the system undergoes some change (even though the change be regarded as only a reinforcement of the pre-existing state).

The minimal components of the A–B–X system, as schematically illustrated in Fig. 1, are as follows:

1. A's orientation toward X, including both attitude toward X as an object to be approached or avoided (characterized by sign and intensity) and cognitive attributes (beliefs and cognitive structuring).

2. A's orientations toward B, in exactly the same sense. (For purposes of avoiding confusing terms, we shall speak of positive and negative *attraction* toward A or B as persons, and of favorable and unfavorable *attitudes* toward X.)

3. B's orientation toward X.

4. B's orientation toward A.

In order to examine the possible relationships of similarity and difference between A and B, we shall make use of simple dichotomies in regard to these four relationships. That is, with respect to a given X at a given time, A and B will be regarded as cathectically alike (++ or −−) or different (+− or −+) in attitude and in attraction; and as cognitively alike or different. We shall also make use of simple dichotomies of degree–i.e., more alike, less alike. We shall refer to lateral similarities of A's and B's orientations to X as *symmetrical* relationships.

This very simple system is designed to fit two-person communication. In the following discussion these additional limitations will be imposed, for simplicity's sake: (*a*) communicative acts will be treated as verbal ones, in face-to-face situation; (*b*) initiation of the communicative act is considered to be intentional (i.e., such acts are excluded as those which the actor assumes to be unobserved); (*c*) it is assumed that the "message" is received–i.e., that the communicative act is attended to by an intended recipient, though not necessarily with any particular degree of accuracy; and (*d*) A and B are assumed to be group members, characterized by continued association.

The assumption that co-orientation is essential to human life is based upon two considerations of complementary nature. First, the orientation of any A toward any B (assuming that they are capable of verbal communication) is rarely, if ever, made in an environmental vacuum. Even in what seems the maximally "pure" case of two lovers oblivious to all but each other, both singly and both jointly are dependent upon a common environment; and their continued attachment is notoriously contingent upon the discovery or development of common interests beyond themselves. It is not certain that even their most person-oriented communications (e.g., "I love you") are devoid of environmental reference. The more intense one person's concern for another the more sensitive he is likely to be to the other's orientations to objects in the environment.

Second, the orientation of any A capable of verbal communication about almost any conceivable X is rarely, if ever, made in a social vacuum. There are few if any objects so private that one's orientations toward them

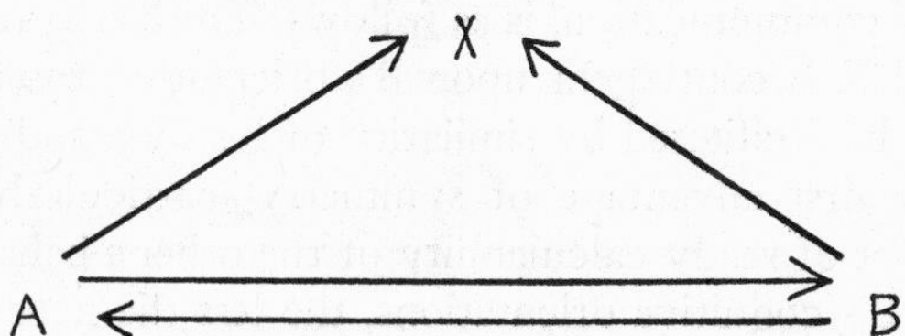


FIG. 1. Schematic illustration of the minimal A–B–X system

are uninfluenced by others' orientations. This is particularly true with regard to what has been termed "social reality" (3); i.e., the less the possibility of testing one's assumptions by observing the physical consequences of those assumptions, the greater the reliance upon social confirmation as the test of what is true and valid. And even when assumptions can be put to the direct test (e.g., the child can find out for himself about the stove which he has been told is hot), social reality is often accepted as the quicker or the safer test. As various linguists have pointed out, moreover, a good deal of social reality is built into the very language with which we communicate about things. Under the conditions of continued association which we are assuming, A and B as they communicate about X are dependent upon each other, not only because the other's eyes and ears provide an additional source of information about X, but also because the other's judgment provides a testing ground for social reality. And to be dependent upon the other, in so far as such dependence influences behavior, is to be oriented toward him.

In short, it is an almost constant human necessity to orient oneself toward objects in the environment and also toward other persons oriented toward those same objects. To the degree that A's orientation either toward X or toward B is contingent upon B's orientation toward X, A is motivated to influence and/or to inform himself about B's orientation toward X. Communication is the most common and usually the most effective means by which he does so.

## SYMMETRY OF ORIENTATION

Much of the remainder of this paper will deal with the relationships between A's and B's orientations toward X, within the postulated A–B–X system. The implications of this model are: (*a*) that while at any given moment the system may be conceived of as being "at rest," it is characterized not by the absence but by the balance of forces; and (*b*) that a change in any part of the system (any of the four relationships portrayed in Fig. 1) may lead to changes in any of the others. We shall also make the assumption (not inherent in the model) that certain forces impinging upon the system are relatively strong and persistent, and that thus there are "strains" toward preferred states of equilibrium.

This assumption, related to the initial one concerning the co-orientation function of communication, is as follows. To the degree that A's orientation toward X is contingent upon B's orientation toward X, A's co-orientation will be facilitated by similarity of his own and B's orientation toward X. The first advantage of symmetry—particularly of cognitive symmetry—is that of ready calculability of the other's behavior; the more similar A's and B's cognitive orientations, the less the necessity for either of them to "translate" X in terms of the other's orientations, the less the likelihood of failure or error in such "translations," and thus the less difficult and/or the less erroneous the co-orientation of either. Second, there is the advantage of validation of one's own orientation toward X; the more similar A's and B's orientations, either cognitive or cathectic (particularly in the many areas where validation is heavily dependent upon "social reality"), the more confident each of them can be of his own cognitive and evaluative orientations. Co-orientation is of course possible with little or no symmetry, but the facilitative value of symmetry for co-orientation is considerable.

If these advantages are commonly experienced as such, communicative acts resulting in increased symmetry are likely to be rewarded, and symmetry is likely to acquire secondary reward value. This is the basis of our assumption of a persistent "strain toward symmetry," under the conditions noted.

These assumptions may now be brought together in terms of the following inclusive postulate: *The stronger the forces toward A's co-orientation in respect to B and X,* (*a*) *the greater A's strain toward symmetry with B in respect to X;* and (*b*) *the greater the likelihood of increased symmetry as a consequence of one or more communicative acts.* The latter part of the postulate assumes the possibility of modified orientations toward X on the part of both A and B, who over a period of time exchange roles as transmitters and receivers of information.

Several testable propositions are derivable from this postulate. First, if the likelihood of instigation to and achievement of symmetry varies as a function of forces toward co-orientation, the latter varies, presumably, with valence of the objects of co-orientation—i.e., of intensity of attitude toward X and of attraction toward B. That is, under conditions such that orientation toward either B or X also demands orientation toward the other, the greater the valence of B or of X the greater the induced force toward co-orientation, and thus the greater the likelihood of both instigation toward and achievement of symmetry.

Such research findings as are known to the writer are in support of these predictions. Experimental results reported by Festinger and Thibaut (5), by Schachter (12), and by Back (1) indicate that attempts to influence another toward one's own point of view vary as a function of attraction. In the second of these studies it is shown that communications within a cohesive group are directed most frequently toward those perceived as deviates, up to a point where the deviate is sociometrically rejected (i.e., attraction decreases or becomes negative), beyond which point communication to them becomes less frequent. It is also shown in this study that frequency of influence-attempting communication varies with degree of interest in the topic of group discussion.

Some of these same studies, and some others, present data concerning symmetry as a consequence of communication. Thus Festinger and Thibaut, varying "pressure toward uniformity" and "perception of homogeneous group composition," found actual change toward uniformity following a discussion to be a function of both these variables, but some change toward uniformity took place in every group, under all conditions. Back found that subjects who started with different interpretations of the same material and who were given an opportunity to discuss the matter were influenced by each other as a direct function of attraction.

Findings from two community studies may also be cited, as consistent with these laboratory studies. Newcomb (10), in a replicated study of friendship choices as related to political attitudes in a small college community, found on both occasions that students at each extreme of the attitude continuum tended to have as friends those like themselves in attitude. Festinger, Schachter, and Back (4), in their study of a housing project, found a correlation of +.72 between a measure of attraction and a measure of "conformity in attitude." No direct observations of communication are made in these two studies; the relevance of their findings for the present point depends upon the assumption that frequency of communication is a function of attraction. This assumption is clearly justified in these two particular investigations, since in both communities there was complete freedom of association. As noted below, this assumption is not justified in all situations.

Other testable propositions derivable from the general postulate have to do with A's judgments of existing symmetry between himself and B with respect to X. Such judgments (to which the writer has for some time applied the term "perceived consensus") are represented by the symbol *B–X*, within A's phenomenal A–B–X system. Such a judgment, under given conditions of demand for co-orientation with respect to a given B and a given X, is a major determinant of the likelihood of a given AtoBreX, since strain toward symmetry is influenced by perception of existing symmetry. Such a judgment, moreover, is either confirmed or modified by whatever response B makes to AtoBreX. The continuity of an A–B–X system thus depends upon perceived consensus, which may be viewed either as an independent or as a dependent variable.

According to the previous proposition, the likelihood of increased symmetry (objectively observed) as a consequence of communicative acts increases with attraction and with intensity of attitude. The likelihood of perceived symmetry presumably increases with the same variables. Judgments of symmetry, like other judgments, are influenced both by "reality" and by "autistic" factors, both of which tend, as a function of attraction and intensity of attitude, to increase the likelihood of perceived consensus. Frequency of communication with B about X is the most important of the "reality" factors, and this, as we have seen, tends to vary with valence toward B and toward X. As for the "autistic" factors, the greater the positive attraction toward B and the more intense the attitude toward X, the greater the likelihood of cognitive distortion toward symmetry. Hypothetically, then, perceived symmetry with regard to X varies as a function of intensity of attitude toward X and of attraction toward B.

A considerable number of research studies, published and unpublished, are known to the writer in which subjects' own attitudes are related to their estimates of majority or modal position of specified groups. Only a minority of the studies systematically relate these judgments to attraction, and still fewer to intensity of attitude. Among this minority, however, the writer knows of no exceptions to the above proposition. The most striking of the known findings were obtained from students in several university classes in April of 1951, in a questionnaire dealing with the very recent dismissal of General MacArthur by President Truman:

| | PRO-TRUMAN *Ss* WHO . . . | ANTI-TRUMAN *Ss* WHO . . . |
|---|---|---|
| attribute to "most of my closest friends" | | |
| pro-Truman attitudes | 48 | 2 |
| anti-Truman attitudes | 0 | 34 |
| neither | 4 | 4 |
| attribute to "most uninformed people" | | |
| pro-Truman attitudes | 6 | 13 |
| anti-Truman attitudes | 32 | 14 |
| neither | 14 | 13 |

If we assume that "closest friends" are more attractive to university students than "uninformed people," these data provide support for the attraction hypothesis. Comparisons of those whose own attitudes are more and less intense also provide support, though less strikingly, for the hypothesis concerning attitude intensity.

Perceived symmetry, viewed as an independent variable, is obviously a determinant of instigation to symmetry-directed communication. Festinger (3), with specific reference to groups characterized by "pressures toward uniformity," hypothesizes that "pressure on members to communicate to others in the group concerning item *x* increases monotonically with increase in the perceived discrepancy in opinion concerning item *x* among members of the group," as well as with "relevance of item *x* to the functioning of the group," and with "cohesiveness of the group." And, with reference to the choice of recipient for communications, "The force to communicate about item *x* to a particular member of the group will increase as the discrepancy in opinion between that member and the communicator increases [and] will decrease to the extent that he is perceived as not a member of the group or to the extent that he is not wanted as a member of the group" (3, p. 8). Support for all of these hypotheses is to be found in one or more of his and his associates' studies. They are consistent with the following proposition: the likelihood of a symmetry-directed AtoBreX varies as a multiple function of perceived discrepancy (i.e., inversely with perceived symmetry), with valence toward B and with valence toward X.

Common sense and selected observations from everyday behavior may also be adduced in support of these propositions. For example, A observes that an attractive B differs with him on an important issue and seeks symmetry by trying to persuade B to his own point of view; or A seeks to reassure himself that B does not disagree with him; or A gives information to B about X or asks B for information about X. From all these acts we may infer perception of asymmetry and direction of communication toward symmetry. Selected observations concerning symmetry as a consequence of communication are equally plentiful; there is, in fact, no social phenomenon which can be more commonly observed than the tendency for freely communicating persons to resemble one another in orientation toward objects of common concern. The very nature of the communicative act as a transmission of information would, on a priori grounds alone, lead to the prediction of increased symmetry, since following the communication both A and B possess the information which was only A's before. B will not necessarily accept or believe all information transmitted by A, of course, but the likelihood of his doing so presumably varies not only with attraction toward A but also with intensity of attitude toward X, since in the long run the more important X is to him the more likely it is that he will avoid communicating with A about X if he cannot believe him. Thus the propositions have a considerable degree of face validity.

But everyday observation also provides instances to the contrary. Not all communications are directed toward symmetry, nor is symmetry an inevitable consequence of communication, even when attraction is strong and attitudes are intense. A devoted husband may refrain from discussing important business matters with his wife, or two close friends may "agree to disagree" in silence about matters of importance to both. People who are attracted toward one another often continue to communicate about subjects on which they continue to disagree—and this is particularly apt to happen with regard to attitudes which are intense, contrary to our theoretical prediction.

In sum, the available research findings and a considerable body of everyday observation support our predictions that instigation toward, perception of, and actual achievement of symmetry vary with intensity of attitude toward X and attraction toward B. The readiness with which exceptions can be adduced, however, indicates that these are not the only variables involved. The propositions, at best, rest upon the assumption of *ceteris paribus;* they cannot account for the fact that the probabilities of A's instigation to communicate about a given X are not the same for all potential B's of equal attraction for him, nor the fact that his instigation to communicate to a given B are not the same for all Xs of equal valence to him. We shall therefore attempt to derive certain further propositions from our basic assumption that both instigation to and achievement of symmetry vary with strength of forces toward co-orientation in the given situation.

## DYNAMICS OF CO-ORIENTATION

The foregoing propositions represent only a slight extrapolation of Heider's general principle (6) of "balanced states" in the absence of which "unit relations will be changed through action or through cognitive reorganization." In a later paper devoted specifically to the implications of Heider's hypotheses for interrelationships among attitudes toward a person and toward his acts, Horowitz et al. (8) note the following possible resolutions to states of imbalance: (*a*) the sign-valence of the act is changed to agree with that of the actor; (*b*) the reverse of this; and (*c*) the act is cognitively divorced from the actor; in addition, of course, the disharmony may be tolerated.

Orientations as attributed by A to B are here considered as equivalent to acts so attributed, in Heider's sense, and symmetry is taken as a special case of balance. Assume, for example, the following asymmetry in A's phenomenal system: +A:X, +A:B, −*B*:*X*, +*B*:*A* (i.e., A has positive attitude toward X, positive attraction toward B, perceives B's attitude toward X as negative, and B's attraction toward A as positive). Any of the following attempts at "resolution," analogous to those mentioned by

Heider, are possible: (*a*) −A:X; (*b*) −A:B, or (*c*) cognitive dissociation. These can occur in the absence of any communication with B. Attempts at harmony (symmetry) may also be made via communications directed toward +*B*:*X*. And, if such attempts fail, the three alternatives mentioned as possible without communication are still available. Finally, there is the possibility of compromise, following communication (e.g., agreement on some mid-point), and the possibility of "agreeing to disagree."

Such acts of resolution are made necessary, according to the present theory, by the situational demands of co-orientation on the one hand and by the psychological strain toward symmetry on the other. But symmetry is only a facilitating condition for co-orientation, not a necessary one. While (as maintained in the preceding propositions) the probabilities of symmetry vary, *ceteris paribus*, with demand for co-orientation, the theory does not demand that a symmetry-directed AtoBreX occur in every instance of strong demand for co-orientation. On the contrary, the theory demands that it occur only if, as, and when co-orientation is facilitated thereby. We must therefore inquire more closely into the nature of the forces toward co-orientation as related to possible forces against symmetry.

One kind of situational variable has to do with the nature of the forces which result in association between A and B. Of particular importance are constrained (enforced) vs. voluntary association, and association based upon broad as contrasted with narrow common interests. The range of Xs with regard to which there is demand for co-orientation is presumably influenced by such forces. The relevant generalization seems to be as follows: *The less the attraction between A and B, the more nearly strain toward symmetry is limited to those particular Xs, co-orientation toward which is required by the conditions of association.* This would mean, for example, that as attraction between two spouses decreases, strain toward symmetry would increasingly narrow to such Xs as are required by personal comfort and conformity with external propriety; similarly, the range of Xs with regard to which there is strain toward symmetry is greater for two friendly than for two hostile members of a chess club.

The problem of constraint has already been noted. In some of the studies cited above it was assumed that frequency of communication varies with attraction, but this is not necessarily true under conditions of forced association. Two recent theoretical treatises deal with this problem.

Homans, one of whose group variables is "frequency of interaction" (though not communication, specifically), includes the following among his other propositions: "If the frequency of interaction between two or more persons increases, the degree of their liking for one another will increase, and vice versa"; and "The more frequently persons interact with one another, the more alike in some respects both their activities and their sentiments tend to become" (7, p. 120). (The latter proposition, which closely resembles the one here under consideration, apparently takes a much less important place in Homans' system than the former.) Almost immediately, however, the latter proposition is qualified by the statement, "It is only when people interact as social equals and their jobs are not sharply differentiated that our hypothesis comes fully into its own." In nearly every chapter, moreover, Homans (whose propositions are drawn *post hoc* from various community, industrial, and ethnological studies) points to the limitations which are imposed by constraining forces—particularly those of rank and hierarchy—upon the relations among attraction, similarity of attitude, and communication.

Blake manages to incorporate these considerations in a more rigorous proposition. Noting that hostility cannot be considered as the simple psychological opposite of positive attraction, he proposes to substitute a curvilinear for Homans' linear hypothesis: ". . . when pressures operate to keep members of a group together, the stresses that drive toward interaction will be stronger in *both* positive and negative feeling states than in neutral ones" (2). This proposition seems consistent with the present argument to the effect that demands for co-orientation are likely to vary with the nature and degree of constraints upon association; hence communicative acts, together with their consequences, will also vary with such constraints.

Another situational variable deals with the fact that, under conditions of prescribed role differentiation, symmetry may take the form of "complementarity" (cf. 11) rather than sameness. For example, both a man and his small son may (following a certain amount of communication of a certain nature) subscribe to the *same norms* which prescribe *differentiated behavior* for man and boy with respect to a whiskey and soda. If the father drinks in the son's presence, there are demands upon both of them for co-orientation; but there is strain toward symmetry only with respect to "the code," and not with respect to personal orientation toward the whiskey and soda. The code becomes the X with regard to which there is strain toward symmetry. In more general terms, *under conditions of differentiation of A's and B's role prescriptions with regard to X, the greater the demand for co-orientation the greater the likelihood of strain toward symmetry with respect to the role system* (rather than with respect to X itself).

A third situational variable has to do with the possibility that symmetry may be threatening. Particularly under circumstances of shame, guilt, or fear of punishment there are apt to be strong forces against a symmetry-directed AtoBreX, even though—in fact, especially when—attitude toward X (the guilty act) and attraction toward B (a person from whom it is to be concealed) are strong. Under these conditions it is the demand for co-orientation which creates the problem; if A could utterly divorce X (his own act) from B, he would not feel guilty. Forces toward symmetry, however, are opposed by counterforces. Demand for co-orientation induces strain toward symmetry, but does not necessarily lead to a symmetry-directed AtoBreX.

A theoretically analogous situation may result from the omnipresent fact of multiple membership groups. That is, strains toward symmetry with $B_1$ in regard to X may be outweighed by strains toward symmetry with $B_2$, whose orientations toward X are viewed as contradictory with those of $B_1$. This is often the case when, for example, two good friends "agree to disagree" about something of importance to both. Thus in one study (14) it was found that those members least influenced by reported information concerning their own group norms were those most attracted to groups whose norms were perceived as highly divergent from those of the group in question.

Communicative acts, like others, are thus subject to inhibition. Such "resolutions" as "agreement to disagree," however, represent relatively stressful states of equilibrium. It is therefore to be expected, in ways analogous to those noted by Lewin in his discussion of the quasi-stationary equilibrium, that A–B–X systems characterized by such stress will be particularly susceptible to change. Such change need not necessarily occur in the particular region of the system characterized by maximal strain.

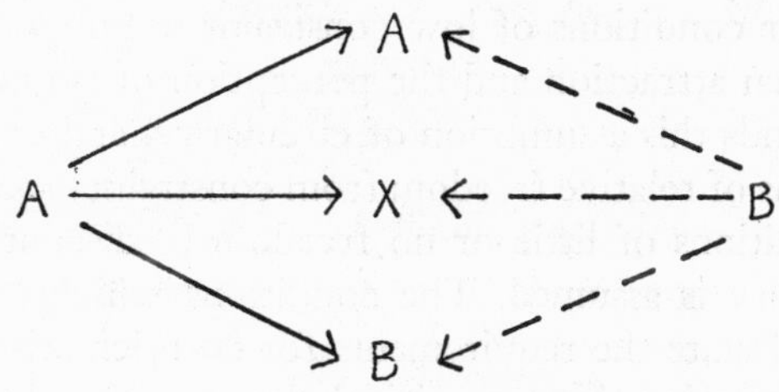


FIG. 2. Schematic illustration of A's phenomenal A–B–X system

The dynamics of such a system are by no means limited to those of strains toward symmetry, but must include changes resulting from acceptance of existing asymmetry. The possible range of dynamic changes is illustrated in Fig. 2. (In this figure, the A and B at either side represent persons as communicators; the A and B in the center represent the same persons as objects of co-orientation. The broken lines represent A's judgments of B's orientations.) Given perceived asymmetry with regard to X, and demand for co-orientation toward B and X, the possibilities for A are such that he can:

1. achieve, or attempt to achieve, symmetry with regard to X
   a. by influencing B toward own orientation,
   b. by changing own orientation toward B's,
   c. by cognitively distorting B's orientation;

2. introduce changes in other parts of the system
   a. modify his attraction toward B,
   b. modify his judgment of own attraction for B,
   c. modify evaluation of (attraction toward) himself (A),
   d. modify his judgment of B's evaluation of himself (B);
3. tolerate the asymmetry, without change.

As suggested by this listing of possible "solutions," the perception of asymmetry, under conditions of demand for co-orientation, confronts A with a problem which he can attempt to solve behaviorally (i.e., by communicative acts) and/or cognitively (i.e., by changing either his own orientations or his perception of B's orientations). Whatever his chosen "solution," it has some effect upon A's phenomenal A–B–X system—either to reinforce it or to modify it. As a result of repeatedly facing and "solving" problems of co-orientation with regard to a given B and a given X, a relatively stable equilibrium is established. If A is free either to continue or not to continue his association with B, one or the other of two eventual outcomes is likely: (*a*) he achieves an equilibrium characterized by relatively great attraction toward B and by relatively high perceived symmetry, and the association is continued; or (*b*) he achieves an equilibrium characterized by relatively little attraction toward B and by relatively low perceived symmetry, and the association is discontinued. This "either-or" assumption under conditions of low constraint presupposes a circular relationship between attraction and the perception of symmetry. The present theory demands this assumption of circularity, and empirical evidence (under conditions of relative freedom from constraint) seems to support it.

Under conditions of little or no freedom to discontinue association, no such circularity is assumed. The conditions which dictate continued association also dictate the requirements for co-orientation, which are independent of attraction. The empirical data suggest that the degree to which attraction is independent of symmetry varies with the degree of *perceived* (rather than the degree of objectively observed) constraint.

## GROUP PROPERTIES

It follows from the preceding assumptions and propositions that there should be predictable relationships between certain properties of any group and variables having to do with communicative behavior within that group. A group's structural properties, for example, viewed as independent variables, may create problems and may provide solutions to other problems of communication. Viewed the other way around, many properties of a group are outcomes of its communicative practices. Evidence from many sources points to distinctive properties of groups which are precisely those which the foregoing considerations would lead us to expect, either as conditions for or as consequences of a given kind and frequency of communicative acts.

Three kinds of properties are briefly noted. Each of them is hypothetically related (either as dependent or as independent variable) to the probabilities of the occurrence of a given kind of communicative act.

1. *Homogeneity of orientation* toward certain objects. All descriptive accounts of interacting groups note this property, in one way or another and by one label or another. As applied to behavior, it does not necessarily refer to similarity of action on the part of all group members, but only of demand or expectation; e.g., all expect each to take his own differentiated role. In order to account for the observed facts it is necessary to make the assumptions (not previously made in this paper) that information may be transmitted in non-verbal ways, and with or without intention to do so—e.g., a person's behavior with regard to a given object informs observers about his orientation to it.

If communication is thus broadly defined, then the degrees of homogeneity of orientation of a given group with respect to specified objects are presumably related to communication variables with respect to those objects. It is not hypothesized that homogeneity is an invariable function of any single index of communication (frequency, for example), but rather that it varies in accordance with the dynamics of A–B–X systems. While there are often extra-group determinants of homogeneity of orientation, it seems reasonable to view this very important group property as an outcome of the conditions and consequences of communicative acts.

2. *Homogeneity of perceived consensus* (i.e., homogeneity of judgments of homogeneity of orientation). This property, though not often specifically mentioned in the literature on groups, is usually implicitly assumed. Most communication presupposes a considerable degree of perceived as well as objective homogeneity of orientation. The very fact of using language or gesture presupposes the assumption of consensus among communicants as to the information transmitted by the use of symbols.

Homogeneity of orientation and of perceived consensus do not, in spite of implicit assumptions to the contrary, have an invariant relationship; judgments of homogeneity may be of any degree of accuracy. If, as in the village reported by Schanck (13), each of many dissenters from a supposed norm believes himself the only dissenter, this state of pluralistic ignorance is an important group property, and is plausibly described by the author as an outcome of certain practices of communication. Any degree of homogeneity of perceived consensus, representing any degree of accuracy, is hypothetically an outcome of previous communicative acts and a determinant of future ones.

3. *Attraction among members*. Relationships of positive attraction of some degree invariably characterize continuing groups under conditions

of minimal constraint, and are commonly found even under conditions of considerable constraint. This is so commonly the case that Homans (7) ventures the almost unqualified hypothesis that "liking" increases with frequency of interaction, and vice versa. Viewed in the light of the hypothetical dynamics of A–B–X systems, Homans' proposition would be amended to the effect that interpersonal attraction varies with the degree to which the demands of co-orientation are met by communicative acts.

These are not, of course, the only group properties of significance, nor are these properties outcomes exclusively of intragroup communication. (Some properties of almost any group, particularly at early stages of its history, derive largely from individual characteristics which its members bring to it.) It appears to be the case, nevertheless, that the hypothetical conditions and consequences of communicative acts are not limited to groups of two, and that some of the important properties of observed groups are consistent with the hypothetical dynamics of A–B–X systems.

## SUMMARY

Communicative acts, like other molar behaviors, may be viewed as outcomes of changes in organism-environment relationships, actual and/or anticipated. Communicative acts are distinctive in that they may be aroused by and may result in changes anywhere within the system of relations between two or more communicators and the objects of their communication. It seems likely that the dynamics of such a system are such that from an adequate understanding of its properties at a given moment there can be predicted both the likelihood of occurrence of a given act of communication and the nature of changes in those properties which will result from that act.

Some of the most significant of group properties are those which, hypothetically, vary with intragroup communicative acts. It should therefore be rewarding to discover whether support for the present hypotheses, as apparently provided by the scattered evidence now available, can be confirmed in more systematic ways. If so, there are promising possibilities of investigating the phenomena of social interaction by viewing them as events within communication systems.

## REFERENCES

1. Back, K. The exertion of influence through social communication. *J. abnorm. soc. Psychol.*, 1951, 46, 9–23.
2. Blake, R. R. The interaction-feeling hypothesis applied to psychotherapy groups. *Sociometry*, 1953, 16, 71–77.
3. Festinger, L. Informal social communication. In L. Festinger, K. Back, S. Schachter, H. H. Kelley, & J. Thibaut, *Theory and experiment in social communication.* Ann Arbor Institute for Social Research, Univer. of Michigan, 1950.

4. Festinger, L., Schachter, S., & Back, K. *Social pressures in informal groups.* New York: Harper, 1950.
5. Festinger, L., & Thibaut, J. Interpersonal communications in small groups. *J. abnorm. soc. Psychol.*, 1951, 46, 92–99.
6. Heider, F. Attitudes and cognitive organization. *J. Psychol.*, 1946, 21, 107–112.
7. Homans, G. C. *The human group.* New York: Harcourt, Brace, 1950.
8. Horowitz, M. W., Lyons, J., & Perlmutter, H. V. Induction of forces in discussion groups. *Hum. Relat.*, 1951, 4, 57–76.
9. Miller, G. A. *Language and communication.* New York: McGraw-Hill, 1951.
10. Newcomb, T. M. *Personality and social change.* New York: Dryden, 1943.
11. Parsons, T., & Shils, E. A. (Eds.) *Toward a general theory of action.* Cambridge: Harvard Univer. Press, 1951.
12. Schachter, S. Deviation, rejection and communication. *J. abnorm. soc. Psychol.*, 1951, 46, 190–207.
13. Schanck, R. L. A study of a community and its groups and institutions conceived of as behaviors of individuals. *Psychol. Monogr.*, 1932, 43, No. 2 (Whole No. 195).
14. White, M. S. Attitude change as related to perceived group consensus. Unpublished doctoral dissertation, Univer. of Michigan, 1953.

# *A Theory of Social Comparison Processes*

LEON FESTINGER

IN THIS paper we shall present a further development of a previously published theory concerning opinion influence processes in social groups (7). This further development has enabled us to extend the theory to deal with other areas, in addition to opinion formation, in which social comparison is important. Specifically, we shall develop below how the theory applies to the appraisal and evaluation of abilities as well as opinions.

Such theories and hypotheses in the area of social psychology are frequently viewed in terms of how "plausible" they seem. "Plausibility" usually means whether or not the theory or hypothesis fits one's intuition or

FROM *Human Relations*, 1954, 7, 117–140. Reprinted by permission of the author and publisher.

The development of this theory was aided by a grant from the Behavioral Sciences Division of the Ford Foundation. It is part of the research program of the Laboratory for Research in Social Relations.

one's common sense. In this meaning much of the theory which is to be presented here is not "plausible." The theory does, however, explain a considerable amount of data and leads to testable derivations. Three experiments, specifically designed to test predictions from this extension of the theory, have now been completed (5, 12, 19). They all provide good corroboration. We will in the following pages develop the theory and present the relevant data.

*Hypothesis I:* There exists, in the human organism, a drive to evaluate his opinions and his abilities.

While opinions and abilities may, at first glance, seem to be quite different things, there is a close functional tie between them. They act together in the manner in which they affect behavior. A person's cognition (his opinions and beliefs) about the situation in which he exists and his appraisals of what he is capable of doing (his evaluation of his abilities) will together have bearing on his behavior. The holding of incorrect opinions and/or inaccurate appraisals of one's abilities can be punishing or even fatal in many situations.

It is necessary, before we proceed, to clarify the distinction between opinions and evaluations of abilities since at first glance it may seem that one's evaluation of one's own ability is an opinion about it. Abilities are of course manifested only through performance which is assumed to depend upon the particular ability. The clarity of the manifestation or performance can vary from instances where there is no clear ordering criterion of the ability to instances where the performance which reflects the ability can be clearly ordered. In the former case, the evaluation of the ability does function like other opinions which are not directly testable in "objective reality." For example, a person's evaluation of his ability to write poetry will depend to a large extent on the opinions which others have of his ability to write poetry. In cases where the criterion is unambiguous and can be clearly ordered, this furnishes an objective reality for the evaluation of one's ability so that it depends less on the opinions of other persons and depends more on actual comparison of one's performance with the performance of others. Thus, if a person evaluates his running ability, he will do so by comparing his time to run some distance with the times that other persons have taken.

In the following pages, when we talk about evaluating an ability, we shall mean specifically the evaluation of that ability in situations where the performance is unambiguous and is known. Most situations in real life will, of course, present situations which are a mixture of opinion and ability evaluation.

In a previous article (7) the author posited the existence of a drive to determine whether or not one's opinions were "correct." We are here stating that this same drive also produces behavior in people oriented toward obtaining an accurate appraisal of their abilities.

The behavioral implication of the existence of such a drive is that we would expect to observe behavior on the part of persons which enables them to ascertain whether or not their opinions are correct and also behavior which enables them accurately to evaluate their abilities. It is consequently necessary to answer the question as to how persons go about evaluating their opinions and their abilities.

*Hypothesis II:* To the extent that objective, non-social means are not available, people evaluate their opinions and abilities by comparison respectively with the opinions and abilities of others.

In many instances, perhaps most, whether or not an opinion is correct cannot be immediately determined by reference to the physical world. Similarly it is frequently not possible to assess accurately one's ability by reference to the physical world. One could, of course, test the opinion that an object was fragile by hitting it with a hammer, but how is one to test the opinion that a certain political candidate is better than another, or that war is inevitable? Even when there is a possible immediate physical referent for an opinion, it is frequently not likely to be employed. The belief, for example, that tomatoes are poisonous to humans (which was widely held at one time) is unlikely to be tested. The situation is similar with respect to the evaluation of one's abilities. If the only use to which, say, jumping ability was put was to jump across a particular brook, it would be simple to obtain an accurate evaluation of one's ability in this respect. However, the unavailability of the opportunity for such clear testing and the vague and multipurpose use of various abilities generally make such a clear objective test not feasible or not useful. For example, how does one decide how intelligent one is? Also, one might find out how many seconds it takes a person to run a certain distance, but what does this mean with respect to his ability—is it adequate or not? For both opinions and abilities, to the extent that objective physical bases for evaluation are not available, subjective judgments of correct or incorrect opinion and subjectively accurate assessments of one's ability depend upon how one compares with other persons.

*Corollary II A:* In the absence of both a physical and a social comparison, subjective evaluations of opinions and abilities are unstable.

There exists evidence from studies on "level of aspiration" which shows clearly the instability of evaluations of abilities in the absence of comparison with other persons (13, 15, 20, 21, 23). The typical situation in an experiment designed to study "level of aspiration" is as follows: a person is given a task to perform which is serial in nature. This may be a series of trials of throwing darts at a target or a series of information tests or a series of puzzles or the like. After each trial the person is told what he scored (how many points he made or how many correct answers or how long it took) and is asked to state what score he expects to get or will try for on the next trial. These experiments have previously been interpreted in terms of goal directed behavior. If we examine the situation closely, however, it is apparent that the individual's stated "level of aspiration" is actually a statement of what he considers a good performance to be. In other words, it is his evaluation, at that time, of what score he should get, that is, his evaluation of his ability. The data show clearly that if the person scores as well as he said he expected to do, he feels he has done well (experiences success) and if he scores less than his "aspirations" he feels he has done poorly (experiences failure) (17).

Let us examine, then, the stability of these evaluations in a situation where the person performing the task has no opportunity for comparison with others. The data from these studies show that the "level of aspiration" fluctuates markedly as performance fluctuates. If the person makes a score better than his previous one, then what was formerly considered a good performance is no longer good and his "level of aspiration" goes up. If his performance drops, his "level of aspiration" drops. Even after a person has had a good deal of experience at a task, the evaluation of what is good performance continues to fluctuate.

Similar instability is found in the case of opinions. When, using the autokinetic effect, persons are asked to make judgments of how far the point of light moves, these judgments continue to fluctuate before there are any comparison persons.[1]

To the extent, then, that there are relevant data available, they tend to confirm *Corollary II A* concerning the instability of evaluations in the absence of comparisons.

*Corollary II B:* When an objective, non-social basis for the evaluation of one's ability or opinion is readily available persons will not evaluate their opinions or abilities by comparison with others.

Hochbaum (18) reports an experiment concerning the effect of knowledge of others' opinions on one's own opinion which corroborates *Corollary II B*. Half of the subjects in this experiment were persuaded by the experimenter that they were extremely good at being able to make correct judgments concerning things like the issue they were to discuss. The other half of the subjects were made to feel that they were extremely

1 Although published material on the autokinetic effect does not present the data in this form, it is clearly shown in special analysis of data from an experiment by Brehm, J. W., A quantitative approach to the measurement of social influence. Honors thesis, Harvard University, 1952.

poor in making such judgments. They were then asked to write their opinions down and were handed back a slip of paper presumably reporting to them the opinions of each other person in the group. In this way the subjects were made to feel that most of the others in the group disagreed with them. Those subjects who were given an objective basis for feeling that their opinion was likely to be correct did not change their opinions very often in spite of the disagreement with others in the group. Those who had an objective basis for feeling their judgments were likely to be poor changed their opinion very frequently upon discovering that others disagreed with them.

*Hypothesis III:* The tendency to compare oneself with some other specific person decreases as the difference between his opinion or ability and one's own increases.

A person does not tend to evaluate his opinions or his abilities by comparison with others who are too divergent from himself. If some other person's ability is too far from his own, either above or below, it is not possible to evaluate his own ability *accurately* by comparison with this other person. There is then a tendency not to make the comparison. Thus, a college student, for example, does not compare himself to inmates of an institution for the feeble minded to evaluate his own intelligence. Nor does a person who is just beginning to learn the game of chess compare himself to the recognized masters of the game.

The situation is identical with respect to the evaluation of opinions. One does not evaluate the correctness or incorrectness of an opinion by comparison with others whose opinions are extremely divergent from one's own. Thus, a person who believes that Negroes are the intellectual equals of whites does not evaluate his opinion by comparison with the opinion of a person who belongs to some very anti-Negro group. In other words, there is a self-imposed restriction in the range of opinion or ability with which a person compares himself.

*Corollary III A:* Given a range of possible persons for comparison, someone close to one's own ability or opinion will be chosen for comparison.

There is some evidence relevant to this corollary from an experiment by Whittemore (24). The purpose of the study was to examine the relation between performance and competition. Subjects were seated around a table and given tasks to work on. There was ample opportunity to observe how the others were progressing. After the experimental session, in introspective reports, the subjects stated that they had almost always spontaneously selected someone whose performance was close to their own to compete against.

*Corollary III B:* If the only comparison available is a very divergent one, the person will not be able to make a subjectively precise evaluation of his opinion or ability.

There is evidence supporting this corollary with respect to abilities but no relevant evidence in connection with opinions has been found.

Hoppe (20) in his experiment on level of aspiration reports that when subjects made a score very far above or very far below their level of aspiration they did not experience success or failure respectively. In other words, this extremely divergent score presented no grounds for self evaluation. Dreyer (5) performed an experiment in which high school children were made to score either: very far above the reported average for boys like themselves; at the reported average; or very far below the reported average. After a series of trials they were asked, "How well do you feel you did on the test?" There were five possible categories of response. The top two were good or very good; the bottom two were poor or very poor. In the middle was a noncommittal response of fair. Both those who scored very far below and those who scored very far above the reported group average gave the response "fair" significantly more often than did those who scored at the reported group average. Also, on the average, the persons who had scored at the reported average felt they had done better than did those scoring far above the group. Again the data support the hypothesis.

We may then conclude that there is selectivity in comparison on abilities and opinions and that one major factor governing the selectivity is simply the discrepancy between the person's own opinion or ability and that of another person. Phenomenologically, the appearance of this process is different for opinions and for abilities but conceptually it is exactly the same process. In dealing with opinions one feels that those with whom one does not compare oneself are different kinds of people or members of different groups or people with different backgrounds. Frequently this allegation of difference, to support the non-comparability, is made together with some derogation. In the case of abilities, the phenomenal process is that of designation of status inferior or superior to those persons who are non-comparable to oneself. We will elaborate on this later.

*Derivation A (from I, II, III)*: Subjective evaluations of opinions or of abilities are stable when comparison is available with others who are judged to be close to one's opinions or abilities.

*Derivation B (from I, II, III)*: The availability of comparison with others whose opinions or abilities are somewhat different from one's own will produce tendencies to change one's evaluation of the opinion or ability in question.

There are also data to show the effect which knowledge of group opinions or group abilities has on the person's evaluations which were initially formed privately. If the evaluation of an opinion or an ability formed in the absence of the possibility of comparison with others is indeed unstable, as we have presumed, then we would expect that, given an opportunity to make a comparison with others, the opportunity would be taken and the comparison would have a considerable impact on the self evaluation. This is found to be true for both abilities and opinions. "Level of aspiration" experiments have been performed where, after a series of trials in which the person is unable to compare his performance with others, there occurs a series of trials in which the person has available to him the knowledge of how others *like himself* performed on each trial (1, 4, 6, 17). When the "others like himself" have scores different from his own, his stated "level of aspiration" (his statement of what he considers is good performance) almost always moves close to the level of the performance of others. It is also found that under these conditions the level of aspiration changes less with fluctuations in performance, in other words, is more stable. When the reported performance of others is about equal to his own score, the stability of his evaluation of his ability is increased and, thus, his level of aspiration shows very little variability. Dreyer, in an experiment specifically designed to test part of this theory (5), showed clearly that the variance of the level of aspiration was smaller when the subject scored close to the group than when he scored far above or far below them. In short, comparison with the performance of others specifies what his ability should be and gives stability to the evaluation.

Festinger, Gerard, et al. (10) find a similar situation with respect to opinions. When a person is asked to form an opinion privately and then has made available to him the consensus of opinion in the group of which he is a member, those who discover that most others in the group disagree with them become relatively less confident that their opinion is correct and a goodly proportion change their opinion. Those who discover that most others in the group agree with them become highly confident in their opinion and it is extremely rare to find one of them changing his opinion. Again, comparison with others has tended to define what is a correct opinion and has given stability to the evaluation. This result is also obtained by Hochbaum (18).

We may then conclude that *Derivations A* and *B* tend to be supported by the available data.

*Derivation C (from I, III B)*: A person will be less attracted to situations where others are very divergent from him than to situations where others are close to him for both abilities and opinions.

This follows from a consideration of *Hypothesis I* and *Corollary III B*. If there is a drive toward evaluation of abilities and opinions, and if this evaluation is possible only with others who are close enough, then there should be some attraction to groups where others are relatively close with respect to opinions and/or abilities. There are data confirming this for both opinions and abilities.

Festinger, Gerard, et al. (10) report an experiment in which after each person had written down his opinion on an issue he was handed back a slip of paper presumably containing a tabulation of the opinions in the group. Some in each group were thus given the impression that most of the others in the group held opinions close to their own. The rest were given the impression that most others in the group held opinions quite different from their own. After the experiment they were each asked how well they liked the others in the group. In each of the eight different experimental conditions those who thought that the others held divergent opinions were less attracted to the group.[2]

The previously mentioned experiment by Dreyer (5) has as one of its main purposes the testing of this derivation in connection with abilities. He used a "level of aspiration" situation and falsified the scores he reported to the subjects so that some thought they were scoring very far above the group, some thought they were scoring very far below the group, while others thought they were scoring about the same level as the average of others like them. After each trial they were asked whether they wanted to continue for another trial or whether they would prefer to stop. The reasoning was that if those scoring well above or well below the group average were not able to evaluate their ability accurately, the situation would be less attractive to them and they would stop sooner. On the average, those scoring very much above the group stop after the fifth trial, while those scoring below or at the average of the group stop after the ninth trial.[3] There is no difference between those scoring at and those scoring well below the average of the group. The derivation in the case of abilities seems confirmed for deviation from the group in one direction then but not in the other. This is probably due to the presence of another pressure which we shall discuss in detail later, namely, the value placed in our culture on being better and better with the result that the subjects scoring below the group wanted to, and felt that they might, improve and achieve comparability with the group average.

This result from the experiment by Dreyer (5) is also corroborated in the previously mentioned experiment by Hochbaum (18). It will be recalled that half the subjects were made to feel that their ability in judging situations of the kind they were to discuss was extremely good and very superior to the abilities of the others in the group. The other half of the subjects were made to feel that their ability was poor and consider-

2 This result is not reported in the article cited. It was obtained by analyzing the data for this particular purpose.

3 It is interesting to note that on this point, the usual theory of level of aspiration (21) would lead to a quite different prediction, namely, that those scoring consistently below the group would stop earliest.

ably worse than the ability of the others in the group. At the end of the experiment all the subjects were asked whether, if they returned for another session they would like to be in the same group or a different group. Of those who felt they were very much above the others in the group, only 38 per cent wanted to return to the same group. Of those who felt that they were considerably inferior to the others, 68 per cent wanted to return to the same group.

With the qualification concerning the asymmetry with regard to abilities the derivation may be regarded as confirmed. We will discuss the unidirectional drive upwards for abilities, which produces the asymmetry, in more detail later.

*Derivation D (from I, II, III)*: The existence of a discrepancy in a group with respect to opinions or abilities will lead to action on the part of members of that group to reduce the discrepancy.

We have stated in *Hypotheses I, II, and III* and in the corollaries to these hypotheses that there is a drive to evaluate accurately one's opinions and abilities, that this evaluation is frequently only possible by comparison with others and that the comparison tends to be made with others who are close to oneself on the particular ability or opinion in question. This implies that the drive to evaluate one's ability or opinion will lead to behavior which will produce for the person a situation where those with whom he compares himself are reasonably close to him, in other words, there will be action to reduce discrepancies which exist between himself and others with whom he compares himself.

Before we can discuss the data relevant to this derivation it is necessary to point out two important differences between opinions and abilities which affect the behavioral manifestations of the action to reduce discrepancies. We will state these differences in the form of hypotheses.

*Hypothesis IV:* There is a unidirectional drive upward in the case of abilities which is largely absent in opinions.

With respect to abilities, different performances have intrinsically different values. In Western culture, at any rate, there is a value set on doing better and better which means that the higher the score on performance, the more desirable it is. Whether or not this is culturally determined, and hence culturally variable, is an important question but one with which we will not occupy ourselves here.[4]

With respect to most opinions, on the other hand, in the absence of comparison there is no inherent, intrinsic basis for preferring one opinion

4 There is some evidence, for example, that among the Hopi Indians this preference for better performance is absent (2).

over another. If we thought of opinions on some specific issue as ranging along a continuum, then no opinion in and of itself has any greater value than any other opinion. The value comes from the subjective feeling that the opinion is correct and valid.

*Hypothesis V:* There are non-social restraints which make it difficult or even impossible to change one's ability. These non-social restraints are largely absent for opinions.

If a person changes his mind about something, deserts one belief in favor of another, there is no further difficulty in the way of consummating the change. It is true that there are sometimes considerable difficulties in getting someone to change his mind concerning an opinion or belief. Such resistance may arise because of consistency with other opinions and beliefs, personality characteristics that make a person lean in one direction or another and the like. But the point to be stressed here is that once these resistances are overcome, there is no further restraint which would make it difficult for the change to become effective.

There are generally strong non-social restraints, however, against changing one's ability, or changing one's performance which reflects this ability. Even if a person is convinced that he should be able to run faster or should be more intelligent, and even if he is highly motivated to improve his ability in this respect, there are great difficulties in the way of consummating the change.

We may now examine the implications of *Derivation D.* Considering *Hypothesis IV* it is clear that the action to reduce the discrepancy which exists is, in the case of opinions, a relatively uncomplicated pressure towards uniformity. When and if uniformity of opinion is achieved there is a state of social quiescence. In the case of abilities, however, the action to reduce discrepancies interacts with the unidirectional push to do better and better. The resolution of these two pressures, which act simultaneously, is a state of affairs where all the members are relatively close together with respect to some specific ability, but not completely uniform. The pressures cease acting on a person if he is just slightly better than the others. It is obvious that not everyone in a group can be slightly better than everyone else. The implication is that, with respect to the evaluation of abilities, a state of social quiescence is never reached.

Competitive behavior, action to protect one's superiority, and even some kinds of behavior that might be called cooperative, are manifestations in the social process of these pressures which do not reach quiescence. We shall now elaborate this further in considering the specific nature of the social action arising from pressures toward uniformity. There are three major manifestations of pressure toward uniformity which we shall list below together with the relevant data.

*Derivation $D_1$:* When a discrepancy exists with respect to opinions or abilities there will be tendencies to change one's own position so as to move closer to others in the group.

*Derivation $D_2$:* When a discrepancy exists with respect to opinions or abilities there will be tendencies to change others in the group to bring them closer to oneself.

Considering *Hypothesis V* in relation to the above two subderivations we can see that a difference is implied between the resulting process for opinions and for abilities. Since opinions are relatively free to change, the process of changing the positions of members of a group relative to one another is expressed in action which is predominantly socially oriented. When differences of opinion exist, and pressures toward uniformity arise, these pressures are manifested in an influence process. Members attempt to influence one another, existing opinions become less stable and change occurs. This process of social influence, as we have mentioned before, ceases if and when uniformity of opinion exists in the group.

When pressures toward uniformity exist with respect to abilities, these pressures are manifested less in a social process and more in action against the environment which restrains movement. Thus, a person who runs more slowly than others with whom he compares himself, and for whom this ability is important, may spend considerable time practising running. In a similar situation where the ability in question is intelligence, the person may study harder. But, needless to say, movement toward uniformity may or may not occur. Even if it occurs, it will take much, much longer than in the case of opinions.

This process would, of course, not be competitive if it were not for the simultaneous operation of the unidirectional push upward which is stated in *Hypothesis IV*. Because of this unidirectional push and the pressure toward uniformity, the individual is oriented toward some point on the ability continuum slightly better than his own performance or the performance of those with whom he is comparing himself. If uniformity concerning an ability were reached this would not lead to a cessation of competition as long as the unidirectional push upward is operating.

There are data which corroborate the two derivations with regard to both abilities and opinions. Back (3), Festinger and Thibaut (9), Festinger, Gerard, et al. (10) and Gerard (14) have shown clearly that the presence of disagreement in a group concerning some opinion leads to attempts to influence others who disagree with them and also to tendencies to change own opinion to agree more with the others in the group. The effect of this process is to have the group move closer and closer to agreement. In groups where uniformity concerning some issue is reached the influence process on that issue ceases.

In the case of abilities the evidence is less direct for a number of reasons. First, there have been fewer studies conducted relevant to this point. Second, since the process resulting from pressure to reduce discrepancies concerning abilities is not clearly shown in a social process, and since it is complicated by the drive to do better and better, it is harder to identify. Some evidence is available from the literature on level of aspiration (21). It has been shown that in most situations, an individual's level of aspiration is placed slightly above his performance. When told the average performance of others like himself, the level of aspiration is generally set slightly above this reported group average. These results are what we would expect if the resolution of the simultaneous unidirectional drive upward and the pressure towards uniformity is indeed a drive to be slightly better than the others with whom one compares oneself. These data can then be viewed as an indication of the desire to change one's position relative to others.

An experiment by Hoffman, Festinger, and Lawrence (19) specifically designed to test parts of the present theory, shows this competitive process clearly. In a performance situation where one of three persons is scoring considerably above the other two, these two can and do act so as to prevent the high scorer from getting additional points. Thus, when the situation is arranged such that the performance of each person is controllable by the others in the group, action is taken to change the position of the members to reduce the discrepancies which exist.

Let us also examine what we would expect of the behavior of someone whose performance is considerably higher than the other members of the group and who has no other possible comparison group to turn to for his evaluation of this ability. Since the others are considerably poorer, they will not effectively serve as a comparison for his own evaluation. The pressure acting on him toward comparability can manifest itself in two ways. It is possible that under these conditions his performance will actually deteriorate slightly over a period of time. It is also possible that he will devote considerable time and effort to trying to improve the performance of the others in the group to a point where at least some of them are close to, but not equal to, him. This could take the form of helping them practice, coaching them, motivating them to improve and the like. Once comparability has been achieved, however, the process should change to the familiar competitive one.

There is some indirect corroboration of this from experimental evidence. Greenberg (16) reports a study in competition in which pairs of children, seated together at a table, were to construct things out of "stones" (blocks) which were initially all in one common pile. Grabbing blocks from the pile was one of the indications of competition while giving blocks to the others was taken as one indication of lack of competition. The author reports the case of two friends, E. K. and H. At a time when E. K.'s construction was clearly superior to that of H., H. asked for "stones" and was freely given such by E. K. Subsequently E. K. asked H. whether or not she wanted more "stones." At the end of the session, although privately the experimenter judged both constructions to be nearly equal, when the children were asked "whose is better?" E. K. said "mine" and H., after a moment, agreed.

From many such pairs the author summarizes as follows: "Sometimes when a child gave another a 'stone,' it was not at all an act of disinterested generosity, but a display of friendly competition and superior skill."

*Derivation* $D_3$*:* When a discrepancy exists with respect to opinions or abilities there will be tendencies to cease comparing oneself with those in the group who are very different from oneself.

Just as comparability can be achieved by changing the position of the members with respect to one another, so can it also be achieved by changing the composition of the comparison group. Thus, for example, if pressures toward uniformity exist in a group concerning some opinion on which there is a relatively wide discrepancy, there is a tendency to redefine the comparison group so as to exclude those members whose opinions are most divergent from one's own. In other words, one merely ceases to compare oneself with those persons.

Here again we would expect the behavioral manifestation of the tendency to stop comparing oneself with those who are very divergent to be different for opinions and for abilities. This difference arises because of the nature of the evaluation of opinions and abilities and because of the asymmetry introduced by the unidirectional push upward for abilities. We will consider these in order.

It will be recalled that opinions are evaluated in terms of whether or not subjectively they are correct while abilities are evaluated in terms of how good they seem. In other words, the existence of someone whose ability is very divergent from one's own, while it does not help to evaluate one's ability, does not make, in itself, for discomfort or unpleasantness. In the case of opinions, however, the existence of a discrepant opinion threatens one's own opinion since it implies the possibility that one's own opinion may not be correct. *Hypothesis VI,* which we will state below, leads us then to expect that the process of making others incomparable (ceasing to compare oneself with others) will be accompanied by hostility or derogation in the case of opinions but will not, generally, in the case of abilities.

*Hypothesis VI:* The cessation of comparison with others is accompanied by hostility or derogation to the extent that continued comparison with those persons implies unpleasant consequences.

Thus, in the case of opinions we expect the process of making others incomparable to be associated with rejection from the group. In the case of abilities, this may or may not be the case. It would be plausible to expect that there would rarely be derogation in making those below oneself incomparable. When making those above oneself incomparable, the presence of unidirectional push upward might lead to derogation in some instances.

The asymmetry introduced in the case of abilities is another difference we may expect to find. While in the case of opinions, deviation on either side of one's own opinion would lead to the same consequences, in the case of abilities there is a difference. The process of making others incomparable results in a "status stratification" where some are clearly inferior and others are clearly superior.

*Corollary VI A:* Cessation of comparison with others will be accompanied by hostility or derogation in the case of opinions. In the case of abilities this will not generally be true.

Festinger, Schachter, and Back (8) and Schachter (22) have shown that when there is a range of opinion in a group there is a tendency to reject those members of the group whose opinions are very divergent from one's own. This rejection tends to be accompanied by a relative cessation of communication of those who are rejected. This is undoubtedly another evidence of the cessation of comparison with those persons.

There are data relevant to this point in connection with abilities from the experiment by Hoffman, Festinger, and Lawrence (19). In this experiment, one out of a group of three persons was made to score very much higher than the other two on a test of intelligence. When the nature of the situation allowed, the two low scoring subjects ceased to compete against the high scorer and began to compete against each other. When they did this they also rated the intelligence of the high scorer as considerably higher than their own, thus acknowledging his superiority. In those conditions where they continued to compete against the high scorer they did not rate his intelligence as higher than their own. In other words, when the situation allowed it they stopped comparing their scores with the score of someone considerably higher than themselves. This cessation of comparison was accompanied by an acknowledgment of the others' superiority. A number of sociometric questions showed no hostility toward or derogation of the high scorer.

Having discussed the manifestations of the "pressure toward uniformity" which arises from the drive to evaluate opinions and abilities, we will now raise the question as to the factors which determine the strength of these pressures.

*Derivation E (from I, II, and III)*: Any factors which increase the strength of the drive to evaluate some particular ability or opinion will increase the "pressure toward uniformity" concerning that ability or opinion.

*Hypothesis VII:* Any factors which increase the importance of some particular group as a comparison group for some particular opinion or ability will increase the pressure toward uniformity concerning that ability or opinion within that group.

To make the above statements relevant to empirical data we must of course specify the factors involved. The corollaries stated below will specify some of these factors. We will then present the data relevant to these corollaries.

*Corollary to Derivation E:* An increase in the importance of an ability or an opinion, or an increase in its relevance to immediate behavior, will increase the pressure toward reducing discrepancies concerning that opinion or ability.

If an opinion or ability is of no importance to a person there will be no drive to evaluate that ability or opinion. In general, the more important the opinion or ability is to the person, the more related to behavior, social behavior in particular, and the more immediate the behavior is, the greater will be the drive for evaluation. Thus, in an election year, influence processes concerning political opinions are much more current than in other years. Likewise, a person's drive to evaluate his intellectual ability will be stronger when he must decide between going to graduate school or taking a job.

The previously mentioned experiment by Hoffman, Festinger, and Lawrence (19) corroborates the *Corollary to Derivation E* with respect to abilities. It will be recalled that this experiment involved groups of three persons who took an "intelligence test." The situation was arranged so that one of the subjects (a paid participant) started out with a higher score than the other two. From then on the two subjects could completely control how many points the paid participant scored. The degree to which they prevented him from scoring points was taken as a measure of the extent to which they were competing against him and hence as an indication of the strength of the pressure toward uniformity acting on them. Half of the groups were told that this test which they were to take was an extremely valid test and hence a good measure of intelligence, an ability which these subjects considered important. The other half of the groups were told that it was a very poor test and the research was being done to demonstrate conclusively that the test was no good. For these subjects their performance was consequently not important. The results showed that the competition with the high scorer was significantly greater for the high importance than for the low importance condition.

Unfortunately there are no relevant data from experiments concerning opinions. The *Corollary to Derivation E* applies to opinions also, however, and is testable.

The data which we have presented refer to changing the position of members in the group. As the pressure toward uniformity increases there should also be observed an increase in the tendency to cease comparison with those who are too different from oneself. Specifically, this would mean that the range within which appreciable comparison with others is made should contract as the pressure toward uniformity increases. This leads to an interesting prediction concerning abilities which can be tested. The more important an ability is to a person and, hence, the stronger the pressures toward uniformity concerning this ability, the stronger will be the competition about it and also the greater the readiness with which the individuals involved will recognize and acknowledge that someone else is clearly superior to them. And just as in influence processes, where, once rejection has taken place there tends to be a cessation of communication and influence attempts toward those who have been made incomparable (10, 22), so we may expect that once inferior or superior status has been conferred, there will be a cessation of competition with respect to those who have been thus rendered incomparable.

Thus, for example, let us imagine two individuals who are identical with respect to some particular ability but differ markedly in how important this ability is to them personally. The prediction from the above theory would say that the person for whom the ability is more important would be more competitive about it than the other; would be more ready to allocate "inferior status" to those considerably less good than he; and would be more ready to allocate "superior status" to those considerably better than he. In other words, he would be more competitive within a narrower range.

*Corollary VII A:* The stronger the attraction to the group the stronger will be the pressure toward uniformity concerning abilities and opinions within that group.

The more attractive a group is to a member, the more important that group will be as a comparison group for him. Thus the pressure to reduce discrepancies which operate on him when differences of ability or opinion exist will be stronger. We would expect these stronger pressures toward uniformity to show themselves in all three ways, increased tendency to change own position, increased effort to change the position of others, and greater restriction of the range within which appreciable comparison is made.

There are a number of studies which corroborate *Corollary VII A* with regard to opinions. Back (3) showed that in groups to which the members were highly attracted there were more attempts to influence others than in groups to which the members were less attracted. This greater exertion of influence was accompanied by more change of opinion in the highly attractive groups. Festinger, Gerard, et al. (10) showed a tendency for members of highly attractive groups to change their opinions more frequently than members of less attractive groups upon discovering that most others in the group disagreed with them. This change of opinion was before any influence had actually been exerted on them by other members of the group. They also found that there was more communication attempting to influence others in the high than in the low attractive groups.

Schachter (22) showed that this same factor, attraction to the group, also increased the tendency to cease comparison with those who differed too much. Members of his highly attractive groups rejected the deviate significantly more than did members of the less attractive groups.

Festinger, Torrey, and Willerman (12) report an experiment specifically designed to test *Corollary VII A* with respect to abilities. If, given a range of performance reflecting some ability, the comparison, and hence the competition, in highly attractive groups would be stronger than in less attractive groups, then this should be reflected in the feelings of having done well or poorly after taking the tests. If *Corollary VII A* is correct we would expect those scoring slightly below others to feel more inadequate in the high than in the low attractive groups. Similarly we would expect those scoring equal to or better than most others to feel more adequate in the high than in the low attractive groups. Groups of four persons were given a series of tests supposed to measure an ability that these persons considered important. One of the subjects was caused to score consistently slightly below the others. The other three were made to score equally well. Those members who were highly attracted to the group, and scored below the others, felt they had done worse than similar persons who were not attracted to the group. Those who were attracted to the group and had scored equal to the others felt that they had done better than did similar persons who were not attracted to the group. Thus the results of the experiment corroborate the corollary for abilities.

*Corollary VII B:* The greater the relevance of the opinion or ability to the group, the stronger will be the pressure toward uniformity concerning that opinion or ability.

The conceptual definition of relevance of an opinion or an ability to a group is not completely clear. There are, however, some things one can state. Where the opinion or ability involved is necessary or important for the life of the *group* or for the attainment of the satisfactions that push the members into the group, the need for evaluation in that group will be strong. Groups will thus differ on what one may call their "realm of relevance." A group of men who meet every Friday night to play poker, and do only this together, will probably have a narrow "realm of relevance." The abilities and opinions for which this group serves as a comparison will be very restricted. The members of a college fraternity, on the other hand, where the group satisfies a wider variety of the members' needs will have a wider "realm of relevance."

In spite of the conceptual unclarity which is involved it is possible to create differences in relevance of an issue to a group which are clear and unambiguous. Thus Schachter (22) created high and low relevance conditions in the following manner. Groups which were to discuss an issue relevant to the group were recruited specifically for that purpose. Other groups were recruited ostensibly for very different kinds of things and on a pretext were asked to discuss the particular issue in question. They were promised this would never happen again in the life of the group thus making this issue of low relevance to that particular group. Schachter found, confirming *Corollary VII B,* that the tendency to reject deviates was stronger in the high relevance condition than in the low relevance condition.

No other evidence bearing on *Corollary VII B* has been located.

Thus far we have discussed only factors which, in affecting the pressure toward uniformity, affect all three manifestations of this pressure in the same direction. There are also factors which affect the manifestations of pressure toward uniformity differentially. We will discuss two such factors.

*Hypothesis VIII:* If persons who are very divergent from one's own opinion or ability are perceived as different from oneself on *attributes consistent with the divergence,* the tendency to narrow the range of comparability becomes stronger.

There is evidence supporting this hypothesis with respect to both abilities and opinions. In the previously mentioned experiment by Hoffman, Festinger, and Lawrence (19) half the groups were told that the three persons in the group had been selected to take the test together because, as far as could be determined, they were about equal in intelligence. The other groups were told that one of the three was very superior to the others. This was reported in a manner which made it impossible for either of the subjects to suppose that he himself was the superior one. In the "homogeneous" condition the subjects continued to compete against the paid participant who was scoring considerably above them. In the condition where they thought one of the others was clearly superior they competed considerably less with the paid participant and tended to compete with each other. In other words, when there was the perception of a difference consistent with the fact that the paid participant was scoring above them, they ceased comparison with him.

There is additional evidence on this point from level of aspiration experiments. Festinger (6) reports an experiment where, on an intellectual task, subjects (college students) were told they were scoring considerably above another group which they ordinarily considered inferior to themselves (high school students) or were told they were scoring considerably below a group which they considered superior to themselves (graduate students). In these circumstances there is practically no effect on the level of aspiration. Thus, the knowledge of this other group's being divergent in a direction consistent with the label of the group had no effect on their evaluation. It is interesting to note in this same experiment that if the reported direction of difference is inconsistent with the level of the group this destroys the incomparability and the effect on the level of aspiration is very great.

The evidence concerning opinions relating to *Hypothesis VIII* comes from experiments reported by Gerard (14) and Festinger and Thibaut (9). In both of these experiments discussions were carried on in a group of persons with a considerable range of opinion on the issue in question. In each experiment, half of the groups were given the impression that the group was homogeneous. All the members of the group had about equal interest in and knowledge about the issue. The other half of the groups were given the impression that they were heterogeneously composed. There was considerable variation among them in interest in and knowledge about the problem. In both experiments there was less communication directed toward those holding extremely divergent opinions in the heterogeneous than in the homogeneous condition. In other words, the perception of heterogeneity on matters related to the issue enabled the members of the groups to narrow their range within which they actively compared themselves with others.

It is interesting, at this point, to look at the data from these two experiments in relation to *Hypothesis III* which stated that the tendency to compare oneself with others decreased as the divergence in opinion or ability increased. In both the Gerard experiment (14) and the Festinger and Thibaut experiment (9) it was found that most communication was directed toward those whose opinions were most different from the others. Since we have just interpreted a reduction in communication to indicate a reduction in comparison with others, it is necessary to explain the overall tendency to communicate most with those holding divergent opinions in the light of *Hypothesis III*.

From *Hypothesis III* we would expect comparison to be made mainly with those closest to oneself. This is indeed true. The support one gets for one's opinion is derived from those close to one's own. However, it will be recalled that, in the case of opinions, comparison with others who are divergent represents a threat to one's own opinion. It is for this reason that communication is directed mainly toward those most divergent but still within the limits where comparison is made. This communication represents attempts to influence them. Reduction in communication to these extreme opinions indicates that the existence of these extreme opinions is less of a threat to one's own opinion. In other words, one is comparing oneself less with them. In the case of abilities we would not expect to find any such orientation toward very divergent persons. Comparison behavior in the case of abilities would follow very closely the simple relation stated in *Hypothesis III.*

*Hypothesis IX:* When there is a range of opinion or ability in a group, the relative strength of the three manifestations of pressures toward uniformity will be different for those who are close to the mode of the group than for those who are distant from the mode. Specifically, those close to the mode of the group will have stronger tendencies to change the positions of others, relatively weaker tendencies to narrow the range of comparison and much weaker tendencies to change their own position compared to those who are distant from the mode of the group.

Some data are available to support this hypothesis, with reference to opinions, from experiments by Festinger, Gerard, et al. (10) and by Hochbaum (18). In both of these experiments some persons in each group were given the impression that the rest of the group disagreed with them while others were given the impression that most of the group agreed with them. In both experiments there was considerably more change of opinion among the "deviates" than among the conformers. In both experiments there were considerably more attempts to influence others made by the conformers than by the deviates. While there exist no adequate data relevant to the tendency to narrow the range of comparison, corroboration is suggested in the experiment by Festinger, Gerard, et al. (10). In this experiment it was found that the deviates actually communicated less to those holding most divergent opinions than to those somewhat closer to their own position. The conformers showed the more familiar pattern of communicating most to those with extremely divergent opinions in the group.

The question may also be raised as to the determinants of the extent to which the group actually does move closer toward uniformity when pressures in this direction exist. In part, the degree of such movement toward uniformity will be dependent upon the strength of the pressures. In part they will be dependent upon other things. In the case of opinions it will be dependent upon the resistances to changing opinions, and upon the power of the group to successfully influence its members. The theory concerning the determinants of the power of the group to influence its members is set forth elsewhere (7). We will not repeat it here since the power of the group to influence its members is relatively unimportant with regard to abilities. The social process itself, no matter how much power the group has, cannot achieve movement toward uniformity on abilities. The power of the group successfully to influence its members will be effective only insofar as changing members' values concerning a given ability and increasing motivations can be effective. With respect to values and motivations concerning the ability the situation is identical with the social process that goes on concerning opinions.

## IMPLICATIONS FOR GROUP FORMATION AND SOCIETAL STRUCTURE

The drive for self evaluation concerning one's opinions and abilities has implications not only for the behavior of persons in groups but also for the processes of formation of groups and changing membership of groups. To the extent that self evaluation can only be accomplished by means of comparison with other persons, the drive for self evaluation is a force acting on persons to belong to groups, to associate with others. And the subjective feelings of correctness in one's opinions and the subjective evaluation of adequacy of one's performance on important abilities are some of the satisfactions that persons attain in the course of these associations with other people. How strong the drives and satisfactions stemming from these sources are compared to the other needs which people satisfy in groups is impossible to say, but it seems clear that the drive for self evaluation is an important factor contributing to making the human being "gregarious."

People, then, tend to move into groups which, in their judgment, hold opinions which agree with their own and whose abilities are near their own. And they tend to move out of groups in which they are unable to satisfy their drive for self evaluation. Such movement in and out of groups is, of course, not a completely fluid affair. The attractiveness to a group may be strong enough for other reasons so that a person cannot move out of it. Or there may be restraints, for one or another reason, against leaving. In both of these circumstances, mobility from one group to another is hindered. We will elaborate in the next section on the effects of so hindering movement into and out of groups.

These selective tendencies to join some and leave other associations, together with the influence process and competitive activity which arise when there is discrepancy in a group, will guarantee that we will find relative similarity in opinions and abilities among persons who associate with one another (at least on those opinions and abilities which are relevant to that association). Among different groups, we may well expect to find relative dissimilarity. It may very well be that the segmentation into groups is what allows a society to maintain a variety of opinions within it and to accommodate persons with a wide range of abilities. A society or town which was not large enough or flexible enough to permit such segmentation might not be able to accommodate the same variety.

The segmentation into groups which are relatively alike with respect to abilities also gives rise to status in a society. And it seems clear that when such status distinctions are firmly maintained, it is not only members of the higher status who maintain them. It is also important to the members of the lower status to maintain them for it is in this way that they can relatively ignore the differences and compare themselves with their own group. Comparisons with members of a different status group, either higher or lower, may sometimes be made on a phantasy level, but very rarely in reality.

It is also important to consider whether or not the incomparability consequent upon group segmentation is a relatively complete affair. The conferring of status in the case of abilities or the allegation of "different kind of people" in the case of opinions may markedly lower the comparability but may not completely eliminate it. The latter is probably the more accurate statement. People are certainly aware, to some extent, of the opinions of those in incomparable groups. To the extent that perfect incomparability is not achieved, this has important bearing on differences in behavior to be expected from members of minority groups. Members of minority groups, if they are unable to achieve complete incomparability with other groups, should be somewhat less secure in their self evaluations. One might expect from this that within a minority group, the pressures toward uniformity would be correspondingly stronger than in a majority group. The minority group would seek stronger support within itself and be less well able to tolerate differences of opinion or ability which were relevant to that group.

In connection with opinion formation, there is experimental evidence that this is the case (14). Subgroups which were in the minority within larger experimental groups showed evidence of stronger pressures toward uniformity within the subgroup than did the majority subgroups. In minority groups where particular abilities were relevant, we would, by the same line of reasoning, also expect stronger pressures toward uniformity and hence fiercer competition with respect to that ability than in majority groups.

We may recall that stronger pressure toward uniformity also implies the existence of stronger tendencies to regard as incomparable those who deviate markedly. Since others are made incomparable with respect to opinions by means of rejection from the group, this gives us a possible explanation of the persistent splitting into smaller and smaller factions which is frequently found to occur in minority groups which are under strong pressure from the majority segments of the population.

## CONSEQUENCES OF PREVENTING INCOMPARABILITY

There are predominantly two kinds of situations in which comparability is forced despite the usual tendencies not to compare oneself with those who deviate markedly. One such situation occurs when the attraction of the group is so strong, for other reasons, that the member continues to wish to remain in the group in spite of the fact that he differs markedly from the group on some opinion or ability. If, together with this state of affairs, he has no other comparison group for this opinion or ability, or if the opinion or ability is highly relevant to that group, then comparability is forced to a great extent. The psychological tendencies to make incomparable those who differ most will still be present but would not be as effective as they might otherwise be.

Under these circumstances where the attraction to the group remains high, the group has power to influence the member effectively and, in the case of opinion difference, we would expect an influence process to ensue which would be effective enough to eliminate the difference of opinion. In short, there would be movement toward uniformity. But what happens in the case of an ability? Here, while the group will probably succeed in motivating the member concerning this ability it is quite likely that the ability itself may not be changeable. We have then created a situation where a person's values and strivings are quite out of line with his performance and we would expect, if he is below others, deep experiences of failure and feelings of inadequacy with respect to this ability. This is certainly not an unusual condition to find.

The other major situation in which comparability is forced upon a person is one in which he is prevented from leaving the group. The theory concerning the effect of this situation on opinion formation is spelled out elsewhere (11). We will touch on the main points here in order to extend the theory to ability evaluation. In circumstances where a person is restrained from leaving a group either physically or psychologically, but otherwise his attraction to the group is zero or even negative, the group does not have the power to influence him effectively. Uniformity can, however, be forced, in a sense, if the group exerts threats or punishment for non-compliance. In the case of opinions, we may here expect to find overt compliance or overt conformity without any private acceptance on the part of the member. Thus a boy who is forced to play with some children whom he does not particularly like would, in such circumstances, where threat was employed, agree with the other children publicly while privately maintaining his disagreement.

Again, when we consider abilities, we find a difference which arises because abilities may be difficult if not impossible to change on short notice. Here the deviating member who is restrained from leaving the group may simply have to suffer punishment. If he deviates toward the higher end of the ability scale, he can again publicly conform without privately accepting the evaluations of the group. If he deviates toward the lower end of the ability scale this may be impossible. Provided he has other comparison groups for self evaluation on this ability he may remain personally and privately quite unaffected by this group situation. While publicly he may strive to perform better, privately his evaluations of his ability may remain unchanged.

## SUMMARY

If the foregoing theoretical development is correct, then social influence processes and some kinds of competitive behavior are both manifestations of the same socio-psychological process and can be viewed identically on a conceptual level. Both stem directly from the drive for self evaluation and the necessity for such evaluation being based on comparison with other persons. The differences between the processes with respect to opinions and abilities lie in the unidirectional push upward in the case of abilities, which is absent when considering opinions and in the relative ease of changing one's opinion as compared to changing one's performance.

The theory is tentatively supported by a variety of data and is readily amenable to further empirical testing. One great advantage, assuming the correctness of the theory, is that one can work back and forth between opinions and ability evaluations. Some aspects of the theory may be more easily tested in one context, some in the other. Discoveries in the context of opinions should also hold true, when appropriately operationally defined, in the context of ability evaluation.

## REFERENCES

1. Anderson, H. H., & Brandt, H. F. Study of motivation involving self-announced goals of fifth grade children and the concept of level of aspiration. *J. soc. Psychol.*, 1939, 19, 209–232.
2. Asch, S. E. Personality developments of Hopi children. Unpublished manuscript referred to in Murphy, Murphy, & Newcomb, *Experimental social psychology*. New York and London: Harper, 1931, 1937 (Rev. Ed.).
3. Back, K. The exertion of influence through social communication. *J. abnorm. soc. Psychol.*, 1951, 46, 9–24.
4. Chapman, D. W., & Volkmann, J. A., A social determinant of the level of aspiration. *J. abnorm. soc. Psychol.*, 1939, 34, 225–238.
5. Dreyer, A. Behavior in a level of aspiration situation as affected by group comparison. Ph.D. thesis, Univer. of Minnesota, 1953.
6. Festinger, L. Wish, expectation and group standards as factors influencing level of aspiration. *J. abnorm. soc. Psychol.*, 1942, 37, 184–200.
7. Festinger, L. Informal social communication. *Psychol. Rev.*, 1950, 57, 271–282.
8. Festinger, L., Schachter, S., & Back, K. *Social pressures in informal groups*. New York: Harper, 1950.
9. Festinger, L., & Thibaut, J. Interpersonal communications in small groups. *J. abnorm. soc. Psychol.*, 1951, 46, 92–100.
10. Festinger, L., Gerard, H., et al. The influence process in the presence of extreme deviates. *Hum. Relat.*, 1952, 5, 327–346.

11. Festinger, L. An analysis of compliant behavior. In M. Sherif (Ed.), *Group relations at the crossroads.* New York: Harper, 1953.
12. Festinger, L., Torrey, J., & Willerman, B. Self-evaluation as a function of attraction to group. *Hum. Relat.*, 1954, 7, 2.
13. Gardner, J. W. Level of aspiration in response to a prearranged sequence of scores. *J. exp. Psychol.*, 1939, 25, 601–621.
14. Gerard, H. The effect of different dimensions of disagreement on the communication process in small groups. *Hum. Relat.*, 1953, 6, 249–272.
15. Gould, R. An experimental analysis of "Level of aspiration." *Genet. Psychol. Monogr.*, 1939, 21, 1–116.
16. Greenberg, P. J. Competition in children: An experimental study. *Amer. J. Psychol.*, 1932, 44, 221–248.
17. Hilgard, E. R., Sait, E. M., & Magaret, G. A. Level of aspirations as affected by relative standing in an experimental social group. *J. exp. Psychol.*, 1940, 27, 411–421.
18. Hochbaum, G. M. Certain personality aspects and pressures to uniformity in social group. Ph.D. thesis, Univer. of Minnesota, 1953.
19. Hoffman, P. J., Festinger, L., & Lawrence, D. H. Tendencies toward comparability in competitive bargaining. *Hum. Relat.*, 1954, 7, 2.
20. Hoppe, F. Erfolg und Misserfolg. *Psychol. Forsch.*, 1930, 14, 1–62.
21. Lewin, K., Dembo, T., Festinger, L., & Sears, P. S. Level of aspiration. In *Personality and the behavior disorders.* Vol. 1. New York: Ronald Press, 1944. Pp. 333–378.
22. Schachter, S. Deviation, rejection and communication. *J. abnorm. soc. Psychol.*, 1951, 46, 190–208.
23. Sears, P. S. Levels of aspiration in academically successful and unsuccessful children. *J. abnorm. soc. Psychol.*, 1940, 35, 498–536.
24. Whittemore, I. C. The influence of competition on performance. *J. abnorm. soc. Psychol.*, 1925, 20, 17–33.

# *PART* II

## THE *Individual* IN *Social Situations*

# Introduction

EACH OF US *intuitively understands the perspective of the individual in a social situation, since it is the same perspective from which each of us views his own world. We may not understand how the situation got to be what it is at present, and we may not be able to anticipate accurately how the action we take now will ultimately affect the situation we will face sometime in the future. Similarly, we may not understand just why we feel as we do in the present, and may have a very poor perception of how others are thinking and feeling. But we all have a feeling that there is a part of the world that is "really real." That part is the fact of our present experience. We may doubt the reality of some of the objects we create through our experience, but that we do experience we "really know."*

*Similarly, most of us have a strong conviction that our experience is an important part or aspect of the process that controls our behavior. We know very well that we do some things unintentionally, that many things go on in our mind and body which we do not ordinarily experience, and that often we wish or will to do something without being able to do so. But nearly every moment of our waking lives convinces us that our experience of deciding to do something or not has a good deal to do with whether or not we later experience ourselves doing it. We feel that what goes on in our experience is a real and important mediating link between the events that we perceive in our situation and the behavior we address to it.*

*Consequently, we are all concerned with the accuracy of our perception—that it should report the world to us now as we shall later find it. Indeed, our concern goes beyond avoiding errors which nature may later point out to us. Most of us realize, though sometimes dimly, that, by acting on our assumptions, we make our world in part, as we go along—particularly that part of it which has to do with our ability to experience and act and the way others will experience and act. These parts of reality are sometimes called "subjective reality" and "social reality."* As W. I. Thomas *so succinctly put it: "If men define situations as real, they are real in their consequences."*

*The line is very dim, at times, between that which is real because the physical events of nature will later convince us; that which is real because we subjectively experience it as so, and act irrevocably upon it; and that which is real because others say it is real and act upon their assumptions. We are all dependent, usually more than we know or care to admit, upon consensus with our fellows in drawing the lines between these different sorts of reality. Even more disturbing—or perhaps hopeful—is the realization that our very ability to experience, to decide, and to control our own behavior through our decisions is dependent in many subtle and involuntary ways on our relationship and interaction with our fellows.*

*This is a problem that is infinitely complex. It is quite as alive in the social sciences as in philosophy and the humanities, though it is not always recognized or stated in quite this form. This is the problem of motivation and social control as seen from the subjective side, from the perspective of the individual in a social situation. The studies in this part are all in one way or another concerned with it. How does the presence or cooperation of others influence learning, problem-solving, evaluating and other "mental activities" which the individual can perform alone? The studies in Chapter 4 link up with some of the earliest research done in the small group field in this area of problems. How does the individual perceive or infer what others are thinking and feeling, and how is this related to his position in the group? This is the theme of the studies in Chapter 5. How much is the individual affected by others in the group, particularly in his overt behavior, and how much does he tend to maintain a consistency of his own and affect others? This is the problem of Chapter 6.*

*The social situation for a given individual may be another individual, or a relationship with a series of other individuals, or it may be, as he conceives it in his own mind, a relationship between himself and the group as a whole. Similarly, in making measurements of perception, liking, disliking, behaving, the individual may be measured against another individual, a series, or against the group average. One can even measure each individual in a group in turn, with each compared to the average of all the others, and still not get beyond the perspective of "the individual" in a generalized sense, compared to "all those others." The work in social perception begins to get beyond this, however. As one obtains data on the prediction of each individual as to how each other individual will rate or choose him, the situation immediately begins to assume complexity. The situation is what it is because each individual makes it so by his choices, which each of the others takes into account in making his predictions. At least two steps of a process of interaction between the individuals is represented, and one is led naturally to the perspective of the group as a system of interaction, the perspective of Part III.*

# CHAPTER 4
# TOGETHER AND APART

## *Group Learning of Nonsense Syllables*

HOWARD V. PERLMUTTER
and
GERMAINE DE MONTMOLLIN

THE EXPERIMENTAL study of the products of small face-to-face groups from a psychological point of view remains relatively unexplored. The focus of the psychologist has been primarily on the performance of the individual in the group, rather than on the psychological products of the group considered as a group.

The early experimentation by Dashiell (2), Travis (8), and others involved a comparison between the measured performances of the individual person when under influences from other persons physically present, with the measured performances in identical functions of the same individual when working alone. These researches on coacting groups did make some real contributions to an understanding of a few of the conditions under which judgment, memory, and learning may take place. They reflected,

FROM *Journal of Abnormal and Social Psychology*, 1952, 47, 762–769. Reprinted by permission of the authors and the American Psychological Association, Inc.

This research was conducted at the Laboratoire de Psychologie Experimentale de L'École des Hautes Études at the Sorbonne under the sponsorship of Professor P. Fraisse.

however, the outlook on group phenomena that Allport expressed in the statement, "There is no psychology of groups which is not essentially and entirely a psychology of individuals" (1).

There are good logical and methodological reasons for examining Allport's statement more critically. While it does represent one point of view still more or less prevalent in contemporary psychology, it is equally felt that Lewin has affirmed the tenability of another more fruitful position. He recommended a theoretical but emphasized an empirical justification of group experimentation. For the purpose of the present study, the following quotation from Lewin will suffice to make this point clear.

> If recognition of the existence of an entity depends upon this entity's showing properties or constancies of its own, the judgment about what is real should be affected by changes in the possibility of demonstrating social properties. . . . The taboo against believing in the existence of a social entity is probably most effectively broken by handling this entity experimentally. . . (4).

The experiments of Lewin, Lippitt, and White (5) and French (3) represented a great advance in the confidence in the reality of social phenomena. Their researches contribute primarily to the understanding of the effects of variation of such group variables as "atmosphere" and frustration on the behavior of the individuals in the group.

There has been relatively little research, however, on the properties of group-qua-group *basic* processes and especially the conditions and laws of change of group *products* such as group-perceived products, group-learned products, and group-memory products. One difficulty may have been the lack of a precise method for evoking a group product. The method of agreement described in the procedure below is an attempt to provide a technique for evoking measurable group product behaviors, such as group-perceived products, group-learned products, etc. The method insures interaction among the members of the group but only *one* product to represent the group.

The previous studies that bear on the study of group basic processes are few. Watson (9) compared group "thinking," that is, the ability to make words out of letters contained in a given word, and found the superiority of group products to the average and the best individual in the group. His groups were groups in which the members had a common goal but, because of the nature of the instructions and the task, interaction among the members was greatly limited.

Shaw (7) conducted a study comparing individuals and small groups in the rational solution of complex problems. She found also the superiority of groups in the ability to solve the problems given. Group activity seemed to insure that the errors made were usually at later stages in the solution of the problem, and that group superiority is in part due to the rejection of incorrect ideas.

These two studies do attempt to examine the properties of group processes and products. But among a number of shortcomings primarily due to the lack of conceptualization of group phenomena, there are noticeable gaps in the explanation of the conditions under which a group "thinks" better or worse than an individual, or one group "thinks" better or worse than another.

A research, using the method of agreement, was conducted by Perlmutter (6) on group-qua-group memory products. In this study the properties of group-qua-group memory products were considered, as well as some analyses of group versus individual memory and the conditions under which each may change.

The present study is a second, now aimed at investigating under experimental conditions the properties of group-qua-group learned products, by repeating learning experiments long associated with individual psychology.

This study aimed at establishing for the specific task and population a "learning" curve of group-learned products. The task of learning a list of nonsense syllables was given to individuals working separately and as a group. The group task required discussion, interstimulation, and a single product agreed upon by the group as representative of it. It called for an interchange of ideas, acceptance, rejection, and interaction that proved to be fairly rich, owing to the ambiguity of the nonsense syllables.

The study examined the learning rate of the group as compared with the individuals, the time required by groups and individuals, and the errors of the group versus the errors of the individual in an attempt to make precise under what conditions and along what dimensions groups differ from individuals on "learning."

## METHOD

### *Subjects*

The *Ss* in this experiment were students at the Sorbonne, in most cases first-year students of psychology. Although most participants were French, *Ss* included Italians, Egyptians, Moroccans, Belgians, and Swiss. All spoke French fluently. There were very rare communication difficulties due to language. The experiments were conducted during two hours. During one part, the group was given a list of 19 two-syllable "nonsense" words to learn as a group; the other part, after a 15-minute rest, required that the individuals work separately but in the presence of one another on an equivalent but different list. The order of procedure and lists were varied systematically. Twenty groups of three persons, homogeneous according to sex, were used (6 groups of males, 14 groups of females). No sex differences in performance were noticed.

## *Materials*

Two equivalent lists of 19 two-syllable nonsense words were used. Their equivalence is demonstrated statistically. There are no differences between groups or individuals using the different lists.

Nonsense syllables were used because the lack of logical associations with each word stimulated discussion. This also made possible the repetition of the experiments with American groups.

## *Working as a Group*

The following instructions were used to evoke a group product during the part of the experiment in which the individuals worked as a group (translation from the French):

The purpose of this experiment is to find how you are going to learn a list of 19 two-syllable nonsense words, working as a group. Your individual results are not of interest; the product of your collaboration, as close as possible, is of primary importance. It is necessary to make the maximum effort to retain all the words as quickly as possible; the order in which you recall them is of no importance.

This is how we are going to proceed: I will present the list to you the first time, each word written on a card, presented separately and regularly. When all the words have been presented, I will go to the blackboard and say "Go." If one of you remembers a word, he says it aloud. I will write it on the blackboard and the other members of the group as well as the ones who gave the original should discuss this and other possibilities, until a group accord is reached. The others should express their opinion as to the exact form of the word. Only one word will be adopted to represent the group. Unanimous agreement is not necessary. It is necessary that you all contribute; the order with which you intervene does not matter. When you have reached a decision as a group, tell the recorder whether you wish to keep the word or not, before passing on to the next word. If after 30 seconds no new word has been presented, the observer will say, "That's sufficient," and then I will present the list a second time followed by a second recall in the same way as with the first recall and so on.

The group was not told there were to be five recalls.

## *Working Individually*

The instructions for the second part of the experiment were given after a 15-minute rest in which the group was asked not to discuss the experiment:

The purpose of the second part of this experiment is to see if you can learn a list of 19 two-syllable nonsense words working alone; we are interested in your results as individuals, and not the product of any kind of collaboration. It is necessary then that during your work you do not display any feelings of success or failure, and if you have the feeling of having learned the list you continue to work like your neighbors. It is necessary that you make the maximum effort to remember the words as quickly as possible, the order with which you remember is not important—this is how we shall proceed. I will present a list a first time, each word written on a card at a regular rhythm. When all the words have been presented, I will say, "Go," and you are to write on the sheets of paper before you the first word in the list that comes to your mind. You are to note with as much care as possible the degree of certitude you have about each word: 9 for absolutely certain the word is correct; 5, some certainty, and 1 if you are quite uncertain but still believe you want to put the word down. It can also occur that you remember a word but you are not certain of it, and think of another that seems more likely. In this case, bar lightly the first word, and write below the one you believe to be better until you reach a certain degree of agreement with yourself. To mark the index of certitude, fold the paper so that the previous words are not visible, and proceed to the next word. After a time when nobody writes for 30 seconds, the experimenter will say, "That is sufficient," and will present the lists again, followed by a second recall, etc.

Again the number of trials (five) was not specified. It is to be noted that after the fifth trial of working as a group, there was an individual recall, and after the fifth trial of working individually, there was a group recall.

The instructions were rarely misunderstood; the most common question, for about 30 per cent of the groups, was: "Can we organize so that A learns 6, B 6, and C likewise?" E then said, "No, we are interested in your collaboration on each word. In the case you suggest, we would be measuring how well person A learned *his* six words, B his six, etc." In all cases the group agreed and the experiment was continued. This, however, does not preclude the possibility of implicit organization.

After the experiments, the groups were asked (*a*) how fatigued they had been, and (*b*) how they had enjoyed working in a group versus working individually.

## RESULTS AND DISCUSSION

In the statistical analysis, the 10 groups and 30 individuals who worked first as individuals working separately and then as a group (to be called I–G groups) were compared with the 10 groups wherein the group worked first and then the individuals in the group worked separately (called G–I groups).

### *Number of Nonsense Words Correctly Recalled Each Trial*

*a.* There is little or no difference between G–I and I–G groups with respect to the number of nonsense words correctly recalled by a group or an individual during each trial (total score). This was the basis for combining the I–G and G–I groups.

*b.* G–I individuals have an average total score significantly greater than I–G individuals. In other words, working in a group first significantly helps the individuals to learn an equivalent list later.

*c.* The total scores of I–G groups average higher than I–G individuals at the .01 level of significance. The I–G group scores are also higher than the best total scores for individuals of each group.

*d.* G–I individuals have a significantly greater total score in the second, third, fourth, and fifth trials. The difference for the first trial is not statistically significant. Furthermore, there is no statistical difference between the G–I groups and the best G–I individual of each group. In fact, in the first two trials, the best individual's average is higher than the group average (see Table 1).

Affective interrelations between the members were important determiners of the group product. Often correct words were rejected by

TABLE 1

*Number of Nonsense Words Correctly Recalled Each Trial*
(Total score)

| | I-G GROUP | | | | | G-I GROUP | | | | |
|---|---|---|---|---|---|---|---|---|---|---|
| TRIAL | AVERAGE OF GROUPS | AVERAGE INDIVIDUAL | $p$ * | AVERAGE OF BEST INDIVIDUAL | $p$ ** | AVERAGE OF GROUPS | AVERAGE INDIVIDUAL | $p$ * | AVERAGE OF BEST INDIVIDUAL | $p$ ** |
| 1 | 5.4 | 2.3 | .01 | 2.4 | .02 | 5.5 | 4.8 | | 5.7 | |
| 2 | 11.4 | 5.4 | .01 | 7.1 | .02 | 10.2 | 8.3 | .05 | 10.7 | |
| 3 | 14.5 | 7.7 | .01 | 10.3 | .01 | 14.8 | 11.3 | .01 | 14.8 | |
| 4 | 16.4 | 9.7 | .01 | 13.0 | .05 | 17.3 | 13.6 | .01 | 17.3 | |
| 5 | 17.2 | 11.4 | .01 | 14.0 | .02 | 18.2 | 14.3 | .01 | 17.1 | |

* Group vs. average individual.
** Group vs. average of best individual.

members of the group when the proposer of the word was in disfavor with the others. On the other hand, the "popular" leader was able to maneuver the group to accept distorted, incorrect words. On a number of occasions groups spent an extremely long time trying to reach a decision about the form of a word and, by doing this, forgot other words.

Practically every group had such situations, some groups more than others. Where the intragroup problems were prominent, the superiority of the group product to the average or best individual product is minimal.

## *Group-Learned Product Curve*

The curve of group-learned products is seen to resemble greatly the curve of individual learning (Fig. 1). This may be interpreted as a point in favor of establishing a more firm analogy between individual learning and group learning, as well as giving some weight to the use of the concept of "group learning curve." The increased acceleration of the curve of group-learned products as compared to the curve of individual learning is a characteristic of group learning. But it is well to emphasize the *conditional* superiority of the group to the individual. One glance at the curve of the best individuals of the G–I groups proves how individuals, with some previous training in a group, can perform as well as groups. This has not been reported previously, but it is evident that there are many instances in life where individuals working separately can produce *better* than a group of persons. In these experiments, in 60 per cent of the G–I groups there were

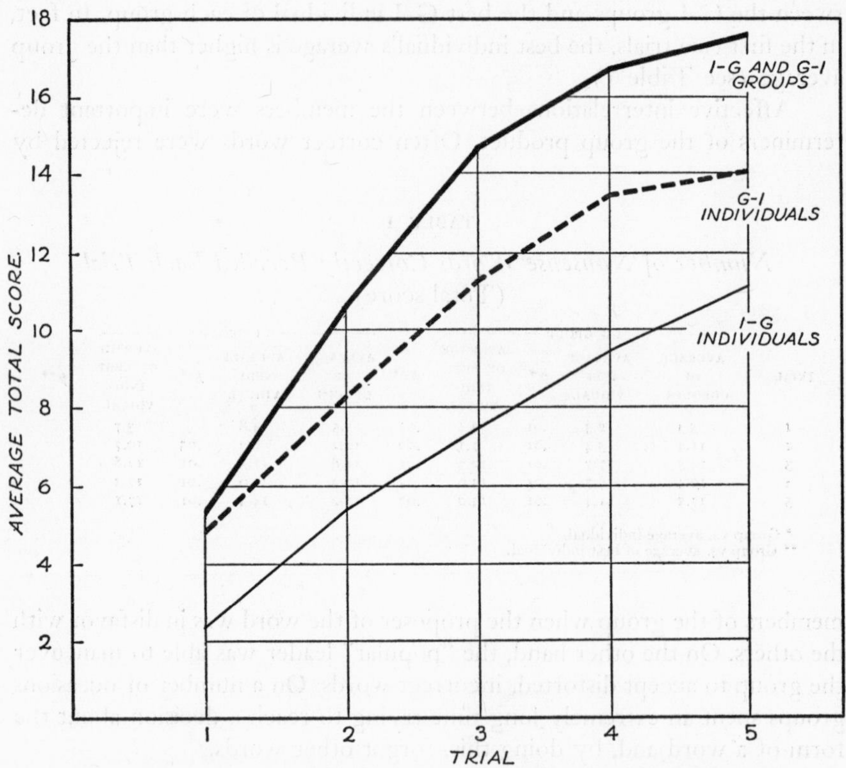


FIG. 1. Average curves of group-learned products and individual learning

individuals who surpassed the group at least three times when working separately. There were cases where all three individuals, when working separately, produced more than the group did during that particular trial. Among the I–G groups, there was one case in which an individual performed better than the group at least three times.

## *Time Required*

*a.* There is little difference between groups (G–I and I–G combined) and individuals with respect to the time required per trial (see Table 2).

*b.* The average time of all the groups is significantly greater in the first three trials, but not in the last two (see Table 2).

TABLE 2

*Time for a Trial*

| TRIAL | AVERAGE FOR I-G AND G-I GROUPS COMBINED | AVERAGE INDIVIDUAL * | *p* |
|---|---|---|---|
| 1 | 6.1 | 3.1 | .01 |
| 2 | 5.0 | 3.7 | .01 |
| 3 | 5.5 | 4.0 | .01 |
| 4 | 4.3 | 4.2 | |
| 5 | 4.1 | 4.1 | |

* Average time for slowest individual.

## *Rate of Recall*

*a.* There is no statistical difference between G–I and I–G groups with respect to the rate of recall. Rate of recall is defined as the total score on a particular trial divided by the time required for that trial.

*b.* G–I individuals have a significantly greater rate of recall than the I-G individuals.

*c.* I–G groups have a greater recall rate than the I–G individuals (on the average) for all trials.

*d.* G–I individuals have a greater recall rate than G–I groups at the first trial. The differences for the second and third trials are not statistically significant. By the fourth and fifth trials, the direction of superiority changes, and the G–I groups surpass the G–I individuals (Table 3).

TABLE 3

*Rate of Recall* *

| TRIAL | I-G GROUP | | | G-I GROUP | | |
|---|---|---|---|---|---|---|
| | AVERAGE OF GROUPS | AVERAGE INDIVIDUAL | *p* | AVERAGE OF GROUPS | AVERAGE INDIVIDUAL | *p* |
| 1 | 1.21 | .78 | .05 | .86 | 1.33 | .02 |
| 2 | 2.97 | 1.57 | .01 | 2.48 | 2.18 | |
| 3 | 2.92 | 2.10 | .01 | 3.42 | 2.80 | |
| 4 | 4.48 | 2.57 | .01 | 8.35 | 3.19 | .02 |
| 5 | 3.87 | 2.91 | .02 | 5.38 | 3.25 | .02 |

* The number of nonsense words correctly recalled for each trial divided by the time required for that trial.

These results indicate that, although groups require more time than individuals during the early trials, during the later trials they not only require equivalent time per trial but recall more correct words than do individuals. This rate of recall is one indication of the superiority of the group procedure. The change in recall rate from the first to the fifth trial is interpreted as an increase in the efficiency of functioning as a group.

The group, from the point of view of total score, resembles the individual more during the early trials. With respect to total time required for recall during the trial, the group seems to resemble the individual more in the later stages.[2]

But the superiority of the rate of recall of the group is further supported by the calculations and qualitative observations on the frequency with which the group adopts deformations of correct words. The group sifts out these incorrect responses, primarily because there is a series of rejections and evaluations of each word before the decision to adopt the word is taken. This corresponds to Shaw's findings in her work on group problem-solving (7). The "critical" forces within a group are greater on the average than the "critical" forces within the individual. The individual is usually less reluctant to put down a deformation of a correct word.

## *Invented Words*

*a.* The slight difference between G–I and I–G groups with respect to the number of invented words is also statistically not significant.

*b.* G–I individuals invent significantly fewer words than I–G individuals (working separately).

TABLE 4

*Inventions*

| TRIAL | I–G GROUP | | | G–I GROUP | | |
|---|---|---|---|---|---|---|
| | AVERAGE OF GROUPS | AVERAGE INDIVIDUAL | $p$ | AVERAGE OF GROUPS | AVERAGE INDIVIDUAL | $p$ |
| 1 | 1.3 | 3.0 | .01 | 2.0 | 1.89 | |
| 2 | 1.0 | 2.98 | .01 | .9 | 2.36 | .01 |
| 3 | 1.8 | 3.5 | .01 | .7 | 2.3 | .01 |
| 4 | 1.2 | 3.29 | .01 | .1 | 1.7 | .01 |
| 5 | 1.0 | 2.89 | .01 | .1 | 1.5 | .01 |

c. I–G individuals invent significantly more words than I–G groups in all five trials. During the first trial there is no statistical difference between G–I groups and G–I individuals working separately, but in the last four trials the G–I individuals invent significantly more words (Table 4).

This means that under some conditions a group invented many more words than a particular individual in the group. The process of inventing a word has to be seen in terms of its dynamic meaning *to the group*. One

2 It is important to note that while the time for individuals has been based on the slowest individual in the group, because of the difficulty in determining when a particular person finished, the difference in time required for the fastest and slowest individual is very small—probably never more than 30 sec. The slow individuals tended to stop working when the others did. This "facilitative" effect has been noted in other studies wherein individuals work individually but in the presence of others. The significance of the results must, however, be restricted to the extent that this variation makes a difference in the calculation of the individual rate of recall.

group, for example, adopted a word *Zevut* in the third trial as being a word in the list presented. After the third trial, a presentation was made in which the correct word, *Zuvat*, was presented. Nevertheless, in the fourth trial and the fifth trial, *Zevut* was unanimously adopted by the group. It is interesting to note that it was not always suggested by the same member of the group. This "hallucination" should be viewed in its context as an attempt to establish a common product, irrespective of the objective reality. It appears to have reflected, in part, a need in the group to have *agreement-on-something*. It appeared in a group that had experienced a number of failures in functioning as a group. The reality-orientation of the group was relaxed in order that this agreement-on-something could be reached. This interpretation is posed as a hypothesis relative to the problem of understanding psychologically the conditions under which a group makes errors, or is "objective."

## *Repetitions*

*a.* The differences between I–G and G–I groups and individuals with respect to the number of words repeated during a single trial are not statistically significant.

*b.* During the first two trials there is no difference between the average number of repetitions of the groups and those by the individuals working separately. But during the last three trials, the group repeats significantly more (see Table 5).

TABLE 5

*Repetitions*

| | I-G GROUP | | | G-I GROUP | | |
|---|---|---|---|---|---|---|
| TRIAL | AVERAGE OF GROUPS | AVERAGE INDIVIDUAL | *p* | AVERAGE OF GROUPS | AVERAGE INDIVIDUAL | *p* |
| 1 | 0.0 | .03 | | .2 | .03 | .01 |
| 2 | .2 | .19 | | .5 | .1 | .01 |
| 3 | .9 | .13 | | 1.6 | .2 | .01 |
| 4 | .5 | .46 | | 1.5 | .3 | .01 |
| 5 | .9 | .39 | | 1.3 | .3 | .01 |

The phenomenon of "repetition" seen from the point of view of the group and the individual-working-separately is a "forgetting" of a previously adopted decision. The task in this experiment required that a list be learned, and also that in each trial the groups (and individuals) know what they have said during that trial, since they do not see the words they have adopted during a given trial. (See *procedure* section above.) It is likely that in many cases the group "automatically" adopted a word suggested by member A, and that later on member B suggested the same word. B's previous agreement with the word when suggested by A for the first time may have been an agreement-for-agreement's sake, designed to speed up the recall process. In a competitively oriented group, however, where the "personal" needs of the members are more important than "group" needs, there is a need to contribute a word, and from the point of view of the contributor, the word presented may be a "new" word since he did not "hear," psychologically, its presentation earlier. The number of repetitions made, it is believed, can often be seen as an index of the lack of psychological communication between the parts, a clue as to the degree of functional dependence between the members of the group.

But it is of utmost importance to note that these were repetitions adopted by the group and hence reflect properties of the group-qua-group, as well as the specific interpersonal relations between members of the group, or the personal motivations of a particular individual in the group. Future experimentation in which control of organization and dynamics of a group is made should attempt to determine conditions under which a group invents or repeats more or less.

## *Evidences of "Implicit" Organization*

A number of groups performed inefficiently because the activity of learning the nonsense words was not organized. In all cases, the groups had no predetermined organization to the extent that there were no defined roles or systems of learning as a group. The most efficient groups, however, showed some kind of organization. The term "organization" is rather crudely used here. It refers to the extent to which there was efficient use of the roles necessary to come up with a group agreement. Members have to suggest, clarify, stimulate, and limit discussion, and call for a "group decision." Inefficiencies in this procedural aspect of the recall limited to some extent the total score of the group.

Sometimes during the recall one member of the group presented the same word on each trial. This "assignment" of words to particular parts of the group was probably unconscious. Most groups professed not to have organized among themselves, and no fixed assignment of several words in the list was noted. Each member of the group did try with various degrees of effort to learn each word, but from the point of view of the individual member, he could relax his attention when a word usually given by another was presented. Most groups reported, for example, that the group task was less fatiguing, even when it came in the second part of the experiment.

## *Individual Recall After Group Recall*

For all groups, an individual recall was taken after the fifth group-qua-group recall. These data shed some further light on the degree of implicit organization and the extent to which one member of the group carried the burden of the group recall.

Generally, there was a great degree of overlap in the words remembered among the members of the group. While one or two words were given special attention by particular individuals, there was general collaboration on the other words. The average difference between the best and the worst individual recalls was 5.1 words.

In only two groups did an individual, during the individual recall after the fifth trial of the group-qua-group recall, reach the group score. No individual surpassed the group score under these conditions.

In addition, the theoretical potentiality of the group was determined by a summation of the number of different words learned by the three different individuals during the individual-working-alone part of the experiments. These results are not clear. There were several groups that could have produced all 19 words if they had pooled their individual resources. There were several others who actually learned 19 words while working as a group, but could not have produced 19 words or their actual group score, even if they had added the different words each learned while working as an individual. Their actual performance exceeded their potentiality.

## *The "Method of Agreement"*

The fruitfulness of the "method of agreement" in experiments on learning is at least indirectly measured by the results of this experiment. Furthermore, the instructions seem to have a clear psychological significance to the groups as well as to the individuals working separately. The groups understood what was meant by working as a group and discussing among themselves until one product, representative of the group as a group, was reached. The participation of each *member*, whether overt or covert, was noted. But there were differences in the amount of agreement that was satisfactory for the group. This was also noted in the individual self-ratings when the individuals worked separately. There were group as well as individual differences in the degree of certitude about words included in each recall. It is possible that the method of agreement sets up analogous "internal situations" for the group considered as a group and the individual considered as an individual.

## *Group Fatigue*

It was noted in the cases of groups who worked as individuals first and as a group second (I–G groups) that there were few instances of fatigue (except in those groups where interpersonal relations were rather strained). The groups reported that they were clearly more fatigued in the first part of the experiment than in the second, even though during the second part of the experiment they were asked to learn another list of two-syllable nonsense words. Future research could point up why a group fatigues less quickly and why, in a few cases, satiation in the group, once begun, was extremely rapid in "snowballing" to such a point that group interest in the task became almost nonexistent.

## *"Group Intelligence"*

The group-learned product curve is often identical to the learned product curve of a poorer member of another group. Clearly there are "low intelligence" groups and "high intelligence" individuals. One adult can solve a problem that thirty children could not even comprehend. Within the adult groups as well, it would be difficult to derive the group "intelligence" from the summation of individual intelligence scores. This is a shortcoming of this research, and of any other that does not control group-qua-group intelligence. It is suggested that a group intelligence test could be constructed using the method of agreement. Until this is done, we are not certain that a group performs well because it is inefficient but very intelligent as a group, or because it is quite unintelligent but very efficient in employing its potentialities.

## SUMMARY

Twenty three-person groups of French-speaking students at the Sorbonne were given the task of learning two equivalent lists of two-syllable nonsense words, working separately but in the presence of the others, and working together as a group with a common goal.

Variation in the order of administration, i.e., whether the individuals first worked separately or first worked in a group, produced differential results: the individuals who worked in the group first had significantly higher total scores and a better rate of recall than did the individuals who worked separately first. These individuals also invented fewer words. There are no statistical differences between individuals who worked first and those who worked second with respect to time required per trial, or between groups who worked first or second with respect to all dimensions (total score, time, rate of recall, inventions, and repetitions). It was concluded that group life can contribute to individual learning of the same kind of task later.

The curve of group-learned products was determined. It is a smooth curve that resembles the curve of individual learning, but is more positively accelerated. In particular cases, a group-learned product curve coincided with an individual learning curve.

Groups were found to be superior to individuals working separately but in the presence of others under special conditions. The group is superior to the average individual in total score but is not significantly different from the average of the best individuals in the groups, if the best individuals have previously worked in a group on a similar task. In seven groups out of 20 instances, there were individuals who surpassed or equalled the performance of the group.

Groups require more time to recall during early trials but have a higher over-all recall rate than individuals.

Under some conditions, a group makes more errors by repeating more words during a particular trial than individuals do, but individuals on the average invent or deform more words than groups.

The conditional superiority of a group is stressed along all dimensions. It is difficult to predict whether groups in particular cases will be superior to particular individuals, will make less errors, or require more or less time. Some of the conditions under which a group may be less efficient were discussed, and analogies were drawn between individual internal processes and group external processes.

## REFERENCES

1. Allport, F. H. *Social psychology*. New York: Houghton Mifflin, 1924.
2. Dashiell, J. F. An experimental analysis of some group effects. *J. abnorm. soc. Psychol.*, 1930, 25, 190–199.
3. French, J. R. P., Jr. Organized and unorganized groups under fear and frustration. Studies in topological and vector psychology, III. *Univer. Ia. Stud. Child Welf.*, 1944, 20, 229–307.
4. Lewin, K. Frontiers in group dynamics. *Hum. Relat.*, 1947, 1, 5–40.
5. Lewin, K., Lippitt, R., & White, R. Patterns of aggressive behavior in experimentally created "social climates." *J. soc. Psychol.*, 1939, 10, 271–299.
6. Perlmutter, H. V. A study of group and individual member products. Unpublished doctor's dissertation, Univer. of Kansas, 1952.
7. Shaw, Marjorie E. A comparison of individuals and small groups in the rational solution of complex problems. In T. M. Newcomb and E. L. Hartley (Eds.), *Readings in social psychology*. New York: Henry Holt, 1947. Pp. 304–315.
8. Travis, L. E. The effect of a small audience upon eye-hand coordination. *J. abnorm. soc. Psychol.*, 1925, 20, 142–146.
9. Watson, G. B. Do groups think more efficiently than individuals? *J. abnorm. soc. Psychol.*, 1928, 23, 328–336.

# *Twenty Questions: Efficiency in Problem Solving as a Function of Size of Group*

DONALD W. TAYLOR and WILLIAM L. FAUST

TWENTY QUESTIONS, popular as a parlor game in earlier years and now popular as a program on both radio and television, involves a type of problem solving that is of considerable interest psychologically.[1] To start the game, the participants are told only whether the object they are to attempt to identify is animal, vegetable, or mineral. In searching for the object which is the solution to the problem, they ask a series of questions, each of which can be answered "Yes" or "No." To find the solution most economically, they must use a high order of conceptualization, gradually increasing the specificity of the concepts employed until they arrive at the particular object.

The game is of psychological interest first of all because it appears to involve a type of problem solving more similar to much problem solving in everyday life than that ordinarily studied in psychological experiments. The solution is obtained not by a series of rigorous well-defined steps. Rather one starts with a general, somewhat vague problem. Questions are asked and information obtained. Upon the basis of this information, new questions are formulated. This procedure continues until the problem is

FROM *Journal of Experimental Psychology*, 1952, 44, 360–368. Reprinted by permission of the authors and the American Psychological Association, Inc.

This experiment was carried out under Project NR 192–018 supported by Contract N6 onr-25125 between the Office of Naval Research and Stanford University. The first author designed the experiment, supervised the analysis of the data, and prepared the present report. The second author conducted the experiment and carried out the analysis of the data. Work on the contract is under the direction of the first author.

1 The idea of using "Twenty Questions" in experimental studies of problem solving is not new. As was discovered after the present study was partly completed, Lindley (3) suggested the use of the game for this purpose in an article published in 1897.

solved. This type of problem solving is also of interest because it seems more similar to much of the problem solving in scientific research than does that involved in problems susceptible of rigorous, deductive mathematical or logical solution.

The use of the game in psychological experiments is recommended by several other considerations: It is quite interesting to college undergraduates; motivation is easily sustained for a period of several days. A very large number of problems of this kind are available. The same problems can be used with children and with adults. The same problems are appropriate for use with individuals and with groups of varying size.

The present experiment, the first in a series planned using the game, was designed to answer three questions: (*a*) How rapidly is the skill involved in the game learned? (*b*) How does efficiency in solving this type of problem vary as a function of the size of the group participating? (*c*) Does improvement in individual performance occur more rapidly with individual practice or with practice as a member of a group?

The second of these three questions is perhaps the most interesting. For many kinds of work, it seems quite reasonable that if a particular job must be completed in a shorter time, the number of people in the group working on it should be increased. It is not clear that increasing the size of a group engaged in solving a problem will necessarily reduce the time required for its solution. Indeed, it appears likely that in some cases it will actually increase the time required. Shaw (4) has presented data which indicate that the performance of groups of four is superior to that of individuals. However, further experimentation with larger samples, varying size groups, and different types of problems is needed to determine adequately the relation between group size and efficiency in problem solving.

## PROCEDURE

A total of 105 students from the elementary course in psychology served as *S*s. The *S*s were assigned by chance to work in solving the problems either alone, in pairs, or as a member of a group of four. There were 15 individual *S*s, 15 groups of two, and 15 groups of four. Each individual or group was given four problems a day for four successive days. On the fifth day, all *S*s worked alone, each being given four problems.

From a longer list of objects originally constructed, 60 were selected for use as problem topics. Included were 20 animal, 20 vegetable, and 20 mineral objects. Excluded were objects which did not clearly fit in only one of the three categories; e.g., hammer was not included because, with a handle of wood and a head of metal, it would be classed as both vegetable and mineral. Also excluded were objects which could not be expected to be familiar to almost every college student. Examples of objects included are: newspaper, Bop Hope, scissors, camel, dime, rubber band.

With four problems a day for five days, a total of only 20 problems was needed for presentation to any particular *S* or group. However, to minimize the possibility that an *S* would have any knowledge of what problem object to expect, it was decided to use a total of 60 different objects. This precaution seemed desirable although the instructions to be given all *S*s specifically requested that they not discuss the problems with other students. It should be added that no evidence was obtained during the course of the experiment to indicate that any *S* had previously heard mentioned a problem object he was to be given.

Since the nature of the learning curve was of interest, it was necessary to control the order of presentation of the problems in such a way that those given on any one day would be equal in difficulty to those given on any other day. In the absence of any measure of the difficulty of the individual problems, the following procedure was employed: The 20 animal objects were listed in chance order, as were the 20 vegetable and the 20 mineral objects. To obtain a group of four for use the first day, the first item was taken from each of the three lists together with the next item from one of the three chosen by chance. Similarly, to obtain four objects for use the second day, the next item was taken from each of the three lists; the fourth item was then obtained by taking the next in order on one of the two lists from which the extra item had not been taken the first day. This procedure was repeated to provide four problems for the third, fourth, and fifth days. A second and a third set of four problems for each of five days were obtained by continuing the same procedure. Next the three lists of 20 were individually reshuffled and the entire procedure repeated to obtain a fourth, fifth, and sixth set.

In the experiment, the first, seventh, and thirteenth individual, pair, or group of four *S*s received the first set of problems. The second, eighth, and fourteenth received the second set, and so on. As a result of this procedure, the order and the frequency of appearance of the problems were the same for individual *S*s as for groups of two or of four.

All *S*s were told that both the number of questions and the time required to reach solution would be recorded, but it was emphasized that number of questions was the more important score. In presenting each problem, *E* stated simply whether the object sought was animal, vegetable, or mineral. Time was measured by means of a stopwatch. A special data sheet was used for groups of two and of four to record which *S* asked each question. To each question, *E* replied "Yes," "No," "Partly," "Sometimes," or "Not in the usual sense of the word." If the question could not be answered in one of these ways or was unclear, *S* was asked to restate it.

The instructions given to groups of two or of four made clear that they might talk freely to each other, reviewing answers to previous questions or suggesting possible questions to ask. It was emphasized that they were not to compete against each other, but were to cooperate as a group to get the answer; they were told that the efficiency of their group would be compared with that of other groups.

As the name of the game indicates, *S*s are traditionally allowed 20 questions in which to obtain the solution. Pretesting showed, however, that with naive *S*s this limit results in a rather large proportion of failures. Accordingly, to simplify the analysis of the data to be obtained, the number of questions permitted

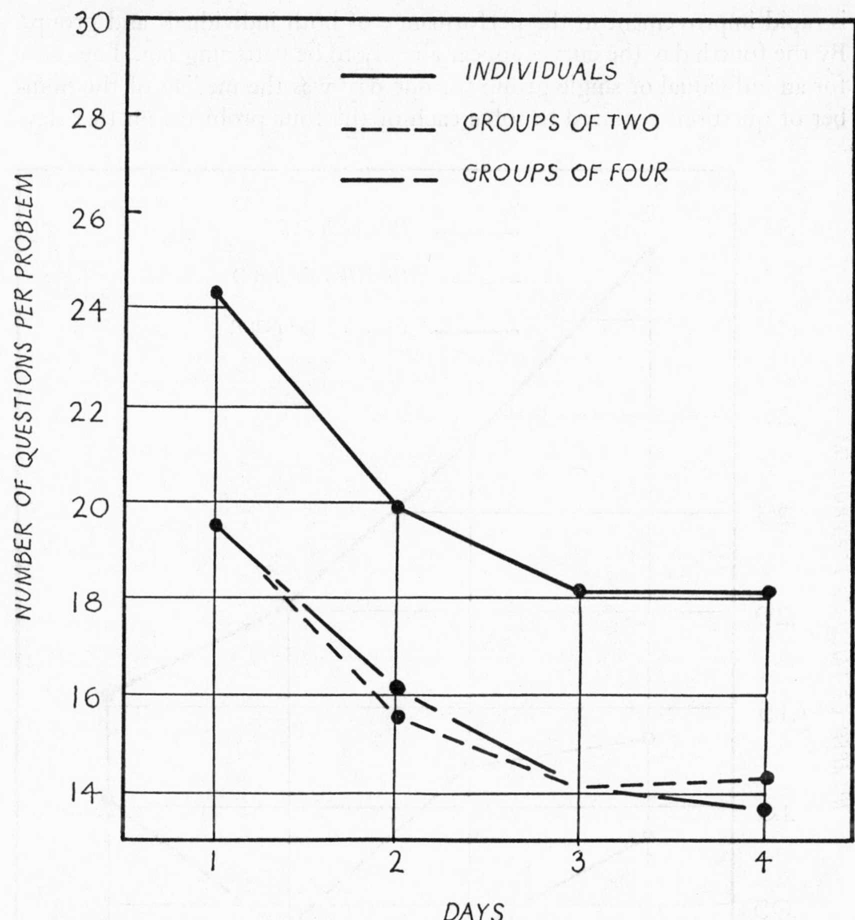


FIG. 1. Number of questions per problem as a function of days of practice and of size of group

was increased to 30. Examination of the distributions of scores obtained suggests that, at least after the first day, the performance of individuals or groups of *S*s who do not reach solution in 30 questions is qualitatively different from that of those who do. The *E*'s impression is that in most cases of failure there was established an incorrect set which was unchanging even in the face of answers irreconcilable with it; it seemed that in such cases the *S*s might easily have asked 50 or 60 questions without solving the problem.

## RESULTS

### *Rate of Learning*

The first question the experiment was designed to answer concerned the speed of learning of the skill involved. The data in Fig. 1 show that there is rapid improvement in the performance of both individuals and groups. By the fourth day the curves appear already to be flattening out. The score for an individual or single group for one day was the median of the number of questions required to solve each of the four problems on that day.

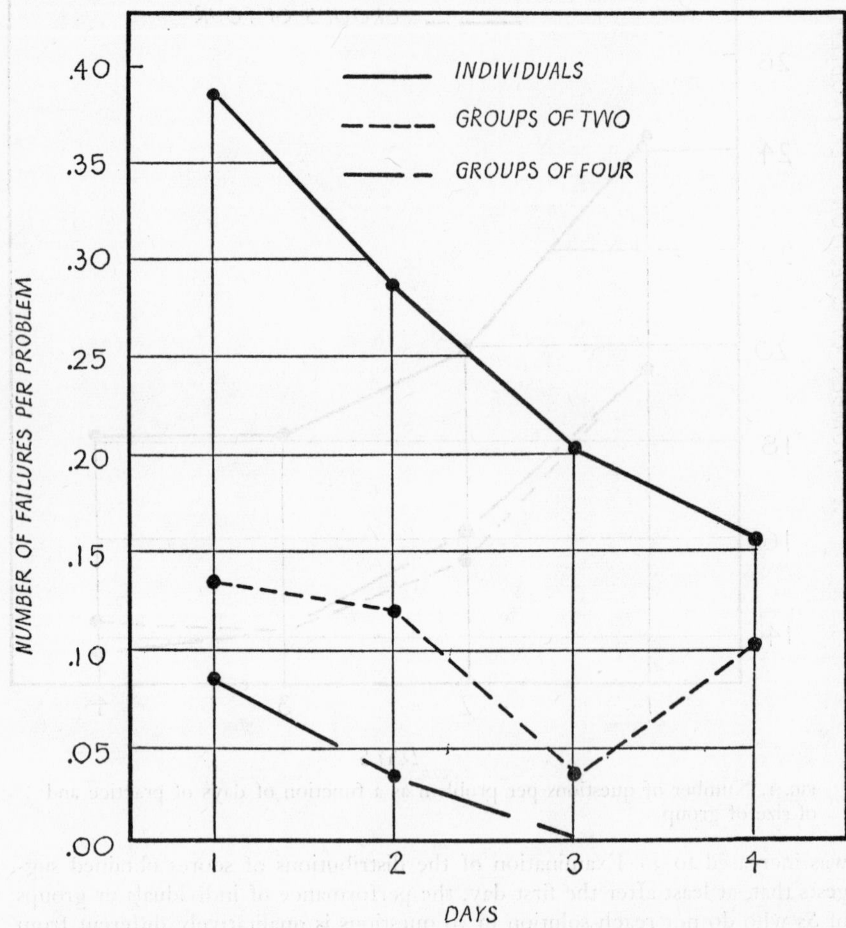


FIG. 2. Number of failures per problem as a function of days of practice and of size of group

The median was used instead of the mean because there were some failures. Each point plotted in Fig. 1 is the mean of these median scores on one day for 15 individuals, or for 15 groups of two or of four. In those few cases where an individual or group failed two or more problems on a single day, the median was obtained by treating the failures as though solution had been reached in 31 questions; the number of such cases was too small to affect the results appreciably; after the first day there were no such cases except among individual *S*s and even there they were rare.

The mean number of failures per problem on each day by individuals or groups is shown in Fig. 2. Thus, for example, on the first day the mean number of failures per problem among the 15 groups of four was .08; in other words, about one-twelfth of the problems were failed. The improvement in performance over four days in terms of number of failures per problem is consistent with that shown in Fig. 1 in terms of number of questions per problem solved.

Figure 3 shows the decrease over four days in the amount of time required per problem. The time required, of course, is somewhat dependent on the number of questions asked, although not entirely so. The score for an individual or single group for one day was the median time required for solution of the four problems. In those few cases where there were two or more failures in one day, the median of the four times was taken simply as obtained; this procedure underestimates somewhat the median time that would have been required to solve all four problems, but as before the number of such cases was too small to affect the general results appreciably.

## *Size of Group*

The second and major question with which the experiment was concerned involved the relation between efficiency in problem solving and size of group. As is evident in Fig. 1, there was no significant difference

TABLE 1

*Values of t for Differences between Mean Scores: Number of Questions Per Problem*

| DAY | INDIVIDUALS VERSUS GROUPS OF TWO | INDIVIDUALS VERSUS GROUPS OF FOUR |
|---|---|---|
| 1 | 2.67 | 2.18 |
| 2 | 2.86 | 1.96 |
| 3 | 2.30 | 2.22 |
| 4 | 2.11 | 2.45 |
| All 4 | 2.64 | 2.62 |

between groups of two and groups of four in terms of the number of questions required to reach solution. The performance of individuals working alone, however, was consistently inferior to that of either size group. The $t$ technique was used to test the difference on each day between the mean score of the 15 individuals and the mean score of the 15 pairs of *S*s, and also that of the 15 groups of four. The values of $t$ obtained are presented in Table 1. With 28 *df*, a $t$ of 2.05 is required for significance at the .05 level and of 2.76 at the .01 level. All of the differences but one are significant at or beyond the .05 level.

A score for all four days was obtained for each individual or single group by taking the median number of questions required to solve the 16 problems. In terms of the means of these scores, the performance both of groups of two and of four is significantly better (.02 level) than that of individuals working alone (see Table 1).

That there were differences as a function of group size in terms of number of failures to reach solution is suggested by Fig. 2. Because of the fact that, as would be expected, the distributions of failure scores were not normal, *t* could not be used to test the significance of these differences. Instead a test described by Festinger (2) was employed. The mean number of failures per problem, all four days included, was for individuals, .26; for pairs, .10; for groups of four, .03. The values of *d* obtained indicate that the difference between individuals and groups of four is significant at well beyond the .01 level; the difference between individuals and pairs and the difference between pairs and groups of four are both significant at about the .02 level.

TABLE 2

*Values of t for Differences between Mean Scores: Time Per Problem*

| DAY | INDIVIDUALS VERSUS GROUPS OF TWO | INDIVIDUALS VERSUS GROUPS OF FOUR | GROUPS OF TWO VERSUS GROUPS OF FOUR |
|---|---|---|---|
| 1 | .85 | 1.14 | .12 |
| 2 | 1.01 | 2.36 | .93 |
| 3 | 2.20 | 2.22 | .06 |
| 4 | 2.15 | 3.49 | 1.90 |
| All 4 | 2.39 | 3.27 | 1.18 |

Differences in mean time to solution among individuals, groups of two, and groups of four may be seen in Fig. 3. Fortunately, the distributions of the median times, of which the individual points plotted in Fig. 3 are the means, were such as to make the use of *t* appropriate in testing the significance of differences between means. Table 2 presents the values of *t* obtained for the various comparisons. As in the case of number of questions required, none of the differences between groups of two and of four is significant. Differences between individuals and groups of two on the third and fourth days are significant at the .05 level; differences between individuals and groups of four on all except the first day are significant at the same level or beyond.

A score for all four days was obtained for each individual or single group by taking the median time required for the 16 problems. The means of these scores were 5.06 for individuals, 3.70 for groups of two, and 3.15 for groups of four. The values of *t* given in Table 2 show that the difference between the first and second mean is significant at the .05 level, and between the first and third mean at the .01 level.

Group performance was superior to individual performance in terms of elapsed time to solution. However, if, instead, an analysis is made in

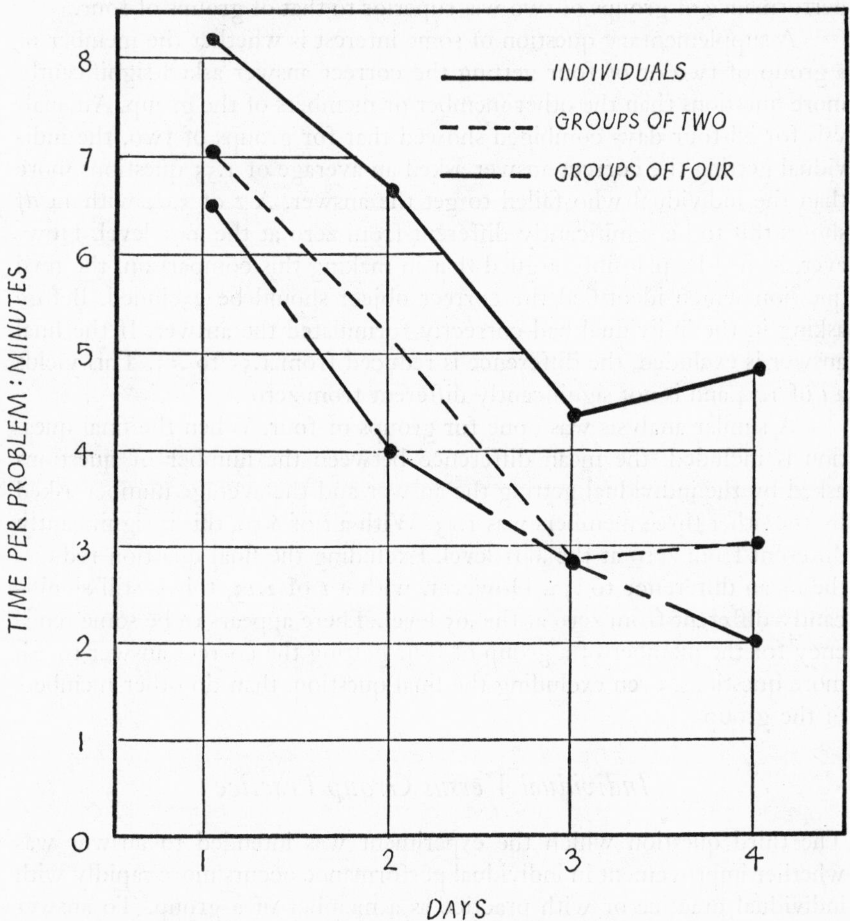


FIG. 3. Time per problem as a function of days of practice and of size of group

terms of number of man-minutes required for solution, the nature of the results obtained changes sharply. The number of man-minutes for a problem will, of course, be equal to the elapsed time multiplied by the number of persons in the group. In terms of man-minutes, the mean of the scores for all four days was 5.06 for individuals, 7.40 for groups of two, and 12.60 for groups of four. Since the variances for these three means were clearly not homogeneous, the use of $t$ was not appropriate for testing the significance of the obtained differences. Instead, $t'$ was employed (1). Both the difference between individuals and groups of two and the difference between groups of two and groups of four are significant at the .02 level. The difference between individuals and groups of four is significant at the .001 level. Clearly, in terms of man-minutes, the performance of individuals was superior to that of groups of two or of four; in addition, the performance of groups of two was superior to that of groups of four.

A supplementary question of some interest is whether the member of a group of two or of four getting the correct answer asked significantly more questions than the other member or members of the group. An analysis for all four days combined showed that for groups of two, the individual getting the correct answer asked an average of 1.55 questions more than the individual who failed to get the answer. A $t$ of 5.04 with 14 $df$ shows this to be significantly different from zero at the .001 level. However, it may be plausibly argued that in making this comparison, the final question which identified the correct object should be excluded. Before asking it, the individual had correctly formulated the answer. If the final answer is excluded, the difference is reduced from 1.55 to .55. This yields a $t$ of 1.74 and is not significantly different from zero.

A similar analysis was done for groups of four. When the final question is included, the mean difference between the number of questions asked by the individual getting the answer and the average number asked by the other three members was 1.53. With a $t$ of 6.50, this is significantly different from zero at the .001 level. Excluding the final question reduces the mean difference to .53. However, with a $t$ of 2.25, this is still significantly different from zero at the .05 level. There appears to be some tendency for the member of a group of four getting the correct answer to ask more questions, even excluding the final question, than do other members of the group.

## *Individual Versus Group Practice*

The third question which the experiment was intended to answer was whether improvement in individual performance occurs more rapidly with individual practice or with practice as a member of a group. To answer this question, all *S*s worked alone on the fifth day. As before, the score for each individual was the median number of questions required to solve the four problems. The mean of these scores for the 15 *S*s who had previously worked alone was 20.8;[2] for the 30 who had worked in pairs, 19.3; and for the 60 who had been members of groups of four, 19.1. None of the differences among these means is significant. Nor were any of the dif-

2 Comparison of this mean for the fifth day with that for the fourth day (20.8 versus 18.1) shown in Fig. 1 may raise the question: Why should the performance on the fifth day be inferior to that on the fourth day in view of the fact that the conditions under which these 15 individuals worked were the same on both days? However, the difference between these two means is not significant ($t = 1.04$).

ferences significant among the corresponding means on the fifth day for number of failures or for time scores. Learning went on as well in groups of two or of four as in individual practice.

## DISCUSSION

The results obtained show that there is rapid learning of the skill involved in the game. The question now arises as to just what it is that is learned. To determine this, a qualitative analysis of the kinds of questions asked on successive days will be necessary. In a second experiment, now in progress, a complete record of all questions asked is being made in order that such an analysis can be carried out.

Group performances were superior to individual performance in terms of number of questions, number of failures, and elapsed time per problem; but the performance of groups of four was not superior to that of groups of two, except in terms of the number of failures to reach solution. Whether one could confidently have predicted such group superiority is questionable: Individual members of the group might have failed to make effective use of the information yielded by questions asked by other members; if this had been the case, the number of questions required by a group would have been larger, rather than smaller, than that required by an individual.

The fact that there were negligible differences between groups of two and of four either in number of questions or in elapsed time strongly suggests that the optimum size group is not larger than four. Proof of this will require further experimentation with other size groups. Additional experiments are also needed to determine whether the optimum size group is similar for other types of problems.

The question may be raised as to why there was a significant difference between groups of two and of four in number of failures to reach solution, this in spite of the fact that there were negligible differences in number of questions or elapsed time. A possible explanation is that increasing the number of participants from two to four reduces the probability of a persisting wrong set resulting in complete failure. For an individual, a wrong set once established may make it impossible to solve the problem. The probability that a wrong set would be established simultaneously for all participants would be smaller for a group of four than for a group of two.

Although group performances were superior to individual performance in terms of elapsed time to solution, the performance of individuals was superior to that of either size group in terms of number of man-minutes required for solution. The practical implications of this fact should not be overlooked. It appears probable that there are many kinds of problems which a group will solve more quickly than an individual. If elapsed time in hours, weeks, or months is the primary consideration, then such problems should be undertaken by groups. However, it appears equally probable that few of those same problems will be solved more efficiently in terms of man-minutes or man-hours by groups than by individuals. If a group of two is to solve a problem more efficiently than an individual in these latter terms, it must solve it in less than half the elapsed time required by the individual. Similarly, a group of four to be more efficient must solve the problem in less than one-fourth the elapsed time required by the individual. The importance of this point appears to be frequently overlooked.

What it is that accounts for the superiority of group as compared to individual performance in terms of number of questions or elapsed time remains to be determined. The suggestion may be made that the superiority of the group is due to the performance of the best member of the group. If one were to pick the most able individual from each of 15 groups of four, it would be expected that the performance of these 15 individuals would be superior to that of 15 individuals chosen by random sampling. The mean number of questions required by groups of four on the fourth day was 13.6. The mean of the best individual performances on the fifth day by former members of each of the 15 groups of four was 14.8, not significantly different from 13.6. This fact would seem to support the suggestion just made. However, this comparison is not fully valid. Which former member of a group of four had the best performance on the fifth day very probably depended partly on ability and to a considerable extent on chance. Selecting the best individual performance from each of the 15 groups thus capitalizes on chance in a way that reduces the mean obtained; it may yet be true that the mean performance of the 15 groups would be superior to that of the best individuals in each of the 15 groups.

That the superior performance of the group is not simply a function of the performance of the best member of the group is suggested by another consideration. If this were the case, then the larger the group, the better on the average should be the performance of the best member on the basis of sampling alone; hence the larger the group, the better should be the performance. The negligible differences obtained between groups of two and of four fail to confirm this expectation.

It may be expected that other factors such as broader range of relevant information, greater flexibility in approach, etc., are at least partly responsible for the superiority of group over individual performance. What these factors are and how they operate to produce an optimum size for a group can be determined only by additional experimentation.

An interesting supplementary question is whether the member of a group who obtains the right answer does so largely because he asks more questions than the other members of the group. The data obtained show that the number of questions asked by the member of a group of two obtaining the correct answer does not differ significantly from the number asked by the other member. A difference significant at the .05 level was found between the number asked by the member of a group of four obtaining the correct answer and the mean number asked by the other three members. However, this significant difference was only a matter of .53 questions per problem. It seems doubtful that getting the right answer is primarily due to the asking of more questions either in groups of two or of four.

The results obtained on the fifth day showed that learning resulting in improvement in individual performance occurred as rapidly with individual practice as with practice as a member of a group of two or of four. This fact, of course, should not be taken to mean that improvement is qualitatively the same under the different conditions. It may or may not be.

## SUMMARY AND CONCLUSIONS

The game of "Twenty Questions" was employed in an experiment on problem solving. A total of 105 *S*s were assigned by chance to solve such problems working either alone, in pairs, or in groups of four. There were 15 individual *S*s, 15 groups of two, and 15 groups of four. Each individual or group was given four problems a day for four successive days. On the fifth day, all *S*s worked alone, each being given four problems.

Both the number of questions and the time required to solve each problem were recorded. Problems not solved in 30 questions were counted as failures.

1. In terms of number of questions, rapid improvement occurred in the performance both of individuals and of groups. By the fourth day, the curves appeared to be flattening out. Similar results were obtained in terms both of number of failures and of time per problem.

2. Group performances were superior to individual performance in terms of number of questions, number of failures, and elapsed time per problem; but the performance of groups of four was not superior to that of groups of two, except in terms of the number of failures to reach solution.

3. In terms of man-minutes required for solution, the performance of individuals was superior to that of groups; the performance of groups of two was superior to that of groups of four.

4. Improvement in individual performance occurred as rapidly with individual practice as with practice as a member of a group.

## REFERENCES

1. Cochran, W. G., & Cox, G. M. *Experimental designs.* New York: Wiley, 1950.
2. Festinger, L. The significance of difference between means without reference to the frequency distribution function. *Psychometrika,* 1946, 11, 97–105.

3. Lindley, E. H. A study of puzzles with special reference to the psychology of mental adaptation. *Amer. J. Psychol.*, 1897, 8, 431–493.
4. Shaw, M. E. A comparison of individuals and small groups in the rational solution of complex problems. *Amer. J. Psychol.*, 1932, 54, 491–504.

# *The Use of Tape Recording to Simulate a Group Atmosphere*

ROBERT R. BLAKE and JACK W. BREHM

THE PRESENT study explores the possibility that tape recordings can be used to communicate to a test subject the experience that he is a participating member of a social group. If this method can be employed to investigate the impact of group membership on individual behavior, its research applications should prove to be numerous.

## THE EXPERIMENT

### *Application of the Method*

To test the feasibility of this approach for a standard problem, a brief description of a study based on the autokinetic phenomenon will be given (1). The situation used is comparable in many respects to that employed

FROM *Journal of Abnormal and Social Psychology*, 1954, 49, 311–313. Reprinted by permission of the authors and the American Psychological Association, Inc.

The study was conducted in the Laboratory of Social Relations, Harvard University, and was sponsored in part by the United States Air Force under contract No. AF 33(038)–12782 monitored by the Human Resources Research Institute. Permission is granted for reproduction in whole and in part by or for the United States Government. The cooperation of the United States Navy in facilitating the conduct of the research is also gratefully acknowledged. The authors express their appreciation to Dr. Henry W. Riecken for his help with design and administrative problems.

by Sherif (2) in his investigation of autokinetic judgments in the group context. The important differences are that (*a*) in our situation the subjects (*Ss*) understand that each is experiencing the same amount of movement, but that they are looking from different observation posts, as would be the case, for example, on shipboard (thus accounting for the fact that they are not physically together); and (*b*) our *Ss* used the millimeter scale, rather than inches, as the unit through which they express their judgments.

As Sherif originally reported, judgments of the movement experienced in the autokinetic situation are responsive to group pressures, the rule being that *Ss*' responses tend to converge on a norm established by the group. Given that finding, it is predicted that the uninstructed *S* experiencing the present situation will tend to locate his judgments somewhere within the range of reports given by the "taped" *Ss*. If he does give responses within this range and if the range used is a most improbable one, as inferred from the frequency with which responses are given within it by *Ss* who judge in a situation without social stimulation, this would constitute evidence for the conformance-producing power of the recorded group situation.

## *Explanation to the Subjects*

After taking him to the darkroom and adjusting his head-set and power microphone, the experimenter (*E*) left, informing *S* that he and the rest of the group who were located in adjoining rooms would be given further instructions over headphones. The *S* was also told that his code letter would be "G." The *E* then returned to the control room, started the tape recorder, and turned on a switch completing the circuit to *S*. The explanation that followed was addressed to the "taped" participants as well as to the uninstructed, critical *S*. The recording ran as follows:

*Experimenter:* All right, here we go. I'm talking to you from our control room. Now I'll tell you all what I want you to do. But first I want to know if you can hear me all right. If you can, please answer okay when I call your code letter. Subject A (okay); subject B (okay); . . . subject E (okay); subject F (okay); subject G (four-second space). All right, that's fine.

Now here's what the experiment is all about. Navy men on board ship or flying occasionally have to judge the distance which a light moves on the horizon. The Navy needs to know how men make such judgments when the conditions are poor—such as when it's dark.

In this experiment each of you will estimate how far a light moves in the dark. You will then report your estimates. As on board ship, you will be able to hear each other's reports. The answers you all give will then be used by our control room to make a single estimate of the distance the light moved. Since a person cannot be very accurate under these conditions, the combined judgments of the group will be much better than the individual reports. It's the group performance which makes the difference between a hit and a miss in this kind of work.

Now here are your instructions. Please listen carefully.

When the experiment begins, a light will appear in front of you. Shortly after it appears it will begin to move. It will only be visible for a few seconds. Your task is to estimate the total distance the light moves. As soon as it stops, you will each be called by your code letter to give your estimate of how far it moved. Give your report in millimeters. (The *S*s were shown a millimeter scale before the beginning of the experiment.)

Are there any questions?

*Subject D:* Yeh, I've got a question. Does this light move the same amount for all of us each time it comes on?

*Experimenter:* Yes, we're doing this just like we did before. Okay? Ready for trial one. (Ten-second space in the tape.) Now give me your reports to the nearest millimeter; first, subject A–(69); subject B . . . subject G–(five-second space). Ready for trial two. (Eight-second space). Etc.

At the end of trial 10, *E* said, "That's the end of this part of the experiment. Please remain in your seats until I bring you a questionnaire to fill out."

The *E* then asked the uninstructed *S* to fill out a questionnaire. After discussion and explanation of whatever part of the experiment he was interested in, *S* was released. As far as could be determined, no one diagnosed the concealed features of the study.

## *Subjects*

The *S*s participating in this study, 84 in number, were drawn from Naval enlistees and Harvard University undergraduates.

## *Experimental Design*

Three sets of conditions using simulated groups and one condition involving judgment in the "alone" situation were employed. The three synthetic conditions involved 10 trials, each consisting of six numerical values spoken by the "participants" as their judgments before the uninstructed *S* was called to give his report. The 10 trials varied in two ways: they had five different ranges and they were built on two different scale centers. In all cases the numerical distances between individual judgments were of equal amounts, and no numerical value was repeated in the same trial. Thus the median and mean coincided at the center for any given scale.

For the *diverging* condition, scale centers alternated from 46 to 57, starting with the low center. The diverging conditions started with a small range, with the range size increasing as the trials progressed. Trial one had a range of 15, trial two of 15, trial three of 20, and so on up to trials nine and ten, each of which had a range of 45. The *converging* condition represents an exact duplication of the diverging one but in reverse since it began with wide ranges and ended with narrow ones. The *nonoverlapping* condition alternated between scale centers of 31 and 52, starting with the high value. However, in this condition ranges alternated from large to small. These ranges were designed in such a way (varying from 5 to 35 in width) that adjacent ranges never overlapped. The composition of each condition is reproduced in Table 1. In the actual experiment, the recorded order of numerical values within each trial was randomized.

The fourth condition, introduced to furnish evidence for judgmental tendencies in the alone situation, provides the control data. Operating under conventional autokinetic conditions, but using exposure periods of the same length as those employed for the simulated group conditions, 27 *S*s simply judged the distance of movement for 10 consecutive trials.

TABLE 1

*Ranges, Scale Centers, and Numerical Values Spoken by Recorded Subjects under the Synthetic Group Conditions*

| CONDITION I * DIVERGING RANGE | | | | CONDITION III NONOVERLAPPING RANGE | | | |
|---|---|---|---|---|---|---|---|
| TRIAL | RANGE | CENTER | STIMULUS VALUES | TRIAL | RANGE | CENTER | STIMULUS VALUES |
| 1 | 15 | 45.5 | 38-41-44-47-50-53 | 1 | 35 | 51.5 | 34-41-48-55-62-69 |
| 2 | 15 | 56.5 | 49-52-55-58-61-64 | 2 | 5 | 30.5 | 28-29-30-31-32-33 |
| 3 | 20 | 46.0 | 36-40-44-48-52-56 | 3 | 30 | 52.0 | 37-43-49-55-61-67 |
| 4 | 20 | 57.0 | 47-51-55-59-63-67 | 4 | 10 | 31.0 | 26-28-30-32-34-36 |
| 5 | 30 | 46.0 | 31-37-43-49-55-61 | 5 | 20 | 52.0 | 42-46-50-54-58-62 |
| 6 | 30 | 57.0 | 42-48-54-60-66-72 | 6 | 20 | 31.0 | 21-25-29-33-37-41 |
| 7 | 40 | 46.0 | 26-34-42-50-58-66 | 7 | 10 | 52.0 | 47-49-51-53-55-57 |
| 8 | 40 | 57.0 | 37-45-53-61-69-77 | 8 | 30 | 31.0 | 16-22-28-34-40-46 |
| 9 | 45 | 45.5 | 23-32-41-50-59-68 | 9 | 5 | 51.5 | 49-50-51-52-53-54 |
| 10 | 45 | 56.5 | 34-43-52-61-70-79 | 10 | 35 | 30.5 | 13-20-27-34-41-48 |

* Condition II is the same as condition I but in reverse sequence.

## RESULTS

Table 2 shows the frequency with which control *S*s gave responses within the range of numbers spoken by the recorded *S*s under each of the three conditions outlined above, as contrasted with the frequency with which uninstructed *S*s located their responses within the same range. It shows that under each of the synthetic group conditions more than 50 per cent of the responses fell within the spoken range of the recorded *S*s, while only about 4 per cent of the responses given under the alone condition were located within the same region. The differences, which are of high statistical significance, point to the conclusion that under each of the three conditions the responses of the uninstructed *S*s operating as members of "synthetic" groups were changed in the predicted direction.

## DISCUSSION AND CONCLUSIONS

In this study a group frame of reference was created for the autokinetic effect solely by auditory stimulation. The reports of all "other" *Ss* were recorded and communicated to the critical *S* over headphones. Eighty-four *Ss* distributed among three experimental and one control condition were asked to give 10 autokinetic judgments. For the experimental conditions, judgment was made after *S* listened to recorded reports from six other people. A control was provided by 27 *Ss*, each of whom made 10 judgments under the nonsocial condition. Owing to effective concealment of the critical feature in the study, the test *Ss* were, as far as could be determined, unaware that the judgments they heard were given by persons not actually present in other rooms.

TABLE 2

*The Frequency of Responses Located Within the Social Range Created by the Simulated (Recorded) Group, Contrasted with the Comparable Frequency for the Nonsocial Situation*

| | CONDITION I | | | CONDITION II | | | CONDITION III | | |
|---|---|---|---|---|---|---|---|---|---|
| TRIAL | CONTROL FREQ. ($N=27$) | EXP. FREQ. ($N=20$) | $p$ | CONTROL FREQ. ($N=27$) | EXP. FREQ. ($N=20$) | $p$ | CONTROL FREQ. ($N=27$) | EXP. FREQ. ($N=17$) | $p$ |
| 1 | 1 | 6 | $<.05$ | 2 | 16 | $<.01$ | 2 | 17 | $<.01$ |
| 2 | 1 | 5 | $<.10$ | 4 | 12 | $<.01$ | 2 | 9 | $<.01$ |
| 3 | 1 | 13 | $<.01$ | 1 | 16 | $<.01$ | 1 | 17 | $<.01$ |
| 4 | 0 | 12 | $<.01$ | 2 | 11 | $<.01$ | 2 | 13 | $<.01$ |
| 5 | 1 | 16 | $<.01$ | 0 | 13 | $<.01$ | 0 | 14 | $<.01$ |
| 6 | 1 | 12 | $<.01$ | 2 | 11 | $<.01$ | 4 | 14 | $<.01$ |
| 7 | 4 | 18 | $<.01$ | 1 | 11 | $<.01$ | 1 | 9 | $<.01$ |
| 8 | 4 | 17 | $<.01$ | 4 | 10 | $<.20$ | 4 | 17 | $<.01$ |
| 9 | 6 | 13 | $<.01$ | 2 | 8 | $<.05$ | 2 | 2 | $>.95$ |
| 10 | 3 | 15 | $<.01$ | 0 | 6 | $<.01$ | 4 | 11 | $<.01$ |

It was hypothesized that under these conditions an *S* would locate his judgments within the range of reports given by the group as a whole. Statistical evaluation indicated that the frequencies of judgments falling within the recorded social ranges were significantly greater for *Ss* who judged with others than they were for those who judged in the alone situation. It may be concluded that pressures to change can be created by skillfully prepared recordings which simulate the conditions of a "live" experimental situation.

These results suggest that the tape method of inducing the experience of group membership may facilitate the conduct of group research in several ways. For example, the conventional procedure of using paid participants entails at least three difficulties: changes within the experimental procedure due to variations in the behavior of participants from time to time, problems of scheduling, and the expense of employing instructed *Ss*. The use of magnetic tape recording eliminates the need for the repeated presence of paid participants, thereby reducing expense and problems of scheduling, and, at the same time, it automatically standardizes the major part of the experimental procedure. It should be clear, of course, that such a procedure imposes constraints on the possibilities of interaction, thus having its own intrinsic limitations.

## REFERENCES

1. Brehm, J. W. A quantitative approach to the measurement of social influence. Unpublished bachelor's thesis, Harvard Univer., 1952.
2. Sherif, M. A study of some social factors in perception. *Arch. Psychol.*, 1935, No. 187.

# CHAPTER 5

# SOCIAL PERCEPTION

## *A Scale for the Measurement of Empathic Ability*

ROSALIND F. DYMOND

IN A PREVIOUS article (2) the writer made some suggestions concerning the importance of the empathic process in the understanding and creation of the state clinicians call "insight." A rudimentary attempt was made to measure the empathic ability of a small group of students and to relate this ability to the degree of insight they had into their interpersonal relations.

Although the term "empathy" has been in the psychological literature for some time, it has had several different usages. For this reason it is important that the term be defined before it is used further. Empathy will be used in this paper to denote the imaginative transposing of oneself into the thinking, feeling and acting of another and so structuring the world as he does.

Recently there have been suggestions from several different sources that empathy may be one of the underlying processes on which our understanding of others is built. This is sometimes phrased as, "fellow-feeling," "social awareness," "sympathy" or "insight." Lois Murphy (4) in her work on the development of sympathy in young children says:

FROM *Journal of Consulting Psychology*, 1949, 13, 127–133. Reprinted by permission of the author and the American Psychological Association, Inc.

In the case of sympathy, probably general thresholds for being affectionate, for seeing similarities between other's situations and our own, and for empathic responsiveness underlie sympathic habits. . . . If we could find measures for susceptibility to empathic responses, if such they be, we might well find the basis for the most important individual differences in sympathy.

In a very different context, Roy G. Hoskins, (3, pp. 102, 165) speaking of schizophrenia says:

It throws open the possibility that the primary defect in schizophrenia, a defect from which the remainder of the symptomatology stems–is inadequate empathy.

Perhaps as fundamentally characteristic as anything about the psychosis is the failure of the subject either to achieve or retain adequate breadth or depth of empathy.

L. S. Cottrell (1, p. 374) in his work on the analysis of situational fields holds that empathy is the basic process in all social interaction.

The impact of one human organism, A, on the activities of another, B, not only stimulates and conditions a response pattern of A to B but also conditions in A the response pattern of B to A as A has perceived that action and vice versa. (This process of responding by reproducing the acts of the other(s) has been referred to by various writers, as, taking the role of the other, identification, introjection, sympathy, empathy or imitation.)

D. L. Watson (5) in his paper on the nature of insight says:

To have correct insight is to share the feeling of him you are observing, to attach the significance appropriate to his part in events.

Although these and others have touched on the importance of the empathic process, there has been little or no systematic work done on the process itself. Many important questions suggest themselves immediately.

1. Can empathic ability be isolated and measured?
2. What is the normal range of the individual differences?
3. Does the development of this ability follow an age curve?
4. What is the relation of this ability to other personality and life history factors, such as intelligence, sociometric position, type of family atmosphere in which the individual was raised, etc.
5. Are there various dimensions to this ability, such as depth, (the degree to which one empathizes with any one individual), and breadth, (the number of individuals with whom one can empathize)?

Before any of the other questions can be dealt with it is necessary that question 1 be answered. A standardized test must be devised which requires the subject to empathize with others and which provides a measure of his accuracy. The remainder of this paper will deal with an attempt to construct such a scale and with the results obtained with it.

The test was made up of four parts, each containing the same six items. In the first part the individual was asked to rate himself, on a five point scale, on each of six characteristics. In the second part he was asked to rate some other individual on the same six traits. In the third he was asked to rate the other individual as he believes this other would rate himself. In the fourth he must rate himself as he thinks the other would rate him. In other words, if two individuals A and B are being tested for their empathy with each other, the procedure would be as follows:

A. Part 1. A rates himself, (A)
  2. A rates B as he (A) sees him.
  3. A rates B as he thinks B would rate himself.
  4. A rates himself (A) as he thinks B would rate him.

B. Part 1. B rates himself, (B)
  2. B rates A as he (B) sees him.
  3. B rates A as he thinks A would rate himself.
  4. B rates himself (B) as he thinks A would rate him.

Therefore a measure of A's empathic ability can be derived by calculating how closely his predictions of B's ratings, (A3 and A4), correspond with B's actual ratings (B1 and B2). Similarly a measure of B's empathy with A can be obtained by calculating how closely his predictions of A's rating, (B3 and B4), correspond to A's actual ratings (A1 and A2).

The six traits which were used as the items in all four parts of the test were:

1. self-confidence
2. superior-inferior
3. selfish-unselfish
4. friendly-unfriendly
5. leader-follower
6. sense of humour

Although the usual objections to such trait-ratings were recognized, this procedure was followed none the less because the ratings were not being used to determine the personality of the subjects nor to determine how accurate the others were in their estimation of this. The test was designed to answer the question how well can the subject transpose himself into the thinking, feeling and acting of the others. If he can do this he should be able to predict how the others will behave in certain defined situations. The situation chosen to test this ability was the subject's ability to predict how others will rate themselves and how they will rate him on these six traits.

The test was designed for use with a social psychology class which was studying the structuring and functioning of groups. There were 53 subjects in all, 29 females and 24 males. The class members were divided in a random way into five groups of seven members each and three groups of six members. All groups were composed of both sexes and in no cases were friends members of the same group. These groups met once a week to discuss and plan a class project. In each case one member was designated Group Observer. The Group Observer took no part in the group's activities, his sole duty being to keep records of how the group structured itself and how it functioned.

The empathy test or Rating Test, as it was called, was first given after these groups had met three times. Each student was required to rate himself on the six characteristics, to rate each of his group members in turn on these traits, and then to make the two types of prediction for each group member: (*1*) how each group member will rate him, and (*2*) how each group member will rate himself. This would seem to require that the individual take the role of the others, or empathize with them in order to see himself as others see him and in order to see others as they look to themselves. Since each rating is made on a five point scale, the test can be scored in terms of the total number of points the individual is in error in his predictions. This was called the Deviation Score and was the one commonly used. Another method of scoring was occasionally used for particular problems. This was called the Right Score and involved counting the number of predictions which coincided exactly with the actual rating.

The first calculation which was made was a comparison of the Right Scores with the number of right predictions which could be expected if chance alone were operating. The number right on each of the two types of prediction (3 and 4) and on both combined was much higher than could be expected if chance alone were the only factor operating in the making of these predictions, (the differences being significant at the 1 per cent level). Therefore it seems likely that this test is measuring some ability, other than chance, to predict what others will do under certain circumstances which involves taking the role of the other or empathizing with him.

In order to discover if the scores would improve as the subjects were in contact with each other over a longer period, the test was given again six weeks later after the groups had met eight times. Table 1 compares the scores obtained on the two tests. Both the Deviation Scores and the Right Scores are quoted although they have opposite interpretations. In terms of deviation the lower the score the more accurate the prediction, whereas in terms of the Right Score the higher score represents the greater accuracy.

An examination of Table 1 shows that some individuals did better on the second test than they had previously, but some did less well. On the whole there was a slight but not significant improvement. Only ten of the fifty-three subjects changed their scores significantly; nine of these were significantly improved and one was significantly poorer. It would appear,

TABLE 1

*A Comparison of the Mean Scores Obtained on Test 1 and Test 2 (Retest)*

| | DEVIATION SCORES | | | RIGHT SCORES | | |
|---|---|---|---|---|---|---|
| | RANGE | MEAN | S. D. | RANGE | MEAN | S. D. |
| Test 1 | 37–70 | 51.3 | 8.0 | 18–39 | 28.8 | 6.5 |
| Test 2 | 29–75 | 48.0 | 9.0 | 18–46 | 31.3 | 7.5 |

then, that the longer contact did not significantly affect the scores and that therefore there was no real increase in the understanding of each other, on the whole, by the group members over this period of time. However when a breakdown was made according to sex an interesting difference was noted.

Although the difference between the males and females was not significant on the first test in terms of either method of scoring, on the second test the females were more accurate than the males in terms of both types of scoring. Also when each sex is considered separately, the males did not increase their scores significantly from Test 1 to Test 2 whereas the females did. Although the females did not have any initial advantage in their ability to empathize with others, for some reason they did, on the whole, learn to understand other group members better over the experimental period, whereas the males did not.

TABLE 2

*Comparison of Mean Scores of Males and Females on Rating Test 1 and Test 2 (Retest)*

| | MEAN DEVIATION SCORE | | MEAN RIGHT SCORE | |
|---|---|---|---|---|
| | MALES | FEMALES | MALES | FEMALES |
| Test 1 | 52.1 | 51.4 | 28.5 | 29.0 |
| Test 2 | 50.9 | 45.6 | 30.0 | 36.0 |

From the Group Observers' reports it was learned that there were large qualitative differences in the groups themselves. Some groups functioned very smoothly, some were deadlocked in struggles for leadership and others were characterized by apathy. A good many of these differences were reflected in the group scores.

Group One was characterized by smooth relationships, a high degree of interest in their project, and a good deal of cooperative effort. Group Eight stood at the other end of the scale. It was broken into two antagonistic factions and accomplished no real work as a result of personal feuding. This group's attempts to empathize with each other were actually less successful, on the average, the second time than the first. This test

TABLE 3

*Mean Scores and Ranking by Groups, Test 1 and Test 2*

| GROUP | TEST 1 | TEST 2 | RANK (1) | RANK (2) |
|---|---|---|---|---|
| 1. | 43.4 | 42.2 | 1 | 1 |
| 2. | 55.4 | 50.5 | 7 | 6 |
| 3. | 52.1 | 42.8 | 5 | 2 |
| 4. | 49.7 | 46.0 | 3 | 3 |
| 5. | 64.5 | 53.7 | 8 | 7 |
| 6. | 50.1 | 47.2 | 4 | 4 |
| 7. | 47.8 | 49.1 | 2 | 5 |
| 8. | 52.5 | 54.1 | 6 | 8 |

does seem to reveal and corroborate in a quantitative manner some of the qualitative differences reported by the Group Observers.

A further calculation was made to determine whether there was any significance to the pattern of the deviations. For the most part the subjects would sometimes overestimate the others in their predictions and sometimes underestimate them so that the deviations did not differ significantly from chance expectancy. However there were some cases in which the errors were so large in one direction as to be significant, (more than 2 S. D.).

There were thirteen individuals in the sample who had distortions in their perceptions of themselves or others, or both, which lasted over the two tests. These people appear to enter their personal relations with a dis-

TABLE 4

*Deviations Significant for Their Consistency of Direction*

| | UNDERESTIMATIONS OF WHAT OTHERS WILL SAY ABOUT: | | OVERESTIMATIONS OF WHAT OTHERS WILL SAY ABOUT: | |
|---|---|---|---|---|
| | THEMSELVES | THE SUBJECT | THEMSELVES | THE SUBJECT |
| Test 1 | 14 | 9 | 4 | 11 |
| Test 2 | 11 | 8 | 6 | 10 |
| Repeats | 4 | 4 | 2 | 5 |

tortion which causes them to feel that others either look down on them or up to them more than they actually do, or that others either think better or worse of themselves than they actually do. This test gives a measure of the direction and extent of these distortions of perception in personal relations which have been recognized in both psychology and common sense as feelings of inferiority or superiority.

One criterion which any new test must meet is that of validity. As this is the only test purporting to measure empathic ability which is known to the author, the simple solution of correlating the results of this test with those obtained with some other test of empathy was inapplicable. The problem of finding some other measure of the ability in question was partially solved by utilizing the same method as reported in the previous paper (2).

Ten subjects from the original sample of fifty-three were asked to take the Thematic Apperception Test (TAT). These subjects were unaware that they represented the five highest and the five lowest scores on the Rating Test. The TAT's were administered by another psychologist (Mrs. Helen Wait), who then turned them over to the author for blind analysis with only an identifying number. The stories were analyzed in terms of how well the subjects took the role or empathized with the characters they introduced into their stories. The five individuals whose scores

TABLE 5

*Correlations of Observers' Rating of Empathic Ability of Their Group Members and the Test Results*

| | CORRELATION COEFFICIENT |
|---|---|
| Observers With High Empathy (in deciles 1–5) N = 4 | r = +.61 |
| Observers With Low Empathy (in deciles 6–10) N = 4 | r = +.14 |

on the Rating Test classified them as highly empathic also rated as highly empathic on the TAT analysis. Four of those whose scores on the Rating Test were very low, also showed low empathy in their stories. Only one whose empathy seemed low on the Rating Test appeared to be highly empathic on the TAT analysis. Although this is hardly sufficient evidence on which to state that this is a valid test of empathic ability, the two types of evidence do tend to corroborate each other.

A further attempt to establish the validity of the test was made by correlating the Group Observers' ratings of the empathic ability of their group members with the test results. This correlation was too low to be of any significance. However when the Observers themselves were divided into two groups according to their empathic ability, an interesting difference was noted.

Although the number of judges is too small for this evidence to be conclusive, Table 5 seems to show that those with good empathic ability are better judges of the empathy of others than those with low ability. A parallel case would be if judges rating the intelligence of others made better judgments when they themselves had good intelligence.

A further criterion which a new test must meet is that of reliability. Actually a high degree of reliability was not anticipated with this test, as it was expected that the scores would change as the individuals got better acquainted. Therefore the correlation of +.60 between Test 1 and Test 2 was not surprising. Although this coefficient is not high enough to warrant the statement that there is good test-retest reliability over this period, it is sufficiently high to say that there is a fairly strong tendency for the empathy ratings to be stable. Since the predictions of what others would say was expected to vary, the individual's own concept of himself was next taken as a measure of the reliability of the test. In other words, it was not expected that the individual's own ratings of themselves would vary

TABLE 6

*Amount and Direction of Change from Test 1 to Test 2 in Concept of Self*

| NO. OF POINTS CHANGED | NO. OF JUDGMENTS CHANGED | PERCENTAGE |
|---|---|---|
| +4 | 2 | .6 |
| +3 | 0 | .0 |
| +2 | 3 | .9 |
| +1 | 50 | 15.8 |
| 0 | 213 | 67.0 |
| −1 | 45 | 14.2 |
| −2 | 5 | 1.5 |
| −3 | 0 | .0 |
| −4 | 0 | .0 |
| | 318 | 100.0 |

very considerably within the six week period. The reliability coefficients of the six items were as follows:

(1) .82; (2) .71; (3) .73; (4) .80; (5) .62; (6) .77.

It is interesting to note that the lowest of these (.62) was the item concerning leadership ability. The individual's own conception of his ability in this regard was subject to some change after being thrown into an unstructured group situation.

Another technique for demonstrating the reliability of the test was to calculate the actual change in number of points of the concept of self. Since fifty-three subjects made six judgments about themselves there was a total of three hundred and eighteen judgments made. Table 6 shows the number of these judgments which were changed and the amount and direction of this change, (on a five point scale).

Table 6 shows that 97 per cent of the judgments that the individuals made about themselves were exactly the same on the second test as on the first or varied only one scale place in either direction. This appears to show a high degree of reliability for these judgments. Although this too fails to be sufficient evidence of the reliability of the test as a whole, it does point to the likelihood of the test meeting this criterion satisfactorily.

To return to the problem of the relation of insight and empathy with which the previous article (2) was concerned, an interesting relationship was noted. At the close of the experiment each subject was asked to rate himself according to his own judgment of the amount of empathy he had in comparison with the others in this experimental group. Each rated himself on a five point scale varying from Very High to Very Low. The group was then divided into deciles according to their scores on the last Rating Test. Next the relation between the individual's self-rating and the

TABLE 7

*Relation of Rating Test Scores and Subject's Own Judgment of His Empathic Ability*

| | HIGH EMPATHY DECILES 1–5 N = 27 | LOW EMPATHY DECILES 6–10 N = 26 |
|---|---|---|
| Ratings Coincide | 33% | 8% |
| Subject 1 scale position off | 41% | 27% |
| Subject 2 scale positions off | 18% | 34% |
| Subject 3 scale positions off | 2% | 27% |
| Subject 4 scale positions off | 0% | 4% |
| | 100% | 100% |

test's rating was determined. Those falling in deciles 1–5 (on the Rating Test) were designated as the High Empathy Group, and those in deciles 6–10 as the Low Empathy Group. The High Empathy Group's ratings of themselves corresponded closer to the test's ratings of them than did those of the Low Empathy Group.

Table 7 shows that 74 per cent of the High Empathy Group placed themselves in the same fifth of the group as the test did or were only one placement off. Only 35 per cent of the Low Empathy Group corresponded to this degree. It seems that those whose empathic ability is high, as measured by this test, have better insight into the fact that they are high, than those who are low have into the fact that they are low. (This, of course assumed the validity of the test.) It seems very likely that the ability to take the role of another, (empathy), is positively related to the ability to understand ourselves, (insight). This latter state seems to involve the ability to stand off and look at ourselves from another's point of view.

To sum up, this paper has reported an attempt to develop a test for the measurement of empathic ability and the results of this test on a group of fifty-three students. Although the work is too preliminary for there to be any final claim made concerning the validity or reliability of the test, the evidence reported does seem to point to this possibility. The ability that is concerned here, seeing things from the other person's point of view, is one in which individuals obviously differ from one another. Some of us are highly sensitive and perceptive of what the other fellow is thinking and how he is feeling, while others are very obtuse and slow about picking up these clues. What accounts for these differences? Can this ability be trained? These are important questions still to be solved. This paper is merely an attempt to define the area as an important one for further study, and to try to provide some techniques for its exploration.

## REFERENCES

1. Cottrell, L. S. The analysis of situational fields in social psychology. *Amer. sociol. Rev.*, 1942, 7, 370–382.
2. Dymond, Rosalind. A preliminary investigation of the relation of insight and empathy. *J. consult. Psychol.*, 1948, 4, 228–233.
3. Hoskins, R. G. *The biology of schizophrenia.* New York: Norton, 1946.
4. Murphy, Lois. *Social behavior and child personality: An exploratory study of some roots of sympathy.* New York: Columbia Univer. Press, 1937.
5. Watson, D. L. On the role of insight in the study of mankind. *Psychoanal. Rev.*, 1938, 25, 358–371.

# *The Relative Abilities of Leaders and Non-Leaders to Estimate Opinions of Their Own Groups*

KAMLA CHOWDHRY
and
THEODORE M. NEWCOMB

ACCORDING to modern social psychological theory, individuals are not selected for positions of leadership merely because they possess personal qualities which fit them for leadership in general. We must, on the other hand, assume that individual characteristics *in a particular*

FROM *Journal of Abnormal and Social Psychology*, 1952, 47, 51–57. Reprinted by permission of the authors and the American Psychological Association, Inc.

The full data upon which this partial report is based are to be found in the first-named author's *Leaders and their Ability to Estimate Group Opinion*, 1948, University of Michigan Library.

*group situation* have something to do with the selection of leaders. Every group is characterized by a set of interests shared by its members, and with regard to these common interests every group has a set of standards which are important determiners of their members' attitudes. Attitudes toward other things, not closely related to the common interests of a particular group, may be expected to be less homogeneous than attitudes toward objects of common interest. It is likely, however, that in every group there is some diversity of attitudes, even with regard to matters of most focal interest in the group.

Other things equal, those members of a group will be most effective leaders who are most familiar with its standards, and most familiar with the degree to which those standards are shared by the group's members. It seems likely, too, that such familiarity with the group is considered desirable by members as they choose their leaders. If so, then chosen leaders should be more accurate than non-leaders in their estimates of the attitudes of other members toward issues relevant to the group's interest. There is no reason, however, to conclude that leaders should judge more accurately than non-leaders the attitudes of members on issues irrelevant to their own groups. On the contrary, if we assume that the characteristics of leaders are more or less specific to particular group situations, we shall expect chosen leaders to be better than average judges of other members' attitudes on relevant, but not on irrelevant issues. It might, of course, turn out that chosen leaders are superior judges of members' attitudes toward irrelevant as well as toward relevant issues; in that event we should have to conclude that leadership is a function of a *general* capacity to judge the attitudes of associates, but not a function of the particular standards of particular groups.

This study therefore attempts to test the hypothesis that chosen leaders of a group are superior to non-leaders in estimating group opinion on issues of high relevance to that group, but not superior to them on issues of little relevance. This hypothesis makes no assumptions as to the components of interest, social skill, or personality dynamics which go to make up ability to judge group opinion. Nothing is hypothesized beyond the covariance of two variables: frequency of being chosen for positions of leadership, and ability to judge group opinion on issues of varying relevance to the group. The confirmation of the hypothesis, however, would tend to support a theory of leadership which presupposes interaction among group members who share interests and standards. The rejection of the hypothesis would tend to support a theory of leadership based primarily upon individual differences in skills and capacities.

The hypothesis is one that can be tested either by creating groups in the laboratory, or by obtaining the appropriate information from "natural," existing groups; only the latter procedure was employed in this study. Four groups were selected upon the basis of the following criteria:

1. That they be organized around definite interest patterns, like religion or politics.

2. That each group provide a basis for face-to-face interaction, so that the phenomena of leadership and isolation could emerge.

3. That the members be sufficiently familiar with each other and the opinions of the group to be able to evaluate group opinion.

4. That each group be an example of a common interest group in our society.

A religious group, a political group, a medical fraternity, and a medical sorority were chosen for the investigation. Each of these four groups satisfied the above criteria, though in varying degrees. The medical fraternity and sorority were somewhat different from the religious and political groups, in having a wider range of common interests and experience. They had in common social as well as medical interests, whereas the political and religious groups, according to available information, were more nearly limited to a single interest.

## METHOD

Each group was administered a different attitude questionnaire which was subdivided into three parts. These three parts were designed to get at three different levels of relevance to the group's common interests. The first part of the questionnaire dealt with issues with which the group was familiar, and which were presumed to be relevant to the group's goals. The third part consisted of issues which were not only little discussed in the group, but which did not seem to be connected with the basic interest pattern of the group. The second part was intermediate in familiarity and relevance.

For the religious group, the first part consisted of items dealing with historic Christian doctrines and practices. The second part included items dealing with the church as a social institution, and the attitudes of Christians toward war. The third part included items dealing with general economic and political issues. Almost all the items in this questionnaire were taken from a previously published "Inventory of Religious Concepts" (1).

For the political group, the first part of the questionnaire consisted of items which the Wallace Progressive group was interested in at that time (1948), and which they were discussing in their meetings. It included such issues as civil liberties, the Palestine question, the Czechoslovakian *coup*, Wallace as a presidential candidate, and nationalization of natural resources. The second part dealt with general economic and political issues, and the third part consisted of items dealing with the church as a social institution, and the attitudes of Christians toward war. The second and third parts of the questionnaire were the same as those used for the religious group.

For the medical fraternity and the medical sorority the items in the first part of the questionnaire were selected (with the help of men and women medical students from other groups) to be representative of those usually discussed in the "bull sessions" of medical students, both men and women. The items dealt with the role of professional women at home, the desirability of medical women as wives, the problems of abortion and euthanasia, of equal opportunity of admission for women and Jews to medical schools, etc. These items were taken from a number of sources, the major one being Kirkpatrick's scale on Feminism (3) and Symonds' Social Attitude questionnaire (5). The second part consisted of general economic and political items, and the third part consisted of religious items dealing with the church as a social institution, and the attitudes of Christians towards war. The second and third parts had also been used in both the religious and political groups.

Sociometric data were also collected in each group according to four criteria of leadership. The questions asked were:

1. Who are the three persons who, in your opinion, are most capable of acting as president of your group?

2. Who are the three persons who, in your opinion, most influence the opinions of the group?

3. Who are the three persons who, in your opinion, are most worthy of acting as representatives of this group to a convention? (The convention was specified according to the nature of the group.)

4. Who are the three persons in this group with whom you would most like to be friends?

Personal information, including name, age, sex, educational status, length of group membership, and positions in previous groups, was also collected.

TABLE 1

*Correlation between the Total and Each of the Four Sociometric Criteria*

| GROUP | CRITERION I | CRITERION II | CRITERION III | CRITERION IV |
|---|---|---|---|---|
| Religious | .95 | .89 | .81 | .67 |
| Political | .96 | .97 | .84 | .95 |
| Fraternity | .87 | .70 | .53 | .86 |
| Sorority | .96 | .93 | .61 | .68 |

Each member of the group was requested to make two replies to every item in the questionnaire. The first was a response indicating his own reaction to the statement by encircling "A" if he definitely agreed, encircling "D" if he definitely disagreed, encircling "a" if he had a tendency to agree rather than disagree, and encircling "d" if he had a tendency to disagree rather than agree, with the statement. Secondly, each member was requested to give the percentage of the group which he believed agreed with the statement. The latter procedure has been used by Newcomb (4) and Travers (6) in their investigations.

From the sociometric data the group status of each individual was determined. Those individuals were arbitrarily designated leaders who received the highest fifth of the total choices on the four criteria. The rest were called non-leaders, and among the non-leaders those who did not receive a single vote on any of the four criteria were termed isolates. The use of total choices for differentiating group status was justified by the high correlation of choices received, according to each of the four criteria. Table 1 gives the correlations between the total and each of the four sociometric criteria, in each of the four groups. All the correlations are significant at high levels of confidence.

### *Measurement of Sensitivity*

To determine the individual's ability to judge group opinion, or his sensitivity to group opinion, a mean error score for each individual was computed, as follows. First, actual group opinion was calculated for each item of the questionnaire by taking the percentage of people who actually agreed to each item. ("Definite agreement" was combined with "tendency to agree.") Secondly, the average error score was calculated for each individual by subtracting his estimate from the actual group opinion concerning each item, and averaging the divergences. The algebraic signs were not taken into consideration because we were not interested in the direction of the error, but only in the magnitude of error.

## RESULTS

### *Comparison of Estimates*

In Table 2 the leaders of each of the four groups are compared to non-leaders and isolates with respect to their ability to evaluate group opinion at the three levels of relevance. The mean error score of the leader group is compared to that of the non-leader and isolate groups, and the significance of difference between the groups is tested.

In the *religious group* on part A (items assumed to be most relevant) the leaders are superior to non-leaders and isolates. The difference between leaders and non-leaders is significant at the .05 level, and between leaders and isolates at the .01 level. On part B (items assumed to be of intermediate relevance) the leaders again have a tendency to be better evaluators than non-leaders and isolates. The difference between leaders and non-leaders is not significant, but the difference between leaders and isolates is significant at the .05 level. On part C (items assumed to be of least relevance) there is hardly any difference in the error scores of leaders, non-leaders, and isolates.

In the *political group* on part A the mean error score of leaders is again the least. The difference between leaders and non-leaders is significant at the .07 level, and between leaders and isolates at the .02 level. On parts B and C there are no significant differences in the mean error scores of leaders, non-leaders, and isolates.

In the *fraternity* on part A the mean error of leaders in evaluating group opinion is less than that of non-leaders or of isolates. The differences in mean error of leaders and non-leaders, and of leaders and isolates, are both significant at the .01 level. On part B the difference between the mean errors of non-leaders is not significant; the difference between leaders and

TABLE 2

*Differences in the Degree to which Leaders, Non-Leaders and Isolates Can Estimate Group Opinion*

| GROUPS COMPARED | A ITEMS | | | B ITEMS | | | C ITEMS | | |
|---|---|---|---|---|---|---|---|---|---|
| | DIFF. IN MEAN ERR. | DIFF. IN STD. ERR. | $t$ | DIFF. IN MEAN ERR. | DIFF. IN STD. ERR. | $t$ | DIFF. IN MEAN ERR. | DIFF. IN STD. ERR. | $t$ |
| *Religious Group* | | | | | | | | | |
| 6 Leaders vs. 20 Non-leaders | 6.13 | 2.52 | 2.38 * | 4.36 | 3.53 | 1.24 | 2.95 | 2.34 | 1.26 |
| 6 Leaders vs. 8 Isolates | 9.00 | 2.96 | 3.04 ** | 9.87 | 3.50 | 2.82 | 2.47 | 2.89 | .85 |
| *Political Group* | | | | | | | | | |
| 5 Leaders vs. 18 Non-leaders | 4.98 | 2.58 | 1.93 | 3.10 | 3.60 | .86 | 2.57 | 4.35 | .59 |
| 5 Leaders vs. 7 Isolates | 9.93 | 3.66 | 2.71 * | 5.32 | 4.64 | 1.16 | 6.09 | 7.00 | .87 |
| *Medical Fraternity* | | | | | | | | | |
| 6 Leaders vs. 24 Non-leaders | 6.76 | 2.50 | 2.70 ** | 2.31 | 2.66 | .86 | 2.80 | 3.02 | .91 |
| 6 Leaders vs. 6 Isolates | 7.22 | 1.71 | 4.22 ** | 6.72 | 2.93 | 2.29 * | 3.10 | 3.01 | 1.00 |
| *Medical Sorority* | | | | | | | | | |
| 8 Leaders vs. 32 Non-leaders | 4.08 | 2.39 | 1.71 | 6.80 | 2.50 | 2.72 ** | 1.23 | 2.77 | .44 |
| 8 Leaders vs. 6 Isolates | 2.67 | 1.98 | 1.35 | 7.66 | 2.73 | 2.81 ** | 2.88 | 4.15 | .69 |

* .05 level.
** .01 level.

isolates is significant at the .05 level. On part C the difference in mean errors is too small to be significant.

In the *medical sorority* on part A the leaders make a smaller average error than non-leaders and isolates, but the differences are not significant. On part B, however, the differences in error scores of leaders and non-leaders, and of leaders and isolates are both significant at the .01 level. On part C the differences in the mean errors of leaders, non-leaders, and isolates are small enough to be accounted for by chance variations.

In the medical sorority we used the same questionnaire as we did for the medical fraternity. The leaders in the fraternity are superior to non-leaders and isolates in their knowledge of group opinion on part A, but this superiority on the same issues is not shown by the sorority leaders. The latter finding is opposite to the hypothetical prediction. On the other hand, the sorority leaders are significantly superior to non-leaders and isolates in their ability to evaluate group opinion on part B. This superiority on part B is not shared by the fraternity leaders. On part C, however, neither the fraternity nor the sorority leaders are better in evaluating group opinion than non-leaders and isolates. There seem to be two possible explanations of this difference of results on parts A and B in the fraternity and the sorority. First, our assumption that the same type of things are familiar and relevant to the fraternity and sorority members may be wrong. It is possible that items on part A were more discussed and more relevant to the members of the fraternity, and the items on part B were more discussed and more relevant to the members of the sorority. Secondly, the fraternity was a much more homogeneous group than the sorority; the sorority included Chinese, Filipinos, Negroes, and South Americans. The fraternity included only white North Americans. It is possible that evaluating group opinion of a homogeneous group is easier than evaluating group opinion of a comparatively heterogeneous one.

In summarizing the results of the four groups in sensitivity to group opinion we may say that, on issues designed to be familiar and relevant to the group (A), the leaders are superior to non-leaders and isolates in their ability to evaluate group opinion, the differences between leaders and isolates usually being greater than between leaders and non-leaders. On issues designed to be relatively nonfamiliar and nonrelevant (C), there are no differences in leaders, non-leaders, and isolates in their ability to evaluate group opinion. On issues intermediate in nature to the above two, there are no consistent results.

## *Supplementary Data from Other Groups*

Data from two quite different groups (Bennington College students and a C.I.O. local) were obtained concerning relevant issues only. In the former group, the mean error score of leaders was smaller than that of both non-leaders and isolates, at the .01 level of confidence. Similar differences were obtained in the C.I.O. group at the .03 level.

## *Chronological Age*

The average age of religious leaders (twenty-six) is about three years greater than that of non-leaders and isolates in the same group, while political leaders are on the average two years younger (thirty) than other members of the same group. Neither of these differences is statistically significant. In the fraternity and in the sorority the average age of leaders (twenty-five) is only a few months greater than that of all other members of the same groups. Chronological age is thus not related to leadership and isolation in these data, and evidently has no relation to ability to evaluate group opinion.

## *Length of Membership in Group*

The longer a person has been a member of a group the more likely it is, other things equal, that he will be able to evaluate group opinion accurately. Is it possible that leaders in these groups were those individuals whose memberships were of relatively long duration, and who, therefore, knew more members and their opinions?

TABLE 3

*Average Months of Membership in Various Groups*

| GROUP | LEADERS | NON-LEADERS | ISOLATES |
|---|---|---|---|
| Religious | 11.5 | 21.2 | 22.5 |
| Political | 5.2 | 4.7 | 8.0 |
| Fraternity | 33.6 | 25.7 | 21.2 |
| Sorority | 30.9 | 29.0 | 25.1 |

Table 3 shows that leaders in the religious group have a shorter period of membership, while leaders in the fraternity and sorority groups have a little longer period of membership in their groups than non-leaders and isolates. In the political group the leaders' length of membership is intermediate between that of non-leaders and of isolates.

Length of membership, in these groups, is not consistently related to leadership and isolation, nor to an individual's ability to evaluate group opinion. Travers' data (6) confirm this finding.

## *Academic Status*

Since all or most members of all groups were college students, it is possible to note whether academic status of a person is connected with his status in the group. The chi-square test of significance was used to test whether graduates and seniors were more often in the leader group than in the non-leader and isolate groups. None of the relationships found was significant, indicating that there is no association between leadership and the academic status of an individual, in these groups.

### *Relations of Elected Positions in Other Groups and Present Status*

The chi-square test was again used to see whether there was any significant association between past and present status. Only in the fraternity and sorority groups did we find that leaders have occupied elected positions in other groups significantly more often than non-leaders and isolates ($p < .02$). The other leadership positions held by fraternity and sorority leaders were (according to own statements) predominantly in social and recreational organizations. Such findings suggest that leadership may be "transferable" among similar kinds of groups.

## INTERPRETATION

It was found that leaders of a group are significantly superior to non-leaders and isolates in their ability to judge group opinion on familiar and relevant issues, the difference between leaders and isolates being usually greater than the difference between leaders and non-leaders. This differential ability on the part of leaders, non-leaders, and isolates to judge group opinion is, however, not evident in unfamiliar or less familiar or less relevant issues.

It is possible that leaders are accorded the leader status because of this superior ability in evaluating group opinion, and that isolates sink into psychological isolation because of this lack of understanding of the group. An alternative explanation might be that leaders have a superior knowledge of the group because of the greater opportunities afforded to them in their official position, since they come into greater contact with the members and can therefore evaluate their opinions better. That familiarity alone is not a sufficient explanation for the greater understanding of leaders is evidenced by a number of facts gathered from other studies, as well as from some of the preceding data.

In the community studied by Jennings (2) some individuals, because of the work situations they had chosen, had greater opportunities of social contact than others. These individuals who had a greater opportunity to know and be known by others were not more often chosen than ones who lacked similar opportunities; 35 per cent (13/37) of the overchosen subjects were individuals of the high opportunity group, whereas 65 per cent

(24/37) attained a similar status without having the same kind of exceptional opportunities.

Further relevant evidence is to be found in the Bennington College data, which show that individuals who later acquire prestige and leadership status are those who possess more than the average amount of sensitivity to group opinion. "Entering freshmen who later acquire leader status have less conservative attitudes than those who are later to achieve little or no prestige. This is significant primarily by way of showing that the histories and the personal characteristics of entering freshmen are such that they are impelled to varying degrees of leadership and prestige, and that *within a few weeks of entering college they have already sized up the dominant community trends*, toward which they adapt themselves in proportion to their habits of seeking leadership and prestige" (4). Those freshmen who had ability enough to "size up" the situation were the individuals who later acquired the leader status.

Group understanding or knowledge, then, seems to be an important factor in the status that an individual may acquire in the group. Understanding or knowledge presupposes communication between individuals, and it seems that some individuals have a better ability to keep these channels of communication open than others. Jennings (2) says, "Each [leader] appears able to establish rapport quickly and effectively with a wide range of other personalities. . . . By contrast, the isolates and near-isolates appear relatively 'self-bound,' unable to bridge the gap between their own personalities and those of other persons."

Also the leaders seem to possess attitudes and personality characteristics which make it possible for them to be in fuller communication with the members of the group. According to Jennings (2), "The overchosen individuals are personalities who are not concerned with personal problems, but direct their energies to group problems. The underchosen individual is self-centered and is not outgoing in emotional expansiveness."

This suggests that certain personality traits of the overchosen make it possible for them to be in fuller communication with the members than can be said of the underchosen. The leaders' thinking is in terms of the group, and this attitude makes it necessary for them to keep the channels of communication open. The isolates, on the other hand, are "self-centered" and "relatively self-bound." Their channels of communication do not operate in both directions, and are often blocked entirely. They are relatively incapable of going out of themselves to understand the groups' problems. There is a lack of group understanding on their part because they fail to establish a two-way communication.

The ability to function as an effective group member would also seem to be related to the ability to perceive the opinions and attitudes of the group. The more awareness an individual has of an environment, the more satisfactorily he can adjust to it, other things equal. Each individual adjusts to the situation according to the way he perceives it, and not as it "really" is. Since the leaders' perceptions of the prevailing attitude trends existing in a group tend to be more realistic than those of non-leaders and isolates, the chances of their adequate adjustment are greater than those of the non-leaders and isolates.

Our evidence, thus interpreted, suggests that group status, understanding, communication, and adjustment are interdependent variables; it seems likely that better understanding, ready communication, adequate adjustment, and high status are apt to be associated, whereas relative lack of understanding and adjustment, blocked communication, and low status are similarly apt to be found together.

It seems reasonable to conclude, therefore, that leaders of groups like these are chosen, in part at least, because of recognized qualities of "sensitivity" to other members of the group. If so, such qualities may or may not be *potentially* of a general nature. That is, the same ability which enables an individual to be a good judge of others' religious attitudes in a religious group might also enable him to be a good judge of political attitudes in a political group. The fact is, however, that leaders excel primarily in judging attitudes of special reference to their own groups. They are not just good judges of others' attitudes in general; if they have the ability to become such all-around good judges, they are not motivated to develop it equally in all directions.

And so we conclude that in groups like these the ability to be a good judge of others' attitudes is a necessary but not a sufficient condition of being chosen for leadership. A further necessary condition is that the ability be demonstrated within the confines of a specific membership-character. Leadership *potentiality* may be adaptable to a wide range of membership characters. But leaders of particular groups seem to be chosen because their potentialities have been developed in particular directions, as called for by the differentiated interests of group members.

## REFERENCES

1. Dunkel, H. B. *General education in the humanities.* Washington, D.C.: American Council on Education, 1947.
2. Jennings, Helen H. *Leadership and isolation.* New York: Longmans, Green, 1943.
3. Kirkpatrick, C. Belief pattern scale for measuring attitudes towards feminism. *J. soc. Psychol.*, 1936, 7, 423–426.
4. Newcomb, T. M. *Personality and social change.* New York: Dryden, 1943.
5. Symonds, P. M. A Social Attitude Questionnaire. *J. educ. Psychol.*, 1925, 16, 316–322.
6. Travers, R. M. V. A study in judging the opinions of groups. *Arch. Psychol.*, 1941, No. 266.

# *Relational Analysis: An Extension of Sociometric Method with Emphasis upon Social Perception*

RENATO TAGIURI

AT A BROAD level of generality, understanding of an interpersonal relationship depends upon the availability of information regarding two of its aspects: the first of these is the nature of the response of each person to the other. The second aspect consists of the *perception* that each person has of the other person's response toward him. The analysis of any interpersonal relationship must consider these two components.

Standard sociometric procedures provide simultaneously two types of data about any member of a group: (a) information about *his* affective response to the others and (b) information about others' affective response to him. Since the latter is the result of the choices and rejections of *all the other* members of the group, one might add that the affective response of the group to the subject has a *consensual* nature. Behavior, however, does not consist of the response to the properties of the stimulus field objectively or consensually specified but, rather, of the reaction to what is perceived [1] by the subject. Therefore, while standard sociometric data constitute very useful information, understanding of behavior in interpersonal situations could be advanced further if, in addition to a consensual view

ABRIDGED from *Sociometry*, 1952, 15, 91–104. Reprinted by permission of the author and publisher.

---

1 "Perception" and "perceiving" in this paper are used in a broad sense to include inferences, and remembered stimuli, not necessarily present at the moment.

of the situation, one had access to information regarding the subject's view of it. One may find, for example, a highly chosen subject making only one choice, or, a highly rejected member making many choices. While various explanations are possible for either instance, the picture would acquire immediate transparence if one knew that this particular popular person is not aware of his success but, on the contrary, perceives himself as highly rejected. Similarly, the surprising response of the rejected subject could be understood better if it became apparent that this subject "felt" highly accepted. It must then be clear that the choice and rejection behavior of members of a group could be better comprehended if, in addition to an objective description of the social field (choices and rejections received by a subject) one also knew how the subject perceived this social field.

*In this paper is described a method by means of which, in a single operation, data on the subject's perception of the situation can be gathered, together with the information usually obtained by standard sociometric procedures.*

The method is an extension of the sociometric choice and rejection technique. The unusual features are the addition of a "guessing," or perceptual procedure and a special method for analyzing and utilizing the data.

## THE "GUESSING" OR PERCEPTUAL PROCEDURE

By a "guessing" procedure is meant that subjects are required to *guess who will choose and reject them* in addition to the usual sociometric choices and rejections made by them. The number of choices, guesses, rejections, and guesses of rejection is left unrestricted. The guessing procedure adds the perceptual component to the standard sociometric method.

## ANALYSIS AND UTILIZATION OF DATA BY MEANS OF A SPECIAL CLASSIFICATION OF DIADIC RELATIONSHIPS

After crosschecking the raw data obtained from each subject with those of every other subject, the following eight categories of information become available on each individual (S):

a. (——>) whom S chose,
b. (——<) who S guessed would choose him,
c. (<——) who chose S,
d. (>——) who guessed that S would choose him,
e. (----->) whom S rejected,
f. (-----<) who S guessed would reject him,
g. (<-----) who rejected S, and
h. (>-----) who guessed that S would reject him.

These eight components of the interaction between a subject and another member of the group will be referred to as "bonds" and will be represented by the symbols in brackets.

Any diad can be described in terms of those affective and perceptual elements of a two-person relationship that are expressed by choice, rejection, and their "guesses," and can be assigned to one of the eighty-one diadic categories possible. These constitute an empirical-theoretical *classification* of relationships between pairs of individuals. This feature of the method accounts for the name Relational Analysis given to it.

Theoretically, the eight bonds would combine in 256 ways.[2] On the logical ground, however, that subjects do not choose as well as reject the same individual, or guess that they are chosen as well as rejected by the same person, one can conclude that the total number of theoretically possible varieties of diads is equal to the sum of all combinations *not* containing incompatible bonds (e.g., choice and rejection). It thus becomes apparent that the most complex relationship is the one with only four bonds, since any fifth bond would be incompatible with one of the other four. This reduces the possible relationships from 256 combinations to 81, including the case where no bonds whatsoever exist between two individuals.[3]

Apart from being a convenient method for ordering the complex data of Relational Analysis this classification has several other useful features:

1. It is a way of describing a person, in terms of his perceived and actual relationships to other group members.
2. It is a method by means of which interpersonal relations between pairs of persons or sub-groups can be systematically classified and analyzed.
3. It provides a systematic way of comparing members of a group to one another.
4. It provides another method for describing, in a limited but important way, the cohesion of a group.
5. Study of deviations from the expected frequencies of the various types of diads have thrown light on certain regularities in the affective and perceptual aspects of interpersonal relationships.

2 $$\sum_{i=0}^{i=8} C_i^8 = 256$$

3 If the focus of attention is on the diad itself rather than on the members of the group, the number of different diads can be considered to be forty-five rather than eighty-one. If, however, the analysis is concerned with the subjects themselves, then it makes a difference whether subject S is related to Other by a choice (S———> O) or by a choice-received (S <———O). From an impersonal point of view on the other hand, the two diads above are identical.

While the purpose of this paper is to present the method, rather than the findings of specific studies in which it was used, it would, however, be difficult to give a clear idea of it without referring to some concrete data.

## BEHAVIORAL AND REALITY DETERMINANTS OF THE PERCEPTION OF AFFECT

Since the focus of this method is upon adding the *perceptual dimension* of interpersonal relations to the information obtained by standard sociometric procedures, the bulk of the research done to date with this technique has been concerned with problems of perception of affect.

Several questions about the determinants of perception of affect can be answered by examining the data collected by means of the present method. In the present context one may speak of *external* determinants, i.e., actual positive or negative responses received, and of *internal* determinants, i.e., the factors within the subject that contribute to the nature of his perceptual hypotheses. The latter are represented in this method by the subject's own feelings (choice and rejection of Other). Internal and external determinants are, of course, conceived as being, by and large, simultaneously active.

We find that individuals have a realistic conception of who chooses them and rejects them. This, of course, is not surprising, since there is more order than chaos in interpersonal relations. According to modern theory, however, the perception of others' response should be a function not only of the behavior of the stimulus person, but also of the needs of the subject himself (1, 2). In other words, one would postulate that, *other things being equal*, the Subject's perception (guess) of Other's positive or negative feelings toward him would be related to the Subject's *own* feelings toward Other; or, that the strongest hypothesis would be the one with most motivational support. This is indeed true, and probably the major contribution of this method is to have permitted a quantitative and unequivocal demonstration of this fact. The relationship between the subject's own affect and the affect perceived by him is discussed more fully in another paper (9).

To give the reader an idea of this striking relationship some data will be presented that are related to it. In *all* groups studied it is found that relationships containing *inter*personally incongruent bonds (e.g., S——> >----O; S——> [<----/>----]O; etc.) constitutes about 18 per cent of all relationships present. Relationships with *intra*personally inconsistent bonds (e.g., [——>/----<] O; S----> [>——/<----]O; etc.), equally likely in incidence, constitute however, *less than 3 per cent* of all relationships. This is one manifestation of the strong congruency between affect and perception discussed above. The tolerance for affective and perceptual inconsistency internal to the person is thus seen to be much lower than the tolerance for a similar inconsistency on reality bases, i.e., between the Subject and Other. The fact that perception of affect is simultaneously well based on reality and strongly determined by the Subject's *own* affects suggests the complex feed-back process of interpersonal actions and reactions leading to the concurrently adept external and internal adjustment. About thirty groups have been studied at the time of this writing and the relationship between perception of affect and affective response has been found to obtain generally, irrespective of the size of the group, the sex and the age of the subjects.

There are individuals who are exceptions to the good reality orientation of most subjects: some feel popular and are not, some feel isolated and are popular, some very grossly *mis*perceive affective responses. But there are practically no cases where there is a persistent lack of consistency in affect experienced for Other and affect perceived from Other.

## RELIGIOUS ETHNOCENTRISM AND ITS RECOGNITION

A study of "recognition" of ethnocentrism between subgroups of adolescent boys in a large preparatory school (5, 9), will be summarized to illustrate the use of Relational Analysis in investigations of relationships *among* subgroups. In this particular case, only choices and guesses were obtained from the 676 subjects, and therefore, the variety of diadic relationships is limited to sixteen types. Criswell (3) among others, has shown that the standard choice-procedure of sociometry can be used to demonstrate cleavages that tend to subdivide groups in terms of some important variable such as sex, color, religion, and so on. Here it was supposed as a matter of course that some religious ingroup preference would appear in the population of the school studied. It was a matter of speculation, however, as to whether the subjects belonging to the different subgroups would be *aware* of the extent of the ethnocentrism of their own and of the other subgroups. Relational analysis answers this question unequivocally for the population studied, in the following manner.

One could assume, if there were *no* religious ingroup preference at all, that the choices allotted by each subgroup would be distributed among all subgroups in proportion to their size. It was found that such was not the case and that each subgroup preferred to choose from among its own members rather than from other subgroups. The choices *received* by the members of each subgroup constitute their social field. The guesses (of choices received) made by each subgroup would then constitute the subgroup's *perception* of the social field. It was found that the allotment of both choices and guesses among subgroups differed from a proportional distribution, but not from each other. In other words, the perception of the social field was congruent with the social field itself. It was concluded that, in general, members of subgroups directed their guesses *as if* they were aware of the actual subgroup preferences present in the population.

## PERSONALITY ADJUSTMENT AND INTERPERSONAL RELATIONS

The relationship between personality adjustment and interpersonal relations was studied on the same group of preparatory school boys (9).

Modern theory of personality holds that personal adjustment is largely a function of "good" development in interpersonal relations; (4, 6, 7, 8, 10, Mowrer, 1950). It was thus postulated that well adjusted and maladjusted boys would differ in the adequacy of their social interaction and that such differences should be reflected in the relational analysis data. Two groups of students were selected from the experimental population: the first one consisted of 15 boys who were being seen by the school psychiatrist ("maladjusted") and the second included 20 students ("well-adjusted") who were outstanding in the sense that they seemed to be able to participate effectively in a variety of activities, from academic work to sports and hobbies.

The "well-adjusted" subjects differed significantly from the "maladjusted" ones in terms of:

a. their actual social situation (actual number of choices received is higher for the "well-adjusted").
b. their perceived social situation (average number of guesses). In other words, the "well-adjusted" "saw" more affection in their environment.
c. their "outgoingness" (average number of choices made).

In all the above instances the "well-adjusted" and the "maladjusted" had means respectively above and below those of the "average" boy in the school. It was concluded that the relationship between efficient psychological functioning and successful interpersonal relations held in this instance. Both groups responded to the perceptual part of the procedure (the "guess") *as if* they were aware of their respectively high and low social success.

The "maladjusted" subjects were also studied in terms of their accuracy in perceiving affect directed toward them. For this purpose they were matched, one by one, to "non-maladjusted" students who were comparable in terms of number of guesses made and number of choices received. The "maladjusted" did not differ at all from the subjects with whom they were matched in terms of their skill in recognizing affect.[4]

4 This finding should not be placed out of this context since its interpretation is complex and partly related to the fact that the very procedure for matching may have caused the selection of a somewhat unusual group of subjects. This matching procedure was necessary since the accuracy of the "guess" is partly a function of popularity as well as of number of guesses made.

REFERENCES

1. Bruner, J. S. Personality dynamics and the process on perceiving. In G. Ramsey, & R. R. Blake (Eds.), *Perception: An approach to personality*. New York: Ronald Press, 1951.
2. Bruner, J. S., & Postman, L. Symbolic value as an organizing factor in perception. *J. soc. Psychol.*, 1948, 27, 203–208.
3. Criswell, Joan H. A sociometric study of race cleavage in the classroom. *Arch. Psychol.*, 1939, No. 235.
4. Freud, S. *The problem of anxiety*. (American Ed.) New York: Norton, 1936.
5. Goodnow, R. E., & Tagiuri, R. Religious ethnocentrism and its recognition among adolescent boys. *J. abnorm. soc. Psychol.*, 1952, 47, 316–320.
6. Horney, K. *Our inner conflicts*. New York: Norton, 1945.
7. Moreno, J. L. *Who shall survive?* Beacon, N.Y.: Beacon House, 1934.
8. Sullivan, H. S. *Conceptions of modern psychiatry*. Washington, D.C.: William Alanson White Psychiatric Foundation, 1947.
9. Tagiuri, R. Related analysis: An extension of sociometric method. Unpublished doctoral dissertation, Harvard Univer., 1951.
10. White, R. W. *The abnormal personality*. New York: Ronald Press, 1948.


# *Assumed Similarity Measures as Predictors of Team Effectiveness*

FRED E. FIEDLER

SMALL groups of individuals, working as teams, committees, or crews, conduct the overwhelming proportion of the nation's civic, industrial, and military business. The effectiveness with which these groups

FROM *Journal of Abnormal and Social Psychology*, 1954, 49, 381–388. Reprinted by permission of the author and the American Psychological Association, Inc.

The research reported here was carried out under Contract N6ori-07135 between the University of Illinois and the Office of Naval Research. The investigations were conducted by a group in which several members of the project staff played a part during various phases. In particular, the writer wishes to express his appreciation to Dr. L. J. Cronbach, then director of the project, and to Messrs. Walter Hartmann, S. A. Rudin, Mrs. Mary E. Ehart, Miss Vivian C. McCraven, and Dr. W. G. Warrington.

function is thus of practical as well as of theoretical concern in our society.

This paper reports a series of related investigations which deal with interpersonal relationships within a team as correlates of the team's total effectiveness.

Certain aspects of interpersonal perception have been investigated in previously published studies on therapeutic relationships (3) and interpersonal relations in a social group (5). These studies present techniques for obtaining the so-called "Assumed Similarity (*AS*) scores," which appear to be correlates of liking and warmth in interpersonal relationships. The present series of investigations relates these interpersonal perception variables to team effectiveness.

A first, frankly exploratory study used 14 high school basketball teams. The most promising measures which emerged from this study were then validated on a second group of 12 high school basketball teams (6). The hypotheses derived from both studies were later tested on teams which differed markedly from the first group, namely, three- and four-man surveying parties (4).

## THE FIRST BASKETBALL STUDY

High school basketball squads are composed of from 9 to 18 players. These are chosen by the coach from a larger pool of interested boys competing for places on the first team. This study was conducted in the Midwest, where basketball is of considerable importance to high school players and coaches and where a large number of teams can be found.

### *The Instrument*

The tests used in the basketball study were forced-choice questionnaires. These questionnaires consisted of 100 descriptive statements grouped into 20 blocks of five statements each. An attempt was made to construct the blocks so that, in the main, statements within each block would be equally acceptable to the subjects (*Ss*), but descriptive of different personality dimensions.

One block of statements is given as an example.

| | MOST | LEAST |
|---|---|---|
| 1*a*. I find it easy to understand what others are trying to tell me. | | |
| *b*. People think I am a hard worker. | X | |
| *c*. I don't mind losing my temper when provoked. | | |
| *d*. I like people who don't worry about me. | | X |
| *e*. People often look to me for leadership. | | |

In a self-description *S* would answer these statements by making an X in the left square opposite the statement which *S* considered *most* characteristic of himself, and an X in the right square opposite the statement he considered to be *least* characteristic of himself.

*Test procedure and instructions.* So-called interpersonal perception scores were obtained by giving each *S* successively three separate questionnaires containing the same blocks of statements. Players were instructed as follows: (*a*) "describe yourself," (*b*) "predict how the person with whom you can cooperate best will describe himself," and (*c*) "predict how the person with whom you can cooperate least well will describe himself."

In addition to these interpersonal perception tests, players named the three team members—not necessarily the best players—with whom they could cooperate best, and the three with whom they could cooperate least well during games.[1]

## Interpersonal Preception Scores

Conventional tests are scored by comparing *S*'s response with the "right" response of a key. Our scores are obtained by comparing two questionnaires of the same person. This comparison yields the so-called "Assumed Similarity" measures listed immediately below. Tentative interpretations are provided which are based in part on evidence from previous studies.

## Assumed Similarity Scores

1. *ASp*—a measure of assumed similarity obtained by comparing (correlating) the *S*'s self-description with his prediction of the self-description of his *positive* choice, the best co-worker. High *ASp* appears to be related to personal liking and perhaps warmth for the chosen person (3, 5).[2]
2. *ASn*—a measure obtained by comparing the *S*'s self-description with his prediction of his *negative* choice. A high *ASn* score may, on the basis of the interpretation above, indicate a feeling of personal closeness and warmth for the negative choice.
3. *ASo*—a measure obtained by comparing *S*'s prediction for his positive choice with his prediction for his negative choice. This measure is interpreted as "set" to differentiate between people. Since *ASn* and *ASo* are highly correlated, we will concern ourselves here only with the scores *ASp* and *ASo*.

## The Criterion

Group effectiveness was measured by proportion of games a team had won. The date used here was December 31, 1951,[3] before many changes in

1 This paper discusses only procedures pertinent to the present hypothesis. A detailed account of the studies is presented in (2, 6, 7, 9).

2 *AS* scores can be computed as correlations or as difference scores. To avoid possible confusion we will in this paper speak of high *AS* as meaning high assumed similarity, i.e., a high correlation between either the self and the predicted self of another person, or between the predicted self-descriptions of two other persons. In terms of *D* scores, this would imply small differences between the two descriptions on which *AS* is based.

3 The original report (5) deals with December 15 as the criterion date. Since some teams had at that time played fewer than 4 games, the December 31 date appears to be a better criterion estimate.

team personnel had taken place and by which time each team had played from 8 to 12 games.

In general, small schools are handicapped by having relatively few eligible students. However, teams generally compete with other neighboring schools of comparable size, thus equalizing some of the differences which would favor large schools. The criterion reliability was estimated by comparing the proportion of games a team had won during the first and second halves of the season. At this time it was possible only to estimate reliability for the second sample which was tested with end-of-season criteria. The corrected criterion reliability estimate for these 12 teams was .88. The corresponding reliability for the December 31 date could not be computed because too few games had been played, but it is undoubtedly lower (7).

## *Relation of Assumed Similarity Measures to Basketball Criteria*

Our hypothesis states that interpersonal perception scores are related to the proportion of games a team wins. We tested whether team members of an effective team will, on the average, perceive each other differently

TABLE 1

*Correlations between the Dec. 31, 1951 Criterion and Interpersonal Perception Scores in 14 Basketball Teams*

| ASSUMED SIMILARITY MEASURE | CORRELATION (rho) MEDIAN SCORE IN TEAM AND CRITERION | SCORE OF MOST PREFERRED CO-WORKER AND CRITERION |
|---|---|---|
| *ASp* | —.25 | —.63 * |
| *ASo* | —.03 | —.69 ** |

* $p < .05$ according to Olds's tables (11).
** $p < .01$ according to Olds's tables (11).
The large number of exploratory tests run on this first sample does not allow interpretation of significance levels. These are here given only as a point of reference.

from members of ineffective teams. Here we correlated the team median of the *AS* scores with the criterion. As can be seen from the second column in Table 1, correlations between the criterion and median scores are generally near zero.

The group may, however, also express its attitude by the type of person whom most members of a team choose as their best co-worker. In order to get at this attitude we considered only the *AS* scores of those members of the various teams which had received the greatest number of "best co-worker" votes. As can be seen in Table 1, this procedure suggests that the *AS* scores of the team's "most preferred co-worker" correlate with the criterion in the negative direction.

In previous studies, high *ASp* seemed to be related to warm, empathic interpersonal relationships. We expected to find these relationships—hence also high *AS*—to be prevalent in effective teams. The present findings are thus in the direction opposite to that which was anticipated. They suggest that the most preferred cooperators in effective teams tend to be somewhat less warm and emotionally less involved with persons whom they choose as work companions than is the case of keymen in less effective teams.

The correlations in Table 1 are, of course, based on a small sample of teams, and on only moderately reliable scores, .62 and .61 for *ASp* and *ASo* respectively (9). In addition, they are the survivors of a considerable number of exploratory measures. A validation attempt, therefore, became essential.

## VALIDATION STUDY ON BASKETBALL TEAMS

The second sample of teams was studied solely for the purpose of testing relationships which were significant at the .05 level in the first study, i.e., on measures *ASp* and *ASo* of the most preferred co-worker.

TABLE 2

*Second Study: Point Biserial Correlations between the Criterion and Assumed Similarity Scores of Most Preferred Co-worker*

| ASSUMED SIMILARITY MEASURE | $r_{\text{pt. bis.}}$ | $t$ | $p$ |
|---|---|---|---|
| *ASp* | —.20 | .53 | |
| *ASo* | —.58 | 2.20 | .03 |

The only major modifications were in the method of choosing teams and testing significance. We selected, toward the end of the season, 9 teams which had had a predominantly winning season and 9 teams which had had a predominantly losing season, and requested their cooperation.[4] These came from the upper and lower third of a roster of over 50 teams. We tested 7 "good" teams and 5 "poor" teams which agreed to cooperate. Since the teams were dichotomously selected, point-biserial correlations were here used to estimate the degree of the relationship. The significance of the difference between the scores of "good" and "poor" teams was tested by the usual *t* test; inspection of the data indicated that the conditions for applying a *t* test were not violated. The small samples and the not very high reliability of the scores suggest caution in interpreting these data.

4 The writer gratefully acknowledges the invaluable assistance received from Clyde Knapp and Harry A. Combes of the University of Illinois.

As can be seen from Table 2, the point biserial correlation between the criterion and *ASo* of the team's most preferred co-worker is —.58. We attempted to validate two measures. Only one of these (*ASo*) reached significance. We are therefore not justified to consider the relation of *ASo* to team effectiveness in basketball as established. *ASp* of the teams' most preferred co-workers did not correlate significantly with the criterion even though the correlation is in the anticipated direction. We have plotted the measures *ASp* and *ASo* of the most preferred team members from good and poor teams. (See Fig. 1.)

| | *ASp* | | | *ASo* | |
|---|---|---|---|---|---|
| Q CORRELATIONS | GOOD TEAMS | POOR TEAMS | Q CORRELATIONS | GOOD TEAMS | POOR TEAMS |
| .55 | | | .55 | | |
| .50 | | | .50 | | |
| .45 | X | XX | .45 | | X |
| .40 | X | X | .40 | | |
| .35 | | | .35 | | X |
| .30 | X | X | .30 | | |
| .25 | | | .25 | X | XX |
| .20 | X | | .20 | X | X |
| .15 | X | X | .15 | X | |
| .10 | | | .10 | X | |
| .05 | | | .05 | X | |
| .00 | X | | .00 | | |
| —.05 | | | —.05 | | |
| —.10 | | | —.10 | X | |

FIG. 1. *ASo* and *ASp* of most preferred co-worker plotted against the criterion in the second sample

In addition, we also computed validities for the end of the season when all league games had been played. These validities are generally lower than those of December 31. It is clear from these data that *ASp* in contrast to *ASo* is not a promising predictor of team effectiveness (7).

## STUDY ON SURVEYOR TEAMS[5]

### *The Hypothesis*

The basketball team studies led to one major hypothesis: *Members of effective teams will prefer co-workers who assume relatively little similarity between the persons whom they choose and those whom they reject as their own co-workers.*

5 The writer is indebted to Prof. M. O. Schmidt, Civil Engineering Department, University of Illinois, whose interest and cooperation made this phase of the study possible.

Since we interpret high *AS* to be indicative of warmth toward, and acceptance of, others we also explored whether team effectiveness and congeniality are negatively related.

The following study was designed to test this hypothesis, and to obtain evidence regarding the additional question.

## *Selection of Groups*

Student surveying parties work in teams of three to four men. The *Ss* were 71 civil engineering students taking a required course in surveying. The course consists of two parts. The first part is taught on the university campus on a full-day basis, lasting three weeks; the second part covers five weeks. This is offered at a university-operated surveying camp in northern Minnesota where students concentrate on field problems in relatively difficult terrain. The camp is almost completely isolated and self-contained. Students as well as faculty members eat, sleep, and work there, and students are under practically continuous supervision of their instructors.

*Organization of the course at camp.* While at camp, the students were divided into six sections, one instructor remaining in charge of each of the sections throughout the camp period. Each section consisted of three or four parties, and each of the parties consisted of three or four men. A total of 22 surveying parties was formed.

*Differences between basketball teams and surveying parties.* Obviously basketball teams differ in many respects from surveying parties. The differences which we considered among the most important are the following:

*a.* Basketball teams require physical coordination, relatively little verbal interaction. Surveying is primarily an intellectual task requiring frequent verbal communication.

*b.* While basketball squads consist of 9–18 members, the surveying parties in our study were no larger than four men.

*c.* Basketball teams work under considerable time pressure. Speed in surveying is only of secondary importance.

*d.* Members of basketball teams are highly identified with the team, and personally involved with their team's success. This identification and involvement is almost completely absent in surveying teams. The students were graded individually, and no benefits were derived from being in a "good" surveying party. This is shown by the fact that none of the students were interested in their instructor's opinion of their *team.*

## *The Instrument*

As in the basketball studies, *Ss* responded to three identical questionnaires, predicting a preferred, and predicting a rejected co-worker. Unlike the forced-choice questionnaires used in the basketball study, the surveyor tests consisted of 60 statements, each of which was to be marked on a seven-point scale ranging from *definitely true* to *definitely untrue.* The statements were pretested on a

180-item questionnaire.[6] Statements were selected on the basis of an item analysis to obtain items with large variances on self-descriptions. Statements such as "I am very discriminating in my choice of friends," "I am not likely to admit defeat," or "when a person is a failure it is his own fault," were used. The instrument presents a considerable improvement over the tests used in the basketball studies. The reliabilities for *ASp* and *ASo* are .83 and .93 respectively (2). In addition, the tests require less time for administration.

By comparing the two tests by means of the statistic *D* (1), it is possible to obtain a score indicating how similarly any two of the questionnaires have been marked.

*Test procedure and instructions.* The instructions and administration of questionnaires followed those of the basketball studies, with a few, relatively minor, exceptions. The *Ss* could predict their preferred and least preferred persons from among those with whom they had previously worked. These did not have to be persons at the camp. The *Ss* again completed sociometrics regarding the three persons within their section (10–15 *Ss*) whom they personally liked most and liked least. They similarly named three *Ss* whom they preferred most, and the three whom they preferred least as co-workers.

## *The Criteria of Effectiveness*

Instructors were asked to rank all teams in their section in terms of the following:

*a. Accuracy* with which surveying jobs were done by various parties.

*b. Speed* with which the jobs were done.

*c. Congeniality* of the teams in terms of lack of conflict and smooth-running field operations.

In addition, students in all sections were asked to "rank all parties in the section from best to poorest." This constitutes our *students' ratings* criterion.[7]

Accuracy is the main criterion in surveying. It was, therefore, the only criterion on which we attempted to validate the hypothesis derived from the basketball study. The one-tailed test of significance was applied, therefore, to the accuracy criterion only. Tests relating to other criteria were exploratory.

Each instructor could rank only the three or four surveying parties in his own section. Ranking of parties from different sections was standardized to permit comparison of all parties. *AS* scores for all 22 teams could then be correlated with the various criteria.

The fact that instructors' frames of reference differ decreases to some

6 We are indebted to Col. R. W. Faubion, Commanding Officer, Det. #3, Human Resources Research Center, Chanute Air Force Base, for permission to pretest this instrument.

7 Students' ratings of Section V could not be used. The *Ss* in that section had been in more than one surveying party, and a number of students rated teams other than the main teams rated by the instructor of that section.

extent the criterion reliability. This would tend to obscure any relationships present, and it would increase the probability of accepting the null hypothesis when a true difference exists. Table 3 presents the intercorrelations of the four criteria used in this study for three- and four-man parties.

## *Relation of Assumed Similarity Measures to Criteria in Surveying*

*The accuracy criterion.* Our major hypothesis states that the assumed similarity of most preferred co-workers in good teams will be relatively

TABLE 3

*Intercorrelations* (r) *of Criteria for Three- and Four-Man Surveyor Teams:* *

| | ACCURACY | SPEED | CONGENIALITY RATINGS |
|---|---|---|---|
| Speed | ·79 | | |
| Congeniality ratings | ·15 | ·52 | |
| Student ratings | —·34 | ·15 | ·39 |

* (See footnote 7.) Based on *N*'s of 22, except correlations with the student rating criterion in which *N*'s = 18.

low. The preferred co-workers in relatively poor teams will have high *ASo* scores.

Our population of teams consists of 22 surveying parties, divided into six different sections. This division presents difficulties in statistical treatment of the data since no criterion was available for comparing teams from different sections. We have here tested the hypothesis by two methods.

*a.* We compare the best and the poorest teams within each of the six sections. We can then ask whether the *AS* scores of the preferred co-worker in the best team from each section are lower than the *AS* scores of the preferred co-worker in the poorest team in each section. Since the two teams for each section are evaluated by the same instructor, the matched *t* test can here be used. This does, however, reduce to 12 the number of teams (cases) used in the analysis. (See Table 4.) As can be seen in Table 4, *ASo* differences are significant. *ASp* shows only a negligible difference.

*b.* A somewhat more satisfactory indication of the *degree* of relation comes from a second analysis. Citerion ratings were converted to *z* scores, and then correlated with the most preferred co-workers' *AS* scores, both *ASp* and *ASo.*

Table 4 also presents the *r*'s between the primary criterion, accuracy, and these two *AS* scores. As can be seen, the hypothesized relationship has been found between the criterion and *ASo* of the most preferred co-worker. Hence, persons chosen as most preferred co-workers in effective (i.e., accurate) teams perceive a greater difference between those whom they prefer and those whom they reject as co-workers than keymen in less accurate teams. The findings thus are consistent with the hypothesis induced from the results which were obtained in the study on basketball teams.

## *The Secondary Criteria*

No significant relation was found between *AS* scores and secondary criteria. The relation between *AS* scores on students' ratings is, however, in

TABLE 4

*Comparison of* AS *of Preferred Co-Workers in Teams Rated Highest and Lowest in Accuracy*

($N = 12$)

| INTERPERSONAL PERCEPTION SCORES | MEAN OF HIGHEST TEAMS * | MEAN OF POOREST TEAMS | $t$ | $p$ | $r$ ($N = 22$) |
|---|---|---|---|---|---|
| *ASp* | 12.96 | 12.24 | .56 | | |
| *ASo* | 20.61 | 15.32 | 3.30 | .025 | —.51 |

* In terms of *D*'s. A high score indicates low assumed similarity.

the opposite direction of those found for accuracy and other criteria based on instructors' ratings. In other words, the students tended to rate those teams as better in which the preferred co-worker assumed relatively high similarity to his negative choice. This appears to lend some support to the interpretation that preference for a person with high *AS* is related positively to congeniality within the team. (See Table 3.)

The relation of congeniality and effectiveness was explored by one further step. An Intrateam Preference Index (*IPI*), defined as an index of congeniality, was devised and correlated with each of our four criterion ratings.

This measure of congeniality is based on the following considerations:

*a.* Each person had rated the other 10–15 members of his section in terms of how well he liked them as co-workers.

*b.* A subject worked in a three- or four-man team. He could choose his preferred co-workers within his own 3- or four-man team, or he could prefer others in his section who were not in the team.

*c.* We assume that a team whose members choose one another is more congenial than one whose members reject one another or choose outsiders.

The measure is computed by the formula:

Intrateam Preference Index (*IPI*) =

$$\frac{\left(\text{choices within} + \text{rejections without}\right) - \left(\text{choices without} + \text{rejections within}\right)}{nk - n}$$

$n$ = number of men within the team
$k$ = number of choices made by each individual

When this Intrateam Preference Index (*IPI*) was correlated with our four criterion ratings, the following relationships appeared: The correlation between accuracy and the *IPI* was negative (—.23), while other criterion ratings correlated positively with the *IPI*. The highest correlation was found between students' ratings and the *IPI* (.37). When we compare the most preferred co-worker's *ASo* scores of teams considered best and those considered poorest by students, we find higher *ASo* for teams rated high by students and lower *ASo* scores (greater perceived difference between most and least preferred work companions) for teams which students rated as poor. This relationship is not statistically significant ($t = 2.24$; $t = 2.57$ is required for significance of .05). The direction would tend to indicate, however, along with our other data, that effectiveness and congeniality may be inversely related in informal teams. This finding is in accord with the findings in the preceding basketball study. Moreover, it is supported by the results in Halpin's recent study of air crew leaders (8) and a paper by Schachter, Ellertson, and McBride on experimentally assembled student groups (10). The results are not in agreement with Van Zelst's study on construction workers (11). All in all, these data suggest that further study is needed to determine whether or not effectiveness and congeniality are inversely related.

## DISCUSSION

Two interpersonal perception scores on assumed similarity were correlated with the criterion in each study. One relation reaches the prescribed significance level every time. The studies thus support the hypothesis that the interpersonal perception variable *ASo* plays a part in group effectiveness.

We feel that the present findings serve primarily to emphasize that research on interpersonal perception in task groups is a fruitful area for continued efforts. This discussion will, therefore, be largely concerned with the implications of these findings for further research.

Let us first examine the measure which yielded significant results.

*ASo*. This score was obtained by comparing *S*'s prediction of his positive choice for work companion with his prediction of his negative choice. It is thus the similarity which *S* assumes to exist between the person with whom he says he can, and the one with whom he says he cannot cooperate. According to our data, the most preferred co-worker in effective teams tends to perceive these two persons as relatively dissimilar. On the other hand, the most preferred co-worker in ineffective teams tends to perceive these persons as relatively similar. Low *ASo* (i.e., large perceived difference between most and least preferred work companions) may, therefore, reflect an evaluative, critical attitude toward others, as contrasted with warm, empathic interpersonal relations. (Further research is needed to clarify the meaning of this measure.) We have found that *AS* tends to correlate positively with reputed therapeutic competence (3); in subsequent studies it was shown that *S*s assume significantly more similarity to a person who is liked than to someone who is relatively disliked (5, 6). Since *ASo* and *ASn* (*AS* to the least preferred) are highly correlated, we believe that the person with low *ASo* is relatively unaccepting, and perhaps rejecting, to the person who is not a good work companion.

*The most preferred co-worker.* While *ASo* in key persons appears to measure relevant factors in team effectiveness, it also points to a phenomenon which may be of more general theoretical importance. Only the scores of the most preferred co-workers correlate with the criterion. When we correlated the team's median *ASo* with the criterion, no significant relationships were found. At present we are inclined to take these results as an indication that members of effective teams use a basis different from that of members of ineffective teams for choosing and rejecting others as cooperators. This interpretation is supported by the positive correlations between *ASo* of the most and of the second most preferred co-workers in basketball teams (.63 and .27 for the first and second samples, respectively). In light of our current interpretation of *ASo*, this would mean that members of effective teams prefer highly task-oriented persons as co-workers. Members of relatively ineffective teams list as their most preferred co-workers the more accepting, relationship-oriented team members. *ASo* in the most preferred team worker is thus possibly an indication of the entire team's attitude toward the task, e.g., an index of the team's morale. Whether or not these relations hold in radically different teams, e.g., formally structured groups, permanent crews, etc., remains to be established.

## SUMMARY AND CONCLUSIONS

The present investigations test the hypothesis that group effectiveness is related to the interpersonal perceptions which members of the group have toward one another.

Interpersonal perceptions were measured by correlating identical questionnaires which subjects were instructed to fill out (*a*) describing themselves, (*b*) predicting the responses of their preferred co-worker, and (*c*) predicting the responses of their rejected co-worker.

The first studies used 14 high school basketball teams, tested at the beginning of the season. A second sample of 7 "good" and 5 "poor" teams was collected toward the end of the season for the purpose of verifying relations identified in the first study. A third sample consisted of 22 surveying teams.

The criterion of basketball team effectiveness was the proportion of games the teams had won (at midseason in the first sample, two weeks before the end of the season in the second sample). The criterion in the surveyor study was the instructor rating on accuracy. There was no correlation between the criterion and the median of any assumed similarity score within a team. The assumed similarity score, *ASo*, of the team's most preferred work companion was negatively correlated with the criterion in all three samples. The finding supports the hypothesis that *ASo* of the most preferred co-worker in surveying, and possibly also in basketball, is related to team effectiveness.

The interpersonal perception scores of the chosen person are believed to reflect his outlook on other persons and on the task. Low *ASo* is thought to reflect lack of emotional involvement with teammates and task-oriented attitudes. The group which chooses a differentiating person as preferred co-worker is thus likely to be more concerned with effective task performance, and correspondingly more successful. Some evidence suggests that the more effective surveying teams tend to be less congenial than relatively ineffective teams.

As in previous studies, we found that Ss assumed greater similarity between themselves and their positive, than between themselves and their negative choices.

## REFERENCES

1. Cronbach, L. J., & Gleser, Goldine C. *Similarity between persons and related problems of profile analysis.* Urbana, Ill.: Bureau of Research and Service, Univer. of Illinois, 1952. (Mimeo.) (Tech. Rep. No. 2, Contract N6ori-07135.)
2. Cronbach, L. J., Hartmann, W., & Ehart, Mary E. *Investigation of the character and properties of assumed similarity measures.* Urbana, Ill.: Bureau of Research and Service, Univer. of Illinois, 1953. (Mimeo.) (Tech. Rep. No. 7, Contract N6ori-07135.)
3. Fiedler, F. E. A method of objective quantification of certain counter-transference attitudes. *J. clin. Psychol.*, 1951, 7, 101–107.
4. Fiedler, F. E. *Assumed similarity measures as predictors of team effectiveness in surveying.* Urbana, Ill.: Bureau of Research and Service, Univer. of Illinois, 1953. (Mimeo.) (Tech. Rep. No. 6, Contract N6ori-07135.)
5. Fiedler, F. E., Blaisdell, F. J., & Warrington, W. G. Unconscious attitudes as correlates of sociometric choice in a social group. *J. abnorm. soc. Psychol.*, 1952, 4, 790–796.
6. Fiedler, F. E., Hartmann, W., & Rudin, S. A. *The Relationship of interpersonal perception to effectiveness in basketball teams.* Urbana, Ill.: Bureau of Research

and Service, Univer. of Illinois, 1952. (Mimeo.) (Suppl., Tech. Rep. No. 3, Contract N6ori-07135.)

7. Fiedler, F. E., Hartmann, W., & Rudin, S. A. *Correction and extension of the relationship of interpersonal perception to effectiveness in basketball teams.* Urbana, Ill.: Bureau of Research and Service, Univer. of Illinois, 1953. (Mimeo.) (Tech. Rep. No. 5, Contract N6ori-07135.)
8. Halpin, A. W. The relation between the crew's perception of the leadership behavior of airplane commanders and superiors' ratings of their combat performance. Paper read at Amer. Psychol. Ass., Washington, D.C., 1952.
9. Rudin, S. A., Lazar, I., Ehart, Mary E., & Cronbach, L. J. *Some empirical studies of the reliability of social perception scores.* Urbana, Ill.: Bureau of Research and Service, Univer. of Illinois, 1952. (Mimeo.) (Tech. Rep. No. 4, Contract N6ori-07135.)
10. Schachter, S., Ellertson, N., McBride, Dorothy, & Gregory, Doris. An experimental study of cohesiveness and productivity. *Hum. Relat.*, 1951., 4, 229–238.
11. Van Zelst, R. H. Sociometrically selected work teams increase production. *Personnel Psychol.*, 1952, 3, 175–185.

# CHAPTER 6 CONSISTENCY OF THE INDIVIDUAL

## *Individual Differences in the Social Atom*

HELEN H. JENNINGS

IN THE AREA of human interrelations—it goes without saying—the individual cannot be studied apart from the other individuals with whom he is interrelated.[1] Hence the problem of studying individual differences here involves not only the individual's emotional-social expression in choice and rejection of others but similarly the expression of other persons towards him. The sum of interpersonal structures resulting from the operation of reactions of choice and rejection centered about a given individual would comprise the individual's social atom, as defined by Moreno.[2] Obviously, if it is desired to study this sociometric unit, the social atom, in a given population, the psycho-social projections in choice and

ADAPTED by the author from Individual differences in the social atom. *Sociometry*, 1941, 4, 269–277. Reprinted by permission of the author and publisher.

1 The experimental material in this report is part of a study investigating individual differences in personal relationships and the character of the choice process (2).

2 Moreno defines the term as the "smallest constellation of psychological relations" comprising the "individual cells in the social universe," and consisting of "the psychological relations of one individual to those other individuals to whom he is attracted or repelled and their relation to him all in respect to a specific criterion" (3, p. 432).

rejection of each member of the population must be secured.[3] Assuming that by a sociometric investigation, the full expression of the members of a population towards one another are secured, the question then is: by what method of analysis can individual differences in the social atom be uncovered?

The method of attack upon this problem which is presented here was preceded by a study of individual differences in various expressions of the choice process in order to ascertain whether or not the various expressions are significantly correlated. If the findings should indicate that individual differences in any aspect of the choice process bear no relation to the differences in other aspects, it would then be futile to pursue a study of the social atom as a structural unit. Then, an investigator would be justified in examining *singly* the expression of the individual towards others and the expression of others towards the individual. Likewise, he would be justified in examining *singly* the expression of positive choice and the expression of rejection. Further, he might disregard whether choice or rejection are reciprocal, and treat as a simple sum the reactions of individuals towards one another.

To investigate the problem, three conditions of experimentation were considered necessary: (*1*) the experiment must test the population studied at two points in time sufficiently distant from each other to admit of structural changes taking place and being recorded; (*2*) the population must be allowed full, spontaneous expression, i.e., no limit must be put on the number of expressions the population gives by specifying a particular number, in order that the whole problem of expansiveness as it affects interrelation systems may be studied; if a given number of choices is specified, as has been done hitherto, it is not possible to study individual differences in expansiveness; and (*3*) negative expressions of rejection should be given the same importance as positive expressions of choice.

A sociometric experiment fulfilling the above conditions was carried out at the New York State Training School for Girls, Hudson, N.Y. The conditions of this experiment allowed unlimited expression of choice and rejection to the test-population comprising 443 persons at the time of Test I (January 1, 1938) and 457 persons at the time of Test II (September 3, 1938), and secured their expressions, positive and negative, towards one another on criteria [4] of significance to this population at two points in time separated by eight months.

3 The writer defines the social atom experimentally as: The constellation of psychosocial projections in positive choice and rejection by and towards the individual as secured under conditions permitting full expression for or against collaborating with others in common life situations (2, p. 324).

4 The criteria for choice and rejection were: (*1*) living in the same housing unit; (*2*) working in the same vocational group; (*3*) spending leisure or recreation together; and (*4*) studying in the same group. The findings relate to the 133 members of the population who were present for both Test I and Test II and living under like conditions in the community on both occasions; the findings are based on their reactions

Some of the findings relative to the choice process have in part been reported elsewhere (1) but may be repeated here as they bear on the present problem.

Choice and rejection as they are expressed by the individual or as they are directed towards him and the reciprocal structures found between the individual and the population indicate that the negative and positive aspects within the choice process are not two separate factors operating independently, either as they emanate from the individual or as they are focussed upon him by the population around him. Instead they form *one* choice process in which the negative and the positive aspects show particular relationships to each other.

Secondly, while the individual in his expression towards others shows increase or decrease on Test II in a manner that is not highly consistent with his expression on Test I, the average change in performance is insignificantly different from zero. (The critical ratio of the difference between the correlated means on the two tests is 1.65 for positive choice by the subject and —.50 for negative choice by the subject.)

Thirdly, the total impress of the individual upon the population, as measured by the sum of positive and negative reactions expressed by others for him, is significantly related at the two time points eight months apart. Fourthly, the positive expression of the population for the individual and the positive expression of the individual for the population shows only a very slight correlation on Test I and is insignificantly different from zero on Test II. This is likewise found for the sum of positive and negative expressions by the individual for the group compared with their expressions, positive and negative, for him, at the two time points. Fifthly, the positive reciprocations of the individual's choice expressions correlate fairly highly with the number of positive expressions for him, and also correlate significantly with the number of his positive choice expressions for others.

In addition to the findings just summarized, various other correlations between one or another aspect of the expression of choice and rejection, examined at the two time points, suggested that the choice process in a community does not vary randomly in its operation: when explored by comparing its expression within a population at one time with its expression at a later time, it is found to be characterized by a *particular manner of operation.*

It therefore appeared that the character of the choice process in its general operation throughout a population must similarly be reflected also in its particularized expression in the social atoms of the individual members of the community who were its "carriers." In the light of the evidence on the choice process it appeared that individual differences in in-

to the total population and the total population's reactions to them, at both periods, on criteria of uniform importance to the total membership.

terrelations within a social atom should be concomitantly examined on each of the six aspects found to be significantly related within the choice process: the positive and negative choice expression *by and towards* the individual together with the mutual expression (reciprocally positive or reciprocally negative) between the individual and others. The problem thus becomes one of examining individual differences in the individual's matrix of relationships in which he is the active focus and comparing it, as one unit, with the matrix formed around other individuals of which they are the active foci.

For this purpose, the positive expression of the subject for others, i.e., the number of individuals chosen by him for inclusion in his life situation, may be called his performance in emotional expansiveness towards others. Likewise the positive expression by others for the subject, i.e., the number of individuals choosing him for inclusion in their life situations, may be called the subject's performance in emotional expansiveness "achieved from" others. The positive reactions by the subject which are reciprocated by positive reactions from the individuals chosen may be called the subject's performance in positive reciprocation. The decision to include the measure of reciprocal reaction as an important performance (just as important as gross reaction by or towards the subject) rests on the finding previously reported that such performance is significantly related to several aspects of interrelations. The negative reactions by and towards the subject and reciprocated rejections may likewise be considered as three further performances in which the subject may be compared with other subjects. Each performance of the subject may then be studied as it ranks in respect to the respective performance of the other subjects, with the mean being taken as dividing subjects who have a plus (+) score in a given performance from subjects who have a minus (−) score in the respective performance. Whatever point is taken, there will be subjects who barely place within a + score or who barely place within a − score.

In the present analysis, it is convenient to describe the scores on positive emotional expansiveness in a given order: first, the expression of the subject towards others (number chosen by him); second, the expression of others towards the subject (number choosing him); and third, the reciprocal expressions between the subject and others (number reciprocating the subject's choice to them). Thus, the subject who has a − score in each of the above performances ranks below the respective average performance of the test-population. It is further convenient to follow the same order in describing the scores on negative reaction. Then, the total six performances may be called for brevity, the choice-and-rejection-pattern of the individual.

The presenting of the findings is simplified by referring to the first three performances (positive choice) as the individual's *choice pattern;* and the latter three performances (negative choice), as his *rejection pat-*

*tern.* Either the choice pattern or the rejection pattern, considered separately, gives a partial picture of the structure of the individual's total constellation given by his choice-and-rejection-pattern as a unit.

The individual may vary from average in a plus or minus direction in three scores on positive expansiveness; hence, there are eight possible choice patterns: −−−, +++, +−+, −+−, −−+, ++−, +−−, and −++. He may likewise vary in the same number of ways on rejection scores; hence, there are eight possible rejection patterns.

As any one of the eight possible choice patterns may be combined with any one of the eight possible rejection patterns, there are 64 technically possible choice-rejection patterns. However, in the test-population, counting both occasions, only 52 choice-rejection patterns appear: 12 do not occur on either Test I or Test II, given eight months later. Of the 64 choice-rejection patterns, only 10 are shown on Test I by five or more individuals; only 10 also are shown on Test II by five or more individuals; and 7 of the 10 are the same patterns. Such a finding was, of course, to be expected; the choice patterns and the rejection patterns cannot have a chance frequency since the choice process is characterized by significant correlations between one or another aspect of emotional expansiveness or of rejection.

The picture of choice-rejection patterns for the subjects as a whole is very complex and cannot be presented within the space limitations of this paper. Some of the findings related to the social atom of individuals while they are in a sociometric "leader-position," contrasted with the social atom of individuals while in a sociometric position of "isolated or near-isolated" will instead be included here as their patterns show a less complicated but equally interesting picture of interrelations.

For the purpose of examining patterns typical for the individuals towards whom the population as a whole shows unusual expansiveness in positive choice and towards whom they show unusually little expansiveness in positive choice, the subjects who respectively rank 1 S.D. above or below the mean may be compared, without regard to whether or not the position occurs on Test I or Test II or is shown by the same individual on both occasions. The position of 1 S.D. above the mean of the population may be referred to as a "leader-position" and that 1 S.D. below the mean of the population, as an "isolated or near-isolated" position, as the individuals occupying the respective positions are found in the one instance to be recognized and given "leadership" by the members of the community and in the other, to be hardly at all recognized even as participants by the population as a whole (2).

There are 43 leader-positions and 41 isolated-or-near-isolated-positions, as defined, found on Test I and Test II, counted together. The number occurring on Test I and Test II is in both instances approximately equal.

TABLE I

*Choice-Rejection Patterns Shown by 41 Isolated-or-Near-Isolated-Positions* *

TEST I AND TEST II

| | | | Positive Choice Pattern | | | | | | | | | |
|---|---|---|---|---|---|---|---|---|---|---|---|---|
| | | | 1 | 2 | 3 | 4 | 5 | 6 | 7 | 8 | | |
| | | | − − − | + + + | + − + | − + − | − − + | + + − | + − − | − + + | TOTAL | PERCENT |
| Rejection Pattern | 1 | − − − | 9 | | | | | | 3 | | 12 | 30 |
| | 2 | + + + | | | | | | | 7 | | 7 | 17 |
| | 3 | + − + | | | | | | | 1 | | 1 | 2 |
| | 4 | − + − | 4 | | | | | | | | 4 | 10 |
| | 5 | − − + | 3 | | | | | | | | 3 | 7 |
| | 6 | + + − | 1 | | | | | | | | 1 | 2 |
| | 7 | + − − | | | | | | | 1 | | 1 | 2 |
| | 8 | − + + | 5 | | | | | | 7 | | 12 | 30 |
| TOTAL | | | 22 | | | | | | 19 | | 41 | |
| PERCENT | | | 54 | | | | | | 46 | | | 100 |

* Ranking 1 S.D. below the mean in choices received: Test I and Test II. Each pattern represents the rank of the individual who shows an "isolated-or-near-isolated-position," as compared with the mean of the test-population (above the mean being indicated by + and below, by −), in three performances: the first + or − in a given pattern represents the individual's expression towards others; the second, the expression of others towards him; and the third, the reciprocal expression between the individual and others. For convenience the patterns are numbered.

Individuals in an isolated-or-near-isolated position could technically place in four possible choice patterns: −−−, +−+, −−+, or +−−. See Table 1. They are found, however, only in two of these patterns: 54 percent show a positive choice pattern of −−− and 4 percent, a positive choice pattern of +−−. They could technically place in any of the eight rejection patterns. Thirty percent show a −++ rejection pattern and 30 percent also a −−− rejection pattern, with the next most frequent pattern of rejection being +++. Their choice-rejection patterns are in order of frequencies: 9 −−− −−− ; 7 +−− +++ ; and 7 +−− −++. Thus only three choice-rejection patterns are found in 56 percent of the instances (23/41).

Individuals in a leader-position could technically place in four possible choice patterns: +++, −+−, ++−, or −++. They are found, however, in 49 percent of the instances to have a +++ pattern, in 35 percent to have a −++ pattern, and only rarely in either of the other two patterns. (See Table 2.) Thus at the time an individual has a leader-position he very likely will place above average in mutual positive choice with other individuals. On the other hand, the greatly above average positive expression of the population towards him may or may not be accompanied by an above average positive expression on his part towards the population. Similarly, as revealed in their positive choice patterns, there appears to be no relation between the extent of choice for others on the part of the individuals towards whom the population shows little if any positive expression: they show about equally often an above and a below average expression.

In marked difference from the isolated-or-near-isolated, the individuals in leader-positions show a +−− rejection pattern in 40 percent of the instances, a pattern shown only in 2 percent of the instances by the former group. Thus, in 40 percent of the instances, the individual in a leader-position in the test-community is above average in the number of persons he rejects while at the same time he is rejected by others to a smaller extent than the average member of the population and likewise has fewer than the average number of mutual rejection structures between himself and others in his constellation of interrelations. Furthermore, if all the patterns containing above average expression of rejection by the individual towards others are added together (rejection patterns #2, #3, #6 and #7 in Tables 1 and 2), it appears that 56 percent of the individuals in leader-positions, as contrasted with 23 percent of the individuals in isolated-or-near-isolated positions, are above average in the number of persons they reject. Thus above average rejection of others is found more often to characterize the interrelation pattern of individuals in the test-population who are very highly chosen by others than those who are very under chosen.

It is notable also that the −++ rejection pattern found for 30 percent of the isolated-or-near-isolated is totally absent for the individuals in

TABLE 2

*Choice-Rejection Patterns Shown by 43 Leader-Positions* *

TEST I AND TEST II

| | | Positive Choice Pattern | | | | | | | | | |
|---|---|---|---|---|---|---|---|---|---|---|---|
| | | 1 | 2 | 3 | 4 | 5 | 6 | 7 | 8 | | |
| | | — — — | + + + | + — + | — + — | — — + | + + — | + — — | — + + | TOTAL | PERCENT |
| Rejection Pattern 1 | — — — | | 4 | | 3 | | | | 6 | 13 | 30 |
| 2 | + + + | | 1 | | | | | | 1 | 2 | 5 |
| 3 | + — + | | 4 | | | | | | | 4 | 9 |
| 4 | — + — | | 1 | | | | | | 1 | 2 | 5 |
| 5 | — — + | | 2 | | | | | | 2 | 4 | 9 |
| 6 | + + — | | | | 1 | | | | | 1 | 2 |
| 7 | + — — | | 9 | | | | 3 | | 5 | 17 | 40 |
| 8 | — + + | | | | | | | | | 0 | 0 |
| TOTAL | | | 21 | | 4 | | 3 | | 15 | 43 | |
| PERCENT | | | 49 | | 9 | | 7 | | 35 | | 100 |

* Ranking 1 S.D. above the mean in choices received: Test I and Test II. Each pattern represents the rank of the individual who shows a "leader-position," as compared with the mean of the test-population (above the mean being indicated by + and below, by —), in three performances: the first + or — in a given pattern represents the individual's expression towards others; the second, the expression of others towards him; and the third, the reciprocal expression between the individual and others. For convenience the patterns are numbered.

leader-positions. The two groups, however, equally often show the −−− rejection pattern (30 percent for either group). The most frequent choice-rejection pattern for the individual in a leader-position is +++ +−−, as compared with the most frequent pattern of −−− −−− found for the individual towards whom the population shows little or no positive choice. Other differences between the two groups of individuals may be seen by inspection of Tables 1 and 2.

It appears that individual differences in pattern within their respective total constellations of interrelations mark the individuals who as a group are shown to be relatively highly chosen members of the population or isolated-or-nearly-unchosen members of the population. Certain of the individual differences are consistently prevalent in their respective patterns. Yet, on the other hand, in still further aspects either group may resemble or differ from the other in its pattern of interrelations. In the latter instances, the aspects of the choice process are apparently not crucially related to the position the individual is accorded by those in contact with him.

The patterns reflect the total impress of others upon the individual and the total impress he in turn makes upon others. The individual differences in structure of constellations of interrelations are seen to be very much more complex than the view permitted by study of the character of the choice process in its general operation, apart from the individuals themselves from whom choice and rejection emanate and upon whom the choice and rejection of others impinge.

The implications of the findings are more fully evident, however, only by inspection of the extent to which individuals in the test-population as a whole are found to have particular patterns and the persistence or the fluctuation these patterns show. The results of this study are reported elsewhere (2). From the few findings presented in this paper, it may be concluded that individual differences in interrelations between well-chosen individuals and individuals who are unchosen-or-nearly-unchosen members of a population appear not to be limited to the contrasting degree to which they are chosen but are reflected in the social atom in such manner that it is structured by various patterns, some typical for the former group and some typical for the latter group.

The conclusion may be drawn that the social atom, for purposes of studying individual differences in interrelations, may be considered a structural unit resulting from the nature of the choice process. If it is a structural unit, in a wider sense than here described, it should be demonstrable that the social atom of *a given individual* as it undergoes change retains some consistency between its "internal structure" at one time and at a second time fairly distant. The evidence from such an analysis indicates this is the case (2).

## REFERENCES

1. Jennings, Helen H. Sociometry and social theory. *Amer. sociol. Rev.*, 1941, 6, 512–522.
2. Jennings, Helen H. *Leadership and isolation.* New York: Longmans, Green, 1943. (2nd Ed. 1950).
3. Moreno, J. L. *Who shall survive? A new approach to the problem of human interrelations.* Collaborator: Helen H. Jennings. Washington, D.C.: Nervous and Mental Disease Publishing Co., 1934.


# *Consistency of Individual Leadership Position in Small Groups of Varying Membership*

GRAHAM B. BELL and ROBERT L. FRENCH

RECENT formulations of leadership behavior have accepted the general principle that leadership depends upon the situation as well as upon the personality of the leader or potential leader (1, 2, 5, 6, 7). Among the types of situational factors which might be assumed to be important for leadership status and behavior are: the nature of the group problem, the personal characteristics of group members, the character of the group's organization, and the external influences acting upon the group. Concerning the effects of variations in these factors, we have, however, relatively little exact information. The present study deals with one of these situational factors, the individuals comprising the group. The study was designed to determine the extent to which individuals maintain consistent leadership status in a series of informal discussion groups made up of different members.

FROM *Journal of Abnormal and Social Psychology*, 1950, 45, 764–767. Reprinted by permission of the authors and the American Psychological Association, Inc.

## PROCEDURE

The Ss were 25 male volunteers from the introductory psychology course. Except for one pair, they were unacquainted at the outset of the experiment. Over a period of six weeks each S participated in six five-man discussions, each discussion group including four other men whom he had not met previously. Thus, in the course of the experiment, each S appeared once and only once with every other S. This arrangement, shown in essentials in Table 1, required a total of 30 group sessions.

The topic for discussion at each meeting was a problem of adjustment confronting one or more persons of college age. Members of the group were given a mimeographed statement of the problem in the form of a short case history. They were instructed to discuss the possible solutions open to the person concerned, arrive at agreement as to what he should do, and submit a short written report of these conclusions. A period of 35 minutes was allowed to accomplish this.

Six problems were used, a different one for each week of the experiment, or, in other words, for each appearance of a given S. The problems were, very briefly, as follows:

Problem I: A college junior acknowledges the wisdom of his extremely dictatorial father but rebels against his demands.

Problem II: A sophomore from a religious, small-town family finds that acceptance in his fraternity depends upon participation in activities which he has been taught to regard as immoral.

Problem III: Jerry, who is attempting to work his way through college and medical school independently of his family, wants to marry Dottie, but will not consent to her working to help out.

Problem IV: On finishing high school Bruce went to work to earn money for college, and soon became a very successful salesman. When he had accumulated enough money, he asked his boss for a leave of absence to go to college, but was turned down and offered a better job.

Problem V: Norma and Joe find, even after separating for a year, that they are still seriously in love, but that marriage continues to appear impossible because of their religious differences.

Problem VI: A student eager for a career as a lawyer feels guilty and resentful toward his elderly father, who persists in endangering his own uncertain health by working beyond retirement age in order to help keep the boy in college.

At the end of each session, the members of the group were asked to nominate a discussion leader for a hypothetical second meeting of the same group. They did this by listing the other members of the group in order of preference on a mimeographed form.

Two observers were present in the room at all sessions. In addition to instructing the Ss, these observers made sound recordings of the discussions and certain additional observations for use in another connection.

## RESULTS

The leadership rankings given by each individual were converted to T-scores by means of Hull's transformation (4). Within each group, the four converted rankings received by each member were averaged to define his leadership status in that group. These five status scores for the five members within one group were then correlated with the averages of their status scores in the other five groups in which they participated. It was assumed that the average of an individual's status scores in the other five groups could be regarded as a measure of his characteristic success as a leader in this type of situation. A correlation between this average and status in the group in question (i.e., a sixth group) may therefore be taken to measure the accuracy with which the characteristic performance of the individual predicts status in a group of novel membership. Application of this procedure to each of the thirty groups yielded thirty correlations as a basis for appraising the average consistency of leadership status.

As Table 1 shows, these correlations ranged between −.03 and +.98, with an average $r$ of .75 (that is, the $r$ corresponding to the mean Fisher $z$). The wide variability in size of $r$ from group to group is not surprising if it is recalled that each correlation is based on five cases.[1] Although the 30 groups cannot be regarded as a series of random samples in a literal sense, it seems reasonable to assume that the systematic recombinations of individuals which the groups represent might approximate in relevant respects the combinations that would be drawn in a series of independent random samples of size 5. The standard error of $z$ where N equals 5 is .71. The standard deviation of the obtained distribution of $z$'s was .76. Granting the foregoing assumption, then, it follows that sampling errors can account adequately for such variations in the size of $r$.

## DISCUSSION

If the average correlation of .75 may be accepted as the best indication of leadership consistency in this type of situation, it would seem that individual characteristics are responsible for somewhat over half (56 per cent) of the variance in leadership status within the average group. Before concluding that the remainder of the variance is attributable to variation in group membership, some attention should be given to other possible sources of status inconsistency in this situation.

Errors of measurement represent one source of variation. By means of the split-half technique, supplemented by the Spearman-Brown proph-

1 As Table 1 also indicates, the design was marred somewhat by 12 cases of subject absenteeism (out of a total of 150 scheduled subject appearances). Due to the intricate character of the design, it was not possible to reschedule the incomplete groups. Analysis revealed no significant difference between complete and incomplete groups with respect to the size of these correlations.

TABLE I

*Summary of Experimental Design and Group Correlations*

| WEEK AND DISCUSSION PROBLEM | GROUP | SUBJECTS | | | | | r ** |
|---|---|---|---|---|---|---|---|
| I | A | 1 | 2 | 3 | 4* | 5* | .26 |
| | B | 6* | 7 | 8* | 9 | 10 | .94 |
| | C | 11 | 12 | 13 | 14* | 15 | .67 |
| | D | 16 | 17 | 18 | 19 | 20 | .94 |
| | E | 21 | 22 | 23 | 24 | 25 | .91 |
| II | F | 1 | 7 | 13 | 19 | 25 | .79 |
| | G | 5 | 6 | 12 | 18 | 24 | .75 |
| | H | 4 | 10 | 11 | 17 | 23 | .93 |
| | I | 3 | 9 | 15 | 16 | 22 | .72 |
| | J | 2 | 8 | 14 | 20 | 21 | .54 |
| III | K | 1 | 9 | 12 | 20 | 23 | —.02 |
| | L | 5 | 8 | 11 | 19 | 22 | .69 |
| | M | 3 | 6 | 14 | 17 | 25 | .52 |
| | N | 2 | 10 | 13 | 16* | 24 | .74 |
| | O | 4 | 7 | 15* | 18 | 21 | .88 |
| | P | 1 | 8 | 15* | 17 | 24 | —.03 |
| | Q | 4 | 6 | 13 | 20 | 22 | .85 |
| | R | 2 | 9 | 11 | 18* | 25 | .98 |
| | S | 5 | 7 | 14 | 16 | 23 | .82 |
| | T | 3* | 10 | 12 | 19 | 21 | .98 |
| V | U | 1 | 10 | 14 | 18 | 22 | .64 |
| | V | 2 | 6 | 15* | 19 | 23 | .34 |
| | W | 3 | 7 | 11 | 20 | 24 | .47 |
| | X | 4 | 8 | 12 | 16 | 25 | .90 |
| | Y | 5 | 9 | 13 | 17 | 21 | .77 |
| VI | Z | 1 | 6 | 11 | 16 | 21* | .97 |
| | AA | 2 | 7 | 12 | 17 | 22 | .19 |
| | BB | 3 | 8 | 13 | 18 | 23 | .96 |
| | CC | 4 | 9 | 14 | 19 | 24 | .75 |
| | DD | 5 | 10 | 15 | 20 | 25 | .80 |

* Subject was scheduled but absent.
** Between status in each group and mean status in the five other groups.

ecy formula, the average reliability of the status scores within the average single group was estimated at .73. The reliability of the average status scores in the other five groups, estimated with the aid of the Spearman-Brown formula, was .93. Correcting the average correlation between the two measures of status for attenuation raises its value from .75 to .91. Since a correlation of .91 implies 83 per cent of variance in common, it may be inferred that 27 per cent of variance in leadership status (or 83 per cent minus 56 per cent) is due to unreliability of the status measures.[2] If this

[2] Unreliability in this case includes two types of errors: (*1*) the error inherent in any individual judgment, and (*2*) disagreement among judgments by members of a group. The latter can of course be regarded as indicating incomplete group integration, but for a status measure based on pooled judgments, it must be viewed in terms of reliability.

interpretation is correct, then at most 17 per cent of the variance in status can be ascribed to changes in group membership. This amount is reduced still further by a type of measurement error not adequately evaluated by the above reliability coefficients, namely the error introduced by the use of ranks and the assumption of a normal status distribution within groups.

Two other possible sources of variation are differential changes in the subjects, and differential effects of the various problems. With respect to the first of these, outside experiences may have produced asynchronous, intra-subject variations in mood and behavior which could affect relative status. Likewise some subjects may have learned more effective leadership techniques during the experiment, while at the opposite extreme others may have become increasingly bored. The problems, even though similar in general character and apparently equal in their effects on groups as a whole, may have differentially affected the contributions of individuals within the groups, and thereby introduced some status inconsistency. All that can be said about these extraneous factors is that our observations yielded nothing to suggest that such effects were extensive.

As a matter of design, it may be noted that rigorous control of the latter factors is impossible where group membership is varied in terms, so to speak, of whole individuals. A control series involving groups of constant membership, although it would take care of the above factors, would introduce the further complication of a developing organization. A better general approach to the study of group composition as a variable in leadership would involve describing composition in terms of patterns of relevant personality traits, and studying experimentally groups constructed to fit predetermined specifications of this sort. Some theoretical and empirical advances will be necessary, however, before this kind of approach can be made very intelligently.

In conclusion, then, it appears that varying group membership in this situation accounts for at most a relatively small portion of the variation in leadership status. Leadership status seems to be rather highly consistent despite the situational changes involved. Obviously this finding cannot be generalized to all types of groups. The groups studied were small, were concerned with a particular type of task, met as a group only once under particular circumstances, and were composed of young men fairly homogeneous in educational background, social class and so on. Some of these distinctive factors, at least, would appear to be relevant to the degree of status consistency that might be expected. Nonetheless, it is of interest to note that roughly the same degree of leadership consistency was found by Gibb (3) when the group task was varied for groups of constant membership. If similar results continue to accumulate for other types of situations, the recent trend toward emphasis upon situational factors in leadership may require some re-evaluation.

REFERENCES

1. French R. L. Morale and leadership. In: *Human factors in undersea warfare*. Washington: National Research Council, 1949. Pp. 463–488.
2. Gibb, C. A. The principles and traits of leadership. *J. abnorm. soc. Psychol.*, 1947, 42, 267–284.
3. Gibb, C. A. *The emergence of leadership in small temporary groups of men*. Unpublished doctor's dissertation, Univer. of Illinois, 1949.
4. Hull, C. L. *Aptitude testing*. Yonkers, N. Y.: World Book Co., 1928.
5. Jenkins, W. O. A review of leadership studies with particular reference to military problems. *Psychol. Bull.* 1947, 44, 54–79.
6. Knickerbocker, I. Leadership: a conception and some implications. *J. soc. Issues*, 1948, 4, 23–40.
7. Stogdill, R. M. Personal factors associated with leadership: a survey of the literature. *J. Psychol.*, 1948, 25, 35–71.

# *Mother-Child Interaction and the Social Behavior of Children*

BARBARA MERRILL BISHOP

AN EXPERIMENT was designed to investigate factors in the interactive relationship between mother and child which might bear on the behavior and social learning of the child. Subjects for the study were 34 mothers and their respective children (17 boys and 17 girls) who attended the Preschool Laboratories of the Iowa Child Welfare Research Station. Ages of the children ranged from 3 years 4 months to 5 years 7 months. Each mother and child was observed for two half-hour sessions on different days in an experimental room which made available an assortment of play equipment for the child and magazines for the mother. The experimenter observed the session from an observation booth fitted with a one-way screen and recorded the behavior of both mother and child every five seconds in terms of a notational system based on a variety of behavior categories. The mothers were told that the purpose of the study was to investigate play behavior of children when adults are present, and that they were free to do as they wished during the period.

FROM *Psychological Monographs*, 1951, 65, No. 11 (Whole no. 328). Reprinted by permission of the author and the American Psychological Association, Inc.

In order to investigate generalization of child behavior from that evidenced with the mother to that shown in social situations with other adults, each child was also tested for two 30-minute sessions, under the same experimental conditions, with a young woman who was socially unfamiliar to him and who has been termed the "neutral adult." The neutral adult was given a frequency range of the main behavior categories within which her behavior toward all the children should fall. Statistical analysis showed that her behavior in all 68 sessions, although somewhat variable, approached as satisfactory a degree of consistency as could be expected in a free-play, interactive situation. A subjective evaluation of her behavior would indicate that qualitatively her manner, attitude, and social responsiveness were constant from child to child.

In order to offset any factors associated with the order in which the child was tested with the adults, the 34 children were divided into two groups matched for age and sex. For one group of children the order of testing was two sessions with the mother, two sessions with the neutral adult; for the other group the order was reversed.

The categories which referred to the behavior of adults included 11 main types: lack of contact, interactive play, teaching, helping, praising, structurizing, directing, interfering, criticizing, cooperation, and non-cooperation. The last six categories were supplemented by numerical ratings expressing the qualitative nature of the behavior evidenced. The following are the categories descriptive of child behavior: bid for attention, bid for physical proximity, directing, interfering, criticizing, indications of anxiety, cooperation, non-cooperation, bid for praise, affection, asking for information, asking for permission, and asking for help. The first eight of these categories were also supplemented by qualitative ratings.

Statistical analysis showed that the mothers evidenced consistent behavior from the first to the second session. The children's behavior was also consistent from the first to the second session with the mother.

Positive correlations indicated that the children reflected directly in their own behavior the mother's use of directing-interfering-criticism, strong stimulation, and suggesting types of control, and also the tendency toward nonacceptance of stimulations.

A high degree of specificity of control, represented by high proportions of directing-interfering-criticism and strong stimulations in the behavior of the mother, showed positive relationships of from .45 to .71 with measures of non-cooperation and of inhibited and reluctant cooperation on the part of the child. Directing-interfering-criticism together with lack of contact from the mother yielded positive *r*'s from .42 to .62 with non-cooperation, with inhibited and reluctant cooperation, with a tendency toward high specificity of control, and with strong and aggressive stimulations and refusals by the child. Positive coefficients of the order of .6 were obtained between the mother's nonacceptance and the child's tendency to give strong and aggressive stimulations and refusals; strong and emotionally toned stimulations by the mother showed positive relationships of from .52 to .71 to negativism and to inhibited and reluctant cooperation on the part of the child.

Correlations ranging from +.43 to +.63 between categories of mother behavior indicated that the mothers who tended to remain out of contact with the child also tended to be more highly specific in their control and more unwilling to accept stimulations when interaction was in progress. Correlations of +.34 to +.44 between categories of child behavior suggested that the children who tended toward high specificity of control also tended to be more negativistic.

Analysis of the child's behavior from the first to the second session with the neutral adult yielded some significant differences. Evidence for generalization of the stimulus properties of the neutral adult from those of the mother was found in the case of the following child behavior categories: strong and aggressive stimulations, inhibited and reluctant cooperation, and non-cooperation. The direction of the change was a progressive increase from first to second session with the neutral adult to the average of the two sessions with the mother. In other words, as the child became more familiar with the neutral adult his behavior approached that displayed toward the mother. The children showed a trend toward differentiation of the stimulus properties of the neutral adult, as compared to the mother, in two types of behavior: asking permission, and directing-interfering-criticism. A decrease in asking permission occurred from the first to the second session with the neutral adult, which showed a correlation of +.41 with a tendency to give a high proportion of strong stimulations on the part of the mother. There was a significant increase in directing-interfering-criticism by the child from the first to the second session with the neutral adult which significantly exceeded in frequency that exhibited in the presence of the mother. This increase yielded positive correlations of from .33 to .42 with directing-interfering-criticism, strong stimulation, and lack-of-contact behavior patterns in the mother.

The order of testing with the adults did not affect these trends.

This study has presented a method for measuring the mother-child relationship under experimental conditions. It has also shown in broad outline some of the relationships which exist between mother and child behavior, viewed in terms of stimulus-response learning theory. Further research is needed to investigate these relationships in more detail and to discover other critical factors in this interactive relationship which are essential to the systematic understanding of personality development.

# Validity and Constancy of Choices in a Sociometric Test

EUGENE BYRD

## PROBLEM

THE PURPOSE of this study is to investigate the constancy of choice behavior as expressed on Moreno's sociometric tests and in a life situation. The degree to which observed choices in the life situation agree with reported choices on the sociometric test, when the criterion of choice is held constant, may be considered a measure of validity. In an effort to determine the degree of change in choice behavior that is known to occur over a period of time, the original sociometric test was readministered shortly following the observation of choosing in the life situation. Lack of validity would be indicated by a change greater than that expected and measured by the test-retest method.

## BACKGROUND AND SETTING OF THE PROBLEM

The Moreno test has found extensive and intensive use in the fields of sociology, psychology, and education. Its fundamental purpose is to measure the social structure of a specified group. The sociometric test accomplishes this by requiring each individual of a specified group to select one or more individuals in that group on the basis of a stipulated criterion of choice. The standard method of obtaining choices in a sociometric test is the question-and-answer method (i.e., the individuals are asked to name their choices). These choices are usually written by the individual or, in cases of young children, may be written by the experimenter. Thus, by simply counting the total number of choices each individual receives from the other members of the group a rank order can be obtained and each in-

FROM *Sociometry*, 1951, 14, 175–181. Reprinted by permission of the publisher.
This study was made in connection with a research project being carried on under a grant from the Research Council of Florida State University.

dividual's relative position in that group may readily be ascertained. This is the basis of the group structure in sociometric studies.

The basic structure may be subdivided into groups of individuals on the basis of the number of choices received. Those individuals who receive the largest number of choices have been designated as *leaders*, *stars*, *most-chosen*, and *most-accepted*. Individuals receiving few or no choices have been called *isolates*, *unchosen*, *rejected*, *least-chosen*, and *least-accepted*. These names refer only to their sociometric status and may or may not agree with other behavioral criteria. One should use caution when using these terms to describe an individual as they are always relative to the group measured and the specific choice criteria used to determine the status. The status of an individual may also change and so an individual who is classified as an isolate on one sociometric test may not be so classified on another test or on the same test at a later date. It is important then to be able to know the degree of stability in sociometrically determined group status.

The following experiment was designed to investigate the validity of a sociometric test as measured by the degree to which observed choices agree with reported choices when the criterion of choice is held constant. In an effort to determine the expected degree of change in choice behavior the original sociometric test was readministered shortly following the observation of choosing in the life situation.

## SUBJECTS

The subjects used in this experiment consist of twenty-seven pupils in the fourth grade class of the Florida State University Demonstration School. All subjects used in computing data were present at the administration of the sociometric tests.

## METHODOLOGY

1. A sociometric test was administered to determine the group status. This test was of the paper and pencil type and the pupils wrote down their choices "privately." A single criterion of positive choice was used. No limit was set on the number of choices that could be expressed.

2. The subjects were next given the opportunity to make their choices in the life situation using the original choice criterion. On the basis of these choices group status was determined as in the sociometric test.

3. After all the subjects had expressed their choices in the life situation the original sociometric test was readministered and group status again determined.

## PROCEDURE

Prior to administration of the first sociometric test the examiner was introduced to the class and with the help of the teacher discussed some of the things the children liked to do. Although the selection of presenting short psychodramas had been pre-selected by the examiner the suggestion of "doing some plays" came from the children themselves. The class then discussed some of the mechanics and manners that would be necessary for such plays. It was decided that the plays could be presented in the classroom with those not participating to act as an audience.

### *Situation I—The Sociometric Test*

The examiner asked all the children to indicate the persons they would choose to be in their play.

When you give your play what classmates would you like to have in it? I want you to write down their names because you know them much better than I do. You may choose anyone you like and as many as you like. Write their names on the piece of paper you have. Miss B________ or I will help you spell any names you need help with.

After the papers had been collected they were told:

You can be thinking about the play you would like to give. It may be about something you have done, something you are going to do, or about something you would like to do if you had the chance. It isn't necessary to write it all out but know what you want to do in case your turn comes first.

No further mention was made of their original choices.

### *Situation II—The Life Situation*

After an interval of four days the dramas were presented at the average rate of two per one hour session; two sessions per week. No sessions were held when there were absences. Each child in turn was asked his choices privately by the examiner in order to obtain a higher degree of individual spontaneity and to avoid influence of a few individuals who exhibited obvious signs of wanting to be chosen in every play. No child with the exception of the last few knew when his turn would come.

After the choices were given, the examiner read off the names and those individuals chosen met in the corner of the room where the theme of the play and assigning of roles were given by each child who did the choosing. The play was then presented to the class. This procedure extended over an interval of eight weeks.

TABLE I

*The Expression of Choices by a Fourth Grade in Three Situations Having the Same Choice Criterion*

| | CHOICES RECEIVED — PUPILS | | | | | | | | | | | | | | | | | | | | | | | | | | | TOTAL CHOICES EXPRESSED SITUATION | | |
|---|---|---|---|---|---|---|---|---|---|---|---|---|---|---|---|---|---|---|---|---|---|---|---|---|---|---|---|---|---|---|
| CHOICES EXPRESSED | AA | A | B | C | D | E | F | G | H | I | J | K | L | M | N | O | P | Q | R | S | T | U | V | W | X | Y | Z | I | II | III |
| AA | | 3 | 123 | | 3 | 123 | 123 | 123 | 1 | | 1 3 | 123 | | 123 | | | | 12 | | | | | | | | | | 8 | 7 | 9 |
| A | 1 3 | | 1 | 1 3 | | 3 | | | | 23 | | 3 | | | | 2 | 23 | | | | 3 | | 23 | | | | | 3 | 4 | 8 |
| B | 123 | 123 | | 1 3 | 23 | 23 | 2 | 1 | | 2 | | 23 | | | | | 2 | | | | | | | | | | | 4 | 8 | 6 |
| C | 1 3 | 123 | | | 1 | 2 | 1 | | | 2 | | | | | 1 3 | 1 | 3 | | | | | | | 23 | | | 23 | 6 | 5 | 6 |
| D | 23 | 23 | 23 | | | 123 | 2 | | 2 | | | 123 | 1 | | | | | 2 | 1 | | | | | | | | | 4 | 8 | 5 |
| E | 123 | 2 | 2 | | 123 | | 123 | 1 | 23 | | | 2 | | | | | | 2 | 1 | | | | | | | | | 5 | 8 | 4 |
| F | 12 | 1 | 123 | | 2 | 23 | | 23 | 23 | | 123 | 23 | | 12 | | | | 23 | | | | | | | | | | 5 | 10 | 7 |
| G | 2 | 1 | | | | | 1 3 | | | | 13 | 2 | | 23 | | | | | | | 2 | | 2 | | | | | 3 | 5 | 3 |
| H | 123 | 12 | | | 23 | 23 | | | | 2 | | 1 3 | | | | | 1 | | | | | | | | | | | 4 | 5 | 4 |
| I | 1 3 | 1 3 | 1 3 | 12 | 1 | 1 3 | | 1 | | | 3 | 1 3 | | | 123 | | 123 | 3 | 3 | 3 | | | | | 3 | | 2 | 10 | 4 | 12 |
| J | 1 | | 3 | | 1 3 | 12 | 2 | 1 3 | 123 | | | 1 | | | | | | 12 | | | | | | | | | | 7 | 4 | 4 |
| K | 123 | 3 | 1 3 | 2 | 123 | 1 | 23 | | 1 3 | | | | | | | | | 12 | | | | | | | | | | 6 | 5 | 6 |
| L | 123 | 123 | 23 | | | | 1 | | | | 1 | 3 | | | 23 | | 2 | | | | 3 | | | | 2 | | | 4 | 6 | 6 |
| M | 1 3 | 123 | 123 | 1 | 123 | 123 | 1 3 | | 1 | 1 | | 123 | | | 2 | | | | | | | | | | | | | 10 | 6 | 7 |
| N | 123 | 123 | 1 3 | | | 3 | | | 123 | 1 | 2 | | 23 | | | | | | | | | 2 | | | 2 | | | 5 | 7 | 6 |
| O | 1 3 | 123 | 123 | 1 | 23 | | | | | | 2 | 23 | | | | | | 23 | | | | 123 | | | | | | 5 | 7 | 7 |
| P | 1 3 | 123 | 1 | | 1 | 1 | | | | 23 | | | 3 | | | 2 | | | | | | | 123 | | | | | 6 | 5 | 5 |
| Q | 123 | 23 | 123 | | 23 | 2 | 12 | | | | 23 | 23 | | 1 | | | | | | | | | | | | | | 4 | 8 | 6 |
| R | 3 | 3 | 1 | 1 3 | 123 | 1 | | | | 3 | | | 3 | | 1 | | 2 | 2 | | 123 | 2 | | | | | 2 | | 6 | 6 | 7 |
| S | | 123 | 1 | 1 | 1 | | | | | 123 | | | | 1 3 | | | | | 123 | | 12 | | | | 123 | | 23 | 9 | 6 | 6 |
| T | 1 3 | 123 | 3 | 1 | | | 23 | | | | | | 1 2 | | | | | | | | | | | | 3 | | | 4 | 3 | 5 |
| U | 3 | 123 | 3 | 1 3 | | | | | 12 | | | | 1 | 2 | 1 | 123 | | 23 | | | | | | | | | | 6 | 5 | 6 |
| V | 1 3 | 1 3 | | 123 | | | | 123 | | 2 | | | 3 | | | | 123 | | | | 3 | | | 2 | | | | 5 | 5 | 7 |
| W | 1 | 12 | 2 | 23 | | 1 | | | | 1 | 1 | | 1 | | 3 | | | 2 | | | 2 | 3 | | | | 3 | 3 | 6 | 5 | 5 |
| X | 1 3 | 123 | 1 3 | 2 | 2 | | | | | 12 | | 2 | | | 2 | | | | | 1 3 | 3 | | | | | | | 5 | 6 | 5 |
| Y | 123 | 123 | 12 | | 2 | 3 | | | | 3 | 3 | | 3 | | | | 23 | 2 | | | | | 2 | | | | | 3 | 7 | 7 |
| Z | 123 | 123 | 123 | 1 | | | | 1 | | 123 | 1 | | 1 | 1 | | 123 | | | | 3 | 1 | | | 1 3 | | | | 12 | 5 | 7 |
| TOTAL CHOICES REC'D I | 21 | 19 | 15 | 11 | 9 | 9 | 7 | 6 | 6 | 6 | 6 | 6 | 5 | 5 | 4 | 3 | 3 | 3 | 3 | 2 | 2 | 1 | 1 | 1 | 1 | 0 | 0 | 155 | | |
| II | 12 | 18 | 11 | 5 | 11 | 9 | 8 | 3 | 6 | 9 | 4 | 10 | 2 | 4 | 4 | 4 | 7 | 11 | 1 | 1 | 4 | 2 | 4 | 2 | 3 | 1 | 4 | | 160 | |
| III | 21 | 20 | 15 | 6 | 10 | 10 | 6 | 4 | 5 | 6 | 6 | 11 | 5 | 3 | 4 | 2 | 5 | 4 | 2 | 4 | 4 | 2 | 2 | 2 | 3 | 1 | 3 | | | 166 |

### *Situation III—The Sociometric Retest*

One week after the last drama was presented a second sociometric test was given. The children were told they would have an opportunity to give another play. The original sociometric test procedure was then repeated.

## RESULTS

The choices made in all three situations are presented in Table 1. The subjects are listed in rank order of choices received on the first sociometric test in Situation I. The vertical columns contain the choices received. The horizontal rows contain the choices expressed. The numbers 1, 2, and 3 indicate the situation in which a choice was expressed. For example, pupil AA chose pupil B in all three situations. These choices are indicated by 1-2-3- under B's name. Since B also chose AA in all three situations these choices are indicated with 1-2-3- under AA's name. Individual totals in each situation, of choices received, and choices made are indicated.

## CONSTANCY OF CHOICE EXPRESSION

The total number of choices made by the group are: Situation 1, 155; Situation II, 160; Situation III, 166. As a group the *number* of choices made tends to remain constant over a two month period.

In order to determine the extent to which the subjects choose the *same* individuals in any two situations a ratio was computed between the number of choices repeated in any two situations and the total number of choices expressed by the group in one of those situations. These results are presented in Table 2.

TABLE 2

*Constancy of Choice Expression as Measured by Repeated Choices*

| SITUATION * | TOTAL NUMBER OF CHOICES MADE BY GROUP | CHOICE REPEATED IN SITUATION | NUMBER | PERCENT |
|---|---|---|---|---|
| I | 155 | II | 73 | 47 |
| I | 155 | III | 89 | 57 |
| I | 155 | II & III | 58 | 37 |
| II | 160 | I | 73 | 46 |
| II | 160 | III | 93 | 58 |
| II | 160 | I & III | 58 | 36 |
| III | 166 | I | 89 | 54 |
| III | 166 | II | 93 | 56 |
| III | 166 | I & II | 58 | 35 |

* Situation I–Sociometric Test
Situation II–Life Situation
Situation III–Sociometric Retest

Of 155 choices expressed in the original sociometric test (Situation I) 73 (47 percent) were reexpressed for the same individuals in the life situation (Situation II). Of 155 choices expressed in Situation I, 89 (57 percent) were reexpressed for the same individuals on the readministration of the sociometric test (Situation III). Of 160 choices expressed in the life situation 93 (58 percent) were expressed for the same individuals on the sociometric retest. Of 155 choices on the original sociometric test 58 (37 percent) were expressed for the same individuals in *both* the life situation and the sociometric retest.

These figures show that as a group about half of the choices expressed are for the same individuals from one situation to another regardless of whether they are written on paper or expressed in a life situation. This would suggest that the choice criterion was not psychologically different between the two situations as reflected by the group. How does this change in expression of choices affect the group status?

## CONSTANCY OF CHOICE STATUS

In order to measure the degree of constancy of the group status from one situation to another the Spearman Rank-Difference correlation method was used.[1] Tied scores were given a common rank equal to the mean of the ranks involved. The coefficients found are as follows:

| | |
|---|---|
| Situation I and II | Rho = .76 ± .09 |
| Situation II and III | Rho = .80 ± .08 |
| Situation I and III | Rho = .89 ± .04 |

If a $t$ ratio of 2.0 is allowed then these three coefficients are not statistically significantly different. The coefficient of .89 ± .04 between the sociometric test-retest is relatively high. It also reflects the change in choice behavior we might expect from the changes observed in the expression of choices. Group status cannot change unless individuals change in their expression of choices. However, it is conceivable and likely that status is more stable than expression of choices. Leaders tend to remain leaders even though their choosers may vary. No attempt is made to demonstrate this hypothesis in this study.

It was stated that in order to measure validity of a sociometric test by observing the choice behavior in the life situation one must be prepared to measure the expected change in choice behavior that would occur during the interval between measurements. If the correlation between the sociometric test-retest is taken as a measure of this change then any increase in

[1] This method yields a coefficient designated by the Greek letter rho. For all practical purposes it is equivalent to the Pearson $r$. In no case does $r$ exceed rho by more than .018. For the formulae and computation of rho and its standard error see Guilford, (1, pp. 227–231).

change in choice behavior due to lack of validity would tend to lower the coefficients of correlation between the sociometric tests and the life situation. It can be seen that these are lower but, as stated, not significantly so. This data suggests that there is little indication that change in choice behavior as measured by a sociometric test is due to lack of validity in the test. The greater part of the change is probably due to the dynamic aspect of choice behavior *per se*. This study should only be considered as exploratory. Only one group of children and one choice criterion were used. Further study is needed using other choice criteria and other groups differing in degree of cohesion before more decisive conclusions regarding the validity of sociometric tests are reached. Other methods of measuring validity that are not influenced by the intrinsic change should be investigated.

## SUMMARY AND CONCLUSIONS

This study investigates the constancy of choice behavior as expressed on Moreno tests and in a life situation using the same choice criterion. This method is offered as an approach to the study of validity in sociometric tests. The sociometric test was readministered after choices were expressed in the life situation to determine the degree of expected change in choice behavior. The results of this study suggest that when a choice criterion has real meaning to the subjects, the degree of change in choice behavior between a sociometric test and a life situation is not significantly greater than that which occurs between a sociometric test and later readministration of the same test. The writer feels that the results of this study support the hypothesis that a sociometric test is valid insofar as the choice criterion has reality value for the subjects.

## REFERENCE

1. Guilford, J. P. *Fundamental statistics in psychology and education.* New York: McGraw-Hill, 1942.

# *Some Consequences of De-Individuation in a Group*

LEON FESTINGER, A. PEPITONE,
and
THEODORE M. NEWCOMB

ANYONE who observes persons in groups and the same persons individually is forced to conclude that they often behave differently in these two general kinds of situations. Casual observation would seem to indicate that one kind of behavior difference stems from the fact that people obtain release in groups, that is, are sometimes more free from restraints, less inhibited, and able to indulge in forms of behavior in which, when alone, they would not indulge.

The most often noted instance of such freedom from restraint is the behavior of persons in crowds. In a crowd, persons will frequently do things which they would not allow themselves to do under other circumstances. In fact, they may even feel very much ashamed later on. Such behavior is not, however, limited to crowds. It occurs regularly in groups of all sizes and of many different types. For example, a group of boys walking down the street will often be wilder and less restrained than any of them individually would be; at an evening party persons who are usually very self-conscious and formal will sometimes behave quite freely; the delegates to an American Legion convention, all dressed in the same uniform manner, will sometimes exhibit an almost alarming lack of restraint. The question with which we will concern ourselves is: *when does this kind of behavior occur and why does it occur?*

There occurs sometimes in groups a state of affairs in which the individuals act as if they were "submerged in the group." Such a state of affairs may be described as one of de-individuation; that is, individuals are

FROM *Journal of Abnormal and Social Psychology*, 1952, 47, 382–389. Reprinted by permission of the authors and the American Psychological Association, Inc.

This study was done at the Research Center for Group Dynamics at the University of Michigan.

not seen or paid attention to as individuals. The members do not feel that they stand out as individuals. Others are not singling a person out for attention nor is the person singling out others.

We would like to advance the theory that, under conditions where the member is not individuated in the group, there is likely to occur for the member a reduction of inner restraints against doing various things. In other words, many of the behaviors which the individual wants to perform but which are otherwise impossible to do because of the existence, within himself, of restraints, become possible under conditions of de-individuation in a group.

If individuals, then, have needs which they are generally unable to satisfy because of the existence of inner restraints against doing certain things, a state of de-individuation in a group makes it possible for them to obtain satisfaction of these needs. A group situation where de-individuation does occur will consequently be more satisfying, other things being equal, than one where de-individuation never takes place. We would expect groups which do occasionally provide conditions of de-individuation to be more attractive to their members.

The satisfaction obtained during states of de-individuation is only one of many kinds of satisfactions which persons obtain in groups. Groups help people achieve goals which require joint or cooperative action, they provide support for opinions and behavior patterns, they sometimes satisfy persons' needs for approval and status, and the like. Many kinds of satisfactions which groups provide and which, consequently, make groups attractive to members may be put into two incompatible classes:

1. *Those which necessitate individuation in the group.* Prestige and status in a group, for example, require singling out an individual and behaving toward him in a special manner. Helping members achieve certain of their goals requires paying attention to the individual and to his particular needs.

2. *Those which necessitate de-individuation in the group.* These are the satisfactions which result from the lessening of inner restraints which we have discussed above.

It is clear that these two classes are incompatible in the sense that groups cannot provide both individuation and de-individuation at the same time. Groups can, however, provide both on different occasions.

Groups which can provide only states of de-individuation are probably not very stable. Crowds are a good example of this kind of group. The momentary and evanescent existence of crowds is probably due to the inability of this type of group to satisfy needs requiring individuation. On the other hand, groups which can provide only conditions of individuation are probably not very satisfying to their members. A group, for example, in which members were constantly being singled out for praise, approval and attention would most likely prove frustrating in the long run. Groups which succeed in being very attractive to their members probably provide both types of situations on different occasions.

As a beginning toward support of this theory concerning the consequences of de-individuation we set out, in the present study, to demonstrate:

1. That the phenomenon of de-individuation in the group occurs and is accompanied by a reduction in inner restraint for the members.

2. That groups in which inner restraints are reduced are more attractive to their members than groups in which this does not occur.

The attempt was made, in a laboratory situation, to provide conditions which would facilitate de-individuation in the group and would also provide adequate opportunities for measurement. To do this, we wanted to create a situation in which there would be a strong force acting on the members to engage in some behavior against which there were strong inner restraints. Under such conditions some groups would be better able to create de-individuation situations than others. If de-individuation in the group did occur it would seem, from our theory regarding the phenomenon, that during such periods of de-individuation individuals in the group would not be paying particular attention to other individuals *qua* individuals. If this were true then, while being attentive to, and consequently well able to remember, what was done in the group, they should be less attentive to and less well able to remember which particular member had done what.

The extent to which inner restraints against engaging in the particular behavior were reduced should be reflected in the extent to which the members showed the behavior in question. This measure would undoubtedly be subject to error because of variation from group to group in the strength of the force acting on the members to engage in the behavior. If, however, we find a positive correlation between the extent to which the behavior in question was produced and the extent to which they were unable to identify who did what, this would be evidence supporting our theory of de-individuation in the group.

In those groups in which the restraints against engaging in the particular behavior were reduced the members would have obtained more satisfaction from the group situation. From our theoretical considerations we would consequently expect that the groups which did provide the conditions for de-individuation would be more attractive to their members.

## PROCEDURE

The subjects (*Ss*) for the study were males who volunteered in various undergraduate classes at the University of Michigan to participate in a group experiment. Seven volunteers were scheduled for each session, but for various reasons (study pressures, forgetfulness, etc.) all seven rarely appeared for the discussion meeting. Our sample consists of 23 groups, ranging in size from 4 to 7.[1]

When they arrived at the discussion room, *S*s were seated around a conference table and were engaged by the observer in mildly cheerful small talk. This procedure was adopted to prevent excessive prediscussion interaction among *S*s which we felt might introduce additional factors.

When all *S*s had arrived, the experimenter (*E*) directed them to print their first names on cards so that each could be identified by the others in the discussion, and then proceeded to read aloud the following statement. The alleged survey and its findings are, needless to say, entirely fictitious.

"The following statement represents a summary of an important research project that has recently come to the attention of psychiatrists and social scientists concerned with problems of personal adjustment among students. Although the results are demonstrably reliable, it is believed that additional implications can be brought to light by having small groups of students discuss their personal views relating to these results.

"A highly representative sample of 2365 students (1133 female and 1232 male) on 14 campuses, from all social-economic classes and several nationality backgrounds, was subjected to an intensive three-week psychiatric analysis consisting of repeated depth interviews and a battery of sensitive diagnostic tests. The results show unequivocally that 87 per cent of the sample possessed a strong, deep-seated hatred of one or both parents, ranging from generalized feelings of hostility to consistent fantasies of violence and murder. A finding of further significance was that those individuals who at first vehemently denied having such hostile impulses or who were unwilling to discuss their personal feelings in the matter were subsequently diagnosed as possessing the most violent forms of hostility. In other words, conscious denial, silence, or embarrassment were found to be almost sure signs of the strongest kind of hatred. Of the 13 per cent in whom no trace of hostility was found, the great majority thought they probably hated their parents and were willing to discuss every aspect of their feelings with the investigator.

"In summary, 87 per cent were found by modern psychiatric techniques to possess deep-seated resentments and hostilities toward one or both parents. Individuals in this category who most vigorously denied that they had such feelings revealed, at the conclusion of analysis, the strongest degree of hatred. Thirteen per cent were found to be free of such aggressive impulses. Most of these individuals at first thought they were basically hostile and were interested in discussing their feelings toward their parents freely.

"Discuss in detail your own personal feelings toward your parents in the light of these results. Try to analyze yourself in such a way as to get at the basic factors involved."

1 Eight female discussion groups were also conducted. These are not included with our experimental sample of male groups because of their considerably poorer memory with respect to who said what during the discussion. The results for these female groups, however, are in the same direction as those herein reported for the males.

The *S*s were each given a copy of the above statement and were asked to start discussing the matter. The discussion lasted 40 minutes.

The discussion material was designed to create conditions in which the phenomenon of de-individuation might occur. The particular topic was chosen because it was felt that most people would have inner restraints against expressing hatred of their parents and, in fact, many would not even want to admit it to themselves. In preliminary experiments, the statement given to *S*s did *not* include the part which indicated that those who initially denied it later turned out to be the ones with the strongest hatred toward their parents. In these preliminary experiments the most frequent occurrence was complete avoidance of the topic they had been asked to discuss. Including this statement provided a force on *S*s to talk about it. In other words, to the degree that *S*s accept the statement, they experience a more or less strong pressure to reveal negative feelings toward their parents. This, together with the inner restraints against saying such things, provided the conditions that we wished to create.

## *Observation Methods*

During the 40-minute discussion an observer categorized statements in terms of whether they reflected positive or negative attitudes toward parents in the present or the past; positive or negative attitudes of others toward their parents; impersonal theories about parent-child relationships; and whether they expressed concern with the interaction of group members and the discussion procedure. Each contribution to the discussion was categorized and recorded next to the name of the person who made it together with the length of the contribution in seconds. Pauses which lasted for 20 seconds or longer were also recorded. In order to permit a detailed analysis of the discussion, the observations were divided into 3-minute sequential frames.

Of particular relevance to the hypothesis being tested are those contributions which expressed existing negative or positive attitudes that the group members have toward their own parents, since from these we can infer the degree to which there was a reduction in the inner restraint against expressing negative feelings.

Experience in our preliminary experiments indicated that each contribution would have to be categorized as an entity. Frequently a statement would begin with the implication that the person loved his parents deeply and end with an explicit denunciation of them. The reverse also appeared quite often—the group member would begin to describe various hostilities he feels toward his parents, only to end with a highly favorable over-all estimate of them. Such examples made it clear that expressions of attitudes toward parents could be coded meaningfully only in terms of the contribution as a whole rather than in terms of specific and often contradictory statements within the contribution. When the observer could not make a judgment of the total unit, that is, whether the basic feeling revealed toward parents was positive or negative, she categorized it as "questionable."

To represent the degree to which inner restraint against expressing "hatred of parents" was reduced in the group, we calculated the difference between the number of contributions which expressed negative attitudes (categorized as *N*) and the number of contributions which expressed positive attitudes (categorized as *P*). The number of *P* contributions was subtracted from the number of *N* contributions because it was felt that *P* contributions were indications of the nonreduction of restraint. The larger the difference, the more successful the group had been in reducing restraint against the expression of negative attitudes toward their parents. Statements categorized as "questionable" were omitted from this calculation. Examples of statements falling into the two major observation categories follow:

Negative Attitudes (*N*)

"Frequently I get very angry at my mother and seemingly there's a good reason; but I don't get angry that way with others."

"There are times when my parents are so stubborn and bull-headed; they think they know best. Sometimes I don't think so."

"No matter how much I try to think that my folks are good to me, the fact remains that they've done me wrong."

Positive Attitudes (*P*)

"I respect my father because he's got a head on his shoulders; he's more of leader and a man."

"I feel toward my father that if I could be half the man he is, I'd be a great success."

"I respect my parents for understanding how important independence is for the person."

The observer [2] was trained intensively in preliminary experiments and in informal practice sessions. To check reliability, the experimenter independently observed one of the discussion groups. Calculating reliability by correlating the number of seconds of *N* in each of the 3-minute observation frames for the two observers yields a coefficient of .91. A correlation could not be computed for *P* because, in that group, it occurred too infrequently. One would expect it to be of comparable magnitude.

## *The Recording of Statements*

To obtain a measure of *Ss*' ability to identify who had said what in the discussion, the experimenter recorded, as nearly verbatim as possible, 10 [3] statements made by the group members during the discussion. The following criteria were employed in selecting these statements from the discussion:

1. The content of the statement should be distinct enough to permit identification of the person who made it, i.e., the statement should be as dissimilar as possible from those made by other group members.
2. The statement should be about a sentence in length.
3. The statement should be grammatically coherent.
4. The 10 statements should come from as many group members as possible.
5. The 10 statements should be distributed over the entire 40-minute discussion period.

2 Miss Dorothy Peterson, a graduate student in the Department of Sociology.

3 In 7 of the groups only 8 or 9 statements were recorded. This was occasioned by a lack of statements which fitted the criteria employed.

At the conclusion of the discussion, *E* made sure that the name cards were visible, and separated *Ss* to prevent copying. He then distributed a form and gave the following instructions:

"I am going to read off some statements that were made in the discussion and some that were not made. If you do not remember the statement having been made, place a check in the first column next to the appropriate number. If you remember the statement, but offhand you do not recall who made it, place a check in the second column next to the appropriate number. Finally, if you recall who made the statement write the first name of that person in the third column. This is not a memory test of any kind, and there is no need to guess." The statements were then read off in the same temporal order in which they were made in the discussion. Interspersed among the 10 statements, in constant order for all groups, were 5 statements that were not made in the discussion. These were included so as to provide a basis for comparing "Identification Errors," i.e., errors in recalling who said what, with "Memory Errors," i.e., errors in remembering the content of the discussion.

The *Ss*' response to the statements were scored in the following way. If, on any of the 10 statements actually made in the discussion, the person failed to recall who had made it or if he attributed the statement to the wrong person, he was given an error. The average number per person of these "Identification Errors" was calculated for each group. Errors of general memory were calculated similarly: Whenever an *S* thought that a given statement had been made which actually had not or whenever an *S* thought that a given statement had not been made which actually had, he was given an error. As with "Identification Errors" these "Memory Errors" were averaged for the group.

The *E*, in recording the statements, frequently had trouble meeting the criteria mentioned above. The statements recorded varied greatly in their identifiability. Sometimes a statement would be recorded and later on others would make very similar statements, thus making the identification ambiguous and difficult for *Ss*. Sometimes, when the discussion was proceeding rapidly the experimenter would not be able to record the statement accurately and consequently the recorded statement would be quite different from what was actually said. To cope with these difficulties some of the statements were eliminated from the analysis when there were good grounds for believing they were poor statements.

The specific criteria used to eliminate the statement were as follows: In groups of five persons or more a statement was eliminated if: (*a*) all or all but one *S* made errors on it, or (*b*) all but two made errors and the *S* who made the statement erred himself.

In groups of four *Ss* a statement was eliminated if all or all but one, including the *S* who made the statement, made errors on it.

When statements had been eliminated the average number of "Identification" (*I*) and "Memory" (*M*) errors was corrected so as to make all groups comparable with respect to number of statements. The correction consisted of multiplying the number of *I* and *M* errors, respectively, by 10 and 15 and dividing by the number of statements actually used in the counting of errors, i.e., the number of statements recorded and not eliminated.

The measure used to represent the ability of the group to identify who said what was the average number of "*I*-errors" minus the average number of "*M*-errors." The average number of "*M*-errors" is subtracted in order to correct for general memory level of the group.

### *The Measurement of Attraction to the Group*

A postsession questionnaire included an item designed to measure the attractiveness of the group for the members. The question and the possible responses are as follows:

"Frankly, how much would you like to return for further discussions of similar topics with this same group (assuming your schedule to be free)?"

...... definitely want to return
...... fairly strong desire to return
...... feel neutral about it
...... fairly strong desire not to return
...... definitely do not want to return

Numerical values were assigned to each alternative (1 for "definitely do not want to return"; 5 for "definitely want to return") and an average attraction score was computed for each group.

### *Explanation to the Subjects*

In each group, after the questionnaire had been administered, *E* explained the purposes of the study in detail to *S*s. They were told that the data presented for the discussion topic were entirely fictitious and the reasons for using it, together with the reasons for the rest of the procedure, were discussed with them. Sufficient time was spent in this manner with each group for them to leave with a good understanding of the experiment. They were also asked not to tell others about the experiment since we did not want future *S*s to know what was going to happen in the group. As far as the experimenters know, *S*s faithfully kept silent about it.

## RESULTS

There are two relationships with which we will be primarily concerned in examining the results of this experiment: (*a*) the relation between the frequency of negative attitudes toward parents revealed in the discussion and the ability to identify who said what, and (*b*) the relation between the frequency of negative attitudes revealed in the discussion and the attractiveness of the group for its members.

### *De-Individuation and Reduction of Inner Restraint*

It will be recalled that our measure of de-individuation in a group was the extent to which the members of the group were unable to identify who said what during the discussion (*I*-errors—*M*-errors). The measure of the extent to which inner restraints were reduced is the frequency of negative attitudes toward parents revealed in the discussion (*N–P*). From the theory we elaborated above we would expect to find them positively correlated.

(*The scatter diagram of the obtained positive correlation between these two variables has been omitted.—Eds.*) The correlation, including all of the groups, is only .22. One of the groups, however, indicated on the figure by an arrow, is considerably off the scale on poorness of identification of who said what. There are grounds for believing that this group was affected by a very different factor, namely, disinterest in the experiment and in the discussion.

The major grounds for asserting this are the great number of pauses in the discussion for this group. Observing pauses only of 20-second duration or longer, this group had a total of over 5 minutes of complete pauses during the 40-minute discussion. No other group had pauses totaling more than one and a half minutes. Most of the groups had no pauses at all lasting as long as 20 seconds.

If we can take this as indicative of disinterest and, consequently, attribute the poor memory in this group to disinterested inattentiveness to people, then, considering how far off the scale of the other groups it is, it may be legitimate to omit this group from the calculations. Omitting this group, the correlation between the two variables is .57. This correlation is significant at the .01 level of confidence. Our further presentation and discussion of the data will omit this deviant group.

It is also instructive to examine the relations between the measure of reduction in restraint and the *I*-errors and *M*-errors separately. We would expect the reduction in restraint to be positively correlated with the average number of *I*-errors alone, although this correlation should be lower because of the uncontrolled general memory factor which enters. The correlation obtained between *N–P* and *I*-errors is .31.

Perhaps a more accurate way to eliminate the general memory factor from this correlation would be to calculate the partial correlation of *N–P* with *I*-errors, holding *M*-errors constant. Table 1 shows the inter-correlations among the three variables involved in this partial correlation.

TABLE 1

*Incorrelation among I-Errors, M-Errors, and N–P*

| | *M*-ERRORS | *N–P* |
|---|---|---|
| *I*-errors | .24 | .31 |
| *M*-errors | | –.39 |

The partial correlation of *N–P* with *I*-errors, holding *M*-errors constant, is .45.

It is interesting to understand why the measure of reduction in restraint (*N–P*) correlates negatively with the number of *M*-errors. This is probably due to the fact that the less the members of a group revealed negative attitudes and the more they tended to skirt the real discussion topic, the less distinctive were the statements which *E* was able to record verbatim during the discussion. Consequently, the greater the number of negative contributions, the better were they able to recall what was said. It is also possible that the greater the extent to which negative attitudes were revealed in the discussion, the more attentive were the members to what was being said and, consequently, the more adequate their memory. It then appears that an increase in the expression of negative attitudes toward parents is accompanied by an increase in the inability to identify who said what, *in spite of* a general improvement in memory.

## *Reduction of Inner Restraint and Attraction to the Group*

Since the reduction of inner restraints allows the group member to behave more freely and to satisfy needs which would otherwise be difficult to satisfy, groups in which reduction of restraint occurs should be more attractive to their members. We should then expect to find a positive correlation between the measure of the reduction of restraint (*N–P*) and the average attraction to the group as measured on the postsession questionnaire. This correlation turns out to be .36, which is significant at almost the 10 per cent level of confidence considering both tails of the probability distribution.

There is evidence, then, supporting the two major derivations stemming from the theory about de-individuation in a group, namely, that it does tend to result in the reduction of inner restraints and that its occurrence does tend to increase the attractiveness of the group for its members.

## SUMMARY

A group phenomenon which we have called de-individuation has been described and defined as a state of affairs in a group where members do not pay attention to other individuals *qua* individuals, and, correspondingly, the members do not feel they are being singled out by others. The theory was advanced that such a state of affairs results in a reduction of inner restraints in the members and that, consequently, the members will be more free to indulge in behavior from which they are usually restrained. It was further hypothesized that this is a satisfying state of affairs and its occurrence would tend to increase the attractiveness of the group.

A laboratory study was conducted to test this theory and the data from this study tend to support it.

# *The Consistency of Subject Behavior and the Reliability of Scoring in Interaction Process Analysis*

EDGAR F. BORGATTA
and
ROBERT F. BALES

WORK carried out by Bales and associates at Harvard has indicated that the *between observer reliability* (for highly skilled observers) by session by scoring category for initiated behavior is acceptably high, with correlations ranging between .75 and .95, depending on the scoring category (2). It may reasonably be inferred that for comparable conditions self-self observer reliability will be equally high or higher. For the self-self observer reliability to be lower, it would require, essentially, that the non-systematic errors of two observers consistently be in the same direction, which is relatively unlikely.

Adequate tests of self-self observer reliabilities will have to wait until series of standardized materials (such as films) are produced for scoring and then rescoring (test-retest). Tests of self-self observer reliability are restricted at present to recordings and written protocols. Experience in both these as reported by Bales and associates is satisfactory, but actual formal tests have been extremely limited since the demands on the observ-

FROM *American Sociological Review*, 1953, 18, 566–569. Reprinted by permission of the authors and publisher.

This research was supported in part by the United States Air Force under contract number AF 33(038)–12782 monitored by the Human Resources Research Institute, Maxwell Air Force Base, Alabama. Permission is granted for reproduction, translation, publication and disposal in whole or in part by or for the United States Government.

ers have been sufficiently great that repeat scoring is ordinarily defined as a luxury item. Repeat scoring by trainees has usually demonstrated satisfactory reliabilities after three to four months of relatively intensive training. In a recent research project with the Air Force, one observer (Borgatta) required estimates of self-self reliability with written protocols. The protocols were responses to the *Conversation Study*, a projective-type form in which ten pictures (depicting three-man groups) are presented and the subject is asked to write the conversation which is going on. The ordinary writing time is two hours. The *Conversation Study* forms of

TABLE 1

| CATEGORY | TEST-RETEST PEARSON R. |
|---|---|
| 1 | .98 |
| 2 | .93 |
| 3 | .96 |
| 4 | .81 |
| 5 | .92 |
| 6 | .96 |
| 7 | .89 |
| 8 | .65 |
| 9 | .83 |
| 10 | .70 |
| 11 | .92 |
| 12 | .88 |
| Total | .92 |

eight subjects were scored and then rescored after an interval of more than four weeks. The scorer had had about four months of training at the time. The Pearsonian correlations are indicated in Table 1. Results of this order, while fairly satisfactory, are not considered to represent the best practically attainable. With greater experience specific improvement would be expected in terms of the establishment of more arbitrary criteria for making decisions, especially in terms of the categories in which known confusion of placement occurs.

It would appear, thus, that researchers may plan to utilize formal scoring techniques such as Bales' Interaction Process Analysis (1) with a reasonable confidence that training will produce observers who are reliable (or consistently arbitrary) in their scoring. A second question of reliability has not been considered in relation to Interaction Process Analysis, and this is that of the reliability of the "test" or *the consistency of the observed phenomena*. In raising this question it should be noted immediately that researchers working with the observation of groups would be greatly disturbed if they found extremely high reliability of the "test" or consistency of the observed phenomena under conditions which they suppose must vary. This is especially obvious in the analysis of phase changes within a given session, session to session changes, and more generally, in the expectations (or hypotheses) concerning the development of structure in the group over time. On the other hand, if common elements exist in the conditions under which the behavior occurs (i.e., the task, subjects, size of groups, etc.), a certain degree of consistency in the interaction pattern may be expected. It is apparent that in this type of study the term "reliability of the test" becomes inapplicable and the more correct identification is the "consistency of the observed phenomena." Few data have been produced in this area, although data which may be so analyzed in the future are currently being collected by Bales. Interest in the consistency of performance of subjects led to a limited treatment of some data in Bales' files. Five sets of data, each consisting of two or four sessions in which the same persons participated were analyzed to ascertain the stability with which each person maintained his position in relation to the other members of the session. In the case of four sessions, sessions 1 and 3, and 2 and 4, were combined directly. (A minor error is introduced in that the sessions were not exactly of the same length. This could have been corrected by conversion to time rates, but the additional work did not seem warranted by the additional accuracy which would have been evident.) The Pearsonian correlations are indicated in Table 2. The variance expected in correlations with such small N's is large, and in addition to this, the number of scores in certain categories is quite small as in the case with category 2. At the same time, the general picture of the correlations indicates that a positive

TABLE 2

| | | | | | |
|---|---|---|---|---|---|
| NUMBER OF PARTICIPANTS (N) | 3 | 5 | 5 | 4 | 5 |
| NUMBER OF SESSIONS | 2 | 2 | 4 | 4 | 4 |
| Category 1 | .40 | —.14 | .58 | .26 | .13 |
| 2 | —.62 | .67 | .94 | —.15 | .50 |
| 3 | .93 | .91 | .70 | .95 | .73 |
| 4 | .26 | .79 | .83 | .84 | —.13 |
| 5 | .87 | .84 | .94 | .91 | .58 |
| 6 | .80 | .79 | .98 | —.01 | .76 |
| 7 | .97 | .39 | .86 | .01 | .33 |
| 8 | .92 | .27 | .99 | .96 | .19 |
| 9 | —.03 | .01 | .33 | .97 | .61 |
| 10 | —.53 | .68 | .69 | .97 | .74 |
| 11 | .02 | .85 | .78 | .89 | .23 |
| 12 | .00 | —.25 | .96 | .00 | 1.00 |
| Total | .99 | .96 | .85 | .92 | .56 |

relationship exists between the behavior of the same subject from one time to another in all the categories. This is not a sufficient test of the stability of individual performance, but is sufficiently good to give the researcher some confidence. The correlations may be viewed as depressed by certain known factors (session to session changes, development of a status hierarchy, task changes, and many additional "interference" factors).

Again, in connection with a research project for the Air Force, a sample of 126 subjects was observed, using Bales' scoring system. The sample was subdivided into 14 batches of nine subjects each. Within a batch of nine, each subject participated in groups of three four times, each session consisting of 48 minutes of observation time. Each subject participated with each of the eight other subjects of the batch of nine, two at a time. Each session was divided into six units of time and two general types of activity as follows:

Actual behavior–get acquainted–six minutes
Actual behavior–plan role playing–six minutes
Role playing behavior–role playing–twelve minutes
Actual behavior–plan role playing–six minutes
Role playing behavior–role playing–twelve minutes
Actual behavior–relax–six minutes

Data were collected by time unit, permitting collation under several plans. The "*actual behavior*" of each subject consisted of four units of six minutes each for each of four sessions (a total of 96 minutes). Each session involved the same type of task, but presented a different *social* situation for the subject since in each session he participated with two new persons for the first time. The 126 subjects may thus be examined under similar conditions for the stability (or consistency) of their social behavior (as scored by the Bales system) which may be attributable to individual personality factors. The stability of subjects was examined by two plans: (1) The patterns of behavior of the subjects in sessions one and three, and two and four, were combined and correlated. In this case we compare the behavior of the same individual in two situations with two other situations, masking changes that may be present within sessions and revealing stability between sessions that may be present (in the behavior of the individual) in spite of the fact that different persons are present in the group. (2) In the second plan we compare the behavior of the same subject in one half of each of the four sessions with his behavior in the other half, thus masking the changes between sessions and revealing the stability over time within sessions when the same two other persons are present. The correlations for initiated actual, initiated role playing, received actual, and received role playing behavior are indicated in Table 3.

The plan (1) correlations are ordinarily lower than the plan (2) correlations. This may be interpreted as evidence for the hypothesis that a

TABLE 3

*Stability of Subjects by Category by Type of Behavior Observed (126 Subjects)*

| | INITIATED ROLE-PLAYING PLAN (2) | INITIATED ROLE-PLAYING PLAN (1) | INITIATED ACTUAL PLAN (2) | INITIATED ACTUAL PLAN (1) | RECEIVED ROLE-PLAYING PLAN (2) | RECEIVED ROLE-PLAYING PLAN (1) | RECEIVED ACTUAL PLAN (2) | RECEIVED ACTUAL PLAN (1) |
|---|---|---|---|---|---|---|---|---|
| Category | | | | | | | | |
| 1 | .38 | .33 | .30 | .23 | .40 | .23 | .28 | .26 |
| 2 | .60 | .15 | .79 | .43 | .30 | .25 | .71 | .14 |
| 3 | .79 | .64 | .76 | .63 | .64 | .22 | .70 | .41 |
| 4 | .50 | .46 | .71 | .61 | .43 | .31 | .59 | .34 |
| 5 | .67 | .47 | .80 | .59 | .56 | .29 | .68 | .49 |
| 6 | .66 | .65 | .72 | .57 | .41 | .28 | .53 | .29 |
| 7 | .49 | .28 | .53 | .53 | .22 | .13 | .18 | .07 |
| 8 | .48 | .46 | .37 | .34 | .21 | .14 | .16 | .09 |
| 9 | .43 | .13 | .21 | .00 | .26 | .08 | .09 | .10 |
| 10 | .47 | .44 | .51 | .32 | .51 | .31 | .54 | .27 |
| 11 | .56 | .34 | .72 | .43 | .56 | .29 | .54 | .36 |
| 12 | .62 | .11 | .61 | .02 | .35 | .13 | .56 | .10 |
| Total | .79 | .63 | .81 | .57 | .57 | .33 | .78 | .50 |

person will be more consistent, given the same amount of time, when interacting with the same individuals than when interacting with different individuals. The stability of subjects shown is sufficient to encourage us to believe that the interaction of an individual, as scored by this system, may tell us something about his personality, in spite of peculiarities due to the fact that he is interacting with particular other persons.

## REFERENCES

1. Bales, R. F. *Interaction process analysis.* Cambridge, Mass.: Addison-Wesley, 1950.
2. Heinicke, C., & Bales, R. F. Developmental trends in the structure of small groups. *Sociometry*, 1953, 16, 7–38.

# *The Dimensions of Syntality in Small Groups*

RAYMOND B. CATTELL,
DAVID R. SAUNDERS, and GLEN F. STICE

## I. HISTORICAL BACKGROUND

HYPOTHESES and experimental designs in group research deal with (a) the properties of groups and (b) the characteristics of individuals, in relation to one another or to various influences. It has astonished the present researchers that many serious writers are apparently prepared to indulge in verbally involved theories without having investigated the first essential fundament in these relations, namely, (a) above—the dimensions along which the attributes of any group are to be quantified. A theoretical statement of this problem was presented by Cattell in 1948 (1) and a demonstration research on 21 groups, of six women in each, was published by Cattell and Wispe (7) shortly afterwards. But otherwise—save for a theoretical appreciation of this work by Gibb (11), Hemphill (12) and Thorndike (18)—social psychology seems to have attempted little progress toward this goal, prior to the present research.

A large-scale investigation on leadership, group structure, and group syntality—of which this is the initial report—was begun immediately after the Cattell-Wispe pilot study, with assistance from the Office of Naval Research. While the pilot study has been criticized (18) for factorizing on a basis of only 21 groups, it was indeed never intended to fix reliably the dimensions of group behavior, but only to call attention to what seemed the best possible methodological solution to the dimension problem, and to explore its technical difficulties preparatory to a research on a larger scale. The studies of Gibb (11) and Hemphill (13) aimed at the

FROM *Human Relations*, 1953, 6, 331–336. Reprinted by permission of the authors and publisher.

The work described in this paper was accomplished under Contract NR 172–369 sponsored by the Human Relations Branch, Office of Naval Research.

same theoretical goal, were also on only a small population of groups, and the latter used rating rather than objective test methods, without the factorial technique here advocated.

Nevertheless, if one is to face squarely the problem which stands athwart the path of progress in group behavior research he must recognize that the dimensionality solution can only be obtained—even for any one sub-species of group—by a research planned and executed over several years with (a) a population of at least seventy groups, (b) a very catholic set of group behavior manifestations, covering at least eighty to a hundred variables, experimentally measured, and (c) a technically adequate factor analysis of this massive data. A consideration of the combination of experimental, statistical and organizational skills required, in relation to the training and resources current in social psychology will perhaps explain why this theoretically so essential experimentation has been so long deferred.

## 2. THEORETICAL BACKGROUND

For the researcher who has not read the growth of theory and research results in this area (1, 2, 4, 6, 7, 11, 12) neither the ensuing account of experiment nor the above historical retrospect can be quite intelligible without a brief section on theoretical background.

Our definition of a group is "an aggregate of organisms in which the existence of all is utilized for the satisfaction of some needs of each." This generally, but not invariably, *includes* the more frequently offered definition as a set of "interacting individuals" (10). The main sub-types of groups to be considered are: (a) overlapping vs. non-overlapping (requiring reference to the degree to which members get the remainder of their satisfactions from other group memberships), and (b) newly-formed vs. traditional. No group, however new, avoids the traditions carried by its members from other groups. These import potential structure which tends quickly to realize itself. Yet we must distinguish between this and the explicit institutions-in-being of a long established group.

Our aim is to establish the chief functionally meaningful group dimensions, but it must be recognized that every factorization or other analysis of dimensions presupposes a defined species—a prior statement of degrees of homogeneity in the population—within which the dimensions obtain. Hemphill's work (13) on the natural history of groups has helped clear the ground for recognizing these species. The species of group we have thought it most desirable to structure in this first application of factor analysis to the field *is that which is most common in all sorts of current small group experimentation* [1] *and may be defined as a face-to-face*

1 And also, as James's survey shows (15), as most common in everyday life situations of committees, neighbor groups, parties, small public meetings, etc. etc.

*group of six to a dozen young men, newly formed and with no tradition other than those potential in their cultural and biological backgrounds, without imposed formal leadership or structure, and motivated by possibilities of common gain amounting to 100 dollars (1948–50 value) through successful group performance in presented problem situations.*

One of the basic concepts of our work is that the description and measurement of a group requires data on three panels: (a) *population characteristics*—the statistics of the distribution of traits of the individual group members as such, e.g., average intelligence; (b) *structure*, e.g., form of leadership, status, roles, interaction, etc., and (c) *syntality*, that which is defined by the attributes of the group *as* a group, i.e., by its measured performances as an integrated whole.

Syntality characteristics, as the Cattell-Wispe exploratory study shows, are likely to be of all modalities—cognitive, temperamental and dynamic. For example, the Cattell-Wispe study indicated a factor of general "group intelligence" similar to individual "g," three factors in the area of morale and group integration, and a dynamic factor of group aggressiveness. It is unitary syntality traits of this kind that we are most concerned to discover, define, and measure, though we are also interested in population and structural measures.

The nature of these dimensions emerges from the cycle of experiment—hypothesis formulation—experiment. In this field, where possible variables are so numerous that hypothesis formation and testing by the usual laws of univariate (dependent-independent variable) experimentation is hopelessly ineffective, we have insisted that the only effective tool is factor analysis, which has already proved itself in the corresponding chaotic field of personality variables. The time for profitable experiment with controlled variables will come when the important dimension variables have been factor-analytically separated out from the vast sea of possible variables—including those which are merely subjectively chosen by some investigators as important.

Nevertheless, some of the hypotheses on which we have chosen our variables have been partly *a priori* concepts. Chief among these are the concept of synergy and the subsidiary concepts of effective synergy and maintenance synergy. If the interest of each member in belonging to a group is represented by an ergic attitude vector (3), then the vector sum of these attitudes of all members represents the total interest which the group can command. The energy of the total interest we have called the group *synergy*. It has a number of important properties, including the fixing of the degree of cohesiveness (10) or viscidity (13) shown by the group. The group synergy is thus likely to be one of the factorial dimensions (functional unities) falling in the dynamic section of the group syntality dimensions. Effective synergy is that portion of group synergy which is devoted to attaining the group goal, while maintenance synergy is the portion utilized in maintaining the group and the group process. These are represented in our variables.

Our aim in the investigation now to be described may therefore be stated as an attempt

(a) to discover in a very catholic and highly varied array of group measurements a more limited, manipulable, representative set of independent primary dimensions of *syntality*, on which further experiments of all kinds by diverse methods of experimentation can be based.

(b) To choose some of our large pool of variables also in terms of our structural and synergy hypotheses so that our factors are also used hypothetico-deductively.

(c) To determine at the same time relations between syntality dimensions and structural and population variables. For each factor is a statement of the extent to which a syntality trait is determined by such structural variables as leadership and sociometric conditions and by the personality characteristics of persons in the group.

## 3. THE EXPERIMENT

We aimed to obtain measures on 100 groups of 10 men each, the men being more varied in intelligence and education than students. Each group was to meet for 3 sessions, of about 3 hours each, of group behavior, spread over a week or two, and in addition the group members were to meet as individuals *before* the group sessions for 2 hours of individual personality and background testing. These main objectives of data gathering were achieved except that through absences of individuals at one group session or another we eventually based our factor analysis on only 80 complete groups. Forty of these were composed of men beginning training in the USAF OCS, at Lackland AFB, twenty of recruits newly arrived at Great Lakes Naval Training Center, and twenty of students in social psychology classes at the University of Illinois. Anyone familiar with this field will recognize that the requirement of completeness of group records makes the collection of adequate numbers of groups particularly arduous in comparison with individual research.

In accordance with our definition of a group as something more than a collection of people in the same room working side by side to please the experimenter, we provided the motive of $100 to be paid to the best group in each consecutive set of 10 groups and *to be obtained only by group, rather than individual, performance.*

As to structure, the first 3 hour session was without explicit injunction to adopt a leader, but, after the experience of this first session, all groups received the experimenter's invitation (accepted without exception) to elect a leader with stated powers, for the better performance of the group in inter-group competition. *The present report deals only with the first sessions of the 80 groups, without formal leadership,* with which the findings of the two later sessions may be contrasted to bring out the developments of syntality with age.

The choice of variables included in the matrix was as follows:

A. *Population Variables.* Measures were taken with a research form of the 16 Personality Factor Questionnaire (8, 9), Forms A and B, 1½ hours, of the primary personality dimensions, including such source traits as general intelligence, surgency, cyclothymia-schizothymia, and emotional stability. The individual measures also included (a) measures on a variety of attitudes and interests before and after group decisions on them, thus comprising both an absolute and a shift score, and (b) the interaction observations, e.g., number of suggestions made, broken down in terms of individuals.

B. *Group Structural Variables.* Here, we aimed at meeting three conditions: 1. to include, as stated at conclusion of the last section, marker variables (5) for the factors already approximately indicated by the Cattell-Wispe study and now presenting hypotheses for testing, 2. to include an extremely varied array, covering also most situations of practical value in every day life group situations, e.g., committee decisions, jury harangues, physical panic situations, group honesty in dealing with other groups, group interests, efficiency in mechanical construction, group learning, constancy of group intentions, etc., 3. to include situations to test hypotheses about the nature of group synergy, effective and maintenance synergy, etc. It will be noticed that in no case are the syntality measures permitted to be mere sums of individual performances.

In regard to the experimental and statistical design the following points are important: (a) Reliability coefficients were planned whenever possible, both to test the consistency of syntality as a concept and also to permit corrections of subsequent factor loadings for attentuation; (b) The total set of variables eventually reached was distributed among the three sessions in such a way as to permit all to be factorized without having too large a matrix, also to permit developmental observations by repetition of some variables and, especially, as a statistical device to permit the three factorizations to be related. The actual situations in which group performance and structure measures were obtained were (note the syntality section of our list begins at 30):

30. *Construction.* A rough diagram, and dowel stick materials sufficient to reproduce it in three dimensions, were presented to the group. It is told that its task is to construct the model building shown in the diagram and that its score for the task will be the time it takes to do it. No instructions are given as to how the task might be accomplished. The group is given a distribution of time scores made by similar groups. Before beginning, it estimates the time that will be required. Upon completion, it is told its time, then asked to repeat the entire process.

31. *Group Judgment.* The group is given, one at a time, four questions of fact (e.g., "What was the ideal minimum subsistence budget in 1939 for a family of four?"). They were allowed two minutes to discuss each and required to submit an answer at the end of that time. They were told that if a correct answer was submitted in less than two minutes, they would receive a bonus that increased as their time shortened.

32. *Attitude.* The subjects were given a 21-item attitude scale consisting of statements taken from the Thurstone scales on birth control, church, war and communism (19). He was asked to indicate his agreement on a seven point scale (ranging from "absolutely certain" to "absurd"). Two of these same statements were later presented to the group as "sentences taken from recent American or foreign newspapers." They were told that the group was to discuss each statement for four minutes during which time they were to try to decide what the statement meant, and how they felt about it. Following each discussion the group voted, by a show of hands, on the same seven point scale, and the mean position of all votes was announced. This average was reported as the "group opinion." At the end of the situation the individual members again indicated their private responses to each question that the group had discussed as a part of the sociometric measurements for that situation.

33. *Guessing Game.* E. answered either "yes" or "no" to questions asked him by the group members. They were instructed to try to discover of what object E. was thinking. They were told that they were limited as to time but not as to the number of questions and that their score was cut more by an excess of questions than by lack of speed. The "objects" varied from an "easy" item (the Eiffel Tower) to a "very difficult" one (the concept of goodness). The time limit (at which penalties began), not told to the group, was three minutes on each item.

34. *Dynamometer.* (This situation was used for the last 40 groups only.) Two steel pipes, 1 inch by 30 inches, were placed one at each end of a dynamometer. The group members were given pieces of canvas to fit over their shoes and were placed on a heavily waxed floor. They were given 30 seconds to get the dynamometer hand as high as possible, and were told that this could best be done by jerking. After trying for 30 seconds their score was read to them, they were asked to estimate what they would do on a repeat performance, then invited to repeat the task.

In a second sub-test the group was instructed to maintain a steady pull for 15 seconds and told that the lowest point to which they allowed their pull to fall would be their score. (A continuous reading was visible.) No practice trials were permitted, but as much time as desired was allowed for planning and organization. Again, following the first performance, an estimate and then a repeat performance was obtained.

35. *Interests.* Immediately after the attitude test was given and just before the group was to begin functioning as a group, each member was asked to indicate privately the relative strength of *his* interests at that moment in a list of 11 activities selected so as to involve as many as possible different basic human needs and to vary in the amount of interaction likely to be involved in doing them. About two hours later the entire group was asked to discuss the same list of possibilities, apparently for the purpose of selecting one of them as a group activity for future meetings. After discussing the possibilities for 6 minutes, the group ranked them in order of preference, and finally cast 100 votes divided among as many activities as it wished. Following this, as a part of the sociometric ratings, the original "interest" form was again filled in by each member privately with instructions to indicate "how you now feel."

36. *Card Sorting.* On the front side of the experimenter's table was placed a sheet of heavy cardboard, 11 by 42 inches, divided into fifteen squares numbered 5, 10 . . . 75. Above some of the squares "red" was printed, above others "black," and above still others there was nothing. On this cardboard, a stack of especially selected playing cards (without face cards) was placed. The group was told that their task was to sort this stack of cards into 15 piles and place each in the appropriate square. They were told that there was a time limit but not what it was (6 minutes) and that their score depended on both speed and accuracy.

37. *Discussion.* The final activity was described to the group as an opportunity for it to discuss what it had done, how it could have done better, what things it found most interesting, what it disliked about the experiment, etc. This discussion was allowed to run for 6 minutes, immediately after which the group ranked its preferences among the various situations which they had done.

## 4. THE FACTOR ANALYSIS AND ITS TABLES

Ninety-three variables, described in *Table 1*, were intercorrelated using the product moment formula. Several of these variables are extracted from the syntality performances listed above, but the latter are separately listed to make abbreviation of *Table 1* possible.

In spite of the attention given the problem in planning the experiment, it was possible to repeat performances under what appeared to be objectively similar circumstances for only a few of the syntality measurements in the matrix. The estimates of reliability of the measures that were obtained are reported in *Table 2*. They were obtained by correlating the measure of performance in Session I with a similar measure of performance from a later session.

TABLE 1

## *List of Variables Describing the Groups* [2]

The first 32 variables are means and variances of the population on the 16 Personality Factor Test (8).

1. PTM: *Friendly cyclothymia v. taciturn schizothymia.* (A) People scoring high on this personality dimension prefer situations involving interaction with people; those scoring low prefer not to deal with people but rather with inanimate objects. (001·1)[3]
2. PTM: *General Intelligence.* (B) The measure used is largely one of analogies and classifications (verbal). (002·1)
3. PTM: *Emotional Maturity v. General Neuroticism.* (C) People scoring high on this measure are not greatly bothered by drives which cannot be satisfied immediately. They do not lean much on defense mechanisms to channelize their basic needs into socially acceptable-behavior patterns as much as do people who are lower on this dimension. (003·1)
4. PTM: *Dominance.* (E) High scores in this dimension are associated with assertiveness in social relations. As measured here this assertiveness tends to be associated with traces of egoism, some person-directed aggression and a lack of inhibition rising from self-consciousness. (004·1)
5. PTM: *Surgency v. Desurgency.* (F) People high on this trait tend to be carefree and enthusiastic, and to enjoy situations in which there is bustle and excitement. People low in this scale are more serious, anxious and reserved and feel more at home in more stable situations. (005·1)
6. PTM: *Positive Character integration.* (G) High scores on this trait are found in people who have interiorized social norms and use them as rules of conduct. They tend to value perseverance and efficiency as ends in themselves. (006·1)
7. PTM: *Adventurous cyclothymia v. self-conscious, withdrawn schizothymia.* (H)

2 The correlation matrix, together with the unrotated factor matrix and the transformation matrix may be obtained by application to the American Documentation Institute, Science Service Bldg., 1719 N. Street Northwest, Washington, D.C., by reference to number 3678.

3 In order to facilitate cross reference between factor analyses in this study an index number was assigned to each measurement, such that the *area* from which the measure comes is indicated by the first digit, the particular measure, and in the case of syntality measures the situation in which it was taken, by the second and third digits. To some extent the mathematical treatment given it is indicated by the numbers, if any, to the right of the decimal point. The convention used is as follows:

000–099. Population measurements (PT), such as mean personality measurements.

100–199. Sociometric measurements (SR), i.e., all ratings made by the group members.

200–299. Observer ratings (OR), of the group or of its members.

300–999. Measurements of group performance.

Mathematical treatment:

·0 A raw score.

·1 A mean.

·2 Variance.

·3 A level of aspiration measurement.

·4 A ratio.

·5 Not used.

·6 An increment, computed by taking the difference between measures of similar performances.

·7 Miscellaneous, locally defined measures making use of special treatments or of selected parts of the available data (see, for example, 201·7).

These index numbers are indicated in parenthesis after the description of each variable.

On this dimension variation is from outgoing sociability, adventurousness and strongly expressed emotional responsiveness, to general shyness and timid withdrawal. (007·1)

8. PTM: *Tender minded sensitivity v. hard headed practicality.* (I) People who score high in this dimension are described as impatient and demanding, but gentle, sensitive and esthetic. The opposites are self-sufficient, tough, practical and realistic. In a college population students studying horticulture and the fine arts have been found to score high while students studying engineering and business administration score low on this factor. (008·1)
9. PTM: *Paranoid suspiciousness v. lack of this trait.* (L) High scores here correlate with jealousy, suspicion and self-centeredness. These people tend to avoid accepting the suggestions of others and devote rather more than the usual amount of time to examining the effects of their behavior in their associates. (009.1)
10. PTM: *Bohemian aggressiveness v. practical concernedness.* (M) The person high in this trait professes a disregard for social norms and for the effect of his behavior upon others, but shows some conversion hysteric behavior. The opposite pole shows anxiety to do the right thing and a tendency to become emotionally involved in what happens to others. (010·1)
11. PTM: *Polished fastidiousness v. rough simplicity.* (N) People who score high in this dimension are socially sophisticated, intellectually trained and aloof. The opposites are clumsy but more warm-hearted. (011·1)
12. PTM: *Worrying, suspicious anxiety v. calm trustfulness.* (O) On this dimension variation is from subjectively felt free-floating anxiety with excessive concern over trivial mistakes, an inability to relax, and an aversion to undertaking any but routine tasks–to the opposite characteristics. (012·1)
13. PTM: *Radicalism v. conservatism.* ($Q_1$) High scores here are associated with a willingness to subject conventions and authority to examination with a possibility of rejecting or modifying them. They also indicate intellectual and "rational" as opposed to concrete and "matter of fact" interests. (013·1)
14. PTM: *Independent self-sufficiency v. lack of resolution.* ($Q_2$) High scores here are made by people who are very self-contained and accustomed to deciding their own fate, with little regard to the reactions of the group. They tend to be task-oriented rather than gregariously oriented. (014·1)
15. PTM: *Deliberate will control v. lack of independence.* ($Q_3$) High scores here indicate people who are "strong willed," restrained, and who consciously maintain long term goals and values. In contrast to people high in $Q_2$ above, these people may *feel* the social pressures and temptations but they reject them if incompatible with the ethical values. (015·1)
16. PTM: *Nervous tension.* ($Q_4$) This dimension is a measure of liability physical symptoms of nervousness especially over-activity of the vegetative nervous system. (016·1)
17. PTV: *Friendly cyclothymia v. taciturn schizothymia.* (A) (001·2) (*This and the scores following through 032 were obtained by computing the squared standard deviation of the distribution of individual group members' scores for personality traits numbers 1 through 16 above.*)
18. PTV: *Population variance. General intelligence.* (B) (002·2)
19. PTV: *Emotional maturity.* (C) (003·2)
20. PTV: *Dominance.* (E) (004·2)
21. PTV: *Surgency.* (F) (005·2)
22. PTV: *Positive character integration.* (C) (006·2)
23. PTV: *Adventurous cyclothymia.* (H) (007·2)
24. PTV: *Tender minded sensitivity.* (I) (008·2)
25. PTV: *Paranoid suspiciousness.* (L) (009·2)
26. PTV: *Bohemian symbolic aggressiveness.* (M) (010·2)
27. PTV: *Polished fastidiousness.* (N) (011·2)
28. PTV: *Worrying suspicious anxiety.* (O) (012·2)
29. PTV: *Radicalism.* ($Q_1$) (013·2)
30. PTV: *Independent self-sufficiency.* ($Q_2$) (014·2)

31. PTV: *Deliberate will control.* ($Q_8$) (015·2)
32. PTV: *Nervous tension.* ($Q_4$) (016·2)
33. SR: *Number of satisfactory co-workers.* Mean number of people which the group members indicate they would like to retain in the group at its future meetings. (101·1)
34. SR: *Number of negative effecters.* Mean number of people which the group members indicate have hindered more than they have helped the group. (*33, 36, 37*) (107·1)
35. SR: *Number of significant members.* Mean number of members without whom the group would have been significantly different. (*37*) (108·1)
36. SR: *Rated enjoyment.* Mean position on an 8 point scale, at which the members rated their enjoyment of the various situations. (*32, 36, 37*) (117·1)
37. SR: *Felt freedom to participate.* Mean position, on an 8 point scale of personal feeling of freedom to bring up objections and partly formulated suggestions. High scores indicate freedom. (*32, 36, 37*) (118·1)
38. SR: *Felt acceptance.* Mean position with regard to how much the individual member felt that he was accepted as a member of the group. High scores indicate felt acceptance. (*30, 31, 32, 37*) (119·1)
39. SR: *Optimsim for group's future interaction.* Mean rating of how well the group will work together in future meetings. High scores indicate judged improvement. (*37*) (122·1)
40. SR: *Commonness of purpose.* Mean rating of the extent to which individual members were striving toward a common end in the group activities. High rating indicates judged commonness of purpose. (*36, 37*) (124·1)
41. SR: *Integration.* Mean rating of extent members felt that they behaved as a unified group, rather than a disjointed collection of individuals. High score indicates rated high integration. (*30, 31, 32, 33, 36, 37*) (125·1)
42. SR: *Satisfaction with overall efficiency.* Mean rating of how satisfied members were with the efficiency with which the group reached decisions. High score indicates satisfactions. (*31, 32*) (126·1)
43. Guessing game: *Total number of questions asked for the "easy" item.* (331a·0)
44. Guessing game: *Total number of questions asked for the difficult item.* (331b·0)
45. Guessing game: *Rate of questioning (seconds per question) for the "easy" item.* (331a·4)
46. Guessing game: *Time required to get answer for the "easy" item.* (332a·0)
47. Card sorting: *Number of stacks correct.* (360·0)
48. Card sorting: *Rate of completion (seconds per stack correctly completed).* (361·1)
49. Discussion: *Speed of ranking.* Time to determine rank order of preferences divided by number of items ranked. (370·1)
50. Interests: *Speed of ranking.* Time required to decide on and rank 11 interest items. (350·0)
51. Interests: *Speed of voting.* Time required to divide 100 votes among the interest alternatives previously ranked. (351·0)
52. Construction: *Planning time.* Total time, for two trials, taken to decide in estimate and to plan attack on the problem. (301·1)
53. Construction: *Decrease in planning time.* Planning time for trial 1, divided by planning time for trial 2. (301·2)
54. Group Judgment: *Accuracy.* Total number of points awarded on the basis of accuracy of answers on 4 questions. (310·1)
55. Group Judgment: *Speed of reaching decisions.* Total time, within allowable limits used for reaching four decisions. (311·1)
56. Construction: *Speed.* Time per unit of work completed. Mean for two trials. (·25) (300·1)
57. Construction: *Learning.* Score 314 computed for each trial separately. Trial then subtracted from trial 2. (304·61)
58. Construction: *Realism of aspiration.* The absolute value for: $A'' - \frac{p' + pa}{2}$. Where $A''$ is the estimate made for trial 2, $p'$ is the first performance and $pa$ is the reported average for other groups. (302·310)

59. Construction: *Optimism of aspiration.* The expression under 58 above, with sign attached. (302·3)
60. Construction: *Inconstancy of aspiration.* Absolute amount of difference between the aspiration estimates. (302·33)
61. Construction: *Absolute level of aspiration.* Sum of the estimates for two trials. (302·34)
62. Discussion: *Rank of preference for construction situation.* (371a·4)
63. Discussion: *Rank of preference for group judgment situation.* (371b·4)
64. Discussion: *Rank of preference for attitude situation.* (371c·4)
65. Attitude: *Group radicalism score.* The group vote (on a seven point scale) with "radical" scored at the 7-end times the Thurstone weight for the statement. Mean of all statements discussed. (320·1)
66. Attitude: *Quantity of change*, without regard to direction, in private responses of individual members following group discussion and vote on the statement. (050·1)
67. Attitude: *Decrease in variance* of the distribution of individual responses following group discussion and vote in the statement. (050·2)
68. Dynamometer jerking pull: *Increase* in level of pull attained for second trial over level for first trial. (340·6)
69. Dynamometer: *Optimism of aspiration.* The algebraic value for (A″ EP/n) where *A″* is the estimate made for the next trial, and *EP/n* is the mean performance for previous trials. No norms were reported and no estimate was made for the first trial. (343a·321)
70. Dynamometer jerking pull: *Total pull.* Highest pull attained in a 30 second period when constant pressure was not required. Mean for two trials. (340·1)
71. Dynamometer sustained pull: *Total pull.* Lowest point to which the dynamometer was allowed to drop during a 15 second period. Mean for two trials. (341·1)
72. Dynamometer sustained pull: *Increase* in level of score 327, computed for each trial separately, of second over first trial. (341·6)
73. OR: Group organization (201·7)
    (All OR's used in this matrix were made at the conclusion of the group meeting).
74. OR: Leadership technique. (202·7)
75. OR: Degree of leadership. (203·7)
76. OR: Orderliness. (204·7)
77. OR: Freedom of group atmosphere. (205·7)
78. OR: Degree of We-feeling. (206·7)
79. OR: Degree of frustration. (207·7)
80. OR: Degree of interdependence. (208·7)
81. Dynamometer sustained pull. *Optimism of aspiration.* (343b·321)
82. OR: Number of members judged to have shown leadership. (250·1)
83. OR: Number of members agreed upon as being principle leaders in at least one situation. (251·0)
84. Interest: *Decrease in variance* of the distribution of individual "investment" following group discussion of the two activities which the group ranked highest in preference. (062·2)
85. Interests: *Persistence of individuality.* The mean investment, following group discussion, by group members in the two choices ranked highest by the group less their investments in the same items *before* the group discussion. (064·1)
86. Interests: *Concentration of resources.* The extent available resources (votes) were concentrated in a single preference, or scattered over many. Measured by multiplying the rank assigned an item by the number of votes given it and summing for all items. (352·71)
87. Interests: *Inconsistency of decisions.* The extent that the rank of the number of votes given in alternative was inconsistent with the rank given the same alternative. Measured by subtracting the votes given each item from the votes given each item ranked higher, then summing all negative results. (352·72)
88. Discussion: *Rank of preference for Guessing Game.* (371d·4)
89. Discussion: *Rank of preference for Dynamometer.* (371e·4)

90. Discussion: *Rank of preference for Interests Situation.* (371f·4)
91. Discussion: *Rank of preference for Card Sorting.* (371g·4)
92. OR: *Motivation* to achieve the group's goal (not necessarily the goal set for the group by the experimenter). (209·7)
93. OR: *Extent group is concerned with procedure,* or of how it should be organized and how it should attack its problem. (213·71)
94. Random number.

TABLE 2

## *Reliability of Group Measures*

| VARIABLE MATRIX NO. | DESCRIPTIVE TITLE | TEST-RETEST RELIABILITY |
|---|---|---|
| 43 | Guessing Game: Number of questions asked for "easy" item | ·01 |
| 44 | ——: Number of questions for "difficult" item | ·32 |
| 45 | ——: Rate of questioning | ·19 |
| 46 | ——: Time to get answer to "easy" item | ·03 |
| 47 | Card Sorting: Number of stacks correct | ·04 |
| 49 | Discussion: Speed of ranking | ·06 |
| 52 | Construction: Planning time | ·53 |
| 53 | ——: Decrease in planning time | ·34 |
| 55 | Group Judgment: Speed of reaching decisions | ·24 |
| 56 | Construction: Speed | ·25 |
| 66 | Attitudes: Quantity of change | ·04 |
| 67 | ——: Decrease in variance | ·18 |
| 70 | Dynamometer, jerking pull: Total pull | ·42 |
| 71 | ——, sustained pull: Total pull | ·31 |
| 84 | Interests: Decrease in variance | ·25 |
| 87 | ——: Inconsistency of decisions | ·08 |

The correlation matrix obtained among the above 94 variables (the 94th is a random variable to test the standard error of a loading) was factor analyzed, using the Thurstone multiple group method, and stable communalities were obtained following four iterations. Fifteen factors were extracted. These factors were then rotated to yield the best possible simple structure. Following 18 overall rotations, involving each of the fifteen factors, and several additional rotations involving slight shifts in the position of individual factors, a reasonably clear simple structure was obtained. At this point the mean percentage of variables which were in the ± ·10 hyperplane, i.e., had correlations of not more than ± ·10 with the factors, was 56 per cent. This figure, showing in the last line of Table 3, compares

TABLE 3

## *The Rotated Vector Matrix*

| | 1 | 2 | 3 | 4 | 5 | 6 | 7 | 8 | 9 | 10 | 11 | 12 | 13 | 14 | 15 | $h^2$ |
|---|---|---|---|---|---|---|---|---|---|---|---|---|---|---|---|---|
| 1 | 17 | −07 | −04 | −04 | 51 | 37 | −15 | −07 | 11 | 16 | 23 | −03 | −03 | −14 | 25 | 64 |
| 2 | 24 | 16 | 19 | 08 | 36 | 21 | 17 | 22 | 05 | 24 | 07 | −05 | 16 | 11 | 05 | 48 |
| 3 | 47 | 21 | −07 | 08 | −01 | −18 | 20 | 30 | 26 | 15 | 09 | 24 | 05 | 02 | −07 | 60 |
| 4 | 30 | 51 | 08 | −16 | 06 | 16 | 07 | 30 | 11 | 06 | −28 | 38 | 02 | −31 | 05 | 84 |
| 5 | −07 | 26 | −12 | −03 | 21 | 06 | 04 | 05 | 60 | −01 | −22 | 17 | 06 | 07 | 02 | 59 |
| 6 | −09 | 62 | −04 | −03 | −19 | −29 | −07 | −06 | 09 | 08 | −25 | −02 | −03 | −03 | 07 | 61 |

THE ROTATED VECTOR MATRIX (*continued*)

| | 1 | 2 | 3 | 4 | 5 | 6 | 7 | 8 | 9 | 10 | 11 | 12 | 13 | 14 | 15 | $h^2$ |
|---|---|---|---|---|---|---|---|---|---|---|---|---|---|---|---|---|
| 7 | 04 | 69 | 04 | 07 | −09 | −21 | 04 | −04 | 36 | −05 | −08 | 22 | −24 | 04 | −03 | 79 |
| 8 | −26 | −11 | 30 | −04 | 31 | 27 | 06 | −13 | 02 | −31 | 17 | −02 | 01 | 08 | −13 | 51 |
| 9 | −85 | 20 | 00 | −01 | −06 | −08 | 04 | 12 | 09 | 04 | −04 | −02 | 09 | 09 | 02 | 82 |
| 10 | −01 | −11 | −24 | 10 | −35 | −01 | −24 | 11 | −10 | 01 | 57 | 02 | 15 | 01 | 29 | 71 |
| 11 | 05 | 48 | −05 | 03 | 09 | −02 | −10 | 08 | 28 | 30 | −01 | 04 | −06 | 04 | 05 | 44 |
| 12 | −46 | −46 | 05 | −11 | −10 | 11 | 03 | 06 | −24 | 12 | 01 | 11 | 10 | −23 | 21 | 66 |
| 13 | −09 | 22 | −08 | 05 | 38 | 16 | 00 | 18 | 01 | 29 | 04 | 15 | 15 | −19 | 07 | 44 |
| 14 | −35 | 29 | −09 | 06 | −07 | −01 | −12 | 10 | 07 | −07 | −12 | 11 | 05 | 28 | −06 | 37 |
| 15 | 03 | 63 | 01 | −06 | −10 | −31 | −01 | 10 | −05 | −06 | −01 | −11 | −13 | 04 | −09 | 56 |
| 16 | −49 | −41 | 00 | 06 | 07 | 13 | 13 | 01 | 06 | 09 | −13 | −04 | 04 | −05 | 07 | 49 |
| 17 | 03 | 08 | −27 | 02 | 28 | 16 | −14 | 09 | −10 | 03 | 19 | 14 | 30 | 10 | 28 | 46 |
| 18 | −04 | −08 | −18 | 03 | −06 | 12 | −14 | 09 | 14 | −36 | −01 | −28 | 02 | 15 | 07 | 34 |
| 19 | 02 | −02 | 02 | 02 | 00 | −12 | 06 | 00 | −08 | −02 | −94 | 09 | 02 | −38 | −04 | 1·06 |
| 20 | 19 | 08 | 15 | 29 | 12 | −06 | −07 | 19 | 16 | 34 | 04 | 00 | 05 | −08 | 31 | 46 |
| 21 | 00 | 06 | 02 | 13 | 50 | 30 | 17 | −00 | −10 | 12 | −08 | 05 | −23 | 16 | −03 | 50 |
| 22 | −26 | 16 | −09 | −10 | 45 | −06 | 28 | 13 | 14 | −06 | −09 | 08 | −10 | −12 | 18 | 51 |
| 23 | 01 | −04 | −12 | −02 | 40 | −01 | −14 | 11 | −08 | 06 | −10 | −19 | 00 | 13 | 33 | 39 |
| 24 | 01 | 08 | 06 | 02 | 10 | −03 | −05 | 01 | 04 | 08 | 11 | 03 | 62 | −12 | 11 | 46 |
| 25 | −02 | 27 | −18 | 03 | 28 | 07 | 06 | −01 | 07 | 01 | −06 | −01 | 54 | −00 | −00 | 49 |
| 26 | 11 | −01 | −28 | −21 | −03 | 04 | 20 | 39 | −10 | −16 | −10 | 28 | 47 | −29 | −03 | 76 |
| 27 | −27 | 06 | 01 | −32 | 09 | 02 | 03 | 34 | 03 | 08 | −05 | −08 | 30 | −16 | −05 | 44 |
| 28 | 06 | −03 | −09 | 05 | −03 | 01 | −20 | 11 | −18 | 13 | −11 | 19 | 11 | −22 | −18 | 26 |
| 29 | −17 | 26 | 12 | 11 | 50 | 16 | 07 | −10 | 07 | 15 | 00 | −13 | 09 | 07 | 03 | 47 |
| 30 | 03 | 41 | −16 | 05 | 22 | 15 | 06 | −02 | −03 | 10 | 08 | 07 | −03 | 05 | 09 | 31 |
| 31 | −20 | 21 | 06 | 13 | −06 | −34 | 10 | −07 | 18 | 34 | −10 | −06 | 09 | −12 | 10 | 43 |
| 32 | −19 | 02 | −05 | 26 | −25 | −28 | 20 | 28 | −08 | 15 | 01 | −01 | 03 | −18 | −00 | 43 |
| 33 | −23 | 23 | 07 | −12 | 13 | −32 | 23 | 12 | 07 | 29 | 14 | −04 | −16 | 01 | −11 | 46 |
| 34 | −28 | 26 | −05 | −02 | 16 | 03 | 03 | 06 | −09 | −19 | −02 | −22 | 38 | 24 | 43 | 66 |
| 35 | 08 | 03 | 08 | −04 | 18 | 08 | 41 | 14 | 18 | −01 | −03 | −01 | 04 | 15 | −13 | 31 |
| 36 | 15 | −01 | −08 | −54 | −10 | −05 | 07 | −24 | 09 | −27 | −06 | −04 | −23 | 04 | −18 | 57 |
| 37 | −18 | −32 | −05 | 35 | 15 | 06 | 06 | 09 | −09 | 18 | 08 | −06 | 08 | 13 | 02 | 35 |
| 38 | 14 | 43 | 17 | −49 | −14 | 06 | −04 | 03 | 08 | −31 | 22 | −03 | −10 | 02 | 10 | 67 |
| 39 | 11 | 03 | −05 | −59 | 03 | −01 | −00 | −12 | −17 | 18 | 07 | 10 | −04 | −05 | 01 | 46 |
| 40 | 02 | 40 | 27 | −52 | 11 | 08 | −12 | 05 | −03 | 20 | 01 | −07 | −03 | −06 | −05 | 59 |
| 41 | 03 | −04 | 05 | −82 | −02 | −10 | 02 | 13 | −04 | 00 | −11 | −05 | −09 | −08 | 00 | 74 |
| 42 | −09 | −05 | −01 | −70 | −15 | 04 | 04 | 02 | −09 | 07 | −07 | −00 | 08 | 16 | 15 | 60 |
| 43 | −01 | 20 | 23 | −07 | 05 | −11 | 15 | −29 | −13 | −32 | 04 | −22 | −09 | −11 | −08 | 42 |
| 44 | −13 | 25 | 06 | 09 | −03 | −23 | 02 | 07 | −15 | −16 | −07 | −14 | −15 | −36 | −34 | 49 |
| 45 | −01 | 20 | 04 | 07 | 09 | 05 | 05 | 60 | −20 | −10 | 12 | −03 | −16 | −01 | −28 | 59 |
| 46 | 01 | −00 | 02 | −08 | 07 | −00 | 05 | −57 | −08 | −27 | 05 | −10 | 00 | −17 | 11 | 47 |
| 47 | −11 | 12 | 02 | 02 | 08 | 01 | 01 | 03 | 07 | 76 | 08 | −37 | −01 | 16 | 06 | 79 |
| 48 | −10 | 03 | 02 | −10 | −16 | −02 | −15 | 07 | 10 | −43 | 04 | 02 | 04 | 12 | 14 | 31 |
| 49 | −07 | 12 | 02 | 06 | 31 | −04 | −09 | −03 | 04 | 06 | −23 | −22 | 41 | 02 | 03 | 41 |
| 50 | −14 | 03 | 03 | −07 | 05 | −06 | 22 | −01 | −12 | 04 | −18 | −12 | −27 | −18 | 09 | 26 |
| 51 | 09 | 06 | −59 | 04 | 12 | 04 | −15 | −06 | −02 | 18 | 11 | −18 | −10 | −05 | 11 | 51 |
| 52 | 03 | 12 | −00 | −02 | −35 | 09 | 56 | 06 | 29 | −03 | −06 | 07 | −09 | −61 | 01 | 94 |
| 53 | 00 | −03 | −02 | −03 | 00 | 53 | 04 | 09 | −31 | −17 | −06 | 22 | 28 | 50 | 05 | 80 |
| 54 | 10 | 06 | −00 | −04 | 45 | 02 | 11 | 19 | −06 | −10 | 08 | −29 | 02 | −06 | 12 | 39 |
| 55 | 05 | −03 | −24 | 11 | −04 | −12 | −00 | −27 | 10 | 02 | −00 | −04 | 01 | −47 | −09 | 40 |
| 56 | −24 | 13 | −03 | −08 | −04 | 25 | 09 | −10 | −16 | −12 | 16 | −12 | −02 | 34 | 28 | 44 |
| 57 | 02 | −02 | 07 | 15 | 06 | 14 | −07 | −09 | 27 | −16 | −12 | −08 | 11 | −10 | −05 | 21 |
| 58 | 05 | −00 | 05 | −02 | 02 | 78 | −13 | −11 | 08 | 04 | 08 | −05 | −03 | 04 | −30 | 75 |
| 59 | 05 | −12 | 02 | 08 | −02 | −80 | −00 | −06 | 08 | −13 | 03 | −11 | 06 | 06 | 08 | 72 |
| 60 | −23 | 00 | 06 | 06 | −40 | −25 | −02 | −08 | 17 | 10 | 08 | −11 | −00 | 01 | 15 | 37 |
| 61 | 13 | −13 | 10 | 11 | −05 | −73 | 05 | 07 | 09 | 06 | −02 | −04 | −09 | −20 | −16 | 69 |
| 62 | 04 | −08 | 05 | −03 | −10 | −00 | 01 | −00 | 04 | −09 | 04 | 80 | −02 | 07 | −15 | 70 |
| 63 | 10 | −65 | 12 | 01 | −13 | −04 | −09 | 02 | 58 | 14 | 05 | −25 | 02 | 17 | −35 | 1·05 |
| 64 | −29 | −11 | 05 | −21 | 11 | −07 | −04 | −05 | −33 | 24 | −07 | −31 | −40 | 03 | 02 | 59 |
| 65 | 12 | −10 | −14 | 08 | 12 | −09 | 03 | 30 | −12 | 12 | −18 | 21 | 07 | 16 | 04 | 30 |
| 66 | 18 | 14 | 00 | −05 | −03 | 15 | −02 | −12 | −25 | −09 | 15 | 29 | 22 | −17 | 07 | 35 |
| 67 | −01 | −11 | 01 | −12 | −27 | −19 | −08 | 16 | −13 | −16 | 12 | 13 | 02 | −01 | −06 | 25 |
| 68 | −08 | 03 | 05 | −04 | 20 | 09 | 37 | −16 | −27 | −09 | 13 | −00 | 14 | 12 | 02 | 35 |
| 69 | −04 | −04 | −36 | −28 | 18 | 22 | −01 | 08 | −52 | 24 | 60 | −04 | 08 | 09 | −06 | 1·01 |
| 70 | 03 | 68 | 05 | −31 | 33 | 07 | 00 | 43 | −04 | 14 | 11 | −00 | −04 | −28 | 40 | 1·13 |
| 71 | 40 | 02 | −20 | −32 | 10 | 01 | 03 | 06 | 57 | −05 | 06 | −34 | −44 | −04 | 07 | 96 |

THE ROTATED VECTOR MATRIX (*continued*)

| | 1 | 2 | 3 | 4 | 5 | 6 | 7 | 8 | 9 | 10 | 11 | 12 | 13 | 14 | 15 | h² |
|---|---|---|---|---|---|---|---|---|---|---|---|---|---|---|---|---|
| 72 | 19 | 21 | −31 | −02 | −24 | 09 | 26 | −08 | −02 | 31 | 38 | 24 | −32 | −09 | −02 | 73 |
| 73 | 42 | 02 | −06 | −02 | 08 | −02 | 62 | 28 | 06 | 01 | −01 | −11 | 07 | −09 | 10 | 69 |
| 74 | 28 | 05 | −02 | −03 | 05 | 21 | −13 | 25 | 09 | 34 | 04 | −10 | 01 | 06 | 07 | 35 |
| 75 | 63 | −14 | 04 | 15 | −02 | 06 | 63 | 09 | −01 | 03 | 08 | 06 | 04 | −06 | 03 | 87 |
| 76 | 53 | −16 | 01 | −09 | 15 | 27 | 17 | 07 | 11 | 08 | −15 | −08 | 23 | −08 | −07 | 56 |
| 77 | 08 | 24 | −08 | −00 | −25 | −05 | 46 | 43 | −35 | 17 | −04 | 40 | −03 | −05 | 13 | 87 |
| 78 | 50 | 07 | −10 | −06 | 19 | −00 | 37 | 46 | −14 | 16 | −09 | 10 | 06 | 00 | 10 | 73 |
| 79 | −53 | 17 | −09 | 01 | 13 | 02 | −24 | −09 | 04 | −45 | 04 | −13 | −19 | 00 | −09 | 67 |
| 80 | 31 | 04 | −08 | −30 | 29 | −03 | 20 | 36 | 08 | −09 | 18 | −19 | 02 | 28 | 03 | 61 |
| 81 | 07 | 11 | −03 | −34 | 09 | 02 | 42 | −09 | −14 | −03 | 16 | −21 | 19 | −28 | 11 | 54 |
| 82 | 16 | 22 | 05 | 08 | −23 | −20 | 03 | 07 | 16 | −29 | 28 | 09 | −19 | 02 | 00 | 41 |
| 83 | 06 | 36 | 21 | 07 | 08 | 06 | 04 | −10 | 09 | −03 | 28 | 03 | −21 | 12 | −01 | 35 |
| 84 | −09 | 01 | 00 | −17 | 11 | −05 | −44 | 07 | −04 | −06 | 05 | 38 | −09 | −16 | 06 | 44 |
| 85 | 16 | 09 | 18 | −03 | 35 | −05 | −54 | −04 | −15 | −18 | 03 | −05 | 16 | −04 | −12 | 59 |
| 86 | 02 | −07 | −87 | 03 | −05 | 04 | 05 | 06 | −07 | 02 | −03 | 03 | 05 | 03 | −01 | 78 |
| 87 | −10 | −05 | −81 | −04 | 07 | −06 | 03 | −06 | 16 | −03 | 04 | −03 | −06 | 12 | −03 | 73 |
| 88 | 02 | 06 | 09 | 09 | −07 | 09 | 05 | −09 | −39 | −00 | −02 | −13 | −07 | 01 | 63 | 62 |
| 89 | −13 | 61 | 07 | 06 | 11 | 33 | 37 | 04 | −34 | −34 | −12 | 07 | 12 | 09 | 37 | 1·07 |
| 90 | 15 | −08 | 05 | 04 | −07 | 03 | 04 | −07 | 04 | 29 | 05 | −41 | −08 | 09 | −23 | 37 |
| 91 | 08 | 16 | −43 | −04 | 15 | −04 | −43 | 13 | −20 | −17 | 12 | 13 | 06 | −29 | 12 | 65 |
| 92 | 46 | 14 | −07 | −11 | 17 | −04 | 40 | 38 | −07 | 02 | 16 | 12 | −07 | −00 | 11 | 65 |
| 93 | 25 | 27 | 07 | 28 | −03 | −06 | 90 | 15 | −00 | −04 | −22 | −16 | −24 | −12 | −11 | 1·22 |
| 94 | −16 | 01 | 01 | −31 | 07 | −08 | 15 | 09 | 05 | −22 | 41 | 10 | −27 | −15 | 15 | 51 |
| ±·10 Hyperplane | 46 | 43 | 67 | 62 | 46 | 57 | 52 | 56 | 53 | 45 | 56 | 49 | 59 | 49 | 56 | 56% |

reasonably favorably with the 65 per cent frequently found in rotations of a varied set of personality variables.

The angles between the rotated factors are shown in *Table 4*.

TABLE 4

*Angles Among Vectors*

| | 1 | 2 | 3 | 4 | 5 | 6 | 7 | 8 | 9 | 10 | 11 | 12 | 13 | 14 |
|---|---|---|---|---|---|---|---|---|---|---|---|---|---|---|
| 1 | | | | | | | | | | | | | | |
| 2 | −27 | | | | | | | | | | | | | |
| 3 | 04 | 16 | | | | | | | | | | | | |
| 4 | 09 | 06 | 03 | | | | | | | | | | | |
| 5 | 12 | −15 | −10 | −22 | | | | | | | | | | |
| 6 | 00 | −04 | 00 | −01 | 06 | | | | | | | | | |
| 7 | 15 | −04 | 07 | 13 | −04 | −05 | | | | | | | | |
| 8 | −03 | 05 | −20 | −29 | 03 | −18 | −03 | | | | | | | |
| 9 | 05 | −05 | 05 | −10 | 01 | −17 | 00 | −12 | | | | | | |
| 10 | 08 | −18 | 04 | 11 | −05 | −11 | 01 | −06 | −10 | | | | | |
| 11 | −13 | 03 | −12 | −03 | −10 | 01 | −16 | −05 | −03 | −07 | | | | |
| 12 | 04 | 01 | −10 | 01 | −33 | 09 | 02 | 03 | −11 | −04 | 01 | | | |
| 13 | 00 | −11 | −08 | −09 | 10 | 03 | −04 | 11 | −01 | 04 | −04 | 00 | | |
| 14 | −17 | −21 | 04 | 02 | −01 | 18 | 03 | −10 | 14 | −04 | 03 | −08 | −03 | |
| 15 | −12 | 16 | −20 | −05 | 20 | −05 | 00 | 08 | −12 | 03 | 14 | −02 | 17 | −14 |

## 5. THE FACTORS AND THEIR MEANINGS

We shall now state the factor patterns found with brief interpretative comments. As usual this will be done by listing the highest 10 per cent or so of the loadings (keeping clear of the lower limit of significance) and attempting to hypothesize what influence could be common to these manifestations. However, systematic hypothesizing and checking will not be attempted until the results for the second and third sessions are also published. The titles given the factors are temporary and aim at maximum *descriptiveness* in a few words.

Three characteristics combine in this factor [*1*]: 1. Population personality characteristics of adventure, vigor, dominance, purposefulness,

FACTOR I

*Vigorous Unquestioned Purposefulness vs. Self-conscious Unadaptedness*

| VARIABLE MATRIX NO. | DESCRIPTIVE TITLE * | FACTOR LOADING |
|---|---|---|
| 7 | PTM Adventurous cyclothymia (H) | ·69 |
| 70 | *Dynamometer,* jerking pull: Total pull | ·68 |
| 63 | *Discussion:* Dislike for Group Judgment Situation * | —·65 |
| 15 | PTM Deliberate Will Control ($Q_3$) | ·63 |
| 6 | PTM Positive Character Integration (G) | ·62 |
| 89 | *Discussion:* Preference for Dynamometer Situation | ·61 |
| 4 | PTM Dominance (E) | ·51 |
| 11 | PTM Polished Fastidiousness (N) | ·48 |
| 12 | PTM Calm trustfulness * (O) | —·46 |
| 38 | SR Felt acceptance by other group members | ·43 |
| 16 | PTM Lack of nervous tension * ($Q_4$) | —·41 |
| 30 | PTV Wide range of Independent self-sufficiency ($Q_2$) | ·41 |
| 40 | SR Commonness of purpose | ·40 |
| 83 | OR Many "principal" leaders | ·36 |
| 37 | SR Members do feel free to participate * | —·32 |

* The title shown here is not necessarily the same as that shown for the same variable in *Table 1*. In this and the following factor loading tables, the descriptive title will in all cases describe the performance of the group, with regard to the variable being measured, which goes along with the positive pole of the factor. Wherever this change in title has been made, it has been indicated by an asterisk (*). The sign of the correlation, however, has not been changed.

orderly, willed application and freedom from anxiety (H, E, G, $Q_3$, N and O—). 2. Self ratings in the group of feeling accepted and of working to a common goal. 3. High performance upon, and a liking for, coordinated vigorous action, with dislike for discussion and ill defined tasks ("Group Judgment"). It resembles Factor V in the Wispe study (7) and, by total sense but not marker variables, the factor of "vigorous, self-willed order" in national culture patterns (2, 6).

The most likely explanation here [*1*] would seem to be that the group performance and the feeling of acceptance in the group arise primarily from the interaction of personalities having these personality factors.

Essentially here [*2*] we have a collection of observer ratings such as would be implied by our hypothesis of synergy. The group appears highly motivated, cohesive, and desirous of a high degree of leadership. "Maintained pull" is perhaps the performance which would be expected most directly to reflect simple high general motivation.

Again [*2*], however, the highest loadings are in population characters and on general principles we would therefore expect these to be the "cause" of the associated group performances. Personality factors of warm-heartedness (L, freedom from paranoia), emotional maturity, and freedom from anxiety and nervous tension are here thrown together, possibly as a second order factor.

Our hypothesis will be that *in neonate groups the immediate determiner of the synergy level is the population personality level in freedom from paranoia, general emotionality, anxiety and tension.* It is interesting that the access of synergy shows itself so early not only in we-feeling and motivation but also in orderliness and the development of leadership.

**FACTOR 2**

*Immediate High Synergy vs. Low Motivation*

| VARIABLE MATRIX NO. | DESCRIPTIVE TITLE | FACTOR LOADING |
|---|---|---|
| 9 | PTM Lack of paranoid suspiciousness * (L) | —·85 |
| 75 | OR High degree of leadership | ·63 |
| 76 | OR High degree of group orderliness | ·53 |
| 79 | OR Low degree of frustration | —·53 |
| 78 | OR High degree of we-feeling | ·50 |
| 16 | PTM Low amount of nervous tension * ($Q_4$) | —·49 |
| 3 | PTM High level of emotional maturity (C) | ·47 |
| 12 | PTM Low level of worrying, suspicious anxiety * (O) | —·46 |
| 92 | OR High level of motivation | ·46 |
| 73 | OR High degree of group organization | ·42 |
| 71 | *Dynamometer:* High score on sustained pull | ·40 |
| 14 | PTM Low level of independent self-sufficiency * ($Q_2$) | —·35 |
| 80 | OR High degree of interdependence | ·31 |

This [*3*] has several variables expressing one meaning of the term democratic: concern with procedure and planning, participation of several significant individuals, freedom of group atmosphere (observed, but not significant in self ratings) and in preservation of individuality of opinions despite group discussion. The validity of the rating on procedure is shown by the loading of the actual measure of time spent planning. This emphasis on procedure seems related also to leadership and organization development, to optimism on dynamometer and to dislike of the exacting task of card sorting. These latter give it a slight resemblance to a former factor (7) of Easy verbal activity vs. Fortitude. At the negative pole is a marked "horde" pattern (3) wherein individuals change their opinions toward those of the group, show increase in homogeneity, and throw themselves into tasks with a sense of urgency and without preamble. The factor has only very slight relation to personality factors (C and M), and

FACTOR 3

### *Democratic, Explicit Procedure-Orientation vs. Horde Urgency*

| VARIABLE MATRIX NO. | DESCRIPTIVE TITLE | FACTOR LOADING |
|---|---|---|
| 93 | OR Much concern with procedure | ·90 |
| 75 | OR High degree of leadership | ·63 |
| 73 | OR High degree of group organization | ·62 |
| 52 | *Construction:* Much time spent in planning | ·56 |
| 85 | *Interests:* Members show much persistence in individuality * | —·54 |
| 77 | OR High degree of freedom of group atmosphere | ·46 |
| 84 | *Interests:* Low decrease in variance of individual investments about group preferences * | —·44 |
| 91 | *Discussion:* Dislike for Card Sorting situation | —·43 |
| 81 | *Dynamometer,* sustained pull: Optimism of aspiration | ·42 |
| 35 | SR Many members rated as making significant contributions | ·41 |
| 92 | OR High degree of motivation | ·40 |
| 89 | *Discussion:* High preference for Dynamometer Situation | ·37 |
| 78 | OR High degree of we-feeling | ·37 |
| 68 | *Dynamometer,* jerking pull: Much increase with practice | ·37 |

must be considered to arise largely from a group structural character of institutionalizing procedure, for this is loaded ·90.

This factor [*4*] is probably of less significance than its rank order indicates, because of spurious correlations among three construction-aspiration variables, which should fall lower in the factor. Its central feature is a schizoid high and unadaptable aspiration level (also in the dynamometer), with rigidity also in starting with little planning and in failing to reduce planning when it proves unprofitable. There is also evidence of low orderliness of procedure but satisfaction with co-workers. Since this factor has the highest loading of the population measure of schizothymia (A—) it may be that the whole pattern is to be ascribed to a summation of such personalities.

FACTOR 4

### *Schizothyme Rigidity vs. Conformity to Circumstances*

| VARIABLE MATRIX NO. | DESCRIPTIVE TITLE | FACTOR LOADING |
|---|---|---|
| 59 | *Construction:* Not optimistic in aspiration * | —·80 |
| 58 | *Construction:* Realistic in aspiration | ·78 |
| 61 | *Construction:* Low absolute level of aspiration * | —·73 |
| 53 | *Construction:* Do most of planning before trial 1 | ·53 |
| 1 | PTM Friendly cyclothymia (A) | ·37 |
| 31 | PTV Narrow range of Deliberate Will Control ($Q_3$) | —·34 |
| 89 | *Discussion:* High preference for Dynamometer situation | ·33 |
| 33 | SR Wish to retain *few* of present members in future meetings | —·32 |
| 15 | PTM Low level of Deliberate Will Control ($Q_3$) | —·31 |

While the measures from the sociometric area tend to overshadow the others, this factor [5] relates every panel of measurement in the present experiment. Because of this, we have rejected the possibility that it might be an artifact arising from some common response set, or treatment of the Likert type continua items used in the ratings, though such an artifact may have served to elevate these loadings.

The three items loading the factor [5] highest have no other significant loadings in the entire matrix. What they seem to have in common is an immediate enjoyment of the group life itself (though the sociometric ratings of actual individuals do not come here). That the ratings represent

FACTOR 5

*High Intrinsic Synergy vs. Low Intrinsic Synergy*

| VARIABLE MATRIX NO. | DESCRIPTIVE TITLE | FACTOR LOADING |
|---|---|---|
| 41 | SR High rated integration | .82 |
| 42 | SR High satisfaction with overall efficiency | .70 |
| 39 | SR High optimism for group's future performances | .57 |
| 36 | SR High rated enjoyment of the group's activities | .54 |
| 40 | SR Much commonness of purpose | .52 |
| 38 | SR Members tended to feel accepted by the group | .49 |
| 37 | SR Members *did not* feel free to participate * | —.35 |
| 81 | *Dynamometer*, sustained pull: High optimism of aspiration | .34 |
| 27 | PTV Wide range in Polished Fastidiousness (N) | .32 |
| 71 | *Dynamometer*, sustained pull: High total score | .32 |
| 70 | *Dynamometer*, jerking pull: High total score | .31 |
| 80 | OR high degree of interdependence | .30 |

more than a subjective feeling, however, is attested by the observer rating of group interdependence and by the dynamometer performances which we have found before to be good indices of group motivation. There are slight personality associations with large scatter on both "Polished Fastidiousness" and dominance, which might mean less individual competitiveness than if the group were homogeneous.

However, though we are dealing with a synergy level pattern, akin to that in factor 1, it seems difficult to ascribe it similarly to personality levels. It must arise from interrelations of persons which generate in some groups a higher level of gregarious satisfactions than exist in others. This source of synergy clearly corresponds to what we have called in our theoretical analysis (1) *intrinsic synergy*, i.e., that synergy which arises from the stimulus of social contacts themselves, and which has also been noted in group data by Hemphill (12).

The characteristics of this factor [6] are a high mean in population intelligence, intellectual interest (possibly radicalism) and cyclothymia; a high scatter in as many as four other factors; a "good" performance in some group work, notably judgment and coordinated action on the dynamometer. Variable 60 in this context may indicate refusal to disregard reported norms in consequence of a single experience and 52 a quick resolution of problems of organization.

This factor [*6*] has considerable resemblance to the largest in our earlier pilot study (7), there labelled *Intelligent "Esprit de corps"* or Morale I. There is the same propensity for intellectual problems, the same intelligent mutual understanding without time spent in discussion (coordination) and the same adaptability, both in group aspiration (*10*) and the adjustment of individual interests to those reached in group discussion (*85*).

FACTOR 6

*Intelligent Role Interaction vs. Low Morale I*

| VARIABLE MATRIX NO. | DESCRIPTIVE TITLE | FACTOR LOADING |
|---|---|---|
| 1 | PTM High Friendly Cyclothymia (A) | ·51 |
| 21 | PTV High Variance, Surgency (F) | ·50 |
| 29 | PTV High Variance, Radicalism ($Q_1$) | ·50 |
| 22 | PTV High Variance, Positive Character Integration (G) | ·45 |
| 54 | *Group Judgment:* High level of accuracy | ·45 |
| 23 | PTV High Variance, Adventurous Cyclothymia (H) | ·40 |
| 60 | *Construction:* Little difference between aspiration estimates * | —·40 |
| 12 | PTM High level of Radicalism ($Q_1$) | ·38 |
| 2 | PTM High Level of Intelligence (B) | ·36 |
| 52 | *Construction:* Little planning * | —·35 |
| 85 | *Interests:* Members show increased preference for the group's choices | ·35 |
| 70 | *Dynamometer,* jerking pull: High total score | ·33 |

Our hypothesis then, which was that these characteristics might arise from a higher intelligence level in the population, is confirmed here to the extent that Personality Factor B is significantly loaded, as found in no other syntality factor. However, since the higher loadings are in *variances* the possible modification must be considered that this higher "group intelligence" arises not only from higher mean population intelligence and information but also from more varied group resources and better "role differentiation."

The group performances outstanding here [*6*] are those which benefit through individuals acting on their own but with awareness of the needs of others and with conscientiousness. Their success comes not from warmth of immediate interaction but from group values in the individuals which cause them to act appropriately in isolation. Performances are unhurried, economical of words but effective. The members are rated as unfrustrated and satisfied with co-workers but they do not feel themselves as highly accepted, while the leadership procedures are democratic and permissive.

FACTOR 7

*Democratic "Savoir Faire" vs. Lack of Self Possession*

| VARIABLE MATRIX NO. | DESCRIPTIVE TITLE | FACTOR LOADING |
|---|---|---|
| 47 | *Card sorting:* High number right | ·76 |
| 79 | OR Low degree of frustration | —·45 |
| 48 | *Card sorting:* High rate of completion * | —·43 |
| 18 | PTV Narrow range of Intelligence (B) | —·36 |
| 89 | *Discussion:* Low preference for the dynamometer situation | —·34 |
| 74 | OR Democratic type of leadership technique | ·34 |
| 20 | PTV Wide range of Dominance (E) | ·34 |
| 31 | PTV Wide range of Deliberate Will Control ($Q_3$) | ·34 |
| 43 | *Guessing Game:* Ask few questions for "easy" items * | —·32 |
| 38 | SR Members do not feel accepted by the group | —·31 |
| 8 | PTM Members tend to be Tender-minded, not Hard headed (I) | —·31 |
| 72 | *Dynamometer* sustained pull: Show increased success with practice | ·31 |
| 11 | PTM High Level of Polished Fastidiousness (N) | ·30 |

A similar factor [7], involving good guessing game performance, a similar dislike of physical performance, high interest in polished, esthetic activity, self criticisms, and insusceptibility to emotional appeal was found in the pilot study (7) and called "Friendly Urbanity, savoir faire vs. Lack of group self-possession." Some observers have wished to call the present factor "Laissez faire" vs. control of individuality. The present title is a compromise, intended to express a bipolarity between independent group respecting action, which is one essence of democracy, and some degree of regimentation required by lack of self possession. It remains for later research to investigate the relation of the two independent dimensions of democratic organization found here—that opposed to urgency (Factor 3) and that opposed to control of individuality (Factor 7)—to the definition used by Lippitt (16) and Lewin and presumably combining these and other meanings of democracy.

The origin of the present pattern [7] can scarcely lie in population

FACTOR 8

*High Verbal Interaction*

| VARIABLE MATRIX NO. | DESCRIPTIVE TITLE | FACTOR LOADING |
|---|---|---|
| 5 | PTM High surgency (F) | ·60 |
| 63 | *Discussion:* Preference for Group Judgment | ·58 |
| 71 | *Dynamometer*, sustained pull: High total score | ·57 |
| 69 | *Dynamometer*, jerking pull: Not optimistic | —·52 |
| 88 | *Discussion:* Low preference for Guessing Game * | —·39 |
| 7 | PTM High level of Adventurous Cyclothymia (H) | ·36 |
| 77 | OR Not a free group atmosphere * | —·35 |

## FACTOR 9

### *Recklessness*

| VARIABLE MATRIX NO. | DESCRIPTIVE TITLE | FACTOR LOADING |
|---|---|---|
| 86 | *Interests:* Group concentrates its resources (votes) on its highest preferences | —·87 |
| 87 | *Interests:* Few inconsistencies in group decisions | —·81 |
| 51 | *Interests:* Short time taken to cast votes * | —·59 |
| 91 | *Discussion:* Low preference for Card Sorting * | —·43 |
| 69 | *Dynamometer*, jerking pull: Not optimistic | —·36 |

personality means, if the loadings of the latter should prove, even with other rotations, to be no higher than here. Yet it is striking that the group characteristics are just those one would expect to be associated with personality factors I— and N+.

This [*8*] is almost certainly a factor arising from a personality factor-surgency. The preferred activities are those involving talking and of high sustained rope pull might well also spring from the high "primitive passive sympathy" (3). It is noteworthy, in view of McDougall's theory of extrovert authoritarianism (17) that this factor contains a negative loading on freedom of group atmosphere.

Some raising of the top loadings has probably occurred here [*9*] through measures being derivative from a single situation. The high groups tend to perform the interest ranking quickly, to concentrate interest on a few alternatives only and to change little from the order assigned earlier. Together with the low optimism and the failure to improve on successive dynamometer pulls, as well as the high level of personality factor I, this suggests a kind of recklessness, but requires more variables to clarify.

This [*10*] is a psychologically consistent pattern of behavior involving a slow rate of questioning, probably a result of the group's taking time to consider and formulate its questions, a quick arrival at the solution, high we-feeling, motivation, etc. It cannot be accounted for by any population

## FACTOR 10

### *Group Elation vs. Group Phlegm*

| VARIABLE MATRIX NO. | DESCRIPTIVE TITLE | FACTOR LOADING |
|---|---|---|
| 45 | *Guessing Game:* Slow rate of questioning | ·60 |
| 46 | *Guessing Game:* Short time taken to get "easy" answer * | —·57 |
| 78 | OR High degree of we-feeling | ·46 |
| 77 | OR High freedom of group atmosphere | ·43 |
| 70 | *Dynamometer*, jerking pull: High total pull | ·43 |
| 26 | PTV Wide variance in Bohemian Symbolic Aggressiveness (M) | ·39 |
| 92 | OR High degree of motivation | ·38 |
| 80 | OR High degree of interdependence | ·36 |

FACTOR 11

*Homogeneity of Emotional Maturity*

| VARIABLE MATRIX NO. | DESCRIPTIVE TITLE | FACTOR LOADING |
|---|---|---|
| 19 | PTV Uniform Emotional Maturity (C) | —·94 |
| 69 | *Dynamometer*, jerking pull: Optimistic aspiration estimate | ·60 |
| 94 | Random number | ·41 |
| 72 | *Dynamometer*, sustained pull: Improvement with practice | ·38 |

characteristic present in the matrix. Our hypothesis is that it is a situationally engendered excitement or elation level.

Perhaps we may infer from this factor [*11*] that when members are more nearly of the same level of emotional maturity they tend to have more confidence in each other (as shown by higher aspiration in a real situation) and are able to learn better. At least it is evident that homogeneity of emotional maturity is an important independent dimension, though its full associations can scarcely be glimpsed with the limited related variables here.

Although loadings below ·40 can only be accepted as suggestive and not as of definite significance, we may include several in these last few factors of smallest variance in order to help our tentative interpretations of the total pattern. Here [*12*] the high groups like construction, dislike attitude, interest and group judgment discussions, and are poor at performances requiring coordination. There is a suggestion of dominant individuals yet of tendency to modify opinions toward the group. Experimenters with experience of many groups, high and low, are inclined to interpret this factor as an evasion of group life, associating the construction preference with impersonal activity, dawdling and horse-play (for which casualness the dominance may be a prerequisite)! It seems a condition in which the individual has not really accepted the group as a means to his ends, and has some similarity to the Withdrawal factor, No. 4, in the pilot study.

FACTOR 12

*Disregard of Group vs. Acceptance of Group Goals*

| VARIABLE MATRIX NO. | DESCRIPTIVE TITLE | FACTOR LOADING |
|---|---|---|
| 62 | *Discussion:* Preference for Construction Situation | ·80 |
| 90 | *Discussion:* Low preference for Interests Situation * | —·41 |
| 77 | OR Free group atmosphere | ·40 |
| 4 | PTM Dominance (E) | ·38 |
| 85 | *Interests:* Members show increased preference for the group's choice | ·38 |
| 47 | *Card Sorting:* Few stacks correct * | —·37 |
| 71 | *Dynamometer*, sustained pull: Low total score * | —·34 |
| 64 | *Discussion:* Low preference for Attitude situation | —·31 |

Here [*13*] we find the existence of wide ranges of individual differences on the personality traits of tendermindedness, suspiciousness and Bohemianism associated with poor performance on the sustained Dynamometer pull, pull learning thereon, taking a long time to reach decisions in the Discussion situation, a dislike of the Attitude situation and a reported feeling that many members hindered the group process.

The performance measures here seem fairly clearly to be consequences of the personality variances which load the factor. These may operate by making it difficult to achieve agreement either as to goals (the slow speed of ranking may be due to this) or as to how to achieve them.

FACTOR 13

*Frustrating Temperamental Heterogeneity vs. Morale from Homogeneity*

| VARIABLE MATRIX NO. | DESCRIPTIVE TITLE | FACTOR LOADING |
|---|---|---|
| 24 | PTV High variance in Tender-Minded Sensitivity (I) | ·62 |
| 25 | PTV High variance in Paranoid suspiciousness (L) | ·54 |
| 26 | PTV High variance in Bohemian symbolic aggressiveness (M) | ·47 |
| 71 | *Dynamometer,* sustained pull: Low score * | —·44 |
| 49 | *Discussion:* Slow speed of ranking preferences | ·41 |
| 64 | *Discussion:* Low preference for Attitude situation | —·40 |
| 34 | SR Many members rated as hindering the group's progress | ·38 |

The factor [*13*] appears to be worthy of careful consideration on the part of those people concerned with assembling teams or work groups, such as small ship or air crews. Thus, grouping people who are alike, whether they are high or low on these three traits, could be expected to result in a reduction in the amount of "personality conflict," as well as in misunderstandings which result from the different perceptual systems associated with different ranges of these scales, and which lead to loss of effectiveness and to accidents. It may be worth pointing out that the fact that these are variance, rather than mean, scores would allow this kind of classification to be done with essentially no attrition.

This factor [*14*] has little variance, but was recognized by participating observers as one of inhibition of verbal interaction presumably through the diffidence of low dominance and large variations in emotional maturity. Discussion activity lags, but manual activities are done quickly, though with little planning and somewhat poor results.

A fifteenth factor, loading liking for guessing game, the presence of many negative effectors and high H variance, also reached simple structure but had little variance left. It is interpreted by group observers as a factor of anarchy and disruptedness, but can be regarded only as a suggestive indication.

FACTOR 14

*Diffidence in Internal Communications*

| VARIABLE MATRIX NO. | DESCRIPTIVE TITLE | FACTOR LOADING |
|---|---|---|
| 52 | *Construction:* Low amount of planning | —·61 |
| 53 | Construction: Planning is done predominantly for first trial | ·50 |
| 55 | *Group Judgment:* Fast in reporting decisions | —·47 |
| 19 | PTV Low variance in Emotional Maturity (C) | —·38 |
| 44 | *Guessing Game:* Ask few questions in trying for "difficult" item | —·36 |
| 56 | *Construction:* Slow rate | ·34 |
| 4 | PTM Low level of Dominance (E) | —·31 |

## 6. SUMMARY

1. A factor analysis of 93 population, structure and syntality variables measured on 80 neonate groups of 10 men each has revealed 15, some of which are recognizably similar to factors indicated in the preliminary pilot study five years ago (7).

2. The striking general feature of these factor patterns is the high loading found in them for population personality variables. One may therefore contingently conclude that the syntality of formally leaderless groups, in their first three hours of existence, when exposed to the same, but very varied, demands, is primarily determined by the pre-group personalities of the component individuals.

3. Of the eight group dimensions in which population personality factors have highest or substantial loadings six are connected with high means —in personality dimensions A, B (Intelligence), F, H, I and L. Two are associated with high population variances (heterogeneity)—in factor C (Emotion stability vs. neuroticism) and the temperament factors I and L.

4. The nature of the *group* factors found with high *individual* personality factor means are entirely psychologically consistent with what is known about these personality factors. For example, high L (Paranoid) powerfully reduces the immediately available group synergy, while high F (Surgency) produces high verbal interaction and group contagion of emotion.

5. The independent dimensions of group variation not associated with population differences can only arise from small, accidental, unintended differences of group experience which have the peculiarity of exaggerating themselves by a feedback mechanism or which for some reason produce, directly, relatively large results. The Group Elation factor may be of the latter kind, as a success-failure consequence. The level of Intrinsic Synergy, and of Acceptance of Group Goals can be envisaged as generated by the former mechanism, through cumulative effects of initial faint attitudes.

It is difficult, however, without further examination of the data, to suggest hypotheses for the generation of the two democracy dimensions. A possibility is that to subjects in different economic circumstances the $100 reward represented different levels of urgency and so differentially reduced, in some groups, the toleration of punctilio in procedure. Such background "situational" differences, not embodied in personality, have not yet been investigated.

6. Some of the syntality factors loaded in population measures present significant correlations among personality factors. It remains to be investigated whether these are (as they could be) the same as the second-order factors found in *individual* psychological research on personality factors, or how far they illustrate the theoretically interesting possibility that certain *combinations* of personality factors in a group uniquely generate group "emergents." For example, the combination (in Factor 13) of high variance in the neurosis-associated I factor with the paranoid L factor can readily be imagined to produce the observed morale-destroying effects in a way not likely from either alone.

7. The concepts of synergy and maintenance synergy, as important dimensions of syntality, are borne out by this analysis, in that cohesion ("we-feeling"), strength of motivation, optimism of aspiration and goodness of performance on non-complex but exhausting tests are shown to go together. However, this synergy pattern is shown to arise from more than one cause. Fuller discussion of dynamic hypotheses regarding these factors is best deferred, however, until further research, now in progress, has confirmed and sharpened the patterns.

The writers wish to express their indebtedness to Dr. Arthur Melton for permission to use Air Force Groups, to the Commanding Officer, Great Lakes Naval Training Center for the use of Navy groups, and to the research assistant, Mr. Adam Miller, for his faithful and skilled work in the IBM factor analyses.

## REFERENCES

1. Cattell, R. B. Concepts and methods in the measurement of group syntality. *Psychol. Rev.*, 1948, 55, 48–63.
2. Cattell, R. B. The dimensions of culture patterns by factorization of national characters. *J. abnorm. soc. Psychol.*, 1949, 44, 443–469.
3. Cattell, R. B. *Personality: A systematic theoretical and factual study.* New York: McGraw-Hill, 1950.
4. Cattell, R. B. New concepts for measuring leadership, in terms of group syntality. *Hum. Relat.*, 1951, 4, 161–184.
5. Cattell, R. B. *Factor analysis for social science.* New York: Harper, 1952.
6. Cattell, R. B. An attempt at more refined definition of the cultural dimensions of syntality in modern nations. *Amer. sociol. Rev.*, 1952.
7. Cattell, R. B., & Wispe, L. G. The dimensions of syntality in small groups. *J. soc. Psychol.*, 1948, 28, 57–78.
8. Cattell, R. B., Saunders, D. R., & Stice, G. *The 16 personality factor questionnaire.* Champaign, Ill.: Instit. Personal. and Ability Tests, 1950.

9. Cattell, R. B., & Meeland, T. Standardization and social validation of the 16PF test on occupational and clinical groups. (In press).
10. Festinger, L. Informal communications in small groups. In H. Guetzkow (Ed.), *Groups, leadership and men.* Pittsburg: Carnegie Press, 1951. Pp. 28–43.
11. Gibb, C. A. The emergence of leadership in small temporary groups of men. Ph.D. Thesis, Univer. of Illinois Library, 1949.
12. Hemphill, J. K. Situational factors in leadership. *Bur. educ. Res. Monogr.*, 1949, No. 31. Columbus: Ohio State Univer.
13. Hemphill, J. K. The measurement of group dimensions. *J. Psychol.*, 1950, 29, 325–342.
14. Hofstaetter, P. R. A factorial study of culture patterns in the U.S. *J. Psychol.*, 1951, 32, 99–113.
15. James, J. A preliminary study of the size determinant in small group interaction. *Amer. sociol. Rev.*, 1951, 16, 474–477.
16. Lippitt, R. Field theory and experiment in social psychology: Autocratic and democratic group atmospheres. *Amer. J. Sociol.*, 1939, 45, 26–49.
17. McDougall, W. *National welfare and national decay.* New York: Methuen, 1921.
18. Thorndike, R. L. Individual differences. *Annu. Rev. Psychol.*, 1950, 1, 87–104.
19. Thurstone, L. L., & Chave, E. J. *Attitude scales.* Chicago: Univer. of Chicago Press, 1929.

# *The Influence of Individual Members on the Characteristics of Small Groups*

WILLIAM HAYTHORN

THERE has been increased emphasis in social psychology recently on the description and measurement of group characteristics. Hemphill and Westie (10) and Cattell and Wispé (6) have been particularly concerned with isolating dimensions along which groups vary. However,

FROM *Journal of Abnormal and Social Psychology*, 1953, 48, 276–284. Reprinted by permission of the author and the American Psychological Association, Inc.

The work described in this paper was done under a contract between the U.S. Navy, Office of Naval Research, and the University of Rochester. This is the eighth paper resulting from that work, and is a revision of a portion of a doctoral dissertation presented at the University of Rochester in 1952 (9). The work was under the general supervision of Dr. Launor F. Carter. Drs. Beatrice Shriver and John Lanzetta rendered invaluable service as observers and informal consultants.

little has been done to relate these group characteristics to the behavior of group members.

Cattell (4) has suggested that leadership be defined in terms of the effect the individual has on group "syntality," and has further hypothesized that each member of a group contributes something to the characteristics of the group. Redl (14) has discussed leadership in terms of the "central person" around whom group formative processes occur, the implication being that the central person is the primary factor in determining the nature of the group.

Other writers (12, 13, 15) in the area of group dynamics have theorized that group characteristics grow out of social interaction in the group, but to the author's knowledge there have been no experimental studies specifically focused on the relationships between the behavior of individual group members and the characteristics of the group. The present study attempts to explore some of these relationships.

## METHOD

In order to isolate the effects an individual has on groups, it is necessary to have him work in several groups with different co-workers. Our experimental design, presented in Table 1, permits isolating the effect each subject (*S*) had on his groups, since each *S* worked in five unique groups; that is, no other *S* worked in more than one of them.

TABLE 1

*Experimental Design*

| SESSION | GROUPS * | | | |
|---|---|---|---|---|
| 1 | ABCD | EFGH | IJKL | MNOP |
| 2 | AEIM | BFJN | CGKO | DHLP |
| 3 | AFKP | BELO | CHIN | DGJM |
| 4 | AGLN | BHKM | CEJP | DFIO |
| 5 | AHJO | BGIP | CFLM | DEKN |

* Letters represent *S*s.

The *S*s were NROTC sophomores, all of whom volunteered and were paid one dollar per hour. They were brought to the laboratory in groups of four and asked to work on three different tasks—reasoning (R), mechanical assembly (MA), and discussion (D). The R and MA tasks are similar to those described in a previous publication (2). That is, the R task involved group solution of syllogistic reasoning problems, and the MA task involved building various structures from precut and predrilled lumber. Both tasks required a high degree of group participation and coordination. For the D task, TAT pictures were presented and the *S*s were asked to compose a story as a group (9, 11). This invariably touched off an active, lively discussion. Group agreement was required.

While the *S*s were working on the tasks, two observers (*O*s) independently watched and recorded behavior by a new recording technique, reported by Carter, *et al.* (3), in which the observers "categorize" and "type out" behavior as it occurs. At the end of each task the *O*s rated the *S*s on twelve behavioral characteristics such as cooperativeness, aggressiveness, and efficiency. Reliability of rating scales ranged from .10 (cooperativeness on the MA task) to .98 with an average reliability of .86.

At the end of the session, both *S*s and *O*s rated the group on eleven group characteristics such as morale, productivity, and cohesiveness. The average interobserver reliability for these ratings was .70, with a range from .20 to .92. The average correlation between ratings by *O*s and by *S*s, which provides another kind of reliability measure, was .64. Although these reliabilities are lower than one would wish, they are considered high enough to make the ratings of some value in an exploratory study such as this one.

In addition, the *S*s were asked to select the best and poorest leaders in the group, as well as the person with whom they liked best to work and the person with whom they liked least to work. Finally, after all groups had been run, *S*s were asked to fill out the Cattell Sixteen Personality Factor Questionnaire (5).

There were, then, the following measures of the behavior of individual group members:

1. The number of choices and rejections received by each *S* from his 15 co-workers on the two choice criteria. Because these were highly intercorrelated, a single measure of choice value was computed for each *S* by simply combining the two measures.
2. The ratings by two independent *O*s of each *S* on 12 variables on each of 3 tasks.
3. The behavioral or interaction categories recorded by *O*s for each *S*.
4. Scores on each of the 16 personality factors of the Cattell questionnaire.

For measures of characteristics of groups in which each *S* worked, two sets of scores were computed:

1. The ratings of group characteristics by each of the *S*'s 15 co-workers were summed. Thus, from Table 1 it can be seen that the average cohesiveness of groups in which subject A worked can be determined by summing the ratings of group cohesiveness by *S*s $B_1$, $C_1$, $D_1$, $E_2$, $I_2$, $M_2$, $F_3$, $K_3$, $P_3$, $G_4$, $L_4$, $N_4$, $H_5$, $J_5$, and $O_5$. The numeral subscripts indicate the session number.
2. The ratings of group characteristics by *O*s were summed over the five groups in which each *S* worked. The average morale, for example, of groups in which subject E worked can be determined by summing the ratings of group morale by the *O*s for groups EFGH, AEIM, BELO, CEJP, and DEKN.

## RESULTS

### *Relationships between Ss' "Choice Values" and Characteristics of Groups in Which They Worked*

Each *S*'s choice value was determined by counting all of the choices received by him from his co-workers, and subtracting from that all the rejections he received. Correlation coefficients between these scores and the average ratings of characteristics of groups in which each *S* worked (described above) were computed, and are presented in Table 2. The correlations with co-workers' ratings of group characteristics indicate statistically significant relationships between the degree to which an *S* was chosen by his co-workers and the extent to which co-workers rated groups in which he worked as high in morale, cooperativeness, cohesiveness, motivation, and interest in job completion. These results suggest

TABLE 2

*Correlations between Subjects' Total Sociometric Scores and Ratings of Characteristics of Groups in which Subjects Worked*

*(N=16)*

| GROUP CHARACTERISTICS RATED | SOURCE OF RATINGS CO-WORKERS | OBSERVERS |
|---|---|---|
| 1. Talkativeness | —.24 | .03 |
| 2. Morale | .68 | .56 |
| 3. Competitiveness | —.10 | —.18 |
| 4. Cooperativeness | .69 | .38 |
| 5. Productivity | .36 | .29 |
| 6. Cohesiveness | .52 | .19 |
| 7. Motivation | .67 | .27 |
| 8. Friendliness | .31 | .09 |
| 9. Activity | .24 | .14 |
| 10. Job Completion | .59 | .49 |
| 11. Social Interaction | .30 | .11 |

$r_{.05} = .49; r_{.10} = .43.$

that individuals who are highly chosen by co-workers "facilitate" group functioning, and that individuals who "depress" group functioning are not generally chosen by other members of the group. A possible alternative interpretation is that, since co-workers' ratings of group characteristics are correlated with co-workers' choices of group members, the results simply reflect halo in the co-workers' ratings. The former interpretation, however, is supported by the statistically significant correlations between *S*s' choice-value scores and ratings by *O*s of group morale and interest in job completion.

## *Relationships between Rated Behavior of Ss and Rated Characteristics of Groups in Which Ss Worked*

The preceding results suggest that highly chosen persons contribute to characteristics indicative of "smooth" group functioning. In order to determine what kinds of *behavior* facilitate or depress each of the group characteristics rated, correlations were computed between the average ratings of each *S* by the *O*s on each of the 12 behavioral traits and the ratings by co-workers of the characteristics of groups in which the *S*s worked.[1]

How the standard error of *r* should be determined is difficult to ascertain. There was an *N* of only 16 *S*s, but each *S* was observed in five different groups. An *N* of 80 gives an underestimation of standard error, since there were not 80 independent measures. An *N* of 16 gives an equally inaccurate overestimate of standard error, since there were 16 clusters of five scores each in the computations. However, since the latter gives a more conservative estimate, it was adopted.

With an *N* of 16 it is obvious that not many of the relationships are statistically significant. However, there are many factors depressing these correlations. For one thing, both sets of ratings include considerable error variance, and no correction for attenuation has been applied. Secondly, the correlations are between ratings of limited aspects of the *S*s' behavior and ratings of equally limited aspects of the group's characteristics. Presumably the *S*'s total behavioral pattern interacts with the total group in a more complicated manner than that indicated by these correlations. In the third place, the correlations indicate relationships between the rated behavior of single *S*s and the rated characteristics of groups in which the *S*s worked. It is more probable that the nature of a group is related to the behavior of all members and to the interaction between members. In view of this, and of the exploratory nature of the study, examining the obtained correlations for any suggested trends seems justified.

To discuss each of the correlations would be a tedious task, and would involve much repetition since the behavioral ratings are not completely independent. Carter and Couch (1) have factor analyzed ratings of similar traits rated under similar laboratory conditions, and have identified three factors which have been labelled Group Goal Facilitation, I; Striving for Individual Prominence, II; and Group Sociability, III. These factor analyses have been done with data from several experiments, using various *O*s and groups of various sizes and structures. There is, therefore, considerable reason to believe that most of the variance in the present 12 traits can be accounted for by the same three factors. Because of this, it is desirable to summarize the present results in terms of the factors.

If attention is directed to only those correlations significant at the .10 level or better, a definite pattern is evident. Of the 35 statistically significant correlations, 27 are between Factor I traits—cooperativeness, prestige, efficiency, and insight—and group characteristics indicating a smooth group functioning. Group morale, for instance, was correlated .66 with individual cooperativeness on the D task, .45 with prestige on the MA task, .52 with efficiency on the MA task, .47 with efficiency on the D task, .48 with insightfulness on the MA task, and .45 with insightfulness on the D task. The only other trait significantly related to group morale was

1 The table of correlations appears in detail in the original article.

leadership (.47 on the D task). This suggests that Factor I behavior as seen by *O*s "facilitated" group morale as seen by co-workers.

Similarly, co-workers' ratings of group cooperativeness correlated .47 with individual cooperativeness on the D task, .42 with prestige on the R task, .47 with prestige on the MA task, .48 with efficiency on the R task, .54 with efficiency on the MA task, .45 with efficiency on the D task, and .53 with insightfulness on the MA task. Factor I behavior, then, apparently facilitated group cooperativeness.

Group motivation correlated .45 with ratings of prestige on the MA task, .54 with efficiency on the D task, and .48 with insightfulness on the MA task. Group interest in job completion correlated .43 with prestige on the MA task, and .45 with insightfulness on the MA task. These findings suggest that individuals whom *O*s rate as efficient, insightful, and having prestige also increase the motivation of other members of the group.

Group talkativeness, which *S*s apparently considered inefficient activity, was negatively related to individual prestige on the R task (−.54) and on the MA task (−.47); to individual efficiency on the R task (−.49), and on the MA task (−.58); and to individual insightfulness on the R task (−.54) and on the MA task (−.54). Factor I behavior on the R and MA tasks significantly "depressed" group talkativeness, as rated by *S*s' co-workers.

Prestige and efficiency on the R task were also positively related to group interest in social interaction (.42 and .49 respectively). It would seem from all these *r*'s that when one member of a group engaged in a high degree of "group goal-facilitating" behavior, the entire group functioned better in terms of the measures obtained.

Group friendliness, however, was negatively related to most of the individual traits rated. Factor II traits—aggressiveness, initiative, confidence, authoritarianism, interest in individual solution, and leadership—tended especially to depress group friendliness. This factor—striving for individual prominence—seems to be somewhat similar to the self-oriented need behavior described by Fouriezos, Hutt, and Guetzkow (7). The finding that such behavior is negatively related to group friendliness is consistent with their finding that such behavior was negatively related to participant satisfaction with the meeting. Particularly relevant here is the correlation of −.56 between interest in individual solution and group friendliness.

There was some tendency for Factor III—sociability—to increase group talkativeness and interest in social interaction but the trend is not very significant statistically.

In summary it can be said that Factor I behavior—group goal-facilitation—was positively related to co-workers' ratings of group morale, cooperativeness, motivation, and interest in job completion. Factor II behavior—striving for individual prominence—tended to be negatively related to group friendliness. Factor III behavior—sociability—tended to be positively related to group talkativeness and interest in social interaction. Other specific findings, such as the correlation of .44 between individual submissiveness and group competitiveness, may suggest possible research leads for the future, but standing alone as they do here does not inspire much confidence in them.

## *Relationships between Personality Factors and Group Characteristics*

It will be recalled that *S*s were given the Cattell Sixteen Personality Factor Questionnaire after all the groups had been run. Correlations were computed between scores on the 16 factors and ratings of group characteristics by *O*s (described above). These correlations are presented in Table 3.

TABLE 3

*Correlations between Sixteen Personality Factor Questionnaire and Ratings of Group Characteristics by Observers*

*(N=16)*

| GROUP CHARACTERISTICS RATED | PERSONALITY FACTORS* | | | | | | | | | | |
|---|---|---|---|---|---|---|---|---|---|---|---|
| | A | C | E | F | G | H | L | M | O | $Q_2$ | $Q_3$ |
| 1. Morale | .24 | .58 | | | | .10 | | | −.49 | −.11 | |
| 2. Competition | −.45 | | | | | | | | | | |
| 3. Productivity | .17 | .48 | −*.16* | −.10 | .19 | | | −.61 | | .14 | .41 |
| 4. Cohesiveness | .37 | | *.26* | .07 | | .29 | −.69 | | −.33 | *.15* | |
| 5. Motivation | | .27 | | −.25 | | | | | −.26 | | |
| 6. Friendliness | | | *.01* | .18 | | .17 | −.57 | | | −.33 | |
| 7. Job Completion | | .43 | −*.21* | −.21 | | | | −.43 | | .00 | |
| 8. Social Interaction | | | *.33* | | | .62 | | | | −.42 | |

$r_{.05}=.49$

* For descriptions of the personality factors, see the text and Cattell (5). Italics indicate cases in which the direction of the relationship was predicted incorrectly.

Before any of the correlations were computed, predictions were made about the directions of the relationships. The predictions were based chiefly on the general hypothesis that more mature, flexible, accepting persons would facilitate effective group functioning. A chi-square test of the hypothesis that there was no relationship between the predicted and computed signs of the correlations yielded a probability value of less than .001. That is, there is very little chance that the number of correct predictions resulted from chance. The alternate hypothesis that the directions of the relationships were predicted more accurately than chance by the general hypothesis stated must be considered tenable. The correlations in Table 3 therefore deserve a closer investigation. Only those correlations for which predictions were made were computed. Cases in which the direction of the relationship was incorrectly predicted are italicized. All of the 10 statistically significant correlations (.10 level) are in the expected directions.

Factor A, Cyclothymia vs. Schizothymia (Cattell's labelling), involves cooperativeness, trustfulness, and adaptability. The correlations are all in the expected directions, suggesting a tendency for groups in which A + *S*s worked to be rated as having high morale ($r$=.24), low competitiveness ($r$=−.45) and high cohesiveness ($r$=.37).

Factor C, Emotional Stability or Ego Strength vs. General Neuroticism, was expected to correlate positively with those group characteristics indicating efficient group functioning. The maturity and stability of high C *S*s were expected to lend stability and efficiency to groups in which C+ persons worked. The correlations between factor C scores and *O*s' ratings of group morale (.58), productivity (.48), and interest in job completion (.43) support these expectations.

Factor E, Dominance or Ascendance vs. Submission, was expected to be related positively to productivity and interest in job completion but negatively to group cohesiveness, friendliness, and interest in social interaction. All five correlations came out contrary to expectations. No satisfactory explanation of this prediction error has been achieved. The *S*s simply did not react to a dominant group member as the experimenter expected.

Factor F, Surgency vs. Desurgency, is said to describe persons "carefree, happy-go-lucky, fond of bustle and excitement, inclined to practical jokes and disinclined to occupations requiring close and accurate work" (5). It was predicted that scores on factor F would be positively related to ratings of group cohesiveness and friendliness, but negatively related to group productivity, motivation, and interest in job completion. The correlations are in the predicted directions, but low and insignificant.

Factor H, Adventurous Cyclothymia vs. Inherent Withdrawn Schizothymia, is described as a measure of the extent to which the respondent likes people. The expectation that factor H scores would be positively related to group cohesiveness and interest in social interaction was strongly supported by the correlations (.29 and .62 respectively).

Factor L, Paranoid Schizothymia vs. Trustful Accessibility, involves paranoid suspiciousness, jealousy, dourness, and rigidity. Persons scoring high on this factor were expected to depress group cohesiveness and friendliness. The correlations (−.69 and −.57 respectively) clearly tend to confirm this expectation.

Factor M, Bohemianism vs. Practical Concernedness, allegedly measures unconventionality, eccentricity and undependability. The M+ individual is described as one who "unconcernedly goes his own way in the community and does not feel much responsibility in practical matters"

(5). The correlations with *Os*' ratings of group productivity (−.61) and interest in job completion (−.43) lend strong support to the hypothesis that "practical, logical, conscientious" persons, low on factor M, facilitate group productivity while M+ individuals depress it.

Factor O, Worrying Suspiciousness vs. Calm Trustfulness, attempts to measure depressive tendencies, moodiness, etc. The correlations between factor O scores and *Os*' ratings of group morale (−.49), cohesiveness (−.33), and motivation (−.26) suggest that O+ persons detract from the pleasant feeling tone of the group.

Factor $Q_2$, Independent Self-Sufficiency vs. Lack of Resolution, is described as a measure of independence and resoluteness. A $Q_2$ person "prefers to work and make decisions in company with other people, likes social approval and admiration," etc. The correlations between factor $Q_2$ scores and *Os*' ratings of group friendliness (−.33) and interest in social interaction (−.42) suggest that individuals who are highly self-sufficient and do not particularly care for social approval tend to depress the social aspects of their groups.

In describing factor $Q_3$, Will Control and Character Stability, Cattell writes that ". . . it has been observed that when people who are high in this factor have been put together in groups, the general efficiency and objectiveness of the group is decidedly higher than in groups that are only average in the factor" (5, p. 16). The correlation (.41) with *Os*' ratings of the productivity of groups in which $Q_3$+ persons worked lends support to the hypothesis that such persons facilitate group productivity.

In summary of the results in Table 3, it seems probable that personality traits involving maturity, adaptability, and acceptance of others tend to facilitate or to be positively related to smooth and effective group functioning, while traits involving coolness, suspiciousness, eccentricity and the like tend to depress smooth group functioning (i.e., to be negatively related to ratings of group morale, cohesiveness, friendliness, etc.). This, of course, represents only a very general summary of the results, but it is felt that more specific conclusions cannot be drawn until much more research has been done. It seems clear, however, that *Ss*' responses to personality questionnaires are related to the effect *Ss* have on small groups, and that the characteristics of small groups are to some degree functions of the personality traits of individual group members.

## DISCUSSION

The preceding results indicate that there are significant relationships between the behavior of individual group members and the characteristics of the total group, and that these relationships can be experimentally isolated. They also support Cattell's hypothesis that "every man in a group is to some extent a leader in so far as every man has some effect upon the syntality of a group" (4, p. 25). The present study suggests the possibility of studying leadership in terms of the relationships between individuals and group characteristics.

The results reported here are considered highly tentative. The lack of previous research in this area and the exploratory nature of this study greatly limit the extent to which the findings can be generalized. Within these limits, however, the following conclusions are considered tenable:

1. It is possible to isolate relationships between the behaviors of individual group members and the characteristics or "syntality" traits of small groups.

2. Individuals who are chosen by co-workers as good leaders or as persons with whom others like to work "facilitate" group functioning, while individuals who "depress" group functioning are not generally chosen by other members of the group.

3. Individual behavior patterns which include cooperativeness, efficiency, and insight—Factor I behavior—tend to "facilitate" or be positively related to effective group functioning as measured by ratings of group morale, cooperativeness, productivity, cohesiveness, motivation, and interest in job completion.

4. Individual behavior patterns which include aggressiveness, self-confidence, initiative, interest in individual solution, and authoritarianism —Factor II behavior—tend to be somewhat negatively related to ratings of group cohesiveness and friendliness.

5. Sociable behavior—Factor III—tends to reduce group motivation and competition, but to increase group talkativeness, friendliness, and interest in social interaction.

6. Personality traits involving maturity, adaptability, and acceptance of others tend to be positively related to smooth and effective group functioning.

7. Personality traits involving suspiciousness, eccentricity, and coolness toward others tend to be negatively related to smooth group functioning.

The results of this study support Cattell's (4) and Gibb's (8) suggestions that leadership be studied as relationships between individual group members and "syntality" traits of the group. At least in small groups of this nature it seems probable that each individual member makes some contribution to the characteristics of the total group. Such contributions can be investigated with a design similar to the one used here. Experimental studies utilizing such a design need to be conducted with a larger number of *S*s, different task situations, larger groups, and more refined measures of personality, behavior, and group characteristics. A knowledge of the effects of behavior of individuals on each other seems essential to an understanding of small group behavior.

## SUMMARY

1. Sixteen male NROTC students met in groups of four. Each *S* worked with each other *S* once and only once, so that each *S* worked in five different groups. Each group worked on a Reasoning (R) task, a Mechanical Assembly (MA) task, and a Discussion (D) task.

2. The *S*s were observed by two independent *O*s who rated individual behavior and group characteristics. The *S*s also rated characteristics of their groups. Sociometric and personality data were obtained.

3. Relationships between measures of individuals and of groups were analyzed. Relationships were found, indicating that individual members significantly affect the characteristics of small groups. In general it was found that effective group functioning was facilitated by cooperativeness, efficiency, and insight, while behavior which we have called "striving for individual prominence" reduced group cohesiveness and friendliness.

4. Significant relationships in the predicted directions were also found between personality measures and ratings of group characteristics, suggesting that mature, accepting persons facilitate while suspicious, non-accepting persons depress group characteristics indicative of smooth functioning.

5. Some of the implications of this study for research on leadership and small group behavior were briefly discussed.

## REFERENCES

1. Carter, L. F., & Couch, A. Factorial studies of the rated behavior of group members. Paper read at East. Psychol. Ass., March 1952.
2. Carter, L. F., Haythorn, W., & Howell, Margaret. A further investigation of the criteria of leadership. *J. abnorm. soc. Psychol.*, 1950, 45, 350–358.
3. Carter, L. F., Haythorn, W., Meirowitz, Beatrice, & Lanzetta, J. Note on a new technique of interaction recording. *J. abnorm. soc. Psychol.*, 1951, 46, 258–260.
4. Cattell, R. B. Determining syntality dimensions as a basis for morale and leadership measurement. In H. Guetzkow (Ed.), *Groups, leadership, and men.* Pittsburgh: Carnegie Press, 1951. Pp. 16–27.
5. Cattell, R. B., Saunders, D. R., & Stice, G. *Handbook for the sixteen personality factor questionnaire.* Champaign, Illinois: Institute for Personality and Ability Testing, 1949.
6. Cattell, R. B., & Wispé, L. G. The dimensions of syntality in small groups. *J. soc. Psychol.*, 1948, 28, 57–78.
7. Fouriezos, N. T., Hutt, M. L., & Guetzkow, H. Measurement of self-oriented needs in discussion groups. *J. abnorm. soc. Psychol.*, 1950, 45, 682–690.
8. Gibb, C. A. The research background of an interactional theory of leadership. *Aust. J. Psychol.*, 1950, 2, 19–42.
9. Haythorn, W. The influence of the individual group members on the behavior of coworkers and on the characteristics of groups. Ph.D. thesis, Univer. of Rochester, 1952.
10. Hemphill, J. K., & Westie, C. M. The measurement of group dimensions. *J. Psychol.*, 1950, 29, 325–342.
11. Henry, W. E., & Guetzkow, H. *Group projection sketches for the study of small*

*groups*. Publication No. 4 of the Conference Research Project. Ann Arbor: Univer. of Michigan, 1949.
12. Northway, M. L., Frankel, E. B., & Potashin, R. *Personality and sociometric status*. Sociometric Monographs, No. 11. New York: Beacon House, 1947.
13. Powell, J. W. The dynamics of group formation. *Psychiatry*, 1948, 11, 117–124.
14. Redl, F. Group emotion and leadership. *Psychiatry*, 1942, 5, 573–596.
15. Slavson, S. R. *An introduction to group therapy*. New York: The Commonwealth Fund, 1943.

# *PART* III

## THE *Group* AS A *System* OF *Social Interaction*

# *Introduction*

WHEREAS *in the preceding part we were viewing the small group from the perspective of an individual facing in the present what to him is a social situation, we now broaden our perspective to take in the perspectives of all the individuals in the group and their reciprocal relations over a longer time span during which the effects of interaction have had a chance to work themselves out. We are now concerned with the processes by which the situation for each individual gets to be what it is, and how the ultimate effects of his action tend to make it remain stable or to change it.*

*The individual may at first see the group as a collection of individuals, all different, or may view the group as a kind of undifferentiated entity, or in both ways at once. But as interaction proceeds, both views become more articulate and refined. One result of interaction is the mutal adjustment of individual perspectives toward a similarity in certain respects, and toward a knowledge of similarity. The content of this overlap in perspectives and expectations we can call the common culture of the group. Another result of interaction, however, is that the members of the group become more differentiated from each other, both as to who does what kind of thing overtly and when, and also as to the picture of the group that each individual carries in his mind. The individual now begins to see himself as having a particular position within a differentiated structure or system of positions.*

*The individual feels himself a part of the group and like all other parts in his orientation to the common culture, but at the same time, different from all other parts both because he has a particular position defined by the common culture, and also because he knows he has a life apart from the group—much or most of himself and his internal life is unknown to the others and is not part of the culture he holds in common with the other members of this particular group.*

*It is not to be supposed that any member of the group pre-visualizes in any detail what the common culture of the group will be. How it devel-*

*ops depends upon many situational factors that exist independently of their representation in the awareness of any of the individuals in the group. For example, the relations of the members in physical space, the size of the group, the constrictions on amount of time available are all important, as shown in Chapter 7, in determining the network of communication—who can interact with whom, how often, and how easily. These factors affect the way the common culture grows, what parts grow at what speed, and also, obviously, the degree of "commonness" that can be achieved, within sub-parts and within the whole. And then, conversely, the nature and content of the common culture reacts back to reinforce, maintain, or change the original constrictions in numerous ways.*

*Communications or interactions in real space and time are the only means by which the common culture can be built. The result is that the physical means for building the common culture always have an economic quality of scarcity relative to the ends sought. There are always problems of allocation and co-ordination, of balance between parts, and of balance in time. Some parts change before other parts change. Time taken for solution of one problem may result in lack of time for solution of some other. Problems of this sort, which may be called problems of equilibrium, are treated in Chapter 8. Many interesting characteristics of groups arise as more or less unforseen and sometimes unconscious attempts to solve problems of this order. In general, the perspective of the individual facing a social situation is not a perspective from which one most clearly sees these problems.*

*It is usually necessary to understand such problems from both individual and system perspectives. One needs to trace the problem to the individual focus to see how it affects the motivation of the individual. Most of the change that takes place in social organization and the building of the common culture comes about because some identifiable person or persons are unhappy with things the way they are. However, it is recognized, when one takes the system perspective, that it is not a sufficient explanation of why change takes place just to understand that someone wants it. On the one hand, one needs to know how it came about that the problem arose for him, and, on the other, one needs to know how it came about that the action he took solved or failed to solve the problem for him and for the other group members.*

*Many attempts by individuals fail to change the system because they do not affect enough other individuals at the same time, or because they affect other parts of the system in unforseen ways. Sometimes actions which seem, from the perspective of the individual actor, to be headed straight toward a goal desirable to the whole group produce a net effect that is precisely the opposite of that intended. The net effects are the final results of the ways in which differentiated parts of a total system interact with each other.*

*Specialization, or role differentiation within the group (Chapter 9), can best be understood when one is able to view it both from the individual and from the system perspective. It is intimately related to the solution of problems of equilibrium. In Chapter 10 leadership is seen as a unique type of specialization, in that it is paradoxically a specialization in generality. The leader is a person who is recognized as specialized in doing whatever has to be done. For this reason, it has been difficult to give leadership an adequate theoretical base, since it is necessary to have some fundamental notion of the problems of groups as systems which change a part at a time and go through cycles in time. The difficulty in defining what the leader does or in constructing a value theory of what he should do is certainly due in part to the fact that the leader is usually required to do different things at different times, according to the condition of the group and its common culture as a system. Our ability to specify what some of these important differences of condition are has improved in the past five or ten years, but one feels that we have only begun to be able to handle the problem empirically. On the one hand, a number of studies, particularly factor analyses, seem to be tending toward some kind of consistency in the specification of three or perhaps four very general factors that are typically associated with leadership, as Carter brings out in his paper. On the other hand, studies of leadership in groups of different kinds, where the norms and values of members are different, tend to come out with results that on the surface appear contradictory. An attempt to reconcile the apparent contradictions, for example, between the findings of Lewin and Lippitt, and those of Berkowitz and Torrance, is most helpful in broadening our perspective.*

# CHAPTER 7 THE COMMUNICATION NETWORK

# *The Spatial Factor in Face to Face Discussion Groups*

BERNARD STEINZOR

## INTRODUCTION

RESEARCH efforts in a new area frequently involve the attempt to identify the variables whose interaction are crucial in determining the events ascribed to the area. Investigators of the field of group dynamics have produced a number of researches designed to describe and demonstrate the degree of significance of such postulated factors. For example, the experiment by Lewin, Lippitt and White (3) first drew attention to the importance of group atmosphere in affecting the behavior of individuals in groups. The series of experiments that have come to be known as the Western Electric studies have shown how group involvement affects the production level of individual workers (4). The studies originating from the Bethel summer workshops on group dynamics are directed toward the formulation of the dimensions of social interaction (1). These studies are also characterized by the fact that many of their findings un-

FROM *Journal of Abnormal and Social Psychology*, 1950, 45, 552–555. Reprinted by permission of the author and the American Psychological Association, Inc.

derline some practical steps a group leader must take if he is to be successful in helping his group achieve some common purpose. The study reported here does indicate one feature which individuals responsible for facilitating group discussion and action should take into account.

While investigating the effect of the intent of verbal behavior in face to face groups (5) this writer observed the behavior of one participant which appeared to be of some relevance to the behavior of the group. In one discussion group which held a series of meetings, a participant was observed changing his seat so that he could sit opposite another member with whom he had previously had a verbal altercation. This action seemed to be in line with the notion that interaction among people was not only affected by the content of what was said but by such non-verbal factors as gestures, posture, and more generally the total physical impression the individuals made on each other. Stated another way, one person will be more likely to interact with another if he is in a good position to see what he does as well as to hear him. The following hypothesis may, therefore, be proposed: seating arrangement in a small, face to face group helps to determine the individuals with whom one is likely to interact.

We might state this more concretely in the following way. In a group composed of say ten members, seated in a circular arrangement, Person *A* will more likely speak following a statement made by Person *D* who sits five seats away than following a statement by Person *B* who sits next to him. We would expect this to happen because we think that people respond to many things in an individual other than the ideas he expresses verbally. If a person happens to be in a spatial position which increases the chances of his being more completely observed, the stimulus value of his ideas and statements increases by virtue of that very factor of his greater physical and expressive impact on others. People sitting next to each other in a circle will probably not observe each other as fully as those sitting further away.

A rather simple test of this hypothesis suggested itself. The seating arrangements of individuals in a face to face group might be obtained and examined for the possibility that people sitting in a position which allows them to observe more of each other's behavior will follow one another in verbal behavior more often than people whose view of each other is limited due to the fact that they sit closer together.

## PROCEDURE

Records of the seating arrangements were available for two groups that had met over a period of weeks in a series of sessions. These groups have been described more completely in a previous publication in which a measure of social interaction was developed and evaluated (5). Group I was composed of nine members and a leader and was a sub-group of a larger class studying counseling methods. Group II was composed of ten members who volunteered as participants in the above described research project. This group did not have a designated leader and the members chose their own topics for discussion. Group I also was permitted to discuss any problem the members wished. The group discussions were electrically recorded so that an accurate picture of the sequence of individual participation on a verbal level was available.

The participants in both groups arranged themselves in a rough circle. Though the distance between the seats was not metrically equal, it was assumed that the assumption of equality would not introduce a serious error. The data were quantified by tallying the number of times persons removed

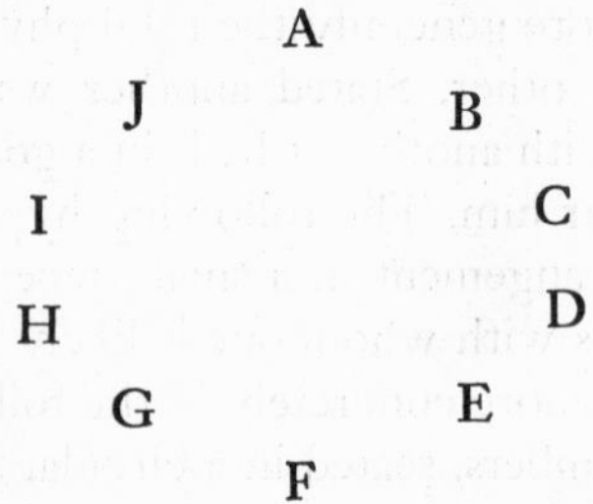


FIG. 1. *An Example of Circular Seating Arrangement for a Group*

from each other by five, four, three, two and one seats followed each other in a verbal remark. Seating distance was thus used as a measure directly proportional to the degree with which the group members could physically perceive one another. Certainly the use of seating distance as such an index isn't feasible when the group is a very large one. For example, in a circle of 50 individuals, a person sitting ten seats away probably can be seen fully as well as a person sitting directly opposite or 25 seats away. The Chi-square technique of calculating the significance of the difference between the observed and expected frequencies was employed. In a group of ten members, the number of times individuals removed from one another by five seats will occur only half as often as individuals removed from each other by any other seating distance. For example, in Fig. 1, A is five seats away from F, but four seats away from E and also from G. To correct for this in the calculation of observed frequencies, the individuals separated by four or fewer seats were divided as to whether they sat to the right or left of the individual whom they followed with a statement. In the example, E is four seats to the left of A, and G four seats to the right. Therefore, this procedure of calculating observed frequencies meant that the number of categories would always be one less than the number of participants in the discussion.

The expected frequency was determined by dividing the total number of remarks by the number of discrete seating categories. In other words, the expected frequency was assumed to be equal for all distances between seats. The calculated Chi-squares were then converted into probability values by means of Fisher's table (2, p. 379).

## RESULTS

Table 1 summarizes the seating distances which yielded Chi-square values significant at .02 level of confidence or better, for 10 sessions of Group I for which data was available and for five sessions of Group II. The last four sessions of Group II were not used because a few of the group members left their seats and moved about a great deal. This was due to the members' decision to serve coffee during the session. Again it should be noted that in this analysis the number of seating distances is equal to the number of participants minus one. It is thus seen that not all members were present at every session.

## DISCUSSION

It is evident from the results presented in Table 1 that the analysis of sequence of statements in terms of the seating arrangements of the participants yields statistically significant results. In only four of the fifteen sessions used in this study do we fail to find a single instance for which the degree of interaction among the members sitting a given number of seats from one another differs significantly from that expected by chance.

TABLE 1

*Seating Distances Yielding Chi-Square Values Significant at at Least the .02 Level of Confidence*

| GROUP I SESSION | 1 | 2 | 3 | 4 | 6 | 7 | 9 | 12 | 16 | 18 |
|---|---|---|---|---|---|---|---|---|---|---|
| No. of possible Distances | 9 | 7 | 9 | 9 | 9 | 9 | 9 | 9 | 8 | 7 |
| Significant Factors * | | | | | | | | | | |
| Plus | 4R | 2L,2R | 5 | — | 3R | — | — | 5,4L | — | 2L |
| Minus | — | 1 | 3L | — | 1L | — | — | 2L,2R | 1R | — |

| GROUP II SESSION | 1 | 2 | 3 | 4 | 5 |
|---|---|---|---|---|---|
| No. of Possible Distances | 9 | 7 | 8 | 7 | 9 |
| Significant Factors | | | | | |
| Plus | 5 | 4 | — | 4 | 4R |
| Minus | 2L | — | — | — | 1L,1R |

* The plus row shows the seating distance in which the observed frequency was much greater than the expected frequency. The minus column indicates the reverse, where the expected frequency was greater than the observed. L stands for left, R for right. This indicates whether the members at a specific seating distance from the others in the group sat to the right or left of the individual whom they followed with a statement.

We find that though significant relationships are found, the significant seating distance is not always the maximal one. The hypotheses stated at the outset predicted that in a small group seated in a circle, the greater the seating distance between two people, the greater the chance that they will follow one another verbally. Though the results are in the expected direction it is also quite clear that, as one may have anticipated, other factors are operating in determining the sequence of statements. Experience in groups tells us that one factor would be the content of a statement and its particular stimulus value for others. Inequality of participation in terms of frequency and length of remarks probably affects the sequence. The intent and attitude of the speaker in making a particular remark has been shown to be related to the intent of the statement of the following speaker (5). The present study does not include an investigation of the effect of some of these factors on the sequence of participation according to the seating arrangement.

One noteworthy trend does appear from an inspection of Table 1. Except for Group I session 16, the seating distance which elicits interaction significantly more often than chance is always greater than the distance in which the interaction occurs significantly less often than chance. Furthermore, if we find the average of the seating distances where the observed degree of interaction is significantly greater than expected by chance, we obtain a mean of 3.6. A mean of 1.2 is found for those seating distances where the expected frequency is greater than actually occurs. These results are in the direction predicted by the hypothesis.

The relationship found in this study is explained as being due to the greater physical and expressive stimulus value a member of a group has for others the more nearly opposite he sits from one in a circle. These results conform to the belief that individuals partaking in a discussion respond to other factors in an individual than the mere content of his remarks. If the results found in this study are confirmed by further investigation of other small discussion groups certain implications are apparent for leadership of such groups. Assuming for a moment that a high level of interaction and a greater extent of participation by members in a group is desirable, the leader may well attend to where specific people sit in a group. It might be desirable, for instance, to have a rather expressive individual sit opposite a rather quiet person. Or the leader might find it helpful to have two people who tend to monopolize the discussion sit next to each other in order to decrease the interstimulation between these two members. The more we learn about the dimensions of group interaction and the dynamics of discussion groups, the more we will be able to adopt the methods and techniques that will help us fulfill the specific purposes for which any group is organized.

REFERENCES

1. Bradford, L. P., & French, J. R. P. (Issue Eds.) The dynamics of the discussion group. *J. soc. Issues*, 1948, 4, No. 2, 1–75.
2. Garrett, H. E. *Statistics in psychology and education.* New York: Longmans, Green, 1939.
3. Lewin, K., Lippitt, R., & White, R. Patterns of aggressive behavior in experimentally created social climates. *J. soc. Psychol.*, 1939, 10, 271–299.
4. Mayo, E. *Human problems of an industrial civilization.* New York: Macmillan, 1933.
5. Steinzor, B. The development and evaluation of a measure of social interaction. *Hum. Relat.*, 1949, 2, 103–121, 319–347.

# *Problem Solving by Small Groups Using Various Communication Nets*

GEORGE A. HEISE
and
GEORGE A. MILLER

A TREND can be discerned in the history of the experimental studies of small groups. Early studies determined that the presence of other people has an effect upon individual performance. Competitive and noncompetitive situations were compared, but social interaction and cooperation was slight (2). More recently the small group has been studied as a unit. The group is given a problem to solve; the discussions of the group are recorded (1), or the efficiency of the group is compared to that of a single individual (6). From Lewin and his followers have come studies of interaction in differently organized groups and of the effectiveness of

FROM *Journal of Abnormal and Social Psychology*, 1951, 46, 327–336. Reprinted by permission of the authors and the American Psychological Association, Inc.

This research was carried out under Contract N5ori-76 between Harvard University and the Office of Naval Research, U.S. Navy (Project NR142-201, Report PNR-93). Reproduction for any purpose of the U.S. Government is permitted.

these groups in coping with various situations. The trend seems to be toward more detailed analysis of the group structure and more interest in the processes of interaction among the members of the group.

Still more precise specification of the group structure and of the kind of interaction has been achieved by Bavelas and his associates. These workers control the channels of communication among the members. Components of the solution are given to each person, but all members of the group must cooperate to reach the correct solution.

In Leavitt's experiment (4), for example, five *S*s were seated around a table, but separated from one another by vertical partitions. Written notes could be passed through slots in the partitions. By varying the slots that were open, the channels among the five could be manipulated into any desired pattern. Four patterns were tested: (*1*) In the *circle* each person could pass notes to the person to his right or to his left; (*2*) the *chain* was identical to the circle except that one more slot was closed, so the *S*s on either side of this closed slot found themselves at the two ends of a chain; (*3*) the Y was a four-member chain, and the fifth *S* could exchange notes only with one of the inner members of this chain; and (*4*) the *wheel* (or X) put one *S* at the center of the net in such a way that he could exchange messages with all the other members, and the other four could not exchange information without passing it through the central member.

Each *S* was given five different symbols out of a possible set of six. The task was for the entire group to discover the one symbol held in common by all five members. Records were kept of speed, errors, and number of messages. At the end of the experimental session the *S*s were given a questionnaire before they talked to each other.

The circle was the most active, erratic, unorganized, and leaderless, but was most satisfying to its members. The wheel was least erratic, required relatively few messages to solve the task, was organized with a definite leader, but was less satisfying to most of its members. The chain and the Y were more like the wheel than like the circle. The member in the central position became the leader, and was more satisfied with his job than were the occupants of peripheral positions. The different communication nets did not differ significantly in the average time it took to solve the problem.

The present experiment is similar in many respects to Leavitt's, although the control of the situation is carried still further. Each *S* is required to reach a solution of the problem. The necessary information is divided equally among the *S*s. Speech, instead of written messages, is the method of communication between group members. However, the content of the messages an *S* can send is restricted and suitable for quantification. The intelligibility of the speech was controlled during a test by controlling the relative intensities of the speech and the noise. These controls permit determination of the dependent variable, group performance, as a function of the independent variables: (*1*) group organization, (*2*) intelligibility of the message, and (*3*) type of problem.

## APPARATUS AND PROCEDURE

### *Nets*

The communication nets were set up as follows. Three *S*s were located in three adjoining rooms. Each *S* had a microphone, amplifier, and earphones. Listening was binaural except when a listener was connected to two talkers; then the listener heard one talker in one earphone and one in the other. The five nets

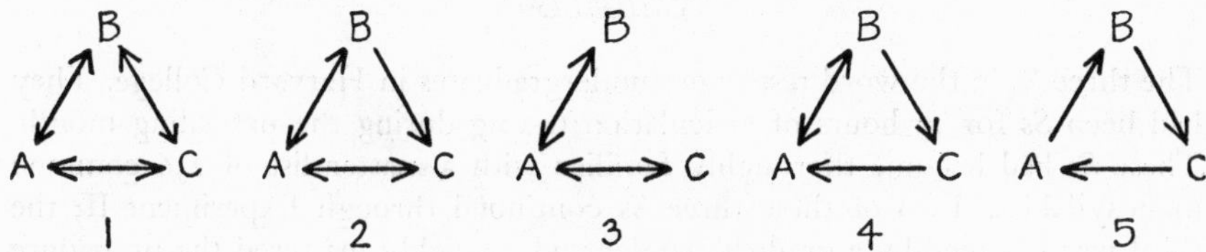


FIG. 1. THE FIVE NETS
The arrows indicate the direction of communication from talker to listener.

tested are shown schematically in Figure 1. The direction of the arrows indicates the channel from talker to listener. A two-headed arrow signifies two-way communication. The nets will be referred to by number, 1 to 5. The subjects will be referred to by letter, *A*, *B*, or *C*, according to the positions indicated in Figure 1. All the channels were free of distortion, and passed frequencies from 200 to 7000 cps.

### *Noise*

Random noise is a shishing sound that has all frequencies of vibration present at equal intensities. Because of the similarity to a white light that has all wave lengths present, such a sound is often called white noise. White noise is a very effective masking sound. This noise was introduced in equal amounts into all the channels. Some noise was always present during the tests in order to mask any airborne sounds that passed directly through the walls.

The intelligibility of speech in the presence of noise is a function of the relative intensities of the speech and the noise, and is independent of their absolute levels over a wide range (3). In order to control the amount of external stress introduced, the speech-to-noise ratio was set to a given value by adjusting the intensity of the noise. Each *S* was given a voltmeter that indicated the intensity of the electrical signal generated by his voice. This meter was used to monitor the speech signal at a constant level (approximately 80 db re 0.0002 dyne/cm$^2$ at the listener's earphones). Use of the meter counteracted the natural tendency of talkers to raise their voices as more noise is introduced. In this way the likelihood of errors could be controlled by the experimenter. Preliminary tests showed that 85 per cent of the monosyllabic words (from a memorized list of 256) could be received correctly at a speech-to-noise ratio of +6 db, 66 per cent at −2 db, and 24 per cent at −10 db.

### *Problems*

The problems were of three kinds. Problems used in Experiment I called for a comparatively stereotyped and unimaginative exchange of isolated words. The problems in Experiment II provided more opportunity for initiative in the construction of sentences. Experiment III was based on a kind of anagram problem. These problems are described in more detail in the discussions of the three experiments.

### *Subjects*

The three *S*s in the word tests were undergraduates in Harvard College. They had been *S*s for 15 hours of articulation testing during the preceding month. These *S*s had become thoroughly familiar with a master list of 256 common monosyllables. Two of these three *S*s continued through Experiment II; the third was replaced by a graduate student who quickly mastered the procedure under the tutelage of the other two. After the first few trials the new member performed as well as the others. Two groups of three naïve *S*s, all graduate students, were recruited for the anagram tests of Experiment III.

## EXPERIMENT I: TESTS WITH WORD PROBLEMS

### *Method*

In order to explain the construction of the word problems, the following terms are defined. (*1*) The *master list* is a set of 256 monosyllables from which all test words were drawn. These 256 words, arranged according to vowel sounds, were placed in easy view of each *S* throughout the word tests. (*2*) The *test list* is a list of 25 words selected at random from the master list. (*3*) The *subject's list* is a list of pairs of words selected at random from the test list. The first step in the construction of a word problem is to assemble a test list of 25 words. Then the pairs of consecutive words from the test list are collected in three sets to form three sub-lists, one for each *S*. Part of a sample test list and the three *S*'s lists derived randomly from it are shown in Table 1. The word pairs are given to the *S*s in their correct order as they appear on the test list.

The problem is to reconstruct the test list in its entirety. Since each *S* has only a part of the information needed for the reconstruction, he is forced to communicate over the net provided. In the example of Table 1, *C* begins by saying "You will write 'south.' " (The carrier phrase "you will write . . ." makes it possible to warn the listeners and to monitor the speech level before the test word occurs.) The word "south" travels through the net until it reaches *B*, who then introduces "though." When "though" reaches *A* he introduces "off," "quiz," "grade." The details of the process are evolved by the *S*s themselves during the preliminary testing, but in this general manner the test list can be patched together. Every *S* must get the entire test list of 25 words before the problem is completed.

Before each test the *S*s were carefully informed about the pattern of channels. They knew that the speech-to-noise ratio was always the same in all channels. Discussion of the roles of members located at different points in the net was discouraged. No suggestions were made about the strategy that the group might employ in solving the problem. The *S*s were not instructed to solve the problem in the shortest possible time; they were told to proceed at a reasonable rate consistent with the accurate reconstruction of the test list by all three participants. The *S*s were permitted to speak only the carrier phrase followed by any number of the words on the master list. A talker was not allowed to indicate to whom he was speaking. These restrictions on the group's vocabulary maintained the intelligibility of their speech at a known, constant level. The order for testing the nets and the positions of the *S*s in the nets was determined by a pre-arranged plan.

TABLE 1

*Sample of Test Material*

***The three subjects received their lists in this form, and attempted to reconstruct the test list cooperatively.***

| TEST LIST | SUBJECT *A*'S LIST | SUBJECT *B*'S LIST | SUBJECT *C*'S LIST |
|---|---|---|---|
| south | though | south | south |
| though | off | though | |
| off | | | plod |
| quiz | off | grade | sniff |
| grade | quiz | act | |
| act | | | pounce |
| dwarf | quiz | sin | rash |
| plod | grade | whiff | |
| sniff | | | rash |
| pounce | act | range | gun |
| rash | dwarf | sledge | |
| gun | | | gun |
| coast | dwarf | wire | coast |
| pig | plod | nine | |
| sin | | | coast |
| whiff | sniff | raid | pig |
| pent | pounce | jug | |
| cook | | | whiff |
| range | pig | shaft | pent |
| sledge | sin | fake | |
| comes | | | sledge |
| fort | pent | fake | comes |
| wire | cook | by | |
| nine | | | etc. |
| etc. | etc. | etc. | |

Four three-hour experimental sessions were required before the group performance stabilized enough to permit satisfactory comparisons of different trials. The times required for completion of the problems decreased steadily during the preliminary period as the *S*s became familiar with the problem and the best procedure on the various nets. The rate of learning was too rapid for accurate assessment of the influence of the experimental variables, although the same general relations obtained as in the later trials that are reported in detail.

The *S*s found the problem an interesting one. Post mortems were a common occurrence after a trial was over, especially when a persistent error had hampered progress. During the trial several spontaneous expressions of agitation were noted. Frustration and irritation were evident on net 5 at the lower signal-to-noise ratios, where correction of errors was difficult and progress was slow. Once, in net 1, an *S* complained that the other two were monopolizing the conversation. In net 3 both subjects *B* and *C* occasionally talked at the same time to a harried subject *A*. Frequent reminders were necessary to prevent the *S*s from raising their voices, thus improving the signal-to-noise ratio, when attempting to correct errors.

By the end of the preliminary period of rapid improvement the group was a smoothly functioning unit within the limits imposed by the three signal-to-noise ratios and the five nets. The *S*s evolved the practice of reporting both members of the word pairs in the same message, which tended to keep all *S*s "up to date" and the words in their proper context.

## Results

The results reported in Table 2 and Fig. 2 were obtained in two three-hour experimental sessions. Three kinds of measures are reported. (*1*) The *time* required to complete the task was measured from the first "You will write . . . ," spoken by the *S* who had the first word, to the point when each *S* had compiled his 25-word list. (*2*) The *accuracy* of the completed list was scored by comparing the *S*'s written record with the test list. (*3*) The *number of words* spoken by each *S* was recorded by him as he said them. The totals for all three gave the number of words the group had spoken in order to solve the problem.

TABLE 2

*Group Scores for Word Problems*

| NET | THEORETICAL MINIMUM NO. OF WORDS | THEORETICAL MINIMUM TIME (in minutes) | PER CENT WORDS CORRECT | | | TOTAL WORDS REQUIRED | | | TIME TO FINISH TASK (in minutes) | | |
|---|---|---|---|---|---|---|---|---|---|---|---|
| | | | +6db | −2db | −10db | +6db | −2db | −10db | +6db | −2db | −10db |
| 1 | 25 | 1.9 | 97.5 | 94.7 | 80.0 | 56 | 68 | 58 | 4 | 5 | 4 |
| 2 | 33 | 2.5 | 97.5 | 94.7 | 86.7 | 75 | 77 | 128 | 6 | 6 | 13 |
| 3 | 42 | 3.2 | 98.7 | 85.4 | 96.0 | 86 | 85 | 112 | 8 | 6 | 9 |
| 4 | 50 | 3.8 | 96.0 | 94.7 | 84.0 | 94 | 186 | 248 | 8 | 13 | 28 |
| 5 | 75 | 5.8 | 96.0 | 90.7 | 82.7 | 122 | 198 | 279 | 8 | 15 | 30 |

A reconstruction of the course of solution would have been possible if the *S*s had written down all the words they said. It proved impossible to write out all the words spoken without destroying the tempo and spontaneity of the group interaction. Hence the *S* was asked to record only the *number* of words he said, rather than the actual words themselves.

The minimum curve plotted in Figure 2A represents the minimum total number of words that the group could say for each *S* to conclude with a reconstruction of the 25-word test list. The calculation assumes no articulation errors by any *S*, and no deviations from the maximally efficient

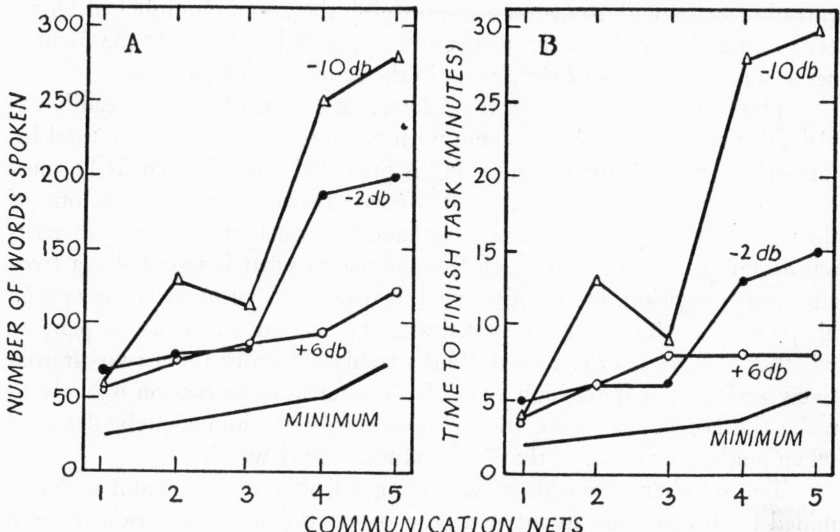


FIG. 2. Performance of the Group on the Word Problems (Experiment I) as a Function of the Communication Net

*Nets are numbered as in Fig. 1. Performance is measured in terms of (A) total words spoken and (B) time required to finish the task. Parameter is signal-to-noise ratio.*

procedure for a particular system. The minimum times of Figure 2B are obtained by dividing the minimum word scores by 13, the average number of words spoken per minute. The similarity between Figure 2A and Figure 2B indicates that the *S*s tended to talk at an approximately constant number of words per minute under all conditions.

It will be noted that the results for a signal-to-noise ratio of +6 are strikingly similar to the minimum curve except for a displacement upwards. Few errors in communication occur at this favorable signal-to-noise ratio. Consequently the difference between minimum and empirical curves indicates a consistent use of surplus words. Unnecessary repetitions and the habit of saying both the words of a pair provided the surplus. The *S*s were not instructed to be economical with words or time.

Figure 2 shows that raising the noise level, with the consequent introduction of errors, accentuates the differences between the systems. The comparative inefficiency of net 5, the one-way closed chain, becomes clear when the noise is introduced. In this net one person's failure to hear correctly a particular word stalls the group's progress; locating the culprit is difficult and correcting him harder still. The same message, containing an error stubbornly introduced by one member and as stubbornly corrected by another may go round and round net 5 before the mistake is finally corrected. Short periods of silence, extremely unusual in other systems, occurred often enough to decrease appreciably the average number of words per minute. The deficiencies of net 5 are present in a less extreme form in net 4, where only one of the *S*s was in the semi-isolated position.

The resistance of net 1 to the deleterious effects of noise is readily explained. Each *S* starts the problem with more than a third of the total information required for solution. He is provided with the words he must contribute and also the words that precede them. Thus in net 1, one of the two listeners to every word must have the word (if it is correct) written down in front of him. Each listener makes what is essentially a two-alternative decision. He decides whether the word he hears is the one on his paper, in which case he introduces the second word of his pair, or whether it is some other word. The articulation score for a two-alternative vocabulary is quite high (5). The listener in this situation is likely to make the correct decision. Incorrect decisions are immediately detected when neither, or both, of the *S*s introduces a next word.

The number of words spoken by a member of the group is determined by his position in the net. The proportional participation of each member is approximately the same as the proportions that can be calculated by considering the most efficient possible solution.

Casual observations indicated that *S*s in different positions in the nets play different roles. The man in position *A* of net 3 is forced by his central position to become a coordinator. He usually warns the other two members at the beginning of a trial, and takes charge of any procedural matters that arise during the trial. When asked at the conclusion of the experiment which position in the network they preferred, all *S*s chose this central position. Isolated positions, of which the clearest example is *C* in net 4, were unpopular with the *S*s, who reported that in these positions they felt left out and unsure of themselves.

A stereotyped procedure, in which the *S* waits passively until he hears the first word of a pair on his list before introducing the second word of his pair, is quite appropriate for the solution of these word problems. The correspondence of the empirical results to the predictions of group performance–predictions based upon the assumption of such machine-like behavior–shows that the word problems did not provide a real challenge for the group's abilities.

## EXPERIMENT II: TESTS WITH SENTENCE PROBLEMS

### *Method*

The sentence problems relied upon verbal context, rather than the repetition of word pairs, to link the contributions of the three members. These problems were less rigidly structured and provided more scope for initiative. The test materials consisted of sentences of 25 words, as simple in thought and expression as possible. For example, "The picture we saw was painted by an old woman who had been taught how to mix the colors by one of the native artists." All sentences used were of approximately equal difficulty and were designed (1) to minimize punctuation, common phrases, and clichés, and (2) to express thoughts unrelated to any particular knowledge possessed by the *S*s. The words in the sentences were commonplace; no proper names and no words longer than three syllables were used.

The words in the sentences were divided into three parts with the aid of a table of random numbers. At the beginning of a trial each *S* received his portion of the words. The words were listed vertically in the order in which they occurred in the test sentence. As before, the task of the group was to reconstruct the original sequence of words in their correct order; each member had to conclude with the complete sentence.

The same five networks and three speech-to-noise ratios were investigated as for the word problems, but more attention was paid to nets 1, 3, and 5, and more data are available for them. The *S*s received the same instructions; they could say as many words as they wished, preceded always by the warning "You will write . . ." The messages actually sent were somewhat longer than they had been for the word problems, because the intelligibility could be raised by placing the words in the context of the sentence.

Sentence building provided a problem that held the *S*'s interest. Each sentence posed a novel problem. Discussions, in which the correct sentence was disclosed and jocular recriminations passed among the *S*s, were unavoidable after trials that were difficult or delayed by errors.

Records were kept of (*1*) the time required to complete the problem, and (*2*) the number of words spoken by each *S*. Accuracy scores were not useful. An *S* could tell when he had the correct sentence by observing that he had 25 words strung together in a reasonable sequence that included, in the proper order, the words he had been given at the outset. The *S*s seldom missed more than one or two words of the test sentence.

### *Results*

Time and total word scores are given in Table 3 and plotted in Figure 3. The results indicate that net 3 is superior to net 1. This superiority is most marked for the unfavorable speech-to-noise ratios, which shows once more that the stress of noise exaggerates differences among the nets.

In net 1 everyone always talks to everyone else. In net 3 a man in the middle is the go-between for the other two. Why is net 1 superior for

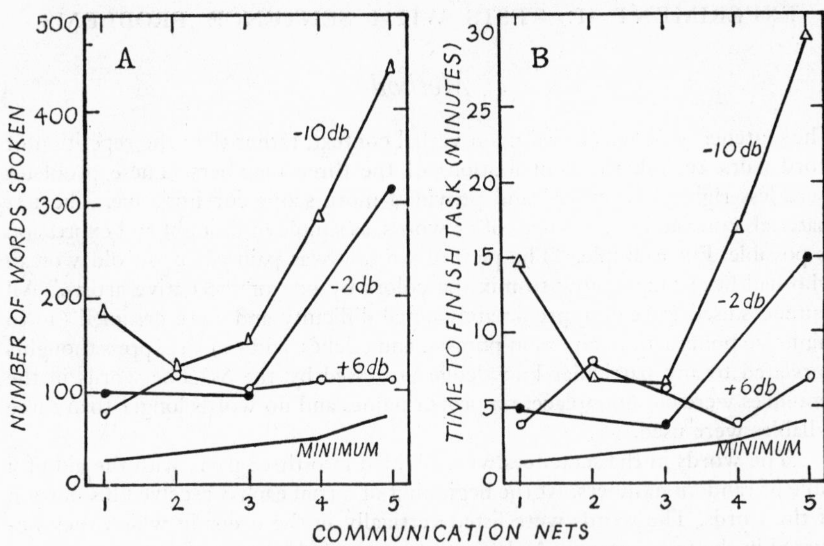


FIG. 3. Performance of the Group on the Sentence Problems (Experiment II) as a Function of the Communication Net

*Nets are numbered as in Fig. 1. Performance is measured in terms of (A) total words spoken and (B) time required to finish the task. Parameter is signal-to-noise ratio.*

word problems but inferior for sentence problems? Apparently the reconstruction of sentences requires more integration of group activity; the central man can coordinate and place in the proper context the words that the *S*s contribute. He is in a position to detect and correct mistaken words and incorrect hypotheses. Conversely, the situation can become chaotic in net 1, for no one organizes the individual contributions. These considerations could mean that the proportional participation of the central man in system three is higher for the sentence problem, where he plays a more significant role, than for the word problem. The individuals' data show, however, that the proportional contributions for the central man are approximately equal for both kinds of problem.

TABLE 3

*Group Scores for Sentence Problems*

| NET | THEORETICAL MINIMUM NO. OF WORDS | THEORETICAL MINIMUM TIME (in minutes) | TOTAL WORDS REQUIRED +6 db | −2db | −10db | TIME TO FINISH TASK (in minutes) +6db | −2db | −10db |
|---|---|---|---|---|---|---|---|---|
| 1 | 25 | 1.4 | 76 | 99 | 186 * | 4 | 5 | 15 * |
| 2 | 33 | 1.8 | 117 | | 121 | 8 | | 7 |
| 3 | 42 | 2.3 | 101 * | 96 | 154 * | 6 * | 4 | 7 * |
| 4 | 50 | 2.8 | 112 | | 287 | 4 | | 17 |
| 5 | 75 | 4.2 | 112 | 315 | 446 * | 7 | 15 | 30 * |

* Averages for two problems.

## EXPERIMENT III: TEST WITH ANAGRAM PROBLEM

### *Method*

The anagram problem was taken from a study by Watson (7). The group was given a word and instructed to form as many anagrams as possible. The test words were *abolished*, *courtesan*, *educators*, *neurotics*, *secondary*, and *universal.* All had nine letters, four vowels, and the consonant *s*. The words formed had to be at least three letters long; singular and plural did not count as separate words; proper nouns and slang were not permitted. The group's goal was to get the largest possible number of words on all three papers; a word could count three times toward the group total if it appeared on all three papers. Communication was not essential for carrying out the task. The extent to which *S*s communicated the words they made up, or heard from other *S*s, was left completely to their own discretion.

The instructions in the use of the equipment were the same as before. Only three nets were tried with anagram problems, nets 1, 3, and 5. Two speech-to-noise ratios, −10 and +6 db, were tested. The group was allowed ten minutes to work on each word. Three practice tests, one with each net, accustomed the *S*s to monitoring their voices and to constructing anagrams.

### *Results*

The results for the last six tests are summarized in Table 4. These figures are the average values obtained for two groups of three subjects.

It is clear from Table 4 that the differences among the nets were small, and that the introduction of noise did not emphasize the differences among

TABLE 4

*Average Group Scores for Anagram Problems*

| NET | TOTAL WORDS CONSTRUCTED | | WORDS SPOKEN | |
|---|---|---|---|---|
| | +6db | −10db | +6db | −10db |
| 1 | 165.5 | 149.5 | 61.5 | 64.0 |
| 3 | 167.0 | 142.5 | 93.0 | 81.0 |
| 5 | 176.0 | 141.0 | 135.5 | 99.0 |

the nets. For this kind of problem, therefore, the pattern of channels among the members of the group has little effect upon the efficiency of the group's performance. The unfavorable speech-to-noise ratio interfered with the group's performance in about the same degree for all nets.

The *S*s marked on their score sheets all the words that they spoke aloud. The total number of words (average for the two groups) that were spoken during the 10-minute tests are shown in Table 4. Fewer words were spoken over the multi-connected net 1 than over the minimally-connected net 5. Intense noise decreased the amount of talking.

In the word and sentence problems of Experiment I and Experiment II, the efficiency of the group depended upon the pattern of channels available for communication among the group members. In the anagram problem, the type of net apparently made no systematic difference in the efficiency of the group. This difference can be explained on the basis of two principal ways in which the word and sentence problems differ from the anagram problems.

1. The information necessary to solve the anagram problem was nonconsecutive and was not divided among the group members. All group members began the problem with identical information which was adequate for the assigned task. In contrast to the word and sentence problems, where the *S* had to wait for the contribution of another group member before he could proceed, the *S* in the anagram problem could work at the task in his own preferred order, at his own optimum speed. Consequently errors and delays in the transmission of words did not appreciably hinder an individual's productivity. The correction of errors, a procedure much easier in some nets than in others, was unnecessary in the anagram problem for keeping the group at work. Errors in the transmission of words frequently stalled progress on the word and sentence problems, however, because an *S* often could not introduce the next word until he had correctly heard the preceding word.

2. The task assigned an *S* in the word and sentence problems was primarily to communicate to the other group members the information that had been presented to him at the beginning of the problem. Consequently, the performance of the group depended in large measure upon the ease of communication. In the anagram problem, however, the *S* himself had to make up the words he sent out. Table 4 shows that *S*s made up about five anagrams per minute, and that not all of these were sent over the communication net. Even the most inefficient system was adequate for this slow rate of output; it is not surprising that no significant differences were observed for the various nets.

## DISCUSSION

A few generalizations can be drawn from these experiments. The relative efficiency of a communication net depends upon the kind of problem the group is trying to solve. The nature of the group's task is the most important variable that remains to be explored. Exposing a group to unfavorable conditions can exaggerate differences in the relative efficiency of different nets. However, if the problem does not require successful communication, the efficiency of the group may be little affected by the net pattern or by noise.

The experimental situation investigated here is considerably more restricted than most of the group situations studied in the laboratory or in the social interaction of day-to-day life. To what extent does this artificiality limit the generality of the results? Some of the limitations of the method can be overcome by modification or enlargement of the equipment. Additional persons, and additional group organizations, can be introduced by adding microphone, loudspeaker, amplifier, and separate room for each person. The size of the group is an important variable that we have not considered here. A switching system can easily be installed that would allow the *S*s themselves to determine the group organization and the recipients of particular messages. Differential noise conditions in the channels can be used to force some of the group members into relatively insignificant roles and to give relative prominence to others. Wire recording can be used for a more thorough analysis of each individual's contribution, the origin of errors, and the progress of problem solution.

Less easily overcome are the limitations imposed by the range of problems appropriate for this experimental situation. Quantification of results is greatly facilitated by restriction of vocabulary and standardized procedure. Since the problem material must all be expressed verbally, the results are perhaps unduly influenced by factors such as verbal context and intelligibility, with a reduction in general applicability to the less restricted life situation.

One thing that is needed is a classification of group problems. What are the significant dimensions of a problem? One obvious dimension is the degree to which the problem is structured. A continuum, based on the degree of structure of the problem, would run from problems so highly restricted that an individual group member could be replaced by a fairly simple robot to the problem faced by a town council deciding whether to raise taxes. The problems devised for these experiments are far toward the structured end of the continuum. At the other end of the scale are problems investigated by the Lewin group, where factors such as the role played by various group members and their personalities, attitudes, and needs were involved explicitly. Many of these factors could be introduced systematically into the intercommunication system employed in this work by a relaxation of curbs on the members' activities, and the setting of more broadly defined tasks.

Other dimensions include such possibilities as the uniqueness of the solution, the initial distribution of information, the number of decisions that someone must make, the rate at which a participant can narrow the range of possible solutions, the position along a competition-cooperation continuum, etc. With a reasonable classification of problems we can begin to relate the problem, the net, and the stress in a systematic way.

It is possible that stress may act as a microscope to magnify differences that otherwise are difficult to measure. How general is the stressful effect of noise? Do other kinds of stress have comparable effects? To what extent can the activity of one member be regarded as a source of stress to another member of the net?

By their careful controls of the conditions under which a group must work, Bavelas and his co-workers have extended the precision of research with small groups. If this precision does not cost too much in validity, we may have a powerful experimental method.

## SUMMARY

The performance of a three-man group was studied for five different communication nets, three signal-to-noise ratios, and three kinds of tasks. The first type of problem was a simple reassembling of a list of standard words. The second type consisted in the construction of a sentence, the words of which had been distributed among the group members. The third type required the group to form anagrams.

For the first type of problem, comparative group efficiency, measured in terms of time or number of words required to complete the task, could be predicted from the net structure. A closed chain in which only one-way communication was possible between any two persons was by far the least efficient; an open chain, which allowed two-way communication between any two adjacent individuals, was intermediate; a closed chain where all members talked and listened to all other members was most efficient. The second type of problem was less rigidly structured and placed a higher premium on the coordination of the group activity. The results were generally similar to those for the first type of problem, except that the open chain, which had a man in a central coordinating position, replaced the two-way closed chain as most efficient. The anagram problem did not require communication; under these conditions there was no large difference among the nets.

Lowering the signal-to-noise ratio introduced errors and increased the time and number of words required to complete the task. For the first two types of problems the stress of noise accentuated the differences between the systems and emphasized the inefficiency of the one-way closed chain. The third problem, where communication was a luxury, was solved equally well over all nets; noise did not accentuate differences.

The performance of a small group depends upon the channels of communication open to its members, the task the group must handle, and the stress under which they work.

## REFERENCES

1. Bales, F. *Interaction process analysis.* Cambridge, Mass.: Addison-Wesley Press, 1950.
2. Dashiell, J. F. Experimental studies of the influence of social situations on the be-

havior of individual human adults. In C. Murchison (Ed.), *Handbook of social psychology*. Worcester, Mass.: Clark Univer. Press, 1935.
3. Egan, J. P. Articulation testing methods. *Laryngoscope*, 1948, 58, 955–991.
4. Leavitt, H. J. Some effects of certain communication patterns on group performance. *J. abnorm. soc. Psychol.*, 1951, 46, 38–50.
5. Miller, G. A., Heise, G. A., & Lichten, W. The intelligibility of speech as a function of the context of the test materials. *J. exp. Psychol.*, in press.
6. Shaw, M. E. A comparison of individuals and small groups in the rational solution of complex problems. *Amer. J. Psychol.*, 1932, 44, 491–504.
7. Watson, G. B. Do groups think more efficiently than individuals? *J. abnorm. soc. Psychol.*, 1928, 23, 328–336.

# *The Distribution of Participation in Small Groups: An Exponential Approximation*

FREDERICK F. STEPHAN
and
ELLIOT G. MISHLER

IN CONTEMPORARY sociological and social psychological theory and research an increasing amount of attention has been given to the functioning of small groups. Many attempts have been made to analyze the interaction that takes place in small group meetings and to discover general principles that appear to determine, or at least influence, the pattern of participation by the various members of the group. The research reported here is devoted to one of the basic aspects of small group research, namely the relative frequency of participation. Specifically, this study concerns the application of a relatively simple mathematical function that appears to express quite well the distribution of participation within a particular type of small discussion group.

In a recent paper (2) Bales suggested that a harmonic distribution

FROM *American Sociological Review*, 1952, 17, 598–608. Reprinted by permission of the authors and publisher.

might serve to approximate the relative frequency of acts of participation among members of small problem-solving groups. The results he obtained, however, indicated that this approximation is not close enough to be fully satisfactory and, for this reason, he concluded that a more complicated model may be necessary for greater precision (2, pp. 466–468).

The proven inadequacy of the harmonic model, however, does not necessitate the use of models of great complexity. A model of comparable simplicity is available which appears to provide a very good representation of data obtained from a variety of small discussion groups. It is a simple exponential model, that had previously been applied by one of the authors to another study of group participation. When it was applied to Bales' published data, it provided a good fit (6). This paper is primarily concerned with the general adequacy of this exponential model for representing other sets of participation data.

## METHODOLOGY

The data presented here are drawn from a project (5) which is part of a general study of the educational process.[1] The findings are based on observations of a total of 81 separate meetings, held by 36 distinct groups, ranging in attendance from four to twelve participants.

The group meetings have certain formal characteristics in common which serve to distinguish them from the problem-solving groups that were studied by Bales. Since the generality of the model is the important consideration, it seems advisable to list these characteristics as specifically as possible. (A more abstract formulation of these conditions, as they affect the applicability of the model, is presented later in the discussion of results.) These common features are:

(*1*) *Social context of the meetings.* The weekly, 50-minute meetings are held at a prescribed time and place in connection with certain courses at Princeton University. The usual expectations, associated with college courses, governing attendance and the fulfillment of assigned work are thus operative here.

(*2*) *Composition of the group.* The members of the group are relatively homogeneous in regard to age, educational training, social background, etc. In addition, membership tends to be restricted to juniors and seniors, increasing the homogeneity within each group in terms of interest and special knowledge.

(*3*) *Role of the leader.* The leader of the group is an instructor in the course. He differs from the other members in his relationship to the group along those social dimensions which are involved in a student's orientation toward a teacher as compared with his orientation toward a fellow student. Although he receives his power ultimately from the outside structure, the leader has considerable freedom to do what he wants in the way he wants. In general, the norms hold that he should be friendly, sociable, and democratic.

1 The Study of Education at Princeton.

(4) *Norms regarding student participation.* The meetings are conducted under the influence of strong traditional attitudes that emphasize discussion by the students and de-emphasize the dominance of the faculty leader in contrast to the usual patterns of lecture, class, and quiz section meetings. They are regarded as an especially valuable part of the education of students. It is expected (by both students and faculty) that all the students will participate actively during each meeting. The leader is expected to stimulate discussion (although specific devices to this end are not prescribed) or at least not to discourage the students from participating. Active participation is regarded as instrumental to the major goal of the meetings.

(5) *Goal of the meetings.* The institutionally defined objective of the meetings is an increase in the members' understanding of assigned course materials. There is a further goal, considered a function of the cumulative effect of many of these meetings in a variety of courses, of an improvement in the general analytical ability of students. It is understood that neither consensus nor action is to be taken as a specific end, although it is recognized that either may occasionally occur as by-products.

The 36 groups whose meetings were observed were a stratified random sample drawn to represent the more than 500 groups that met weekly in the Fall term of 1950. Two variables were used to stratify the population: the department of instruction and the time (day and hour) at which the group met. An additional restriction provided that no single leader (instructor) was represented more than once in the sample. It is assumed that there was no important systematic bias in the types of content discussed, styles of leadership exercised, or kinds of student members in the sample groups.

There are two important methodological differences between the procedure for recording participation and that developed by Bales (1). The basic unit of participation tallied by the observers is the word, sentence, or longer statement of an individual that follows such a participation by one member and continues until it is terminated by an appreciable pause or by the participation of another member. In other words, an individual's uninterrupted contribution is taken to be one participation. However, if there was a clear change of content during the course of a lengthy contribution, it was taken to be the beginning of a new unit of participation. If Bales' procedure had been used, these units of participation would have been divided into elementary "acts" each consisting of a simple sentence or equivalent meaningful expression. What is recorded here as one unit of participation would be recorded by Bales as many times as the number of "acts" it contained.

In the present study, the observers interrupted their recording of participation periodically to make other observations. They did this after each series of participations that totalled 50 units or covered a period of 15 minutes, whichever limit was reached first. This interruption of the recording lasted for less than five minutes, and was devoted to rating certain general aspects of group activity.[2] As soon as the ratings were completed the observers resumed the regular recording of participation. This sequence continued throughout the meeting. The participation records are, therefore, a sample rather than a full record of the meeting. Although systematic evidence was not collected, informal reports by the observers and certain other data indicate that this sampling procedure did not present a distorted picture of the distribution of the participation of members of the group during the entire period.

The differences between this approach and that of Bales have been cited in some detail. If results of both approaches can be described by the same simple model, these differences lend added significance to this finding.

Participation in the discussion groups was observed and recorded by 18 student observers. Each of them had a minimum of about 15 hours of experience in the development and use of the procedure before he started the regular observation of the sample groups. The reliability among observers was investigated by having pairs of observers record the same discussion meeting.*

## PARTICIPATION DATA AND THE EXPONENTIAL FUNCTION

The data recorded by the observers were tabulated for each individual at a meeting and then the individuals were ranked according to the number of units of participation that were contributed by them. The tabulations for all meetings of the same size were then combined by adding the counts of units of participation for the members that had the same ranking. The result is given in column 3 of Table 1. Each individual was also ranked according to the number of units of participation that were directed to him. The tabulations of these units for all groups of the same size were combined according to this second ranking and appear in column 7 of Table 1.

Graphs of relative participation plotted against rank are similar to those reported by Bales (2) and are therefore omitted from the present paper. The decrease in rate from the leader to the highest ranking student becomes somewhat sharper as one goes from smaller to larger groups. It was found that the percentage distributions could be approximated by an exponential function,

$$p_i = ar^{i-1}, \qquad (1)$$

where $p_i$ is the estimated percentage for students ranked $i$, $r$ is the ratio of the percentage for any rank to the percentage for the next higher rank, and $a$ is the estimate for students ranked 1. The variation of $r$ and $a$ with the size of the group will be discussed later.

2 These ratings are related to the larger study noted above and will not be reported here. Cf. Mishler, (5).

* Discussion of reliability of observers has been omitted. (Eds.)

TABLE I

*Distribution of Participation by and to Members of Small Discussion Groups* *

*(Data combined for all meetings of the same size, participations to the group omitted)*

| | | *Participations originated by the member* | | | | *Participations directed to the member* | | | |
|---|---|---|---|---|---|---|---|---|---|
| *Size and number of meetings* | *Rank of the member* | *Partici-pations* | *Per cent* | *Esti-mated percent-age* | *Differ-ence* | *Partici-pations* | *Per cent* | *Esti-mated percent-age* | *Differ-ence* |
| (1) | (2) | (3) | (4) | (5) | (6) | (7) | (8) | (9) | (10) |
| Six | | *2951* | | *36.9* | | *2951* | | *28.8* | |
| (17) | L | 1261 | 42.8 | 44.8 | +2.0 | 1402 | 47.5 | 47.5 | 0.0 |
| | 1 | 704 | 23.8 | 23.0 | −0.8 | 471 | 15.9 | 16.2 | +0.3 |
| | 2 | 455 | 15.4 | 14.3 | −1.1 | 272 | 9.2 | 9.1 | −0.1 |
| | 3 | 297 | 10.0 | 8.9 | −1.1 | 162 | 5.5 | 5.1 | −0.4 |
| | 4 | 175 | 5.9 | 5.6 | −0.3 | 90 | 3.0 | 2.9 | −0.1 |
| | 5 | 59 | 2.0 | 3.5 | +1.5 | 39 | 1.3 | 1.6 | +0.3 |
| Seven | | *1999* | | *30.3* | | *1999* | | *21.9* | |
| (15) | L | 912 | 45.6 | 45.8 | +0.2 | 933 | 46.6 | 46.5 | −0.1 |
| | 1 | 416 | 20.8 | 20.1 | −0.7 | 287 | 14.5 | 14.1 | −0.4 |
| | 2 | 245 | 12.2 | 13.2 | +1.0 | 167 | 8.3 | 9.1 | +0.8 |
| | 3 | 175 | 8.6 | 8.8 | +0.2 | 118 | 5.9 | 5.8 | −0.1 |
| | 4 | 119 | 5.9 | 5.8 | −0.1 | 82 | 4.1 | 3.8 | −0.3 |
| | 5 | 86 | 4.2 | 3.8 | −0.4 | 55 | 2.6 | 2.4 | −0.2 |
| | 6 | 46 | 2.4 | 2.5 | +0.1 | 27 | 1.3 | 1.6 | +0.3 |
| Eight | | *2042* | | *31.9* | | *2042* | | *22.0* | |
| (14) | L | 803 | 39.2 | 39.9 | +0.7 | 946 | 46.3 | 46.0 | −0.3 |
| | 1 | 434 | 21.2 | 21.3 | +0.1 | 266 | 12.9 | 14.1 | +1.2 |
| | 2 | 294 | 14.3 | 14.2 | −0.1 | 218 | 10.6 | 9.0 | −1.6 |
| | 3 | 184 | 8.9 | 9.5 | +0.6 | 105 | 5.1 | 5.8 | +0.7 |
| | 4 | 140 | 6.6 | 6.3 | −0.3 | 87 | 4.1 | 3.7 | −0.4 |
| | 5 | 98 | 4.8 | 4.2 | −0.6 | 49 | 2.3 | 2.4 | +0.1 |
| | 6 | 55 | 2.6 | 2.8 | +0.2 | 32 | 1.5 | 1.5 | 0.0 |
| | 7 | 34 | 1.6 | 1.9 | +0.3 | 17 | 0.7 | 1.0 | +0.3 |

* a. The percentages for participations *to* within each size of meeting (columns 8 and 9) do not total 100. This is due to the fact, noted previously, that the percentage of participation *to* the group has been omitted.

b. The numbers in *italics* in columns 3 and 7 are the total number of participation units recorded. The totals in column 7 include participations directed *to* the group as a whole. These totals were the basis on which the percentages of total in columns 4 and 8 were calculated.

c. The numbers in *italics* in columns 5 and 9 are the percentages that would be estimated for the leader by extrapolation from the exponential model.

NOTE: Data for groups of 4, 9, 10, 11, and 12 are omitted. (Eds.)

In the fitting of his function, the percentages by and to the leaders and to the group were omitted from the distributions. There were several reasons for this step. First, they differed from the students in knowledge of the subjects under discussion, experience in discussion, etc. Second, they had different functions to perform in the meeting, a different role to play.

Third, it was deemed a sufficient first step to find a function that fitted the student members' participation rates, without the addition of another function for the leaders' roles.

In order to give what was judged to be appropriate weight to the fit for large and for small percentages, the function was fitted to the data by minimizing the sum of squares of deviations of the logarithms of the estimated percentages from the logarithms of the observed percentages, each square being weighted by the observed percentage. That is, the quantity to be minimized was:

$$\Sigma\, p_i[\log p_i - \log(ar^{i-1})]^2$$

where $p_i$ is the percentage observed for the members ranked *i.* It was not possible to establish a defensible probability model for maximum likelihood estimates or a more rational formulation of least squares procedure. The selection of this basis for fitting was to a degree arbitrary but it appears to be justified by the closeness of fit that was attained. It led to the following equations:

$$(2)\ \log a = \frac{CD-BE}{AC-B^2} \quad (3)\ \log r = \frac{AE-BD}{AC-B^2}$$

$$\text{where } A = \Sigma\, p_i,\ B = \Sigma\, ip_i,\ C = \Sigma\, i^2p_i,$$

$$D = \Sigma\ (p_i \log p_i),\ E = \Sigma\ (ip_i \log p_i)$$

These equations were solved for each distribution of percentages. Then estimates were computed from equation (*1*) and entered in columns 5 and 9 of Table 1.

To complete the estimates, a percentage was added for the leaders in each distribution that brings the total to 100 per cent. It may be compared with the figure above it, in italics, which is the percentage that would be estimated for the leader according to the exponential function, when he is assigned rank 0.

The percentages computed from the exponential function agree remarkably well with the actual percentages, except for the estimates for the leader. Considering participation *by* a member, 62 of the 72 differences in column 6 are less than one percentage point, positive or negative. For participation *to* a member, 59 differences are less than one percentage point, either way. There is a little evidence of systematic error, primarily a tendency toward negative errors in the middle rankings and positive errors for the very lowest ranks.

Table 2 presents the ratios ($r$ in equation 1) that were used for computing the percentages and an approximation to them by two linear functions of the size of the meeting.

The ratios appear to increase with the size of the meeting in fairly close conformity to the linear functions. Thus, men of adjoining rank tend to have more nearly equal rates of participation as the size of the meeting increased.

The parameter, $a$, also changes in a fairly regular way with the size of the meeting. It can be represented by such an empirical function as $a_n = 234/(n+4)$, for participations by the member, and $a_n = 157/(n+4)$, for participations to the member.

## DISCUSSION OF RESULTS

The findings presented above suggest that the simple exponential model may be applicable for describing the distribution of participation in other types of small groups. The problem now becomes one of discovering the conditions under which the model may be expected to remain applicable (i.e., of "explaining" this empirical law). Such an analysis should also be helpful in specifying those factors which influence the size of the ratio in

TABLE 2

*Ratios $r_n$ Used in Estimating Participations and Approximations by Linear Functions of the Size of the Meeting*

| SIZE OF MEETING, $n$, INCLUDING LEADER | PARTICIPATION BY A MEMBER * | | PARTICIPATION TO A MEMBER † | |
|---|---|---|---|---|
| 4 | .589 | (.590) | .566 | (.582) |
| 5 | .611 | (.607) | .638 | (.596) |
| 6 | .623 | (.624) | .563 | (.610) |
| 7 | .661 | (.641) | .643 | (.624) |
| 8 | .667 | (.658) | .640 | (.638) |
| 9 | .668 | (.676) | .656 | (.652) |
| 10 | .694 | (.693) | .667 | (.666) |
| 11 | .710 | (.710) | .682 | (.680) |
| 12 | .727 | (.727) | .686 | (.694) |

* Approximation using $r_n = .522 + .0172\ n$ is shown in parentheses.
† Approximation using $r_n = .526 + .0140\ n$ is shown in parentheses.

the exponential equation. A great deal of research may be necessary before this problem can be solved. As a step toward formulating hypotheses, the authors will set forth some of their thoughts about the essential conditions.

It would appear that, within the general context of a face-to-face group oriented toward some common problem or content, the fit of the model to the data may be a consequence of the following conditions:

1. There is a distribution of what might be labeled "verbal participation potential" among the participants present at a meeting. The genesis of this potential, i.e., whether it is a personality characteristic or situationally induced, is not relevant here although it would seem to be a fruitful area for investigation. The inequality among the participants in this respect is the important factor rather than the reasons for this inequality. One qualification should be suggested, although it will not be elaborated

in this paper. That is, that the differences among the participants should not be of such a nature as to divide them into two or more distinct groups characterized by markedly different systems of participation relationships. If this restriction does not hold, the variation involved in the distribution of participation may be more abrupt than the model can handle. The potential of a given member of the group may vary during the meeting and be affected by the influences to which he is subjected, but it is essentially a compounded resultant of individual factors. The data that are yielded by observation of participation reflect average differences in potential.

2. There is no systematic regulation of the "free competitive expression" of "verbal participation potentials." For example, neither the leader nor the group attempts to control the rates of participation by specifying when an individual may participate or by regulating the distribution of relevant information.
3. The members are relatively undifferentiated in regard to the roles they play in the discussion, except for the differentiation that results from the relative strength of their verbal participation potentials. There is no set of structured differentiated roles that has a major effect on the distribution of participation. In the groups described above there was always present, of course, a clearly differentiated leader role. This is not an exception to the general rule, however, since the leader's participation was calculated residually and not directly by the formulae. This device permits one to use the model in concrete instances where there is such a well-differentiated role.

It is believed that the groups from which the data were drawn fulfilled these conditions. The evidence is, however, inferential rather than direct. The controls which were exercised in drawing a sample, the manner in which the group discussions were conducted, and the processes of observing and tabulating the data operated to ensure that there was no systematic selection in terms of "verbal participation potential" or the possibilities for the "free expression" of this potential. The general norms for student behavior also served to mitigate against any well-defined role structure among the members.

The results presented in Table 2 suggest that under these conditions the size of the group is a major determinant of the ratio, $r_n$, in the exponential function that fits the participation relationships of the members.

In groups of a given size it might be expected that the ratio will vary with changes in some of the conditions noted above. For example, the effect of selecting members on the basis of factors closely associated with their verbal participation potentials is revealed by an experiment conducted by the Study of Education.[3] Two groups were formed from students who had been observed in discussion groups during the preceding

3 The data on high and low participating groups are drawn from unpublished work by Bray (3).

term. One of the groups consisted of individuals who had shown high rates of participation and the other of individuals who had shown low rates. This selection not only established a substantial difference between the two experimental groups in their average previous rate of participation, but it narrowed the range of verbal participation potential within each group. The results of applying the model to data drawn from two meetings of each of these groups are shown in Table 3.[4]

The exponential model is found to hold for these data also. Although one might have expected the homogeneity within each of the groups to have the same effect on the ratio, i.e., to increase it in both instances, it

TABLE 3

*Participation by Individuals in High- and Low-Participator Groups*

| | MEETINGS OF HIGH-PARTICIPATOR GROUP | | | MEETINGS OF LOW-PARTICIPATOR GROUP | | |
|---|---|---|---|---|---|---|
| RANK OF MEMBER | PER CENT OF TOTAL | ESTIMATED PERCENTAGE | DIFFERENCE | PER CENT OF TOTAL | ESTIMATED PERCENTAGE | DIFFERENCE |
| L | 30.1 | 30.0 | −0.1 | 42.3 | 40.3 | −2.0 |
| 1 | 19.1 | 19.0 | −0.1 | 28.3 | 26.7 | −2.0 |
| 2 | 14.9 | 15.2 | +0.3 | 12.9 | 15.1 | +2.2 |
| 3 | 11.7 | 12.1 | +0.4 | 8.9 | 8.6 | −0.3 |
| 4 | 10.1 | 9.7 | −0.4 | 4.0 | 4.9 | +0.9 |
| 5 | 9.3 | 7.8 | −1.5 | 3.6 | 2.8 | −0.8 |
| 6 | 4.7 | 6.2 | +1.5 | 0.0 | 1.6 | +1.6 |
| Ratio, $r_7$ | | .799 | | | .567 | |

appears that there have been opposite effects. Members of adjacent ranks in high-participator groups seem to be more like each other; those in low-participator groups to be less like each other.

One source for this difference lies in the original selection of members. The members of the high-participator group were more homogeneous with regard to their previous rankings than were the members of the low-participator group. It was possible to recruit the former group from men who had been in the first to the fourth rank in their prior meetings; for the latter group it was necessary to select from men in a broader range of prior ranking that extended from the sixth to the fourteenth.

While the range of previous ranking was reduced for both groups by the process of selection, it was compressed to one-quarter of the original range for the high-participator group, while for the low-participator group it was compressed only one-half. This difference in the degree of

4 These meetings were chosen because they permitted comparison of meetings at which the size of the group was the same. Other meetings were observed at which the attendance was greater or less than seven. Some of them did not conform as closely as these to the exponential function, usually because of definite factors that tended to structure the discussion, such as assignment of reports to be presented by one or more members.

homogeneity in prior ranking is assumed to have produced a corresponding difference between the two groups in their range of verbal participation potentials and hence in their respective ratios, *r*, in the subsequent meetings. On this assumption the ratio for the low group should be roughly the square of the ratio for the high group and it is nearly so.

This explanation is by far the simplest one but does not sufficiently account for the fact that the low-participator ratio is also lower than that found in non-selected groups of the same size where one would normally expect to have even greater initial variation among the members. It may be that the nature of the participation pattern among those with low verbal participation potentials is such that a low ratio would result even though homogeneity were increased. It may be that here one finds some evidence that the fit of the exponential is defective beyond a certain degree of approximation. Further research is needed to separate out the effects of homogeneity from the effects of average strength of verbal participation potential, and to bring to light other factors that should be incorporated into the model.

One further illustration of the effect of various factors on the ratio in the exponential function is provided by a study of experimental groups at another university that compared two situations in which the behavior of the leader was markedly different.[5] For present purposes, the two styles of leader behavior might be described as active and passive. In the former instance the leader played a major role in the discussion through his own contributions. In the latter, the leader merely introduced the subject for discussion and permitted the group to function with a minimum of interference. The members within each group were heterogeneous in regard to a personality dimension usually labeled "ascendance-submission." That is, within each group the members represented a range of scores from high to low on personality tests considered to measure this variable. The groups under different leaders had similar membership in terms of this variable. They were not selected on any other variable. "Ascendance-submission" is not equivalent to "verbal participation potential," but it was found to have consistent though low correlations with actual participation.

In comparison to the groups in the last illustration, these groups appear to be relatively heterogeneous in regard to verbal participation potential and functioned under two different leader styles. Table 4 shows the results of applying the model to data drawn from three meetings of passive-leader groups and four meetings of active-leader groups.[6]

The ratios for the two styles of leadership are higher than the ratio

5 These data are drawn from an unpublished study in which the distribution of participation was an important but not primary focus. Cf. G. Mishler, (4).

6 The unit of participation counted in these groups differs from that used for the other groups reported in this paper. Briefly, a contribution could be assigned to from one to twelve separate problem-solving categories. Each assignment to a category constituted a unit of participation.

for the seven-man groups in Table 2 but differ very little between themselves. The different leadership styles did, of course, produce different effects. There was, quite obviously, a large difference between the proportions of total participation contributed by the members in each of the groups. The leadership styles did not differentially affect the participation relationships among the members. (Nor were these relationships significantly different from those holding among members in groups where leader styles were not altered in any systematic way.)

TABLE 4

*Participation by Members of Discussion Groups Under Passive and Active Leadership*

| GROUP WITH PASSIVE LEADER | | | | GROUP WITH ACTIVE LEADER | | | |
|---|---|---|---|---|---|---|---|
| RANK OF MEMBER | PER CENT OF TOTAL | ESTIMATED PERCENTAGE | DIFFERENCE | RANK OF MEMBER | PER CENT OF TOTAL | ESTIMATED PERCENTAGE | DIFFERENCE |
| 1 | 34.3 | 33.0 | −1.3 | L | 52.8 | 52.5 | −0.3 |
| 2 | 23.3 | 22.9 | −0.4 | 1 | 16.3 | 15.6 | −0.7 |
| 3 | 14.3 | 15.9 | +1.6 | 2 | 8.9 | 11.2 | +2.3 |
| 4 | 9.9 | 11.1 | +1.2 | 3 | 8.8 | 8.0 | −0.8 |
| L * | 7.8 | 7.7 | −0.1 | 4 | 6.8 | 5.7 | −1.1 |
| 6 | 6.1 | 5.4 | −0.7 | 5 | 4.4 | 4.1 | −0.3 |
| 7 | 4.2 | 3.8 | −0.4 | 6 | 2.0 | 2.9 | +0.9 |
| Ratio, $r_7$ | | .696 | | | | .717 | |

* In this instance, inasmuch as the leader did not have a role which differentiated him markedly from the other members, his participation was computed directly rather than residually.

To understand why a difference, which might have been expected, failed to appear, one may refer back to the previously listed conditions which were considered responsible for the fit of the model and for the derived ratios.

It would appear that in both the active- and passive-leader groups, the three required conditions were fulfilled. To the extent that the personality dimension of ascendance bears some relationship to participation (and as a minimum it may be said with assurance that heterogeneity in the former is not likely to produce homogeneity in the latter), the groups were heterogeneous in regard to verbal participation potential. Second, there were no clearly differentiated roles by which the members were distinguished from each other.

Third, although the active leader was indeed active, none of his activity was directed towards controlling "who" spoke during the time when he himself was not speaking. Although he controlled the content and contributed over half the total number of participations, he recognized whomever wanted to speak and neither attempted to stimulate nonparticipators nor ignore over-participators. There was, therefore, no systematic regulation of the "free competitive expression" of the "verbal participation potentials" present in the active-leader groups; and most certainly not in the passive-leader groups.

The last discussion raises an important point which should be borne in mind in research with different styles of leadership (whether autocratic *vs.* democratic, or directive *vs.* non-directive, etc.). The areas of group functioning to which the leader is to be systematically oriented (whether content, distribution of participation, etc.) must be specified if one is to understand the effects of alterations in leader styles. As has been pointed to above, marked differences in certain aspects of leadership behavior do not produce differences in the participation relationships of members when the leaders have not also been differentially oriented to the latter dimension.

Finally, it may be said that the usefulness of the model extends beyond its utility for describing the distribution of participation in small groups. Its fit in these cases is a function of certain theoretically postulated conditions. These conditions all refer essentially to groups which are unstructured, i.e., where a pattern of interaction is permitted to develop spontaneously.

Where the data do not fit or where the ratios are considerably different from what might be expected, this is a cue to search for the conditions which are responsible for these alterations. One cannot, with this model alone, develop a full theory of group functioning. The results of applying it, however, may stimulate work of this kind in other areas and so serve to further the development of a more complete and more adequate theory.

## SUMMARY

A simple exponential model is fitted and is found to describe adequately the distribution of participation among the members of small groups. Where three conditions are fulfilled: a range of verbal participation potential among the members, no systematic interference with the "free competitive expression" of these potentials, and a lack of well-differentiated roles among the members—then the size of the group is found to be an important parameter affecting the size of the ratio in the basic equation. That is, as groups increase in size members of adjacent ranks become more like each other in their relative rates of participation.

The model is applied to other data where the conditions appear to vary from those required. Its fit in these cases is discussed along with suggestions for further research which develop out of these new applications.

## REFERENCES

1. Bales, R. F. *Interaction process analysis.* Cambridge, Mass.: Addison-Wesley, 1950.
2. Bales, R. F., et al. Channels of communication in small groups. *Amer. sociol. Rev.*, 1951, 16, 461–468.

3. Bray, D. W. A comparison of precepts composed of low and high participating students. Study of Education, 1950. (Unpublished).
4. Mishler, E. G. Ascendant and submissive members and leaders: Their interaction in group discussion. Occasional Paper of the Conference Research Project. Univer. of Michigan, 1950.
5. Mishler, E. G. The Princeton preceptorial system. (In preparation).
6. Stephan, F. F. The relative rate of communication between members of small groups. *Amer. sociol. Rev.*, 1952, 17, 482–486.

# *Interaction of Individuals in Reconstituted Groups*

EDGAR F. BORGATTA
and
ROBERT F. BALES

## INTRODUCTION

THE RESULTS of this study indicate that it may be possible to use diagnostic sessions to estimate characteristic rates of particular individuals and from this information to predict certain aspects of performance of groups reconstituted from these individuals. Conversely, it may be possible to predict certain aspects of performance of the individual in a particular group if we have estimates of the characteristic performance of each of the individuals based on previous diagnostic sessions.

FROM *Sociometry*, 1953, 16, 302–320. Reprinted by permission of the authors and publisher.

This research was supported in part by the United States Air Force under contract number AF 33 (038)–12782 monitored by the Human Resources Research Institute, Maxwell Air Force Base, Alabama. Permission is granted for reproduction, translation, publication and disposal in whole and in part by or for the United States Government.

We are indebted to the research staff at Maxwell Air Force Base, which assisted in the collection of data.

We are also indebted to Richard Mann for his assistance in the devising of the arbitrary classification used in this paper, and to Jonathan Robbin for his constant attention to the accuracy of the data.

Evidence is presented that each individual who is a prospective member of a group can usefully be regarded as having a characteristic rate of interaction, and a characteristic upper bound, with a tendency to increase his rate to his upper bound, depending upon opportunity. The rate actually achieved by a given man in a group is an inverse function of the characteristic rates of his co-participators. The total rate achieved by a given group is in part a function of the summed characteristic rates of the participants. However, the total rate of a given group is also a function of the degree of differentiation of the characteristic rates of the individuals composing it.

For both groups and individuals, qualitative differences of performance are associated with differences in interaction rates. For individual persons, specialization on the side of task leadership is generally associated with high interaction rate. Persons with relatively lower rates tend to assume residual roles of supporting, modifying, qualifying, or rejecting. Persons with the lowest rates may be excluded or withdrawn, will tend to show high rates of tension, and may not contribute substantially either to the task or to the support of co-participators.

## THE SAMPLE AND THE DATA

The data are obtained from observation of 166 sessions of three-man groups. One hundred twenty-six enlisted Air Force personnel were divided into fourteen batches of nine men each. Each batch of nine men was organized and reorganized into twelve three-man groups in such a way that each subject participated in four of the sessions and participated with each other subject in his batch only one time.[1] The design attempted to limit the contact of subjects with each other before the sessions. Subjects had equal experience at each stage of testing. Each session was 48 minutes long. The behavior observed was classed under two headings according to the type of task: *Actual Behavior* (24 minutes which included time spent getting acquainted, planning role playing sessions, and discussion) and *Role Playing Behavior* (24 minutes which consisted of role playing two scenes planned by the participants themselves). The social behavior of the participants (the interaction) was observed and classified according to Bales' categories of interaction process analysis.[2] The data will be treated as two sets of 166 sessions each.

1 Two sessions were lost in the scheduled 168 total since one subject went AWOL on a second day of testing.

2 Bales, (1). Briefly, the categories in this observation system may be identified as follows: Categories 1, 2 and 3, showing solidarity, tension release, and agreement; categories 4, 5 and 6, giving suggestion, opinion, and orientation; categories 7, 8 and 9, asking for orientation, opinion, and suggestion; and categories 10, 11 and 12, showing disagreement, tension, and antagonism. The first three and the last three categories are known as the positive and negative social-emotional categories, respectively. The central six categories are known as the task categories.

Greater detail on the characteristics of the sample and session organization will be found in two previous articles (2, 3). Problems of scoring reliability and consistency of subject behavior, and task and experience as factors in the interaction of these groups are considered in these articles. High scorer reliability and a reasonable range of consistency of subject behavior were reported. Interaction differences by task between *Actual Behavior* and *Role Playing Behavior* were manifest.

## OBSERVATIONS OF INDIVIDUALS

Since we have four independent observations (sessions) in which each individual has participated, we have taken his average performance in these as the best available estimate of his characteristic interaction behavior.[3] On this basis of classification, and further, considering the ranking of the individual in his batch of nine, we have arbitrarily placed the subjects into five classes. The operations were as follows: A frequency distribution of the initiated behavior (total rates) of the 126 subjects was arbitrarily cut into three intervals. The arbitrary cuts were made on a basis that gave a relatively symmetric distribution of persons around the middle cell in both the Role Playing and the Actual Behavior. In the sessions of Actual Behavior 49 individuals were classed as High initiators, 34 Middle, and 43 Low. In the sessions of Role Playing Behavior, 40 were classed as High, 31 Middle, and 55 Low. It should be noted that the median initiator for the Role Playing set is lower in rate than the median initiator for the Actual Behavior set. The second point of reference used in the arbitrary classification is the cut nearest the mean score of the set. The third reference point in the classification is the ranking of the individual within his batch of nine persons.

The arbitrary definitions of the five classes are:

H The person is above the Middle initiators, and among the top four in the batch of nine persons from which he is drawn.

h The person is above the mean, and among the top five in the batch of nine from which he is drawn.

l The person is below the mean, and among the lowest five in the batch of nine from which he is drawn.

L The person is below the Middle initiators, and among the lowest four in the batch of nine from which he is drawn.

M The residual individuals are classed as M, which stands for mixture and is given a middle value.

Under these definitions we get the following distributions of persons. In the Actual Behavior set: H=46, h=19, M=4, l=15, L=42. In the Role Playing Behavior set: H=36, h=21, M=8, l=10, L=51. This distribution

3 Actually, there is a minor restriction of independence since a person's co-participators are chosen from his batch of nine persons rather than the total sample.

is approximately that which was desired, that is, one which would allow us to expect to find at least a few cases of groups composed of three participants at the same extreme.

Having a classification of individuals on the basis of an estimate of their characteristic behavior, we would like to know how well these estimates would predict the outcome of sessions of three-man groups composed of different combinations of these individuals, and further, the influence on the characteristic performance of the individual that participation with two other persons (of known characteristics) would have. To do this, the most rigorous research design would require that we again reconstitute our sample into three-man groups (again restricting contact before sessions) if we wish to maintain independence in our predictions in all possible ways. In our design, one would actually have used the first three sessions to predict the fourth, and thus satisfy the rigorous requirement at the cost of fewer cases. However, since we have not used information concerning the *rate of the group* in our derivation of types of persons and types of groups, we have not lost independence of prediction in this sense, and we decided to proceed with the larger available N of all sessions (166).

In analyzing the composition of groups we have made use of an arbitrary weighting of individuals according to their classification, i.e., H=4, h=3, M=2, l=1, L=0. This allows us, for example, to classify sessions according to the total weight of the participants (or mean weight). The distribution of sessions by types of groups, and by total weight, is given in Table 1.

## TWO HYPOTHESES ON INTERACTION RATE OF THE GROUP

Two hypotheses were formulated before the analysis of the data. The first was that *the total interaction rate* (number of acts per unit time) *of the group is correlated with the total of the weights associated with the characteristic performance of the individuals composing the group.* This essentially states that individuals will tend to be relatively stable in their rate of participation, irrespective of the group they happen to be in from session to session. The weights have been indicated in Table 1, and these were correlated directly to the total interaction rates of the groups. The correlations (product moment) were .38 for the Role Playing Behavior set and .40 for Actual Behavior set. Both these results are significant at the .05 level with N=166, and we do not reject the hypothesis.

The second hypothesis stated that *the greater the differentiation of the group, the higher the interaction rate of the group.* Any definition of differentiation would be arbitrary, and the decision here was to use the amount of deviation from the maximally differentiated type, HML, as our

TABLE I

*Distribution of Sessions by Characteristics of Participants. Role Playing and Actual Behavior, Arranged by Total Weight of Participants*

| TYPE OF GROUP | TOTAL WEIGHT OF PARTICIPANTS | NUMBER OF SESSIONS OBSERVED ROLE PLAYING BEHAVIOR | ACTUAL BEHAVIOR |
|---|---|---|---|
| HHH | 12 | 2 | 3 |
| HHh | 11 | 5 | 8 |
| Hhh | 10 | 5 | 4 |
| HHM | 10 | 4 | 3 |
| hhh | 9 | 1 | — |
| HhM | 9 | 3 | 3 |
| HHl | 9 | 5 | 10 |
| HMM | 8 | 1 | — |
| hhM | 8 | — | — |
| Hhl | 8 | 2 | 9 |
| HHL | 8 | 18 | 26 |
| hMM | 7 | — | — |
| hhl | 7 | — | — |
| HhL | 7 | 16 | 20 |
| HMl | 7 | — | 4 |
| hMl | 6 | 1 | 1 |
| hhL | 6 | 4 | 3 |
| MMM | 6 | — | — |
| HML | 6 | 11 | 2 |
| Hll | 6 | 1 | 2 |
| hML | 5 | 4 | 1 |
| HlL | 5 | 8 | 17 |
| hll | 5 | 1 | — |
| MMl | 5 | — | — |
| HLL | 4 | 24 | 17 |
| hlL | 4 | 13 | 8 |
| Mll | 4 | — | — |
| MML | 4 | 1 | — |
| hLL | 3 | 17 | 12 |
| MlL | 3 | — | 1 |
| lll | 3 | — | — |
| MLL | 2 | 5 | 1 |
| llL | 2 | — | 2 |
| lLL | 1 | 7 | 2 |
| LLL | 0 | 7 | 7 |
| Total | | 166 | 166 |

measure of lack of differentiation.[4] The differentiation scores of the groups were correlated to the total interaction rates of the groups. The correlations were .14 for Role Playing and .22 for Actual Behavior. The correlation for Role Playing is just short of significance at the .05 level. We again do not reject the hypothesis.

4 This measure has an equivalent but reversed form which may be computed as follows: Find the minimum number of unit changes to reduce the group type to an undifferentiated form (e.g., to lll or MMM). To this number add 1 if the reduced form is lll or hhh, and add 2 if reduced form is MMM.

Since the measure of differentiation and the total weight assigned to the group type are independent, we may ask the question: How much of the variance in the total interaction rates of the groups may be accounted for just on the basis of these two measures? Again, using unit sized arbitrary weights with the base at zero (the simplest weighting), the total weight scores and the differentiation scores were added and correlated to the total interaction rates of the groups. The correlations were .39 for Role Playing Behavior set and .45 for Actual Behavior set, showing a small improvement in the prediction by using the two independent measures. The improvement could be greater with more sophisticated weighting, but here it is enough to demonstrate that these two factors alone will account for about 15 to 20 per cent of the variance.

The analysis is parallel in Role Playing and Actual Behavior, and the results are parallel. The Role Playing, however, apparently does not show the relationships tested as clearly as the Actual Behavior. The differences between these classifications are not significant. However, if such differences continued to occur, one area which would be suggested for further investigation is the influence of the roles participants assign to each other (or the roles assigned to them) on the interaction rate of the group. On an *a priori* basis, it might be expected that mis-matching of persons to roles would create tensions which would interfere with their ability to participate.

## TWO HYPOTHESES ON INTERACTION RATES OF INDIVIDUALS

One of the crucial problems in the composition or reconstitution of groups (that is, assessment of individuals and assignment of them to new groups) is the effect that it will have on the particular individual to be placed with others of given characteristics. For example, group psychotherapists often face the problem of whether to compose groups of patients for homogeneity or heterogeneity on any of several characteristics. With regard to interaction rates, should low participators be put with low participators in order to minimize competition between them and raise their interaction rates? Or, should they be put in with high participators in order to stimulate them to greater activity? Conversely, should very high participators be put with very high participators to increase competition and lower their interaction rates? If they are put with low participators will it bore them into inactivity? Two hypotheses were advanced relevant to this problem: First, it was expected that *when all high interactors participate together, they depress each other's activity*. Second, it was expected that *when all low interactors participate together, they depress each other's activity*. The first hypothesis was based on reasoning concerning an upper limit for the group interaction rate, and the second hypothesis was based on the lack of stimulation and elicitation of response expected in such groups.

For each individual a weight has been assigned on the basis of his characteristic performance over the four sessions (H = 4, h = 3, etc., as described above). In a given session this individual participates with two co-participants. The weights designating the characteristic performance of each of these two individuals are added to find the "total weight of the co-participants."

For each of the five classifications of group members for both Role Playing and Actual Behavior, the total weight of the co-participants was correlated to the interaction rate of the group member. The coefficients are summarized in Table 2.[5]

TABLE 2

*Coefficients of Correlation between the Interaction Rate of the Group Member and the Total Weight of His Co-participators*

| | r (PRODUCT MOMENT) | NUMBER OF CASES |
|---|---|---|
| Actual Behavior Group Member | | |
| H | —.78 | 181 |
| h | —.74 | 76 |
| M | —.34 | 16 |
| l | —.27 | 60 |
| L | —.55 | 165 |
| | Sum | 498 |
| Role Playing Behavior Group Member | | |
| H | —.78 | 141 |
| h | —.91 | 83 |
| M | —.90 | 40 |
| l | —.34 | 32 |
| L | —.88 | 202 |
| | Sum | 498 |

The data confirm the first hypothesis, namely, that in sessions composed of all high participators, the group members depress each other's activity. The second hypothesis is emphatically rejected. In sessions composed of all low participators the group members do not depress each other's activity. The relation found, however, is an unusually stable one. Namely, *irrespective of the person's characteristic performance, and irrespective of the type of behavior (Role Playing or Actual), the rate of initiation of behavior of the group member will be an inverse function of the average characteristic interaction rate of his co-participants.*

5 Detailed tables showing the average raw and percentage profiles of initiated behavior for each type of person by each type of group, for Role Playing and Actual Behavior are not included for reasons of space.

The high coefficients of correlation and their replication indicates that a large amount of the variance is under control for prediction. While a number of explanations might be advanced for this extremely stable finding, the following seems to fit the data most reasonably.

For any group, given a set period of time, there exists an upper bound to the amount of interaction that can take place in the group and still preserve adequate communication, no matter how high the characteristic rates of the individuals may be. That individuals stay within such bounds may be viewed as a minimum condition of cooperation. The fact that the highest participators tend to depress each other may be due in part to this upper bound. This factor, however, does not explain why, when three characteristically low interactors are put together, they do not automatically rise to the mechanical upper bound. We infer, therefore, that the participation of a given individual is not infinitely elastic, that is, associated with his characteristic rate is an upper bound *for him* which appears to operate no matter how much opportunity he has to participate. We have already shown that a considerable part of the variance in the total interaction rates of groups may be accounted for by the simple addition of the characteristic rates of the constituent individuals. This could not be true unless such individual bounds existed. However, the inverse relation shown in Table 2 cannot be explained by either of these boundary conditions. It appears that no matter what the characteristic rates of the individuals may be, a competitive situation exists. This is to say that, in the absence of resistance, *the individual tends to his maximum rate*. The amount of resistance is determined by the characteristic rates of the coparticipants.

## QUALITY OF INTERACTION ACCORDING TO RATE OF THE INDIVIDUAL

Since we know that the gross rate of interaction of the individual differs according to the rates of the other individuals who happen to be in the group with him, it is important to ask: What happens to the quality of the individual's participation when he is put in a group where his characteristic rate is depressed? What happens when he is in a group where he is allowed (or encouraged) to increase his participation? Or, in general, what is the typical quality of interaction for persons of different characteristic rates?

The categories in terms of which the observations were made give a qualitative breakdown as indicated in footnote 3. Table 3 shows the average raw rate of activity in each of the twelve categories for individuals of each type, H, h, M, l, and L, in the Actual Behavior sets. These rates are also given as percentages of the total rate. Table 4 shows the same breakdown for the Role Playing sets. The second half of each of these tables gives an

TABLE 3

*Average Raw and Percentage Profiles of Initiated Behavior by Type of Person, Actual Behavior*

*All Cases (Regardless of Types of Co-participators):*

| TYPE OF PERSON | H | h | M | l | L |
|---|---|---|---|---|---|
| NO. OF CASES | 181 | 76 | 16 | 60 | 165 |
| CATEGORY | | | | | |
| 1 | 2.4 ( *2.0*) | 2.5 ( *2.5*) | 2.6 ( *2.6*) | 2.5 ( *2.8*) | 1.9 ( *2.7*) |
| 2 | 6.1 ( *5.0*) | 5.8 ( *5.8*) | 6.6 ( *6.7*) | 7.8 ( *8.6*) | 4.7 ( *6.7*) |
| 3 | 9.3 ( *7.7*) | 9.3 ( *9.3*) | 13.9 (*14.0*) | 9.0 ( *9.9*) | 7.9 ( *11.3*) |
| 4 | 7.3 ( *6.0*) | 6.2 ( *6.2*) | 5.6 ( *5.6*) | 5.3 ( *5.8*) | 3.8 ( *5.4*) |
| 5 | 35.6 ( *29.4*) | 25.7 ( *25.5*) | 26.3 (*26.5*) | 24.8 ( *27.3*) | 16.8 ( *24.0*) |
| 6 | 44.0 ( *36.4*) | 35.0 ( *34.7*) | 30.6 (*30.8*) | 27.3 ( *29.9*) | 21.4 ( *30.5*) |
| 7 | 7.4 ( *6.2*) | 7.6 ( *7.5*) | 7.1 ( *7.1*) | 6.4 ( *7.0*) | 5.2 ( *7.4*) |
| 8 | 2.4 ( *2.0*) | 2.0 ( *2.0*) | 2.2 ( *2.2*) | 1.3 ( *1.5*) | 1.4 ( *2.0*) |
| 9 | 0.9 ( *0.7*) | 0.8 ( *0.8*) | 0.7 ( *0.7*) | 0.5 ( *0.5*) | 0.6 ( *0.9*) |
| 10 | 1.1 ( *1.0*) | 1.1 ( *1.0*) | 0.6 ( *0.6*) | 0.8 ( *0.9*) | 0.5 ( *0.8*) |
| 11 | 4.3 ( *3.5*) | 4.6 ( *4.6*) | 3.0 ( *3.0*) | 5.3 ( *5.8*) | 5.8 ( *8.3*) |
| 12 | 0.1 ( *0.1*) | 0.2 ( *0.2*) | 0.1 ( *0.1*) | 0.1 ( *0.1*) | 0.1 ( *0.1*) |
| Total | 120.9 (*100.0*) | 100.8 (*100.1*) | 99.3 (*99.9*) | 91.1 (*100.1*) | 70.1 (*100.1*) |

*Those Cases where Average Weight of Co-participators is High:*

| TYPE OF PERSON | H | h | M | l | L |
|---|---|---|---|---|---|
| NO. OF CASES | 58 | 28 | 10 | 28 | 69 |
| CATEGORY | | | | | |
| 1 | 2.7 ( *2.3*) | 2.2 ( *2.6*) | 2.6 ( *2.7*) | 3.1 ( *3.6*) | 1.9 ( *3.0*) |
| 2 | 7.1 ( *6.1*) | 5.9 ( *6.9*) | 7.6 ( *7.9*) | 8.6 ( *9.9*) | 4.3 ( *6.8*) |
| 3 | 9.7 ( *8.4*) | 8.3 ( *9.7*) | 14.9 ( *15.5*) | 8.0 ( *9.2*) | 7.2 ( *11.4*) |
| 4 | 6.6 ( *5.7*) | 5.1 ( *6.0*) | 5.1 ( *5.3*) | 5.4 ( *6.2*) | 3.2 ( *5.0*) |
| 5 | 35.2 (*30.3*) | 20.6 ( *24.1*) | 26.3 ( *27.4*) | 24.3 ( *27.9*) | 16.3 ( *25.7*) |
| 6 | 39.1 (*33.7*) | 29.6 ( *34.6*) | 26.7 ( *27.8*) | 24.1 ( *27.7*) | 19.3 ( *30.4*) |
| 7 | 8.0 ( *6.9*) | 6.9 ( *8.1*) | 6.7 ( *7.0*) | 6.7 ( *7.7*) | 4.7 ( *7.4*) |
| 8 | 2.1 ( *1.8*) | 1.6 ( *1.9*) | 1.9 ( *2.0*) | 1.1 ( *1.3*) | 1.3 ( *2.1*) |
| 9 | 0.7 ( *0.6*) | 0.6 ( *0.7*) | 0.5 ( *0.5*) | 0.6 ( *0.7*) | 0.5 ( *0.8*) |
| 10 | 1.1 ( *0.9*) | 1.2 ( *1.4*) | 0.9 ( *0.9*) | 0.9 ( *1.0*) | 0.4 ( *0.6*) |
| 11 | 3.6 ( *3.1*) | 3.6 ( *4.2*) | 2.8 ( *2.9*) | 4.1 ( *4.7*) | 4.3 ( *6.8*) |
| 12 | 0.1 ( *0.1*) | 0.0 ( *0.0*) | 0.1 ( *0.1*) | 0.1 ( *0.1*) | 0.0 ( *0.0*) |
| Total | 116.0 (*99.9*) | 85.6 (*100.2*) | 96.1 (*100.0*) | 87.0 (*100.0*) | 63.4 (*100.0*) |

indication of "what happens when a man is put with high co-participators," (i.e., with two co-participators whose total weight is 5, 6, 7, or 8). (What happens when a man is put with low co-participators is, of course, just the reverse.)

Note first what happens to the total rates of participation. In general, under all conditions, the total rate declines as we go from High to Low. (This, of course, is expected from the original definition of types.) In every case, the total rate of a given type of man decreases when he is in a group with high co-participators. This is also expected from the findings in Table 2.

TABLE 4

*Average Raw and Percentage Profiles of Initiated Behavior by Type of Person, Role Playing Behavior*

*All Cases (Regardless of Types of Co-participators):*

| TYPE OF PERSON | H | h | M | l | L |
|---|---|---|---|---|---|
| NO. OF CASES | 141 | 83 | 32 | 40 | 202 |
| CATEGORY | | | | | |
| 1 | 0.8 ( *0.7*) | 0.6 ( *0.6*) | 0.5 ( *0.6*) | 0.8 ( *0.8*) | 0.5 ( *0.8*) |
| 2 | 2.2 ( *1.7*) | 1.7 ( *1.7*) | 2.6 ( *2.9*) | 1.8 ( *2.0*) | 2.0 ( *3.1*) |
| 3 | 9.8 ( *7.8*) | 10.6 (*10.7*) | 13.5 ( *14.9*) | 10.7 (*11.8*) | 8.6 (*13.0*) |
| 4 | 3.8 ( *3.1*) | 2.3 ( *2.3*) | 2.8 ( *3.1*) | 2.8 ( *3.0*) | 1.9 ( *2.9*) |
| 5 | 53.8 (*42.9*) | 38.9 ( *39.1*) | 34.9 ( *38.6*) | 38.9 (*42.7*) | 27.0 (*41.1*) |
| 6 | 39.5 (*31.5*) | 31.6 ( *31.8*) | 23.6 ( *26.1*) | 25.4 (*27.8*) | 16.0 (*24.3*) |
| 7 | 5.5 ( *4.4*) | 4.0 ( *4.0*) | 5.9 ( *6.5*) | 3.4 ( *3.7*) | 3.0 ( *4.6*) |
| 8 | 6.3 ( *5.0*) | 6.1 ( *6.1*) | 3.8 ( *4.2*) | 4.6 ( *5.0*) | 3.4 ( *5.2*) |
| 9 | 0.2 ( *0.1*) | 0.4 ( *0.4*) | 0.3 ( *0.3*) | 0.2 ( *0.2*) | 0.1 ( *0.2*) |
| 10 | 1.8 ( *1.4*) | 1.3 ( *1.4*) | 1.3 ( *1.4*) | 0.9 ( *0.9*) | 0.8 ( *1.3*) |
| 11 | 0.8 ( *0.6*) | 1.5 ( *1.5*) | 1.2 ( *1.3*) | 1.5 ( *1.6*) | 1.9 ( *2.9*) |
| 12 | 0.8 ( *0.7*) | 0.5 ( *0.6*) | 0.1 ( *0.1*) | 0.3 ( *0.4*) | 0.3 ( *0.5*) |
| Total | 125.3 (*99.9*) | 99.5 (*100.2*) | 90.5 (*100.0*) | 91.3 (*99.9*) | 65.5 (*99.9*) |

*Those Cases Where Average Weight of Co-participators is High:*

| TYPE OF PERSON | H | h | M | l | L |
|---|---|---|---|---|---|
| NO. OF CASES | 42 | 23 | 9 | 10 | 61 |
| CATEGORY | | | | | |
| 1 | 0.7 ( *0.6*) | 0.4 ( *0.5*) | 0.7 ( *0.9*) | 0.4 ( *0.7*) | 0.6 ( *1.1*) |
| 2 | 1.9 ( *1.7*) | 2.7 ( *3.3*) | 2.8 ( *3.6*) | 0.8 ( *1.1*) | 2.2 ( *3.9*) |
| 3 | 10.6 ( *9.3*) | 10.7 (*13.1*) | 13.3 ( *16.9*) | 8.1 ( *11.5*) | 7.9 ( *14.1*) |
| 4 | 3.3 ( *2.9*) | 2.2 ( *2.7*) | 2.4 ( *3.1*) | 2.8 ( *4.0*) | 1.3 ( *2.3*) |
| 5 | 48.4 ( *42.3*) | 33.0 (*40.6*) | 25.9 ( *33.0*) | 31.5 ( *44.7*) | 22.2 ( *39.5*) |
| 6 | 35.4 ( *30.9*) | 22.3 (*27.4*) | 23.2 ( *29.6*) | 19.5 ( *27.7*) | 13.5 ( *24.0*) |
| 7 | 4.8 ( *4.2*) | 2.8 ( *3.4*) | 4.4 ( *5.6*) | 2.1 ( *3.0*) | 3.6 ( *6.4*) |
| 8 | 5.5 ( *4.8*) | 4.1 ( *5.0*) | 3.2 ( *4.1*) | 3.2 ( *4.5*) | 2.8 ( *5.0*) |
| 9 | 0.1 ( *0.1*) | 0.1 ( *0.1*) | 0.1 ( *0.1*) | 0.0 ( *0.0*) | 0.1 ( *0.2*) |
| 10 | 2.2 ( *1.9*) | 1.6 ( *2.0*) | 1.3 ( *1.7*) | 1.1 ( *1.6*) | 0.6 ( *1.1*) |
| 11 | 0.6 ( *0.5*) | 1.1 ( *1.4*) | 1.1 ( *1.4*) | 0.5 ( *0.7*) | 1.2 ( *2.1*) |
| 12 | 1.0 ( *0.9*) | 0.3 ( *0.4*) | 0.1 ( *0.1*) | 0.5 ( *0.7*) | 0.2 ( *0.4*) |
| Total | 114.5 (*100.1*) | 81.2 (*99.9*) | 78.5 (*100.1*) | 70.5 (*100.2*) | 56.2 (*100.1*) |

If the quality of participation did not change according to changes in the total rate, we should expect the changes in each category to be proportional to those in the total rate. In other words, the rate in each category should decrease proportionately as we go from High to Low, and also as we compare the performance of a man under average conditions with his depressed performance when with high co-participants.

From an examination of the tables it may be seen that this is not the case. With minor exception, the task categories 4, 5, and 6 decrease more rapidly than expected. Low men are not only lower absolutely than High men in giving orientation, opinion, and suggestion, but they spend proportionately less of their own participation time in this type of activity. The other task categories asking for orientation, opinion, and suggestion, again with minor exception, decrease about as expected. Asking questions is about as characteristic of High men as of Low men, though possibly for different reasons.

One notable increase of rates occurs. Category 11, showing tension, actually *increases*, both absolutely and proportionately, as we go from High men to Low men. It might be suggested that this is an artifact of scoring, since "awkward pauses" and hesitations are scored in this category, and one might thus expect more scores in category 11 for Low persons. However, this cannot possibly be a simple relationship, since we find that while the total interaction rate of Role Playing is lower than that of Actual Behavior, the amount of tension shown is also consistently lower. Not only are the differences quite clear and consistent, but they are perfectly in line with the hypothesis very generally held, that tension is associated with reality pressures of the task and tends to be lowered in the non-threatening atmosphere of role playing.

This hypothesis, if sound, also serves to explain another curious thing about the rates of tension, namely, that when a man is put with high co-participators, his rate of showing tension *does not increase*, as we might expect on the basis of a "competition" hypothesis. Rather his rate of showing tension decreases disproportionately fast. It may very well be that with two high co-participators in the group who can provide adequate resources for the solution of task problems, the anxiety associated with reality pressures is decreased. The data indicate that High men as well as Low men show lower tension rates when two high co-participators are present. This is consistent for *both* Actual Behavior and Role Playing. A hypothesis which rests on a notion of "shared confidence" rather than one which views tension simply as a result of "competition" and "getting crowded out of the discussion" seems to be necessary to explain this finding. It still remains true, however, that Low men show higher rates than High men, and so we are not able to dispense with the competition hypothesis. We conclude that both types of factors are operating. It may be quite important, in composing groups, to recognize that "sharing in the success of the group as a whole" may operate to offset the increased tension of the lower participators in the group resulting from their "unsuccessful competition" within the group. This way of looking at the problem is compatible with the notion that *differentiation of member rates* rather than uniformity *is associated with an over-all optimization of tension level.* (Earlier in this paper we have taken H M L as the maximally differentiated group and found that high differentiation is associated with high interaction rate.)

Although the absolute rates of disagreement and antagonism in the groups of this study are very low as compared to other groups that have been observed with the same method, there is some indication that these categories decrease more rapidly than expected by the hypothesis of decrease proportionate to total rate, as we do from High men to Low. Disagreement and antagonism are less inhibited types of negative reaction than is showing tension. Previous studies have tended to show that when tension is high, disagreement and antagonism tend to be low, and vice versa, as if they were alternate forms (passive and active) of the same general negative attitude. This inverse relationship among the variables may be seen in the comparisons of the Role Playing Behavior and Actual Behavior in Tables 3 and 4. It is perhaps worth noting that while the data are not unambiguous, there is an indication that in the Role Playing Behavior individuals tend to increase their rate of disagreement when put with high co-participators. This again would be consistent with the theory that in the role playing normal inhibitions are to some extent relaxed.

The changes in positive reactions as we go from High man to Low do not generally tend to decrease as fast as the proportionality hypothesis would require. Indeed, there is a strong suggestion that men in the middle positions (h, M, l) tend to be higher than either extreme. This is very possibly a result of the differentiation of roles which occurs when one person (in this case H) begins to specialize more heavily in the task categories. When this happens, a situation is created in which another person may specialize in endorsement and encouragement of the task efforts of the first man. These two, then, may form a complementary pair, distributing the major portion of the interaction between them. In a three-man group, if this happens, the third man may to some extent be excluded from the interaction. This interpretation of our findings is consistent with the earlier report by Mills concerning supportive behavior in three-man groups (4).

In the over-all picture of changes we find that decrease in total rate tends to be associated primarily with decrease in the task area, in particular, in giving orientation, opinion, and suggestion. If a man has a high characteristic rate and is granted the opportunity to go ahead, he is likely to do so by increasing his participation in the task areas. Since adequate integration of the group requires that task efforts receive response (supporting, modifying, qualifying, rejecting), the lower members tend to fall into the residual roles, and their rates in the social-emotional area tend to become proportionately higher than for the task specialist. Withdrawal, loss of involvement, or passivity, of course, are also residual roles and may result in a lowering of all rates for the person, including those in the social-emotional area, with the possible exception of showing tension. There is some evidence in our data that the Low man shows this tendency. The person who wishes to compose groups for special purposes may thus be able to control to some extent the *qualitative role* an individual may take, aside from his general tendencies, by placing him with other persons of higher or lower characteristic rates.

Conversely, if one knows that the placement of a given person relative to the others is likely to subject him to pressures to assume a given qualitative type of role, it may be desirable and possible to assess his aptitude or preference for this type of role ahead of time.

## QUALITY OF INTERACTION ACCORDING TO RATE OF THE GROUP

In the last section we examined changes in the quality of participation of characteristically High men compared to Low under the hypothesis that changes in the categories would be proportional to changes in the total rate of interaction. It was found that the changes were not proportional. On the contrary, a *qualitative* differentiation of roles appeared. The qualitative differentiation that appeared, however, was the same in the Role Playing as in the Actual Behavior. There were absolute differences according to task, but aside from these, the qualitative differences from High men to Low were relatively constant over the tasks. Essentially, this may be interpreted to mean that there is a tendency for persons to fulfill the *same roles relative to each other* within the group if their relative total rates are the same, in spite of changes of task. There are probably tasks of such great divergence in character that this tendency will not be manifest. However, in the composing of groups, it is important to recognize the existence of this tendency since it implies that there are pressures for members to take different qualitative roles, other than those related to the technical demands of the task.

Another problem in composing groups is the quality of participation of groups with high interaction rate as compared to those with low interaction rate. Should one attempt to compose a group for a high total rate? If there are changes in quality of interaction from high groups to low groups, are they the same as those found from High men to Low? Tables 5 and 6 show the average rates in the qualitative categories of all groups, as compared to the twelve highest and the twelve lowest groups. Percentages of total rates are also shown. (All groups will serve as the reference point of change.) Again, if the quality of participation did not change, we would expect the changes in each category to be proportional to the changes in the total rate of the group.

It is seen that again the proportionality hypothesis does not fit the data. Perhaps the most notable departures from this hypothesis are in category 11, showing tension, category 9, asking for suggestion, category 4, giving suggestion. Each of these categories actually *shows an increase in the absolute rate* in the Role Playing Behavior as we view the trend from high groups to low groups. The same thing is found in the Actual Be-

TABLE 5

*Average Raw and Percentage Profiles of Initiated Behavior for All Groups, and for the Twelve Highest and Twelve Lowest Groups, Actual Behavior*

| TYPE OF GROUP | HIGHEST | TOTAL | LOWEST |
|---|---|---|---|
| NO. OF CASES | 12 | 166 | 12 |
| CATEGORY | | | |
| 1 | 9.7 ( *2.7*) | 6.8 ( *2.3*) | 4.7 ( *2.3*) |
| 2 | 25.6 ( *7.1*) | 17.3 ( *6.0*) | 6.6 ( *3.2*) |
| 3 | 39.3 ( *10.8*) | 27.0 ( *9.3*) | 13.8 ( *6.7*) |
| 4 | 20.8 ( *5.8*) | 16.9 ( *5.8*) | 14.3 ( *7.0*) |
| 5 | 104.3 ( *28.8*) | 79.2 ( *27.3*) | 45.6 ( *22.3*) |
| 6 | 116.3 ( *32.1*) | 98.0 ( *33.8*) | 63.7 ( *31.2*) |
| 7 | 22.5 ( *6.2*) | 19.7 ( *6.8*) | 16.7 ( *8.2*) |
| 8 | 7.6 ( *2.1*) | 5.6 ( *1.9*) | 3.1 ( *1.5*) |
| 9 | 1.3 ( *0.3*) | 2.2 ( *0.7*) | 2.3 ( *1.1*) |
| 10 | 3.6 ( *1.0*) | 2.6 ( *0.9*) | 1.0 ( *0.8*) |
| 11 | 11.1 ( *3.1*) | 14.7 ( *5.1*) | 31.9 ( *15.6*) |
| 12 | 0.3 ( *0.1*) | 0.3 ( *0.1*) | 0.2 ( *0.1*) |
| Total | 362.2 (*100.1*) | 290.1 (*100.0*) | 204.2 (*100.0*) |

TABLE 6

*Average Raw and Percentage Profiles of Initiated Behavior for All Groups, and for the Twelve Highest and Twelve Lowest Groups, Role Playing Behavior*

| TYPE OF GROUP | 12 | TOTAL | LOWEST |
|---|---|---|---|
| NO. OF CASES | HIGHEST | 166 | 12 |
| CATEGORY | | | |
| 1 | 1.7 ( *0.5*) | 2.0 ( *0.7*) | 1.8 ( *0.9*) |
| 2 | 11.5 ( *3.3*) | 6.1 ( *2.2*) | 2.3 ( *1.2*) |
| 3 | 38.9 ( *11.0*) | 29.7 ( *10.8*) | 24.9 (*12.5*) |
| 4 | 6.6 ( *1.9*) | 7.8 ( *2.8*) | 9.5 ( *4.8*) |
| 5 | 159.1 ( *45.0*) | 114.5 ( *41.4*) | 77.3 (*38.8*) |
| 6 | 99.5 ( *28.1*) | 80.0 ( *29.0*) | 56.5 (*28.4*) |
| 7 | 14.3 ( *4.0*) | 12.2 ( *4.4*) | 4.0 ( *2.0*) |
| 8 | 16.8 ( *4.8*) | 14.1 ( *5.1*) | 8.3 ( *4.2*) |
| 9 | 0.1 ( *0.0*) | 0.5 ( *0.2*) | 1.3 ( *0.6*) |
| 10 | 3.2 ( *0.9*) | 3.6 ( *1.3*) | 3.7 ( *1.8*) |
| 11 | 1.9 ( *0.5*) | 4.4 ( *1.6*) | 8.8 ( *4.3*) |
| 12 | 0.3 ( *0.1*) | 1.5 ( *0.5*) | 0.8 ( *0.4*) |
| Total | 353.8 (*100.1*) | 276.5 (*100.0*) | 198.9 (*99.9*) |

havior, with the exception of category 4, giving suggestion, but even in this case the rate of decrease is slower than expected. If the rate of giving suggestion alone is considered, one might suppose that the low groups are more resourceful in dealing with the task than are the high groups. When the high rate of tension and asking for suggestion is considered, however, the indication is one of relative anxiety about the task and an inability to deal with it. In the Actual Behavior, categories 1, 2 and 3, showing solidarity, tension release, and agreement decrease at a rate faster than expected as we go from the high groups to the low. This fits with the picture of relative difficulty in arriving at a satisfactory solution of the task problem. In composing groups one may need to take care that the group has sufficient resources for dealing with its problem (particularly if he has put low interactors together with the hope of minimizing competition).

The task may make an important difference at this point, however. In the Role Playing Behavior we note that categories 1 and 3 decrease at a slower rate than expected. Further, category 10, showing disagreement, *increases in absolute rate* as we go from high groups to low groups. This does not change our interpretation of ineptness as associated with the low groups. It appears that in the Role Playing situation where a person may feel less threatened, as inability to cope with the task becomes evident, more random behavior occurs (more ill-considered suggestions), and is responded to in a less inhibited way, with rates in categories 3 and 10 (agreement and disagreement) proportionately higher than expected. Category 7, asking for orientation, apparently shows a difference in pattern between the Role Playing and the Actual Behavior, at least for the lowest groups. In the Actual Behavior the lowest groups are disproportionately high in asking for orientation, while in the Role Playing, they are disproportionately low. It seems reasonable to associate the high relative rate of asking for orientation with the greater reality pressures of the Actual Behavior for task solution. It may be noted that this relatively high rate of asking for orientation is not accompanied by a proportionately high rate of giving orientation, category 6. This is congruent with the notion that the lowest groups are low also in ability or resources for dealing with the factual and logical aspects of the Actual problem. The same types of pressures apparently do not exist as strongly in Role Playing.

The differences between the two tasks may be approached directly in terms of the profile of all groups taken together for each type of task. The absolute rate of interaction is lower in Role Playing. One possible interpretation of this difference is that the persons are generally more relaxed in the Role Playing, that is, under less pressure to get a specific decision made within a strict time limit. The qualitative differences are consistent with this notion. In the Role Playing there is less tension, more negative affect in categories 10 and 12, which suggests less inhibition. The Role Playing shows higher rates in asking for opinion and giving it, relative to questions and answers of orientation and suggestion, which again suggests a more affective and less guarded attitude. In the Actual Behavior the planning problem apparently tends to exert pressures toward more concrete specificity and emotional neutrality in remarks addressed to the task.

The Actual Behavior sets were not given over entirely to planning, however. Part of the task in these sets was "getting acquainted," so that they were actually mixtures of two tasks. This probably accounts partly for the fact that categories 1 and 2, showing solidarity and tension release, are higher for the Actual Behavior sets. Another factor is that the final period of Actual Behavior for each group was a permissive period of discussion of the two role playing sessions that had gone before, and a certain amount of joking and laughing occurred. Similarly, between the two role playing sessions, as tension built up, there were also occasional breaks of tension release in "kidding" concerning assignment of roles for the next session. In general, it may be remarked, high rates of joking and laughing cannot be taken at face value as signs of low tension. They should be considered in the context of the task and the rates in other categories, particularly category 11.

Finally, it is worth pointing out that the qualitative differences between high *groups* and low *groups* are not the same as the qualitative differences between High *men* and Low *men*. The differences between High men and Low men we attribute to their relative position with regard to each other in particular groups. The differences between high groups and low groups we attribute to the relation between the resources present in the group as a whole relative to the demands of the task. It is possible that resources of the group as a whole tend to be additive in relation to the task demands made on the group as a whole, but the evidence appears very strong that the qualitative tendencies of particular persons are not additive in the same sense. The constellation of positions within the group appears to be a complex interactive result of system formation.

## SOME IMPLICATIONS FOR THE COMPOSITION OF GROUPS AND DEVELOPMENT OF LEADERSHIP

In composing groups, optimum composition presumably depends upon the ends one has in view. At least three types of purposes may be distinguished: (*1*) Accomplishment of an immediate task, with all other goals secondary, (*2*) accomplishment of a task or a series of tasks, extended over a period of time within which the development of a satisfactory social organization is a critical factor, and (*3*) training of personnel for improving individual performance in a given role.

For the realization of objective (*1*), technical ability in relation to the task at hand may call for selection of individuals according to this criterion alone. With regard to interaction rate, this might involve putting together all high participators with high technical ability. The risks of this procedure are that the social organization may be unstable and unsatisfactory for the participants.

Where a stable and satisfactory social organization is critical, as in objective (*2*), the optimum composition of the group, aside from technical requirements, would seem to call for a *gradient* of characteristic rates among the members, with personality characteristics which would incline them to take the roles likely to develop from their relative positions by activity rate. Thus, a mis-matched group might be one in which the person with the highest characteristic activity rate prefers specialization in the social-emotional area rather than the task area. Such a person, on the other hand, might be optimally located in a group where one other member had an activity rate at least as high or higher, and preference for the task area. In the first group the morale of the person might be as high as in the second, but the task performance of the first group might be unnecessarily low. We have found that there is a positive correlation between differentiation (existence of a gradient) and activity rate of the group. On the other hand, we have also noticed that the very lowest persons are likely to be excluded or withdrawn. This would suggest that one should not compose for a gradient so steep that the middle persons exclude the lowest even from the residual supportive roles. There is some indication that the lowest man inevitably suffers from his unfavorable location, but it is also indicated that this may be compensated for to some extent by his identification with the success of the group as a whole.

Finally, (*3*) when the major objective of composing the group is the training of individual personnel for improved performance in a specific role, particularly the task leadership role, one will probably wish to compose for a gradient much as in the case of (*2*) above, with special attention to the position of the individual to be trained. Presumably, practice in a given role is necessary for improved performance, and practice is available only if the person is properly located with reference to his co-participators. Simple rotation of personnel in a given group, where each is instructed (or admonished) to take the role of leader will probably not be as effective as the recomposition of the group in such a way that the person to be trained for task leadership is the person with the highest characteristic rate in the group. If only simple rotation is used, it may well be that what will occur is that the "natural" task leader will be more indirect in his leadership, i.e., the leadership becomes "hidden." Our findings indicate that this is true even though role playing is employed. Role playing as the group task may, however, aid in reducing reality pressures, lessening tension, lowering inhibitions, and promoting a more relaxed atmosphere in the group as a whole. This may be particularly valuable where the characteristic interaction rates of all the members of the group are on the low side. Role players, provided they are able to adjust the quality and rate of their interaction sensitively enough, may be used as co-participants for a given person, in lieu of actual reconstitution of groups.

REFERENCES

1. Bales, R. F. *Interaction process analysis.* Cambridge, Mass.: Addison-Wesley, 1950.
2. Borgatta, E. F., & Bales, R. F. Task and accumulation of experience as factors in the interaction of small groups. *Sociometry*, 1953, 16, 239–252.
3. Borgatta, E. F., & Bales, R. F. The consistency of subject behavior and the reliability of scoring in interaction process analysis. *Amer. sociol. Rev.*, 1953, 18, 566–569.
4. Mills, T. M. Power relations in three-person groups. *Amer. social. Rev.*, 1953, 18, 351–357.

# *Size of Group as a Factor in the Interaction Profile*

ROBERT F. BALES
and
EDGAR F. BORGATTA

THIS is a report of the effects of group size on the kind of social interaction of members within the group. The report has two major purposes. The first purpose is to analyze certain observed variations in social interaction by group size in order to develop and systematize a set of substantive hypotheses about the effects of group size. Group size has been a focus of interest in the social sciences for a very long time, and the present study draws on earlier theory and research for many of the basic hypotheses advanced.[1]

This report is the first of several on a study of group size. The research was facilitated by the Laboratory of Social Relations, Harvard University. The planning and execution of the larger study was done by a team of researchers, who have consulted and advised on the present report. The team includes Philip E. Slater, Arthur S. Couch, Bernard P. Cohen, Nathan Altshuler, Richard D. Mann, and in the early stages, Christoph M. Heinicke. Later reports will appear under the authorship of various members and pairs of the research team. We are grateful to Hugh Williams and Jonathan Robbin for work on the extensive computation required for this report.

1 One of the reports in the planned series will present a review of the hypotheses contained in the literature on group size, and consider their relation to the hypotheses and findings of the study as a whole. Citations are therefore omitted in this report.

The second purpose is to present basic data from which interaction norms for further diagnostic and experimental purposes can easily be prepared. A series of groups of sizes two through seven were observed using Bales' method of interaction process analysis (1).[2] According to this method every observed act of verbal and non-verbal communication between members is classified into one of twelve categories, which in turn combine into four major types. *Questions* consist of asking for orientation, opinion, and suggestion (categories 7, 8, and 9). *Problem Solving Attempts* consist of giving orientation, opinion, and suggestion (categories 6, 5, and 4). *Positive Reactions* consist of showing agreement, tension release, and solidarity (categories 3, 2, and 1). *Negative Reactions* consist of showing disagreement, tension, and antagonism (categories 10, 11, and 12). The person who performs the act, and the person(s) to whom it is addressed are also recorded. A number of studies have been completed using this method and there is a need for norms in a standard test situation in order to extend its usefulness as a diagnostic device.

## THE SAMPLE AND THE DESIGN

The members of the groups were all male students drawn from the university employment office and paid for their time. No special attempt was made to compose groups of given characteristics, except that the requirement was made that members should not know each other previous to the first meeting. Pairs who were previously acquainted were put in separate groups. Persons who said they could not continue for the full four sessions were rejected. A number of groups were lost nevertheless, because of unavoidable drop outs. New groups were run to replace the broken groups. Groups of each size, two through seven, were observed. Each group of persons met for four sessions, each session with the identical membership. There were four groups of each size. The total number of persons participating was thus 108, and the total number of sessions from which data are drawn was 96.[3]

## THE TASK OF THE GROUPS

The task of each session was the discussion of a human relations case, a five page presentation of facts about a problem facing an administrator in his organization. Members were given copies of the case separately, to

2 Bales was the only observer present through the entire series, which required more than two years to complete. A second observer was nearly always present, and data on reliability will be the subject of one of the reports of the series. In order to avoid the introduction of variability due to change in scorers, Bales' observations alone were used for this study.

3 At a late stage of analysis, it was found that the coded information was improperly entered for one six man group. As necessary, the data for the six man groups are reduced in this presentation.

read ahead of time, and were told that although each was given accurate information, we intended to leave them uncertain as to whether they each had exactly the same range of facts. The cases were collected after they had been read by the members individually, to prevent direct comparison of typed copies, although members were allowed to take notes. The task defined for each session was to assemble the information, to discuss why the people involved were behaving as they did, and to decide what should be recommended as action for the solution to the problem presented. Four quite similar cases were used to provide each group with a different but comparable task each session.[4] For each group size, a Latin square design was utilized to randomize any possible effect on developmental trends in the groups because of the particular human relations cases used. The groups were asked to time themselves to 40 minutes, and to dictate the group solution for the sound record in the final one or two minutes of the meeting. There was some variation in the time taken, since the groups were not arbitrarily stopped at the 40 minute limit.

## TRANSFORMATION OF THE DATA

The data consist originally of a raw number of acts recorded in each of the twelve categories, called a raw profile, per member, per session. Profiles for sessions and groups are obtained by adding the appropriate raw member profiles. For the analysis, any raw profile to be examined, whether of an individual or a group, is then converted to a percentage profile by finding the percentage of the total number of acts in the profile that is contained in each of the twelve categories. This operation thus standardizes all profiles for time differences and for differences in the total number of acts contained in the profile. Certain effects which might be called artifacts result from this procedure, as will be pointed out in the analysis.

Time rates would be preferable for certain purposes, but since we desired to study variability as well as means, of categories, individuals, groups, and sessions, percentage rates have a certain advantage. Time rates for most of the categories do not give normal distributions. Percentage rates, however, can be converted to distributions that are approximately normal, by the arcsine transformation. The square root of each percentage rate is transformed to its corresponding arcsine angle.[5] The distribution

4 Copies of the four cases and complete instructions to subjects will be provided to persons who may wish to use them as tasks for various experimental or diagnostic purposes. The task and instructions were prepared in such a way as to provide a basic situation for which norms could be constructed, and within which a large number of experimental variations could be introduced.

5 This procedure is described simply in Snedecor (7). In our analysis the transformation was done by using the first five steps of the approximation series. The degree of accuracy obtained is sufficient for our purposes.

of these angles has asymptotic normal properties. These properties are desirable for the comparisons we wish to make, since the effects of skewness on estimates of variability are minimized as the distribution approaches normality. Preliminary examination indicates that without the transformation, the means of the time rate distributions in certain of the categories place severe restrictions on the variance. With the transformation this restriction is at least reduced, since the mean and variance of the normal distribution are independent.

The numbers in all the tables thus represent the arcsine equivalents of the original percentage rates. Those who wish to prepare norms in easily used form can do so by transforming the arcsine numbers back to percentage rates. Cutting points above and below the mean can be obtained by finding the standard deviation indicated in the proper table, adding the desired number of standard deviation units to the arcsine mean, above and below, and then transforming these numbers back to percentage equivalents.

## THREE KINDS OF EFFECTS OF SIZE

In speculating about the possible effects of group size on interaction patterns, at least three kinds of effects might be expected. First, there may be some effects which vary directly with size. For example, if there is an absolute time limit for a meeting, it is obvious that the talking time available for each person decreases as the group size increases. Second, there may be some effects which are uniquely associated with a group of a given size. For example, in a group of size two it is impossible to form a majority except by unanimity. Third, there may be effects which are associated with the way a group can be divided into sub-groups. It has often been said that it is wise to appoint a committee with an odd number of members so that a division of the group into two equal and opposed subgroups is impossible. Thus, there may be some effects associated with groups of odd and even numbers of members.

Each of the tables which follows shows rates of interaction for groups of sizes two through seven. Each table will be examined first for trends by size, then for any indication of a unique size, and finally for effects of odd and even number of members. Hypotheses suggested by the data will be stated. Differences which are found significant will be indicated by asterisks as explained in a footnote.[6] In general, the level of significance

6 Tests of significance were computed only for the statements which are followed in the text by the number of the category involved. All statements of this kind, however, were tested. Absence of asterisks thus means that a test has been made but the relationship does not satisfy the .05 significance requirements. One or more asterisks indicates significance at the .05 level on some relevant comparison. The comparison

will be .05 on a two tailed test. Our discussion, however, will not be confined only to those differences which are found significant. Since our object is to develop an integrated set of hypotheses, and the number of groups of each size studied is relatively small, we wish to take advantage of every lead provided by the data, even though the effect may be slight. While some of the hypotheses might reasonably be accepted on the basis of the interaction data alone, additional evidence will be brought to bear in later reports which will include other kinds of measurements as well.

TABLE I

*Mean Profile of N Individuals, by Group Size*

| GROUP SIZE | 2 | 3 | 4 | 5 | 6 | 7 |
|---|---|---|---|---|---|---|
| N | 8 | 12 | 16 | 20 | 18 | 28 |
| CATEGORY | | | | | | |
| 1 | 9.2 | 9.1 | 10.3 | 9.7 | 11.2 | 10.5 |
| 2 | 11.2 | 11.4 | 12.8 | 14.2 | 18.4 | 16.6 |
| 3 | 27.2 | 27.0 | 22.3 | 23.1 | 21.6 | 21.3 |
| 4 | 14.3 | 13.5 | 13.7 | 15.9 | 18.4 | 19.2 |
| 5 | 31.7 | 34.0 | 35.0 | 32.0 | 32.1 | 31.2 |
| 6 | 25.3 | 23.3 | 23.7 | 26.6 | 24.1 | 25.7 |
| 7 | 12.0 | 10.2 | 10.5 | 10.2 | 10.2 | 10.1 |
| 8 | 9.8 | 8.5 | 8.2 | 8.5 | 7.4 | 7.1 |
| 9 | 5.2 | 5.9 | 5.0 | 6.4 | 4.6 | 5.9 |
| 10 | 10.2 | 15.6 | 19.9 | 14.5 | 17.7 | 16.4 |
| 11 | 12.4 | 8.6 | 10.0 | 9.1 | 6.3 | 6.6 |
| 12 | 1.0 | 3.5 | 5.2 | 3.3 | 3.9 | 3.8 |

Note: The profile of each individual is the sum over four sessions of his raw profile in each session, converted to a percentage profile and transformed to arcsine equivalents.

## TRENDS ACCORDING TO SIZE

The mean profile of initiated behavior for individuals by group size is indicated in Table 1. When the size of the group increases, showing tension release * (category 2) and giving suggestion * (category 4) show emphatic increases. Showing solidarity (category 1) appears to increase somewhat with group size, and if groups of size two are excluded from consideration, giving information * (category 6) also appears to increase. Showing tension * (category 11) shows an emphatic decrease with increase in group

made varies by the proposition to be tested. The number of asterisks indicates the type of comparison, as follows:

* Size 3 compared to size 7
** Smaller sizes compared with larger sizes
*** Size 2 compared to size 3
**** Sizes 4 and 6 compared with sizes 3, 5, and 7
***** Size 2 compared to sizes 4 and 6
****** A given size compared with all other sizes

size, and decreases are also visible in showing agreement * (category 3) and asking for opinion ** (category 8). Again, if groups of size two are disregarded, giving opinion ** (category 5) shows a decrease when the group size increases.

Most of the trends observed appear to be results of two gross factors. The first is that the relative talking time available per member decreases as size increases. The second is that each person is confronted with an absolutely larger number of persons as size increases. Each is under pressure to maintain a more or less adequate relationship with each other. Thus as size increases, each member has more relationships to maintain, and less time to do so. Some time might be gained by increasing rates of activity; however, the requirements of effective communication place limits on this source of gain. In a previous study we have shown that members of three man groups adjust their activity rates to each other as if there were an upper limit to the total activity rate for the group as a whole (4).

The relative lack of time in which to build an argument may account for the increase in giving suggestion, and also the decrease in both asking for and giving opinion. Giving suggestion is a more direct response to the demands of the task than is giving opinion. When time is at a premium members may feel under pressure to take the most direct approach, and suggestions may be made without taking time to justify them with opinions or to ask others for their opinions. It may also be that the larger group represents a more formidable sanctioning system than the smaller one, and as a result evaluative statements may be inhibited. This might also account for the relative increase in giving orientation since one may state the facts in his possession with less fear of disapproval. The relative increase in giving orientation may also be due in part to a "round robin" procedure of stating facts which results in considerable repetition of detail. Similarly, giving suggestion may increase as a result of the emergence of repetitive patterns built around the necessities of coordinating the activities of more persons. If true, the larger groups should show more procedural suggestions, as distinguished from content suggestions.

The requirement that persons greet each other pleasantly and make some attempt to establish their solidarity presumably applies about equally strongly to all groups in our sample. Since the number of relationships increases very rapidly with the size of the group, the proportion of time devoted to this business might be expected to be greater as size increases. It may be pressure of this kind that results in the trend toward increase in showing solidarity in the larger groups.

A general result of the time pressure and the larger number of persons is that the number of persons who participate at absolutely low rates will be increased. Those who participate minimally tend to be forced more and more toward types of behavior which can be performed simultaneously with others and thus do not compete for time. Simply listening, of course, is the prime example, but this is not scored directly. The other two main types of activity which can be performed without time competition are showing tension (by withdrawal, nervous mannerisms, or awkward pauses that occur for the group as a whole) and showing tension release (primarily through laughter of the group as a whole).

According to the scoring system used, activities such as awkward pauses or laughter which involve the group as a whole are credited separately to each individual. Thus, when the raw profiles of low participators are converted to percentage profiles, these types of activities are apt to show up as particularly prominent. In Table 1 it is seen that showing tension release does indeed show a marked increase by size, which is probably due to the presence of more minimal participators. However, the increase is not as large as would be expected if this were the only factor operating. Apparently there is a counter factor which results in fewer occasions of general laughter in the larger groups.

By the same reasoning one would expect showing tension to increase as the size of the group increases, but, in fact, there is a marked decrease. This may be due partly to the fact that the observer is too busy to note the signs of tension which do occur, but probably this is not the whole explanation. It is suggested, rather, that the increased number of persons has two effects which may tend to minimize certain types of tension. First, in the larger groups the role requirements for task completion and adequate group maintenance may be allocated over a larger range of persons, so that there is more likelihood that the necessary roles will be performed by some persons without difficulty. Second, and this is really the other side of the coin, the larger size group permits relative anonymity for persons who might be prone to show tension if forced into greater involvement.

The drop in rate of showing agreement is possibly related to the increase in time pressure. Just listening may be a form of tacit agreement. If the responsibility of the formal show of agreement falls to the more active members of the group, again, the minimal participators, especially in the larger groups, will residually have little agreement scored. For the larger groups, which have more minimal participators, this may result in low rates of showing agreement on the mean profiles.

## UNIQUE ASPECTS OF TWO MAN GROUPS

Inspection of Table 1 for the possibility that any given size may show unique characteristics strongly suggests that size two is unique. The mean profile for groups of this size has a notably high rate of showing tension *** (category 11), and at the same time low rates of showing disagreement *** (category 10) and antagonism *** (category 12). Asking for orientation *** (category 7) is uniquely high, and although giving orientation (category 6) is not uniquely high, it is somewhat higher than would be expected from extrapolating the trend for the remaining group sizes. Similarly, giving opinion (category 5) although not uniquely low, is lower than would be expected from extrapolation. Asking for opinion (category 8), on the other hand, is uniquely high. Giving suggestion (category 4) is somewhat on the high side in the sense that it deviates from an otherwise perfectly clear and consistent trend seen in the remaining group sizes.

Most, if not all, of the unique features of the interaction profile of the two person group may be associated with one major feature which distinguishes it from groups of all other sizes. This is the fact that in a group of two it is impossible to form a majority except by unanimity. Either person in the diad possesses power to influence the decision by withdrawal or veto. Neither person is able to influence the other by bringing a majority to bear against him. In this sense there is no public opinion or group sanction to which either can appeal. Similarly, there is no good office, mediator, or arbitrator for the differences. Consequently, each person is under pressure to behave in such a way that the other will not withdraw and will continue to cooperate even though he may have to yield a point at a given time. Essentially, this is the problem of allowing the co-participant to "save face" when he does yield a point. The dominant person is thus under pressure to avoid the implication of superiority, and to persuade the other by gentle and self-effacing means.

The low rates of showing disagreement and antagonism and the high rates of asking for information and opinion are reasonably associated with the necessity of a gentle, persuasive approach. The high rate of showing tension is probably associated both with the delicate balance the dominant person tries to maintain and with the tendency to withdraw used as a power device by the less dominant person. The concentration on giving orientation and relative avoidance of giving opinion may be a device used for the neutralizing of the evaluative implications of what is said or suggested, by sticking to that which is most self evident and incontrovertable. The relatively high rate of giving suggestion, if indeed the rate is high, may reflect the development of procedural suggestions to handle the high tension. It is of some interest that there is high rate of asking for opinion and that this is not accompanied by a correspondingly high rate of giving opinion. This suggests, again, the hesitancy to respond in terms which are evaluative.

## DIFFERENCES IN GROUPS OF ODD AND EVEN NUMBER OF MEMBERS

In the presence of trends which are appreciable and vary directly with group size, complicated by the unique character of size two, any effects which are due to odd and even number of members are likely to be masked to some extent. If the effects are systematic and distributed with some strength, however, they may be discernible in terms of peaks and troughs. Such regular effects appear in Table 1 as follows: excluding size two, groups with even numbers of members (sizes 4 and 6) are high in showing disagreement **** (category 10) and antagonism **** (category 12), and are low in asking for suggestions **** (category 9). The data also suggest that the even groups may be higher in showing solidarity (category 1), and possibly lower in showing agreement (category 3).

The unique character of the two man group may be viewed as the result of the restriction that the group may subdivide in only one way. Groups of larger sizes may also have special characteristics due to the ways in which they may subdivide, but obviously, all sizes above two may subdivide in a number of ways which increases very rapidly as size increases. Groups of even numbers, however, can divide into two equal parts, in which case there is no majority. In such splits each person has an ally and may maintain the hope of achieving a majority. Consequently, there is not the same stringent pressure to avoid overt conflict as in the two man group.

It may be, thus, that even numbered groups will persist in deadlock whereas odd numbered groups will more easily break into a majority and a minority and so arrive at a decision sooner. The observed differences between groups of odd and even number of members (excluding the special case of size two) are consistent with this theory. The disagreement and antagonism are presumably the overt manifestation of the conflict, and the relative lack of asking for suggestion and showing agreement are consistent with a state of conflict. There is no obvious reason why showing solidarity should be higher for the groups of even number.[7]

## VARIABILITY OF GIVEN INDIVIDUALS OVER SESSIONS

For each individual the standard deviation over the four sessions in which he participated was computed. The mean standard deviation for individuals, by size of group, is presented in Table 2.

Examination of this table indicates that, essentially, all categories show a tendency toward greater variability for each individual's performance as the size of the group increases.** This allows for at least two interpretations. The first and most obvious is that the larger groups partition scores among a greater number of persons, and thus the estimates of

7 One hypothesis is that the members within a faction may show more solidarity to each other in the face of an external threat. However, this is a very tenuous ad hoc hypothesis. In contrast, the hypothesis that groups of even size would show less agreement and more disagreement and antagonism was stated in a theoretical memorandum prepared in advance of the research. This prediction, however, did not recognize size two as a special case.

one session are less reliable than for smaller sizes. This is particularly true for the low interactors in the large group, where a relatively small number of acts shifting for a category may make a considerable shift in the percentage profile.

A second possibility is that there may be more shifting of roles in the larger groups, due to the larger number of persons among whom roles

TABLE 2

*How the Profile of an Individual Varies over Successive Sessions: The Mean for N Individuals of the Standard Deviation of Each Individual over Four Sessions, by Group Size*

| GROUP SIZE | 2 | 3 | 4 | 5 | 6 | 7 | |
|---|---|---|---|---|---|---|---|
| NUMBER OF INDIVIDUALS OR OF STANDARD DEVIATIONS | 8 | 12 | 16 | 20 | 18 | 28 | MEAN |
| CATEGORY | | | | | | | |
| 1 | 2.5 | 2.8 | 3.4 | 4.0 | 5.6 | 4.1 | 3.7 |
| 2 | 2.5 | 2.9 | 3.0 | 3.8 | 5.8 | 7.3 | 4.2 |
| 3 | 2.3 | 2.9 | 2.9 | 2.6 | 3.8 | 3.7 | 3.0 |
| 4 | 2.6 | 2.5 | 3.7 | 3.4 | 3.7 | 4.9 | 3.5 |
| 5 | 2.4 | 2.9 | 3.2 | 2.6 | 3.6 | 4.0 | 3.1 |
| 6 | 2.3 | 2.4 | 3.6 | 3.1 | 4.1 | 4.6 | 3.4 |
| 7 | 2.3 | 2.1 | 3.4 | 2.7 | 2.5 | 3.3 | 2.7 |
| 8 | 1.6 | 2.3 | 2.2 | 2.7 | 3.5 | 3.6 | 2.7 |
| 9 | 1.6 | 1.7 | 2.7 | 2.8 | 3.0 | 3.6 | 2.6 |
| 10 | 1.6 | 3.4 | 3.0 | 2.7 | 3.3 | 3.5 | 2.9 |
| 11 | 2.4 | 2.2 | 4.3 | 3.7 | 3.2 | 3.7 | 3.3 |
| 12 | .5 | 2.5 | 3.0 | 2.3 | 2.3 | 2.2 | 2.1 |
| MEAN | 2.0 | 2.5 | 3.2 | 3.0 | 3.7 | 4.0 | |

Note: The standard deviations are based on the four profiles of each individual which have been converted to percentage profiles and transformed to arcsine equivalents.

may be allocated. If particular profiles are associated with particular roles for which there is some evidence (2, 3, 6), the greater variety of roles a person may hold would contribute to the greater variability of performance.

Probably both these factors are operating. A preliminary check of the data indicates that at least the first can be demonstrated to be a significant factor. The proportion of responses in category five (or six) is known to be highly correlated (usually about .80) with the total interaction rate. If persons are chosen for their interaction level by the proportion of acts in category five (or six), then examination of the standard deviations indicates that persons with high proportions of category five (or six) have less variability in the other categories. Thus, high variability is associated with persons of lower interaction rate, those who have fewer scores in each category. The larger groups will have relatively more low participators than the smaller.

The two man groups appear to have uniquely low variances in showing disagreement *** (category 10) and showing antagonism *** (category 12). While the low variance of showing antagonism may be accounted for by the fact that the mean is extremely low and may place an automatic restriction on the variance, this will not account for the low variance in showing disagreement. The low variability here indicates that the constraint on overt negative reactions characteristic of the two man groups operates consistently through sessions.

The odd and even effect above size two is not marked, but there is some indication that the mean variability of the even groups is slightly higher than might be expected. This would only be inconsistent with the interpretation that even size groups are prone to conflict if there is the expectation that conflict is continuous over sessions. If the amount of conflict changes from session to session according to changes in task or session order, we would expect the variability in individual profiles as shown.

## VARIABILITY AMONG INDIVIDUALS

The standard deviations of profiles among all individuals of a group size are given in Table 3. The profile for a given individual is based on the sum of his four single session profiles.

Trends in this table are not clearly marked. The apparent reason for this is that the odd and even effect is so prominent. Making allowance for size two and the odd and even differences, consistency of trends is observable. The variability among individuals in showing tension release (category 2) and giving suggestion ** (category 4) increases with increasing size, while showing agreement (category 3), disagreement (category 10), showing tension ** (category 11) decrease.

The increase of variability among members in showing tension release is probably accounted for by the fact that when laughter occurs for the group as a whole, each individual is credited for an act in that category. When the raw profiles are converted to percentage profiles, this affects the profile of the low participators more than that of high participators. Thus, since the range of total interaction rates of participation in the large groups is larger, the members will diverge more from each other with the increase in size.

The increasing variability among members in giving suggestion does not have a parallel explanation. It is probably due to an actual increase in the degree to which certain members rather than others specialize in this activity. Giving suggestion is probably the most characteristic behavior of the person who specializes in the solution of the task problem and is associated with the subject's own attribution of leadership. This change by size, thus appears to be some evidence that as size increases, the probability of a clear cut differentiation between leader(s) and followers increases.

The decreasing difference between the percentage profiles of different individuals in showing agreement, disagreement, and tension indicates perhaps that these are types of activity in which specialization does not tend to take place as the size increases. On the contrary, this seems to

TABLE 3

*How the Profiles of Different Individuals Vary from Each Other: The Standard Deviation of Individual Profiles, by Group Size*

| GROUP SIZE | 2 | 3 | 4 | 5 | 6 | 7 | |
|---|---|---|---|---|---|---|---|
| NUMBER OF INDIVIDUALS | 8 | 12 | 16 | 20 | 18 | 28 | MEAN |
| CATEGORY | | | | | | | |
| 1 | 3.9 | 3.5 | 2.5 | 3.4 | 2.7 | 3.7 | 3.3 |
| 2 | 3.6 | 4.8 | 2.4 | 6.6 | 3.9 | 6.7 | 5.0 |
| 3 | 9.5 | 5.3 | 2.9 | 4.7 | 2.6 | 4.3 | 4.4 |
| 4 | 3.1 | 2.0 | 2.6 | 2.7 | 3.5 | 3.1 | 2.9 |
| 5 | 6.4 | 4.7 | 2.5 | 4.7 | 1.6 | 4.5 | 3.9 |
| 6 | 2.1 | 3.8 | 1.1 | 5.7 | 1.9 | 3.6 | 3.2 |
| 7 | 3.1 | 2.1 | 2.3 | 1.8 | 2.4 | 2.4 | 2.3 |
| 8 | 3.5 | 2.1 | 2.7 | 2.2 | 1.7 | 3.0 | 2.5 |
| 9 | 1.2 | 1.5 | 2.6 | 1.6 | 1.4 | 1.9 | 1.8 |
| 10 | 3.7 | 4.6 | 2.5 | 3.8 | 1.6 | 3.7 | 3.3 |
| 11 | 3.4 | 3.9 | 3.3 | 3.0 | 2.8 | 2.9 | 3.1 |
| 12 | 1.7 | 3.6 | 2.2 | 3.4 | 3.5 | 3.6 | 3.2 |
| MEAN | 3.8 | 3.5 | 2.5 | 3.6 | 2.5 | 3.6 | |

Note: The profile of each individual is the sum over four sessions of his raw profile in each session, converted to a percentage profile and transformed to arcsine equivalents.

point to the fact that as the groups grow larger, the participation of members in these categories is a function of their general participation. Some people agree, disagree, and show tension more than others, of course, but not disproportionately more in relation to their total interaction. It may very well be that in the larger groups the relative anonymity and lack of pressure to participate unless one wishes to do so, underlies all three of these decreasing trends. One does not need overtly to agree or disagree unless he is specifically addressed or wishes to enter the conversation. Similarly one can escape more or less successfully into anonymity and relative non-participation without remaining in the focus of a tense situation.

Groups of size two appear to be unique in the amount of variability among individuals. Every category except asking for suggestion and showing antagonism shows higher variability than one might expect, particularly when compared to other even groups.***** The mean variability is higher than for any other size. The hypothesis which would account for the low variability in showing antagonism has already been stated earlier. The high variability of the other categories suggests that in two man groups there is a very strong tendency for the roles of the two individuals to become differentiated from each other, presumably in a complementary way. The plainest clue, perhaps, is the high variability in giving opinion and showing agreement. Presumably one person tends to give most of the opinion, and the other tends to give most of the agreement. More generally, probably, one person tends to gravitate toward a more active initiating role, while the other tends to be more passive and spends more of his time reacting. In this respect, at least, there is a certain similarity between size two and the larger sizes with their tendency to differentiation into a leader(s) and followers structure.

The most striking feature of Table 3 is the difference between odd and even size groups. Excluding size two it is seen that the profiles of individuals tend in general to be more like each other in the groups of even size than in the groups of odd size. The tendency toward similarity (low variability) appears particularly in all types of positive reactions, showing solidarity,**** tension release,**** and agreement **** (categories 1, 2 and 3), in giving opinion **** and orientation **** in the task area (categories 5 and 6), and in showing disagreement **** (category 10). Giving suggestion (category 4) is the only type of activity in which the differences between persons appear more marked in the even groups.

The combination of categories in which variability among individuals is low is congruent with the hypothesis of more occasions in the groups of even size when the members split into two equal parts, in conflict with each other, and unable to break the deadlock. Protracted argument tends to increase the rates of disagreement and giving opinion, and to decrease the rates of positive reactions, at least during the period of the conflict. The more general the conflict, the more equal the participation rates of members may become, and the more similar they become in their concentration on disagreement and opinion. The only fact that does not fit into this picture is that the effect of similarity through competition does not appear in the category of giving suggestion. If anything, the converse is true. This effect may be connected in some way with the emergence of a specialized mediator or arbitrator who tries desperately, after a long period of deadlock or in the final few minutes of a session, to force a final formulation of the decision for the experimenter, even though it is not basically acceptable to the members. This hypothesis, however, is tenuous.

## VARIABILITY OF GIVEN GROUPS OVER SUCCESSIVE SESSIONS

The average standard deviation of a group over four sessions is shown for groups of each size in Table 4. Only a few trends are discernable. The mean variability of all categories shows a minor upward trend with group size. Showing solidarity ** (category 1) increases slightly, and showing tension release ** (category 2) increases more prominently.

TABLE 4

*How the Profile of a Group Varies over Successive Sessions: The Mean for Four Groups of the Standard Deviation of Each Group over Four Sessions, by Group Size*

| GROUP SIZE | 2 | 3 | 4 | 5 | 6 | 7 | |
|---|---|---|---|---|---|---|---|
| NUMBER OF GROUPS | 4 | 4 | 4 | 4 | 3 | 4 | MEAN |
| CATEGORY | | | | | | | |
| 1 | 2.1 | 2.3 | 2.5 | 1.9 | 2.9 | 2.9 | 2.5 |
| 2 | 2.1 | 2.5 | 2.8 | 2.7 | 5.1 | 5.6 | 3.5 |
| 3 | 1.5 | 2.3 | 2.0 | 2.0 | 2.0 | 2.2 | 2.0 |
| 4 | 2.1 | 1.6 | 3.3 | 1.0 | 2.7 | 2.4 | 2.2 |
| 5 | 1.9 | 2.0 | 1.7 | 1.2 | 2.3 | 2.7 | 2.0 |
| 6 | 1.3 | 1.8 | 2.3 | 1.7 | 2.4 | 2.3 | 2.0 |
| 7 | 1.6 | 1.1 | 1.9 | 1.4 | 3.3 | 1.2 | 1.8 |
| 8 | 1.1 | 1.0 | 1.3 | 1.2 | .9 | .7 | 1.0 |
| 9 | 1.3 | 1.0 | 1.8 | .6 | .8 | 1.2 | 1.1 |
| 10 | 1.3 | 2.6 | 2.0 | 1.4 | 2.0 | 2.1 | 1.9 |
| 11 | 1.7 | 1.2 | 2.9 | 2.8 | .8 | 1.3 | 1.8 |
| 12 | .4 | 2.7 | 2.4 | 2.0 | 2.2 | 1.5 | 1.9 |
| MEAN | 1.5 | 1.8 | 2.2 | 1.7 | 2.3 | 2.2 | 2.0 |

Note: The standard deviations are based on the four profiles of each group, which have been converted to percentage profiles and transformed to arcsine equivalents.

The larger variability between sessions in the larger groups in showing solidarity is probably related to the necessity of getting acquainted. Greetings, introductions, and friendly social remarks are generally scored as showing solidarity. The problem of getting acquainted is presumably greatest in the first session, and since a greater proportion of time may be spent in this activity, this would produce variability by session for all groups. In the larger groups there are more people to get acquainted initially, and thus the variability between sessions due to this effect would be expected to be greater among the larger groups.

Showing tension release has been demonstrated to increase through successive sessions (2, 3, 4, 5, 6), and thus variability by session is especially characteristic of this category. It should be noted that the mean variability of this category is the highest of all categories taken over all groups. Since laughter of the group as a whole is credited to each member individually, a general laugh in the larger groups will produce a more marked change in the rate for the category than in the smaller groups. And since this category of activity tends to increase through successive sessions, the variability by sessions will be more marked in groups of larger sizes.

As to effects connected with a unique size, size two evidences the low variance expected in showing disagreement (category 10), and particularly in showing antagonism ****** (category 12). Of more interest, in view of previous theory and research, is that size three shows a uniquely high variance over sessions in these same two categories. Size three has often been thought to be peculiarly "unstable" in some sense or other, connected with the fact that in case of disagreement of two members, the third has it within his own power to form a majority by combining with one other, whereas in case of the agreement of two, the third is left almost powerless, whether he agrees or disagrees. Formation of a majority is particularly damaging to the unity of the whole group, since whenever it appears it tends to isolate one member who is left with no support. Whether this member then elects to give in, or to fight it out against an alliance which has already solidified, probably depends upon the relative dominance of the member in terms of status and personality.

Thus, the amount of disagreement in the group profile for the period of a given coalition could be markedly influenced by the propensity of the isolated member to handle his difficulty in an active or a passive manner. If any given coalition persisted over sessions with little or no disagreement to give the isolated member a chance to combine with one and isolate the other, the session to session variance would be expected to be small. But it is not small—rather, it is uniquely large. The inference that appears most plausible, then, is that the coalitions tend to be fragile, changing from session to session, and that the amount of disagreement and antagonism in a given session varies according to whether a coalition forms, and if so, whether the isolated member is active or passive. If this were the case, variability of sessions would be the result for showing disagreement and antagonism (categories 10 and 12) in the three man groups.

The effects of odd and even sizes are seen most clearly in the mean variability for each size, without regard to particular categories. Sizes four and six (the even sizes excluding the special case of size two) show higher variability over sessions than odd sizes. The categories which contribute most to this variance are giving suggestion **** (category 4), giving orientation (category 6), and asking for orientation **** (category 7). One possible explanation is that during actual periods of conflict, the rates in these categories tend to fall, as more time is taken up with disagreement and giving opinion. Suggestions are rejected and are not allowed to build up as the argument regresses to opinion and counter opinion. Matters of factual information are neglected because the heat of the argument interferes with the degree of objectivity or emotional neutrality required to make facts seem effective and important. There may be a growth curve over sessions, however, in the degree to which these types of activity are utilized in an attempt to get around disagreement by procedural suggestions and concentration on facts. Or this may happen periodically. In either case, variability between sessions would be the result, only providing these activities are low for certain sessions.

## VARIABILITY AMONG GROUPS

The variability of the profiles of different groups is represented in Table 5 by the standard deviation of the four groups of each size, averaged through the sequence of four sessions.

Showing tension release ** (category 2), giving opinion ** (category 5), and giving orientation ** (category 6) show fairly clear increasing

TABLE 5

*How the Profiles of Different Groups Vary from Each Other: The Mean for Four Sessions of the Standard Deviation of Each Session over Four Groups, by Group Size*

| GROUP SIZE | 2 | 3 | 4 | 5 | 6 | 7 | |
|---|---|---|---|---|---|---|---|
| NUMBER OF SESSION ORDERS FOR WHICH A S.D. WAS COMPUTED AND ON WHICH THE MEAN IS BASED | 4 | 4 | 4 | 4 | 3 | 4 | MEAN |
| CATEGORY | | | | | | | |
| 1 | 4.2 | 3.2 | 2.9 | 2.9 | 3.2 | 3.0 | 3.2 |
| 2 | 3.3 | 4.3 | 3.4 | 6.0 | 5.0 | 5.0 | 4.5 |
| 3 | 2.9 | 2.9 | 2.7 | 3.4 | 3.3 | 1.9 | 2.9 |
| 4 | 2.6 | 2.3 | 3.4 | 1.4 | 4.4 | 2.3 | 2.7 |
| 5 | 2.4 | 2.3 | 2.9 | 3.8 | 5.1 | 4.8 | 3.6 |
| 6 | 1.5 | 2.3 | 2.2 | 4.5 | 4.5 | 3.0 | 3.0 |
| 7 | 1.3 | 1.5 | 1.9 | 1.2 | 2.3 | 1.2 | 1.6 |
| 8 | 2.5 | 1.6 | 1.2 | 1.5 | 2.1 | 1.2 | 1.7 |
| 9 | 1.8 | 1.6 | 1.6 | .8 | 1.5 | .9 | 1.4 |
| 10 | 3.6 | 3.5 | 2.3 | 2.7 | 3.4 | 2.2 | 3.0 |
| 11 | 3.5 | 1.3 | 3.3 | 2.3 | 2.3 | .8 | 2.3 |
| 12 | 1.6 | 3.1 | 2.7 | 2.8 | 3.0 | 3.5 | 2.8 |
| MEAN | 2.6 | 2.5 | 2.5 | 2.8 | 3.4 | 2.5 | 2.7 |

Note: The standard deviations are based on the group profiles of the four separate groups on a given session, e.g., four separate groups on their first session. Each raw group profile was converted to a percentage profile and transformed to the arcsine equivalent.

trends by size. The reason for the greater variability between larger groups in showing tension release is probably the same as indicated previously—namely, that general laughter produces a number of scores equal to the number of persons in the group, thus affecting the profiles of larger groups in a more marked manner than in smaller groups. Whatever variability there is between groups, then, is emphasized progressively more as the number of members increases. The greater variability of the larger groups in giving orientation is probably the effect of the more or less mechanical procedure adopted by some (but not other) groups of "going around" the whole circle of members in the reporting of the facts of the case given to them. Whenever this device is adopted, it tends to increase the rate of the group as a whole in the category of giving information, in a degree which is proportionate to the number of members. Insofar as members fail to stick strictly to giving information on the "round robin" and include an admixture of opinion, this procedure would also increase the variability between groups in a more marked way for larger groups in giving opinion.

So far as effects of unique sizes are concerned, neither size two nor size three show evidence of unusual variability among groups, except for the low variability for two man groups of showing antagonism ****** (category 12), with which we have already dealt. Size seven, however, shows uniquely low variability among groups in showing agreement ****** (category 3), showing tension ****** (category 11), and showing disagreement (category 10). Showing disagreement, however, is not so clearly defined as the others, and is included because of the consistency of the argument that follows. These are the same three categories, it will be recalled, on which individuals showed decreasing variability with group size. The hypothesis advanced earlier was that these are categories in which specialization by role tends not to occur in the larger groups, and participation in these categories tends to be a function of the total rate of the participant. If this is the case, then the group rates in these categories would tend to be functions of the group total rates. It will also be remembered from Table 1 that the rates of agreement and showing tension show a decreasing trend by group size, and there is some indication that showing disagreement as well may be undergoing a general decrease from an earlier high point. It may be that these categories are approaching a minimum operating rate no longer associated with role specializations. While data are not available it is possible that with further increase in size, others of the categories might also tend toward such an operating minimum, and so reduce the variability among groups. This might be the case with asking for suggestions (category 9). It is noticed that the mean variability for size seven is lower than the two preceding sizes, and as low as that of any other size. This may be the point at which such a trend begins to become visible.

Effects of odd and even size are not marked in this table, except for giving suggestion **** (category 4) and asking for orientation **** (category 7), which are high in the even groups. The variability of these two categories was also high over sessions, as shown in the previous table. The hypothesis advanced there, was that these are types of activity which tend to decline during periods of conflict, and this hypothesis holds with equal plausibility as an explanation of the variability between groups. Conflict is not supposed to be a feature of every group of even size. The hypothesis is rather that even size simply increases the probability of longer periods spent in deadlock if deadlocks occur. This should increase the variability among groups.

## VARIABILITY OVER SESSIONS COMPARED TO VARIABILITY AMONG GROUPS

Finally, we call attention to a finding which bears on the question of whether groups of these sizes and short duration develop and maintain structural features through time which distinguish one group from another. A positive answer is inferred directly from the fact that the mean variability over all categories and sizes of groups is substantially lower over sessions than among groups.

## REFERENCES

1. Bales, R. F. *Interaction process analysis: A method for the study of small groups.* Cambridge, Mass.: Addison-Wesley, 1950.
2. Bales, R. F. The equilibrium problem in small groups. In T. Parsons, R. F. Bales, & E. A. Shils, *Working papers in the theory of action.* Glencoe, Ill.: Free Press, 1953. Pp. 111–161.
3. Bales, R. F., & Slater, P. E. Role differentiation in small groups. (To be published.)
4. Borgatta, E. F., & Bales, R. F. Interaction of individuals in reconstituted groups. *Sociometry*, 1953, 16, 302–320.
5. Heinicke, C. M., & Bales, R. F. Developmental trends in the structure of small groups. *Sociometry*, 1953, 16, 7–38.
6. Mann, R. D. The relation of informal status to role behavior in small discussion groups. Unpublished honors thesis, Harvard College, 1954.
7. Snedecor, G. W. *Statistical methods.* (4th Ed.) Ames, Ia.: Iowa State College Press, 1946.

CHAPTER 8

# INTERACTION AND EQUILIBRIUM

## Some Effects of Feedback on Communication

HAROLD J. LEAVITT
and
RONALD A. H. MUELLER

### INTRODUCTION

THE EXPERIMENTS reported here are concerned with the transmission of information from person *A* to person or persons *B*. Our problem deals with only one of the many relevant variables, the variable of feedback. The question becomes: how is the transmission of information from *A* to *B* influenced by the return of information from *B* to *A*? It is apparently taken for granted in industry, in the lecture hall, and in radio that it is both possible and efficient to transmit information from *A* to *B* without simultaneous feedback from *B* to *A*. On the other

FROM *Human Relations*, 1951, 4, 401–410. Reprinted by permission of the authors and publisher.

Readers familiar with the recent work of Professor Alex Bavelas and his group at M.I.T. will doubtless correctly recognize that many of the theoretical and experimental ideas in this research had their origins in that group. We are most grateful to Dr. Bavelas for both his direct and indirect help.

hand, the information theories of the cyberneticists and, to some extent, trial and error concepts in learning theory suggest that for *A* to hit successfully some target, *B*, requires that *A* be constantly informed of *A*'s own progress. The servomechanism needs a sensory system that is capable of transmitting cues about the errors of its own motor system. The human being learning some motor skill apparently utilizes the same process. But when the human being (*A*) seeks to transmit information to another human being (*B*), *A*'s own sensory system is hardly an adequate source of information *unless B* takes some action which will help *A* to keep informed of *A*'s own progress. If *A* were trying to hit *B* with a brick, *A*'s eyes combined with an inactive *B* would probably be adequate to permit *A* to hit his target after several trials. But if *A* seeks to hit *B* with information, he will probably be more successful if *B* helps to provide some cues which *A*'s own sensory system cannot pick up directly. In other words, where communication between *A* and *B* is the goal, feedback, in the form of verbal or expressive language, should make for greater effectiveness.

If we take the human memory mechanism into account, we need not require that there be *contemporaneous* feedback between *A* and *B*. It may not even be necessary that there be any feedback from $B_2$ if feedback from a similar $B_1$ has already occurred. The practice sessions of the past may have provided enough feedback to permit one to hit his present target accurately. Language, for example, may be thought of as a tool originally learned with feedback, but currently useful in a multitude of situations without simultaneous feedback to help us at least to get within range of our targets. But if the material to be communicated is relatively new and relatively precise, previously learned language may not be enough. Accurate transmission may require some additional contemporaneous feedback.

In addition to this hypothesis that contemporaneous feedback should increase the accuracy of transmission of information from *A* to *B*, is the hypothesis that the completion of the *AB* circuit produces other effects on the *AB* relationship. Feedback from both *A* and *B* can increase the certainty of *B* that he is getting the intended information, and the certainty of *A* that he is getting it across. This increase in certainty, assuming motivated participants, should have some effect on feelings of frustration or achievement and, hence, on the feelings of hostility or security that pervade the relationship.

Our purpose, then, in these experiments is to try to test these hypotheses; to try to determine experimentally the effects of feedback (or the absence of feedback) on certain kinds of *A* to *B* communications.

## EXPERIMENT I

### *What Are the Effects of Progressive Levels of Feedback?*

We chose as our material-to-be-communicated in these experiments a series of geometric patterns. The patterns were all composed of six equal rectangular elements, but the relationships of the elements to one another differed from pattern to pattern (see *Fig. 1A* for sample pattern). *A*'s (the instructor's) job was to describe orally one of these abstract patterns

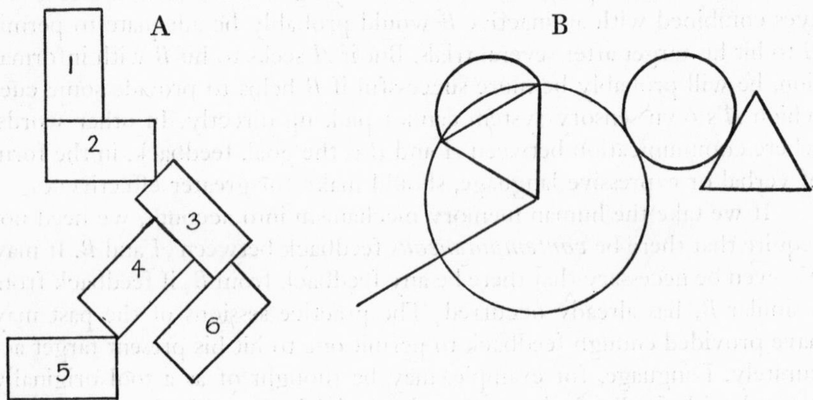


FIG. I. Sample Problems
A. Sample of problems used in Experiment I. B. Sample of problems used in Experiment II.

to the members of his class as accurately as possible, accuracy to be measured from the students' reproductions of the described (but unseen) patterns.

Two instructors were used, and four groups of students (total student N = 80), with each instructor describing four patterns to each student group. There were four conditions of feedback: 1. *Zero feedback* in which instructors sat behind a movable blackboard to describe the patterns. No questions or noises were permitted from the students. 2. The *visible audience* condition in which students and instructor could see one another but no speaking by students was allowed. 3. A *yes-no* condition in which the visible audience was permitted to say only yes or no in response to questions from the instructor. And 4. a *free feedback* situation in which students were permitted to ask questions, interrupt, etc.

With the use of a kind of Latin Square arrangement it was possible then to have each instructor use each condition of feedback in a different order. (See *Table 1.*)

Besides reproducing the test patterns, students were asked to estimate their confidence in the correctness of their answers and, after the last pattern, to indicate the feedback condition they found most comfortable. We also timed the description of each pattern.

All students were given the same instructions at the beginning of the class period. They were told that the experiment was a test of their ability to understand instructions, and that they were to work as rapidly and as accurately as possible. Both instructors had had some previous experience in describing similar patterns, and both had participated in the construction of the test patterns.

Students' papers were scored for accuracy on a scale from 0 to 6. A particular rectangular element was scored correct if it bore the correct relationship to the preceding element. The first element was scored correct if it was correctly oriented on the page.

TABLE I

*Design of Experiment I*

| *Pattern No.* | *1* | *2* | *3* | *4* | *5* | *6* | *7* | *8* |
|---|---|---|---|---|---|---|---|---|
| Class 1: | zero | V–A | Y–N | free | zero | V–A | Y–N | free |
| | (Instructor X) | | | | (Instructor Y) | | | |
| Class 2: | V–A | Y–N | free | zero | V–A | Y–N | free | zero |
| | (Instructor Y) | | | | (Instructor X) | | | |
| Class 3: | Y–N | free | zero | V–A | Y–N | free | zero | V–A |
| | (Instructor X) | | | | (Instructor Y) | | | |
| Class 4: | free | zero | V–A | Y–N | free | zero | V–A | Y–N |
| | (Instructor Y) | | | | (Instructor X) | | | |

## *Results*

### 1. ACCURACY

The mean accuracy score for *all* patterns increased steadily from *zero* to *free feedback*. With *zero feedback* the mean was 4·7 out of a possible 6. The range of means for the eight different patterns given under this condition was 3·1 to 5·9. Under the *visible audience* condition the mean score was 5·3 with a range from 4·5 to 5·9. Under the *yes-no* condition the mean score was 5·5, the range 5·0 to 5·8. With *free feedback* the mean was 5·6 and the range 5·1 to 6·0.

### 2. CONFIDENCE LEVEL

Students' estimates of their own accuracy correlated closely with actual accuracy. For all patterns the mean confidence levels were: *zero feedback*, 4·6; *visible audience*, 5·3; *yes-no*, 5·6; *free feedback*, 5·5. No effects of experience could be detected. There was a tendency to favor one instructor for the *free feedback* situation and the other for all others. These differences were slight and may indicate a differential skill on the part of the instructors in handling the different feedback conditions.

#### 3. TIME

The mean time required to give instructions under the four conditions were: *zero feedback*, 229 seconds; *visible audience*, 249 seconds; *yes-no*, 316 seconds; *free feedback*, 363 seconds. Any decrease in time with experience is once again obscured by differences in difficulty. No clear-cut differences between instructors were apparent.

#### 4. OTHER OBSERVATIONS

Both instructors noticed some rather interesting behavior under certain conditions. When using *free feedback*, both found that on some occasions the students utilized their opportunities to speak by speaking aggressively and with hostility. There were comments like: "That's impossible"; "Are you purposely trying to foul us up?"; "You said left, it has to be right"; and so on. These comments even flowed on to students' papers, when they wrote beside their patterns such comments as: "The teacher made mistakes on this one, I didn't." These hostile reactions seemed to occur only when the *free feedback* condition *followed* other conditions. Both instructors noticed too that their *free feedback* experience stood them in good stead in the *zero feedback* situations. A student in the *free feedback* situation might say, "Oh, it looks like an L." In the next use of that pattern the instructors would find themselves saying, "It looks like an L."

### *Commentary*

Although these data indicate that *free feedback* does yield more accurate results than the other conditions, some new questions arise. Can it not be argued that the *free feedback* method is more effective simply because it requires more time? Would the time required decrease if *free feedback* were used continuously? Does the *free feedback* method always put the teacher on the spot? Will he be attacked for his errors or lack of knowledge? Though free feedback may be helpful at first, is it of any use after the student and the teacher have had an opportunity to straighten out their language difficulties? Can the teacher improve just as much after a series of experiences without feedback as after a series with feedback? Can we show continuous improvement in the course of several trials without feedback?

## EXPERIMENT II

### *Feedback vs. No Feedback*

In an attempt to answer some of these questions we designed another series of experiments that seemed to permit the most efficient use of our limited supply of instructors and students. The purpose of these experiments was to compare the two extreme conditions, *free feedback* and *zero feedback*, over a longer series of trials.

## *Method*

Using eight new geometric patterns, all made up of six elements (see *Fig. IB*), we selected ten instructors and ten separate groups of students, the groups ranging in size from six to twenty-four. Five of the instructors were members of the English Department at the Institute, one taught German, one economics, and three psychology. Four of the classes were speech classes, six were general psychology. For *three* pairs of instructors the procedure was as follows:

Instructor *A* faced class *A* with four patterns in sequence and *zero feedback*. Then instructor *B* faced class *A* with four new patterns in sequence and *free feedback*. Instructor *A* then faced class *B* with his original four patterns and *free feedback*. Then instructor *B* faced class *B* with his original four patterns and *zero feedback*. For the other two pairs of instructors the procedure was reversed, instructor *A* beginning with *free feedback*.

We again asked for confidence levels, from both the students and instructors.

## *Results*

### 1. OVERALL

The results of this experiment bear out the trend of the first. The mean student accuracy score for all *zero feedback* trials was 5·2 of a possible 6; the mean with *feedback* was 5·9. These means represent the students of ten instructors. The ranges for individual instructors were, with *zero feedback*, 3·8 to 5·8; with *free feedback*, 5·6 to 6·0. This difference between these means is significant at the 1% level.

In students' confidence in their results, the data again correlate closely with accuracy. The mean for *zero feedback* is 5·0 with a range from 3·5 to 5·7, while for *free feedback* the mean is 5·8 and the range 5·4 to 6·0. These differences are also significant.

In terms of time required to describe each pattern, *free feedback* remains a more time-consuming process. The average time for *zero feedback* is 166 seconds with a range from 60 to 273. For *free feedback* the average time is 284 seconds with a range of 193 to 423. These differences too are significant.

Finally in our measure of teacher confidence, means were 4·5 with *zero feedback* and 5·0 with *free feedback*, with respective ranges of 2·5 to 5·5 and 4·5 to 5·8. In all cases instructors were *less* confident than their students.

In every case individual instructors changed in the same direction as the means. Every instructor got better results with feedback than without, and every instructor took longer with feedback than without.

### 2. EFFECTS OF EXPERIENCE

In *Figure II* are shown curves representing the changes in accuracy from pattern to pattern. Each instructor, you will recall, described four patterns in sequence under conditions of *zero feedback* and then *free feedback.*

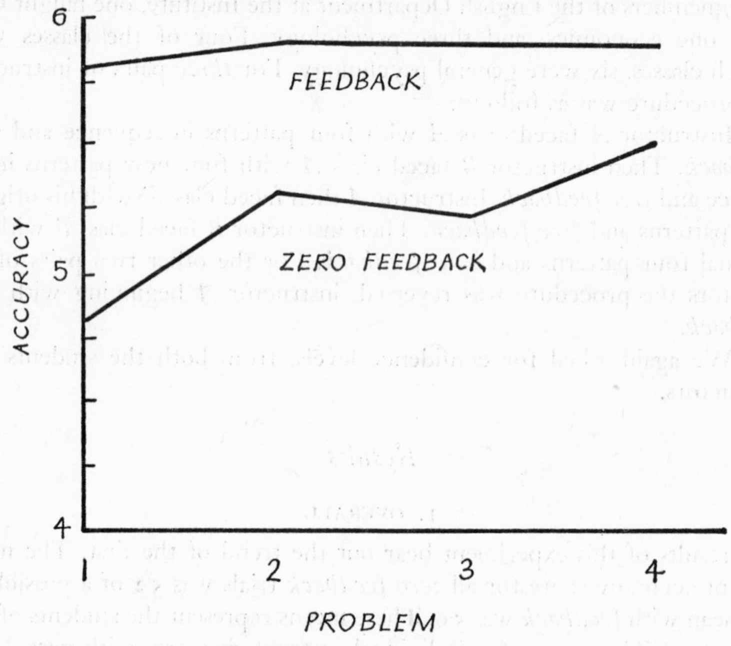


Fig. II. Accuracy

Each point represents the mean of 10 groups.

From these accuracy curves one can see that *free feedback* starts at almost the maximum level and stays there. *Zero feedback* changes in the direction of greater accuracy from trial to trial.

As far as time (*Fig. III*) is concerned, the reverse is true. *Zero feedback* remains more or less constant, while *free feedback* time *declines progressively*.

There is at least one other way of analyzing the data that provides some rather interesting results. Our experimental design supplied us with data for all combinations of (a) inexperienced (with these patterns) and experienced instructors, and (b) inexperienced and experienced classes, working (c) with and without feedback. The data broken down this way indicate that instructors' experience is the most significant factor present. Differences between experienced and inexperienced instructors are always greater than between experienced and inexperienced classes. This difference holds for *zero feedback* only, since with *free feedback* there are no perceptible differences among any of the different conditions.

### 3. OTHER OBSERVATIONS

One of our hypotheses in these experiments centered on the effects of feedback on the relationship between sender and receiver. We have no quantitative data that are relevant to this hypothesis, but we do have some

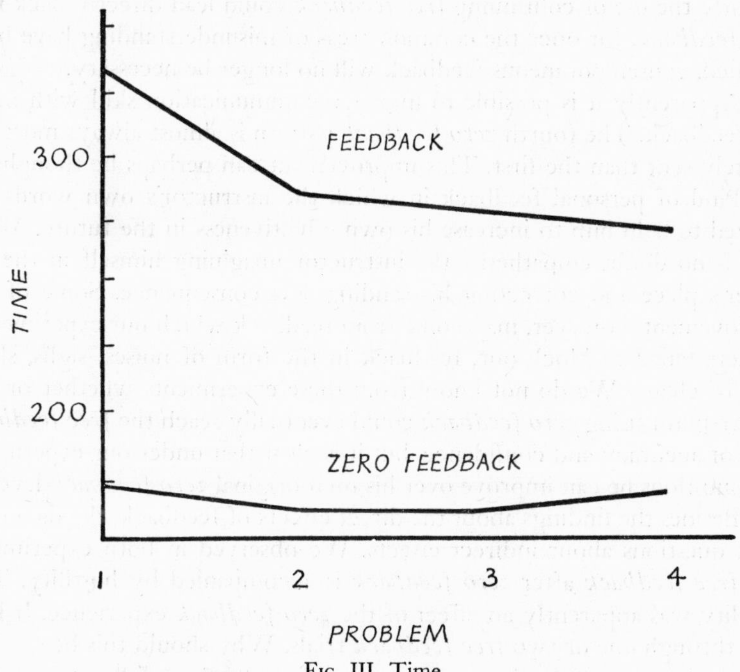


Fig. III. Time

Each point represents the mean of 10 groups.

observations that were astonishing in their consistency. These observations amounted to this. When an instructor faced a new class with *free feedback*, he got fairly rational feedback. That is, the students asked questions or asked for elaboration or repetition of a point. But when an instructor faced a class that had just been exposed to a *zero feedback* session, the instructor got an attack. The students asked lots of questions, but with barbs and implications about the instructor's (in)ability to do his job. The new instructor had innocently opened Pandora's box. This hostility did not last through more than one or two patterns, nor did it prevent the majority of students from expressing a preference for the *free feedback* method.

## *Commentary*

In a sense these experiments demonstrate the obvious. When a receiver *B* is free to ask questions he can get a better understanding of what the sender *A* is trying to communicate. Moreover, with *free feedback* both the sender and the receiver can feel, correctly, more confident that they have respectively sent and received accurately. *Free feedback* requires more time, but there is some evidence that this time differential decreases with increased understanding between the sender and the receiver. Apparently the use of continuing *free feedback* could lead directly back into *zero feedback*, for once the common areas of misunderstanding have been clarified, contemporaneous feedback will no longer be necessary.

Apparently it is possible to improve communication skill with minimal feedback. The fourth *zero feedback* pattern is almost always more accurately sent than the first. This improvement can perhaps be thought of as a kind of personal feedback in which the instructor's own words are utilized to help him to increase his own effectiveness in the future. Much of it is no doubt empathetic, the instructor imagining himself in the receiver's place and correcting his sending as a consequence. Some of the improvement, however, may come from feedback which our experimental barriers failed to block out; feedback in the form of noises, sighs, shuffling of chairs. We do not know from these experiments whether or not an instructor using *zero feedback* could eventually reach the *free feedback* level of accuracy and confidence, but it is clear that under our experimental conditions he can improve over his own original *zero feedback* level.

Besides the findings about the direct effects of feedback, the data raise some questions about indirect effects. We observed in both experiments that *free feedback* after *zero feedback* is accompanied by hostility. This hostility was apparently an effect of the *zero feedback* experience. It lasts only through one or two *free feedback* trials. Why should this be so? We believe that the mechanism centers around the notion of "certainty." In our attempts to satisfy our needs we must be as certain as possible that we are successful. Uncertainty is frustrating. Without feedback uncertainty is prevalent.

In the same vein we noted that instructors' confidence is lower than students' confidence. We suggest that the instructor can be satisfied only by knowing that the receiver is getting the proper information. But the receiver can be satisfied by comparing his own work with the sender's directions. The receiver then has more information available against which to check his own progress toward his goal. Hence he can be more certain of his progress. But the sender is not sure of what the receiver is receiving. He can get *some* information with feedback, but almost none but his own empathy without feedback. Hence his certainty and confidence are low. These differential feelings of certainty, adequacy, and hostility seem to us to be the most significant differentials between our *free feedback* and *zero feedback* systems.

## SUMMARY AND CONCLUSIONS

Since the scope of this research has been limited by the utilization of one kind of problem, one kind of sender-receiver situation, and a relatively short series of experiences, our conclusions must be severely circumscribed.

To summarize, we found that, within narrow limits: 1. a completion of the circuit between sender and receiver (feedback) increases the accuracy with which information is transmitted. 2. Feedback also increases receiver and sender confidence in what they have accomplished. 3. The cost of feedback is time. But the difference in time between *free feedback* and *zero feedback* appears to decrease. 4. A sender and a receiver can improve without what we have defined as feedback experience. 5. *Free feedback* experience improves subsequent *zero feedback* trials measurably. 6. Sender experience contributes more than receiver experience to improved accuracy of communication. 7. *Zero feedback* engenders some hostility in the receiver that becomes clearly perceptible when the situation *changes* from *zero* to *free feedback*. This hostility is short-lived, lasting through only one or two *free feedback* trials. 8. *Zero feedback* engenders doubt in the sender.

These findings support the hypothesis that *free feedback* is an aid to accuracy in interpersonal communication. *Free feedback* seems to permit the participants to learn a mutual language, which language once learned may obviate the necessity for further feedback.

The findings also support the hypothesis that the presence or absence of feedback affects the sender-receiver relationship. *Zero feedback* is accompanied by low confidence and hostility; *free feedback* is accompanied by high confidence and amity.

# *The Equilibrium Problem in Small Groups*

ROBERT F. BALES

THE PURPOSE of this paper is to present certain empirical findings from the program of observation of small groups at the Harvard Laboratory of Social Relations and to discuss their relevance to the theory of equilibrium developed elsewhere.

## METHOD

Some of these findings have been published previously, and the reader is referred to these earlier articles for details omitted here (1, 3, 4, 5). It will also be assumed that the reader is familiar with the method of observation, recording, and analysis used in the direct study of the interaction process as it takes place in our small laboratory groups (2). The observation categories are shown in Table 1. Certain aspects of their theoretical grounding in the general theory of action have been discussed earlier.

## CONDITIONS OF OBSERVATION

A number of different types of groups have been observed, in natural as well as laboratory settings, and some of the generalizations to be discussed

ABRIDGED from T. Parsons, R. F. Bales, and E. A. Shils, *Working papers in the theory of action.* Glencoe, Ill.: Free Press, 1953. Pp. 111–161. Reprinted by permission of the author and publisher.

The research reported in this paper was facilitated by the Laboratory of Social Relations, Harvard University. The funds for the observation project now in progress are provided by the RAND Corporation, Santa Monica, California. I am indebted to Philip E. Slater, Research Assistant in the Laboratory of Social Relations, especially for work on the latter parts of this paper on problems of role specialization, and more generally for the many stimulating discussions we have had on the research as a whole. Similarly, I owe much to Christoph Heinicke, Social Science Research Council Fellow, for initial insights on the nature of the status struggle as it appears through the series of meetings of our groups. This phenomenon will be described in later papers.

were obtained before the present observational series was begun. For purposes of exposition, however, it will be simpler to confine the description of the conditions under which the generalizations hold best to the series of groups now under observation since these groups were specifically set up to epitomize the appropriate conditions.

Groups of sizes two through ten are under observation in the present series. Data for sizes three through six have been gathered. The groups are experimental discussion groups, each group meeting for four meetings. The subjects are all males, Harvard undergraduates, who are obtained through the Harvard employment service and typically do not know each other prior to the first meeting. In each of its four meetings, the group examines and discusses a "human relations case." A different case is used for each of the four meetings. Each case is a summary of facts, five pages in length, about a person in an administrative setting who is having some kind of difficulty with the men under him, and has some superior putting pressure on him to get some technically important job done. The summaries for a given case discussion are distributed separately to the subjects. After each member has read his summary the actual typed copy of the case is collected from each by the experimenter. The manner of presentation is such that the subjects are made specifically uncertain as to whether or not they possess exactly the same facts, but are assured that each does possess an accurate, though perhaps incomplete, factual summary.

The subjects are asked to consider themselves as members of the administrative staff of the central person in the case. He has asked them to meet and consider the case. He wishes an answer to two questions: (*1*) why are the persons in the case behaving as they do, and (*2*) what should he do about it. The members of the discussion group are asked to come to their decision in forty minutes. No leader is appointed. The host experimenter leaves the room. The discussion is observed through a one-way mirror and sound recorded. The interaction is observed and recorded in the categories shown on Table 1. After the meeting the members fill out a questionnaire asking certain questions about their reactions, their satisfaction, their relations to each other, and their opinions about their discussion group.

This particular concrete task has certain abstract characteristics which are important in eliciting a range of diversified behavior. The problems of *orientation*, *evaluation*, and *control* are each to a major degree unsolved at the beginning of observation. More specifically:

(a) With regard to *orientation*, members of the group have some degree of ignorance and uncertainty about the relevant facts, but individually possess facts relevant to decision. Their problem of arriving at a common cognitive orientation or definition of the situation must be solved, if at all, through interaction.

(b) With regard to problems of *evaluation*, the members of the group ordinarily possess somewhat different values or interests and the task is such that it involves several different values and interests as criteria by which the facts of the situation and the proposed course of action are to be judged. The problem of arriving at common value judgments necessary to a concrete plan must be solved, again, if at all, through interaction.

(c) With regard to problems of *control*, (that is, attempts of the members to influence directly the action of each other and arrive at a concrete plan) the acceptance of the task sets up in most instances a moderately strong pressure for group decision, with the expectation that the excellence of the decision can and will be evaluated by each of them as well as by the experimenter, so that the decision will affect their status. There are a number of possible alternative decisions or solutions, with uncertain degrees of potential frustration or satisfaction associated with various choices.

These abstract conditions, with emphasis varying according to circumstances, are met in very much this form and emphasis in a great many group conferences, work groups, committees, and the like. When group problems or tasks lack or greatly minimize any of the three abstract characteristics described above (a, b, c) we speak of them as being "truncated." When these three characteristics are all present and marked, we speak of the problem as "full-fledged." We have felt that full-fledged problems give us a better opportunity to explore the range and interconnections of various sorts of social behavior, and so have begun to develop empirical norms and a body of theory around this particular set of conditions as a standard diagnostic task. Once this baseline has been established, other sets of conditions expected to have different results can be described as modifications or accentuations or reversals of the laboratory conditions. The more we learn about the typical effects of the particular diagnostic *task* we employ, the more we are able to use discrepancies from our typical base-line patterns of observed interaction as diagnostic indicators of the *personalities*, *culture*, and *role organization* of the participants, since these are all sets of conditions which influence the way interaction actually goes.

Under each mode of analysis discussed below some of the main uniformities of behavior we have found will be compactly stated. Space does not permit the presentation of the evidence in detail. In general, the patterns described and illustrated can be understood to refer to approximate or average uniformities in aggregates of large numbers of group meetings under randomly varying external conditions, and in addition, they can be understood to hold more uniformly and in particular under the full-fledged conditions of the standard diagnostic task described above.

## THE PROFILE OF ACTIVITY AND THE EQUILIBRIUM PROBLEM

One of the interesting characteristics of interaction is the distribution of total number of acts among the twelve categories, according to quality. A distribution of this kind in percentage rates based on the total is called a profile. An illustrative comparison of group profiles of two five-man groups working on the standard diagnostic task is shown in Table 1.

TABLE I

*Profile of a "Satisfied" and a "Dissatisfied" Group on Case Discussion Task*

| | MEETING PROFILES IN PERCENTAGE RATES | | | |
|---|---|---|---|---|
| TYPE OF ACT: | *Satisfied* * | *Dissatisfied* ** | *Ave. of the two* | *Ave. rates by Sections* |
| 1. Shows Solidarity | .7 | .8 | .7 | |
| 2. Shows Tension Release | 7.9 | 6.8 | 7.3 | 25.0 |
| 3. Agrees | 24.9 | 9.6 | 17.0 | |
| 4. Gives Suggestion | 8.2 | 3.6 | 5.9 | |
| 5. Gives Opinion | 26.7 | 30.5 | 28.7 | 56.7 |
| 6. Gives Orientation | 22.4 | 21.9 | 22.1 | |
| 7. Asks for Orientation | 1.7 | 5.7 | 3.8 | |
| 8. Asks for Opinion | 1.7 | 2.2 | 2.0 | 6.9 |
| 9. Asks for Suggestion | .5 | 1.6 | 1.1 | |
| 10. Disagrees | 4.0 | 12.4 | 8.3 | |
| 11. Shows Tension | 1.0 | 2.6 | 1.8 | 11.4 |
| 12. Shows Antagonism | .3 | 2.2 | 1.3 | |
| PERCENTAGE TOTAL | 100.0 | 100.0 | 100.0 | 100.0 |
| RAW SCORE TOTAL | 719 | 767 | 1486 | |

* The highest of sixteen groups. The members rated their own satisfaction with their solution after the meeting at an average of 10.4 on a scale running from 0 to a highest possible rating of 12.

** The lowest of sixteen groups. Comparable satisfaction rating in this group was 2.6.

In the present illustration the "satisfied" group attained a higher rate of suggestions, more often followed by positive reactions and less often by negative reactions and questions than did the "dissatisfied" group.

The profiles produced by groups, however, are not completely and radically different from each other. The profile produced by the average of these two illustrative groups is more or less typical of averages of larger aggregates under laboratory standard conditions. Attempted Answers, that is, giving orientation, opinion, and suggestion, are always more numerous than their cognate Questions, that is, asking for orientation, opinion, or suggestion. Similarly, Positive Reactions, that is agreement, showing tension release, and solidarity, are usually more numerous than Negative Reactions, i.e., showing disagreement, tension, and antagonism. Intuitively one would feel that the process would surely be self-defeating and self-limiting if there were more questions than answers and more negative reactions than positive.

On the average, for groups we have examined, the relations of amounts by Sections are about as they are in the illustration. The relations between the amounts can be viewed as the final result of a repetitive series of cycles, each of which consists of: (*1*) an initial disturbance of the system (precipitated by the introduction of a new idea, or opinion, or suggestion into the group) followed by (*2*) a "dwindling series of feedbacks" and corrections as the disturbance is terminated, equilibrated, or assimilated by other parts or members of the system. Attempted Answers, or as one might call them for the moment, "Initial Acts," account for a little over half (or 57 percent) of the total activity, with Positive and Negative Reactions and Questions accounting for the other half, roughly.

Looking at the *Reaction* side alone, and assuming it to be 50 percent of the total, about half the reactions (or 25 percent of the total) are Positive and presumably terminate the disturbance introduced by the initial action. The other half of the time the Reaction fails to terminate the disturbance. Of this non-terminating portion again, about half (or 12 percent of the total) are Negative Reactions, which typically precipitate another Attempted Answer, thus beginning a repetition of the cycle. Of the remaining hypothetical 13 percent or so, about half (or 7 percent) are Questions, which also typically precipitate another Attempted Answer. If about 7 percent of Attempted Answers are in direct response to Questions, these might well be called "Reactions," thus leaving the relation of "Initial Acts" to "Reactions" about 50-50, as assumed above. One might say that quantitatively (as well as qualitatively, by definition) interaction is a process consisting of action followed by reaction. The balance of action with reaction is one of the equilibrium problems of the system.

## ACT TO ACT TENDENCIES AND THE EQUILIBRIUM PROBLEM

A more detailed understanding of the equilibrating tendencies by which the characteristic profile arises may be obtained by examining the frequencies with which each type of activity tends to be followed by each other type. Two input-output matrices showing these act-to-act tendencies are presented in Tables 2 and 3. These particular matrices were obtained by tabulation from the interaction tapes of the total sixteen sessions of the four five-man groups of the present observation series. The total number of output acts occurring after each input type of act is considered as 100 percent, and the probabilities for each type of output act are derived by a percentage breakdown.

It will be noted that two matrices are presented, one called a Matrix of Proactive Tendencies, and the other a Matrix of Reactive Tendencies. A single matrix could be produced, of course, by omitting this distinction, but such a matrix would ignore the fact that the action "changes hands" at certain points, from one member to another. And this fact is crucial, since the equilibrium problem of social systems is not simply one of a certain "balance" in the relation of qualitatively different types of acts to each other, as shown by the profile. It is at the same time, and just as intrinsically, a problem of a certain balance in the way in which these activities are distributed between separate members. The distinction between "proaction" and "reaction," for the matrices presented, hinges on the member-to-member oscillation of activity. Very simply, an act which is a direct continuation by the *same* member who has produced the last act is called "proactive." An act which follows immediately the last act of *another* member is called "reactive."

The distinction is based on a suggestion by Murray:
"I . . . suggest . . . that the term *proaction*, in contrast to *reaction*, be used to designate an action that is not initiated by the confronting external situation but spontaneously from within. An action of this sort is likely to be part of a serial program, one that is guided by some directional force (aim) which is subsidiary to a more distally oriented aim. As a rule, a proaction is not merely homeostatic, in the sense that it serves to restore the organism to a previously enjoyed equilibrium or state of well-being. If successful, it results in the addition or production of something–another bit of physical construction, let us say, or more money in the bank, or greater social cohesion, or another chapter of a novel, or the statement of a new theory. The integrates of serials, of plans, strategies, and intended proactions directed toward distal goals constitute a large portion of the ego system, the *establishment* of personality which inhibits impulses and renounces courses of action that interfere with progress along the elected paths of life" (10, pp. 439–440).

The operational definition of the distinction for purposes of tabulating from interaction records does not correspond perfectly to Murray's theoretical distinction, but the basic idea is the same. In face to face interaction it is true by and large that the first act of a person following the last act of some other is "provoked" by the last act of the other as the "stimulus" and thus has a "reactive" quality. Conversely, it is sufficiently true that as a person continues talking his activity tends to change to a "proactive" quality, directed adaptively and instrumentally to the achievement of more distant aims. The activity is now *directed toward* the external confronting situation, including the situation external to the group as a whole, rather than immediately *initiated by* it, as in the "reactive case." It might be noted in passing that the term "initiation of action" is ambiguous, in that it is often defined empirically as the total of *all* types of activity "given out"

TABLE 2

*Matrix of* Proactive *Tendencies: Output Probabilities for a Given Input. 16 Meetings of 5-Man Groups*

| CATEGORY OF PRIOR ACT (Input Type) | CATEGORY OF FOLLOWING ACT (Output) | | | | | | | | | | | | TOTAL PERCENT |
|---|---|---|---|---|---|---|---|---|---|---|---|---|---|
| | 1 | 2 | 3 | 4 | 5 | 6 | 7 | 8 | 9 | 10 | 11 | 12 | |
| 1 SHOWS SOLIDARITY, raises other's status, gives help, reward: | — | 6.8 | 9.1 | 22.7 | 29.5 | 18.2 | — | 4.5 | 2.2 | — | — | 6.8 | 99.8 |
| 2 SHOWS TENSION RELEASE, jokes, laughs, shows satisfaction: | 1.6 | 37.5 | 1.6 | 6.3 | 21.9 | 9.4 | .8 | 1.6 | 2.3 | 3.1 | 3.9 | 10.2 | 100.2 |
| 3 AGREES, shows passive acceptance, understands, concurs: | 3.0 | 4.6 | 6.6 | 9.7 | 41.6 | 22.1 | 2.8 | 2.1 | .7 | 5.1 | .8 | .8 | 99.9 |
| 4 GIVES SUGGESTION, direction, implying autonomy for other: | 2.6 | 4.8 | 1.6 | 55.6 | 19.3 | 9.6 | 1.0 | 2.6 | .6 | 1.0 | 1.0 | .3 | 100.0 |
| 5 GIVES OPINION, evaluation, analysis, expresses feeling, wish: | 2.3 | 4.4 | 1.6 | 5.0 | 60.1 | 17.0 | 1.8 | 4.4 | .7 | .9 | 1.4 | .3 | 99.9 |
| 6 GIVES ORIENTATION, information, repeats, clarifies, confirms: | .2 | 2.1 | .2 | 3.4 | 22.6 | 61.4 | 4.7 | 2.8 | 1.3 | .4 | .8 | .2 | 100.1 |
| 7 ASKS FOR ORIENTATION, information, repetition, confirmation: | 1.1 | 1.1 | 1.1 | 6.5 | 19.4 | 38.7 | 21.5 | 7.5 | 1.1 | 1.1 | 1.1 | — | 100.2 |
| 8 ASKS FOR OPINION, evaluation, analysis, expression of feeling: | — | 3.2 | — | 9.7 | 31.2 | 26.9 | 4.3 | 19.4 | 2.2 | 2.2 | 1.1 | — | 100.2 |
| 9 ASKS FOR SUGGESTION, direction, possible ways of action: | 3.2 | 6.5 | — | 16.1 | 22.6 | 19.4 | 3.2 | — | 19.4 | 6.5 | — | 3.2 | 100.1 |
| 10 DISAGREES, shows passive rejection, formality, withholds help: | 1.2 | 2.5 | 1.6 | 6.6 | 51.4 | 21.8 | 4.1 | 2.5 | .8 | 1.6 | 5.3 | .4 | 99.8 |
| 11 SHOWS TENSION, asks for help, withdraws "Out of Field": | — | 4.2 | 2.1 | 8.3 | 45.8 | 35.4 | — | 2.1 | — | — | 2.1 | — | 100.0 |
| 12 SHOWS ANTAGONISM, deflates other's status, defends or asserts self: | 5.9 | 27.5 | — | 5.9 | 19.6 | 7.8 | 5.9 | 2.0 | — | — | 3.9 | 21.6 | 100.1 |

TABLE 3

*Matrix of* Reactive *Tendencies: Output Probabilities for a Given Input. 16 Meetings of 5-Man Groups*

| CATEGORY OF PRIOR ACT (Input Type) | CATEGORY OF FOLLOWING ACT (Output) 1 | 2 | 3 | 4 | 5 | 6 | 7 | 8 | 9 | 10 | 11 | 12 | TOTAL PERCENT |
|---|---|---|---|---|---|---|---|---|---|---|---|---|---|
| 1 SHOWS SOLIDARITY, raises other's status, gives help, reward: | 28.4 | 11.9 | 3.0 | 13.4 | 14.9 | 11.9 | 4.5 | 4.5 | — | 3.0 | 1.5 | 3.0 | 100.0 |
| 2 SHOWS TENSION RELEASE, jokes, laughs, shows satisfaction: | .7 | 68.2 | 3.2 | 3.1 | 10.2 | 6.7 | 2.2 | 1.5 | .3 | 1.7 | .6 | 1.5 | 99.9 |
| 3 AGREES, shows passive acceptance, understands, concurs: | .6 | 2.7 | 15.9 | 8.5 | 40.8 | 21.4 | 2.3 | 3.0 | .9 | 2.7 | 1.0 | .2 | 100.0 |
| 4 GIVES SUGGESTION, direction, implying autonomy for other: | 1.3 | 6.7 | 46.0 | 8.6 | 9.2 | 8.8 | 2.3 | 1.5 | 1.5 | 12.4 | 1.3 | .4 | 100.0 |
| 5 GIVES OPINION, evaluation, analysis, expresses feeling, wish: | .6 | 4.3 | 48.9 | 2.2 | 19.2 | 6.3 | 2.3 | 2.8 | .3 | 11.8 | .6 | .6 | 99.9 |
| 6 GIVES ORIENTATION, information, repeats, clarifies, confirms: | .6 | 5.8 | 35.0 | 3.6 | 15.2 | 24.0 | 5.6 | 1.3 | .4 | 5.7 | 1.1 | 1.7 | 100.0 |
| 7 ASKS FOR ORIENTATION, information, repetition, confirmation: | — | 1.0 | 5.6 | .7 | 10.0 | 73.7 | 5.6 | 1.0 | .3 | 1.6 | — | .7 | 100.2 |
| 8 ASKS FOR OPINION, evaluation, analysis, expression of feeling: | 1.5 | 5.4 | 9.2 | 2.4 | 45.9 | 13.2 | 10.7 | 3.0 | .5 | 4.4 | 2.0 | 2.0 | 100.2 |
| 9 ASKS FOR SUGGESTION, direction, possible ways of action: | — | 13.2 | — | 35.8 | 28.3 | 9.4 | 1.9 | 1.9 | — | 3.8 | 3.8 | 1.9 | 100.0 |
| 10 DISAGREES, shows passive rejection, formality, withholds help: | .3 | 6.6 | 12.4 | 5.2 | 25.0 | 13.5 | 3.6 | 2.0 | .3 | 24.2 | 3.9 | 3.0 | 100.0 |
| 11 SHOWS TENSION, asks for help, withdraws "Out of Field": | 4.1 | 7.2 | 5.2 | 2.1 | 39.2 | 22.7 | 2.1 | 4.1 | — | 4.1 | 9.3 | — | 100.1 |
| 12 SHOWS ANTAGONISM, deflates other's status, defends or asserts self: | 1.0 | 18.1 | 4.8 | 3.8 | 12.4 | 11.4 | 1.0 | 3.8 | — | 5.7 | 1.9 | 36.2 | 100.1 |

by a specific individual, but usually carries the theoretical *connotation* of "proaction."

The Matrix of Proactive tendencies shows very clearly that when the same person continues talking, after having given an act of orientation, opinion, or suggestion, the probability is very high that he will continue with the same type of activity (probabilities of about .61, .60, and .55) presumably in a connected "serial program," to use Murray's term. When he does not continue with the same precise category of activity, the probability is still relatively high that he will carry on in one of the three types called Attempted Answers. If his preceding act was a Question of some type, and he continues himself instead of yielding the floor to some other, the highest probabilities are that he will either repeat or go directly ahead with an Attempted Answer. Indeed, the tendencies to continue proactively in the Attempted Answer area are very strong, even when the member has begun his participation with a Reaction to the other. As we all know, an act of agreement is often a way of "getting one's foot in the door" in order to go ahead and present one's own ideas. And similarly, when one has given a disagreement, he is very likely to go ahead and "tell why." In both of these cases, the tendency to present the argument in terms of "opinion" rather than "facts" is notable.

If the preceding Reaction was far over on the affective side, however, there are appreciable tendencies for the member to continue in the affective area. If one's former act was a display of antagonism, the present act is likely to be another, unless it passes over into tension release, either of which is more probable than a direct return to the task area. Similarly, when the last act was one of tension release, the next act is likely to be *another* act of tension release, and the tendency to continue with an act of antagonism (possibly a joking one) is still appreciable. Once such a cycle of antagonism and tension release is set in motion, it appears to have a tendency to continue until presumably the major potential of implicit tension is "bled off" to a substantially lower level. Similar cycles also appear between showing solidarity and showing tension release, although they do not appear on this matrix because of our scoring convention (now changed) of scoring "jokes" in category two, as well as laughs. We now score the jokes themselves in either category one, or category twelve, according to whether the butt of the joke is outside the immediate group, or a member of it. This convention appears to us now to more satisfactorily represent affective dynamics of the process, but as a result of the change we obtain considerably more scores in category one than previously, and a few more in category twelve. The implication of the scoring change is simply that we now assume, on the basis of experience and intuition, that one of the reasons the number of acts in these two categories was formerly so low (of the order of one or two percent) is that in our particular type of groups, the management of positive and negative affect is typically accomplished in a "joking" rather than in a "serious" manner. Whether joking or serious, however, these cycles of affective activity, once started, have a tendency to "carry on," just as do the "serials" of instrumental-adaptive activity.

As we think of the matter, the instrumental-adaptive activity of the preceding participant tends to build up tensions in the present participant to some point where he enters the process and changes to activity of an expressive-integrative relevance, which tends to "bleed off" the tension to some point at which he changes the focus himself and continues again with instrumental-adaptive activity. *The problem of equilibrium is essentially the problem of establishing arrangements (or an "orbit of activity") whereby the system goes through a repetitive cycle, within which all of the disturbances created in one phase are reduced in some other.* The dilemma of all action systems is that no one disturbance can be reduced without creating another.

The individual personality is such an action system, and some of its cyclical tendencies can be seen in the Proactive Matrix. The combination of two or more personalities in interaction, however, is also an action system. Indeed, this is the level on which the systematic properties can be seen most fully articulated in overt observable behavior. The "switch-over" from reactive to proactive behavior can be seen in the individual person as he continues his participation, but the switch-over from proactive to reactive is most notable at those junctures in the process when the action changes hands. What happens to the quality of action when the action changes hands may be seen in the Matrix of Reactive Tendencies.

When the prior act of another member has been an Attempted Answer, the highest probabilities are that the present act will be a Positive Reaction, specifically an agreement, rather than a continuation in the task area, although there are appreciable tendencies for the reacting person to continue directly with further opinion or information. Probabilities of positive reactions (for these groups) far outweigh probabilities of negative reactions, and this is generally true, though occasionally we observe groups where it is not the case.

Theoretically, we tend to assume that a preponderance of positive reactions over negative is a *condition* of equilibrium or maintenance of the steady state of the system. The reasoning goes something like this: We assume that the instrumental-adaptive goals of the system involve the maintenance of a certain level of accomplishment output, and that this level *tends to fall* without the constant application of effort, energy, and activity applied successfully to the realities of the external situation. But the level of *accomplishment* can not be maintained for long without also maintaining the level of diffuse *satisfaction,* which depends upon the achievement of expressive-integrative goals. The full stable "orbit" will have to include tension release, gratification, and a feedback of positive sanctions to the person(s) performing the instrumental activities, in such a way as to "reinforce" them (in the learning theory sense), either in keeping them doing what they are doing, or in keeping them generalizing appropriately from their former accomplishments. Negative reactions tend to inhibit the behavior which preceded, but do not provide the basis for establishing a stable, positively defined orbit. Nor does generalization from negative reactions help appreciably in finding a positively defined orbit. It simply tends to cancel out or inhibit possible untried orbits, while the unstable "seeking" or "trial and error" fluctuation of the system continues.

Furthermore, each failure, and each negative reaction, tends to result *in its own right* in disturbance, and thus reduces the satisfaction levels directly. Assuming a quantitative equivalence of units of action observed (a shaky, but not inconceivable assumption), one might conclude that at least one positive reaction would be required for each negative reaction, simply to counteract the disturbances introduced by the negative reactions. On these assumptions, if positive reactions are only equal to negative reactions, the system barely manages to counteract the disturbances introduced by the "friction" of its own controlling apparatus, and the accomplishment and satisfaction levels will tend to sink because of lack of effort and instrumental activity applied constructively and successfully to the situation of the system. One concludes that the accomplishment and satisfaction levels can only be maintained in a steady state if an orbit is found in which positive reactions preponderate over negative. The degree to which they must do so in order to maintain steady levels will then depend upon such factors as levels of expectation or aspiration, the stringency of situational demands, and the abilities or resources of the actors in relation to aspirations and situational demands.

One obvious inference from this theoretical formulation is that the levels of satisfaction of members at the end of a problem-solving attempt will be a function of the degree to which positive reactions have outweighed negative reactions during the process. The two illustrative profiles given earlier demonstrate this relation. There are a considerable number of ways of constructing single indices from the balance of rates in the profiles which give reasonably good predictions of satisfaction. We do not yet know which of these is best in general. Several we have tried tend to yield correlations with average satisfaction at the end of meetings ranging from about .6 to .8.

Another possible inference is that the satisfaction ratings of individual members will tend to be a function of the preponderance of positive reactions received over negative reactions received by that member. We have not thoroughly explored this hypothesis as yet, but there are some indications that higher status members tend to receive higher relative proportions of positive reactions, and in general have higher satisfaction ratings.

The degree of satisfaction, we believe, as a working hypothesis, tends to be highest with the members of highest status, and to grade down as status grades down. On the basis of the theory, however, one should definitely not expect perfect correlations, either between total group profiles and average post-meeting satisfactions, or between positive reactions received by individual members and their individual post-meeting satisfactions. The reason is that starting levels are typically not known, and that other factors such as stringency of situational demands, abilities or resources of the members, and the content and stringency of levels of expectation or aspiration are believed to be involved also. Much work remains to be done in this direction.

On the Matrix of Reactive Tendencies it will be noted that the tendency to reply to an Attempted Answer of the other with a Positive or Negative Reaction increases from a prior act of giving orientation to one of giving opinion, to one of giving a suggestion. One might say that the "urgency" of giving a Positive or Negative Reaction increases as the proaction becomes more "directive" or "constricting." An act of giving orientation has only a probability of about .06 of provoking a disagreement. An act of opinion, however, has a probability of about .12 and an act of suggestion has a little higher probability. But an act of suggestion is a little less likely than an act of opinion to provoke an agreement. If one makes an index by representing the probability of disagreement as a percentage of the probability of agreement the index rises from .16 in response to an act of orientation, to .24 in response to an act of opinion, to .26 in response to an act of suggestion. The difference between the last two is very small, but in the expected direction. It should be pointed out that on the Proactive Matrix the probability that a member will follow a disagreement with an act of opinion is very high, .51. Consequently, the replies to opinion on the Reactive Matrix are often replies to an opinion which was in support of a still prior disagreement. If one took the trouble to segregate those cases where the acts of orientation, opinion, and suggestion are given without prior disagreement, it is likely that the differences between them would be greater.

The notions that proaction is likely to provoke reaction, that the probability of reaction increases as the process passes from problems of orientation, to evaluation, to control, and that the reaction will tend to swing to the negative side as the implications of the acts become more "directive" and "constrictive" are fundamental to the theory of equilibrium problems in small groups. The problem appears in many guises, and solutions are worked out in many directions, as will appear later in the discussion of the way in which participation tends to get distributed between members, the way in which quality of activity tends to move through a series of phases constituting a closed cycle in time, the way in which number of members affects the process, the way in which differentiated roles tend to appear, and the way in which the structure of roles tends to shift through a series of meetings.

On the Matrix of Reactive Tendencies the probabilities that a Question from the other will provoke a complementary or cognate Attempted Answer are seen to be very high. There is perhaps nothing very remarkable about this, but it does provide evidence of a kind of "reasonable continuity" in the process—the persistence of the system in an instrumental-adaptive direction of movement, once started, in spite of the fact that the action changes hands from one member to another. Questions provide a means of turning the process into the instrumental-adaptive direction of movement, with a low probability of provoking an affective reaction, and are an extremely effective way of turning the initiative over to the other.

Our impression is, however, that in our groups the number of questions which arise out of a self-conscious anticipatory attempt to guide the process in this way is comparatively small. They probably appear more often after strains arise out of earlier failures, as a result of disagreement, argument, and "backtracking" from premature attempts to proceed more "directively." Questions provide a "neutral way out"—a "patch up" procedure of last recourse when negative reactions are anticipated if one goes ahead himself. At least this way of looking at the process gives a reasonable explanation as to why the rates of Questions are in general so low (about half that of Negative Reactions). Questions constitute the last of the "dwindling series of feedbacks" mentioned earlier, and tend to be called into play only after more direct and obvious feedback controls have failed to equilibrate the system. Since they tend to prevent the asker from going ahead to give his own ideas, they provide little opportunity to raise one's status, but rather hand this opportunity over to the other. Thus, one might suppose, where competition is high (as it is generally in our initially leaderless groups) there will be a tendency to avoid them except as a last resort. Those who have a fixed high status, and those who have essentially accepted a low status, can "afford" to ask Questions, but not those who are in the thick of competition.

The tendency for antagonism to provoke antagonism is even more marked when the action changes hands (in the Reactive Matrix) than when the same person continues (in the Proactive Matrix). Similarly, in the Reactive Matrix, showing solidarity tends to provoke a like Reaction. Either type of marked affect tends to lead to tension release, and this type of activity, when once tripped off, is more likely to continue than any other type. "Laughter is contagious" as the saying goes. In the present context it is another instance of the tendency of the system, once started, to continue in a given direction of movement until checked by other factors. It is interpreted as a mechanism by which massive changes in the tension level take place in a short length of time, and typically appears only periodically, with intervening periods of tension build-up, as will be pointed out later in the discussion of phase movement.

The interpretation of the rate of tension release for given groups is a vexed problem. According to our present thinking, a "moderate rate" (around 7 or 8 percent) is associated with successful equilibration after normal hazards. Very low rates lead us to expect high residual tension, and very high rates lead us to look for extraordinary sources of tension. Levels of satisfaction as measured by post-meeting questions would appear to give us some entree to this problem, but the complex determinants of satisfaction have already been pointed out.

These problems of interpretation are general, however, not specific to certain types of acts or results of acts. The whole implication of an equilibrium theory as an interpretive device is that the determinants of any part of the process, or any result of it, are complex, and should be sought in some kind of complicated balance of the system as a whole, rather than in a maximization or minimization of supposedly isolated factors. The understanding of a *repeated* phenomenon in this type of approach lies in showing how it fits into a system, or constellation of interlocking systems, as one link in a closed, repetitive cycle of activities or orbit which constitutes the moving steady state of the system as its equilibrium is persistently disturbed and reestablished.

## THE WHO-TO-WHOM MATRIX AND THE EQUILIBRIUM PROBLEM

A further unfolding of the equilibrium problem may be seen by a closer examination of the way in which participation tends to be distributed among members. The total number of different possible combinations of who is speaking and to whom for a given time period is called a "who-to-whom matrix." The scoring system recognizes acts addressed to the "group as a whole" as well as to specific individuals.

An aggregate matrix of a collection of 18 sessions of six-man groups (all types of activity) is presented in Table 4 as an illustration. The aggregate matrix is produced by rank ordering the members of each separate session according to the total amounts of participation given out, and then summing together all rank one men, all rank two men, all rank one men speaking to all rank two men, etc.

The pattern of distribution is different in detail under different conditions. For example, groups with no designated leader generally tend to have more equal participation than groups with designated leaders of higher status. However, in spite of these differences, the distribution of total amounts of participation of each member, as well as the pattern of who talks how much to whom, (and how, qualitatively) seems to be subject to system-influences, which tend to produce similarities from group to group, and some regular gradations by group size.

These generalizations may be illustrated in part by reference to Table 4. If the personnel are arrayed in rank order according to the total amount they speak ("basic initiating rank") we then find that they are spoken to in amounts proportionate to their rank order. Roughly speaking, each man receives back about half as much as he puts out in total. It will be remembered that something like half of all interaction is "reac-

TABLE 4

*Aggregate Who-to-whom Matrix for 18 Sessions of Six-Man Groups,* All Types of Activity*

| RANK ORDER OF PERSON ORIGINATING ACT | SPEAKING TO INDIVIDUALS OF EACH RANK: 1 | 2 | 3 | 4 | 5 | 6 | TOTAL TO INDIVIDUALS | TO GROUP AS A WHOLE | TOTAL INITIATED |
|---|---|---|---|---|---|---|---|---|---|
| 1 | | 1238 | 961 | 545 | 445 | 317 | 3506 | 5661 | 9167 |
| 2 | 1748 | | 443 | 310 | 175 | 102 | 2778 | 1211 | 3989 |
| 3 | 1371 | 415 | | 305 | 125 | 69 | 2285 | 742 | 3027 |
| 4 | 952 | 310 | 282 | | 83 | 49 | 1676 | 676 | 2352 |
| 5 | 662 | 224 | 144 | 83 | | 28 | 1141 | 443 | 1584 |
| 6 | 470 | 126 | 114 | 65 | 44 | | 819 | 373 | 1192 |
| Total Received | 5203 | 2313 | 1944 | 1308 | 872 | 565 | 12205 | 9106 | 21311 |

* These groups were observed before the standard laboratory task was evolved. The general features of the standard task groups are similar.

tive" and each man spends a certain portion of his time reacting to the initial acts of others. The amount of time spent reacting to specific other individuals rather than proacting to the group as a whole, however, differs according to the rank of the member. The profiles of participants tend to change systematically as we proceed downward in rank. High ranking men tend to have more proactive Attempted Answers in their profiles and to address more acts to the group as a whole than lower ranking men, while low ranking men have more "Reactions," both positive and negative, and address more of their acts to specific individuals. Quantitative differentiation in participation is accompanied by, or is symptomatic of, qualitative differentiation of roles of members. For example, the top man tends to give out more information and opinion to specific individuals than he receives, while, on the contrary, low men give out more agreement, disagreement, and requests for information than they receive.

If this is true one might expect quantity of participation to be related to the status hierarchy of the members. We typically find that the order produced by ranking individuals according to their "basic initiating rank" on total amounts of participation is fairly highly correlated with the order produced by their own ratings of each other as to "productivity," i.e., who has the best ideas, and who does the most to guide the discussion effectively. Similar findings are reported by Norfleet (11) and Bass (6) with correlations of about .95 in each case. Strodtbeck (13) finds in addition a fairly dependable connection between amount of activity given out and probability of winning in contested decisions, which is a kind of measure of power or influence. The empirical correlation between status in some generalized sense and amounts of participation given out and received seems to be pretty well established, but perfect correlation is definitely not to be expected in general.

Such approximate generalizations, once established, can typically be used to produce further valuable diagnostic information, as will be shown later. Any specific group, or some particular types of groups, may present exceptions, in one or more particulars, depending on the conditions operating. Exceptions to the empirical rule give the investigator the cue to look for exceptional conditions. For example, we have often found particular exceptions to the expected correlation between amount given out and amount received in cases where one of the members disagrees with the others persistently, and so tends to attract or receive a disproportionate amount of communication. Festinger and Thibaut (7) have produced this effect experimentally. We have found similar exceptions to the generalization when two highly interactive and agreeing members form a sub-group or coalition vis-a-vis a third neglected or rejected member.

Size of group is obviously an important condition affecting the distribution of activities. From present indications it appears that the top man in groups larger than five or so tends to speak considerably more to the group as a whole than to specific individuals in the group, as in Table 4. All other members tend to speak more to specific individuals (and particularly to the top man) than to the group as a whole. Each man tends to speak to each other man in an amount which is a probability function of both his own rank on outwardly directed remarks, and the rank of the other on the receiving of communication (8). As groups increase in size, a larger and larger proportion of the activity tends to be addressed to the top man, and a smaller and smaller proportion to other members. In turn, as size increases, the top man tends to address more and more of his remarks to the group as a whole, and to exceed by larger amounts his proportionate share. The communication pattern tends to "centralize," in other words, around a leader through whom most of the communication flows.

But if the situation is one in which *inter*action is expected by the participators, there would seem to be a top ceiling for the top man somewhere around 50 percent, apparently connected with the general tendency for interaction under such expectations to come to a system-closure, such that each "action" of one member, as it were, tends to be countered with a "reaction" from some other. Even if the top man is initiating most of the action, he still has to expect that he will receive a "feedback of reactions," both of a positive and negative sort, that will tend to equal the amount of action he initiates. It may very well be that the expectation of "equality" which is so often present in groups of our culture, refers rather to this over-all balance of action and reaction than to an equality of amounts of output of all members, which in practice, is never found.

Thus it can be seen that the differentiation between members as to specialized roles and status, is intimately related to the equilibrium problem. The tendency for the system, once started, to continue moving in the same direction until checked by opposing forces, is reflected in the tendency of given members to continue proacting until checked by other members. Negative Reactions appear to act as such a check, presumably through learning mechanisms. Their regular appearance should be viewed as a check on the widening of status differences, as well as a result of "objective mistakes" and task attempts which fail to appeal on other grounds. But if, as we have hypothesized, the system cannot maintain a steady state without a preponderance of positive reactions over negative, then in the equilibrated system more task attempts will be rewarded than punished, and they will be attempts by specific persons.

Here enters the crucial importance of "generalization" in the learning theory sense. Insofar as a given person "gets on the right track" and receives Positive Reactions from other members, he will be reinforced in his direction of movement, and will tend to keep on talking. He will "generalize" from the premises, logical and emotional, which underlay his original successful attempt. This is the "growing point" of the system of common symbols or group culture, as well as of role differentiation. And reciprocally, the other members will "generalize" from his earlier attempts, gratifying in some sense to them, to an expectation of further effective behavior on his part. The member begins to build a "specialized role." Insofar as the activity he performs is felt to be important in terms of the functional problems of the group, its goals and value norms, the "status" of the member will begin to rise. There will be a "generalization" from the specific *performance* of the person to a *qualitative ascribed* "position" in the group which bears a rank relation to other positions similarly developed. It is apparently in some such terms that one may understand the tendencies toward gross differentiation of amounts of participation given and received, the qualitative differences by rank, and above all, the emergence of a "top man" in larger groups, with an amount and quality of activity radically discontinuous with the more or less equal rank intervals between the other men. A system can not achieve a steady state without generalization, but the operation of generalization produces a differentiation of roles which introduces new strains. The price of accomplishment is differentiated status.

It should not be assumed, however, that once generalization in its various aspects has resulted in an ascribed status and role for a man, that his position is now stable. There are apparently a number of ways in which it may be undermined and subject to later shifts, two of which may be mentioned as likely. The first is that the effects of his role-specialized behavior, even if it does not change, put other members under ambivalent strains of some sort which gradually lead them to shift their perception of, attitudes toward, or behavior addressed to him. The second is that the psychological effects of holding a given position may result in gradual *changes* in his behavior (either by "overconfidence," "dissatisfaction" or in some other way) which finally "break through" stereotyped perceptions of his previously established role and become obvious to the other members, with a resulting shift in their attitudes toward him. In other words, the problem of equilibrium is relevant on the more macroscopic levels of role structure and in longer changes over time, as well as on the more microscopic levels we have so far discussed. The unfolding of the equilibrium problem on these levels will be discussed later in this paper. First, however, it may be useful to present, in a very tentative way, a sample of the type of statistical models we have been "playing with," which ignore these more macroscopic equilibrium problems of larger scale "social structure change."

## A STATISTICAL MODEL FOR EXPLORING THE MATRIX EQUILIBRIUM PROBLEM

Some characteristics of the hypothetical learning process just described can be formalized slightly in terms of a statistical model. The model presented below is the fifth of a series of models which have been informally explored and discarded as their deficiencies forced to clearer awareness the sorts of assumptions which appear to be necessary to "reproduce" the characteristics of the average process as we have found it empirically. The present model has been barely explored as yet, and is by no means expected to be the last of the series. It is presented simply as another step in what is hoped to be the right direction. This model which we call $T_5$ (T for "temporary") takes the act-to-act tendencies represented by the Proactive and Reactive Matrices as given, makes certain additional assumptions about the effects of learning mechanisms and generalization as discussed above, and attempts to determine whether, if these givens and assumptions are true, the who-to-whom matrix we find for groups of each size will turn out to be the equilibrium state of the system.

No formal mathematics have been employed. The model is set up for easy "Monte Carlo" calculation. The results to be obtained are thus exceedingly "approximate." They have been quite adequate however, to show that previous models could not possibly be satisfactory, and this is all that is required for progress. To lighten the boredom we have typically employed an actual group of people, each of whom is given an identical set of Proactive and Reactive Matrices (thus erasing all "personality differences") and a table of random numbers. The process proceeds by a series of probability choices according to a set of "Rules of Order" administered by the experimenter. Still another person takes down the scores as they are determined by the probability choices, and these scores are later tabulated and analyzed just as we analyze actual scores. To forestall any misunderstanding it may be repeated: the group of people is in no sense necessary—the whole operation is defined by rules and probability choices and can be performed by a single statistical clerk. However, to do the calculation as a game gives an excellent setting for spotting specific deficiencies and artificialities of the model.

For use in the model, the probabilities in the Proactive and Reactive Matrices given earlier are translated into spans of random numbers, so that one can make a probability choice by drawing from a table of random numbers. For example, take the probabilities for what happens next following an act in Category 1 in the Proactive Matrix. The probabilities add to 1.000. Random numbers 001 to ’000 are taken to represent this range. The probability that the output act will be in Category 1 is zero on the table, so no random number span is assigned. The probability that the output will be in Category 2 is .068, so the span of random numbers from 001 to 068 is taken to represent this probability. The probability of an output in Category 3 is .091, so the span of random numbers from 069 to 159 is taken to represent this probability, and so on.

## *Model $T_5$*

The first two elements of the model are the two act-to-act matrices, represented in terms of random numbers, as explained:

*The Matrix of Proactive Tendencies*
(See Table 2)
*The Matrix of Reactive Tendencies*
(See Table 3)

The next two elements of the model are two tables which represent, not the *tendencies*, as above, but the *opportunities* arising out of the status order, and modified by a "learning" process, as explained in the Rules of Order.

### *The Table of Proactive Opportunities*

This table contains a set of probabilities, one for each man, adding to 1. Initially each man's probability is $\frac{1}{N}$, where N = number of members in the group. However, Man 1 is designated for purposes of this model as "Leader," and he is given special treatment as indicated later. In the event a man's probability is to be increased, as under Step 8 in the Rules of Order, a suitable operator is applied which increases the probability of the given man and decreases the probability of each of the others, with the probabilities still adding to 1 after the operation.

Practically, the change will be accomplished in this Model $T_5$ by the following crude method. A set of numbered tags will be used, the numbers indicating the identification numbers of the members. Initially an equal number of tags (say 10) will be put in a hat for each man. When a probability choice is to be made, a tag will be drawn, and then returned. When a man's probability is to be increased, a single tag bearing his number will be added to those already in the hat.

Mathematically, this is a very awkward operator. However, with the present mechanical method the operation is very easily performed.

## *The Table of Reactive Opportunities*

This table contains a set of probabilities, one for each man, adding to 1. Each man's probability will be set at $\frac{1}{N}$, where N = number of members in the group. These probabilities are not changed.

Practically, the probabilities will be represented by the assignment of an appropriate span of random numbers to each man, and the choices will be made from a random number table.

Following is the Table to be used for a six man group:

| RANDOM NUMBERS: | | MAN DESIGNATED: |
|---|---|---|
| 001–167 | = | 1 |
| 168–333 | = | 2 |
| 334–500 | = | 3 |
| 501–667 | = | 4 |
| 668–833 | = | 5 |
| 834–1000 | = | 6 |

## *Rules of Order for $T_5$*

### PROACTION

1. A man is chosen from the table of *Proactive* Opportunities (it may be any man) and the Process goes to Step 2.
2. The quality of the man's proaction is chosen by probabilities from his Matrix of Proactive Tendencies, from the row of the preceding input act * and the Process goes to Step 3.

(* Note: If there was no preceding act—that is, if the present act is the first of the run—the present act is arbitrarily chosen as an act in Category 6.)

3. The proaction is delivered to a given target as follows:
   a. If the man *just received a Positive Reaction* (or if his present act is the first of a run) the present act is delivered to the *group as a whole*, and the Process goes to Step 4.
   b. If the man has *just given a Positive Reaction*, and he is now continuing, the present act is now delivered to the *group as a whole*, and the Process goes to Step 4.
   c. If the man has *just given an Attempted Answer, a Question, or a Negative Reaction to a specific individual or to the group as a whole*, the present act is now delivered to the same target, and the Process goes to Step 4.

CHOICE OF PROACTION OR REACTION

4. The number of a man is drawn by probabilities from the Table of *Proactive* Opportunities, and a decision is made as follows:
   a. If the number of the man is that of the man who *just spoke*,* he is allowed to *continue Proaction* and the Process returns to Step 2.
   (* Note: If the group as a whole delivered the last act (as in Category 2) any man drawn may be considered as having just spoken.)
   b. However, if the number is *different* from that of the man who just spoke, he is now required to *stop speaking* and another man is chosen to *continue with a Reaction*, as the Process goes on to Step 5.

REACTION

5. The man who just spoke is *excluded* from the *Table of Reactive Opportunities* and a *different* man is chosen from this Table by probabilities. The Process then goes to Step 6.

6. The quality of the man's Reaction is chosen from his Matrix of Reactive Tendencies, from the row of the preceding input act, and the Process goes to Step 7.

7. The reaction is delivered to a given target as follows:
   a. The act is delivered *to the man who just spoke*, and (unless the exception under "b" applies) the Process goes to Step 8.
   b. If the act under "a" is an act in Category 2 (Tension Release) each other man in the group is allowed to deliver an act in Category 2 to the same man, (but the receiver of these laughs does not deliver such an act to himself). The Process then goes on to Step 8.

REWARD AND PUNISHMENT

8. Depending upon the quality of the act, and who receives it, the Table of Proactive Opportunities may be changed as follows:
   a. If the "*Leader*' receives the act, *regardless of its quality*, he is "re-

warded" by an increase in his probability of speaking again in the Table of Proactive Opportunities, and the Process goes to Step 4.

b. If any other member receives the act, a change may be made or not, as follows:
   1. If he receives a *Positive Reaction*, he is rewarded, as above, and the Process goes to Step 4.
   2. If he receives a *Negative Reaction*, he is punished by a decrease in his probability of speaking again in the Table of Proactive Opportunities, and the Process goes to Step 4.
   3. If he receives a *Question or an Attempted Answer*, no change is made, and the Process goes to Step 4.

This particular model has not been in existence long enough at the point of this writing to provide data which might be presented. However, it includes one feature which previous models did not contain—the fact that one person is designated in the very beginning as "Leader." It also assumes that there will be no change in leadership, and indeed, that the equilibrium problems of role organization, once roles get specialized, are much simpler than we know them in fact to be. Some of these problems will be discussed later.

The "Leader" is rewarded by an increase in probability of speaking *each* time he speaks, regardless of the response. All other men are rewarded when they receive a positive response, and punished by a decrease in probability when they receive a negative response. All men are started equal, but with say 10 tokens each, so that one punishment does not extinguish the probability of speaking again.

The "rationalization" of the model, so far as it goes, is this: Any model generally similar to this one, so far as I can see, will only produce the aforementioned radical discontinuity between the top man and the others if the top man is somehow singled out for distinctive treatment. Otherwise he can not get so far ahead as he actually does. Of course the probabilities of speaking could be set on an empirical basis, but this would defeat the purpose of the model, except as a device for obtaining sampling distributions. It is hoped that there is some set of assumptions which will regulate the process in such a way that the empirical gradients will appear as an equilibrium state of the system. The problem is to discover some such set of assumptions.

One possible procedure is to employ further matrices which members use in speaking to the top man. This would involve constructing such matrices so that the probability of the top man receiving agreement (rather than disagreement) is enhanced, or even set to the point where disagreement is not received. However, empirically we know that the top man *does* receive disagreement—in fact he receives, absolutely, more than any other member, just as he receives absolutely more agreement. His ratio of agreement to disagreement may, however, be somewhat higher than other members.

This will come about automatically, however, I think, for the rest of the members on the gradient, if not the leader, by the working of the model. That is, a man obtains the opportunity to go ahead by receiving agreement. Those who go ahead will have higher totals of amounts given out—or vice versa, those who are found with higher amounts given out will also be found to have received more agreement, since that is the mechanism by which they got ahead. All will be held down by disagreement however, to some extent, with the exception of the top man. He will receive the full probability of agreement in the model, whereas the others will all have been held down.

The reward of the top man each time he speaks can be given some rationalization in various ways. One can assume that the leader is the man who is speaking as the expression of a self-consistent set of norms, and is internally rewarded by the "knowledge that he is right," no matter what response comes from others. For the same reason, he can receive disagreement and antagonism without abandoning his self-initiating and self-rewarding tendencies. If his status is the highest in the group, and he is the source of authority, it is as if he "can do no wrong" and disagreements from other members are taken simply as signals that they are confused, in error, or deviant. It is then the leader's job to "remain steadfast," and to correct the deviance by his own consistent attitude and administration of rewards and punishments. So long as his status is the highest in the group, his positive and negative responses function as rewards and punishments to the other members, but not vice-versa.

The original sources of such a position might be assumed to be various. They might proceed from some initial positive affective reactions of the members to the leader. The leader in this case is the major target of positive affect in the group—the "sociometric star." They might proceed from the identification of the leader with a set of norms or a coherent symbol system, where both the leader and the members identify with the symbol system and the leader is identified by the members as the "true spokesman and interpreter" of the symbol system. Both of these sources would involve a kind of "generalization" of response. In the first case affective responses of liking are organized by generalization so that the leader is persistently "liked" in spite of variability of his behavior. In the second case affective responses of evaluation and of agreement with verbal or symbolic propositions are generalized in such a way that new propositions appropriately linked with (or "deduced from") the existing symbol set are also felt to compel agreement.

There is a third case, perhaps, where one might say that whatever will tend to "insulate" a given man from the ordinary influences men have on each other by reward and punishment will tend to produce an

"Archimedean Point" for change and readjustment of the system around the unyielding and stable element. The psychotic or semi-psychotic personality, or the rigidly neurotic one can thus be seen to answer the formal requirements perhaps as well as the former cases. By extension one might say that if one wishes to move a system as a leader, he must be able to "take it"—i.e., take disagreement and antagonism, without reacting in the usual way. The refusal of the therapist to assume a full reciprocity of relation with the patient is a case that is formally similar, in this "immovable" quality. The therapist often differs from other leaders and influencers of behavior, however, in that he takes a "passive" immovable role rather than an "active" one, as in the case of the charismatic leader.

The preliminary character of this speculation is obvious. In fact, it clearly overlooks the complications introduced by the fact that the role of "Leader" in the sense of the man with "the best ideas" or who "does most to guide the discussion" tends *not* to be the sociometric star, as will appear later in this paper. This model, $T_5$, is simply not complicated enough to handle this problem. Perhaps it will suggest, however, the way in which an effort toward more formal models can play a part in clarifying the assumptions involved in the type of equilibrium theory toward which we are aiming, and give some inkling as to how they may be handled formally as they get too complicated for intuitive grasp.

## PHASE MOVEMENT AND THE PROBLEM OF EQUILIBRIUM

Changes in quality of activity as groups move through time in attempting to solve their problems may be called phase patterns. The pattern of phases differs in detail under different conditions. However, these changes in quality seem to be subject to system-influences which produce similarities from group to group. An increase of task-oriented activities in the early parts of a meeting, that is, Questions and Attempted Answers, seems to constitute a disturbance of a system equilibrium which is later redressed by an increase in social-emotional activities, that is, both Positive and Negative Reactions.

Part of our observations prior to the development of the standard diagnostic task were kept by time sequence. Each available meeting was divided into three equal parts, and the amount of each type of activity in each part of each meeting was determined. The meetings were divided into two kinds: those which were dealing with full-fledged problems (essentially problems of analysis and planning with the goal of group decision as described for the standard diagnostic task), and those dealing with more truncated or specialized types of problems. Those groups dealing with full-fledged problems tended to show a typical phase movement through the meeting: the process tended to move qualitatively from a *relative* emphasis on attempts to solve problems of *orientation* ("what is it") to attempts to solve problems of *evaluation* ("how do we feel about it") and subsequently to attempts to solve problems of *control* ("what shall we do about it"). Concurrent with these transitions, the relative frequencies of both *negative reactions* (disagreement, tension, and antagonism), and *positive reactions* (agreement, tension release, and showing solidarity), tend

CHART I

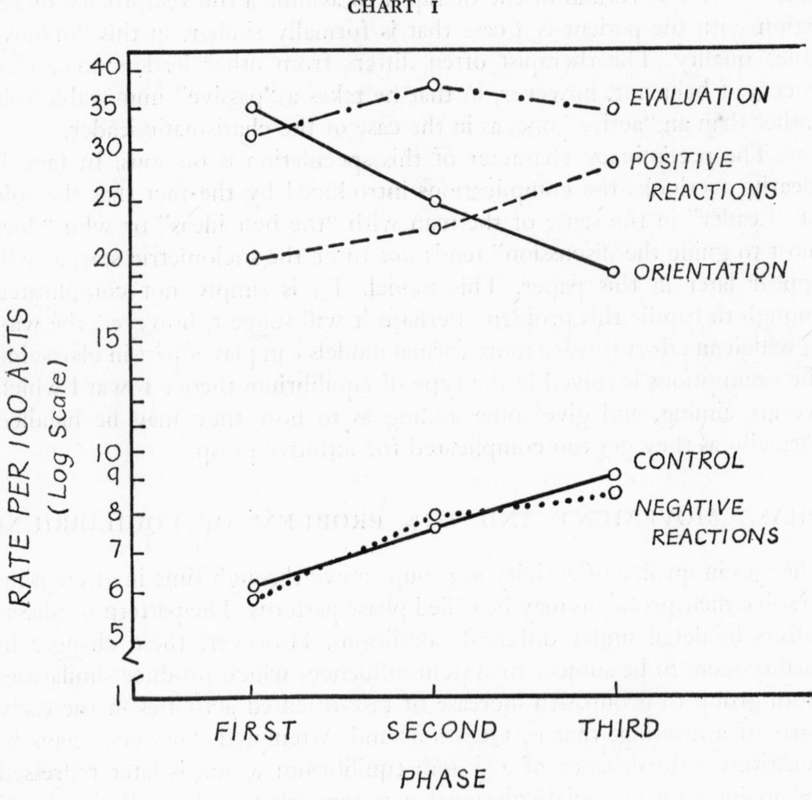


to increase. Chart I presents the summary data for all group sessions examined in the phase study.

The underlying theory as to why the phase movement just described is characteristic of full-fledged conditions is again a system-equilibrium rationale. An individual may be cognitively oriented to a situation and speak of it to others in cognitive terms without committing himself, or the other when he agrees, either to evaluation of it, or an attempt to control it. But in speaking to the other in evaluative terms he attempts to commit both himself and the other to some assumed previous orientation, and further, if he suggests a way to control the situation by joint cooperative action, he assumes both previous orientation and evaluation. When the problems of arriving at a common orientation and evaluation of the situation have not been substantially solved by the group members, attempts at control will meet with resistance on the part of the others and frustration on the part of the person attempting to exercise the control. Probably generally, unless there are contrary cultural, personality, or group organizational factors, the interacting persons tend to avoid or retreat from this frustration-producing type of interaction by "back-tracking" toward orientation and evaluative analysis until the prior problems are solved.

In addition to their task problems, the members of any cooperating group have problems of their social and emotional relationships to each other to solve and keep solved. Efforts to solve problems of orientation, evaluation, and control as involved in the task tend to lead to differentiation of the roles of the participants, both as to the functions they perform and their gross amounts of participation. Some major features of this differentiation have already been described in the presentation of findings about the matrix. Both qualitative and quantitative types of differentiation tend to carry status implications which may threaten or disturb the existing order or balance of status relations among members. Disagreement and an attempt to change existing ideas and values instrumentally may be necessary in the effort to solve the task problem but may lead, nevertheless, to personalized anxieties or antagonisms and impair the basic solidarity of the group.

This impairment, or the threat of it, we may assume, tends to grow more marked as the group passes from emphasis on the less demanding and more easily resolved problems of cognitive orientation on to problems of evaluation, and still more acute as it passes on to its heaviest emphasis on problems of control. It will be recalled that this notion appeared earlier in the examination of act-to-act tendencies. This assumption seems to be a more generalized way of stating the findings of certain other studies. For example, Lippitt (9) found negative reactions to autocratic control or leadership in boys' clubs under certain conditions, while Rogers (12) and his associates tend to find a minimization of negative reactions on the part of clients when the counselor confines himself to nondirective (or, in our categories, orienting rather than evaluating or controlling) types of activity. The present assumption may be regarded as a generalization of this connection between degree of control and negative reactions, so that it is viewed as applying to different points in the process of the same group, not simply to differences between groups. Thus, a series of changes in the social-emotional relationships of the members tend to be set in motion by pressures arising initially from the demands of the external task or outer situation. These social-emotional problems tend to be expressed in overt interaction as they grow more acute—hence the increasing rate of negative reactions.

However, at the extreme end of the final period, assuming that the members' attempts at control over the outer situation and over each other are successful and a final decision is reached, the rates in Categories 1, 2, and 3 also rise to their peak. In other words, one might expect the successfully recovering group to confirm its agreement and to release the tensions built up in its prior task-efforts, repairing the damage done to its state of consensus and social integration. We note joking and laughter so frequently at the end of meetings that they might almost be taken as a signal that the group has completed what it considers to be a task effort, and is ready for disbandment or a new problem. This last-minute activity completes a cycle of operations involving a successful solution both of the task problems and social-emotional problems confronting the group. The apparent incongruity of predicting a peak for both negative and positive reactions in the third phase is thus explained. Negative reactions tend to give way to positive reactions in the final part of the crudely defined third phase.

## CHANGES IN ROLE STRUCTURE AND THE EQUILIBRIUM PROBLEM

We now consider a series of role changes which take place on "the next rung up" the ladder of microscopic-to-macroscopic contexts in which the general theory of action systems can be applied. Changes in quality of act from one act to the next are on a very microscopic level as to time span involved. Changes in rates of acts of various types through the course of a single meeting are on a more macroscopic level. As we have seen, very much the same sort of general system theory can be applied to both, with proper allowance for changes in conditions which will surely be characteristic of any shift up or down on the microscopic-macroscopic ladder. We now proceed up another rung of the ladder to consider changes that take place from meeting to meeting in a time span of four meetings. And for the present analysis, we shift from a primary emphasis on consideration of interaction rates to a consideration of more "generalized" or partially "structured" roles as reflected in post-meeting ratings and choices of members by each other. Much more detailed treatment of changes within the four meeting time span, using interaction rates as well as post-meeting measures will be given in later publications.

The essential rationale for the ratings and choices we ask members to make at the end of meetings is rooted back in the four types of system problems, the "dimensions" along which system change takes place—the instrumental, adaptive, integrative, and expressive. For present purposes we link the instrumental and adaptive dimensions together to obtain one "pole" of specialization: the instrumental-adaptive pole. On the other side we link the integrative and expressive dimensions together to obtain the integrative-expressive pole.

Toward the instrumental-adaptive pole we distinguish two types of roles: The first is a role emphasizing specifically task-oriented achievement addressed to the problems of the external situation confronting the group. In terms of the type of task we give our groups, this role appears to be fairly well defined operationally by answers to the question: "Who contributed the best ideas for solving the problem? Please rank the members in order. . . . Include yourself." The second type of instrumental-adaptive role we distinguish is one which emphasizes regulation or management of the group process in the service of task oriented achievement—a role approximating that of "chairman" or perhaps in a more general sense that of "executive," (as contrasted with that of "technical specialist" which is the first type of role above). We attempt to get at the second type of role by the question: "Who did the most to guide the discussion and keep it moving effectively? Please rank the members in order. . . . Include yourself."

Toward the integrative-expressive pole we also distinguish two subtypes of roles, but this time according to a "positive-negative" distinction rather than according to an "external-internal" distinction as above. The questions we ask here are fairly orthodox sociometric choice questions—essentially "Who do you like in rank order" and "Who do you dislike in rank order," although we ask them in a somewhat more complicated way that would take unnecessarily long to describe here. Detailed description of scoring methods will also be omitted—by inverting ranks it is possible to obtain high scores for top ranking men and low scores for low ranking men. This is done for greater intuitive ease in grasping the meaning of the data. I shall refer to high ranking men as "receiving the most votes," sacrificing accuracy a bit to convenience.

Now, according to the line of thought embodied in the sample statistical model for reproducing the matrix, and its "rationalization," one might make the following sorts of inferences: Since a man may receive agreement for advancing ideas which appeal to other members, or for making neutral suggestions with procedural content rather than task content, or simply because people like him emotionally, and since agreement tends to encourage a man to go ahead and talk more, we might suppose that such men would tend to have high rates of participation. Conversely, since disagreement tends to discourage a man from talking, and since disagreement is often a manifestation of dislike, we might suppose that dislikes would tend to center around men with low rates of participation. And since the model makes no assumptions about the incompatibilities of these various roles (excepting the incompatibility of Liking and Disliking) we might suppose that the same man—"The Leader"—might receive the most votes on all three roles—Best Ideas, Guidance, and Best Liked, and that another man—"The Scapegoat"—at the bottom of the heap might receive the fewest votes on all three of these virtuous roles, but the most on Dislikes. The simplest assumption is that the votes on each of these roles will grade according to Basic Initiating Rank—the rank on total amounts of participation given out. Such a group we might call a "simply organized group," meaning that no matter what criterion of status were chosen, it would place the men in the same rank order of relative status. Now those who are acutely aware of the lack of such perfect integration of various criteria of status in larger social systems will be likely to suspect that small groups will not be so "simply organized" either. Nevertheless, we had evidence of some appreciable degree of positive correlation of these various status criteria with Basic Initiating Rank, and the hypothesis of the "simply organized group" was adopted as a working hypothesis for the first ordering and examination of the data.

Our first major insight with regard to what we now regard as a basic problem of role structure was obtained from a tabulation of data from twelve meetings of five-man groups (twelve instead of sixteen because of absences in four meetings). No distinction was made as to which meetings in the series of four were represented. The identity of men was not preserved from meeting to meeting. We simply took each meeting, listed the men in rank order of total amounts of participation given out, and recorded "the number of votes received" on each role. Then the data for all rank one men on total acts initiated were pooled, and so for all rank two men, and so on for the five. The fact that Joe Smith might have been rank one man in the first meeting, rank two man in the second, and so on, was ignored. The data are represented in Chart 2.

First it may be noted that there is a general gradation of votes on Best Ideas and Guidance by Basic Initiating Rank as expected by the working hypothesis. Second, note that these two curves are very close together and move in the same way, indicating the relative lack of segregation of these roles from each other. But there is a departure from the prediction of the working hypothesis: on both curves the second man is unaccountably low.

But a more serious departure from the prediction is in terms of the curve on Likes. There the top man is unaccountably low, and the second man is highest in the group—by an insignificant margin, but still enough to give birth to the idea: can there be any connection between the fact that the second man, who is unaccountably low on Best Ideas and Guidance, is also Best Liked? Can it be that he is avoiding too heavy participation in the instrumental-adaptive area? Can it be that the man who is participating most heavily and is receiving the most votes on Best Ideas and Guidance is provoking dislikes and losing likes? Here we note the Dislike curve. Contrary to the prediction of the working hypothesis, the top man receives *most* Dislikes, and they grade down by rank—until we come to the bottom man, and here the curve shows an upturn. The upturn is consistent with the scapegoat hypothesis.[1] Looking again at the Like curve, we note that although the second man is receiving more likes than the top man, actually both are depressed in terms of an expectation of an evenly graded curve. The new hypothesis is strengthened: there must be something about high participation and specialization in the technical and executive directions which tends to provoke hostility.

CHART 2

"Total Number of Votes Received" on each of four roles, pooled for men of each basic initiating rank as of each meeting. (Data from twelve assorted meetings of four five-man groups.)

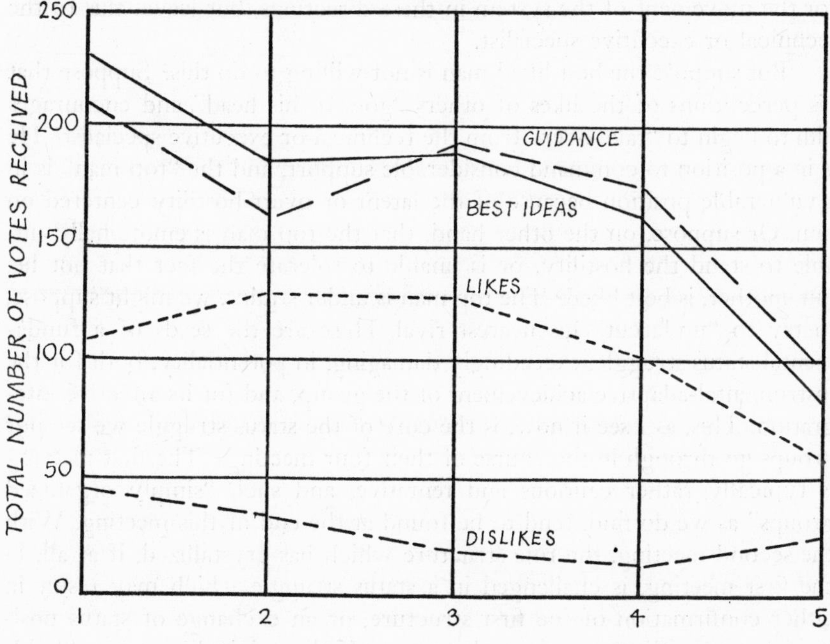


Here I think it can be seen that we are dealing with the same equilibrium problem encountered before in attempting to understand the uniformities of the profile, the matrix, and the phase movement. Movement in the instrumental-adaptive direction tends to upset the equilibrium of the system, and recovery mechanisms must be worked out if the system is to turn full cycle and regain equilibrium. The more "directive" and "constricting" the quality of activity, the more likely it is to arouse negative reactions. If a man begins to specialize noticeably in this direction, the

[1] Similar curves are found in 3 and 4-man groups. The 6-man groups introduce a special complication at a level of subtlety which is inappropriate to these preliminary generalizations.

negative reactions tend to be centered on him. The displacement of hostilities on a scapegoat at the bottom of the status structure is one mechanism, apparently, by which the ambivalent attitudes toward the instrumental-adaptive specialist—the "top man"—can be diverted and drained off. The centering of positive affect on a secondary man is another mechanism by which the solidarity of the group—its integration as a collectivity of persons—can be re-established. Such a man can be warm, receptive, responsive, and rewarding, can "conciliate" and "bind up the wounds," without diverting the movement of the system too far from the kind of movement in the instrumental-adaptive direction which is also felt to be necessary. He can do this because he does not assume the "responsibility" for the movement of the system in these directions, but leaves this to the technical or executive specialist.

But suppose the best liked man is not willing to do this? Suppose that his perceptions of the likes of others "goes to his head" and encourages him to begin to "take over" from the technical or executive specialist? He is in a position to command considerable support, and the "top man" is in a vulnerable position because of the latent or overt hostility centered on him. Or suppose, on the other hand, that the top man is emotionally unable to stand the hostility, or is unable to tolerate the fact that not he, but another, is best liked? The top man is under strains, we might suppose, to try to "undercut" his nearest rival. Here are the seeds of a fundamental status struggle, exceedingly damaging, in potentiality, both for the instrumental-adaptive achievement of the group, and for its affective integration. This, as I see it now, is the core of the status struggle we see our groups go through in the course of their four meetings. The first meeting is typically rather cautious and tentative, and such "simply organized groups" as we do find, tend to be found at the end of this meeting. With the second meeting, the role structure which has crystallized, if at all, in the first meeting, is challenged in a status struggle which may result in either confirmation of the first structure, or an exchange of status positions between the top two or three men. If the original structure "holds up," the group may begin to "level out," and the status struggle slacks off. If a new man comes to the top, the *new* structure is challenged in the third meeting. Some groups apparently arrive at a fairly stable differentiated structure, others never do. Things go "from bad to worse," with a last meeting that breaks records for disagreement, antagonism, tension, perhaps tension release, and other signs of serious strains and an inability to achieve an equilibrated role structure. However, the stable structure is never, in our data, a "simply organized" one. It is rather one in which differentiated roles have appeared, in which one specialist "undoes" the disturbance to equilibrium created by another, and in turn is dependent upon another to remove the strains he himself creates—the total constellation of specialists being one which allows or aids the system to establish a full orbit in its dimensions of necessary movement.

Furthermore, there are probably "typical" solutions which tend to be found with considerable frequency, and may in older and more permanent types of groups, give rise to cultural arrangements and supporting symbol constellations including explicit ritual. Three constellations which are exceedingly ubiquitous, in a cross-cultural sense, come to mind as possibly significant in this connection. They are incest taboos, totem taboos and rituals, and scapegoat patterns. In the experimental small-group setting, of course, nothing concretely resembling these exceedingly complicated and elaborate cultural complexes appears, but certain functional equivalents may be possible.

There is some reason to believe that one possible arrangement by which the status struggle between the top instrumental-adaptive leader and the best liked man can be prevented or stabilized is the formation of a kind of "coalition" between them, such that the two tacitly agree, as it were, not to undercut each other, which is to say, not to be "seduced" into attempting to form a coalition with lower status members in order to displace each other. If such a coalition can be formed, it becomes quite difficult for lower status members to revolt, unseat the top men, or develop the norms of the group in any different direction.

Does this bear any resemblance, in functional terms, to the incest taboo as a cognate mechanism in the nuclear family? Is the incest taboo, at least in certain of its aspects, a kind of coalition between the father (in some family systems comparable to the senior technical and executive specialist) and the mother (similarly often the first major target of positive affect)? Such a coalition could be a powerful mechanism for forcing the socialization of the child, by putting him in a position where he must accept the authority and values of the father in order to obtain gratification, rather than allowing him to retain and overdevelop an affectively gratifying relation to the mother which would leave him insufficient incentive to acquire the skills, values, and other characteristics of the adult role. It may well be, I think, that the ubiquity of the incest taboo as it applies in the nuclear family, is simply another case of the much more general equilibrium problem.

Similarly with totem taboos and rituals. This is not the place for an adequate attempt to examine the problem, but the killing of the totem on certain ritual occasions is certainly suggestive of a ritual display of aggression against the principal authority figures, and the eating of the totem can be viewed as an "undoing"—a reacceptance of the target of aggression after all. In some cases, as Frazier documents at length, the king himself is killed—the king becomes the scapegoat. In many other cases, as we know, some low status person or group is victimized. These facts are well known, and on one level, fairly well understood. The only new emphasis here, if any, is the suggestion that these patterns, culturally elaborated and various in form, can be viewed as particular cases of mechanisms relevant to the much more general problem of equilibrium, which has cognates on every level, from the most microscopic to the most macroscopic.

## REFERENCES


1. Bales, R. F. A set of categories for the analysis of small group interaction. *Amer. sociol. Rev.*, 1950, 15, 257–263.
2. Bales, R. F. *Interaction process analysis: A method for the study of small groups.* Cambridge, Mass.: Addison-Wesley, 1950.
3. Bales, R. F. Some statistical problems of small group research. *J. Amer. statist. Assn.*, 1951, 46, 311–322.
4. Bales, R. F., & Strodtbeck, F. L. Phases in group problem solving. *J. abnorm. soc. Psychol.*, 1951, 46, 485–495.
5. Bales, R. F., Strodtbeck, F. L., Mills, T. M., & Roseborough, Mary E. Channels of communication in small groups. *Amer. sociol. Rev.*, 1951, 16, 461–468.
6. Bass, B. H. An analysis of leaderless group discussion. *J. appl. Psychol.*, 1949, 33, 527–533.
7. Festinger, L., & Thibaut, J. Interpersonal communication in small groups. In L. Festinger, et al., *Theory and experiment in social communication.* Ann Arbor: Research Center for Group Dynamics, Univer. of Michigan, 1950. Pp. 37–49.
8. Keller, J. B. Comment on "Channels of communication in small groups." *Amer. sociol. Rev.*, 1951, 16, 842–843.
9. Lippitt, R. An experimental study of authoritarian and democratic group atmospheres. *Stud. Topolog. Vector Psychol., Univer. Ia. Stud. Child Welf.*, 1950, 16, No. 1.
10. Murray, H. A. Toward a classification of interactions. In T. Parsons, & E. A. Shils (Eds.), *Toward a general theory of action.* Cambridge, Mass.: Harvard Univer. Press, 1951. Pp. 434–464.
11. Norfleet, Barbara. Interpersonal relations and group productivity. *J. soc. Issues*, 1948, 4 (2), 66–69.
12. Rogers, C. R. Counselling and psychotherapy: New concepts in practice. Boston: Houghton Mifflin, 1942.
13. Strodtbeck, F. L. Husband-wife interaction over revealed differences. *Amer. sociol. Rev.*, 1951, 16, 468–473.

# *Task and Interaction Process: Some Characteristics of Therapeutic Group Discussion*

GEORGE A. TALLAND

BALES' (1) *interaction process analysis* furnishes a valuable technique for analyzing and also for constructing models of small group functioning. Records based on problem-solving discussions in the laboratory have suggested to Bales (2) certain significant empirical uniformities in group interaction which, for heuristic purposes, he treats as a closed system. To the extent that such situational variables as membership composition, motivation, expectancies, task set and conditions of performance differ from those in the laboratory debate, predictions can be made about the areas and directions in which the process of interaction will deviate from Bales' model in other types of group discussion.

Psychotherapy groups, for instance, differ from experimental problem-solving groups in several clearly marked respects. They meet in order to discover problems rather than to solve one neatly formulated for their attention; they neither have to reach a solution nor must they finally close a case unresolved at the end of a meeting. Insofar as the psychotherapeutic technique stresses spontaneity, the discussion is allowed a free course, wheras in the laboratory its trend is implicitly determined by the task even in the absence of directive chairmanship. Finally, discussing a hypothetical or didactic case and a transient acquaintance do not lead to deep emotional involvements that occur when patients grapple with their own

ABRIDGED from *Journal of Abnormal and Social Psychology*, 1955, 50, 105–109. Reprinted by permission of the author and the American Psychological Association, Inc.

The author wishes to express his appreciation of the valuable help and constructive criticism he received from Dr. R. F. Bales of Harvard University in this research which was carried out at the University of London Institute of Psychiatry, Maudsley Hospital.

and each other's personal problems, baring their inmost thoughts and experiences week after week in intimate fellowship. Consequently the process of interaction would be expected to differ in the two situations, and more particularly in such dynamic aspects of the model as the phase sequence of acts indicated by and the equilibrium properties of the interaction system inferred from observations made in laboratory debates.

By analyzing the proportionate shares within the total interaction of acts registered as informative, evaluative or control, Bales and Strodtbeck (3) traced a consistent shift of emphasis in the course of a typical problem-solving discussion. Dividing meetings into three phases, orientation reached its peak in the first, evaluation in the second, control in the third. Since these groups are instructed to reach some solution by the end of a meeting and since each member enters with some piece of information on the case, which he may believe to be different from and complementary to his fellow members' information, the phase sequence is logically indicated. In therapy groups the pressure of time is much milder and the problems, so far from being clearly formulated at the outset, are expected to emerge as the discussion proceeds; the meeting, however, is unlikely to conclude with a solution or control of these problems. The probability of the problem solving phase sequence occurring here is therefore, no higher than that of any other or of no phase sequence whatever.

Bales' (2) other dynamic principle of the interaction process conceives of the group discussion as progressing by cycles, each of which begins with the introduction and ends with the resolution of a disturbance. His empirical findings closely correspond to the theoretical model which, here again, is logically dictated by the situation. If problem-solving groups are to succeed within the time available for discussion, they must indeed proceed in this manner; they cannot leave unresolved a conflict over a relevant issue and they cannot well afford to discuss irrelevances. In problem-solving debates the aim is to resolve a disturbance initially introduced by the experimenter; in therapy groups the very purpose of the discussion is to maintain disturbance at a level throughout, and to bring it back to that level if it has flagged. The patient must talk or listen to talk about disturbing personal problems; in order to benefit by group therapy he must be emotionally involved in it. If, as it periodically happens, the discussion drops below the required degree of affective involvement and consequent disturbance, the therapist regards this event as a manifestation of resistance, and not as a state of equilibrium to be maintained. In these groups therefore, the sequel to an initial act is not necessarily nor preferably an equilibrating response. Disturbances are introduced all the time to provide the groups with tasks and are generated spontaneously through personal interaction. Therapy groups are not unique in this respect; many political, committee or board meetings start with little more than a formal agenda, and would soon peter out if some disturbance were not introduced into them by personal interaction, or do come to a premature end for the lack of it.

## SUBJECTS: PROCEDURE

As part of a research on psychotherapy groups, interaction process analysis was applied to four groups, of 6 to 8 members excluding the therapist, during the first eight weeks of therapy. Observations made over a total of 18 meetings, each lasting 90 minutes, were analyzed for the purposes of the present report. The groups met once weekly at the Maudsley Hospital, London, and were conducted by psychiatrists according to the principles of *group analytic psychotherapy* (4, 6). Their members were outpatients suffering from psychoneuroses; they were between 23 and 45 years of age, of high average or higher intelligence, the men in most instances clerical workers, the women with few exceptions not occupied outside their homes.

Records of interaction were kept according to Bales' (1) method, but only of verbal acts. Although all observations were made while the meeting was in progress, those registering tension and tension release were not thought to be sufficiently reliable, and these categories were therefore entirely omitted. The very scarce antagonistic acts were bracketed with disagreements. For the analysis of phase sequences the interaction records were divided into three equal time sections, each representing a thirty minute phase of a meeting. In the final analysis the corresponding phases of the 18 meetings were summated, as were the records of entire meetings, according to a classification of acts (3) into orientation, evaluation, control, positive and negative reactions, and further also attempted answers and questions. Each of these categories was tested for the presence of a consistent phase sequence by chi square, using frequency data.[1] The null hypothesis was formulated in two versions: (a) that in a given category the absolute frequencies of acts vary from phase to phase only within the limits of chance; (b) that the phase to phase variation of frequencies expressed as proportions of the total acts per phase, is within the limits of chance at the one per cent level of confidence. It was thought necessary to apply the test in both these versions, because the meetings were divided into phases by the clock and not by parcelling out the total of acts into three equal shares.

The prediction that in psychotherapy groups discussion does not tend

1 Bales and Strodtbeck (3) used rankings of phases in preference to frequency values, and tested goodness of fit to prediction by the number of transpositions required. This method may give undue importance to numerically small differences, and moreover in the final analysis allows equal weight to all the categories, however small or large their share in the total interaction. In the present study this method would have had the additional disadvantage of providing no information beyond the finding that one particular phase sequence does not apply.

towards equilibrium was tested by fitting the category profile based on observed data to that of Bales' theoretical model.

## RESULTS

Average frequencies of acts per phase in therapy groups are given in Table 1 according to the combined categories used by Bales and Strodtbeck.

It is quite apparent that positive reactions, attempted answers and questions keep on a level throughout, and indeed the observed frequencies fit an equal threefold division more closely than could happen by chance once in a hundred instances, testing either version of the null hypothesis.

TABLE 1

*Phase Movement of Categories*

| | MEAN FREQUENCIES PER PHASE | | |
|---|---|---|---|
| | I | II | III |
| Positive reactions | 15.56 | 16.89 | 15.33 |
| Control (suggestions) | 6.44 | 10.72 | 8.33 |
| Evaluation (opinions) | 45.11 | 54.73 | 59.50 |
| Orientation | 170.46 | 159.68 | 159.57 |
| Negative reactions | 3.56 | 5.50 | 5.78 |
| Attempted answers | 199.79 | 203.12 | 204.95 |
| Questions | 22.22 | 22.00 | 22.45 |

The upward trend of negative reactions and the steep rise of control acts from the first to the second phase, followed by a partial relapse, deviate significantly from a distribution of equal frequencies, once again testing either statement of the null hypothesis. The steady increase of opinions and the initial decline of orientation to a level maintained through the second and third phases, are significantly different as deviations from the null hypothesis, in form (a) at the 2 per cent, in form (b) at the 1 per cent level of confidence.

Although trends indicated by distributions of frequencies summated over 18 meetings are of some interest, much significance should not be attached to these results. They are not typical of single meetings in the sense of being modal. Indeed, the meeting to meeting variability is so high that, even choosing the criterion of ranking phases, not a single occasion could be shown as exemplifying the phase pattern typical of the summated records in each of the categories. Bales and Strodtbeck's method of counting the transpositions required to bring rankings of phases on actual frequencies in line with the norm, necessitates at least three steps in every instance. Since the norm derived from the summated data allows for a maximum of two transpositions in one category (orientation) and three each in another three categories, each of the 18 meetings observed deviates in its phase pattern from the norm to an extent which is beyond chance, even at the five per cent level of confidence.

Whilst the theory of phase movement was derived from the analysis of actual sequences, the equilibrium principles of group interaction are based on hypothetical sequential patterns. Bales' (2) theoretical model assumes that, in a group which maintains equilibrium, half the total acts are

TABLE 2

*Category Profiles*

| CATEGORIES | PERCENTAGE RATES OF ACTS | | | | | |
|---|---|---|---|---|---|---|
| | THEORETICAL * EQUILIBRIUM | | LABORATORY GROUPS | | THERAPY GROUPS | |
| | | REACT. | | REACT. | | REACT. |
| Showing solidarity | 3.8 | | 3.42 | | 2.0 | |
| Showing tension-release | 7.7 | | 5.97 | | — | |
| Agreement | 15.2 | | 16.54 | | 4.8 | |
| | | 26.7 | | 25.93 | | 6.8 |
| Giving suggestion | 7.6 | | 7.94 | | 3.5 | |
| Giving opinion | 30.4 | | 30.06 | | 20.2 | |
| Giving orientation | 15.3 | | 17.89 | | 59.2 | |
| | | 6.7 | | 6.97 | | 8.5 |
| Asking for orientation | 3.8 | | 3.53 | | 5.5 | |
| Asking for opinion | 1.9 | | 2.39 | | 2.3 | |
| Asking for suggestion | 1.0 | | 1.05 | | 0.7 | |
| | | 6.7 | | 6.97 | | 8.5 |
| Disagreement | 7.6 | | 7.78 | | 1.8 | |
| Showing tension | 3.8 | | 2.66 | | — | |
| Showing antagonism | 1.9 | | .73 | | — | |
| | | 13.3 | | 10.67 | | 1.8 |
| Total | 100.0 | | 99.96 | | 100.0 | |
| | | 53.4 | | 50.54 | | 25.6 |

* The theoretical values postulated for interaction tending towards equilibrium and the percentage rates of categories in problem-solving groups are based on records as yet unpublished by Dr. Bales. The latter represents averages of 96 meetings, each lasting 40 minutes.

reactive, and half of these in turn close a cycle while the remaining half start new cycles. Empirical data are so interpreted as to class all positive and negative reactions by definition as reactive, and the former also as closing a cycle. Questions and an equal number of attempted answers, i.e., those given in direct reply to questions, are also regarded as reactive. Taking this principle of classification, the category profile observed in Bales' laboratory groups closely fits the model; that characteristic of therapy group discussion, however, does not. The two category profiles expressed in percentage rates are compared in Table 2.

The most striking difference between the two profiles is the overwhelmingly large share taken up by orientational acts in therapy groups. This finding is, of course, entirely in agreement with the nature of the task this group performs, and has in itself no decisive bearing on the problem of equilibrium. Taking all the acts which according to Bales' model are reactive, the total amounts to little over a quarter of the entire interaction. The omission of nonverbal acts may account for some of the discrepancy between the profiles of the two types of group, though this would not alter the balance in favor of new disturbances as against equilibrating responses, since in psychotherapeutic discussion acts indicating tension outweigh those of tension-release. Interaction analysis thus confirms the theoretical argument that termination of disturbance occurs far less frequently in therapy than in problem-solving groups. Whether we accept the value of 6.8 as the percentage of positive reactions, or correct it for the omission of records of tension-release, it falls far below a quarter of total interaction. It is also worth noting that most acts of solidarity are expressions of identification and are typically followed (in 69 per cent of all instances) by acts of orientation, i.e., some elaboration of the information on which identification is based, and would therefore carry on the disturbance or start a new one. Also 41 per cent of all agreements are followed by negative responses, questions or opinions, and cannot therefore be considered as acts resolving a disturbance. In fact, analysing actual sequences of acts, it appears that only 61 per cent of all positive reactions, i.e., 3¼ per cent of the total interaction and about half the opinions, i.e., those followed by positive responses or orientation, are likely to close a cycle. This would allow for little over 13 per cent of the total as acts terminating a disturbance.

## SUMMARY

The weekly discussions of four therapy groups were recorded by the method of *interaction process analysis.* It was predicted that, though structuring similar to that found in problem-solving groups would take place, the dynamic pattern of the process would be characteristically different in these groups, in accordance with their different task and conditions of discussion. More particularly, the research tested the hypotheses that (*1*) the control-oriented phase sequence of interaction does not apply to therapeutic group discussion, and (*2*) there is no tendency to establish equilibrium in successive cycles.

Analysis of quantified records confirms the predictions that in therapy groups there is no consistent progress from orientation through evaluation to control within single meetings, and that there is a tendency to keep disturbance at a certain level.

## REFERENCES

1. Bales, R. F. *Interaction process analysis: a method for the study of small groups.* Cambridge, Mass.: Addison-Wesley Press, 1950.
2. Bales, R. F. The equilibrium problem in small groups. In T. Parsons, R. F. Bales, &

E. A. Shils, *Working papers in the theory of action.* Glencoe, Ill.: The Free Press, 1953. Pp. 111–161.

3. Bales, R. F., & Strodtbeck, F. L. Phases in group problem solving. *J abnorm. soc. Psychol.*, 1951, 46, 485–495.
4. Foulkes, S. H. *Introduction to group-analytic psychotherapy*. London: Wm. Heinemann Medical Books, 1948.
5. Talland, G. A. The working system of psychotherapy groups. *Group Psychother.*, 1954, 7, 67–80.
6. Taylor, F. K. The therapeutic factors in group-analytical treatment. *J. ment. Sci.*, 1950, 96, 967–997.

# CHAPTER 9 ROLE DIFFERENTIATION

# *Husband-Wife Interaction over Revealed Differences*

FRED L. STRODTBECK

IN THE course of a series of pilot studies of power, or influence, in small group situations a procedure has been developed, called the revealed difference technique, which has shown promise in a first application to husband-wife interaction. In the attempt to validate the results obtained by this technique, use has been made of similar groups in different cultures. The following paper is organized in a form to emphasize how this methodological innovation and the technique itself grew from successive sequences in which pilot findings led to further research operations.

### BACKGROUND

During 1948–49 a series of groups were observed engaged in decision-making. An effort was made to determine some of the correlates of dif-

FROM *American Sociological Review*, 1951, 16, 468–473. Reprinted by permission of the author and publisher.

Data for this paper were collected under the auspices of the Comparative Study of Values Project being conducted by the Social Relations Laboratory, Harvard University, with the assistance of the Rockefeller Foundation and the Peabody Museum.

ferential ability to persuade others in accordance with the actor's desires. In one instance, four mathematics students were requested to recommend jointly the best of three possible solutions to particular problems. While these students were in the process of developing consensus they were asked to record privately the alternative they personally favored. Thus, the experimenter was provided with a continuous means of relating a type of private opinion to public behavior. The experimentation indicated that the ultimate decision could be most accurately predicted by simply weighting the privately pre-determined opinion of each participant by the total time he had spoken during the experimental interaction. This finding was duplicated in various groups who worked at the task of jointly selecting the best move in a chess problem. This simple answer did little, however, to recapture the subtlety and complexity of social interaction as it is generally understood.

We recognized that we had up to this time worked with *ad hoc* groups which had no group structure at the beginning of the observation period and no expectation of participating with one another at a later time. The problems they had considered were delimited and specific; the nature of their arguments and responses was highly structured. On the basis of this analysis, we were led to consider experimentation with groups whose members approached the opposite extreme of broad common interests, daily contact, and permanence—so-called primary groups.

Among the various types of primary groups that might profitably be studied, husband-wife dyads were selected because of the ease of replication of these units. Each couple was asked to pick three reference families with whom they were well acquainted. The husband and wife were then separated and requested to designate which of the three reference families most satisfactorily fulfilled a series of 26 conditions such as: Which family has the happiest children? Which family is the most religious? Which family is most ambitious? After both husband and wife had individually marked their choices they were requested to reconcile their differences and indicate a final "best" choice from the standpoint of their family. For the first ten couples studied, this pooling took place with the experimenter out of the room and under conditions such that the couple did not know they were being observed or having their voices recorded. Their lack of knowledge of the observation was ascertained after the session, at which time their permission to use the material in a scientific inquiry was obtained.[1] The anticipated experimental difficulties—(a) producing "polite" interaction because of the intrusion of the experimenter, and (b) structuring the task to such a degree that the mode of interaction would be highly determined—were judged to have been satisfactorily avoided.

1 Ursula Marsh, Donald Michael, Theodore M. Mills, and Herbert Shepard were joint participants in this phase of the research.

Omitting, for present purposes, a discussion of the content of the recorded protocols, it was found that women won 47 of the contested decisions and men, 36. In six of the eight cases in which there was a difference both in number of decisions-won and in talking-time, the spouse who talked most won the majority of the decisions. At this time there was no basis for appraising whether the women had won slightly more decisions because they had known more about the types of information under discussion, or whether the decision winning represented, as we had hoped, the operation of structured power relations in an area in which both participants were equally informed. The observed margin by which the women exceeded the men was not significant—a result which might have been much more valuable if we had predicted it in terms of independent knowledge of the equalitarian characteristics of the married veteran couples used in the sample. In short, further application was necessary to determine whether the technique was a valid method of indicating in any more general sense the balance of power between participants.

A field study was designed to throw further light on this problem. Three communities were selected which presumably differed in terms of the degree to which the wife was favored by the cultural phrasing of power. The communities were at the same time sufficiently small to increase greatly the probability that both spouses would be adequately, if not equally, informed concerning the behavior of the reference couples. The technique as described above was applied to ten couples from each of these cultures. It was proposed that the conformity of the experimental results with the a priori cultural expectations be taken as a crude measure of the validity with which the technique reflected power differences.

## DESCRIPTION OF CULTURES

The cultures which were selected for study are geographically adjacent communities in the Arizona–New Mexico area. Briefly described, the groups are Navaho Indians; dry farmers from Texas who have recently homesteaded in the area; and early settlers who utilize a dam operated under the supervision of the Mormon church. These communities will be described in detail in forthcoming publications of the Comparative Study of Values Project.[2] For present purposes the communities will be designated Navaho, Texan, and Mormon. A brief recapitulation of power attributes of the culturally legitimized role of women in each culture is presented below.

The young Navaho man, who marries a girl from a moderately successful family, typically leaves his own family and resides with the girl's

2 Clyde Kluckhohn gives a brief description of the Navaho studies which are now considered a part of this project in the introduction to *Gregorio, the Hand Trembler* (5).

family and works under her father's direction until he has established himself as a responsible person. When this change of residence is made, the man leaves his sheep with his own family of orientation and his work activities result in little immediate increase in his own holdings. The children are considered a part of the wife's consanguine group, and marriages are generally unstable. Both men and women own sheep, but the women do the processing of wool into rugs and blankets. This assures the women a regular income throughout the year. The man has greater earning power when he performs wage work, but the wage work opportunities are scarce and seasonal. The man is considered the head of the household, but the relative economic independence of the wife and her close integration with her own consanguine group effectively limit his exercise of power. All but one of the ten Navaho couples studied maintained Navaho religious practices, the one exception was a recent convert to a fundamentalist church now proselytizing in the area.

The Texan group is composed of migrants who came from Eastern Texas during the drought and depression of the early 1930's. With minor exceptions the households are farms on contiguous sections headed by persons who as young adults made the earlier move, or by their older children who have more recently married. Due to the short growing season and lack of rainfall, the cultivation of pinto beans has developed into the major cash crop. The ten couples who participated in this study were members of the ranking Presbyterian clique in the community.[3]

The ten couples selected for study in the Mormon village were chosen from the most active participants in the affairs of the local church. Religious teachings which exercise a pervasive effect upon local social organization specifically stress the role of the husband as the head of the family. The position of the church is stated in different ways in quotations similar to the following:

> There must be a presiding authority in the family. The father is the head, or president, or spokesman of the family. This arrangement is of divine origin. It also conforms to the physical and physiological laws under which humanity lives. A home, as viewed by the Church, is composed of a family group, so organized as to be presided over by the father, under the authority and in the spirit of the priesthood conferred upon him (8, p. 81).
>
> This patriarchal order has its divine spirit and purpose, and those who disregard it under one pretext or another are out of harmony with the spirit of God's laws as they are ordained for recognition in the home. It is not merely a question of who is perhaps best qualified. Neither is it wholly a question of who is living the most worthy life. It is a question largely of law and order, and its importance is seen often from the fact that authority remains and is respected long after a man is really unworthy to exercise it (7, p. 359).

3 A forthcoming publication by Evon Z. Vogt will describe the social organization of this community in detail.

Corresponding prescriptions for the wife's role emphasize that she should above all else be a mother, for "motherhood is the noblest, most soul-satisfying of all earthly experiences." Mormonism has a this-worldly orientation, divine grace is attained through effort, and the symbol of progress is the advancement the man makes in the priesthood and in extending his flocks and fields. The woman is not eligible for membership in the priesthood and her status is coupled with that of her husband both in her present life and in the next, by the regular Temple marriage. From the incomplete evidence now available, Mormon women of this community do not appear to have important land-holdings nor independent sources of income, and accounts of women's participation in church activities confirm the correspondence of women's current attitudes with the church writings quoted above. The historic emphasis by Brigham Young and others on woman's education and political participation was always hedged by the general reservation that motherhood should not be interfered with—the women of the community in question strongly emphasize this reservation.

In Navaho mythology and folklore the actions imputed to women contrast sharply with the emphasis of Mormon theology. For the Navaho the women become major charismatic figures.[4] Marriage customs are also consistent with this conception of the Navaho woman as an active and demanding person. On the morning after a Navaho wedding the groom runs a foot race with his bride. The cultural interpretation is that "the one who wins will become rich" (6, p. 141). This practice is quite different from the familiar custom in which the bride is passively carried over the threshold, and it is also a commentary on the independence of the economic fortunes of Navaho marriage-mates.

In summary, the favored position of the Navaho woman in contrast to the Mormon woman was judged in terms of economic, religious, and kinship considerations to be quite unequivocal. Between Texan and Mormon women there is less difference, but in terms of holding church office and the present possession of productive land and semi-professional jobs, the women in the Texan community appear to be more favored than the Mormon women. On the basis of this analysis it was predicted that Navaho women would win the highest percentage of the decisions and the Mormon women the smallest.

4 These include Changing Woman, Spider Woman and Salt Woman. Blessing Way, the most frequently repeated ceremonial, stresses that each of the four poles of the hogan represent still different female divinities. Kluckhohn and Leighton comment that this practice "speaks volumes for the high place of women in the traditional conceptions" (4, p. 56).

## EXPERIMENTAL PROCEDURE

The area under study had no electrification, and since it was impractical to attempt to bring the subjects to an observation room, the field sessions of the experimental procedure were recorded by portable sound equipment powered from a truck. Although the subjects were separated from the experimenter and other persons, they knew that their voices were being recorded. The task was explained to the Navahos by an interpreter. An appropriate picture was presented for each question and underneath the illustration there were pockets representing the three reference couples. The Navaho would place his marker in the pocket which represented the couple of his choice. In those instances in which there had been a difference between the choice of the man and wife, the illustration was presented again to the two of them with their markers in separate pockets. They were requested to combine their markers in the position which best represented their joint opinion. Some questions were changed somewhat by translation into Navaho; for example, the question, "Which family is the most religious?" became "Which family follows the 'Navaho Way' best?" It was not felt that these changes would significantly modify the results here presented. These recordings were transcribed and, in the case of the Navaho, translated into English.

TABLE 1

*Decisions Won, by Spouse and Culture*

| CULTURE | NUMBER OF COUPLES | DECISIONS WON BY: HUSBAND | WIFE |
|---|---|---|---|
| Navaho | 10 | 34 | 46 |
| Texan | 10 | 39 | 33 |
| Mormon | 10 | 42 | 29 |

The written protocols were analyzed to determine the number of acts used by each participant and the distribution of these acts in terms of interaction process categories.[5] This information plus knowledge of the number of decisions won by each participant provides the basis for the analysis presented below.

## FINDINGS

We present in Table 1 the sum of the decisions won by the husbands and wives in each of the three cultures. The appropriate null hypothesis is compounded of two elements: (a) the proposition that the Mormon

5 For a description of the categories used see Bales, (1).

wives win an equal or greater number of decisions than their husbands (p=.007); and (b) the proposition that Navaho husbands win an equal or greater number of decisions than their wives (p=.16). Since the combined probability associated with these two propositions is less than .01, we reject the null hypothesis and conclude that we were able to predict the balance of decision-winning from our study of the comparative social and cultural organization of the groups from which our sample was drawn.

Having to this limited degree established the validity of the technique, we are encouraged to inquire further into elements of behavior in the small group situation which are linked with decision-winning. Our earlier experience had indicated a very strong relationship between decision-winning, or leadership, and talking-time in *ad hoc* groups of four persons.[6] In the present instance two-person primary groups are involved. From a broader study of the rank characteristics of participants in groups ranging in size from two to ten persons it is known that differentiation in speaking-time in two-person groups is relatively less than it is in larger groups, hence it is probable that the relation between speaking-time and decision-winning is less clearly defined in two-person than in larger groups (2). There was no compelling rationale for predicting the effects of the primary relationships upon "speaking and decision-winning." By combining the ten cases observed at Cambridge with the thirty cases from the field and eliminating the six cases in which the decisions were split evenly, we obtain the thirty-four cases compared in Table 2. The null hypothesis of independence between talking most and winning may be rejected at the .05 but not the .01 level.

TABLE 2

*Decisions Won and Talking-Time for 34 Married Couples*

| SPOUSE WHO TALKED MOST | SPOUSE WHO WON MOST: HUSBAND | WIFE |
|---|---|---|
| Husband | 14 | 5 |
| Wife | 5 | 10 |

To approach a more systematic description of the interaction characteristics of the spouse who talks most, we have selected the 24 cases in which there was a significant difference between the number of acts originated by the husband and the wife. We find that the most talking spouse tended more frequently to *ask questions*, carry out *opinion and analysis*, and make *rewarding remarks*. As Simmel suggested, in a dyad there can be no coalitions—the speaker does not have alternative audiences, so the

6 Bass reports a correlation of .93 between the time a participant in an eight-man group spent talking and the votes he received from observers for having demonstrated leadership (3).

"threat of withdrawal" is generally a more compelling adjustmental device in two-person than in larger groups. While we do not as yet have norms by group size for category usage on a common task, the unexpected finding in the present study that the most active participant is significantly high in question-asking gives us further insight into how withdrawal is anticipated and prevented. The finding that the frequency of opinion and analysis acts is higher for the most talking person is in agreement with Bales' notion that acts of this type have a central generative function which results in their being heavily represented in the profile of the most talking person in groups of any size.

The categories which discriminate the profile of the least talking participants are, in order of magnitude, the following: simple *acts of agreement*, *aggressive acts* designed to deflate the other actor's status, and simple *disagreements*. Taken together, these characteristics suggest the passive agreeing person who from time to time becomes frustrated and aggresses.

Concerning cultural differences in category usage, the Navahos gave *opinion*, *evaluation*, and *analysis* acts during the solution of their differences only one-half as frequently as the Mormon and the Texan group. As a result they required on the average fewer acts per decision (8 in contrast with 30 for the other groups) and the reasoning and persuasion in their protocols seemed extremely sketchy. They did not emphasize the arguments that might bear upon the issue, they tended to reiterate their choices and implore the other person to "go with them;" "go together," or simply consent. This is in marked contrast with the other couples who appeared to feel that they had to give a reasoned argument to show that they were logically convinced, even when they were giving in to the other person. It is a matter for further research to determine if other "traditional" people show a similar tendency to minimize analysis in social problem solving.

For the Texans it was a rational exercise, sometimes directly commented upon, to see that the decisions came out even, the standard deviation between spouses in decisions won was only 1.3. The Mormons were less concerned with equality, the comparable figure is 2.1, and among the Navaho there were marked differences between spouses, the standard deviation being 5.1.

## SUMMARY

The essence of the revealed difference technique here described consists of: (a) requesting subjects who have shared experiences to make individual evaluations of them; and then, (b) requesting the subjects to reconcile any differences in interpretations which may have occurred. It has been shown that the disposition of these reconciled decisions is related both to power elements in the larger social and cultural organization and amount of participation in the small group situation. It is believed that other couples as well as parent-child, foreman-worker, and similar relationships may be profitably studied with the technique, since it appears not only to reveal the balance of power, but also to produce a sample of interaction in which modes and techniques of influence can be studied by methods of content and process analysis.

## REFERENCES

1. Bales, R. F. The analysis of small group interaction. *Amer. sociol. Rev.*, 1950, 15, 257–264.
2. Bales, R. F., Strodtbeck, F. L., Mills, T. M., & Roseborough, Mary E. Channels of communication in small groups. *Amer. sociol. Rev.*, 1951, 16, 461–468.
3. Bass, B. M. An analysis of leaderless group discussion. *J. appl. Psychol.*, 1949, 33, 527–533.
4. Kluckhohn, & Leighton. *The Navaho.* Cambridge, Mass.: Harvard Univer. Press, 1947.
5. Leighton, A. H., & Leighton, D. C. *Gregorio, the hand trembler.* Papers to the Peabody Museum, Cambridge, Mass., 1949.
6. Reichard, Gladys A. *Social life of the Navaho Indians.* New York: Columbia Univer. Press, 1928.
7. Smith, J. F. *Gospel doctrine.* Salt Lake City, 1929.
8. Widtsoe, J. A. *Priesthood and church government.* Salt Lake City, 1939.

# *The Family as a Three-Person Group*

FRED L. STRODTBECK

AT DIFFERENT centers and in different disciplines small group research has grown at a rapid rate during the past five years. The limited empirical character of most of these studies has enabled their authors to attain what for students of social behavior is an enviable level of rigor, but a central question remains: How far may we generalize these results? The objective of the present paper is to test the appropriateness of certain propositions concerning ad hoc three-person groups by the use of father, mother and adolescent son subject groups. Insofar as our work is carefully done, our results should contribute to the understanding of the extent to which propositions concerning ad hoc three-person groups may be extended to family groups, and to a more limited degree, to other groups with prior common experience and expectations of continued relations.

Our procedure for obtaining a sample discussion between a father, mother, and adolescent son was, very briefly, as follows: Each family is visited at home. We explain that we are interested in the way a family considers questions which relate to the son's selection of his occupation. To help the family recall specific topics which they may have previously

FROM *American Sociological Review*, 1954, 19, 23–29. Reprinted by permission of the author and publisher.

This report was prepared as part of the project, "Cultural Factors in Talent Development" supported by the Social Science Research Council from funds granted to it by the John and Mary R. Markle Foundation for research on the early identification of talented persons.

Bernard C. Rosen, Florence Sultan, George Psathas, and Leslie L. Clark are appreciatively acknowledged as project members and Ann Dennison, Bob Ellis and William Vosburg for their assistance in the collection and analysis of these data. Yale University, where this work was conducted, actively supported every phase of the project and this assistance is also gratefully acknowledged.

With regard to this particular paper, the author is indebted to T. M. Mills for a most constructive criticism of the first draft.

discussed, we ask the father, mother and son to check independently one of two alternatives to 47 items of the following type: [1]

(a) A teen-agers' hobby club plans to enter their models in a state-wide contest. Some of the boys want to put the models up under the club's name and win honor for the club as a whole. Others want to put the models up under each boy's name so that each can gain individual honor. Which plan should they adopt?

(b) Two fathers were discussing their boys, one of whom was a brilliant student and the other an athlete of great promise. In general, some people feel one father was more fortunate and some the other. Do you think the father with the *athletic* son or the father with the *studious* son was most fortunate?

(c) Some people believe that a father should be prepared to speak to a son as a father and direct the son's behavior so long as the son lives, others believe the son should be accepted as completely independent of his father's direction after 18 or 21. Which would you tend to agree to with regard to a boy in his late 20's?

While our introductory remarks are being made in the home, we request permission to set up our portable tape recorder. After the 47 item questionnaire has been checked, we have the family fill out still another similar questionnaire so that we will have time to sort through their responses. We select three items which represent a potential coalition of the type in which the mother and father have taken one alternative and the son another; three with mother-son paired against the father; and three with father-son paired against the mother. We then present the family successively with these nine disagreements rotating the isolate role. They are asked to talk the question over, understand why each person chose the alternative he did, and, if possible, select one alternative which best represents the thinking of the family as a whole. While this discussion takes place, the experimenter withdraws to another room, operates the controls on the sound equipment, and tries to keep any other member of the family from overhearing or interrupting the interaction. During May and June of 1953 we obtained 48 cases in this manner.

Concerning the selection of the 48 cases, three criteria were considered: ethnicity, the families were predominantly second generation (the son, third) divided equally between Jews and Italians; socioeconomic status (SES), equal numbers of high, medium and low; and the son's achievement, half of the boys were underachieving in school and half were overachieving as determined by a comparison of grades and intelligence test performance. By sampling from a frame of more than a thousand 14 to 16 year old boys in New Haven public and parochial schools it was possible to work out a factorial design of the following type:

1 These items have in large part been adapted from questions originated by the Social Mobility Seminar at Harvard, conducted by Samuel A. Stouffer, Talcott Parsons and Florence R. Kluckhohn.

| SES | JEWS | | ITALIANS | |
|---|---|---|---|---|
| | OVER | UNDER | OVER | UNDER |
| High | 4 | 4 | 4 | 4 |
| Medium | 4 | 4 | 4 | 4 |
| Low | 4 | 4 | 4 | 4 |
| | | | TOTAL | 48 |

The recordings averaged about 40 minutes in length. The interaction analysis consisted of breaking the on-going discussion into units, or acts; identifying the originator and target of each act; and assigning each act to one of Bales' 12 categories which are identified in our discussion of the index of supportiveness below (1).

One primary objective of the present paper is to compare our results with those of Mills who, working with student volunteers, asked them to create from three pictures a single dramatic story upon which all agreed (8). The comparison requires that we utilize jointly the information concerning the originator and target of each act, as well as the category in which it is placed, to form an index which reflects the tendency of a particular actor, number 1, to give positive responses to the attempts at problem solution by another actor, number 2. The following steps are involved in arriving at the index of supportiveness:

(a) Sum together the acts in the following categories which have been originated by person number 1 and directed to number 2:

1. SHOWS SOLIDARITY, raises other's status, gives help, reward
2. SHOWS TENSION RELEASE, jokes, laughs, shows satisfaction
3. AGREES, shows passive acceptance, understands, concurs, compiles

(b) Subtract from the above sum the number of acts originated by number 1 and directed to number 2 in these categories to form the numerator of the index:

10. DISAGREES, shows passive rejection, formality, withholds help
11. SHOWS TENSION, asks for help, withdraws "Out of Field"
12. SHOWS ANTAGONISM, deflates other's status, defends or asserts self

(c) Divide the above numerator by the number of acts originated by number 2 in the following categories:

4. GIVES SUGGESTION, direction, implying autonomy for other
5. GIVES OPINION, evaluation, analysis, expresses feeling, wish
6. GIVES ORIENTATION, information, repeats, clarifies, confirms
7. ASKS FOR ORIENTATION, information, repetition, confirmation
8. ASKS FOR OPINION, evaluation, analysis, expression of feeling
9. ASKS FOR SUGGESTION, direction, possible ways of action

(d) The result, multiplied by 100, is $I_{12}$, the index of support of person 1 of person 2. Between three persons, six index values are produced. To simplify our reference to this set of values we organize it in a matrix, placing the person with the largest number of acts originated in the first row and column and the person with the least number of acts originated in the last row and column. To illustrate this convention see Table 1. To form Table 1 we have taken the median of the corresponding cells for the 48 discussions in each of the six positions. In parenthesis we show the value Mills obtained when he carried out these steps for his 48 groups.

Mills makes the following observation with regard to Simmel's having anticipated the pattern of support which Mills found: [2]

"The highest rates of support are those exchanged between the two more active members and the rates are very nearly the same . . . All other distributions of rates are significantly different from these two. This is to say that, as far as exchange of support is concerned, the relationship between these two members is sharply differentiated from the other relationships. The results for this sample confirm Simmel's observation. The two more active members form the pair and the least active member is the relatively isolated third party."

TABLE 1

*Median Index of Support, Families Compared with Ad Hoc Student Groups* *

| RANK OF INITIATOR | RANK OF RECIPIENT | | |
|---|---|---|---|
| | 1ST | 2ND | 3RD |
| 1st | | −6 (12) | −5 (7) |
| 2nd | −5 (11) | | −5 (7) |
| 3rd | 3 (4) | −2 (2) | |

* Mills' values for ad hoc student groups are given in parenthesis.

For Mills the 1−2 value is 12 and the 2−1 value is 11, which are higher than the other cell values and similar. In our data the 1−2 value is minus 6 and the 2−1 value is minus 5—these do not differ significantly from the other values. By correlating the sets of medians in particular cells of Table 1, we may compare the relative magnitudes of our values to Mills' without regard for the difference in means. We obtain a rho of −.67. Neither the inspection of the corresponding cells of the two most speaking participants nor the correlation over the whole table can be interpreted as a confirmation of Mills' results on ad hoc groups. Whether the significantly lower mean level of the index of support can be accounted for by the differences in our tasks or by a lesser emphasis on polite behavior on the part of family groups we, of course, can not say.

We are indebted to Mills for the following typology for classifying the individual matrixes. He suggests that we look at the index of support, $I_{12}$ and $I_{21}$. These indices are then compared with the medians for the $I_{12}$ and $I_{21}$ positions, and the experimenter indicates + if the value is above its corresponding median and − if it is below, the following results:

2 Mills and Simmel's thesis treating of the partition of three into two and one is most effectively stated by von Wiese (12, p. 525).

| $I_{12}$ | $I_{21}$ | SUPPORT TYPES |
|---|---|---|
| + | + | solidary |
| + | − | contending |
| − | + | dominant |
| − | − | conflicting |

For our data $I_{12}$ is minus 6 and $I_{21}$ is minus 5.

Mills finds that when the two high ranking participants have a solidary relationship, both the intake and output of support for the low man is lower than in any other circumstances. Our data are not in accord with his finding (see Table 2). The lowest value in any row would have been in

TABLE 2

*Median Index of Support for Cells Involving the Low-Ranking Participant*

| MATRIX CELL | SUPPORT TYPE ++ (17) | +− (8) | −+ (7) | −− (16) |
|---|---|---|---|---|
| 1 to 3 | —05 | 12 | 08 | —11 |
| 2 to 3 | 03 | —10 | —08 | —07 |
| 3 to 1 | 03 | —02 | 08 | 01 |
| 3 to 2 | 00 | 02 | —03 | —05 |

the solidary (++) column if our data had corresponded to Mills' finding. It may be seen that no one of the four cells involved fulfill this requirement.

Mills goes further to say,

"Not only is this determined position of the third party as weak as a power position can be (when the relation between the two principles is solidary) but it is likely that the power interests involved in it are inversely related to the interests of the other member. The stronger the coalition, the weaker the position of the third man, and vice versa."

Unfortunately Mills had no measure of power other than participation. With our data, to form a "power" score, we arbitrarily give two points to each decision. If the isolated person persuades the others he is given two points and they receive none; if he holds them off and no decision is made, he is given one point and the other two get .5 each; if the isolated person is persuaded by the other two, they receive one point each and he receives nothing. Thus, for nine decisions there is a total of 18 points. Under random expectations the mean for each participant would be six.

In our experiment we find that if one attempted to predict power, as measured in this way, from participation he would account for less than three tenths of the variation, though the correlation is significant in the .5

to .6 range. We therefore have attempted to test Mills' statement by comparing the mean power score computed by the system explained above for the first, second and third most-speaking participant for each of the four support types. It may be seen from Table 3 that the low man does not appear to be conspicuously worse off in the solidary (+ +) type. There is no significant gap between his power and that of the man in the second position whereas there is such a gap between the low and middle man in the contending (+ −) and dominant (− +) support types.

In three of the four support types the most-speaking person wins the largest share of the decisions and in all cases the least-speaking person wins

TABLE 3

*Mean Decision-Winning Power by Participation Rank and Support Type*

| RANK | SUPPORT TYPE ++ (17) | +− (8) | −+ (7) | −− (16) |
|---|---|---|---|---|
| 1st | 8.0 * | 6.3 | 8.0 | 8.3 |
| | ... | | ... | ... |
| 2nd | 5.2 | 6.6 | 5.5 | 4.9 |
| | | ... | ... | |
| 3rd | 4.8 | 5.0 | 4.5 | 4.8 |

* The value 8.0 indicates that the most-speaking participants in solidary (+ +) groups won on the average 8.0 of the 18 possible points. The dots in the columns indicate significant gaps.

least. We have found the means for the rank positions within three of the support types to be heterogeneous and the gap between the first and second most-speaking person significant at the .05 level or less.[3] There is a reversal of power scores between the first and second rank position in the contending (+ −) pattern.

One of the observations in Mills' article with broad implications for a theory of group process dealt with the stability of the participation patterns through time. His measure of stability was a comparison of the participation rank in the first third of his sessions with the participation rank in the last third. His conclusions are as follows:

"In summary, there is one pattern where all positions are stable; there is another where all positions are unstable; and in the others, the strongest position is stable while the others fluctuate. The significantly stable pattern is the *solidary* (++) one, which, as we have seen, tends to develop into the fully differentiated, interdependent pattern called the *true coalition.* The significantly unstable one is the *conflict* (−−) pattern which is notable for its lack of interdetermination."

3 For similar findings see Hare (4, 5), Strodtbeck (11), French (3), and, if it may be inferred that an instructor has more power than students, Stephan & Mishler (10).

From this comment and study of other portions of the text it is our guess that Mills would rank the support types: solidary (+ +), contending (+ −) and dominant (− +) tied, and conflict (− −) lowest regarding their implication for participation stability. For our data we have the relative participation for three decisions each with the father, mother and son as isolate—a total of nine. To parallel Mills procedure and stratify the incidence of the isolate role, we sum the first three decisions and compare with the sum of the last three decisions. The father, mother, and son are the isolate once in each group. By considering the rank for the first three decisions as the criterion ranking, we can compare the consistency of participation within the four support types by use of Kendall's S (see Table 4) (7). Corresponding values from Mills' study are given in parentheses.

TABLE 4

*Stability of Rank Between First and Third Phase* *

| REQUIRED VALUES | SUPPORT TYPE + + | + − | − + | − − |
|---|---|---|---|---|
| S | 344 (278) | 62 (62) | 0 (122) | 96 (62) |
| M | 17 (15) | 8 (9) | 7 (11) | 16 (13) |
| $S_{.05}$ | 102 (90) | 48 (54) | - (66) | 90 (78) |
| P(S) | <.05 (<.05) | <.05 (<.05) | >.05 (<.05) | <.05 (>.05) |

* Mills' values for ad hoc groups given in parentheses.

In this instance our findings partially correspond to Mills'. Our most stable group is the solidary (+ +), but our least stable is not the conflicting (− −). The dominant (− +) has less stability than the conflicting, but since there are only seven cases this apparent reversal of order must remain in doubt.

Mills includes in his paper certain observations on the temporal shifts of support patterns. He finds that the solidary (+ +) patterns in the first phase tend to persist into the third whereas other patterns more frequently shift toward solidarity (+ +) or conflicting (− −). Mills refers to these two latter patterns as *terminal* patterns. Unfortunately our data were not tabulated so that this comparison could be made at a modest cost. We do note however that one might infer from Mills' comments that primary groups with a much longer period in which to stabilize their interaction would tend to be more concentrated in the (+ +) and (− −) categories. While our distribution of cases is in line with this expectation,

| | |
|---|---|
| + + | 17 (15) |
| − − | 16 (13) |
| + − | 8 (9) |
| − + | 7 (11) |

the observed differences are not statistically significant.

## DISCUSSION

Any given hour of face to face interaction can be categorized in many different ways. Even a simple system such as Bales', which extracts only a small portion of the available information, results in units which can be recombined to form a number of measures or indices. The net effect of this latitude in analysis is to provide a very large set of potential hypotheses which may be tested. Since this is the case, special precautions must be taken against errors of the first kind—the rejection of the null hypothesis when the hypothesis is in fact true.

To avoid errors of the first type some workers only report relationships which they have demonstrated several times and others report, or write as if they are reporting, only those relationships they have deduced, predicted, or anticipated in advance of the experiment. In the present context Mills has used still a third alternative. He reported his basic operations in detail, he carefully specified the particular characteristics of his group, and he was completely candid in noting that his findings arose from what we have come to call "blind analysis" notwithstanding the fact that they had in part been "adumbrated" by Simmel. Mills' treatment invited comparison, and although we had collected our three-person interaction for a different purpose, comparison was easily made.

The subjects we used were related in a particular and pervasive way—they were a family. There was every reason to believe that after the experimental session was over they would pick up their daily relations very much as they had been in the past. Their actions in the experimental session proceeded on a broad basis of common knowledge and their behavior in the experimental situation could very well have consequences in their interpersonal relations at a later time.

The tendency for a three person group to break into a pair and another party, which was the central theme of Mills' analysis, would seem to run counter to certain expectations we associate with a family. Crudely expressed, parents give succorance to children contingent upon the child's conforming to selected rules of behavior. This elemental aspect of the relationship becomes greatly elaborated. By adolescence one is tempted to believe that a son has moved into a position where his censure of parents may be fully as effective a control mechanism as parents' censure of the son. Competition for sexual favors is regulated by incest proscriptions. The action of one family member in the community is not without implications for other family members. In short, three family members may, in many important ways, reward one another and accept responsibility for one another's well being. No member can easily withdraw from the relationship. From considerations of this order one can form a strong common sense basis for the expectation that the division of the trio into two and one will be attenuated in families in contrast with ad hoc groups and in this way account for the disparity between our data and the expectations based on Mills' findings relative to the distribution of support.

An alternative explanation for the disparity can be based upon the task we've set for our subjects. There were nine specific decisions, each person had three isolated and six coupled coalitions and the group was instructed to try to achieve consensus. This shifting of coalitions would strike at the stability of relations which might have grown if only one task were involved, hence the task also might have caused the departure from Mills' distribution of support findings which we report in Table 1.

The effects of our using a task different from Mills' are not entirely negative. We were enabled by virtue of our decision-winning measure to test a proposition concerning the relative power of the low man in the solidary (+ +) group which had not been tested with equal directness by Mills. It is plausible to believe that the members of the major coalition in a solidary (+ +) family would not pool their power against the low man to the same degree as would an ad hoc group. While the evidence we present is in line with such an expectation, the proposition at issue cannot be firmly established until it has been demonstrated, in accordance with Mills' expectations, that the low ranking participant in ad hoc solidarity (+ +) groups is in fact less powerful than the low ranking member in groups with other support characteristics.

A point of correspondence between Mills' study and the present, which encourages one to believe that it is fruitful to think in terms of a common process underlying both primary and ad hoc group interaction, relates to the stability of the participation ranks. In both studies it is demonstrated that the solidary (+ +) pattern results in the most stable participation ranks. In this manner support type takes its place along with previously published discussions of the phase hypothesis (2), status struggle (6), and equilibrium problem (9, pp. 111–163), as one of a series of more or less cumulative increments in our understanding of factors which influence participation stability.

In conclusion, we have attempted to assess the appropriateness for families of propositions derived from the study of ad hoc three-person groups. We do not find in families the regularities in the distribution of support which Mills' reported, nor do we confirm the tendency for solidary high-participating members to dominate the decision-making which Mills anticipated would materialize. We do find in families, like many other groups, decision-making power is associated with high participation. We confirm Mills' finding that when the two most active members are solidary in their relation to one another the stability of their rank participation is high, but we do not find that when the two most active members are in conflict, the stability is as low for families as he found it to be for ad hoc groups.

## REFERENCES

1. Bales, R. F. *Interaction process analysis.* Cambridge, Mass.: Addison-Wesley, 1950.
2. Bales, R. F., & Strodtbeck, F. L. Phases in group problem solving. *J. abnorm. soc. Psychol.*, 1951, 46, 485–495.
3. French, R. L. Verbal output and leadership status in initially leaderless discussion groups. *Amer. Psychologist*, 1950, 5, 310–311.
4. Hare, A. P. Interaction and consensus in different sized groups. *Amer. sociol. Rev.*, 1952, 17, 261–267.
5. Hare, A. P. Small group discussions with participatory and supervisory leadership. *J. abnorm. soc. Psychol.*, 1953, 48, 273–275.
6. Heinicke, C., & Bales, R. F. Developmental trends in the structure of small groups. *Sociometry*, 1953, 16, 7–39.
7. Kendall, M. G. *Rank correlation methods.* London, 1948.
8. Mills, T. M. Power relations in three-person groups. *Amer. sociol. Rev.*, 1953, 18, 351–357.
9. Parsons, T., Bales, R. F., & Shils, E. A. *Working papers in the theory of action.* Glencoe, Ill.: Free Press, 1953.
10. Stephan, F. F., & Mishler, E. G. The distribution of participation in small groups: An exponential approximation. *Amer. sociol. Rev.*, 1952, 17, 598–608.
11. Strodtbeck, F. L. Husband-wife interaction over revealed differences. *Amer. sociol. Rev.*, 1951, 16, 468–473.
12. von Wiese, L. (translated by H. Becker) *Systematic sociology*, 1932.

# *Some Consequences of Power Differences on Decision Making in Permanent and Temporary Three-Man Groups*

E. PAUL TORRANCE

MOST of the sociological and social psychological studies of the consequences of power differences on decision making have been concerned either with communities, large organizations, temporary groups,

FROM *Research Studies, State College of Washington*, 1954, 22, 130–140. Reprinted by permission of the author and publisher.

or artificially created groups without histories of interaction. The present study deals with decision making in permanent groups with uniform, well-established, and clear-cut hierarchical structures. A number of studies suggested that the consequences may be due as much to patterns of behavior developed as a result of interaction as to power itself. For this reason, a second aspect of the study is concerned with a comparison of the decision making behavior of permanent groups with that of similarly constituted temporary groups.

## SUBJECTS

It was found that B-26 combat crews are particularly well suited for the purposes of the study. A B-26 crew is composed of three men: a pilot, a navigator and a gunner. The pilot as the aircraft commander has final authority to make crew decisions regardless of differences in rank. The navigator is a commissioned officer and may even outrank the pilot; he makes many decisions and as a commissioned officer may exercise certain power over the gunner, an enlisted man. He may be overruled by the pilot and in many ways occupies a status inferior to that of the pilot. The gunner is definitely the "low man on the totem pole." He is an enlisted man and has relatively little power over the two officers.

The permanent crews had been together for several months and had reached the final stage of their crew training before entering combat. The temporary groups were drawn from the same type of personnel. They were only regrouped so that no man was on a crew with a member of his regular crew. For each set of three crews, the following pattern was followed in the regrouping.

CREW A: Pilot 1, Navigator 2, Gunner 3
CREW B: Pilot 2, Navigator 3, Gunner 1
CREW C: Pilot 3, Navigator 1, Gunner 2

## EXPERIMENTAL DESIGN

Each of the 62 permanent and 32 temporary crews was administered four decision-making problems varying in nature and difficulty. Both individual and group decisions were required. A crew description and decision making questionnaire were administered the permanent crews. The procedures used in reaching the decisions were also studied, using the Bales categories (1).

The first problem was the Maier Horse-Trading Problem (5):

"A man bought a horse for $60 and sold it for $70. Then he bought it back for $80 and sold it for $90. How much money does he make in the horse trading business?"

Each individual was first asked to write on a slip of paper his solution without conferring with anyone. Crew members were then asked to confer to reach a crew decision.

The second problem required the subjects to estimate the number of dots on a 16″ x 21″ card with 3155 black dots scattered evenly but not geometrically over a white background. The card was exposed for 15 seconds and then each subject was asked to write his individual estimate on a slip of paper. They were then asked to confer to decide upon the best estimate. Finally, each man was asked to write on a slip of paper the number of dots he personally *really* thought there were.

The sketch of the conference group in the Michigan Group Projection Sketches (4) was used in the third problem. The subjects were instructed to write within a five-minute limit a story about the picture. They were asked to write what they thought was going on in the picture, what had been going on, and what the outcome would be. After the individual stories had been collected, the subjects were asked to agree upon and write within a ten-minute limit a crew story about the same sketch.

The fourth problem was a survival situation in which the crew had been downed in enemy territory. After two days, one of the members of the crew had been slowing down the attempts to reach safe territory, estimated to be about 40 miles away. He had developed severe blisters on his feet and felt that he was nearing exhaustion. He does not believe that he can continue and urges the other two men to go ahead without him. The crew was instructed to designate one member to act as the man who insists on giving up, and to make its decision as it would in an actual situation.

After the four decision-making problems, a very brief questionnaire regarding their reactions to the fourth decision-making situation was administered, along with a question concerning their attitude toward being transferred to another crew.

## ANALYSIS OF DATA AND RESULTS

### *Horse-Trading Problem*

Only about three different answers are possible on the Horse-Trading Problem: \$0, \$10, and \$20. If any member of the group has the correct answer, the solution is so simple and obvious that his answer is usually accepted, if it is really considered by the group. This makes it very easy to determine influence and failure to influence. For example, in one crew, the pilot's answer was \$0, the navigator's was \$20 and the gunner's was \$10. The crew correctly decided upon \$20. It may thus be assumed that the navigator influenced the decision. If the crew had decided upon \$0, it might have been assumed that the pilot influenced the crew to accept an incorrect answer while the navigator failed to influence the crew to accept a correct answer.

In the permanent crews, 31 percent of the pilots, 50 percent of the navigators and 29 percent of the gunners had the correct answer. As shown in Table 1, the pilots are most successful and the gunners least successful in influencing the crew to accept their correct solutions. Only 6 percent of the pilots, compared with 20 percent of the navigators and 37 percent of the gunners, failed to influence the crew to accept their solutions when they had the correct answer (differences all significant at the 5 percent level of confidence).

When temporary crews were compared with permanent crews, it is found that the temporary crews had a higher percentage of correct answers than did the permanent crews (78.2 percent against 60.4 percent with the difference significant at the 10 percent level of confidence). Some understanding of the dynamics emerges when failure to influence is analyzed by crew position as shown in Table 1. In the temporary crews, the effects of status differences seems to have been diminished and all members less frequently fail to influence when they have the correct answer (significant at better than the 10 percent level of confidence).

TABLE 1

*Percentage of failures to influence to accept correct answer on horse-trading problem in permanent vs. temporary crews*

| | CREWS | |
|---|---|---|
| | PERMANENT (N = 62) | TEMPORARY (N = 32) |
| Pilots | 6.0 | 0.0 |
| Navigators | 20.0 | 10.5 |
| Gunners | 37.0 | 12.5 |

These findings support the contention of Heinicke and Bales (3) that in groups with a history of development, the opinions and suggestions of high status members tend to be accepted and these individuals no longer have to do much to win their point. It further supports their contention that the high status individual responds favorably most often to members of the group close to him in prestige while suggestions of members of less importance are often passed over.

## *The Dot Test*

Success or failure in influencing the group estimate on the Dot Test is less easy to trace than in the Horse-Trading Problem. It can be traced with reasonable certainty, however. In one crew, the pilot's estimate was 800, the navigator's was 2,000, the gunner's was 8,000 and the crew's was 2,500.

It seems fairly reasonable to argue that the navigator exerted the greatest influence. Following the principle illustrated by this example, the results shown in Table 2 were obtained. There is a tendency for the gunner, the least powerful member of the crew, to exert the least influence on the crew's decision. When he had the best answer, he failed 64 percent of the time to exert a dominant influence, compared with 46 and 50 percent for the navigators and pilots respectively (difference significant at the 10 percent level of confidence). Only 11.3 percent of the gunners as compared with 21 and 14.5 percent of the pilots and navigators respectively influenced the decision when they had poor answers (differences not statistically significant).

TABLE 2

*Consequences of Power Differences on Influence of Crew Decision on Dot Test*

| | PERCENTAGES | |
|---|---|---|
| POSITION | TIMES HAD BEST ANSWER BUT FAILED TO INFLUENCE | TIMES INFLUENCED DECISION WITH POOR ANSWER |
| Pilots | 50.0 | 21.0 |
| Navigators | 46.1 | 14.5 |
| Gunners | 64.0 | 11.3 |

When permanent crews are compared with the temporary crews, essentially the same effect is found.

Evidence presented by the writer in a previous study (6) indicates that a very important aspect of decision making is the degree to which the members accept the decisions made by the crew. Greater acceptance of crew decisions characterized the more effective crews in survival training and in combat. In the present study, a measure of acceptance of the crew's decision was obtained by computing the difference between the crew's estimate and the individual's estimate made after the crew decision. The results in Table 3 show a consistent, though not statistically significant (except in the case of pilots vs. gunners), effect of power differences

TABLE 3

*Mean deviancy scores between crew estimates and individual estimates after the crew decision*

| | CREWS | |
|---|---|---|
| | PERMANENT | TEMPORARY |
| Pilots | 686.20 | 444.63 |
| Navigators | 888.03 | 825.16 |
| Gunners | 1151.90 | 946.93 |
| Crews | 908.71 | 738.91 |

on the degree to which the decision was accepted. These results suggest the possibility that individuals low in status tend to resist accepting the group's decisions, possibly as a consequence of their not participating more fully in the decision-making process and in not having their ideas considered more adequately.

When the acceptance scores of the permanent crews are compared with those of the temporary crews, it is found that essentially the same picture occurs. A consistent, though not statistically significant, trend occurs for the members of temporary crews to accept more fully the crew decisions.

## *Conference Group Story*

Since individuals wrote their stories about the conference group sketch before the crew story, it is possible to develop an index of influence for each person. In each case, the five most salient aspects of each story were identified and then the individual stories were checked for the presence of these same five aspects. If all five aspects are common to the crew and individual stories, a score of "5" was assigned; if four aspects are common, a score of "4" was given, etc. If four or five aspects were common, it was considered that the individual exerted a strong influence on the crew's decision. If three elements were common, the individual was considered to have exerted "some influence." Less than three common aspects was considered as evidence of little or no influence.

The results, shown in Table 4, indicate that the members of permanent crews influenced the crew's decision according to the power structure (differences significant at better than the 5 percent level of confidence).

TABLE 4

*Consequences of Power Differences on Influence on Decision Concerning Story about Conference Group*

| | PERCENTAGES | | |
|---|---|---|---|
| DEGREE OF INFLUENCE | PILOTS | NAVIGATORS | GUNNERS |
| Strong influence | 58.7 | 37.7 | 0 |
| Some influence | 23.4 | 26.9 | 23.2 |
| Little or no influence | 17.0 | 34.6 | 78.6 |

Permanent and temporary crews were compared on the basis of the percentages of those who exerted little or no influence, or failed to influence. Results, presented in Table 5, indicate that the same trend holds in temporary as in permanent crews. A striking fact is that there is a consistent tendency for fewer in all positions to fail to influence the decision (difference for gunners significant at the 5 percent level of confidence).

Differences in perceptions of group functioning as measured by content analyses of the conference stories are too complex to be discussed in this paper, but one aspect of this analysis supports the hypothesis that the low status member of the group does not feel free to disagree and therefore withholds his ideas. Only 46 percent of the gunners, compared with 70 percent of the navigators and 72 percent of the pilots perceive disagreement in the conference group (difference significant at the 5 percent level of confidence). In the temporary groups, the gunners perceived as much disagreement as did the other members of the crew.

TABLE 5

*Percentage of failure to influence conference group story decision in permanent vs. temporary B–26 crews*

| | CREWS | |
|---|---|---|
| | PERMANENT (N = 62) | TEMPORARY (N = 32) |
| Pilots | 17.0 | 9.4 |
| Navigators | 34.6 | 25.0 |
| Gunners | 76.9 | 53.1 |

## *Survival Problem*

In the survival problem, influence was studied through participation analysis and the questionnaire administered after the crew decision. Both amount and type of participation were considered. Amount of participation was computed by adding the number of interactions credited to each individual. The navigators contributed 40.7 percent of the total participations in contrast to 34.1 and 25.2 percent for pilots and gunners respectively (differences significant at the one percent level of confidence).

The interaction seems to be most clearly represented by the percentage in each position who interacted one or more times in each category. The results, presented in Table 6, indicate that certain types of interaction tend to characterize the occupants of each position. From these data, the pilots appear to show more solidarity; do less joking and laughing; give more suggestions, opinions, evaluations, and information; do more asking for suggestions and less withdrawing from the field. The navigators tend to do less agreeing, more disagreeing, less asking for information, and more asking for opinions. The gunners manifest less show of solidarity, do more joking and laughing, offer fewer suggestions and opinions, give less orientation and information, do more asking for orientation and information, do less asking for suggestions, and show more tension and withdrawal from the field.

Responses to the decision-making questionnaire are summarized in Table 7. According to self reports, the pilots and gunners make less effort to influence the crew's decision than the navigators (significant at the one percent level of confidence). Very few of them, however, feel that they influenced the decision greatly (difference in percentages between pilots and navigators significant at the one percent level of confidence). None of

TABLE 6

*Consequences of Status Differences on Participant Roles in Crew Decision in Survival Problem*

| CATEGORY | PERCENTAGE PARTICIPATING IN CATEGORY | | |
|---|---|---|---|
| | PILOTS | NAVIGATORS | GUNNERS |
| 1. SHOWS SOLIDARITY, raises other's status, gives help, reward | 29.6 | 17.2 | 12.0 |
| 2. SHOWS TENSION RELEASE, jokes, laughs, shows satisfaction | 37.0 | 41.4 | 48.0 |
| 3. AGREES, shows passive acceptance, understands, concurs, complies | 48.1 | 44.8 | 48.0 |
| 4. GIVES SUGGESTIONS, directions, implying autonomy for other | 92.5 | 82.7 | 44.0 |
| 5. GIVES OPINION, evaluation, analysis, expresses feeling, wish | 96.3 | 82.7 | 76.0 |
| 6. GIVES ORIENTATION, information, repetition, confirmation | 81.5 | 72.4 | 56.0 |
| 7. ASKS FOR ORIENTATION, information, repetition, confirmation | 25.9 | 20.7 | 40.0 |
| 8. ASKS FOR OPINION, evaluation, analysis, expression of feeling | 33.3 | 44.8 | 24.0 |
| 9. ASKS FOR SUGGESTIONS, direction, possible ways of action | 25.9 | 13.8 | 8.0 |
| 10. DISAGREES, shows passive rejection, formality, withholds help | 25.9 | 41.4 | 24.0 |
| 11. SHOWS TENSION, asks for help, withdraws out of field | 3.7 | 10.3 | 16.0 |
| 12. SHOWS ANTAGONISM, deflates other's status, defends or asserts self | 0.0 | 3.7 | 3.7 |

the gunners felt that they had greatly influenced the decision. Probably as a result, fewer of the gunners and navigators completely agreed with the decision (difference significant at the one percent level of confidence).

The subjects were also asked how they felt about being transferred to another crew. Of the navigators, 28.1 percent, compared with 8.3 of the pilots and 10.5 percent of the gunners, stated that it would not matter greatly if they were transferred (difference between navigators and pilots and gunners combined, significant at the one percent level of confidence). This is another indication of the navigator's relatively poor identification

TABLE 7

*Consequences of Power Differences on Decision-making Behavior According to Individual Declarations*

| ATTITUDE OF BEHAVIOR | PERCENTAGE PILOTS | NAVIGATORS | GUNNERS |
|---|---|---|---|
| Made little effort to influence decision | 43.8 | 28.1 | 55.3 |
| Had most influence on decision | 41.7 | 8.8 | 0.0 |
| Complete agreement with decision | 77.1 | 59.6 | 52.6 |
| Complete satisfaction with decision | 89.6 | 86.0 | 84.2 |

with the crew. The gunners, on the other hand, seem to be better satisfied with their roles, even though they make little effort to influence crew decisions. It might be inferred that their status needs are not as great as those of the navigators.

Unfortunately, the temporary crews cannot be compared with the permanent crews on the aspects just discussed because of incompleteness of data. They can, however, be compared in regard to the characteristics of the decisions submitted. The results of the categorization of decisions, presented in Table 8, indicate that the temporary groups more frequently make sequential decisions which require testing and revision. The meaning of this becomes clearer when it is noted that more of the permanent crews decided to keep the ailing crew member with them in spite of all circumstances. They simply did not even entertain the notion that this might not be possible. Their decisions were therefore presented as final and not needing future revision in harmony with reality events. Of the permanent crews, 93.7 percent manifested much concern for keeping the

TABLE 8

*Comparison of Type of Decision Made in Survival Problem by Permanent vs. Temporary Crews*

| CHARACTERISTIC OF DECISION | PERCENTAGES PERMANENT N = 48 | TEMPORARY N = 32 | *t*-RATIO | LEVEL OF CONFIDENCE |
|---|---|---|---|---|
| Sequential decision | 43.8 | 75.0 | 3.03 | <.01 |
| Decision to keep crew together in spite of everything | 70.8 | 56.2 | 1.33 | <.20 |
| Concern for keeping crew together, if possible | 93.7 | 71.8 | 2.27 | <.05 |
| Administration of first aid (physical) | 50.0 | 31.3 | 1.71 | <.10 |
| Administration of first aid (psychological) | 35.4 | 28.1 | 0.68 | .50 |

crew together, whereas only 71.8 percent of the temporary crews showed such a concern. The permanent crews also tended to mention provision for first aid and attempts to bolster the ailing member's morale. This finding might be accepted in support of Cartwright and Zander's (2, p. 74) hypothesis that willingness to endure pain or frustration for the group is a possible indication of the group's cohesiveness. This, of course, does not answer questions concerning the quality of the decisions. This willingness to endure pain or frustration for the group may in some instances be taken too far and result in blindness to the realities of the situation. This, in fact, is the major reason for difficulties in developing adequate criteria for assessing the quality of the decisions. It is, nonetheless, important to recognize the operation of the phenomena which have just been described.

## SUMMARY

In this paper, an attempt has been made to study some of the consequences of power differences on decision making in permanent groups with well-defined power structures and to compare these effects with those obtained in similarly constituted temporary groups. B-26 combat crews were chosen for study.

Each of 62 permanent crews and 32 temporary crews were administered four decision-making problems of varying nature and difficulty: Horse-Trading Problem, Dot Test, Conference Group Projection Sketch, and a survival problem. Both individual and group decisions were elicited.

An attempt was made to study the "influence" and "failure to influence" of each group member. On all four problems, influence was directly and clearly in accord with the power structure of the group. In general, the effects were somewhat lessened in the temporary crews. On the Horse-Trading Problem, this resulted in a greater percentage of correct crew decisions in the temporary groups. In the Dot Test, evidence was found to indicate that the less powerful members of the crew do not accept the crew's decision as completely as does the more powerful member. The perceptions of the Conference Group Picture suggest that the least powerful member of the group does not feel free to disagree with the more powerful members. Interaction analysis reveals that certain types of interaction tend to characterize occupants of each position. Navigators make more effort to influence the decision but feel that they have little influence on the decision and do not agree with it completely. The gunners make little attempt to influence the decision, recognize the fact that they influence the decision very little, and tend not to accept it completely. In the survival problem, the permanent crews show much concern for keeping the crew together at any sacrifice while the temporary crews are more willing to leave the ailing member behind. The former are also more concerned about giving the ailing member physical and psychological first aid.

Solutions of temporary groups are less absolute and final and provide more frequently for sequential decisions.

## REFERENCES

1. Bales, R. F., & Strodtbeck, F. L. Phases in group problem solving. *J. abnorm. soc. Psychol.*, 1951, 46, 485–495.
2. Cartwright, D., & Zander, A. F. *Group dynamics research and theory*. Evanston, Ill.: Row, Peterson, 1953.
3. Heinicke, C., & Bales, R. F. Developmental trends in the structure of small groups. *Sociometry*, 1953, 16, 7–38.
4. Henry, W. E., & Guetzkow, H. Group projection sketches for the study of small groups. *J. soc. Psychol.*, 1951, 33, 77–102.
5. Maier, N. R. F., & Solem, A. R. The contribution of a discussion leader to the quality of group thinking: The effective use of minority opinions. *Hum. Relat.*, 1952, 5, 277–288.
6. Torrance, E. P. *Crew performance in a test situation as a predictor of field and combat performance.* HFORL Report No. 33. Washington, D.C.: HFORL, Bolling Air Force Base, 1953.

# *Recording and Evaluating the Performance of Individuals as Members of Small Groups*

LAUNOR F. CARTER

THE MANY techniques for assessing individuals range from the simplest paper and pencil devices to intensive clinical appraisal. In the past few years there has been increasing interest in evaluating individuals in small group situations. Such assessment is thought to allow an exceptional opportunity to evaluate certain characteristics which are uniquely prominent in group interaction.

The major problem to be discussed in this paper attempts to answer one question, namely: What are the characteristics which can be evalu-

FROM *Personnel Psychology*, 1954, 7, 477–484. Reprinted by permission of the author and publisher.

ated by observing people interacting? In the use of small group observational techniques it seems probable that some such process as the following often occurs. The experimenter has a hypothesis he wishes to investigate. He desires to test this hypothesis in terms of variables he thinks observable in group behavior, and proceeds to develop a list of rating categories. Thus, in a study of leaders' behavior, my colleagues and I (1) attempted to rate nineteen variables such as the individual's cooperation, efficiency, confidence, prestige, insight, initiative, and leadership. During the last war the OSS Assessment Staff (7) tried to rate ten variables such as effective intelligence, leadership, interest, motivation, energy, and initiative. Recently, Hemphill and Coons (4) described leaders' behavior in terms of nine dimensions. Wherry (6) has described Army officers' behavior in terms of thirteen dimensions. Each group of investigators has attempted to examine "logically" the dimensions of behavior which might be observed, and then to build some instruments for recording this behavior. While good semantic distinctions can be made among quite a large number of supposed dimensions of behavior, the major theme of this paper will be that the actual number of dimensions which can be assessed is quite small. It will be contended that in assessing the behavior of individuals participating in small groups or situational tests, probably only three or at most four independent dimensions of behavior can be evaluated.

There are a number of empirical studies which support such a view. Arthur Couch and I (3) have some evidence suggesting that only three factors are needed to account for the variance obtained in ratings made on nineteen variables. We asked observers to make ratings on aggressiveness, cooperativeness, sociability, leadership, submissiveness, authoritarianism, task orientation, talkativeness, and many other logically distinguishable characteristics. It soon became apparent that our observers could not clearly distinguish nineteen independent characteristics in the subjects' behavior, although a logically sound case could be made that each variable represented a somewhat different way of behaving. Our problem was to discover how many psychologically independent factors need be defined to account for the variance in the nineteen ratings.

College men were formed into groups of eight or four members, and run on three different tasks: a reasoning task, a mechanical assembly task, and a discussion task. Some of the groups were run in emergent situations, and others in situations where the leader was appointed. At the end of each task, two independent observers rated the subject on the nineteen variables. Tables of intercorrelations of the trait characteristics for groups run under these conditions were obtained and factor analyzed. The main question we wished to answer was: How many factors are needed to account for most of the variance contained in the nineteen ratings?

In spite of considerable variation in group size, kind of task, and leadership practice, essentially the same factorial structure was found in each

TABLE I

*Dimensions of Individual Behavior Observable in Small Groups*

| INVESTIGATOR | FACTOR I | FACTOR II | FACTOR III |
|---|---|---|---|
| *Couch and Carter* | INDIVIDUAL PROMINENCE | GROUP GOAL FACILITATION | GROUP SOCIABILITY |
| (Small groups. Ratings.) | Authoritarianism<br>Confidence<br>Aggressiveness<br>Leadership<br>Striving for recognition | Efficiency<br>Cooperation<br>Adaptability<br>Pointed toward group solution | Sociability<br>Adaptability<br>Pointed toward group acceptance |
| *Sakoda* | PHYSICAL ENERGY | INTELLIGENCE | SOCIAL ADJUSTMENT |
| (OSS data. Various situations. Over-all ratings.) | Energy and initiative<br>Physical ability<br>Leadership | Effective intelligence<br>Observing and reporting<br>Propaganda skills | Social relations<br>Emotional stability<br>"Security" |
| *Hemphill and Coons* | OBJECTIVE ATTAINMENT | GROUP INTERACTION FACILITATION | MAINTENANCE OF MEMBERSHIP |
| (Leader's behavior described by group members and leaders.) | "Related to output"<br>"Initiation and organization" | "Enable group members to recognize their function" | "Behavior which is socially agreeable to group members" |
| *Wherry* | FORCEFUL LEADERSHIP AND INITIATIVE | PROPER ATTITUDE TOWARD JOB | SUCCESSFUL INTERPERSONAL RELATIONS |
| (Items describing Army officers' behavior completed by other officers.) | Bold<br>Forceful<br>Not timid<br>Quick to take the lead | Sincere<br>Helpful<br>Cooperative | Genial<br>Cordial<br>Well liked |
| | JOB COMPETENCE AND PERFORMANCE<br>Competent<br>Alert<br>Persevering | | |
| *Clark* | INDIVIDUAL PERFORMANCE | GROUP ORIENTATION | SOCIAL RELATIONS |
| (Sociometric items from combat squads.) | Scrounger<br>Squad leader<br>Cheerful | Helpful<br>Work with<br>Patrol with<br>Share bunker with | Go on pass with |
| SUMMARY DESCRIPTION | INDIVIDUAL PROMINENCE AND ACHIEVEMENT | AIDING ATTAINMENT BY GROUP | SOCIABILITY |

analysis. In all the analyses, three factors emerged. Table I shows the items which have higher loadings for each factor. The name given each factor is in capital letters, while the ratings identifying the factor appear under the factor name. This factorial composition came out essentially the same for eight independent analyses of group situations which differed in size, kind of task, and leadership structure. From an inspection of the factor loadings and their structure, the factors were identified as follows:

*Factor I: Individual Prominence*—the dimension of behavior which is interpreted as indicating the prominence of that individual as he stands out from the group. The behavior associated with the traits of aggressiveness, leadership, confidence, and striving for individual recognition seems to have a common element which is interpreted as the member's attempting to achieve individual recognition from the group.

*Factor II: Group Goal Facilitation*—the dimension of behavior which is interpreted as being effective in achieving the goal toward which the group is oriented. Efficiency, adaptability, cooperation, etc., all seem to have a common element which facilitates group action in solving the group's task.

*Factor III: Group Sociability*—the dimension of behavior which is interpreted as indicating the positive social interaction of an individual in the group. The traits heavily loaded in this factor—sociability, striving for group acceptance, and adaptability—all have a common element which represents a friendly interpersonal behavior pattern of the individual toward the other group members.

The work of other investigators supports such a three dimensional interpretation. A short review of several relevant reports follows. The OSS Assessment Staff rated each participant on ten different variables. When Sakoda (5) factor analyzed the table of intercorrelations for these ratings, he also found that three factors accounted for the ten rating variables. His results are indicated on the table. While Sakoda has named these dimensions somewhat differently than we have, they seem to be similar in composition.

Hemphill and Coons (4) have recently published a monograph in which they describe the behavior of leaders. First they constructed a large number of items and had various group members rate the behavior of their group leaders. They also had leaders rate their own behavior. Members of the research staff then sorted the behavior descriptions into ten *a priori* dimensions. These dimensions were factor analyzed, and again three factors were obtained as indicated in the table.

Likewise in a study by Wherry (6), a limited number of dimensions were found. Several hundred Army officers each rated an immediate subordinate on 292 items describing the characteristics of the subordinate. The items were then sorted into thirteen logically distinct categories. The relationship of the items in these thirteen categories was analyzed by the Wherry-Gaylord Iterative Process. Wherry says, "After approximately four iterations in each case, the staff was surprised to discover that the items selected on the thirteen scales fell roughly into three groups or patterns." Feeling that more dimensions should be found, Wherry performed additional analyses. He reports, "Iteration of the (new) group of items resulted in a subtest which contained several new items. It was also tending to iterate toward one of the three groups, but iteration was stopped before it reached that stage. . . ." Here again, as can be seen in the table, three factors were found while a weak fourth one may have emerged.

Last winter a group led by Rodney Clark (2) studied rifle squads on the main line of resistance in Korea. As a part of the study, each squad member made sociometric choices relative to ten different activities. The choices were tabulated by item and the intercorrelation between types of activities obtained. As shown in the table, three factors were obtained, although the third factor is not well defined.

These studies point forcefully to the conclusion that descriptions of the behavior of individuals working in groups can be categorized into three dimensions. These same dimensions seem to be found whether the descriptions are made from the immediate observation of people working together, or from sociometric material, or from one individual describing the past behavior of another. It is quite possible to logically distinguish among a large number of disparate categories describing such behavior, but when reports of actual observations are obtained they can all be adequately included in three dimensions. It seems that these three dimensions can be described as follows:

FACTOR I: *Individual Prominence and Achievement*

These are behaviors of the individual related to his efforts to stand out from others and individually achieve various personal goals.

FACTOR II: *Aiding Attainment by the Group*

These are behaviors of the individual related to his efforts to assist the group in achieving goals toward which the group is oriented.

FACTOR III: *Sociability*

These are behaviors of the individual related to efforts to establish and maintain cordial and socially satisfying relations with other group members.

The implication of these conclusions for the rating of individuals in situational tests seems clear. Whatever system of rating is to be used, it should be designed to obtain a reliable estimate of each individual's behavior relative to these three factors. A large number of techniques have been employed to describe individuals' behavior in small groups. These techniques include subjective descriptions, rating scales, descriptive items, and recordings of the minutia of behavior. No general statement regarding the best methods can be made since the technique to be used depends upon the purpose for which the assessment is made and the degree of training and competence of the observers. Unfortunately, time does not permit a discussion of the advantages and limitations of the different systems.

There will be objection that, if assessment is to be made on the basis of the three factors proposed, it will not be possible to make statements regarding many customarily rated qualities, such as leadership, for example. After all, the impetus for situational testing has developed from leadership assessment. The results cited indicate that leadership is not a unitary trait, rather the behaviors usually subsumed under the term leadership seem to involve loadings on both Factor I, Individual Prominence, and Factor II, Group Goal Facilitation. In the Couch and Carter study the largest leadership loading was on Factor I, with a smaller loading on Factor II. In Sakoda's study, leadership was about equally loaded on these two factors, as it was in Clark's study. Leadership did not show a significant loading on the third factor, Group Sociability, in any of these studies. Thus it appears that leadership is not a single basic dimension but a composite of behaviors related to individual prominence and achievement, and of behaviors related to assisting the group in achieving group goals.

In conclusion, it seems apparent that the interaction behavior of individuals involved in small group situations can be adequately described by three factors. Using these three factors simplifies the conceptual problem of describing individual behavior, and may also clarify thinking regarding such concepts as leadership.

## REFERENCES

1. Carter, L. F., Haythorn, W., Meirowitz, B., & Lanzetta, J. The relation of categorizations and ratings in the observation of group behavior. *Hum. Relat.*, 1951, 4, 239–254.
2. Clark, R. A. Analyzing the group structure of combat rifle squads. *Amer. Psychol.*, 1953, 8, 333.
3. Couch, A., & Carter, L. F. A factorial study of the rated behavior of group members. Paper read at meeting of Eastern Psychological Association, March 1952.
4. Hemphill, J., & Coons, A. *Leader behavior description.* Columbus: Personnel Research Board, Ohio State Univer., (undated).
5. Sakoda, J. M. Factor analysis of OSS situational tests. *J. abnorm. soc. Psychol.*, 1952, 47, 843–852.
6. Wherry, R. J. *Factor analysis of officer qualification form QCL–2B.* Columbus: Ohio State Univer. Research Foundation, 1950.
7. Office of Strategic Services Assessment Staff. *Assessment of men.* New York: Rinehart, 1948.

# *Role Differentiation in Small Groups*

PHILIP E. SLATER

SMALL group research provides a most fruitful meeting-ground for psychological and sociological thinking. Few fields of study lend themselves so easily to this dual perspective. The concept of "role" holds a potentially strategic position in this rapprochement, but its rather indiscriminate use has thus far seemed to create as much confusion as enlightenment in the small group area.

We might define a role as a more or less coherent and unified system of items of interpersonal behavior. With even this minimal definition it becomes apparent that role performance in the small group situation will have both consequences which are important to the functioning of the group in which the role is performed, and personal consequences of importance to the individual who performs it. Similarly, an individual may be motivated to perform a role both by specific inducements offered by the group, and by more general needs operating within the individual himself.

The rather general failure to consider simultaneously both of these aspects of role performance has constituted a very real stumbling-block in small group research. This paper will attempt to illustrate the way in which consideration of both psychological and sociological factors may aid in the interpretation of tendencies for members of small experimental groups to behave in systematically differentiated ways. Our research in this area [1] has been centered around five problems:

1. To what extent do group members distinguish between different

FROM *American Sociological Review*, 1955 (in press). Reprinted by permission of the author and publisher.

This research was carried out under the direction and guidance of Robert F. Bales. The larger project of which this study was a part was facilitated by the Laboratory of Social Relations, Harvard University. Funds were supplied by the RAND Corporation, Santa Monica, California.

1 The theoretical assumptions underlying this research are discussed elsewhere (2, 3).

*kinds* of favorable evaluations of their fellow group members, or, conversely, to what degree do they tend to rank fellow members similarly on criteria assumed to be different? A consistent tendency for subjects to rate one man high on one criterion and another man high on a second criterion would constitute prima facie evidence for the existence of a set of differentiated roles, at least in the minds of the subjects themselves.

2. What effect do repeated interactions have upon such discriminations? Since randomly composed laboratory groups are rather ephemeral organizations, it might be assumed necessary for some time to elapse before even a crude protoype of the elaborate kind of differentiation found in permanent groups would appear.

3. How do individuals differentiated by their fellow group members differ in their behavior? How can we characterize this behavior, and how do these characterizations relate to the criteria upon which the individuals were rated?

4. How do such individuals respond to each other? Do differentiated "specialists" cooperate or compete with each other?

5. What is the relationship of personality factors to role differentiation? Are there factors which predispose an individual to assume a particular role? What is the effect upon the group as a whole of variations in the motivations of various "specialists"?

## PROCEDURE

The sample consisted of 20 groups of from three to seven men each, with four groups of each size. Each group met four times, so that a total of 80 meetings was studied. The groups were composed of paid male undergraduates at Harvard who knew each other only casually, if at all, prior to the first meeting. They were told that we were engaged in the study of group discussion and decision-making, and that we would observe them through a one-way mirror. Each subject was given a five-page factual summary of an administrative problem which they were asked to solve as a group, assuming the role of administrative staff to the central authority in the case under discussion. They were given 40 minutes to discuss the case and decide (a) why the persons involved in the case were behaving as they did, and (b) what the central authority should do about it. A new case was used for each meeting. The subjects' remarks during the discussion were classified according to Bales' set of interaction categories (1). Following each session the subjects filled out a questionnaire which included the following questions:

(a) Who contributed the best ideas for solving the problem? Please rank the members in order. *Include yourself.*

(b) Who did the most to guide the discussion and keep it moving effectively? Please rank the members in order. *Include yourself.*

(c) How well did you personally like each of the other members? Rate each member on a scale from 0 to 7, where zero means "I feel perfectly neutral toward him," and seven means "I like him very much." [2]

At the end of the fourth session an additional question was asked:

(d) Considering all the sessions, which member of the group would you say stood out most definitely as a leader in the discussion? How would you rank the others? *Include yourself.*

These questions, along with the Bales interaction scores, constituted the major source of data for this study.

Prior to analysis of the data, each of the 20 groups was assigned to one of two classes, according to whether the members showed high or low agreement on their responses to questions (a) and (b) above. This procedure was followed on the basis of findings by Heinicke and Bales that these two types of groups showed different developmental characteristics (6). It was felt that role differentiation might take different forms in groups with varying degrees of agreement on status ratings.

The measure used to represent agreement on status ratings is based on Kendall's "Coefficient of Concordance" (8, 10) which he calls "W." It is obtained from a matrix of rankings, each individual (placed in vertical order on a series of rows) ranking each individual (placed in horizontal order on a series of columns). In Kendall's formula:

$$W = \frac{12\,S}{m^2\,(n^3 - n)}$$

where $S$ equals the sum of the squares of the deviations of the column totals from the grand mean, and $n$ equals the number of individuals ranked by $m$ observers. In our rankings $n = m$, since everyone in the group ranks everyone, including himself. When agreement is perfect, W is equal to one; when there is no agreement, W is equal to zero.

W indices obtained from the rankings made on questions (a) and (b) were averaged, and the resulting mean called the "Index of Status Consensus." When the average Index of a group over all four meetings was .500 or above the group was classified as a "High" group. When the Index was below .500 the group was classified as a "Low" group.

## SPECIALIZATION AS PERCEIVED BY SUBJECTS

Subjects in this sample may be ranked in five different ways for each session. From the interaction scores it was possible to rank order the men according to who talked the most, and who *received* the most interaction. From the post-meeting questions it was possible to rank order the men on the perceived quality of their ideas, their perceived ability to guide the

2 A different form of question was used for some of the earlier groups, but both forms were reduced to rank orders for the present study.

discussion, and their personal popularity. Our interest in role differentiation stemmed from the relationships of these rank orders to each other.

A simple method of seeking out tendencies toward specialization consists of counting the number of times a man with top rank on any one of these five measures holds top rank on none of the other measures. Such a man might be considered a "specialist," and if such "specialists" are found in one characteristic more often than in the others, this characteristic might be considered a specialized one.

Table 1 indicates that there are more cases in which the Best-liked man holds top ranking in only that one characteristic than cases of any

TABLE 1

*Number of Sessions * Out of a Possible 80 in Which a Given Person Holds Top Position in One and Only One Rank Order Out of Five Possible Rank Orders.*

| | | |
|---|---|---|
| Talking | T | 11.0 |
| Receiving | R | 10.5 |
| Ideas | I | 12.0 |
| Guidance | G | 11.6 |
| Liking | L | 30.4 |
| TOTAL | | 75.5 |

* The decimals arise from ties in rankings.

other sort of isolated prominence. The difference between this characteristic and the other four is significant at the .001 level, using a Chi-square test. Popularity is apparently a relatively specialized achievement.

Further information may be obtained by proceeding in the obverse manner and asking rather, how often does the same person in a particular group hold top position on two characteristics? Table 2 shows, for each pair of characteristics, the percentage of cases in which such coincidence occurs.

Table 2 indicates that for both High and Low status-consensus groups, Popularity is least often associated with other characteristics. The difference is significant at the .01 level in both cases, using a Chi-square test. Marked differences between High and Low groups appear, however, when we examine the table further. The two participation measures, Talking and Receiving, are significantly less often associated with Ideas in the Low groups than in the High (.01 level), and Ideas and Guidance are significantly less often associated with Liking (.01 level). In other words, in the High groups high participation (Talking and Receiving) is associated with high rated task ability (Ideas and Guidance), but neither is strongly associated with Popularity. In the Low groups the association of high rated task ability with popularity is even lower (less in fact than chance expectancy), while the association of high participation with high rated task ability tends to break down.

Note that Talking and Receiving are strongly associated in both High and Low groups, as are Ideas and Guidance. This fact perhaps justifies the groupings made above, which will be used throughout this section wherever they seem to be appropriate.

These techniques for determining the amount of specialization among these various characteristics are not entirely satisfactory, since they deal only with the top man on each rank order. To meet this problem, mean

TABLE 2

*Percentage of Total Number of Sessions (80) in Which the Same Person Holds Top Position in Two Rank Orders at the Same Time.*

HIGH STATUS-CONSENSUS GROUPS

| | T | R | I | G | L |
|---|---|---|---|---|---|
| Talking T | | 51.3 | 63.3 | 36.5 | 20.5 |
| Receiving R | | | 53.3 | 39.0 | 34.3 |
| Ideas I | | | | 56.3 | 32.0 |
| Guidance G | | | | | 45.5 |
| Liking L | | | | | |

LOW STATUS-CONSENSUS GROUPS

| | T | R | I | G | L |
|---|---|---|---|---|---|
| Talking T | | 52.5 | 43.7 | 40.0 | 32.0 |
| Receiving R | | | 28.7 | 42.5 | 37.0 |
| Ideas I | | | | 50.0 | 16.5 |
| Guidance G | | | | | 20.0 |
| Liking L | | | | | |

rank order correlations [3] between all pairs of characteristics were computed, and are shown on Table 3.

First, as we might expect from Tables 1 and 2, the correlations between Liking and the other four characteristics are the lowest correlations in both the High and Low group matrices. Second, the tendency for amount of participation and rated task ability to be highly correlated in the High groups and poorly correlated in the Low groups is even more sharply outlined in Table 3 than in Table 2.[4]

3 The use of rank order correlations here involves serious statistical problems, due to the small sizes of our groups. Clearly a *rho* drawn from a three-man group means very little, and *rhos* from even the larger sizes are not too reliable. In dealing with this problem two different techniques were used: (a) Median values were computed; (b) Means based on the raw *rhos* of all but the three-man groups were computed. While these methods yielded identical results, neither is entirely satisfactory, and we suggest that the reader accept these findings with reserve.

4 All of the correlations in the Low groups are in fact lower than those in the High groups, a result which is not surprising in view of the fact that low agreement between

Differences between the correlations in Table 3 were tested in the following manner: the 10 correlations in each matrix were divided into three sets, with the Talking-Receiving and Ideas-Guidance correlations in the first set, the four correlations between the participation measures and the rated task ability measures in the second set, and the four correlations between Liking and the other measures in the third set. The three sets were then tested against each other by means of sign tests. Note that in the first set the correlations are high in both High and Low groups, in

TABLE 3

*Intercorrelations between Talking, Receiving, and Ratings on Ideas, Guidance, and Liking. Mean Rank Order Correlations of 64 Sessions (Size 3 Excluded).*

HIGH STATUS-CONSENSUS GROUPS

| | | T | R | I | G | L |
|---|---|---|---|---|---|---|
| Talking | T | | .88 | .80 | .75 | .38 |
| Receiving | R | | | .74 | .74 | .46 |
| Ideas | I | | | | .83 | .41 |
| Guidance | G | | | | | .49 |
| Liking | L | | | | | |

LOW STATUS-CONSENSUS GROUPS

| | | T | R | I | G | L |
|---|---|---|---|---|---|---|
| Talking | T | | .69 | .48 | .51 | .10 |
| Receiving | R | | | .44 | .52 | .16 |
| Ideas | I | | | | .71 | .14 |
| Guidance | G | | | | | .27 |
| Liking | L | | | | | |

the second set they are high in the High groups and relatively low in the Low groups, while in the third set they are relatively low in both.

In the High groups there was no significant difference between the first two sets. The first set was significantly higher than the third set, at the .01 level, and the second set was significantly higher than the third at the .05 level. In the Low groups the first set was significantly higher than the second and the second significantly higher than the third, both at the .01 level.

raters is equivalent to low reliability of measures, which would tend to produce lower correlations in the Low groups. All of the differences between High and Low groups in Table 3 are significant at the .05 level or better, with the exception of the Talking-Receiving correlations (which are not based on ratings), the Ideas-Guidance correlations, and the Guidance-Liking correlations. It is notable, however, that Ideas and Guidance are very highly correlated even in the Low groups, and this fact, along with the existence of several High group-Low group differences which are not based upon ratings, suggests that unreliability of Low group measures plays little part in the creation of qualitative differences between High and Low groups.

Popularity, then, again appears to be the most specialized characteristic, regardless of the degree of status-consensus in the group. In Low status consensus groups, however, the tendency for Liking to separate itself from other characteristics is stronger, and seconded by the dissociation of rated task ability from amount of participation.

In summary, role differentiation in the High groups seems to be bipartite, with an active "task specialist" and a Best-liked man. In the Low groups it tends to be tripartite (as well as more extreme), with an active participator who is neither well-liked nor highly rated on task ability, a more passive task specialist who is not well-liked, and a popular individual who is neither active nor highly rated on task ability.

## CHANGES OVER TIME

Common sense and sociological folklore would lead us to expect that any tendency toward role specialization in these groups would increase over time, as the group became more highly "organized" or "structured." This expectation is fulfilled. Table 4 shows the number of times in each meeting

TABLE 4

*Percentage of Cases in Which the Same Man Holds Top Position on Like Ranking and Idea Ranking at the Same Time, by Sessions.**

| SESSIONS | | | |
|---|---|---|---|
| 1 | 2 | 3 | 4 |
| 56.5 | 12.0 | 20.0 | 8.5 |

* The trends for High and Low groups are identical.

in which the top man on Ideas is also Best-liked. Table 5 shows the number of times in each meeting in the Low groups in which the top man on either participation measure is also top man on either task ability rating. The trend in Table 4 is significant at the .01 level, the trend in Table 5 at the .05 level, using Chi-square tests.[5]

The selection of Ideas rather than Guidance as the task ability measure in Table 4 is based upon the fact that it is in general less highly correlated with Liking, and thus in some sense "purer." Guidance and Liking do tend to correlate less with the passage of time, but the trend is more gradual, as we might expect.

## ROLE DIFFERENTIATION AND LEADERSHIP

At the end of the fourth session, after differentiation has become well-developed, our subjects are asked to rank each other on the most general-

5 Computations using mean *rhos*, in the manner of Table 3, yield similar results.

ized of criteria, leadership. What is the relationship of this ranking to the five more specialized ones?

This relationship may be determined by finding the top man on each measure for all four sessions taken together, and then computing the percentage of cases in which top rank on leadership coincided with top rank on each of the five other measures. The results were as follows: Guidance 80 per cent, Receiving 65 per cent, Ideas 59 per cent, Talking 55 per cent, and Liking 25 per cent.[6] A Chi-square test showed Liking to coincide significantly less often (at the .01 level) with leadership than the other four characteristics. The Best-liked man is in fact chosen leader no more often than would be expected by chance.[7]

TABLE 5

*Percentage of Cases in Low Status-consensus Groups in Which the Same Man Holds Top Position on a Participation Measure (Talking or Receiving) and a Task Ability Measure (Ideas or Guidance) at the Same Time *, by Sessions.*

| SESSIONS | | | |
|---|---|---|---|
| 1 | 2 | 3 | 4 |
| 55.0 | 28.7 | 41.3 | 30.0 |

* Using the mean of the four possible combinations.

Yet, strangely enough, leadership is most *strongly* associated with those measures which are in turn most strongly correlated with popularity, namely, Receiving and Guidance (see Tables 2 and 3). This fact seems less strange if we consider the generalized character of Leadership. Subjects choosing a leader must take into account a wider range of abilities and virtues than in deciding who has the best ideas or whom they like best. The chosen leader of a group is perhaps the man who has the highest hypothetical *combined* rating on all possible characteristics related to the group's purposes and needs. The man so chosen is not likely to be *dis*liked, nor to have unacceptable Ideas nor to be unable or unwilling to participate in the discussion. Hence those measures which are themselves more general, that is, related to a wider range of abilities, will correlate more highly with leadership. Tables 2 and 3 suggest that Guidance and Receiving are more general in this sense than their counterparts, Ideas and Talking.

6 There were no important differences between High and Low groups.

7 Computations using mean rank order correlations between Leadership and the five other characteristics yield the same results.

## BEHAVIORAL DIFFERENCES BETWEEN IDEA MEN AND BEST-LIKED MEN

Thus far we have dealt with the differentiation of task ability and popularity primarily as perceived by the subjects. We might now ask, is this trend a reflection of actual behavioral differences between the perceived "specialists," or have our subjects merely been gripped by some sort of sociological delusion while making their ratings? What, for example, does a Best-liked man *do*?

TABLE 6

*Composite Profiles in Percentages of 44 Top Men on Idea Ranking and 44 Top Men on Like Ranking for the Same Sessions.*

| | INTERACTION CATEGORY | INITIATED | | RECEIVED | |
|---|---|---|---|---|---|
| | | IDEA MEN | BEST-LIKED MEN | IDEA MEN | BEST-LIKED MEN |
| AREA A: | 1. Shows Solidarity | 3.68 | 4.41 | 2.57 | 3.15 |
| *Positive* | 2. Shows Tension Release | 5.15 | 6.98 | 7.95 | 9.20 |
| *Reactions* | 3. Shows Agreement | 14.42 | 16.83 | 23.29 | 18.27 |
| AREA B: | 4. Gives Suggestion | 8.97 | 6.81 | 7.01 | 7.22 |
| *Problem* | 5. Gives Opinion | 32.74 | 28.69 | 25.52 | 31.09 |
| *Solving* | 6. Gives Orientation | 18.54 | 17.91 | 14.06 | 14.54 |
| *Attempts* | | | | | |
| AREA C: | 7. Asks Orientation | 3.04 | 3.71 | 3.62 | 2.80 |
| *Questions* | 8. Asks Opinion | 1.84 | 2.94 | 1.94 | 1.74 |
| | 9. Asks Suggestion | .93 | 1.33 | .85 | .84 |
| AREA D: | 10. Shows Disagreement | 8.04 | 7.60 | 10.65 | 9.35 |
| *Negative* | 11. Shows Tension Increase | 1.92 | 2.16 | 1.59 | 1.35 |
| *Reactions* | 12. Shows Antagonism | .73 | .63 | .95 | .45 |

In order to compare the Bales' interaction profiles of Idea men and Best-liked men, the following procedure was followed: (a) All sessions in which the Best-liked man also held top rank on Ideas were eliminated. (b) All sessions in which ties for top rank occurred in either ranking were eliminated. The raw profiles of the remaining 44 matched pairs of Idea men and Best-liked men were added together, and percentage profiles computed, as shown in Table 6.[8]

The most salient general difference in Table 6 is the tendency for the Idea man to initiate interaction more heavily in Area B (Problem Solving Attempts) and the Best-liked man in Area A (Positive reactions). The Idea man also seems to disagree somewhat more, and show a little more antagonism, while the Best-liked man asks more questions and shows more tension. On the Receiving end, the situation is largely reversed, with the Idea man receiving more agreement, questions, and negative reactions,

8 Although some suggestive variations in these differences appear when the sample is divided into High and Low group pairs, the major outlines are the same.

while the Best-liked man receives more problem solving attempts, and more solidarity and tension release. The general picture is thus one of specialization and complementarity, with the Idea man concentrating on the task and playing a more aggressive role, while the Best-liked man concentrates more on social-emotional problems, giving rewards and playing a more passive role.

The problem of testing the significance of these differences is a vexed one, in view of the interdependence of the categories. Several different techniques have been utilized, the most satisfactory of which has been the use of category indices based upon the raw profiles of each man.[9] If, for example, we wish to test the apparent tendency for Idea men to interact more in Area B and Best-liked men in Area A, we simply divide the number of scores each man has in Area A by his score in Area B, and compare the resulting indices of the two types of men. Best-liked men should and do have significantly higher indices than Idea men (at the .01 level, using a sign test).

Another index may be constructed by simply placing in the numerator all categories in which the Best-liked man initiated more interaction and in the denominator all categories in which the Idea man initiated more. The same procedure may be followed for the Receiving profiles. On both of these indices the Best-liked man is significantly higher (at the .01 level).

The principal drawback of these indices is that they fail to show us which categories are most crucial in differentiating Idea from Best-liked men. Unfortunately, there is no satisfactory solution to this problem, in view of the statistical difficulties mentioned above. Comparing raw scores in each category would be fruitless, since the Idea men have a somewhat higher total rate of participation and will therefore tend to show larger scores in every category. Percentage profiles for each man may be computed, and percentage scores in each category compared, but this exacerbates problems of interdependence and distribution. In order to give some clue, however, to the relative importance of the various categories in differentiating Idea men from Best-liked men, sign tests were performed on individual percentage profiles, category by category, for interaction initiated by each type of man. These showed categories 2, 3, 4, 5, 8, and 11 as the strongest differentiating categories.[10] Grouping categories by area, however, produces differences stronger than those generated by any of

9 Such a technique gives equal weight to each man, contrary to the composite profiles in Table 6, which, since they lump together all acts of all men, give greater weight to those men whose total rate of participation is higher. As a result, some differences which seem negligible in Table 6 are actually very consistent, and vice versa.

10 A study by Richard Mann (9), performed on a different sample, showed almost identical results for a slightly different type of comparison. Mann used not top men, but all men, comparing those who had higher ratings on task ability than on Liking with those who had higher Liking ratings than task ratings.

the component categories, with the single exception of Area D. In other words, Area A differentiates Idea men from Best-liked men better than Categories 1, 2, and 3 taken individually, Area B better than categories 4, 5, and 6 taken individually, and Area C better than categories 7, 8, and 9 taken individually. In Area D, grouping does not seem meaningful, since the three categories do not tend in the same direction. The tendency for the Idea men to initiate more in categories 10 and 12, however, is so weak that it may almost be discounted.

These findings indicate that qualitative differentiation in the subjects' ratings of each other is accompanied by qualitative differentiation in the overt behavior of the subjects rated, such that Idea men tend to specialize in active problem-solving attempts, and Best-liked men in more reactive, less task-oriented behavior. The apparent complementarity of these two patterns suggests that a large share of the group's interaction may take place directly between the two "specialists." Since both are by definition highly valued in one way or another by the group, a high rate of interaction between them would be an indication that this relationship constitutes some sort of focal point in the group, and that the welfare of the group may be to some extent dependent upon the strength of this relationship. It would, therefore, be useful to know whether or not the two men interact more with each other than with other members.

Table 7 shows the extent to which this interaction preference existed. The tendency seems sufficiently marked, especially in the High groups, to justify the conclusion that the relationship is quantitatively important, though not always dominant in the group. Since the total amount of participation of the Best-liked man averages no more than the average for all men, the findings in Table 7 suggest that his interaction is concentrated around the Idea man to a greater extent than that of the other group members. In other words, although there may be men in the group who interact in general more heavily than the Best-liked man, they do not engage the Idea man in interaction to the same degree.

Some evidence also exists indicating that the relationship between the two "specialists" tends on the whole to be the most positive in the group, especially in the High groups. Comparing the ratings each subject gave to each other subject on the question "How well did you personally like each of the other members?", we find that:

(a) The Best-liked man tends to give the Idea man a rating higher than the average of the other group member ratings of the Idea man. This difference is significant at the .01 level, using a sign test.

(b) The Best-liked man gives the Idea man a rating higher than his mean rating of other group members (significant at the .05 level).

(c) The Idea man gives the Best-liked man a rating higher than the average of the other member ratings of the Best-liked man in the High groups (significant at the .05 level) but not in the Low.

(d) The Idea man gives the Best-liked man a rating higher than his mean rating of other group members (significant at the .01 level).

We thus have the rather interesting picture of a respected task-oriented group member who is at best only moderately well-liked, receiving strong support from a perhaps more socially-oriented member who is the most popular man in the group, and with whom the task-oriented

TABLE 7

*Interaction between Top Ranking Men on Ideas (I) and Top Ranking Men on Being Liked (L).*

| CHARACTERISTIC OF INTERACTION OBSERVED | PERCENTAGE OF CASES IN WHICH CHARACTERISTIC OCCURRED | | SIGNIFICANCE LEVEL FOR HIGH AND LOW GROUPS COMBINED |
|---|---|---|---|
| | HIGH GROUPS | LOW GROUPS | |
| I interacted with L more than he did with any other number. | 44.7 | 48.0 * | ** |
| I interacted with L more than any other member interacted with L. | 52.6 * | 50.0 * | *** |
| L interacted with I more than he did with any other member | 73.7 *** | 52.0 ** | *** |
| L interacted with I more than any other member interacted with I. | 57.9 * | 30.0 | * |
| Percentage expected by chance | 28.9 | 26.0 | |

Level of significance:
No asterisk: not significant
*: .05
**: .01
***: .001

member forms a close and active relationship. Qualitative differentiation seems to be associated, then, with cooperation. Quantitative differentiation, i.e., differentiation along any single status dimension, may well be associated with more competitive responses.

## PERSONALITY FACTORS IN DIFFERENTIATION

The data from which this study was drawn includes little material which bears directly upon an analysis of personality characteristics. An indirect source of material, however, appears in the subjects' ratings of each other on the question, "How well did you like each of the other members?" Many subjects tend to give all other members the same rating on this question. Since these subjects also tend to rate highly, they are saying, in effect, "I like everyone." Such undifferentiated ratings constitute about one-fifth of all the ratings in the sample, but they are not by any means divided equally among different types of subjects. Best-liked men are the most frequent non-differentiating members, Idea men the least frequent. The difference between them is significant at the .05 level, using a Chi-square test. Top Guidance, Talking, and Receiving men fail to differentiate about as often as the sample as a whole.

There is also a striking difference between High and Low status-consensus groups on the distribution of undifferentiated ratings. In the High groups, subjects who refuse to differentiate their ratings tend to be persons with low status, i.e., persons who do not hold top rank on any of the five characteristics mentioned above. In the Low groups, non-differentiating persons tend to be high status persons. This tendency is significant at the .01 level, using a Chi-square test.

TABLE 8

*Mean Scores on 30-Item F-Scale for Top Men on Five Characteristics and Leader, in High and Low Groups.*

| | HIGH GROUPS | LOW GROUPS | ALL GROUPS |
|---|---|---|---|
| Leader | 76.2 | 85.2 | 80.7 |
| No. 1 Guidance | 88.7 | 79.2 | 83.9 |
| " 1 Receiving | 83.3 | 94.2 | 88.7 |
| " 1 Talking | 74.9 | 103.8 | 89.3 |
| " 1 Ideas | 82.3 | 101.2 | 91.7 |
| " 1 Liking | 91.1 | 99.9 | 95.5 |

The meaning of this tendency to make undifferentiated ratings will perhaps become more clear if we examine its relationship to the only direct measure of personality characteristics available, i.e., subject scores on the California F-Scale. A 30 item F-Scale was given to 62 of the 100 subjects in the sample, with differentiating raters receiving a mean F-score of 85, and non-differentiating raters a mean score of 103. The difference is significant at the .001 level, using a standard t-test.

High F-scores would thus be expected to distribute themselves much as do the undifferentiated Liking ratings. Mean F-scores of all top-ranking men in High and Low groups are shown in Table 8, and three types of differences are immediately apparent. First, top men in High groups generally have lower F-scores than top men in Low groups. This tendency is significant (at the .01 level) only in the case of Talking and Ideas, however. Second, Idea men have significantly lower scores than Best-liked men (.05 level) in the High groups, though not in the Low. Third, there is a tendency for top men on what have been described as more generalized characteristics, namely, Leadership, Guidance, and Receiving, to have lower F-scores than top men on the more specialized characteristics, Talking, Ideas, and Liking. This difference is significant at the .05 level.

Both relatively high F-scores and undifferentiated ratings may be interpreted as reflecting a tendency toward a rigid and oversimplified approach to interpersonal relations. Fine perceptual discriminations, or flexible and situationally-determined behavior, are perhaps not to be expected from subjects falling into this category.[11] Their behavior will be determined rather by chronic, compulsive responses to inner needs, such as the need to be accepted and loved, the need to deny negative feelings toward members of one's own group, and so forth.

When we recall that Low groups are more sharply specialized than High groups, and that the Best-liked role is the most specialized of all our measures, it becomes clear that the common factor in all these findings is a strong relationship between this personal rigidity and specialization. The sharper the role differentiation in the group, or the more specialized the role played by the individual, the greater the rigidity in the personality or personalities involved.

## DISCUSSION

According to Barnard (4), the survival of any organization depends upon its ability to solve two problems: the achievement of the purposes for which the organization was formed, and the satisfaction of the more immediate needs of the members of the organization. On the small group level, Bales (1, p. 10) makes a related distinction between the problems of the group involving goal achievement and adaptation to external demands, and problems involving internal integration and the expression of emotional tensions. The first group of problems he calls Adaptive-Instrumental problems, the solution of which demands activity in the Task area. The second he calls Integrative-Expressive problems, the solution of which demands activity in the social-emotional area. Bales goes on to emphasize the difficulties inherent in attempting to solve both groups of problems at the same time.

Similar difficulties arise when the same *individual* attempts to take an active lead in solving these problems simultaneously. In large organizations, e.g., the solution of Integrative-Expressive problems is in large part left to the leaders of informal groups, the importance of which Barnard and others have emphasized (4, pp. 223–224; 7, pp. 48 ff.).

We have found that the most fundamental type of role differentiation in small experimental groups is the divorcing of task functions from social-emotional functions. Presumably, the ideal leader of a small group would be sufficiently skillful and flexible to alternate these types of behavior in such a way as to handle both problems, and maximize his status on all possible dimensions. He would be able to make both an active, striv-

11 An inference which might also be made on the basis of the high negative correlation between F-score and intelligence.

ing response to the task and a sympathetic response to the individual needs of group members. He would be a high participator, well-liked, rated high on task ability, and eventually chosen leader.

Such individuals are rare. They appear occasionally in High status-consensus groups, almost never in Low. It is possible that the absence in the Low groups of anyone approaching this ideal type is responsible for their low status-consensus. Where a group must choose between individuals who are in different ways one-sided and limited in their capabilities, agreement on ratings will be difficult to attain.

There are at least two kinds of reasons for the rarity of such men. First, there are sociological factors, revolving around the non-compatibility of the task and social-emotional roles. Adaptation to pressures from outside the group, such as are created by a task which must be performed, involves, by definition, change. The individual who presses toward solution of a task inadvertently forces those around him to make continual minor adjustments in their behavior, and to continually re-examine their ideas and values, in the light of these external demands. The individual who concerns himself with internal social-emotional problems, on the other hand, is supportive in his responses to the ideas and behavior of those around him, and continually reaffirms their dominant values. The orientation of the task specialist is thus more technological, that of the social-emotional specialist more traditionalistic. It is presumably the latter type of behavior which seems more appealing to members called upon to indicate whom they personally like best.

This is not to say that the task specialist will actually be disliked, but rather that his task emphasis will tend to arouse some negative feelings—feelings which may not be expressed, and which will never outweigh his value to the group in the minds of its members. Such feelings merely neutralize any strong positive feelings other members may hold toward him. Only in the Low groups are task specialists actually *un*popular, and this phenomenon is perhaps expressive of the rigidity with which Low group task specialists perform their role.

The second set of reasons may be called psychological. These have to do with the individual's predisposition to assume a particular role. Men who are Best-liked, e.g., may "have to be liked," and may achieve prominence in this role because of the ingratiating skills they have acquired during their lives in bringing this desired situation about. Avoidance of conflict and controversy may be a felt necessity for this type of person—hence, his behavior will show nothing that could be a source of disharmony. He will avoid even the thought that he might like some of his fellow members better than others. His rate of interaction will be average—not too high, not too low. He will in fact retire into the conventional safety of the "average Joe." He may even avoid the performance of task functions altogether, because of the personal threats which task activity might hold for him. Instead, he will express the group's feelings and questions, and place its stamp of approval upon what has already come to pass.

The task specialist, on the other hand, may assume this role only because of an unwillingness or inability to respond to the needs of others. A compulsive concentration on an abstract problem will serve as an intellectual shield against the ambiguity of human feelings. Needs to express hostility may be channeled into aggressive and dogmatic problem-solving attempts.

When these motives determine the assumption of a specialized role in a group, the outlook for this group would seem to be poor. The F-score data suggests that such motives may in fact determine the behavior of specialists in Low status-consensus groups.

It is even possible that the presence, in a group, of individuals with motives of this sort *creates* low status-consensus. The difficulty of choosing between inadequate specialists has already been mentioned. Furthermore, it seems reasonable to expect that rigidity in the personality structure will be associated with rigidity in the value structure of the individual concerned. The F-scale is in fact founded on this assumption. Such absolutistic value systems, rigidly held and zealously defended, will impede the formation of any kind of consensus, particularly consensus on the relative emphasis the group should place upon task and social-emotional activities.

The way in which this kind of consensus in turn determines the degree of consensus on a particular rating may be illustrated by considering again the process of choosing a leader. It was suggested above that the man chosen as leader is that individual who is felt to possess those qualities which best serve to satisfy *both* the task and social-emotional problems of the group. Since different groups emphasize task and social-emotional problems in varying proportions, the attribution of leadership will depend not only upon the choice of one person over another but also upon the differential stress placed upon these group problems by the group. The group problems might thus be conceived as factors, with weights assigned to them by the group according to some elementary kind of value consensus. One group, e.g., might attribute leadership on the basis say, of .7 task ability, .3 likeability; another might reverse the weights.[12] The fact that Liking coincides so seldom with Leadership suggests that in our sample social-emotional skills are not highly valued, and are given a low weight. This may be due to the heavy task demands placed upon the group by the experimental situation, or to the emphasis placed upon task ability and achievement by our culture.

In any case, Leadership will be attributed to that member who has the highest combined rating on these and perhaps other factors. But if

12 This discussion of leadership as a fused role is founded on suggestions by Arthur Couch. A factor analysis of leadership variables by Couch and Carter (5) produced factors closely related to those discussed here.

implicit agreement on weights is lacking, each rater will be making a qualitatively different evaluation, and Leadership consensus becomes almost impossible.

Similarly, in making more specialized evaluations, a rater must decide what a specialist is supposed to do before deciding how well he does it. If there is no agreement in a group about what a given role should include, then roles will be performed in accordance with individual norms, and evaluated in terms of personal criteria. Agreement on role definitions is thus hindered by rigid value systems at the very time when the inflexibility characteristic of specialists operating under these conditions makes this agreement all the more imperative.

In this discussion we have isolated three types of role structure:

1. The rare case in which a single leader performs all functions and differentiation does not occur. This is a High group phenomenon.

2. The case in which moderate specialization arises simply because the specialists lack the exceptional talent necessary to counteract the sociological pressures toward differentiation. Choice of role is undoubtedly determined by personality factors as well as situational factors, but such preferences will not be immutable. This is the more common case in High groups.

3. The case in which extreme specialization is brought about by psychological as well as sociological pressures. Specialization is sharp and disruptive, due to the fact that it springs from an overdetermined response to inner needs rather than a flexible response to the needs of others, or to the demands of an ever-changing task situation. Specialists perform in a particular role because they "have to" rather than because it is useful or desirable. This is a Low group phenomenon.

Thus while differentiation occurs in both High and Low status-consensus groups, it seems to occur for different reasons. It is only the depth and breadth of the differentiation which will supply an immediate clue as to which kinds of reasons are operating. One final example of this duality of meaning is the highest participator, who has not been considered in much of the foregoing analysis.

It will be recalled that in High groups, the highest participator usually receives the highest rating on task ability. Approval and acceptance of his ideas perhaps encourages him to participate more heavily, and also generates his high rating. In Low groups, the highest participator is far less often rated highly. He apparently does not adjust his amount of participation to the approval and acceptance he receives, but persists in interacting despite their absence. His participation time is determined by his own aggressiveness, by insensitivity rather than responsiveness to feedback from others. In keeping with the motivations of other Low group specialists, he talks, not because it is helpful to the group for him to do so, but because he has to.

In short, Low group specialists are going through many of the same motions as High group specialists, but their needs and purposes differ. It would seem likely that double entendres of this sort constitute a major factor in obscuring the complexity of small group relationships.

## REFERENCES


1. Bales, R. F. *Interaction process analysis: A method for the study of small groups.* Cambridge, Mass.: Addison-Wesley, 1949.
2. Bales, R. F. The equilibrium problem in small groups. In T. Parsons, R. F. Bales, & E. A. Shils, *Working papers in the theory of action.* Glencoe, Ill.: Free Press, 1953. Pp. 111–161.
3. Bales, R. F., & Slater, P. E. Role differentiation in small groups. In T. Parsons, R. F. Bales, et al., *Family, socialization, and interaction process.* Glencoe, Ill.: Free Press, 1955.
4. Barnard, C. I. *The functions of the executive.* Cambridge, Mass.: Harvard Univer., 1938.
5. Carter, L. F. Leadership and small group behavior. In M. Sherif, & M. O. Wilson (Eds.), *Group relations at the crossroads.* New York: Harper, 1953, Pp. 257–284.
6. Heinicke, C., & Bales, R. F. Developmental trends in the structure of small groups. *Sociometry*, 1953, 16, 7–38.
7. Homans, G. C. *The human group.* New York: Harcourt Brace, 1950.
8. Kendall, M. G. *Rank correlation methods.* London, 1948.
9. Mann, R. D. The relation of informal status to role behavior in small discussion groups. (Unpublished honors thesis, Harvard Univer., 1954.)
10. Taylor, F. K. Quantitative evaluation of psychosocial phenomena in small groups. *J. ment. Sci.*, 1951, 97, 690–717.

# CHAPTER 10
# LEADERSHIP

## An Experimental Approach to the Study of Autocracy and Democracy: A Preliminary Note

KURT LEWIN and RONALD LIPPITT

IF ONE hopes to investigate experimentally such fundamental socio-psychological problems as: group ideology; conflicts between and within groups; types of their spontaneous substructuring; the stability of various spontaneous group structures versus structures created by external authority; minority problems; renegade, scapegoat, double loyalty conflicts—one has to create a setup where group life might be studied under rather free but well defined conditions. Instead of utilizing the groups in schools, clubs, factories, one should create groups experimentally because only in this way the factors influencing group life will not be left to chance but will be in the hands of the experimenter.

However, one should break away from the rather narrow aspect of studying the effect of the group influence on the individual (e.g., the effect of various groups on the suggestibility of the individual) as the main problem; one should consider not only one effect of a given social situation

FROM *Sociometry*, 1938, 1, 292–300. Reprinted by permission of Mrs. Gertrude W. Lewin and the publisher.

(e.g., the influence on productivity). Rather one should try to approach an experimental procedure: (a) where group life can proceed freely; (b) where the total group behavior, its structure and development can be registered. Any specific problem such as group ideology should be approached in the experimental setup and in the analysis of the data as a part of this greater whole.

Such data might always be analyzed with a double frame of reference, that of the individual group member and of the group as a dynamic unity.

The main interest of the present preliminary study is to develop from this point of view techniques to investigate "democracy" and "autocracy" as group atmospheres.

Two experimental mask-making clubs of ten and eleven year old children were selected from a group of eager volunteers of the fifth and sixth grades of the University Elementary School. A preliminary sociometric survey, following Moreno's technique, was made of the affinities and rejections existing in the two classrooms. With a sociogram of each group at hand the groups were selected (one from each schoolroom) from the available volunteers so that the groups would be as nearly equated as possible on the number and potency of friendship and rejection relationships, and on general popularity and leadership characteristics of the members. Instead of choosing a clique of close friends five children were chosen in each case who had expressed little relationship with each other, either in the school situation or in playing together in non-school groupings. It was believed that any inter-personal relations that developed during the life of the club could then be more closely correlated to the common life space of the new group membership.

In a ten minute preliminary meeting with each group the leader made it clear that the aim of the club would be to make theatrical masks (a new activity for all of the children); that the masks would belong to the group as a whole; and that one mask would be made at a time rather than each individual making one by himself. Two half-hour meetings a week were held with each group, the same experimenter being the leader in both clubs.

It is methodologically meaningless in studying democracy and autocracy experimentally to be guided mainly by the question: What is "the" prototype of democracy and which is the "true" autocracy. One should realize from the start that there are many varieties of such atmospheres. The experimental approach can only try to attack one case at a time. What type of democracy should be chosen should be less guided by the tendency to copy some historically given case than by the attempt to realize those types of group atmospheres which promise the best insight into the underlying dynamics and laws. Only the insight into these laws, and not the search for a prototype, will enable us to answer the question of what are the common properties and individual differences of autocracies and democracies.

With such a point of view the experimenter attempted to differentiate the atmospheres of the two groups chiefly in the following ways:

| AUTHORITARIAN | DEMOCRATIC |
|---|---|
| *1. All determination of policy by the strongest person (leader).* | *1. All policies a matter of group determination, encouraged and drawn out by the leader.* |
| *2. Techniques and steps of attaining the goal (completed mask) dictated by the authority, one at a time, so that future direction was always uncertain to a large degree.* | *2. Activity perspective given by an explanation of the general steps of the process (clay mould, plaster paris, papier mache, etc.) during discussion at first meeting. Where technical advice was needed the leader tried to point out 2 or 3 alternative procedures from which choice could be made.* |
| *3. The authority usually structured autocratically the activities of each member—the task and whom to work with.* | *3. The members were free to work with whomever they chose and the division of tasks was left up to the group.* |
| *4. The dominator criticized and praised individual's activities and remained aloof from group participation. He was always impersonal rather than outwardly hostile or friendly (a necessary concession in method).* | *4. The leader attempted to be a group member in spirit but not in the actual work. He gave criticism and praise, generally in regard to the group as a whole.* |

It is obvious that with voluntary group participation, and with the cooperation of the school system radically autocratic methods would not be utilized. A congenial extra-group relationship was maintained with all of the children during the entire course of the experimental sessions. The attempt was to make the authoritarian atmosphere as much more autocratic than the schoolroom as the democratic one was freer than the schoolroom.

During the series of twelve meetings for each group four trained observers made observational records, synchronized in minute units, of a varied nature. These techniques are here described very briefly:

1. A quantitative running account of the social interactions of the five children and leader, in terms of symbols for ascendant, submissive, and objective (fact-minded) approaches and responses, including a category of purposeful refusal to respond to a social approach.

2. A quantitative group structure analysis minute by minute with running comments to give a record of: activity subgroupings (e.g. three

of the children are busy mixing plaster of paris, one is tearing up paper towels for papier mache, and the fifth is working on the clay mould. This would be a 3-1-1 group structure with three subgroups. One individual may be a subgroup.); the activity goal of each subgroup; whether the subgroup was initiated by the leader or spontaneously formed by the children; and ratings on the degree of interest and unity of each subgroup.

3. Running comments and ratings indicating shifts of interest from minute to minute for each member (from complete involvement in the club activity to "out-of-the-field" preoccupations).

4. A stenographic record of conversation.

5. To the observers' records outlined above was added a post-meeting writeup by the leader of his impressions gathered from the more intimate contacts with the children.

Laid side by side these records give a rather complete minute by minute, meeting by meeting picture of the ongoing life of the group. A wide variety of quantitative and qualitative analyses are possible. Below are listed a few upon which we have already made some progress:

1. The total volume of social interactions broken down into ascendant, submissive, objective, and ignoring behavior.

2. The volume and types of social interactions between subgroups as compared to those within subgroups.

3. Analysis in terms of individual activity curves of these same data.

4. The stability of group structure and of specific subgroupings under varied conditions.

5. The influence on unity and stability of structure of leader-initiated and spontaneous subgroupings.

6. Analysis of stenographic records in terms of such categories as hostility; attention demands, resistant behavior, hostile and objective criticism, expression of competition and cooperation, amount of dependence on authority, expressions of "I-centeredness" (ego-centrism) versus "we-centeredness" (group spirit), etc.

7. Analysis of gradients of activity such as increase of hostility, and volume of total activity.

8. Changes of interest in terms of such related factors as group stability, outbreak of hostility, and standards of production.

The first purpose of this technique of observation is to record as fully and insightfully as possible the total behavior of the group. This is a distinct break away from the usual procedure of recording only certain symptoms which are determined in advance. It is an attempt to apply the same "total behavior" methodology in social psychology which has proven fruitful in a number of investigations into individual psychology (i.e. Dembo's study on anger, Karsten's of psychological satiation, and that of Dembo and Barker on frustration), and which is a logical procedure for the "field theoretical" approach in social psychology.

The second point we wish to stress is that exact quantitative records become valueless if one loses sight of the meaning which the single action had within the total setting. It is therefore most important to have some complete characterization of the atmosphere as a whole. The necessary quantitative analysis (choice of items, classification of items, and statistical combinations) should always be made in view of these larger wholes.

The comprehensiveness of these data makes it possible to follow up with re-analysis new clues which arise from time to time as to behavioral relationships. It is our belief at the present time that this "total behavior" technique, combining strands of all degrees of quantitativeness and qualitativeness offers the most hopeful methodology yet developed for the experimental study of group life. The possibility of focusing numerous strands of evidence upon one or two focal points corrects to some extent for the necessity of working with such a number of variables as the social situation presents.

An interesting set of problems has arisen in the statistical analysis of social interactions which has led to the development of an embryo "mathematics of group life." It became obvious that before statements could be made about the relative amount of interactions between members of in-groups under various circumstances or between members of out-groups, it was necessary to take into account the possibilities of in- and out-group communication in each type of group structure. For example, it is clear that if all members were working on isolated individual bits of activity there could be no in-group relationships for no subgroup would have more than one member. If all five children were united in one activity unity there would be no possibility of interactions with an out-group member. In case the total group were divided into two subgroups these possibilities are different in case the two subgroups contain 4 and 1 children, or 3 and 2 children.

It is necessary then to compute the possibilities of in- and out-group communication for each possible group structure. In case the total group contains 5 individuals the following 7 group structures are possible:

5, 4-1, 3-2, 3-1-1, 2-2-1, 2-1-1-1, 1-1-1-1-1

The formula for computing in-group interaction possibilities (*ip*) and out-group interaction possibilities (*op*) for any given group structure may be stated simply:

$$ip = a\,(a-1) + b\,(b-1) + \cdots r\,(r-1)$$
$$op = m\,(m-1) - ip$$

where *a*, *b*, . . . *r* are the number of members in the various subgroups coexisting in a particular group structure and where *m* is the total number of members in the group.

In our case we find the following interaction possibilities:

Possible group structures

| | 5 | 4-1 | 3-2 | 3-1-1 | 2-2-1 | 2-1-1-1 | 1-1-1-1-1 |
|---|---|---|---|---|---|---|---|
| *ip* | 20 | 12 | 8 | 6 | 4 | 2 | 0 |
| *op* | 0 | 8 | 12 | 14 | 16 | 18 | 20 |

Weighting these possibilities by the time that each group structure existed we get an index with which to measure the relative in-group, out-group, and total social interactions in the authoritarian and democratic atmospheres. We can use the following formula for the total in-group interaction possibilities ($\Sigma ip$) during a given period of group life:

$$\Sigma ip = ip(A) \cdot t(A) + ip(B) \cdot t(B) + \cdot \cdot \cdot + ip(L) \cdot t(L)$$

where $A$, $B$, . . . . . . . , $L$ are the various types of group structure which came up during that period; $t(A), t(B), \ldots t(L)$ the duration of each group structure; $ip(A), ip(B), \ldots ip(L)$ their in-group interaction possibilities.

The total out-group possibilities ($\Sigma op$) is:

$$\Sigma op = op(A) \cdot t(A) + op(B) \cdot t(B) + \cdot \cdot \cdot + op(L) \cdot t(L)$$

The total social interaction possibilities ($\Sigma sp$) is:

$$\Sigma sp = \Sigma ip + \Sigma op$$

Ex: If, during a certain club meeting the structure was 4-1 for 5 minutes, 3-1-1 for 10 minutes, and 2-1-1-1 for 10 minutes the formulation of the index would demand this computation:

$$\Sigma ip = 12 \times 5 + 6 \times 10 + 2 \times 10 = 140$$
$$\Sigma op = 8 \times 5 + 14 \times 10 + 18 \times 10 = 360$$
$$\Sigma sp = 140 + 360 = 500$$

The computation of these interaction possibilities seems an essential step in the experimental treatment of group relationships. It makes possible also the correction for missing members now and then over a series of club meetings.

There is little space in this note for an adequate exposition of the analyses which have been completed on the lives of these two experimental clubs. In summary form the findings indicate that:

1. A higher state of tension existed in the atmosphere of the autocratic group. A number of findings focus on this point: (a) a much higher volume of social interactions (55% more) in spite of the fact that the ongoing activity demanded less communication than in the democratic group; (b) a less stable group structure was maintained; (c) more ascendance and less submissiveness and objectivity of members toward each other; (d) the development of two scapegoats during 12 meetings; (e) about 30 times as much hostility expressed between members as in the democratic group.

2. More cooperative endeavor emerged in the democratic group;

(a) a much higher incidence of offering and asking for cooperation; (b) many more occurrences of praise and expressions of friendliness.

3. More expression of an objective attitude in the democratic group: (a) many more constructive suggestions offered; (b) more give and take of objective criticism without personal involvement.

4. Constructiveness was higher in the democratic group: (a) superiority of the group products; (b) more careless and unfinished work in the autocratic group; (c) greater incidence of constructive suggestions in the democratic group.

5. The feeling of "we'ness" was greater in democracy, and that of "I'ness" was greater in the authoritarian group as shown by test situations and by analysis of the stenographic records.

6. The group structure was more stable and tended to maintain a higher degree of unity in the democratic group. When the authority withdrew his influence on the situation the group structure tended toward disorganization in the autocratic group.

7. Twice in the autocratic group a situation arose where the group combined its aggression against one individual, making him a scapegoat. In both cases the scapegoat quit the group. No such lack of harmony existed in the democratic group.

8. The feeling for group property and group goals was much better developed in the democratic group as shown by test situations and the stenographic accounts.

9. Following the one exchange of group members which was made there was a decrease in dominating behavior for the child transferred to the democratic group and an increase in like behavior for the child changed to the authoritarian group.

It seems necessary to reiterate that a number of these specific results, which will be tabulated more fully when further analysis is completed, may be due to the particular types of autocratic and democratic atmospheres developed in these groups. For instance there would probably not be such an overt expression of hostility in most cases of authoritarian group atmosphere, for it would be suppressed. This "steam valve" of free expression was purposely left open however in this investigation because it was hoped it would prove a good measuring stick for the record of tension when it existed. This seems to have been the case. The thoughtful establishment of such test areas seems at the present to be a very fruitful procedure. Only further research, some of which is already under way, with a variety of groups and leaders will make possible a more assured statement as to the common factors in these dynamic relationships. These new experiments indicate, for example, that the dynamic differences between free and authoritarian atmospheres present quite a different picture in case the freedom of the group swings from democratic group determination to anarchic individualism.

A more sociological survey of the atmospheres of the other groups (e.g. family, school) in which the children have membership-character will also need to be made for clues as to the influence of overlapping group memberships upon the development of the experimental group ideology. New methods of experimental manipulation are also being developed as we become more oriented to the nature of the task.

# *A Further Investigation of the Criteria of Leadership*

LAUNOR F. CARTER, WILLIAM HAYTHORN, and MARGARET HOWELL

IN A PREVIOUS paper Carter and Nixon (1) have reported the results of a study of the relationship between four criteria of leadership ability for three different tasks. From their work with high school students they drew two major conclusions: first, that leadership in certain intellectual and clerical situations tends to be independent of leadership performance in mechanical assembly tasks; second, that there was not a high relationship between assessments of leadership based on leaderless-group situations, on supervisor's ratings, on student nominations, and on participation in extracurricular activity.

Since these results were based on high school students observed for only a relatively short period of time a new experiment was designed to determine if the above conclusions would be supported when based on a different group of subjects studied more intensively. The scope of the work was expanded by increasing the number and diversity of the work-tasks used in the leaderless-group technique and by increasing the number

ABRIDGED FROM *Journal of Abnormal and Social Psychology*, 1950, 45, 350–358. Reprinted by permission of the authors and the American Psychological Association, Inc.

The work described in this paper was done under a contract between the U.S. Navy, Office of Naval Research and the University of Rochester.

of criteria used. In the current work assessments were obtained from use of the leaderless group technique, from nominations, from faculty members, from the subject's friends and from an evaluation of their past leadership activities. The results of this more intensive investigation will be reported by discussing each of the different criteria separately and then considering the interrelations between the criteria.

## THE LEADERLESS GROUP WORK-TASK CRITERION

The basic method common throughout the use of the leaderless-group technique is the setting up of miniature work-tasks similar to actual problems to be faced later in real life by the members of the group. Several individuals are introduced into these situations without an appointed leader and careful note is made of the group interaction and leadership behavior of those involved. It is hoped that those demonstrating leadership behavior in such "artificial" miniature situations will later perform similarly when faced with real leadership problems. More extensive accounts of the methods used in a variety of situations can be found in 1, 3, 4, and 6.

### *Work-Tasks and Observation Technique*

In the present study six different types of work-tasks were used. A short description of each follows:

THE REASONING TASKS. Each subject was handed a card containing four "given statements" for a syllogistic reasoning problem. The group as a whole received a paper containing statements which were to be marked true, false, or indeterminate, in terms of the given statements. The subjects were allowed to tell each other their given statements but could not show the cards to one another. Group agreement was required.

THE INTELLECTUAL CONSTRUCTION TASKS. The group was given a diagram of a field or court, such as a basketball court. Some dimensions were given and others had to be determined from known relationships. The group plotted the court on the floor with string and scotch tape.

THE CLERICAL TASKS. The subjects were asked to sort a large number of cards by several breakdowns. The requirements were such that considerable coordination between different sortings of the cards was required.

THE DISCUSSION TASKS. Group discussion was required in the acceptance or rejection of some questions, such as: "Resolved: the recent election of Harry Truman as President will help continue the present high level of national prosperity." A written conclusion was to be composed.

THE MOTOR COOPERATION TASK. The motor cooperation task involved the use of the spiral-ball apparatus devised by French (2). By tipping the apparatus the subjects tried to roll the ball to the top of the spiral. The closest cooperation and coordination between the subjects was required to accomplish this purely motor task.

THE MECHANICAL ASSEMBLY TASKS. The subjects were furnished with a very general diagram of the object they were to assemble. They built such things as bridges, backstops, goal posts, etc., using bolts and pre-cut and pre-drilled lumber.

## SUMMARY AND CONCLUSIONS

Five different criteria of leadership ability were investigated. These five criteria included use of the leaderless-group technique, the nominating method, ratings by faculty members, ratings by friends, and the assessment of leadership in previous extracurricular and out-of-school activities.

The reliability of ratings made by observers from the leaderless-group situations was quite high. There was some indication that as the number of people observed increased, the reliability of the ratings decreased. The coefficients of attenuation between a session involving groups of four subjects and later sessions involving these same subjects averaged .65.

The correlations between the leadership ratings given the subjects on six different kinds of tasks were computed. Almost all of the coefficients were positive, indicating a certain generality of leadership performance from task to task. At the same time there were noticeable groupings of relationships between certain tasks. By the use of factor analysis it was indicated that there were two different kinds of tasks apparently calling for different leadership abilities. These two factors were called an "intellectual leadership" factor and a "doing things with one's hands leadership" factor.

On two occasions the subjects nominated from their members the men they thought would be the best and the poorest leaders. These nominations were quite reliable. The nominations were made with regard to six different tasks. Again the intercorrelations between the tasks were positive; factor analysis revealed essentially the same pattern of leadership factors as was determined from the ratings made by the observers in the leaderless-group sessions.

The ratings by faculty members and by friends proved to be quite unreliable. In contrast, the reliability obtained from high school faculty members' ratings, using the same technique, had been fairly high in a previous study. The difference in reliability appears to be due to the fact that in the high school study all of the subjects were rated by the same judges whereas in the college study a large number of different judges was required to obtain the ratings. The subjects' past leadership performance was assessed from their activities and positions of leadership in clubs, social groups, extracurricular activities, etc.

Intercorrelations between these five criteria of leadership tended to be quite low. The average correlation between the leaderless-group ratings and the nomination scores, our two most reliable criteria, was .39. These results would tend to indicate that the generality of studies of leadership is limited by the nature of the particular criterion used.

The results of this study correspond closely with that of a previous study using high school subjects.

## REFERENCES


1. Carter, L. F., & Nixon, M. An investigation of the relationship between four criteria of leadership ability for three different tasks. *J. Psychol.*, 1949, 27, 245–261.
2. French, J. R. P. Organized and unorganized groups under fear and frustration. In *Studies in topological and vector psychology*. Iowa City: Univer. Iowa Press, 1944.
3. Gellhorn, W., & Brody, W. Selecting supervisory mediators through trial by combat. *Publ. Admin. Rev.*, 1948, 8, 259–267.
4. Taft, R. Use of the "group situation observation" method in the selection of trainee executives. *J. appl. Psychol.*, 1948, 32, 581–587.
5. Williams, S. B., & Leavitt, H. J. Group opinion as a predictor of military leadership. *J. consult. Psychol.*, 1947, 11, 283–292.
6. Office of Strategic Services Assessment Staff. *Assessment of men.* New York: Rinehart, 1948.


# *The Sociometry of Leadership in Temporary Groups*

CECIL A. GIBB

## INTRODUCTION

LEADERSHIP is such a common phenomenon of experience and is so frequently spoken of that there is ordinarily little conscious awareness of the variety of social relationships the term embraces. A moment's thought, however, reveals the diversity of leaders and of leader-follower relations in the culture. Few words in the English dictionary have a greater variety of meanings than does the verb "to lead."

In its dictionary sense, however, leadership is usually defined, in what might be called a social-dynamic sense, as "the exercise of authority and influence." But there is almost general agreement in the psychological lit-

FROM *Sociometry*, 1950, 13, 226–243. Reprinted by permission of the author and publisher.

erature of the last few years that the exercise of authority and influence varies qualitatively as the group-dynamic relations between the influencer and the influenced vary from rigid to more free structuration. Cowley (2) drew attention to such a distinction by differentiating headmen from leaders. Pigors (12) differentiated between these two forms of social influence by defining as domination that "process of social control in which accepted superiors assume a position of command and demand obedience from those who acknowledge themselves as inferiors in the social scale, and in which, by the forcible assumption of authority and the accumulation of prestige, a person (through a hierarchy of functionaries) regulates the activities of others for purposes of his own choosing." Many observational studies have confirmed the need for this kind of distinction with consequent restriction of the definition of leadership. Anderson (1), studying the social behavior of young children, distinguished dominative from integrative modes of behavior. The former involved the use of commands, threats and attacks on the personal status of the individual; while the latter entailed explaining the situation to the other person, and by means of this, getting voluntary cooperation. Steward and Scott (14), observing the behavior of a herd of goats, reported that there was no more than chance correlation between leadership and dominance. They suggested, in fact, that these two phenomena are the result of two separate learning processes which are not associated. They pointed out also that their results agreed with similar experiments done on human subjects (e.g., Anderson) and that it was therefore possible to conclude, tentatively at least, that the lack of correlation between dominance and leadership is a general phenomenon independent of cultural factors.

In the more restricted sense required by this differentiation leadership is best defined, by Pigors, as "a concept applied to the personality-environment relation to describe the situation when one, or at most a very few, personalities are so placed in the environment that his or their will, feeling, and insight direct and control others in the pursuit of a common cause (12)." Leadership is, then, to be understood as rather more than taking initiative, planning and organizing, as more than a positional relationship. Leadership implies a particular dynamic relationship between the leader and his followers. The chief characteristics of this relationship are: (a) an influence hierarchy; (b) integrative cooperative behavior; (c) mutual interaction and stimulation; and (d) the absence of a fixed social structure which maintains an individual's status in this hierarchy after he has ceased to perform the functions upon which the status originally rested.

One further distinction, employed in this report, is that between the leader of a group and that person who may be called (following R. B. Cattell) its socio-center. The latter term is used to fit the general terminology of Moreno (11) from whose work it derives. Jennings (7, 9), in particular, has done a great deal of very significant work in the field of leadership using the techniques of sociometric choice. By this method, however, the most chosen individual or the person who has highest "choice-status" is, by definition, a leader. It will, of course, sometimes be the case that this "leader" will also meet the criteria of the definition of leadership advocated above. But there is no reason why this should always be so. Thus it seems desirable to call this most chosen person a socio-center and to leave open to investigation the relation between the roles of socio-center and leader. A further advantage of this terminology is that socio-center and "isolate" are more logical opposites than are Jennings' leader and isolate. The terms leader and follower may then be counterposed in such a way that both represent distinct but related social roles. The isolate is not necessarily, of course, a follower, any more than the socio-center is necessarily a leader. It is one of the objects of this report to examine the relation between sociometric choice-status and leadership in temporary groups of men.

Before this may be done, however, there is a further concept, introduced by Jennings (9), which requires exposition and testing. This is the distinction between socio-groups and psyche-groups. Socio-groups are defined (9) as those "where sociometric structure is based on a criterion which is *collective* in nature." Thus sociometric choice based upon the criterion of wishing to work in a common unit defines a socio-group. On the other hand psyche-groups are those "where sociometric structure is based on a strictly private criterion which is totally personal in nature." Associating or indicating a desire to associate in leisure time is such a criterion. Further, it is suggested by Jennings (9) that "the tele between persons in respect to collaborating with one another in socio-groups may be called sociotele," and "the tele between persons in respect to associating with one another in psyche-groups may be called psychetele, since it is founded upon response towards associating or not associating with others in a purely personal matter, and concerns no situation common to all the members." Jennings has contended that there is very little overlap between these two groups, that there are few common choices by any individual on psychetelic and sociotelic bases. This contention has been submitted to a preliminary experimental test in temporary groups.

## THE PRESENT INVESTIGATION

In the course of a comprehensive study of group behavior and of the emergence of leaders in small temporary groups of men (5) [1] an investigation has been made of the degree of overlap between socio-groups and psyche-groups and of the extent of correlation between sociocentral and leadership status. For the purpose of the larger study small aggregations

1 Conducted under the general direction of Raymond B. Cattell at the University of Illinois and with the cooperation of Glen F. Stice.

of ten men were brought together in a particular way, under certain controlled conditions. These individuals were motivated generally to cooperate by the offer of financial rewards and by their needs to fulfill requirements of study courses, as part of which participation in this program was required. Men were allocated to aggregations, as nearly as possible, on the basis of their being unknown to one another, but with no other criterion of selection. Each aggregation was directed to a variety of activities so chosen that they found interaction expedient or essential and so formed a group. Ten such groups were established among male students of psychology classes at the University of Illinois and twenty among male candidates of the Air Force Officer Candidate School at Lackland Air Force Base.[2]

Each of these groups met in three three-hour sessions. This was necessary in order to have the group in existence long enough for leadership to emerge and for the members to become aware of the group as a functioning unit. It was necessary that each session be of sufficient duration to permit participation in a number of different activities and that there be a sufficient number of sessions to permit variation of the leadership structure. The design was such that in the first session leadership was left unstructured completely. It was a "leaderless" session, and the only leadership present was that which occurred spontaneously in the group. Where the group did not, of its own accord, reach the conclusion that a leader would help in planning the second session, it was suggested to them, at the end of session one, that they might select a leader for session two. When they reported for the second session an opportunity was given to reconsider this leader-choice and to elect another leader if they cared to do so. Whether this offer of change was accepted or not, another similar opportunity was offered about halfway through session two. Again, at the conclusion of this session the group was offered a change of leader in that it was asked to select a leader for session three. At the beginning of the third session a reminder was given concerning this choice and the person so chosen was then directly addressed and told that he was the leader and that he could use that office as he saw fit. Throughout session three the experimenter dealt directly with this leader in a way that had been carefully avoided up to that time.

Within this structural framework each session was planned to include a varied program of activities so that situations would occur characterized variously by demands upon: (i) cognitive abilities; (ii) social skills; (iii) special interests; (iv) group cohesion; (v) previous leadership experience, etc. Detailed descriptions of these activities and of the many measures

2 The writer wishes to express his thanks to instructors and students at the University of Illinois and to Officers and Candidates of the Air Force O.C.S., whose cooperation made possible this research. Thanks are due, too, to those members of the 3309 Research and Development Squadron who assisted, and to senior administrative officers whose approval was a prerequisite to the program.

made of: (a) personal characteristics of members; (b) inter-member relationship patterns; (c) physical equipment; and (d) the behavior of the group as a group need not be given here.

Both to gather information to be used in a study of syntality correlates of leadership (5) and to explore the foundations of some of the findings of Jennings (8, 9) a number of sociometric questions were put to participants of this program as each separate activity was completed and at the end of each session. Thus among some fifteen questions to be answered after each session were placed one (sociotele) which asked each participant to indicate those members of the group he would like to have remain in the group for future repetitions of the particular activity, or for other similar activities, and also to indicate (by circling a number) those members he would prefer to have allocated to another group; and another (psychetele) by which participants were asked: "If you were to choose personal friends from among this group which members would you choose?"

With the object of casting some light on problems already raised implicitly in what has been said above, two other questions of the general sociometric type were put to participants. After each session participants were asked a question designed to discover their judgments of behavior influencing the group. This question was: "Some groups are so closely knit that the removal of any one person changes its complexion. For which persons, if any, in this group, would this be the case?" Further, in the second and third sessions, during which they were more or less aware of leadership, at the conclusion of the construction situation participants were asked whom they would judge to have been leaders in this situation. This activity of constructing a wooden model was chosen as the vehicle for this question because it was known to involve several difficulties, was expected to afford a good opportunity for leadership to occur, and since it was an active participation task, rather than a verbal one, it was anticipated to be one in which leadership could be relatively reliably judged both by independent observers and by participants. While this latter expectation was realized the former was not. This situation did not reveal a great deal of leadership but what was revealed was reliably rated. Thus, while it did not turn out to be the best situation for this question, it was not the worst choice for the purpose. Experience with student groups, however, led to a slight re-wording of this question and its re-location at the end of the final session.

## DISCUSSION OF RESULTS

### (i) *Socio-group and Psyche-group*

One test of Jennings' claim that there are, in a group, few common choices based upon social, common criteria and purely private criteria, may be made by examining the extent of overlap of socio-centers based upon the sociotelic and psychetelic questions quoted in the previous section. Upon examination of the distribution of choices based upon each question, it was found that their shapes suggested the normal curve and that six or more choices in each group of ten men would conveniently define a socio-center. Since the assumption of normality seemed justified and the criterion choice score determining a socio-center was so chosen as to divide the distributions near their medians, the tetrachoric correlation coefficient has been chosen as an adequate index of the relation between any pair of choices.

TABLE I

*Reliability Coefficients * for Sociometric Questions*

| | SESSIONS COMPARED | | | |
|---|---|---|---|---|
| | 20 OFFICER CANDIDATE GROUPS | | | 10 STUDENT GROUPS |
| QUESTION | I-II | I-III | II-III | II-III |
| A. Sociotelic–Future working together | .45 | .50 | .66 | .78 |
| B.14. Psychetelic–Personal friends | 0 † | 0 † | .80 | .78 |
| B.6. Influence | .77 | .64 | .83 | .78 |

* Tetrachoric coefficients with sectioning at the median.

† This question was not asked in session I since time had scarcely been sufficient to form judgments concerning the friend potentialities of members.

First, as an indication of the reliability of the sociometric test, choices indicated on the sociotelic and the psychetelic questions respectively, were compared from one session to another. In particular sessions two and three were chosen for this purpose on the assumption that by this time members had some knowledge of one another. (See Table 1.)

For the sociotelic question the tetrachoric correlation coefficient between sessions two and three was 0.78 ± .09 [3] for the ten student groups and 0.66 ± .075 for the twenty O. C. S. groups. Similarly choices made in response to the psychetelic question, concerning choice of personal friends, in the two sessions were corrected and the coefficients were 0.78 ± .09 for the student groups and 0.80 ± .06 for the O. C. S. groups.

Tetrachoric intercorrelation of choices for the psychetelic and sociotelic questions could not be calculated for session two with student groups since no persons were chosen on a psychetele basis who had not been chosen on a sociotele basis. In this session with the criterion mentioned, there were 75 socio-centers on a sociotele basis. There were but 34 socio-centers on a psychetele basis and every one of these was included among the sociotelic socio-centers. Using the notion of common elements (10) a

3 The figure given thus in each case is the standard error of the appropriate tetrachoric coefficient when both dichotomies are at the medians. Since some variation from median sectioning does occur this figure is approximate only.

coefficient may be estimated at 0.67. This situation was almost duplicated in the third session with student groups where there were 60 sociotelic socio-centers and 44 psychetelic socio-centers of which 38 were common. This situation gave a tetrachoric correlation coefficient of 0.70 ± .10. With the O. C. S. groups in session two $r_{tet}$ for these two sets of socio-centers was again 0.70 ± .07 and in session three $r_{tet}$ was 0.81 ± .05.

These two sets of data confirm Jennings' (9) claim that "the structures built by sociotele are in general larger in size (quantitatively 'take in' more individuals) than the structures built by psychetele." On the other hand, since the correlations between sociotele and psychetele choices are comparable with the "reliability" coefficients of the sociometric tests, it must be concluded that Jennings' claim of "very little overlap" is not confirmed.

The significance for this comparison of the temporary nature of the present groups is not known. It would be a reasonable guess that as individuals came to know each other in more detail there might be less overlap between sociotelic and psychetelic structures. But it is interesting that within the narrow confines of this study the degree of overlap *increased* between the second and third sessions, from 45 per cent to 50 per cent for students and from 50 per cent to 66 per cent for officer candidates.

In attempting any interpretation of these findings it must be remembered that these were relatively small homogeneous groups observed over the period of group formation. As group self-consciousness increased and the group members perceived the group as achieving something, positive group feeling increased and this may well be a common factor in determining both sociotele and psychetele choices. Further, preparedness to accept an individual as a personal friend on short acquaintance is different from the actual designation of friends after longer association. But it is difficult to assess the force of accidental situational factors and of opportunity in the long-term choice of friends, and consequently it is not possible to choose between these criteria in the determination of the overlap between socio-group and psyche-group. On the face of the evidence here presented, in temporary, traditionless groups, at least, there is considerable overlap between sociotele and psychetele choices. It would still be true as Jennings (9) contends that "the psychetele pattern of a social atom cannot be predicted from its sociotele pattern," though it might be anticipated that such prediction would be a possibility if the sociometric test could be modified to respond more sensitively to differences in degree of feeling.

### (ii) *Leadership and Sociometric Choice-Status*

The primary concern of this study, however, is with the sociometric conception of leadership. Jennings (8) claims to have shown that prominence and choice status in the socio-group are a "reflection of demonstrated capacities to affect favorably the social milieu of the group." Choice status in the psyche-group is apparently less closely associated with behavior influencing the group but represents rather "capacities to 'accept' the milieu of the group" (9). In either case "leadership" and choice-status are indentified and the inverse of leadership is isolation. Jennings says those persons who are much chosen are leaders because they "count," because they "set the tone for the group in large measure." Some of them, she says, "may function chiefly as steadiers or moral support for the others, some may lead in ideas and activities, and some may be wanted on account of a special aptitude." And again (9) she writes, "While the varieties of styles of leadership (and of isolation) are many, nevertheless a number of characteristics of leader individuals stand out as common attributes. The social milieu is 'improved' from the point of view of the membership through the efforts of each other. Each widens the area of social participation for others (and indirectly his own social space) by his unique contribution to this milieu. Each leader seems to sense spontaneously when to censure and when to praise and apparently is intellectually and emotionally 'uncomfortable' when others are 'left out,' and acts to foster tolerance on the part of one member towards another." A footnote recognizes that other patterns of behavior are also found among leaders.

The point here is that, on this purely verbal level, Jennings' description appears to characterize leaders as defined in this paper as well as she claims it describes leaders by sociometric choice, i.e. socio-centers. As the writer interprets Jennings, she first meant that the much chosen individual, the socio-center, affected the group milieu because, by virtue of her choice position, she provided telic linkages with other group members. If one can think of direct and indirect influencing behavior, this would be relatively indirect. But Jennings also ascribes direct influencing to these socio-centers and thus suggests an hypothesis of some identity between them and leaders as rated by external observers using the definition of this paper. One may hypothesize also some identity between socio-centers derived from the sociotelic and psychetelic questions already examined and those derived from additional questions which imply influence and leadership criteria.

### (A) LEADERSHIP RATINGS COMPARED WITH SOCIOTELIC AND PSYCHETELIC CHOICE

The first of these hypotheses has been examined by comparing sociotelic and psychetelic sociocentrality with leadership ratings for the sessions as a whole. These criterion ratings have been obtained by regarding as leaders only those group members who were "chosen" for leadership in a majority of situations in all sessions by both of the non-participant observers. Estimates of the reliability of these ratings have been made in two ways.

First, inter-observer correlations have been calculated session by session for each group. These have been found to be 0.92, 0.77, 0.74 for the student groups in successive sessions, and 0.60, 0.60 and 0.68 for the O. C. S. groups in corresponding sessions. Second, for O. C. S. groups observer identifications over the whole period have been correlated and a coefficient of 0.80 has been obtained. This latter figure is the best available estimate of the inter-observer consistency which constitutes "reliability" for this criterion rating. Again tetrachoric correlation has been used since the assumptions of normality of the traits are quite well met here.

TABLE 2

*Correlations * between Sociometric Choices and Leadership Ratings*

| QUESTION | 20 OFFICER CANDIDATE GROUPS SESSION | | | 10 STUDENT GROUPS SESSION | |
|---|---|---|---|---|---|
| | I | II | III | II | III |
| A. Sociotelic–Future working together | .44 | .40 | .59 | .20 | .36 |
| B.14. Psychetelic–Personal friends | 0 | .46 | .45 | .32 | .41 |
| B.6. Influence | .77 | .80 | .77 | .88 | .86 |
| B.15. Leaders as judged by participants | 0 | 0 | .80 | 0 | .75 † |

* Tetrachoric coefficients.
† Construction situation only.

The correlations are as set out in Table 2. Between rating as a leader and sociotelic choice $r_{tet}$ is found to be 0.20 ± .16 in session two and 0.36 ± .15 in session three for student groups; while for O. C. S. groups the corresponding values are 0.40 ± .10 and 0.59 ± .08. The suggestion, inherent here, that the coefficient tends to rise between the second and third sessions, may have very considerable significance for Jennings' contentions. While, at this stage of mutual knowledge, there is little similarity between sociotelic choices and leader ratings, it may be that the two become more alike as group members become more familiar with each other.

Correlations between psychetelic choice and leader ratings are found to be 0.32 ± .15 and 0.41 ± .14 for student groups in sessions two and three respectively. Again, the corresponding coefficients for the officer candidates are 0.46 ± .09 and 0.45 ± .09 respectively. The suggestion of increasing correspondence just noted for sociotelic choice is not present here for psychetele. Whether sociometric choices or ratings of leadership by non-participating observers most nearly indicate "true" leadership cannot be told; but it must be recognized that they are not, in this study at least, representing the same things.

### (B) LEADERSHIP RATINGS COMPARED WITH SOCIOMETRIC "INFLUENCE" CHOICES

Further light on these facts is obtained from participants' responses to the "influence" question included in this investigation. As indicated earlier participants were asked a question designed to get at judgments of behavior influencing the group "milieu." This question was: "Some groups are so closely knit that the removal of any one person changes its complexion. For which persons, if any, in this group would this be the case?" After an examination of the distribution of identifications ("choices") on this question the socio-center criterion score was set at five choices or more rather than five plus, as it had been for the more directly sociometric questions. The nature of this question was evidently such as to encourage fewer identifications than did the two questions discussed above, in spite of the fact that an individual was himself available for identification on this question in a way that he could not normally be for the other questions.

The tetrachoric correlations between identifications on this milieu-influencing criterion and leadership ratings are, for student subjects 0.88 ± .06 in session two and 0.86 ± .06 in session three. Officer candidates yield coefficients of 0.80 ± .05 for session two and 0.77 ± .06 for session three. These coefficients are considerably and statistically significantly different from the values, given in sub-section (A) above, of the correlations between leadership ratings and sociotelic and psychetelic choices. This fact suggests that participants in a group do recognize and can identify those members who primarily determine group behavior and group atmosphere but they do not necessarily choose these persons to be members either of a socio-group or of a psyche-group.

### (C) "INFLUENCE" IDENTIFICATIONS VERSUS SOCIOTELIC AND PSYCHETELIC CHOICES

Identifications based on the "influence" question have been correlated (tetrachoric) with sociotelic and psychetelic choices. For student data this analysis was made for the third session only. It is found that $r_{tet}$ for the sociotelic choices and "influence" is 0.53 ± .13 and that for the psychetelic choices is 0.30 ± .15. For O. C. S. groups a more complete analysis was made and there tetrachoric coefficients for the sociotelic choices and influence identifications are 0.38 ± .10, 0.46 ± .09 and 0.65 ± .075 respectively for the three sessions. For psychetelic choices and influence identifications the coefficients are 0.54 ± .09 and 0.64 ± .075 for sessions two and three respectively. (See Table 3.)

The implication of these data would seem to be that in the minds of group members in a program of this nature socio-centers whether based upon sociotele or psychetele are not identified with those persons who are recognized as "counting" and as most affecting the group "milieu." Since in sub-section (B) above some evidence has been presented to suggest that participants responding to this "influence" question do identify "leaders" as they are identified by non-participating observers, the evidence of this section indicates that *socio-centers are not necessarily leaders.* Certainly these two concepts are not coincident.

On the other hand, the consistent tendency for these coefficients to increase as the period of association increases does suggest that there may be a tendency towards Jennings' notion that in a larger, well-established group, the sociotelic and psychetelic questions identify leaders well enough. This hypothesis gives rise to the question whether there may be found some systematic shift over these three sessions. (Do the leaders become the socio-centers or do the socio-centers become the leaders?) The

TABLE 3

*Correlations between Sociotelic and Psychetelic Choices and Other Forms of Leader Identification*

| Identification | SOCIOTELIC QUESTION SESSION | | | PSYCHETELIC QUESTION SESSION | | |
|---|---|---|---|---|---|---|
| A. STUDENT GROUPS | I | II | III | I | II | III |
| Observer ratings of leadership (overall) | | .20 | .36 | | .32 | .41 |
| "Influence" question | | | .53 | | | .30 |
| "Leaders" in construction | | | .25 | | | .36 |
| B. O.C.S. GROUPS | | | | | | |
| Observer ratings of leadership (overall) | .44 | .40 | .59 | * | .46 | .45 |
| "Influence" question in appropriate session | .38 | .46 | .65 | * | .54 | .64 |
| Leaders in session III | | | .59 | | | .65 |

data have been examined from this point of view and it is found that the tetrachoric "reliability" coefficients of the three questions concerned are as given in Table 1; and the respective correlations with leadership ratings are as given in Table 2.

These data suggest somewhat greater consistency for the "influence" question and indicate that this question identifies leaders earlier and more consistently than either sociotelic or psychetelic questions. One implication of the figures might be that the people who "count" by their influencing the group milieu tend to be chosen more readily as work companions (sociotele) when their influence is recognized and when the group settles down to working together in a more matter-of-fact way. Examining the several choices and identifications group by group suggests that the increasing coincidence is due largely to a general shrinkage of the number of socio-centers on sociotelic and psychetelic criteria, in which the "influencing" persons tended to retain their choice-status better than others. There is nothing here to suggest why this should have occurred, though one might hazard a guess that participants may have become increasingly aware of the experimental interest in leadership in the study and may have endeavored to make their own records "look better" by choosing only those whom they expected the observers would also choose on quite different criteria. In other words, there is a possibility that choices became less genuine. "Reliability" coefficients, however, offer no support to this hypothesis.

(D) LEADERSHIP JUDGMENTS OF PARTICIPANTS AND OBSERVERS

As already indicated, participants in the student groups were asked, at the conclusion of the construction situation in both the second and third sessions, whom they would judge to have been leaders in this situation.

The analysis of data derived from this question must begin by noting that in some 30 per cent of cases the respondents replied that there was no leadership. This may be contrasted with the fact that the observers never agreed that there was no leadership in the construction situation. However, when the remaining participants' recognition of leadership is correlated with observer ratings the coefficient obtained is 0.75 ± .10. Further the correlation in the third session between choices on this question and those on the sociotelic question was 0.25 ± .16 and with those on the psychetelic question was 0.36 ± .15. Considering the brevity of this one situation these figures are consistent with the finding (see Table 2) that these sociometric choices are correlated with the leadership ratings of observers, in the same situation, 0.36 and 0.41 respectively.

O. C. S. groups were asked, at the end of the third session, to identify the leaders for the whole session. Bearing in mind the leadership design of this session, which was to have one leader throughout, it is necessary to comment here that this never occurred in practice. Though there was this designation of an official leader, and thus, of the elements of an "official" influence structure, this was quickly forgotten in the course of the group's activities, and leadership was determined by the relation between group needs and individual ability, as much in this session as in either sessions one or two (cf. 4, 13). The distribution of "choices" on this question was such that five or more "choices" were taken as indicative of leader selection by participants. The corresponding criterion among the ratings was agreement between the two observers. With these criteria and for this session observers' identifications of leaders varied from two to seven in any one group, while participants identifications ranged between three and six. The tetrachoric correlation between the two sets of identifications is 0.80 ± .05.

For these groups, and for this third session, the correlation between the sociotelic question and the identification of leaders was 0.59 ± .11; and for the psychetelic question $r_{tet}$ was 0.65 ± .10. In this case the comparison of these coefficients with the corresponding correlations with observer ratings, reveals that for sociotele the results are identical. For psychetele the association with participants' leader identifications is considerably closer than that with observer ratings.

In Table 3 have been drawn together the coefficients of correlation between the sociotelic and psychetelic questions and all the other identifications made in this study. Viewed in contrast with the last two rows of Table 2, this would suggest that "leadership" is not identified in the minds of participants with either socio-group choice or psyche-group choice and further question is cast upon this common sociometric identification. When asked simply to indicate leaders, without being given any definition of leadership for the purpose, participants did so with a fair degree of validity—.80 if observers' ratings can be regarded as a criterion of leadership. This would, in fact, tend to reinforce any argument that observers' ratings may be regarded as such a criterion and that socio-centers are not necessarily leaders.

#### (E) "STATUS-SCORES" AND LEADERSHIP RATINGS

Recently French and Eng (3) defined "status-scores" in terms of the number of choices received minus the number of rejections received on a sociometric test. Using these scores French and Eng found a number of significant correlations with leadership behavior. Since data was readily at hand in part of the present study to examine this status-score against a different, and rather more stable, criterion of observer ratings, this was done for student groups, for status-scores derived from the sociotelic question.

The distributions of status-scores, for both leaders and non-leaders, approximate normal, so that again tetrachoric correlation has been used as an estimate of the relation. The coefficient obtained has a value of 0.44 ± .14 which compares well with results reported by French and Eng for socio-group scores with such categories of behavior as dominance, generosity, fairness, purpose, etc. The present finding, however, but slightly favors these "status-scores" over the more usual "choices." The size of the correlation coefficient is still so small as to indicate that "status-scores" and leadership ratings have little variance in common.

### (iii) *The Value of First Impressions*

#### (A) "FIRST IMPRESSION" AND PSYCHETELIC CHOICE

As indicated above sociometric questions were also asked after each specific situation was completed. The first situation of the first session was usually construction, but sometimes it was a situation known as "group judgment" in which the group was asked by discussion to derive answers to several questions of fact. In either case the situation took no more than fifteen minutes to complete, and these were, of course, the first fifteen minutes of acquaintance. At this stage participants were asked to indicate the two members of the group they liked most because of the kind of persons they appeared to be and also the two liked least. Since participants were, in general, previously unknown to one another, the responses to this question at this time must therefore have represented first, or very early, impressions. Consequently it has been of some interest to correlate these responses with the indication of willingness to choose friends within the group, made at the conclusion of the third session, that is after some ten hours of formal association, probably longer when casual meetings coming to the group and leaving the building are considered.

The relation between the two sets of responses has been estimated by tabulating friend choices and not-friend choices against most liked, not mentioned and least liked. Both of these distributions may be conceived as really normal. Therefore a tetrachoric correlation coefficient may be regarded as a more appropriate summarizing statement of the relation than a contingency coefficient would be. Thus the "not-mentioned" category has been thrown first to one side, then to the other, and two tetrachoric coefficients found.

For the 10 student groups these two coefficients agreed very closely, the one being 0.30 and the other 0.28. Since the number of judgments upon which this calculation is based is approximately 900, this is a highly significant value and is consistent with the value of $P < .001$ obtained by the chi square test.

The 20 O. C. S. groups give tetrachoric coefficients of 0.31 and 0.45 (average $r_{tet} = .38$) for the correlation between first impression and choice of friends. This again is highly significant.

The significance of these values does not mean, of course, that this correlation coefficient is high. It cannot be said that first impression is a close function of final willingness to choose friends or vice versa, but there is a considerable relation between them.

### (B) "FIRST IMPRESSION" AND LEADERSHIP RATINGS

It is to be expected that these first impressions would bear less relation to leadership ratings than to friend choice since the latter was made by the same individuals on much the same criterion. Nevertheless, it was thought worthwhile to investigate the correlation between first impression and leadership rating. The procedure was exactly as for the previous comparison.

Chi square was again significant at or beyond the .001 level. Again, tetrachoric correlation has been used putting scores of the "not-mentioned" category first with "most liked" and then with "least liked." For student groups in the first case the coefficient given was 0.20 and in the second case 0.10. Regarding the mean of these as a summarizing coefficient the value is 0.15 which is significant at the .01 level. Corresponding values of the coefficient for O.C.S. groups were 0.10 and 0.25 respectively. The summarizing value in this instance is thus 0.17 which is again statistically significant.

These results indicate that there is no close relation between ultimate leadership in a small temporary group and making a favorable impression very early in the group's association. On the other hand, the correlation is significantly positive and thus suggests that something of leadership has already emerged when a first impression is recorded.

## SUMMARY AND CONCLUSIONS

Small temporary traditionless groups, each of ten men, have been formed for the purposes of experimentation with factors associated with emerging leadership. Ten such groups were composed of male students at the University of Illinois and twenty of male O.C.S. cadets at Lackland Air Force Base. Among the many aspects of group and group-member behavior which has been observed and assessed by non-participant observers, ratings were made of the leadership behavior of each participant. These ratings have been based upon a definition of leadership as an inter-individual relation of influence, voluntarily accepted by the influenced person, in which leader and follower mutually stimulate one another and in which the relationship is not maintained beyond its mutual usefulness by a rigid social structure.

At the same time participants have completed a number of sociometric "tests" in which both sociotelic and psychetelic choices have been called for, among others specifically introduced here. Relations among these sociometric tests and between them and leadership ratings have been examined. Centrally, the relations between the sociometric definition of "leader," (or what has here been called "socio-center") and the "influence" definition employed in the observer ratings, and in two of the introduced sociometric devices, have been examined.

Both sociotelic and psychetelic types of sociometric test have a session two-session three reliability coefficient in the range 0.72 to 0.78, the psychetelic choices being rather more consistent. The introduced "influence" question had a reliability of approximately 0.80. Intercorrelation between sociotelic and psychetelic choices was approximately 0.70.

The correlation between sociotelic choice and leadership ratings is shown in Table 2 from which it may be seen that a value of approximately 0.45 will represent this relation. Similarly the correlation between psychetelic choice and leadership ratings may be said to be approximately 0.42. The implication is that these two concepts, while overlapping, are not identical.

When participants were asked a sociometric question which implied the "influence" criterion, correlation with observer ratings of leadership was approximately 0.80. And when participants were asked directly whom they regarded as having been leaders, the correlation with observer ratings was again 0.80. But this same question correlated only 0.25 and 0.36 with sociotelic and psychetelic choices respectively, for student groups; and 0.59 and 0.65 respectively for O.C.S. groups. Despite these slightly higher values for O.C.S. groups it seems safe to conclude that sociotelic and psychetelic choices are not identified in the minds of participants with leadership.

The correlation between leadership ratings and socio-group "status-scores," as defined by French and Eng, was examined in ten groups, and found to be 0.44. The indication is that these two have little variance in common and that these status-scores are not superior to sociotelic choices in their correlation with leader identification by external observers.

Another form of sociometric question has been used to study the value of first or early impressions. It was found that correlations between first impression and final willingness to choose as friends, and between first impression and leadership ratings, are so low as to indicate that there is no close relation between these. But the fact that these coefficients were significantly positive may suggest that something of the value one individual has in the eyes of another, which must partially determine his leadership status, is already evident at the stage of a first impression.

In drawing conclusions from this study, it must be remembered that these were temporary, artificial and traditionless groups; and that this quality alone may be sufficient to explain what differences there are between these findings and those of the sociometrists, particularly Jennings. Nevertheless, there can be little doubt but that real groups have been formed here and that data derived from them may have real significance in understanding the dynamics of more well-established groups. In a sense this has been a group embryological study which can illuminate the dynamics of formed groups much as embryology contributes to the study of anatomy and physiology.

Some of the sociometric findings are clearly confirmed. For example, it is clear that structures built by sociotele are more inclusive than those built by psychetele. On the other hand, the sociometric concept of leadership as roughly identical with sociocentrality is brought under fire. The evidence suggests that leadership defined in terms of influencing behavior cannot be measured by sociometric tests using either sociotelic or psychetelic criteria. The fact that participants (for whom leadership was not defined) identify "leaders" in a closely similar way to observers (for whom leadership was defined as a voluntary influencing relationship) indicates that this definition does no violence to common sense and that, in fact, this is the relation which is generally conceived as that of leadership. Further, the lower correlations between these identifications and the sociotelic and psychetelic choices is indication enough that, in the minds of these participants, they were not choosing leaders in making those choices.

An additional fact is that participants in responding to a question, in which the influence criterion is implied, but not stated and in which the notion of leadership is not introduced, did identify leaders much as did external observers. The implication of this fact is that the sociometric technique is applicable to the identification of leaders but that sociotele and psychetele are not adequate criteria.

Finally, and in summary, it may be said that participants in such groups as these understand the relation of leadership and that if adequately questioned they can identify leaders in the group with both reliability and validity.

## REFERENCES

1. Anderson, H. H. Domination and integration in the social behavior of young children in an experimental play situation. *Genet. Psychol. Monogr.* 1937, 19, 343–408.
2. Cowley, W. H. Three distinctions in the study of leaders. *J. abnorm. soc. Psychol.* 1928, 23, 144–157.
3. French, R. L., & Eng. Value categories differentiating leaders and isolates in adolescent boys' groups. Paper read at Midwestern Branch of A. P. A. meetings in Chicago, 1949.
4. Gibb, C. A. Principles and traits of leadership. *J. abnorm. soc. Psychol.* 1947, 42, 267–284.
5. Gibb, C. A. The emergence of leadership in small temporary groups of men. *Ph.D. Thesis Univer. of Illinois*, 1949.
6. Guetzkow, H. *University of Michigan Conference Research Report.* April 1948.
7. Jennings, Helen H. *Leadership and isolation.* (1st Ed.) New York: Longmans, Green, 1943.
8. Jennings, Helen H. Leadership and sociometric choice. In Newcomb & Hartley (Eds). *Readings in social psychology*. New York: Holt, 1943.
9. Jennings, Helen H. Sociometry of leadership. Beacon House, 1947. *Sociometry Monogr.* No. 14.
10. McNemar, Q. *Psychological statistics.* New York: Wiley, 1949.
11. Moreno, J. L. *Who shall survive?* Washington, D.C.: Nervous & Mental Disease Publishing Co., 1934.
12. Pigors, P. *Leadership or domination.* London: Harrap, 1935.
13. Sherif, F. *An Outline of social psychology*. New York: Harper, 1948.
14. Stewart, J. C. & Scott, J. P. Lack of correlation between leadership and dominance in a herd of goats. *J. comp. physiol. Psychol.* 1947, 40, 255–264.

# *Sharing Leadership in Small, Decision-Making Groups*

LEONARD BERKOWITZ

SOCIAL scientists engaged in research in the area of leadership have approached the exceedingly complex problems in this area from many different directions. The personalities of the leaders (2) and of the followers (12) have been investigated, as have the behavioral characteristics of elected or sociometrically chosen leaders (8) and of institutionalized or designated leaders (13). But despite the approach used, as Katz indicates (9), the present trend is to emphasize the relational aspects between the leader and his group. The characteristics of the leader, whether personality-wise or behavioral, become significant only in terms of the leader's group. A leader's behavior, thus, may or may not satisfy the needs of the group, and a group member's behavior may or may not be in conformity with the traditions of his group.

In this sense, training in "democratic" leadership may not benefit the leaders of certain groups, particularly if those groups have learned to expect and adjust to, or even require, more "authoritarian" leadership practices. "Democratic" leadership may affect the group adversely (for example, in terms of criteria such as satisfaction with the group meeting) because it is not in keeping with the group's needs and expectations. The present study does not test the efficacy of "democratic" groups as contrasted with "authoritarian" groups. However, one aspect of "democracy"

FROM *Journal of Abnormal and Social Psychology*, 1953, 48, 231–238. Reprinted by permission of the author and the American Psychological Association, Inc.

This study is part of a larger series of investigations undertaken by the Conference Research project at the University of Michigan. Thanks are due to the project staff, and to Drs. R. W. Heyns and H. Guetzkow in particular, without whom this study would not have been possible, and to Dr. Daniel Katz and the members of my doctoral committee for their helpful suggestions. An overview of some of the general findings of the project is presented elsewhere (11). The full data upon which this report is based are to be found in the author's dissertation, Some Effects of Leadership Sharing in Small, Decision-Making Conference Groups, 1951, University of Michigan Library, and in the reports of the Conference Research project (1).

in groups may be described in terms of leadership sharing. We may define a "democratic" group as one in which many members may influence the group in the course of its goal setting and goal achievement. French has pointed out (5) that many conditions may intervene to affect the relationship between group "democracy" and criteria of group effectiveness. One such condition may have to do with the expectations of the groups.

Very broadly, then, this is the problem with which we are presently concerned. What happens when the functions of the institutionalized or designated leader are shared by others in the group?

## METHOD

The present study is based on the methodology and many of the hypotheses developed by the Conference Research project. The most extensive study undertaken by the project was a field observation of 72 conferences in government and industry. The present report is concerned with a small part of the data collected in the course of this study.

### *The Data*

Of the 72 conference groups in the sample, 42 were industrial in nature, i.e., they were conference groups in organizations devoted to manufacturing. Fourteen were business groups from organizations engaged in retailing, banking, newspaper publishing, and hotel enterprises. The remaining 16 came from federal and local governmental organizations. The size of the groups ranged from 5 to 17 members with a mean of 9 members, and the duration of the conferences was from 16 to 191 minutes. Many of these groups, furthermore, were composed of members having high status in their organizations. Of particular relevance to the present study is the chairman's status relative to the mean status of the group as measured by distance on the organizational chart from the head of the organization. Only 9 of the chairmen are at or below the mean level of the group; the great majority of the 72 chairmen are thus above the mean of the group in organizational status. Lastly, the sample of conferences was restricted to those primarily decision-making in nature.

### *Methods of Data Collection*

Three observers, each with a specific area of interest, were present at all the meetings. The independent measures used in the present study were largely obtained from the records of one of these observers. The task of this individual, the "problem-solving coder," was to code the remarks of the participants according to the problem-solving category system developed by Heyns (7). In essence, the observer noted every participation—the total speech of an individual from the time he started to speak until the next person spoke—breaking each down into the categories it included.

Upon the completion of the meeting, each conference member was given a five-item questionnaire attempting to assess his satisfaction with various aspects of the meeting. Some of these ratings, all highly intercorrelated, were later averaged to form a measure of the group's satisfaction with the conference. After these ratings were collected—but before they were examined—the observers left the meeting room and immediately made a series of 54 ratings describing the interactions among the conference participants. The final source of data came from interviews with the participants within 48 hours after the meeting. Among other things, the data gathered at this time had to do with the members' perceptions concerning the interactions within the group.

## *The Measures*

In general, the functions or behaviors going to make up the role of the conference chairmen are behaviors either directly influencing the group to follow him or behaviors facilitating this influence. Previous exploratory work carried out by the project led to the development of hypotheses as to what some of these behaviors might be, and measures of these were used as the independent variables in the present study. The meaning of these variables is twofold. In a sense they are two sides of the same coin. The variables have to do with the extent to which conference leadership is shared by members other than the designated leader, the chairman. When the chairman is said to be firmly in control over the group's procedure, it is also implied that there are few other group members attempting to influence the course of the meeting. Again, the greater the proportion of solution proposing contributed by the other conference members the smaller the proportion of all the solution proposing accounted for by the chairman. The independent variables are as follows:

1. *Leader Control of Process*—postmeeting observer rating. This item refers to the leader's control over the *manner* in which the group went about handling its problems, and not the content of the problems.

2. *Leader Permissiveness in Content*—postmeeting observer rating. This measure is a rating of the designated leader's restrictiveness in the area of the *content* of the group's problems.

3. *Functional Differentiation of the Leader*—postmeeting observer rating. This has to do with whether or not the conference chairman behaved differently from the other group members by performing somewhat unique functions. A separate analysis has revealed that there were generally two or more behavioral leaders among the group members when the chairman was rated low on this item. Thus, the more the designated leader was differentiated from the others, the more the leadership functions were centered in him alone.

4. *Percentage of Member Participation*—observer tally made during the meeting. This is the percentage of all the participation in the group that was accounted for by the members other than the chairman.

5. *Percentage of Functional Units to the Leader*—observer tally made during the meeting. Within each participation a group member may perform several different functions: he may propose a solution to the group's problems (solution proposing), develop and enlarge upon the solution (development giving), and seek further comments from the others (development seeking). Furthermore, each of these functional units may be directed to a different member.

This, then, is the proportion of the total number of functional units contributed by the group members which were directed to the chairman.

The following 3 variables have to do with the functional units or categories within the participations. In computing the following scores we used the proportion of all the units within any one category that were accounted for by the members other than the chairman.

6. *Percentage of Goal Setting by Members.*
7. *Percentage of Solution Proposing by Members.*
8. *Percentage of Summarizing by Members.*

Three of the dependent measures used in the Conference Research field study are employed here. They are designed to assess some of the more important outcomes of conferences: the cohesiveness of the group, the members' satisfaction with their meeting, and the productivity of the meeting.

1. *Cohesiveness.* The series of experiments carried out by the Research Center for Group Dynamics (3, 4) have demonstrated the theoretical importance of this construct. The present definition is the sum of five highly interrelated observer ratings of the attractiveness of the group situation, e.g., the pleasantness of the group atmosphere, the degree of personal liking, etc.

2. *Satisfaction with the Conference.* This is a mean of five highly interrelated ratings made by the conference participants at the conclusion of their meeting or shortly thereafter. These include: satisfaction with the decisions arrived at, satisfaction with the leader, satisfaction with the group's process, etc.

3. *Productivity.* The operational definition of productivity is the proportion of agenda items completed of those brought up for consideration. This information was obtained from the tallies made by one of the observers in the course of the meeting.

## RESULTS

### *Relationships Over All Groups in the Sample*

Table 1 reveals the correlations between the measures of leadership sharing and the three criteria. The results with the group's satisfaction with its meeting are fairly clean cut. The more the chairman is the sole major behavioral leader the more satisfied the group with its conference. This can be seen in the following correlations. Satisfaction increases: the more the chairman controls the group's process, the more functionally differentiated he is, and the greater the proportion of functional units addressed to him. Satisfaction also increased the less the members participate relative to all the participating done in the group, and the less they do of all the solution proposing done in the group.

But although the conference groups in the present sample tend to be less satisfied when leadership is shared—when others besides the chairman perform leadership functions—it appears that productivity does not suffer. The indices of leadership sharing bear no relation to the proportion of agenda items completed of those considered.

The only leadership measure significantly related to the ratings of cohesiveness was the rating of the leader's permissiveness in the area of the content of the group's problems. The more permissive the leader the higher the rating of group cohesiveness. Just as good a case may be made for saying that permissiveness produces cohesiveness as for saying that cohesiveness gives rise to permissiveness. It is likely that both are correct, that allowing the group freedom to express opinions can both result from and enhance the attractiveness of the group situation.

TABLE 1

*Correlations between Criteria and Measures of Leadership Sharing for All 72 Groups*

| MEASURE | COHESIVENESS | SATISFACTION WITH CONFERENCE | PRODUCTIVITY |
|---|---|---|---|
| Leader control of procedure | .04 | .29 * | −.09 |
| Leader permissiveness in content | .57 ** | −.04 | .05 |
| Functional differentiation of leader | .15 | .33 ** | −.04 |
| % Participation by members | −.17 | −.38 ** | −.20 |
| % Functional units to leader | .10 | .31 ** | .13 |
| % Goal setting by members | −.02 | −.23 | .06 |
| % Solution proposing by members | .01 | −.30 ** | −.15 |
| % Summarizing by members | −.24 | −.18 | −.03 |

* Significant at the 5% level of confidence.
** Significant at the 1% level of confidence.

## *The Effects of Situational Factors*

It is not possible to go into all of the additional "breakdowns" carried out to test the effects of situational conditions upon the above relationships. For example, they suggested that there are "negative reactions"–lowered cohesiveness and satisfaction–to leadership sharing in both more and less permissively led groups.

Although there is more sharing of the leadership functions in the more permissive situations, the chairman's control of process, the extent to which he is functionally differentiated from the others in the group and the percentage of units addressed to him tend to be positively correlated (statistically significant or almost so) with cohesiveness and member satisfaction in both the more permissively led and the less permissively led groups. Similarly, the proportion of all the participations in the group accounted for by members is related to decreased cohesiveness and satisfaction under both types of conditions. This is shown in Table 2.

It should be pointed out that though the results indicate that the present groups want behavioral control by the socially recognized conference

TABLE 2

*Correlations between Criteria and Measures of Leadership Sharing for Groups Contrasted on the Chairman's Permissiveness in the Content of the Group's Problems*

| MEASURE | *N* | | COHESIVENESS | | SATIS. WITH CONF. | | PRODUCTIVITY | |
|---|---|---|---|---|---|---|---|---|
| | HI PERM. | LO PERM. | HI PERM. | LO PERM. | HI PERM. | LO PERM. | HI PERM. | LO PERM. |
| Leader control of process | 39 | 33 | .38 * | .21 | .44 ** | .18 | .08 | —.22 |
| Functional differentiation of leader | 39 | 33 | .37 * | .24 | .49 ** | .18 | .14 | —.18 |
| % Participation by members | 39 | 33 | —.43 ** | —.29 | —.35 * | —.46 ** | —.23 | —.25 |
| % Functional units to leader | 39 | 33 | .27 | .22 | .27 | .37 * | .15 | .17 |
| % Goal setting by members | 37 | 32 | —.14 | —.16 | —.14 | —.38 * | .12 | —.05 |
| % Solution proposing by members | 39 | 33 | —.39 * | .02 | —.18 | —.47 ** | —.17 | —.23 |
| % Summarizing by members | 30 | 23 | —.06 | —.30 | .03 | —.38 | .11 | —.14 |

* Significant at the 5% level of confidence. ** Significant at the 1% level of confidence.

leader, they do not indicate that they want substantive control over what should or should not be said.

An attempt was made to determine whether the negative effects of sharing could be attributed to those groups having an opposing relationship with the chairman. That is, is the lessened satisfaction due to the fact that the sharing may be done in opposition to the chairman?

The 72 groups in the study were subdivided into three categories. (*a*) Those groups having no consistent leadership sharers, as indicated by a high rating on the continuum of functional differentiation of the chairman. There is evidence indicating that there were more emergent leaders the lower the rating of designated leader differentiation. (*b*) Those groups having a somewhat lower rating on the differentiation of the chairman scale, but who appeared to be in a positive, supporting relationship with the chairman. These are termed the *positive-sharing* groups. (*c*) Those groups having consistent leadership sharers, but who were in less of a supporting relationship with the chairman. These groups are termed the *negative-sharing* groups.

The positive-sharing groups were differentiated from the negative-sharing groups on the basis of the ratio of supporting to supporting-plus-opposing interchanges with the chairman. It was reasoned that this proportion of supporting remarks to and from the chairman could serve as an indication of the extent of the group's supporting relationship with the chairman. Those groups having a higher proportion of supporting interchanges are more likely to be in a positive, supporting relationship with the chairman.

Several conclusions may be drawn from the correlations shown in Table 3. We can organize them in terms of the relationships with the criteria. But what seems to be generally indicated by the results is that there is little evidence that the type of relationship with the chairman is of primary significance in determining the correlation between the measures of sharing and the criteria.

1. Cohesiveness.

*a*. The leader's permissiveness in the content of the group's problems is positively related to the rating of group cohesion in the less supporting, negative-sharing group as well as in the more supporting, no-sharing and positive-sharing groups.

*b*. Despite the general supporting relationship with the chairman in the positive-sharing groups, the group attractiveness tends to decrease the more the members participate relative to the chairman and the less they address their remarks to the chairman.

2. Satisfaction with the conference.

*a*. The greater the proportion of the total number of participations accounted for by the members other than the chairman, and the less clearly the chairman is the major behavioral leader by being functionally

TABLE 3

*Correlations between the Criteria and Measures of Leadership Sharing for the Three Kinds of Sharing Groups*

| MEASURE | KIND OF GROUP | COHESIVENESS | SATISFACTION WITH THE CONFERENCE | PRODUCTIVITY |
|---|---|---|---|---|
| Leader control of process | o sharing | .02 | .12 | —.13 |
| | + sharing | —.10 | .32 | .17 |
| | — sharing | .31 | .22 | —.10 |
| Leader permissiveness in content | o sharing | .64 ** | .03 | .11 |
| | + sharing | .43 | —.12 | .02 |
| | — sharing | .59 ** | .01 | —.06 |
| Functional differentiation of leader | o sharing | —.36 | .13 | —.08 |
| | + sharing | .29 | .54 * | .41 |
| | — sharing | .52 * | .20 | —.06 |
| % Participation by members | o sharing | —.14 | —.15 | —.15 |
| | + sharing | —.54 ** | —.47 * | —.42 |
| | — sharing | —.24 | —.59 ** | —.33 |
| % Functional Units to leader | o sharing | —.13 | .12 | .01 |
| | + sharing | .50 * | .31 | .30 |
| | — sharing | .22 | .58 ** | .52 * |
| % Goal setting by members | o sharing | .14 | —.05 | —.32 |
| | + sharing | —.25 | —.15 | .24 |
| | — sharing | —.13 | —.31 | —.18 |
| % Solution proposing by members | o sharing | .03 | —.45 * | —.35 |
| | + sharing | —.32 | —.04 | —.09 |
| | — sharing | .12 | —.25 | —.31 |
| % Summarizing by members | o sharing | —.22 | —.36 | —.09 |
| | + sharing | .02 | —.16 | —.15 |
| | — sharing | —.48 * | —.02 | —.23 |

* Significant at the 5% level of confidence.
** Significant at the 1% level of confidence.

differentiated from the rest of the group the less the group's satisfaction in the more supporting positive-sharing groups.

In general, then, the indications are that cohesiveness and member satisfaction may be lessened by leadership sharing even though the group is in a supporting relationship with its designated leader, the chairman.

## *Correlations with the Sharing Measures in Groups Contrasted on the Urgency of Their Problems*

Unlike the correlations in the groups contrasted on the permissiveness of the leader, and the relationship between the group and its leader, there is evidence that the urgency of the group's problems may affect the reactions to the sharing of leadership. The groups in the present sample were "broken down" into groups with more and less urgent problems, depending upon the mean of the members' ratings on this scale. Judging from the correlations (not given here) with the urgency scale, we might characterize the groups with urgent problems as being more motivated, and with this motivation focused on the reaching of definite problem decisions. There is also a tendency for these groups to have greater interdependence among the members.

The correlations shown in Table 4 fairly clearly indicate differences in relationships with the sharing measures in the more and less urgent situations. For one thing, the results suggest that the designated leader's control over the group and his being functionally differentiated from the rest of the group are related to group cohesiveness and satisfaction only when the problems confronting the group are not pressing ones. These correlations are significantly different from the *r*'s in the more urgent situations. The percentage of all the participations accounted for by the members is negatively related to cohesiveness and satisfaction in only the less urgent situations, but the differences in correlation are not significant.

It is also interesting to note that the relationships with the percentage of all the solution proposing accounted for by the members vary depending upon the urgency of the group's problems. This measure is *negatively* related to cohesiveness and member satisfaction in the less urgent situations, but *positively* related to cohesiveness in the more urgent situations. This difference is statistically significant. Last, the chairman's permissiveness is positively related to the cohesiveness of the group only in the more urgent situations. This difference in correlations is also statistically significant.

## DISCUSSION

Over all groups in the present population and in several different situations, leadership sharing is associated with lessened group cohesion and lessened satisfaction with the conference. Although we have no direct evidence on this matter, these results would appear to suggest that the present groups have an expectation maintaining that the designated leader, the chairman, is to be the major behavioral leader in the group. Group members performing leadership functions are then reacted to negatively if their behavior is seen as challenging the position of the chairman as the group's major behavioral leader. This hypothesis does not deny that there may be other causes for negative reactions to the sharing of leadership functions; members perform these functions when they attempt to influence the group, and the group may not agree that the influence attempt is in the proper direction. However, if there is the tradition we have hypothesized, it will tend to act like any social norm and nonconformists will be rejected.

Other investigations undertaken by the Conference Research project lend some support to this *post hoc* hypothesis. One of these was an interview study of executives in 75 business and governmental organizations; the other was an experiment carried out at the University of Michigan. One of the conclusions from the interviews was stated as follows: "Most

TABLE 4

*Correlations between the Criteria and Measures of Leadership Sharing in Groups Contrasted on the Urgency of Their Problems*

| MEASURE | *N* | | COHESIVENESS | | SATIS. WITH CONF. | | PRODUCTIVITY | |
|---|---|---|---|---|---|---|---|---|
| | HI URG | LO URG | HI URG | LO URG | HI URG | LO URG | HI URG | LO URG |
| Leader control of process | 35 | 37 | —.27 | .34 | —.04 | .59 ** | —.17 | —.23 |
| Leader permissiveness in content | 35 | 37 | .79 **† | .26 | .12 | —.19 | .17 | .05 |
| Functional differentiation of leader | 35 | 37 | .02 | .32 | .06 | .68 **† | —.16 | .09 |
| % Participation by members | 35 | 37 | —.01 | —.34 * | —.26 | —.51 ** | —.05 | —.30 |
| % Functional units to leader | 35 | 37 | .06 | .15 | .31 | .32 | .09 | .17 |
| % Goal setting by members | 33 | 36 | —.00 | —.02 | —.02 | —.22 | .02 | .11 |
| % Solution proposing by members | 35 | 37 | .30 | —.37 *† | —.17 | —.39 * | —.00 | —.18 |
| % Summarizing by members | 27 | 27 | —.26 | —.23 | —.18 | —.36 | —.20 | .11 |

* Significant at the 5% level of confidence.
** Significant at the 1% level of confidence.
† Correlation significantly different from other correlations at the 1% level of confidence.

of the executives felt that what occurs in a conference is primarily the responsibility of the leader. When asked what they thought were the important factors in obtaining a successful conference, 86 per cent of their replies were in terms of factors which ordinarily are controlled by the leader before the conference begins" (10, p. 16). Few executives considered motivational factors. "The paucity of comment on this score clearly reflects the executive's conception of conferences as serving only his administrative needs" (10, p. 16). We may readily infer from this that the present population of groups can be characterized as having customary leader control and leader dominance.

Results from the experiment mentioned above also suggest a fairly widespread tradition concerning the role of the conference chairman. If there is such a tradition, one that has the properties of a group norm, we might predict that violators of the tradition would tend to be rejected by the group. There is evidence on this point in the experiment conducted by Heyns (6).

Heyns set up two divergent leadership styles: "positive" and "negative" leadership. The "positive" leader performed functions related to group maintenance and goal attainment while the "negative" leader not only failed to perform these functions, but attempted "to create the impression that one part of the group was working at cross purposes with other parts." The obtained correlations suggest, in part, that when the designated leader does perform leading functions, performance of these behaviors by members other than the leader tends to result in these members being rated by the group less acceptable both as a person and as a participant. However, when the leader is inactive and nonhelpful, "responsibility for behaviors which are accepted as leader behaviors tends to make one perceive unity and feel accepted both as a person and as a participant" (6, p. 115). In other words, those members who acted like leaders when the designated leader performed his functions tended to be rejected, while they were not rejected when the designated leader failed to perform the functions associated with his role.

In the two populations considered, then, college students in experimental situations and executives in business, government, and industry, the groups behaved *as if* they wanted the designated leader to be the sole major behavioral leader. In somewhat different terms, they may have expected a role differentiation with the chairman's role being clearly differentiated from the members' roles. The conditions under which the field study and experiment were conducted suggest a possible limiting condition for this expectation. In both cases the designated leaders were clearly of a higher status level than the majority of the group members. (The departmental chairman was the leader of the experimental groups.) Desire to maintain this hierarchical structure—not to have rivalry with the high status leader—may thus account for the present results.

The evidence reported in this paper also suggests two types of conditions that may affect the group's reactions to violations of this expectancy. In the Heyns' experiment there are indications that the hypothesized group tradition becomes less important when the designated leader does not perform the functions associated with his role. The members who attempt to fill the "gap" left by the chairman are not rejected by the group.

This expectancy may also be less important when there are urgent problems confronting the group, according to the results of the field study presented above. It will be recalled that cohesiveness and satisfaction tend to decrease the less differentiated the chairman is from the other group members, the more the members participate relative to the chairman, and the less the chairman controls the group's process—but only when the group's problems are not too urgent. On the other hand, there are positive relationships with the permissiveness of the leader and the percentage of all the solution proposing done by the members when the group's problems are relatively urgent. The group's motivation to reach a problem solution as quickly as possible thus appears to be stronger than its motivation to conform to the expectancies concerning role differentiation. Not only does leadership sharing fail to lessen cohesiveness and member satisfaction in the more urgent conditions, but the leader's permissiveness and the proposing of solutions by the members tends to make for more attractive group situations.

The present results point up the necessity of considering the relational aspects of leadership. In the present case, the effects of leadership sharing cannot be fully understood without taking into consideration the relationship between this sharing and the expectancies and motivations of the group.

## SUMMARY

Seventy-two groups of small decision-making conferences in business, industry, and government were studied by a team of observers. The conference participants filled out a brief questionnaire upon the completion of the meeting and were later interviewed. Correlational analysis was applied to the data obtained from the observers and the conference participants. The following hypotheses were developed to explain the results:

1. There is a general expectation in the present population of groups maintaining that the socially designated leader, the chairman, should be the sole major behavioral leader. In other words, there appears to be an expectancy of role differentiation between the designated leader and the group members with each performing somewhat unique functions.

*a.* Leadership sharing by members other than the designated leader tends to be related to a decrease in group cohesiveness and satisfaction with the meeting over the entire sample of groups, and in groups with more and less permissive leaders.

*b.* These results also hold in groups contrasted on whether the leadership sharing is generally supporting or less supporting of the chairman.

2. Leadership sharing is not generally reacted to negatively in groups with urgent problems. It may be that the group's motivation to reach an adequate problem solution as quickly as possible lessens the importance of the hypothesized group tradition.

Some other investigations undertaken by the Conference Research project are cited to support the hypothesis of an expectancy of role differentiation in the present population.

## REFERENCES


1. Conference Research project. Dittoed reports, University of Michigan, 1948–1951.
2. Cowley, W. H. Traits of face-to-face leaders. *J. abnorm. soc. Psychol.*, 1931, 5, 304–313.
3. Festinger, L., *et al. Theory and experiment in social communication.* Ann Arbor, Michigan: Univer. of Michigan Press, 1950.
4. French, J. R. P., Jr. Organized and unorganized groups under fear and frustration. *On authority and frustration: Studies in topological and vector phychology.* III. Iowa City: State Univer. of Iowa, 1944.
5. French, R. L. Leadership and the authoritarian-democratic dimension. Paper read at Amer. Psychol. Ass., State College, Pa., September, 1950.
6. Heyns, R. W. Effects of variation in leadership on participant behavior in discussion groups. Unpublished doctoral dissertation, Univer. of Michigan, 1948.
7. Heyns, R. W. Functional analysis of group problem-solving. Dittoed report Conference Research, Univer. of Michigan, 1948.
8. Jennings, H. In T. M. Newcomb and E. L. Hartley (Eds.), *Readings in social psychology.* New York: 1947. Pp. 407–412.
9. Katz, D. Social psychology and group processes. In C. P. Stone (Ed.), *Annual review of psychology.* Vol. II. Stanford: Annual Reviews, 1951. Pp. 137–142.
10. Kriesberg, M. Executives evaluate administrative conferences. *Advanced Management*, March, 1950, 15–17.
11. Marquis, D. G., Guetzkow, H., Heyns, R. W. A social psychological study of the decision-making conference. In H. Guetzkow (Ed.), *Groups, leadership and men.* Pittsburgh: Carnegie Press, 1951. Pp. 55–67.
12. Sanford, F. H. *Authoritarianism and leadership.* Philadelphia: Institute for Research in Human Relations, 1950.
13. Shartle, C. L. Leadership and executive performance. *Personnel*, March, 1949, 370–380.

# *Small Group Discussions with Participatory and Supervisory Leadership*

A. PAUL HARE

THE PURPOSE of this research was to repeat with a different age-group an experiment by Preston and Heintz (2) which showed that participatory leadership was more effective than supervisory leadership as a technique in producing change of opinion in small discussion groups of college students.[1]

## METHOD

A number of troops of Boy Scouts in a summer camp were told a story about a camping trip which would require each boy to travel alone through unknown country. They were then asked to rank 10 items of camping equipment in the order of their importance for such a trip. Next the troops were divided into groups of a leader and five followers for a 20-minute discussion period during which each leader recorded his group's decision concerning the importance of the items of camping equipment. Just before the discussions the leaders were taken aside and given instructions for participatory or supervisory leadership. After the discussions each individual ranked the equipment again and recorded his reactions to the discussion and to the leader on a questionnaire.

In addition to computing the rank-order correlations used by Preston and

FROM *Journal of Abnormal and Social Psychology*, 1953, 48, 273–275. Reprinted by permission of the author and the American Psychological Association, Inc.

Abstracted from Hare, A. P. A study of interaction and consensus in different sized discussion groups. Unpublished doctor's dissertation, University of Chicago, 1951. Pp. 144–168.

1 The writer is indebted to Professor Preston for suggesting this research and for providing material and advice in the early stages of the experiment.

Heintz, within each group the average correlation of all rank orders, $r_{av}$, was computed before and after discussion (3, pp. 372–375).

The questionnaire was modified so that instead of reporting on influence, satisfaction, etc., the Scouts were asked to report good and bad things about the leadership and to describe what they would have done if they had been the leader.

## *Subjects*

The subjects (*Ss*) were Boy Scouts who attended a Philadelphia Scout Camp during the summer of 1949. Since the Scouts usually came to camp with their home troops the members of all but one of the discussion groups knew each other the year round. The average age of the followers was 13 years. The leaders, boys from the same troop who had had some leadership experience, averaged 14 years.

## *A Nonrandom Factor in the Sample*

For each group led by a supervisory leader there was not always another group from the same troop led by a participatory leader. As a result, 6 pairs of the groups in the sample were matched and 3 were unmatched; that is, they came from different troops. When the amount of change in opinion ($\bar{r}_{av}$ before–$\bar{r}_{av}$ after) was compared for the matched and unmatched groups a significant difference was found,[2] indicating a greater similarity in the amount of change in consensus when the supervisory and participatory groups come from the same Scout troops than when they come from different troops.

TABLE 1

*Average Correlation of All Rank Orders for Followers before and after Discussion*

| LEADER TYPE | NUMBER OF GROUPS | $\bar{r}_{av}$ BEFORE | AFTER | *Diff* | *t* | *p* |
|---|---|---|---|---|---|---|
| Supervisory | 9 | .28 | .65 | .37 | 4.18 | $<.01$ |
| Participatory | 9 | .27 | .81 | .54 * | 3.85 | $<.01$ |

* This value for the difference between the $\bar{r}_{av}$ before and after discussion is similar to that obtained in an experiment by the *E* (1) in another camp using participatory groups of the same size.

## RESULTS

A comparison of the means of the average correlation of all rank orders ($\bar{r}_{av}$) before and after discussion indicates that there is a significant change in the amount of agreement in each type of group as a result of the discussion (Table 1). Furthermore, the amount of change in the participatory groups (.54) is greater than the amount of change in the supervisory

2 In this experiment a result is considered significant if it has a probability of $<.10$ of occurring by chance.

groups (.37), although the difference is not significant, having a probability of >.30 of occurring by chance.

The resemblance between the initial and group ranking, $\bar{r}'_{12}$ (Table 2), is higher in every case than that reported by Preston and Heintz, suggesting that there is more initial agreement among Boy Scouts concerning camping equipment than among college students concerning the desirability of presidential candidates.

The average correlation of the group and final ranking, $\bar{r}'_{23}$, is also higher in every case than the corresponding correlation obtained by Preston and Heintz with the participatory followers showing significantly more agreement with the group ranking than the supervisory followers.

TABLE 2

*Rank Correlations as a Function of Leadership Techniques and the Role of the Individual*

| SUBJECTS | *N* | $\bar{r}'_{12}$ | $\bar{r}'_{23}$ | $\bar{r}'_{13}$ |
|---|---|---|---|---|
| Leaders | | | | |
| Supervisory | 9 | .50 | .80 | .72 |
| Participatory | 9 | .77 | .98 | .78 |
| Followers | | | | |
| Supervisory | 36 | .55 | .86 | .61 |
| Participatory | 36 | .56 | .96 | .60 |

The participatory leaders have a significantly higher correlation for $r'_{12}$ than do either the supervisory leaders or participatory followers, which, when combined with a high $r'_{23}$ and $r'_{13}$, suggests that they influenced the group decision. This result, which is not obtained by Preston and Heintz, is, however, consistent with the way the discussions were conducted. Most of the Boy Scouts participating in this experiment were very interested in the subject for discussion. (In some cases the arguments touched off by the "camping game" continued for several days.) For this reason, the participatory leaders were generally anxious to give their views as well as to insure an equal chance for everyone else. On the other hand, the supervisory leaders who were specifically told to stay out of the discussion had little chance to influence the group. They tend to have the least agreement with the group ranking after discussion as well as a high degree of consistency between their initial and final rankings.

The data in Table 3 supplement those given in Table 1 by providing another measure of the change in opinion which results from the two types of leadership. In every case the difference between the $\bar{r}'_{13}$ and $\bar{r}'_{23}$ is negative, indicating that the correlation between the initial and final rankings is smaller than the correlation between the group and final rankings. The difference is significant for all but the supervisory leaders. This suggests that each of the other three types of group members tends to be influenced more by the group ranking than by his initial ranking. Participatory leaders and followers show relatively more agreement with the group ranking than do the supervisory leaders and followers. Both the $r_{av}$ and the $r'$ data tend to substantiate the finding of Preston and Heintz that group activity under participatory leadership is more productive of change of opinion.

TABLE 3

*Correlation between Group and Final Rankings Compared with Correlation between Initial and Final Rankings*

| SUBJECTS | $\bar{r}'_{13}-\bar{r}'_{23}$ * | $t$ | $df$ | $p$ |
|---|---|---|---|---|
| Leaders | | | | |
| Supervisory | −.20 | −.52 | 16 | >.50 |
| Participatory | −.95 | −3.93 | 16 | <.01 |
| Followers | | | | |
| Supervisory | −.52 | −3.93 | 70 | <.01 |
| Participatory | −.96 | −6.55 | 70 | <.01 |

* Differences are the equivalents of differences in $z$ functions.

## Questionnaire Responses

A summary of the responses to the questionnaire given after the final ranking indicates that participatory *Ss* are generally better satisfied with the decision made by their group than are the supervisory *Ss*. The differences between leaders and followers of each type, while not significant, are consistent with the findings of Preston and Heintz.

On the three 160-mm. linear rating scales all subgroups rate their group discussions as generally friendly and enjoyable, as interested in the task, and as efficient and productive. Although Preston and Heintz report statistically significant differences in the responses in the direction of more enjoyable, interesting, and efficient discussion in the participatory groups, a series of $t$ tests reveals no significant differences in the present experiment. The fact that differences are not reported may be due to a tendency for 13-year-old boys to withhold unfavorable comments about their peers from an adult experimenter. This same tendency toward a positive report is evident in the responses to open-end questions included to provide some descriptive data about the effects of the two types of leadership style. No matter what the leader style, the boys tried to say something good about it.

## SUMMARY

When 13-year-old boys were used as *Ss* in an experiment which compared the effects of supervisory and participatory leadership on group judgment in discussion groups of five members, the results generally substantiated the findings of a similar experiment using college-age *S*s. The data indicated that participatory leadership was more effective than supervisory leadership as a technique for changing opinion. In addition, the participatory leader generally had more influence on the group, a result not obtained with college *S*s. Although participatory *S*s were generally better satisfied with the results of the group decision than were the supervisory *S*s, the differences were not statistically significant.

## REFERENCES

1. Hare, A. P. A study of interaction and consensus in different sized groups. *Amer. sociol. Rev.*, 1952, 17, 261–267.
2. Preston, M. G., & Heintz, R. K. Effects of participatory vs. supervisory leadership on group judgment. *J. abnorm. soc. Psychol.*, 1949, 44, 345–355.
3. Woodworth, R. S. *Experimental psychology*. New York: Henry Holt, 1938.

# *Methods of Conducting Critiques of Group Problem-Solving Performance*

E. PAUL TORRANCE

THE PURPOSE of this study is to evaluate the relative effectiveness of four alternative methods for conducting brief critiques of a short problem-solving exercise designed to assist groups (air crews) to function more effectively as groups.

In many training situations, both military and civilian, it is necessary to conduct brief on-the-spot critiques of a group's performance. Instructors of the Advanced Strategic Air Command Survival School, the scene of the present study, are faced with this problem many times during the course of the field training of each crew they instruct. In all of these

FROM *Journal of Applied Psychology*, 1953, 37, 394–398. Reprinted by permission of the author and the American Psychological Association, Inc.

situations, there is the problem of how much guidance by the instructor or expert produces the best results. Can a crew effectively criticize itself and improve its problem-solving performance, or is the assistance of the expert necessary? When the expert conducts the critique, should he be the evaluator or should he keep the locus of evaluation within the crew?

## THEORETICAL CONSIDERATIONS

Much has been written in the areas of counseling and guidance and industrial training about techniques applied to the individual to bring about proper evaluation and improved adjustment or performance. One set of considerations deals with the locus of evaluation. One group, of which Rogers is the chief spokesman, holds that only when the locus of evaluation is in the individual does real growth and development take place (20). According to this theory, an evaluation by an expert or an evaluation resulting from a test would remove the locus of evaluation from the individual and would not result in development and growth. Essentially the same theory is represented in the work of Cantor (1, 2), Maier (14), Lippitt (12), French (4), Katzell (10), Haas (5), and others.

If one were to apply this theory to the problem of critiques, the superior method would be expected to be one in which the leader assumes a non-evaluative role and stimulates the group to evaluate its performance and discover improved methods.

A second set of considerations centers about the role of group decision in changing behavior. Recent findings in industrial research and nutritive education research (6, 8, 11) indicate that group discussion as such results in very little change in behavior, while group decision as a component of group discussion brings about considerable change. In these experiments, scientifically developed information was given by the expert as it was needed but the decision was left to the group. Haire (6) points out, however, that group decision does not work with passive or apathetic groups, although its use almost always stimulates a desire for participation and eventually changes the apathy.

A number of experiments have explored situations and leadership techniques which set up resistance or retard growth, and others which win acceptance or stimulate growth. The problems of resistance have been treated by Zander (22), Torrance (20) and Coch and French (3). All emphasize the importance of respecting the individuals or groups involved. A variety of methods are discussed by Maier (14, 15, 16), Cantor (1, 2), Haas (5), Haire (6), Lippitt (12), and Rogers (18). There seems to be agreement that improved performance does not result merely through reading or hearing lectures. More active participation methods, such as through discussion and role playing procedures, are required.

The skill of the leader must also be considered as a factor. A series of experiments conducted by Maier (17, p. 170) showed that "a leader, if skilled and possessing ideas, can conduct a discussion so as to obtain a quality of problem-solving that surpasses that of a group working with a less skilled leader and without creative ideas. Further, he can obtain a higher degree of acceptance than a less skilled person."

Maier concludes, however, that "even an unskilled leader can achieve good quality solutions and a high degree of acceptance" using democratic leadership. In another experiment (16), he demonstrated the superiority of the permissive discussion leader over the self-critique discussion with an observer present. Maier maintains that the major part of the difference was due to the relatively greater influence exerted by individuals with minority opinions in the "leader" groups than in the "observer" groups. "A discussion leader can function to up-grade the group's thinking by permitting an individual with a minority opinion time for discussion" (16, p. 287).

## METHOD AND PROCEDURE

### *Subjects*

The subjects of the experiment were 57 combat air crews undergoing training at the Strategic Air Command's Advanced Survival School at Stead Air Force Base, Nevada. Most of these crews were B-29 (11 men) crews, but a few B-50 (10 men) and B-36 (usually about 15 men) crews were also included. Most of the crews had been functioning as crews for about four months, although some had been together for two or more years.

### *Problem-Solving Exercises*

Two of the Intellectual Talents Tests (401-B and 701-X) developed by the Human Resources Research Laboratories were used. Both tests are thought to tap common-sense judgment and are alike in that each presents the examinee with problem-situations too complex for solution by any step-by-step logical reasoning process and requires the examinee to select the most essential or most critical of the many elements presented in the problem-situation. The problem-situations are rather commonplace and can be solved on the basis of knowledge gained from background experiences common in most persons' lives. Differences in the 401-B and the 701-X are that the 701-X consists of a larger number of shorter problems and permits an unlimited number of choices.

### *Experimental Procedures*

The crews were tested in tents measuring 16 feet by 32 feet on the first day of their training. Each crew was first given an orientation regarding the nature and purpose of the test. Following this, each member of the crew was asked to make an estimate of his crew's performance. The first problem-solving test was then administered, after which a post-test estimate of crew performance was obtained from each crew member.

Following this, a critique of the first problem-solving performance was conducted by one of the following methods:

1. Unstructured non-authoritarian or crew-centered critique: The crew was asked to evaluate and discuss its own performance. Discussion was centered on both the decision as to method and the way it was reached, as well as the way the decision was executed. The experimenter tried to stimulate discussion and encourage crew members to evaluate their performance, but the experimenter did not evaluate their performance. The experimenter accepted questions but referred them back to the crew. The attitude of the experimenter was definitely non-authoritarian. Techniques used were similar to those described by Cantor (1, 2), Maier (14), and Rogers (19).

2. Directive or expert critique: The experimenter diagnosed the performance of the crew according to a set of 13 rating scales (listed later), pointed out ineffective procedures, and suggested ways of improvement. He stated that through research, certain characteristics have been found to differentiate between crews which operate effectively and those which do not. The analysis included both the way the group went about making its decision and what they decided, as well as how they worked together to carry out the decision.

The experimenter took a very active role, assuming the role of the "expert." He tried, however, to give his advice in the most tactful way possible. He, nonetheless, gave definite evaluations and advice. The experimenter accepted questions and answered them as an "expert."

3. No critique: The experimenter went ahead and administered the California F-Scale which required about 15 minutes, before administering the second problem-solving test.

4. Self-critique: Time was allotted for a critique and the experimenter left the tent, returning after 15 minutes.

5. Structured non-authoritarian or crew-centered critique: The experimenter used the set of rating scales as a guide in getting the crew to evaluate itself and discover more effective ways of performing. The locus of evaluation was still within the crew, however.

Following the 15 minute critique period, the second problem-solving test, the 701-X, was administered. The rules were the same as for the first problem except that the time limit was ten minutes.

## *Observations and Ratings*

After each of the two problem-solving tests, the experimenters completed a set of five-point rating scales following a set of descriptive scales on each of the following characteristics: (*1*) Organization of manpower; (*2*) Selective use of personnel; (*3*) Supervision; (*4*) Participation in decision-making; (*5*) Acceptance of suggestions or criticisms; (*6*) Consideration of available time; (7) Checking work; (*8*) Leadership function; (*9*) Survey of the situation; (*10*) Understanding instructions; (*11*) Group atmosphere; (*12*) Speed of reaction to the problem situation; and (*13*) Officer-airmen relations.

## RESULTS

A problem-solving score was computed for each crew on both of the problem-solving tests, using the scoring formulae already in use for these tests. A performance rating was also computed for each crew on both of the problem-solving situations by adding the thirteen ratings made by the examiner. In order to hold constant scores and ratings for the first problem-solving test and to determine if the variance in scores and ratings is due to the method of conducting the critique, analyses of co-variance were then carried out both for ratings and for scores. Using the ratings, the variance for critique methods was found to be statistically significant at the one per cent level of confidence ($F = 4.968$). Using problem-solving scores, however, the variance was not statistically significant at less than the five per cent level of confidence ($F = 1.957$). Because of the small number of crews critiqued by each experimenter by each method, it was not possible to compute the interaction of experimenter and critique method.

Crews participating in the unstructured non-authoritarian critique were combined with those participating in the self-critique and crews participating in the expert critique were combined with those participating in the structured non-authoritarian critique in order to study the effect of structure vs. non-structure in critiques. Analysis of co-variance revealed that the variance due to structure is significant at the five per cent level both for ratings ($F = 5.664$) and for scores ($F = 5.124$). Analysis of co-variance also showed that the variance due to different experimenters is not statistically significant ($F = 0.429$) for ratings and for scores.

In order to study relative improvement in performance which might be attributable to differences in methods of conducting critiques, each crew was ranked in order from one to fifty-seven on each of the four variables (score on 401-B, score on 701-X, ratings on 401-B performance, ratings on 701-X performance). Crews were then divided equally into a most improvement category and a least improvement category on ratings and on scores. Table 1 shows the percentage falling into each category according to method of conducting the critique for both ratings and scores.

The *t*-test of significance of differences in percentage reveals the superiority of the expert critique over the non-authoritarian critique (significant at the .001 level of confidence), no critique (significant at the .01 level), and the self-critique (significant at the .02 level). The differences in percentages between the expert critique and the structured non-authoritarian critique are not statistically significant. The latter tends to be more frequently followed by improvement than are the unstructured non-authoritarian critique (significant at the .01 level of confidence), no critique (significant at about the .10 level of confidence), and the self-critique (not statistically significant).

The situation in regard to improvement on problem-solving scores is about the same as for ratings, except that the superiority of the expert critique is not as clear. The *t*-test of significance of the difference in percentage shows that the expert and structured non-authoritarian methods are superior to the unstructured non-authoritarian, the self-critique and no critique at about the .02 level of confidence. The unstructured non-authoritarian method and the self-critique appear to have no superiority over no critique.

TABLE I

*Comparison of Effectiveness of Methods of Conducting Critiques*

| BASIS OF COMPARISON | EXPERT CRITIQUE (11 *crews*) | STRUCTURED NON-AUTHORITARIAN CRITIQUE (11 *crews*) | SELF-CRITIQUE (12 *crews*) | UNSTRUCTURED NON-AUTHORITARIAN CRITIQUE (11 *crews*) | NO CRITIQUE (12 *crews*) |
|---|---|---|---|---|---|
| Percentage showing "most improvement" in standing on scores | 73 | 73 | 33 | 36 | 33 |
| Percentage showing "most improvement" in standing on ratings | 91 | 64 | 50 | 9 | 33 |

## DISCUSSION

The fact that the structured non-authoritarian is superior to the unstructured non-authoritarian method and that the expert method is not superior to the structured non-authoritarian method would suggest that the locus of evaluation is not important in the type of critique studied in this experiment. Of course, it may be that even though the "expert" makes evaluations, the crew still makes its own evaluations and does not surrender its evaluative function to the expert as readily as some might suppose. A close examination of crews subjected to the expert method and making little improvement indicates that some of the evaluations given by the "expert" were definitely rejected by the crew. The crucial thing may be the giving of evaluations that can be accepted rather than the giving or not giving of evaluations.

The issue of group decisions does not become crucial in this experiment since in every case the decision was left to the crew, although that decision may have been made by one person, usually the aircraft commander. In using the unstructured non-authoritarian, however, it was observed by almost all of the experimenters that a crew would recognize and discuss improved solutions and even appear to give general approval to these solutions. Yet, when the time came to decide how to organize for the second problem, the Aircraft Commander would simply say,

"We'll do it the same way we did the other one." This may explain why this method is not more effective than no critique of any kind.

In regard to the overcoming of resistance, the less structured methods are least effective. It must be mentioned, however, that some of the crews which made the most outstanding improvement were crews using the self-critique. The difficulty is that not all crews are able to look objectively at their performance and discover more effective ways of working together. Most crews seem to require enough structure or guidance to assure that their evaluations and considerations will be concerned with the salient elements. This does not in any way deny the importance of the participation and involvement of the group. It does, however, emphasize the importance of the "expert" and the nature of the role he must play in order to be effective where single trial, immediate performance is concerned.

Although the variation due to experimenter differences was not significant, differences in the success of experimenters were observed. For example, 70 per cent of the crews critiqued by two of the experimenters were in the "most improvement" category while only 25 per cent of the crews of another experimenter were in this category (significantly different at about the 5 per cent level of confidence). The least well trained experimenter differed very little from the best trained experimenters.

The results would appear to have important implications for training of many types, especially training of the on-the-job variety in industry, education, and the military services. Although there are a number of questions which need to be subjected to further study, the results of this study seem to point the way to using structured critiques where decisions are still left to the group, where final evaluation is left to the group, but where the trainer can help guide the evaluative process. This study also suggests several directions for further research which are being pursued through a series of additional studies now under way. These studies are concerned with the role of the expert, the decision-making techniques of the group's usual leader, spread of learning within the group, and transfer of learning to more different situations.

## SUMMARY

A total of 57 combat air crews undergoing survival training were divided randomly into four experimental groups and one control group. Each experimental group was administered a problem-solving test, critiqued according to one of four methods, and then administered a second problem-solving test. The control group was given no critique between the two problem-solving tests.

Crews obtained scores on both of the problem-solving tests and ratings of manner of performance on both of the tests.

Analysis of co-variance indicates statistically significant variances in ratings due to method of conducting critiques. Analysis of co-variance indicates statistically significant variance in both scores and ratings due to structuring the critique but no statistically significant variance due to experimenters.

Crews critiqued according to the more highly structured methods are more frequently followed by "greater improvement" than are crews critiqued according to the less highly structured methods. Crews participating in the unstructured non-authoritarian and the self-critique do not perform significantly better than crews receiving no critique.

## REFERENCES

1. Cantor, N. *The dynamics of learning.* Buffalo, N.Y.: Foster and Stewart, 1946.
2. Cantor, N. *Learning through discussion.* Buffalo, N.Y.: Human Relations for Industry, 1951.
3. Coch, L., & French, J. R. P. Overcoming resistance to change. *Hum. Relat.*, 1948, 1, 512–532.
4. French, J. R. P. Field experiments: changing group productivity. In J. G. Miller (Ed.), *Experiments in social process.* New York: McGraw-Hill, 1950.
5. Haas, R. B. Action counseling and process analysis; a psychodramatic approach. *Psychodrama Monogr.*, 1948, No. 25.
6. Haire, M. Some problems of industrial training. *J. soc. Issues*, 1948, 4, 41–47.
7. Hendry, C. E., Lippitt, R., & Zander, A. Reality practice as educational method. *Psychodrama Monogr.*, 1947, No. 9.
8. Hendry, C. E. *A decade of group work.* New York: Association Press, 1948.
9. Human Resources Research Laboratories. *Intellectual Talents Tests 701-X and 401-B.* Washington, D.C.: HRRL, Bolling Air Force Base.
10. Katzell, R. A. Testing a training program in human relations. *Personnel Psychol.*, 1948, 1, 319–329.
11. Lewin, K. Group decision and social change. In T. M. Newcomb, & E. L. Hartley (Eds.) *Readings in social psychology.* New York: Holt, 1947.
12. Lippitt R. An experimental study of the effect of democratic and authoritarian atmospheres. *Univer. Iowa Stud. Child Welf.*, 1940, 16, 43–195.
13. Lippitt, R. *Training in community relations.* New York: Harper, 1949.
14. Maier, N. R. F. *Principles of human relations.* New York: Wiley, 1952.
15. Maier, N. R. F., & Zerfoss, L. F. MRP: a technique for training large groups of supervisors and its potential use in social research. *Hum. Relat.*, 1952, 5, 177–186.
16. Maier, N. R. F., & Solem, A. R. The contribution of a discussion leader to the quality of group thinking: the effective use of minority opinions. *Hum. Relat.*, 1952, 5, 277–288.
17. Maier, N. R. F. The quality of group decisions as influenced by the discussion leader. *Hum. Relat.*, 1950, 3, 155–174.
18. Rogers, C. R. *Client-centered therapy.* Boston: Houghton Mifflin, 1951.
19. Rogers, C. R. Divergent trends in methods of improving adjustment. *Harvard Educ. Rev.*, 1948, 38, 209–219.
20. Torrance, E. P. The phenomenon of resistance in learning. *J. abnorm. soc. Psychol.*, 1950, 45, 592–597.
21. Torrance, E. P., & Levi, M. *Crew performance in a test situation as a predictor of performance in the field.* Stead Air Force Base, Nevada: HRRL Detachment No. 3, 1952.
22. Zander, A. Resistance to change–its analysis and prevention. *Advanc. Mgmt.*, 1950, 15, 9–11.

# *Some Findings Relevant to the Great Man Theory of Leadership*

EDGAR F. BORGATTA, ARTHUR S. COUCH,
and
ROBERT F. BALES

## INTRODUCTION

A CENTRAL area of research and theory in social psychological science, particularly in group dynamics and small group research, is that of "leadership." The interest apparently lies in the expectation that the "effectiveness" of group performance is determined in large part by the leadership structure of the group. Effective performance is usually defined by the joint occurrence of high task accomplishment and high satisfaction of members of the group.

There are at least six types of thinking about the optimum leadership structure of the group for effective performance. (*1*) The most effective group is the one which has the most adequate all-around leader ("great man"). (*2*) The most effective group is the one in which all members have been chosen according to ability for the specific task. (*3*) The most effective group is the one in which members are selected on the basis of their sociometric choices of each other as co-workers. (*4*) The most effective group is the one in which the various qualities of task ability and social ability are distributed among the members to allow or encourage role differentiation and division of labor. (*5*) The most effective group is one in which members are similar in values or some critical area of values.

FROM *American Sociological Review*, 1954, 19, 755–759. Reprinted by permission of the authors and publisher.

This research, carried out at the Harvard Laboratory of Social Relations, was supported in part by the United States Air Force under Contract A33 (038)-12782 monitored by the Human Resources Research Institute. Permission is granted for reproduction, translation, publication and disposal in whole and in part by or for the United States Government. We are grateful to Hugh Williams for assistance in computations.

(*6*) The most effective group is the one in which members are selected primarily on the basis of compatibility of personality characteristics, such as authoritarianism, major mechanisms of defense, ascendance-submission, etc.

Our concern here is in exploring some aspects of the first principle which we arbitrarily call the "great man theory of leadership." This is probably the oldest of the six theories and one which has received attention throughout the centuries. Such attention is understandable when one considers that history is frequently written from the reference point of "great men." It is equally understandable in terms of the implicit ease with which manipulation is possible if the organizational performance is determined by the single person in the top position. Much psychological research, assuming the great man theory, has been oriented to the problems of selecting persons who are best fitted for a top position of leadership. However, tests of the great man theory which involve the performance of groups rather than the consistency of the leader's behavior are relatively absent in the literature.

## PROCEDURE

The data to be presented, bearing on the great man theory, are based on 166 sessions of three man groups.[1] The subjects (N = 126) were male enlisted Air Force personnel assigned to the research project on temporary duty. They were recruited from different organizations, and acquaintance was minimal. The purpose of the testing was represented to the subjects as being the observation of how small groups work together, and presumably, this observation was to take place when they did some role playing. However, they were also observed in periods during which they planned the role playing session and periods of informal participation. It is this data which is analyzed in this experiment. Each of these 166 sessions was 24 minutes long. Every person participated in four sessions with two new co-participants in each session. The differences in enlisted grade were controlled by assignment of subjects to session with persons of their own status.

## DESIGN

Couch and Carter (6) have demonstrated in a factor analysis of the rated behavior of individuals in group interaction that three orthogonal factors

1 Other aspects of this research have been reported in other papers. Problems of reliability of scoring and consistency of subject performance were discussed in Borgatta & Bales (5). Problems concerning the effect of task differences of experience, and the "accumulation of a common culture" are discussed in Borgatta & Bales (4). The effects of participation with various types of co-participants, and a rationale for reconstituting groups are presented in Borgatta & Bales (3). The relationships among sociometric measures, interaction performance, ratings by superiors, intelligence, and selected variables are discussed in Borgatta (2).

account for the major portion of the variance in these ratings. The factors have been identified as: (*1*) *Group goal facilitation;* (*2*) *Individual prominence;* and (*3*) *Group sociability*. More simply, the factors may be identified as Task ability, Individual assertiveness, and Social acceptability. For this study, using the Couch and Carter experience, along with that accrued from other sources, we attempted to measure the factors as follows:

FACTOR I: *Task ability*—(a) leadership rating received from co-participants on a task criterion; (b) the I.Q. score as measured by the Science Research Associates Primary Mental Abilities.

FACTOR II: *Individual assertiveness*—the total activity rate of the individual in terms of the number of initiated acts per unit of time (using Bales' category system 1).

FACTOR III: *Social acceptability*—the sociometric popularity as determined by choices received on a criterion of "enjoyed participation with."

It is our notion that a *great man* would need to possess each of the three independent qualities to a substantial degree. With this fusion of qualities the great man is able to satisfy the major role demands and personality needs of group members. In this study we have defined the great man in terms of a product of the four measures mentioned above. The product of the scores is used rather than a sum to emphasize the requirement of a *simultaneous* occurrence of the qualities. Some sample computations of the product index used are shown in Table 1.

*Great men* were selected on the basis of their performance in the first session. The top eleven such persons were chosen, each participating in a separate group. That is, there was no case of two great men together in a first session. Our choice of eleven persons was arbitrary and based on the assumption that only about the top tenth of the total sample would satisfy the criterion of "greatness." In the three subsequent sessions when two great men participated together, that three-man group was eliminated from the sample; this reduced our number from 33 to 25. We did this because the term "great man group" implies a group with a *single* great man as all-around leader.

Before examining other hypotheses, a point of concern for this study is whether a person who performs as a great man in the first session does so by virtue of the particular composition of his group, or whether it is a function of relatively stable characteristics of his personality which determine his "greatness" in any group in which he participates. If there is no stability in performance, our subsequent hypotheses are meaningless.

We have no post-meeting estimates of productivity or satisfaction. However, we have indices of interaction in the group which have face validity as bearing on productivity and satisfaction.

(a) For the satisfactory performance of a group in relation to a complex or general task, a large number of suggestions which are acceptable to the group must be made. An index which is a reasonable *a priori* estimate of this kind of task facilitation is the simultaneous presence of high rates of giving suggestion and showing agreement in the group as a whole.

TABLE I

*Some Sample Factor Product Indices*

| SUBJECT IDENTIFICATION | FACTOR I TASK ABILITY | | FACTOR II INDIVIDUAL | FACTOR III SOCIAL | PRODUCT INDEX |
|---|---|---|---|---|---|
| (ordered by index) | (a) Leadership | (b) I.Q. (percentile) | (c) Assertiveness | (d) Acceptability | (a) (b) (c) (d) (in 1,000's) |
| 1 | 4 | 97 | 161 | 2 | 124.9 |
| 2 | 4 | 96 | 145 | 2 | 111.4 |
| 3 | 4 | 98 | 126 | 2 | 98.8 |
| 4 | 4 | 81 | 152 | 2 | 98.5 |
| 5 | 4 | 78 | 151 | 2 | 94.2 |
| 6 | 3 | 88 | 175 | 2 | 92.4 |
| 7 | 4 | 78 | 135 | 2 | 84.2 |
| 8 | 4 | 96 | 106 | 2 | 81.4 |
| 9 | 4 | 68 | 144 | 2 | 78.3 |
| 10 | 4 | 70 | 121 | 2 | 67.8 |
| 11 | 4 | 54 | 145 | 2 | 62.6 |
| . | | | | | |
| . | | | | | |
| . | | | | | |
| 102 | 1 | 4 | 117 | 2 | 0.9 |
| 103 | 3 | 2 | 94 | 1 | 0.6 |
| 104 | 1 | 4 | 46 | 2 | 0.4 |
| 105 | 1 | 1 | 99 | 2 | 0.2 |
| 106 * | 0 | 8 | 75 | 0 | 0.0 |
| 107 | 0 | 1 | 25 | 1 | 0.0 |
| 108 | 0 | 12 | 16 | 0 | 0.0 |
| . | | | | | |
| . | | | | | |
| . | | | | | |

* There were twenty-one persons with a product-index of 0.

Again, for this index we use a product relationship so that both must be high in order for the index to be high. The total number of suggestions was multiplied by the total number of agreements (Bales' category 4 times category 3). This gives a rough measure of the degree to which a given group reaches consensus on proposed solutions to the task problem.

(b) A high rate of showing tension (Bales' category 11) is a fairly direct indication of difficulty in the interaction process. It is usually a sign of anxiety and withdrawal from participation by the individual. High rates of showing tension in the group are probably associated with low satisfaction, although the relationship may not be linear.

(c) An indication of a friendly atmosphere in a group is a high rate of interaction in the positive social emotional categories, showing solidarity and showing tension release. In this case, our measure is the sum of these (Bales' category 1 plus category 2), indicating the amount of warmth expressed in the group.

## HYPOTHESES

Hypothesis (*1*): *Great men* will tend to remain *great men* over a series of sessions.

Hypothesis (*2*): Sessions in which *great men* participate will have a higher product rate of suggestion and agreement (index: time rate of giving suggestion times rate of giving agreement).

Hypothesis (*3*): Sessions in which *great men* participate will have lower time rates of showing tension than those in which they do not participate.

Hypothesis (*4*): Sessions in which *great men* participate will have higher time rates of showing solidarity and tension release than those in which they do not participate.

## *Results*

Hypothesis (*1*): The top eleven persons (of a total sample of 123) defined by the product index of the first session were followed through the subsequent sessions, and the frequency with which they appeared within the top eleven ranks of the product index in the second, third and fourth sessions was noted. Of the eleven persons, eight were in the top ranks in the second and third sessions, and seven were still in top rank in the fourth session, which is a remarkably stable performance. This pattern, based on Chi Square tests, is significant beyond .001 level. The hypothesis is emphatically supported.

The results of the remaining hypotheses are presented in Table 2.

Hypothesis (*2*): When the first sessions in which the great men participated were examined, it was found that they were significantly higher than the residual category of first sessions in terms of the product rate of agreement and suggestion. When subsequent sessions in which they participated were examined, it was found that the product index of agreement and suggestion for the sessions remained significantly higher than those in which the great men did not participate. The hypothesis is emphatically supported.

Hypothesis (*3*): Sessions from which great men were selected showed less tension than the residual first sessions as expected. The difference in the predicted direction was significant when subsequent sessions in which great men participated were compared to those in which they did not. The hypothesis is supported.

Hypothesis (*4*): When the first sessions in which great men participated were compared with the remaining first sessions with regard to amount of positive affect shown, it was found that the "great man" sessions were significantly higher. In the subsequent sessions the difference remained significant. The hypothesis is emphatically supported.

TABLE 2

*Mean Rates of Interaction for Great Man Groups and Non Great Man Groups: Identification of Great Men Based on First Session*

| | SESSION 1 | SESSIONS 2, 3, 4 |
|---|---|---|
| Product Rate of Giving Suggestion and Agreement: | | |
| Great Man Groups | 867 (N = 11) | 530 (N = 25) |
| Non Great Man Groups | 566 (N = 31) | 362 (N = 95) |
| (value of t) | (5.98)* | (2.43)* |
| Rate of Showing Tension | | |
| Great Man Groups | 9.4 (N = 11) | 11.7 (N = 25) |
| Non Great Man Groups | 14.1 (N = 31) | 16.4 (N = 95) |
| (value of t) | (1.41) | (1.79)* |
| Rate of Showing Solidarity and Tension Release | | |
| Great Man Groups | 39.6 (N = 11) | 28.6 (N = 25) |
| Non Great Man Groups | 19.7 (N = 31) | 22.2 (N = 95) |
| (value of t) | (3.98)* | (1.65)* |

* $\alpha \leq .05$, one tail test.

## DISCUSSION

The stability with which great men, chosen on the basis of their first session performance, retain top position in subsequent groups is impressive.

To the extent that our hypotheses are supported, it is suggested that great men selected on the basis of their first session continue to have an influence on the relatively superior performance of the groups in which they subsequently participate.

The evidence is quite clear that those groups containing a great man have higher product-rates of giving suggestions and agreements. Insofar as one has any reason to believe that this is related to the quality of solutions, the "productivity" of these groups is likely to be increased relative to the groups without great men.

To the extent that a lack of showing tension is an indication of smooth functioning, groups with great men appear to show less inhibited response to the task situation with less anxiety and withdrawal from active participation. This may indicate greater satisfaction with the group. Further evidence of this is seen by the greater amount of positive social emotional behavior, reflecting friendly interpersonal relationships among the members of the group.

Thus, it may be said that great men tend to make "great groups" in the sense that both major factors of group performance—productivity and satisfaction of the members—are simultaneously increased.

## CONCLUSION

In general, the great man principle of group composition appears to have much to recommend it. Further study [3] should focus on testing some of the underlying assumptions of the various principles of group composition, especially in terms of the differential effect of the leadership structures on group performance.

## REFERENCES

1. Bales, R. F. *Interaction process analysis*. Cambridge, Mass.: Addison-Wesley, 1950.
2. Borgatta, E. F. Analysis of social interaction and sociometric perception. *Sociometry*, 1954, 17, 7–32.
3. Borgatta, E. F., & Bales, R. F. Interaction of individuals in reconstituted groups. *Sociometry*, 1953, 16, 302–320.
4. Borgatta, E. F., & Bales, R. F. Task and accumulation of experience as factors in the interaction of small groups. *Sociometry*, 1953, 16, 239–252.
5. Borgatta, E. F., & Bales, R. F. The consistency of subject behavior and the reliability of scoring in interaction process analysis. *Amer. sociol. Rev.*, 1953, 18, 566–569.
6. Carter, L. F. Leadership and small group behavior. In M. Sherif, & M. O. Wilson (Eds.), *Group relations at the crossroads*. New York: Harper, 1953. Pp. 257–284.

3 A study is now in progress under the direction of Robert F. Bales in which groups composed according to the role differentiation principle will be compared with groups composed according to the great man rationale.

# *PART* IV
# *Annotated Bibliography*

# *Introduction*

THE LITERATURE *on small groups is now extensive. In the past ten years or so it has shown a phenomenal growth. Contributions have come from many sources in the behavioral sciences, and the literature is scattered over a large range of journals and books. For the bibliography which follows we have tried to draw together the more relevant references and to annotate briefly the nature of the content or findings. In spite of their brevity, we believe that the annotations can be read with profit as a review of the empirical base of the field, and that they will help to place the studies included in this book in a larger perspective.*

*As a further aid we have prepared a topical index to the bibliography. The index lists items in the bibliography according to the types of variables studied, the methods used, and various other characteristics likely to be of interest to the reader. In some cases the topical index adds to the information included in the annotation.*

*The bibliography represents a selection of 584 titles taken largely from a bibliography of about 1400 titles published by Strodtbeck and Hare.*[1] *About 300 titles in the larger bibliography were not available because of publication in foreign journals or for similar reasons, and hence had to be omitted without examination. The Strodtbeck and Hare bibliography lists titles from 1900 to January, 1954, and the present bibliography extends this canvass of the literature through July, 1954.*

*We have tried to select from the larger list those articles which dealt most specifically and concisely with small groups, as distinguished from those which present material of more general psychological or sociological interest without a particular small group reference. We have chosen those which have as a major aim the advancement of scientific knowledge about small groups as distinguished from those which concentrate on application. Finally, we have tried to give preference to original contributions to the*

1 Fred L. Strodtbeck and A. Paul Hare, Bibliography of Small Group Research, *Sociometry*, 1954, 17, 107–78.

*field as distinguished from later secondary treatments or summaries of already published material. Any such process of selection is likely to involve biases and errors, and, admittedly, we have been more concerned with errors of inclusion than errors of omission. We hope that interested readers will help us to enlarge and improve the bibliography for later revisions.*

# *Bibliography*

AN ARTICLE *which is reprinted in this volume is indicated by the italic page number in parentheses at the end of the reference. Articles reprinted in other books of readings are indicated by the bibliography number which follows the reference.*


1. Abel, Theodora M. The influence of social facilitation on motor performance at different levels of intelligence. *Amer. J. Psychol.*, 1938, 51, 379–389.

   *In two levels of subnormal girls, those of lower intelligence benefit less from working in pairs, although both groups profit quite consistently.*

2. Adams, S. Status congruency as a variable in small group performance. *Soc. Forces*, 1953, 32, 16–22.

   *Social relationships and personal emotional states are in a positive linear relation to the status congruency of a group (degree of consistency between status hierarchies, i.e., the older man should have higher status in the formal line organization), but technical performance improves for a time and then deteriorates as status congruency increases.*

3. Albert, R. S. Comments on the scientific function of the concept of cohesiveness. *Amer. J. Sociol.*, 1953, 59, 231–234.

   *In a comment on Gross and Martin "On group cohesiveness" the need for the concept of cohesiveness is questioned.*

4. Allport, F. H. The influence of the group upon association and thought. *J. exper. Psychol.*, 1920, 3, 159–182. (*31*)

   *Group presence speeds free association, with efficiency in inverse correlation to degree of mechanical nature of task, and an inverse correlation between individual's association speed and the amount of group influence on him. In group more associations are suggested by surroundings, while individually there are more personal associations. In reasoning, group stimulates more conversational, expansive expression, while the individual alone is more logical.*

5. Allport, F. H. *Social psychology*. Boston: Houghton Mifflin, 1924.

   *The individual in his social aspects and social behavior comprise the two main divisions of the book, including a section devoted to together and apart experiments and a discussion of the nature of face to face groups.*

6. Alpert, B., & Smith, Patricia A. How participation works. *J. soc. Issues*, 1949, 5 (1), 3–13.

*Participation, involving destructuring and restructuring individual viewpoint, requires both emotion and intellect in its three stages (definition, discussion, and action). Thus, there are two types of faulty participation: formalistic (unemotional) and anarchic (unanalytic).*

7. Anderson, C. A. An experimental study of "social facilitation" as affected by intelligence. *Amer. J. Sociol.*, 1929, 34, 874–881.

*The presence of a group is found to generally facilitate performance, but with bright students performance is sometimes inhibited. Fast workers tend to be more accurate and respond more to the presence of a group. Greater accuracy is evident in the presence of a group.*

8. Anderson, H. H. An experimental study of dominative and integrative behavior in children of pre-school age. *J. soc. Psychol.*, 1937, 8, 335–345.

*Nursery school children in an orphanage are more dominating and show less integrating behavior than those in the orphanage not attending school (controls). Slight positive correlation is found between integrative behavior and age.*

9. Anderson, H. H. Domination and integration in the social behavior of young children in an experimental play situation. *Gen. psychol. Monogr.*, 1937, 19, 341–408.

*Dominating behavior and integrative behavior are observed by pairing nursery school children in an experimental play situation. Children from a public nursery school have a higher rate of interaction, are more integrative and less dominating than children from an orphanage nursery school. Mental age tends to correlate positively with integrative behavior, negatively with dominating behavior. Domination in one member of the pair is associated with domination in the other, integration with integration.*

10. Anderson, H. H. Domination and social integration in the behavior of kindergarten children and teachers. *Genet. psychol. Monogr.*, 1939, 21, 287–385. (See # 31.)

*A measurement of domination and integration by observing kindergarten teacher's contact with children showed more contacts with boys, negative correlation with age, and positive correlation with mental age. A positive relationship exists between teacher's dominative and integrative contacts. Measurement of domination and integration of kindergarten children in an experimental situation showed boys more dominating with boys than are girls with girls. Where teachers had more dominating contacts, children had more integrative contacts with each other.*

11. Ansbacher, H. L. The history of the leaderless group discussion technique. *Psychol. Bull.*, 1951, 48, 383–391.

*Early use of the leaderless group discussion technique for selecting leaders for the German military is outlined.*

12. ARGYLE, M. Methods of studying small social groups. *British J. Psychol.*, 1952, 43, 269–279.

*Problems of experimental design and generalization from results are described. Experimental studies are reviewed briefly.*

13. ARRINGTON, RUTH E. Time-sampling studies of child behavior. *Psychol. Monogr.*, 1939, 51, No. 2.

*Children are observed in order to test the applicability of an observational recording technique to different age levels and to situations differing in degree of structuralization. Time sampling method of controlled observations is used, as well as a category system. Language data revealed definite developmental patterns but physical contact records do not. There was individual variation in amount of time spent in working.*

14. ARRINGTON, RUTH E. Time sampling in studies of social behavior: A critical review of techniques and results with research suggestions. *Psychol. Bull.*, 1943, 40, 81–124.

*The literature is reviewed describing the use of short observation periods with some type of category system, primarily in the area of child study.*

15. ARSENIAN, JEAN M. Young children in an insecure situation. *J. abnorm. soc. Psychol.*, 1943, 38, 225–249.

*Security in children is found to be related to the presence of a familiar adult, and insecurity tends to diminish with familiarity with the situation.*

16. ASCH, S. E. *Social Psychology*. New York: Prentice-Hall, 1952.

*An examination of fundamental concepts of social psychology in terms of Gestalt theory. One section is devoted to the effects of group conditions on judgments and attitudes.*

17. BABCHUK, N., & GOODE, W. F. Work incentives in a self-determined group. *Amer. sociol. Rev.*, 1951, 16, 679–687.

*A case study of a sales group in a department store finds low morale a result of a strongly individualistic orientation, and that cooperation and assumption of the decision-making functions created high morale. However, morale and production level are independent variables.*

18. BACK, K. W. Interpersonal relations in a discussion group. *J. soc. Issues*, 1948, 4, 61–65.

*Two discussion groups are compared. Changes over time are found in the amount of work centered activity, emotional participation, and the recipients of interaction.*

19. BACK, K. W. Influence through social communication. *J. abnorm. soc. Psychol.*, 1951, 46, 9–23. (See #507.)

*When high and low cohesive groups (strength of the forces acting on the members to remain in the group) for each of three kinds of "attraction to the group" conditions are compared, it is found that the greater the cohesiveness of the group the greater is the amount of influence exerted on the members. Members of high cohesive groups, irrespective of the nature of the attraction to the group, are less resistant to their partner's attempt to influence them and themselves attempt to exert more influence than the members of low cohesive groups.*

20. Bales, R. F. A set of categories for the analysis of small group interaction. *Amer. sociol. Rev.*, 1950, 15, 257–263.

    *Preliminary norms for the interaction process analysis are presented.*

21. Bales, R. F. *Interaction process analysis: A method for the study of small groups.* Cambridge, Mass.: Addison-Wesley, 1950. (*127*)

    *A comprehensive report of the development of a category system for interaction observation. Exploratory hypotheses about the character of interaction are presented, as well as preliminary data on cumulative norms for the observation system. The theoretical nature of social interaction is considered in terms of the objectives of small group experimentation.*

22. Bales, R. F. Some statistical problems in small group research. *J. Amer. Statist. Ass.*, 1951, 46, 311–322.

    *Statistical problems in the handling of data gathered from interaction observation, particularly problems of interdependence of observation, are discussed.*

23. Bales, R. F. The equilibrium problem in small groups. In T. Parsons, R. F. Bales, & E. A. Shils, *Working papers in the theory of action.* Glencoe, Ill.: Free Press, 1953. Pp. 111–161. (*424*)

    *The study of small groups is considered in the broad framework of general sociological theory. The concept of equilibrium is discussed in terms of problems of continuity of interaction, the development of structure, and the achievement of relatively stable systems. Data are presented which are interpreted in terms of the theoretical assumption of a system tending to equilibrium.*

24. Bales, R. F. In conference. *Harvard Bus. Rev.*, 1954, 32, 44–50.

    *Generalizations from laboratory research are applied to the business conference.*

25. Bales, R. F., & Borgatta, E. F. A study of group size: Size of group as a factor in the interaction profile. (*396*)

    *Data derived from a comprehensive study of group size indicate at least three major effects: (a) size as a variable; (b) odd and even number of persons; and (c) unique characteristics of certain sizes.*

26. Bales, R. F., & Slater, P. Role differentiation. In T. Parsons, R. F. Bales et al., *Family, socialization, and interaction process.* Glencoe, Ill.: Free Press, 1955.

    *The degree of consensus on status ranking is critical to the structure and development of a group. High status consensus generally is a function of consensus in critical values, yet there is usually ambivalence concerning the task specialist even in high consensus groups. The leader combines the two specialized functions (likeability and task ability).*

27. Bales, R. F., & Strodtbeck, F. L. Phases in group problem solving. *J. abnorm. soc. Psychol.*, 1951, 46, 485–495. (See # 115.)

*The patterns of interaction of small discussion groups are examined in terms of three time periods (phases). Systematic and consistent differences in the phases are suggested.*

28. Bales, R. F., Strodtbeck, F. L., Mills, T. M., & Roseborough, Mary E. Channels of communication in small groups. *Amer. sociol. Rev.*, 1951, 16, 461–468. Also: Bales, R. F. Reply to Keller's comment. *Amer. sociol. Rev.*, 1951, 16, 843.

*When the participants in small discussion groups are ranked by the total number of acts they initiate, they also tend to have the same rank for the number of acts they receive, address to specific other individuals, and address to the group as a whole.*

29. Barker, R. G. The social interrelations of strangers and acquaintances. *Sociometry*, 1942, 5, 169–179.

*Immediate response to others is not random. The author finds agreement in choices made by "group" members.*

30. Barker, R. G., Dembo, Tamara, & Lewin, K. Frustration and regression: an experiment with young children. *Univer. of Iowa Stud. Child Welf.*, 1941, 18, No. 1.

*Children (two to five years old), are observed in a free play and a frustration situation. Amount of escape behavior is positively correlated to amount of barrier behavior (attention to the barrier separating child from desirable toys) and amount of both is an index of frustration. In frustration, freedom of expression and frequency of happy actions decrease; masking of social behavior, unhappy actions, and restless, aggressive actions increase. Constructive play is lower (regression) in frustration.*

31. Barker, R. G., Kounin, J. S., & Wright, H. F. (Eds.) *Child behavior and development.* New York: McGraw-Hill, 1943.

*A collection of essays reporting substantive findings and methodological advances in the study of the child. Several essays deal with observation techniques and methods of analysis of social interaction.*

32. Barnard, C. I. *The Functions of the executive.* Cambridge, Mass.: Harvard Univer. Press, 1938.

*A theory of formal organization, authority, and the general nature of cooperative systems is presented. Informal organization is considered.*

33. Bass, B. M. An analysis of the leaderless group discussion. *J. appl. Psychol.*, 1949, 33, 527–533.

*Time spent talking in leaderless discussion group is found to correlate with leadership status as rated by an observer.*

34. Bass, B. M. Situational tests: II. Leaderless group discussion variables. *Educ. psychol. Measmt.*, 1951, 11, 196–207.

*Amount of participation in leaderless discussion group correlates with observers' ratings of desirability of the participant as a job candidate.*

35. Bass, B. M., & Coates, C. H. Forecasting officer potential using the leaderless group discussion. *J. abnorm. soc. Psychol.*, 1952, 47, 321–325.

*Leadership in initially leaderless group discussions is found a valid predictor of leadership in training performance.*

36. Bass, B. M., & Klubeck, S. Effects of seating arrangement on leaderless group discussions. *J. abnorm. soc. Psychol.*, 1952, 47, 724–727.

*Little effect of seating on final leadership rating received was found.*

37. Bass, B. M., McGehee, C. R., Hawkins, W. C., Young, P. C., & Gebel, A. S. Personality variables related to leaderless group discussion behavior. *J. abnorm. soc. Psychol.*, 1953, 48, 120–128.

*In a sample of 140 girls rated for leadership in (seven person) "leaderless discussion groups" the Rorschach was found to discriminate the top ten girls from the bottom ten girls. The authors find results on relationship of leadership ratings to the Guilford-Zimmerman Temperament Survey and the F Scale to be consistent with previous theory and research.*

38. Bass, B. M., & Norton, Fay-Tyler, M. Group size and leaderless discussions. *J. appl. Psychol.*, 1951, 35, 397–400.

*Observers reached maximum agreement on leadership assessment, and their ratings showed the greatest absolute variance in leadership assigned (stratification) in groups of size 6 as opposed to sizes 2, 4, 8, and 12. There was a significant decline in the mean leadership assessment earned by participants as size increased.*

39. Bass, B. M., & Wuster, C. R. Effects of the nature of the problem on LGD performance. *J. appl. Psychol.*, 1953, 37, 96–99 (also see 100–104).

*Stability of leadership is found when problems of initially leaderless discussion groups are changed and when the composition of the groups are changed. Status of supervisors in an oil company correlates with leadership in discussion of relevant topics. Leadership ratings in the discussion groups also correlate with aptitude tests on supervisory ability.*

40. Bassett, R. E. Cliques in a student body of stable membership. *Sociometry*, 1944, 7, 290–302.

*Clique structure, leadership, and differentiation of role by sex are analyzed.*

41. Bates, A. P. Some sociometric aspects of social ranking in a small, face-to-face group. *Sociometry*, 1952, 15, 330–341.

*Some support is found for the hypothesis that persons in high status replicate the norms of the group. Sociometric status is related to frequency of interaction.*

42. Bavelas, A. Morale and the training of leaders. In G. Watson (Ed.), *Civilian Morale.* New York: Reynal & Hitchcock, 1942. Pp. 143–165.

*Attitudes, techniques, and morale are more decisive for leadership than is personality. Experimental change of these factors in a three man group of poor playground leaders, led permissively, raised the morale of leaders and children.*

43. Bavelas, A. A mathematical model for group structures. *Appl. Anthrop.*, 1948, 7, 16–30.

*A mathematical model based on Lewin's topological concepts (e.g., connectedness, region, boundary) is developed and illustrated.*

44. Bavelas, A. Communication patterns in task oriented groups. *J. Accoustical Soc. of Amer.*, 1950, 22, 725–730. (See # 115.)

*The effects of restrictions on communication are explored. Research in the area is briefly reported.*

45. Beaver, Alma P. A preliminary report on a study of a preschool "gang." In Dorothy S. Thomas (Ed.), *Some new techniques for studying social behavior*. New York: Teacher's Coll., Columbia Univer., 1929. Pp. 99–117.

*An observation of a "gang" of three pre-schoolers concentrates on initiation of action, cohesion, and acceptance or rejection of other children.*

46. Beaver, Alma P. The initiation of social contacts by pre-school children. *Child Develpm. Monogr.*, 1932, No. 7.

*The number and percentage of social contacts verbalized increases with age.*

47. Becker, H., & Useem, Ruth H. Sociological analysis of the dyad. *Amer. sociol. Rev.*, 1942, 7, 13–26.

*A broad consideration of dyadic relationships is presented with a classification of basic dyads (after Von Wiese and Becker). The applicability of sociometric techniques is examined in the light of previous and current theory.*

48. Bell, G. B., & French, R. L. Consistency of individual leadership position in small groups of varying membership. *J. abnorm. soc. Psychol.*, 1950, 45, 764–767. (275)

*When 25 male subjects are combined in 30 discussion groups, the leadership rank for each individual is found to be consistent for the five groups in which he participated. The authors conclude that situational factors may not be important.*

49. Bell, G. B., & Hall, H. E. The relationship between leadership and empathy. *J. abnorm. soc. Psychol.*, 1954, 49, 156–157.

*Both Dymond and Kerr empathy test scores taken in five (and four) member initially leaderless groups have a significant positive correlation to leadership peer ratings.*

50. Bender, I. E., & Hastorf, A. H. The perception of persons: Forecasting another person's responses in three personality scales. *J. abnorm. soc. Psychol.*, 1950, 45, 556–561.

*A positive correlation is found between forecasts of one's scores (forecast by others) and the scores actually made. Accuracy of forecast does not appear to be general since accuracy of forecast for one individual does not mean accuracy of forecast of others, and since accuracy of forecast in one subject matter does not mean accuracy of forecast in another (although a positive relationship may exist in all events to forecast comparisons). Projection is seen to operate as an important factor in forecasting.*

51. BENNE, K. D., & LEVIT, GRACE. The nature of groups and helping groups improve their operation. *Rev. educ. Res.*, 1953, 23, 289–308.

*Nine approaches in research on the nature of groups are described, and the literature which has implications for helping group operations is reviewed.*

52. BENNE, K. D., & MUNTYAN, B. *Human relations in curriculum change.* New York: Dryden, 1951.

*Change in curriculum, seen as involving changes in the knowledge, values, skills, and relations of the people concerned, raises questions about the nature, technology, ethics, and methodology of change in social groups. In a collection of selections from articles on group development, hypotheses are advanced concerning conceptual tools to analyze change-situations, groups, and group methods in curriculum change, democratic ethics and management of change, and discipline for leadership in curriculum change.*

53. BENNE, K. D., & SHEATS, P. Functional roles of group members. *J. soc. Issues*, 1948, 4 (2), 41–49.

*Roles for members of discussion groups are classified under the headings (a) group task roles, (b) group building and maintenance roles, and (c) individual roles.*

54. BERELSON, B. *Content analysis in communication research.* Glencoe, Ill.: Free Press, 1952.

*Content analysis as a technique is discussed in detail, including its use in inferring the psychological state of the communicant.*

55. BERENDA, RUTH W. *The influence of the group on the judgments of children.* New York: King's Crown Press, 1950.

*An individual child, opposed by 8 classmates giving unanimous, incorrect judgments on simple perceptual material, tends to change his judgment in the direction of the majority. (This result correlates negatively with age, but there is no relation with IQ or with personality traits.) The younger child, confronted with a task on which the teacher gives the wrong answer, changes judgment, while older children in the same position become more cautious and accurate. A minority of 8 children, confronted with a majority of children giving non-uniform wrong answers, show strong tendency to follow when line-length judged was long (unambiguous), but no such tendency when the line was short (ambiguous). This influence was stronger with children under 10 years old, and in classes where the teacher had never assumed effective control. A small majority in opposition to a unanimously wrong majority shows no change in judgment if the objective situation is clearly struc-*

*tured. If it is ambiguous, correct majority judgment may be a new frame of reference for the minority, but wrong judgments will not affect minority judgments.*

56. Berkowitz, L. Sharing leadership in small, decision-making groups. *J. abnorm. soc. Psychol.*, 1953, 48, 231–238. (*543*)

*In 72 conferences in business, industry, and government, leadership sharing is found to be negatively related to cohesion and satisfaction unless the group has an urgent problem.*

57. Bernhardt, K. S., Millichamp, Dorothy A., Charles, Marion W., & McFarland, Mary P. An analysis of the social contacts of pre-school children with the aid of motion pictures. *Univer. Toronto Stud. Child Develpm.*, 1937, No. 10.

*The motion picture technique proved superior to observers' recording of social contacts and behavior of pre-school children of three age groups in revealing differences in rank of each individual though not in overall group comparisons. In terms of the frequency of social contacts, little difference was noted in three age groups, but qualitatively there are age-increase tendencies to restrict social contact, to prefer certain types of contact, and to increase pattern complexity.*

58. Beum, C. O., Jr., & Brundage, E. G. A method for analyzing the sociomatrix. *Sociometry*, 1950, 13, 141–145.

*A method of matrix arrangement maximizing the principal diagonal and producing a canonical form is described. It has the advantage over the Forsyth and Katz method of being an iterative rather than a trial and error procedure. Iteration may be long, however.*

59. Biber, Barbara, Murphy, Lois B., Woodcock, Louise P., & Black, Irma S. *Life and ways of the seven-to-eight year old.* New York: Basic Books, 1952. (2nd Ed.)

*An intensive study is made of ten seven year olds in a school situation. Anecdotal and verbatim records are made during regular school activities, experimental situations, and standard performance tests. The skills, attitudes, language, thinking and other aspects of social behavior are described for the group in general and a case history presented for each child.*

60. Bieri, J. Changes in interpersonal perceptions following social interaction. *J. abnorm. soc. Psychol.*, 1953, 48, 61–66.

*Social interaction results in a significant increase in perception of others as similar to self.*

61. Bion, W. R. Experience in groups: I. *Hum. Relat.*, 1948, 1, 314–320.

*A case study of a therapy group illustrates the difficulty of introducing meanings which a group will not accept and that the emotional life of the group members interferes with the solution of intellectual problems.*

62. Bion, W. R. Experiences in groups: II. *Hum. Relat.*, 1948, 1, 487–496.

*The group is described as an interplay between individual needs, group mentality, (anonymous expression of individual opinion), and group culture, (the momentary structure, organization, and occupation of the group).*

63. Bion, W. R. Experiences in groups: III. *Hum. Relat.*, 1949, 2, 13–22.

*Three basic assumptions characterizing group culture and mentality (dependence, fight-flight, and pairing) are defined and illustrated.*

64. Bion, W. R. Experiences in groups: IV. *Hum. Relat.*, 1949, 2, 295–303.

*In the dependent state group members expect the leader to solve their problems. Other vocal members are seen as rivals of the leader and are suppressed. The problem of hatred of learning by experience is also discussed.*

65. Bion, W. R. Experiences in groups: V. *Hum. Relat.*, 1950, 3, 3–14.

*Members of a work group act on one basic assumption to suppress the activity of the other two basic assumptions. Author posits prototypes of his three basic assumptions of groups (flight-fight, pairing, dependence) which he calls protomental (matrix in which physical and psychological are undifferentiated). This protomental system is then applied theoretically to the occurrence of physical diseases and to the evaluation of money, in order to test its possible use as a predictive concept.*

66. Bion, W. R. Experiences in groups: VI. *Hum. Relat.*, 1950, 3, 395–402.

*Each individual has some degree of readiness (valency) to enter into combination with the group in making and acting on the basic assumptions. The group with the basic assumption of dependence will choose, in an unstructured, spontaneous situation, its most ill member as leader. The group must then oscillate from the recognition that its leader is disordered, to the belief that he is the dependable leader. The group tries to overcome this disruptive oscillation by absorption of external groups.*

67. Bion, W. R. Experiences in groups: VII. *Hum. Relat.*, 1951, 4, 221–227.

*When development is demanded of a group, resistance is set up and a schism may occur between the sub-group which appeals to tradition in opposition to advance, and the sub-group which, ostensibly supporting advance, is so exacting that it ceases to recruit new members. In a summary, the author's theory is compared with that of Freud, McDougall, and LeBon.*

68. Bion, W. R. Group dynamics: A review. *Int. J. Psychoanal.*, 1952, 33, 235–247.

*The author's views of group functioning are summarized with special reference to psychoanalytic assumptions.*

69. Bishop, Barbara M. Mother-child interaction and the social behavior of children. *Psychol. Monogr.*, 1951, 65, No. 11 (Whole No. 328). *(280)*

*Using a set of categories and observation in short time intervals, mother-and-child and neutral adult-and-child were each observed for two half-hour sessions. Consistency of behavior was found for mothers and for children over the two sessions, and, when interacting with the neutral adult, children tended in time to simulate their pattern with their mothers. Negative behavior on the part of the mother (directing-interfering-criticizing) was associated with negative responsiveness in the child (inhibition, reluctance, or non-cooperation).*

70. Blake, R. R. The interaction-feeling hypothesis applied to psychotherapy groups. *Sociometry*, 1953, 16, 253–265.

*When pressures holding a member in a "free" system of group psychotherapy are strong, interaction communication will be greater in both positive and negative affect, than in neutral states. Although problems arise in measuring feelings and quantifying interaction, Relational Analysis and Interaction Process Analysis are procedures which could supply these data.*

71. Blake, R. R., & Brehm, J. W. The use of tape recording to simulate a group atmosphere. *J. abnorm. Soc. Psychol.*, 1954, 49, 311–313. (*220*)

*Subjects acting as members of synthetic groups (tape recorded responses) are influenced by the group in their judgments of an autokinetic phenomenon.*

72. Block, J. The assessment of communication: Role variations as a function of interactional context. *J. Pers.*, 1952, 21, 272–286.

*A case study of personality and role differences of one subject using a sentence sorting technique.*

73. Block, J., & Block, Jeanne. An interpersonal experiment on reactions to authority. *Hum. Relat.*, 1952, 5, 91–98.

*Subjects responding to a suggestion of the experimenter to continue the task tended to be less ego-controlled, more ethnocentric, and slow to structure an ambiguous situation.*

74. Blumer, H. Psychological import of the human group. In M. Sherif, & M. O. Wilson (Eds.), *Group relations at the crossroads.* New York: Harper, 1953. Pp. 185–202.

*Human association should be studied as a moving process in which the participants note and gauge each other's actions, inhibiting, encouraging, and guiding themselves accordingly; it should not be conceived in terms of culture, social structure, or role playing.*

75. Bogardus, E. S. Group behavior and groupality. *Sociol. soc. Res.*, 1954, 38, 401–403.

*The term groupality is suggested to include both universal and unique aspects of groups.*

76. Bonney, M. E. A sociometric study of the relationship of some factors to mutual friendships on the elementary, secondary, and college levels. *Sociometry*, 1946, 9, 21–47.

*Pairs of mutual friends in elementary and secondary schools and college are compared with pairs of children in which friendship is not reciprocated. Little or no relationship is found between mutual friendship and academic achievement, intelligence, interests, and personality. Some positive relationship is found between mutual friendship and socio-economic background and with a friendship scale developed by the author.*

77. Bonney, M. E., & Powell, J. Differences in social behavior between sociometrically high and sociometrically low children. *J. educ. Res.*, 1953, 46, 481–495.

*Differences in social behavior in 5 of 25 categories are found between ten sociometrically high and ten sociometrically low children in the 1st grade. Highly acceptable children are more conforming, smiling, and cooperative and less likely to play alone.*

78. Bonney, M. E., Hoblit, R. E., & Dreyer, A. H. A study of some factors related to sociometric status in a men's dormitory. *Sociometry*, 1953, 16, 287–301.

*Peer acceptance is due to responses to total personalities rather than to certain traits, although some traits are more characteristic of highly chosen personalities.*

79. Borgatta, E. F. An analysis of three levels of response: An approach to some relationships among dimensions of personality. *Sociometry*, 1951, 14, 267–316.

*The behavior of subjects is compared in interaction (situations involving subject, role player, and experimenters), in role playing, and on a paper and pencil test (Rosenzweig). Holding the scoring categories constant, it is found that prediction is not justified across the levels. For this group of subjects, it is found that a significant increasing trend in profanity is from actual behavior, to role playing, to paper and pencil. Using a general measure of distance, role playing is found to be closer to actual behavior than is paper and pencil. A system of personality classification based on norms and trends developed from the observation of different levels, which would be applicable both to normals and deviants, is proposed.*

80. Borgatta, E. F. A diagnostic note on the construction of sociograms and action diagrams. *Group Psychother.*, 1951, 3, 300–308.

*An article presenting suggestions for choice criteria and diagram construction. Emphasizes readability (how to reduce the number of crossing lines) and sub-group structure.*

81. Borgatta, E. F. Analysis of social interaction and sociometric perception. *Sociometry*, 1954, 17, 7–31.

*Sociometric perception literature is reviewed. A study is reported involving measures of sociometric leadership and choice, perception, interaction, intelligence, ratings by superiors, background factors, a projective test, and others.*

82. Borgatta, E. F., & Bales, R. F. The consistency of subject behavior and the reliability of scoring in interaction process analysis. *Amer. sociol. Rev.*, 1953, 18, 566–569. (*300*)

*Evidence is presented of the effective reliability of a behavioral category scoring system in terms of trained scorers. Subjects observed tended to be consistent in their behavior, but more so when participating with the same coparticipants than with different sets of coparticipants.*

83. BORGATTA, E. F., & BALES, R. F. Task and accumulation of experience as factors in the interaction of small groups. *Sociometry*, 1953, 16, 239–252.

*Development of structure over sessions in groups (previously reported by Heinicke and Bales) is examined in terms of groups in which a new structure is required (by design). The latter groups apparently do not develop a "common culture base" and a tendency to more unrestrained social emotional participation does not develop. High tension in the second or an early session, a "crisis" either over status or understanding task, is present for both groups. Role playing apparently does not involve members as much as the discussion and planning sessions, and tension decreases with session order—a facilitation or learning effect.*

84. BORGATTA, E. F., & BALES, R. F. Interaction of individuals in reconstituted groups. *Sociometry*, 1953, 16, 302–320. (*379*)

*The total interaction rate of the group is correlated with the characteristic performance of the individuals composing the group, and with the differentiation of the group membership. The rate of initiation of behavior of the person is an inverse function of the characteristic rate of his coparticipants. Qualitative differences in performance are found between high and low participators, and between high and low participation groups, but the differences in participators and groups are not the same. Three objectives of composing groups are noted.*

85. BORGATTA, E. F., COUCH, A. S., & BALES, R. F. Some findings relevant to the great man theory of leadership. *Amer. sociol. Rev.*, 1954, 19, 755–759. (*568*)

*Leaders who excel in popularity, task ability, and activity simultaneously tend to hold their leadership in groups of different composition (with similar task). Indirect evidence indicates that groups they participate in may show more productivity and less dissatisfaction.*

86. BOTT, HELEN McM. *Method in social studies of young children.* Toronto: Univer. of Toronto Press, 1933.

*Literature on observations of pre-school children is reviewed with a discussion and selection of categories, quantitative measures, recording, measurement of reliability, and expression of results.*

87. BOVARD, E. W. Group structure and perception. *J. abnorm. soc. Psychol.*, 1951, 46, 398–405. (See # 115.)

*Group centered classes (high intercommunication) show more initial dispersion and more shift toward the norm in judging length of rectangle than do leader centered classes. Groups judge, are told results, and then rejudge.*

88. BOVARD, E. W. The experimental production of interpersonal affect. *J. abnorm. soc. Psychol.*, 1951, 46, 521–528.

*In a comparison of two group centered (high intercommunication) classes and two leader centered classes, higher affect ratings and greater dispersion of these were found in the group centered classes.*

89. BOVARD, E. W. Conformity to social norms and attraction to the group. *Science*, 1953, 118, 598–599.

*In an experiment of guessing the number of dots in a square, it was found that the amount of convergence on the norm for 23 small groups did not correlate with the amount of liking of the members for the group. The author concludes that it does not appear that attraction for the group is a determinant of social conformity.*

90. Brofenbrenner, U., & Newcomb, T. M. Improvisations—an application of psychodrama in personality diagnosis. *Sociatry*, 1948, 1, 367–382.

*Based on OSS experience, the technique of "improvisations" is detailed. It involves two subjects in a partially structured interpersonal relationship designed to produce emotional involvement. The utility of this for personality diagnosis is indicated. Six standardized conflict situations for diagnosis and hypotheses as to crucial aspects for clinical observation are presented.*

91. Brown, J. C. An experiment in role-taking. *Amer. sociol. Rev.*, 1952, 17, 587–597.

*Sixteen students were tested in groups of four for the quality of performance in role playing of four situations. Each performed roles of others (who were known to them). Males tended to perform roles of other males better than females, and vice versa. Males appeared to be more perceptive of the roles of females than vice versa.*

92. Buhler, Charlotte. Social behavior of the child. In C. A. Murchison (Ed.) *A handbook of child psychology*. Worcester, Mass.: Clark Univer. Press, 1931, 392–431.

*Social behavior of the child may be organized about the developmental aspect or the aspect of social types and situations. Helplessness, need, companionship, common interest, desire for information or discussion, are inducements to group formation and development of social behavior. Types of social behavior in the normal family and in different cultural situations are also illustrated.*

93. Buhler, Charlotte. *The child and his family*. New York: Harper, 1939.

*Observational description of the social behavior of children.*

94. Burchard, E. M. L., Michaels, J., & Kotkov, B. Citeria for the evaluation of group therapy. *Psychosom. Med.*, 1948, 10, 257–274.

*A review of the literature emphasizing different approaches and expectations associated with group therapy.*

95. Burgess, E. W., & Cottrell, L. S. *Predicting success or failure in marriage*. New York: Prentice Hall, 1939.

*In a study of 526 married couples, the following findings are reported: 1) wives make the major adjustment in marriage, 2) affectional relationships of childhood condition the love life of the adult, 3) socialization of the person is significant for adjustment in marriage, 4) the economic factor per se is not significant for adjustment, 5) sexual adjustment is mainly a result of psychogenetic development and cultural conditioning of attitudes toward sex, and 6) pre-marital prediction of adjustment is feasible.*

96. Burnham, W. H. The hygiene of home study. *Pedag. Sem.*, 1905, 12, 213–230.

*A review of early together and apart experiments.*

97. Burrow, T. The group method of analysis. *Psychoanal. Rev.*, 1927, 14, 268–280.

*Man, as a societal animal, requires therapeutic analysis within the group situation, where his realization of others' similar problems resolves his resistances, and where a consensual scientific approach replaces society's and the psychoanalyst's enforcement of secrecy on the neurotic patient.*

98. Burton, A. The influence of social factors upon the persistence of satiation in pre-school children. *Child Develpm.*, 1941, 12, 121–129.

*When presented with an associate, a child who was bored with a task will resume activity up to 43% of a previous period of high motivation.*

99. Burtt, H. E. Sex differences in the effect of discussion. *J. exper. Psychol.*, 1920, 3, 390–395.

*Group discussion increased tendency to change one's decision, but change is wrong as often as it is right. There is no appreciable sex difference in profiting from discussion.*

100. Byrd, E. A study of validity and constancy of choices in a sociometric test. *Sociometry*, 1951, 14, 175–181. (*283*)

*A fourth grade class of 27 children was given a sociometric test, then given the actual opportunity to choose in the life situation (for acting in a play), and then later retested with the sociometric test. The degree of change from test to life situation was not found to be significantly greater than from test to retest in terms of number of choices common to the two conditions, and status from condition to condition appeared to be equally stable.*

101. Campbell, D. T. *A study of leadership among submarine officers.* Columbus, Ohio: The Ohio State University Research Foundation, 1953.

*The effective leader shows consideration for needs of his subordinates. This type of behavior is most typical of those in the higher status positions.*

102. Carr, L. J. Experimental sociology: A preliminary note on theory and method. *Soc. Forces*, 1929, 8, 63–74.

*Experiences during the first year of experimental sociology at the University of Michigan illustrate the thesis that interactions are observable, related to controllable factors, and have an organic nature.*

103. Carr, L. J. Experimentation in face-to-face interaction. *Amer. Sociol. Soc. Papers*, 1930, 24, 174–176.

*Since interaction is an unconscious by-product of situational adjustment, it may be studied by setting up problems to be solved by a group, recorded by mechanisms which are out of sight, and charted under carefully observed conditions.*

104. CARTER, L. F. Leadership and small-group behavior. In M. Sherif, & M. O. Wilson (Eds.), *Group relations at the crossroads*. New York: Harper, 1953. Pp. 257–284.

*The major determiners of group behavior are the abilities and personalities of group members, the influence of the tasks and goals of the group, and the structural and traditional factors. Examples of research are given.*

105. CARTER, L. F. Recording and evaluating the performance of individuals as members of small groups. *Personnel Psychol.*, 1954, 7, 477–484. (*492*)

*Interaction behavior of individuals in small groups is grossly (adequately) described by three factors (replicated factor analyses): individual prominence and achievement, aiding attainment by the group, and sociability.*

106. CARTER, L. F. Some research on leadership in small groups. In H. Guetzkow (Ed.), *Groups, leadership and men: Research in human relations*. Pittsburgh: Carnegie Press, 1951. Pp. 146–157.

*Findings from research on criteria for judging leadership ability, and leadership as a function of the task, of personality, or the formal group structure, are summarized.*

107. CARTER, L. F., HAYTHORN, W., & HOWELL, MARGARET. A further investigation of the criteria of leadership. *J. abnorm. soc. Psychol.*, 1950, 45, 350–358. (*523*)

*Leadership ratings given to subjects in six tasks (four and two man groups) correlated positively with two groupings (factor analysis) of intellectual leadership and doing-with-one's-hands leadership. Nominations (sociometric choices) corresponded to the ratings given, and showed the same two groupings. Faculty (college) ratings, best friends' ratings, and positions held did not intercorrelate highly with each other or with observer ratings and nominations. Analysis is parallel to a previous study, and it is possible that faculty ratings will be more meaningful where the same faculty members rate all persons (as in high school study).*

108. CARTER, L. F., HAYTHORN, W., MEIROWITZ, BEATRICE, & LANZETTA, J. A note on a new technique of interaction recording. *J. abnorm. soc. Psychol.*, 1951, 46, 258–260.

*The stenotype machine is proposed for recording purposes in the use of a category system.*

109. CARTER, L. F., HAYTHORN, W., MEIROWITZ, BEATRICE, & LANZETTA, J. The relation of categorizations and ratings in the observation of group behavior. *Hum. Relat.*, 1951, 4, 239–254.

*Both categories and ratings yield* reliable *results. Ratings tend to be positively intercorrelated, as do behavioral observation categories. Reliabilities are related to task and group size.*

110. CARTER, L. F., HAYTHORN, W., SHRIVER, E., & LANZETTA, J. The behavior of leaders and other group members. *J. abnorm. soc. Psychol.*, 1951, 46, 589–595. (See # 115.)

*Unique behavior of leaders is seen, particularly in analyzing the situation and initiating required action. Leaders who "emerge" in a group are more authoritarian than those initially appointed. Task is an important factor in determining behavior of leader and group.*

111. CARTER, L. F., & NIXON, MARY. Ability, perceptual, personality, and interest factors associated with different criteria of leadership. *J. Psychol.*, 1949, 27, 377–388.

*Leadership ratings in three tasks, derived in four independent ways, are examined in terms of primary abilities, personality, and interest tests.*

112. CARTER, L. F., & NIXON, MARY. An investigation of the relationship between four criteria of leadership ability for three different tasks. *J. Psychol.*, 1949, 27, 245–261.

*Four criteria of leadership are found to be only slightly related. The intellectual and clerical tasks appear different from the mechanical assembly task.*

113. CARTWRIGHT, D. Achieving change in people: Some applications of group dynamics theory. *Hum. Relat.*, 1951, 4, 381–392.

*Eight generalizations are given for changing people through groups.*

114. CARTWRIGHT, D. Emotional dimensions of group life. In M. L. Reymert (Ed.), *Feelings and emotions.* New York: McGraw-Hill, 1952. Pp. 439–447.

*Discussion of the ways in which individual security can be affected by group membership such as means of need satisfaction and frustration, and as a primary determinant of self-esteem. Review of experimental literature in this area.*

115. CARTWRIGHT, D., & ZANDER, A. F. (Eds.) *Group Dynamics: Research and Theory.* Evanston, Ill.: Row, Peterson, 1953.

*A set of readings consisting of 41 essays in this field, six of which are written for the text by the editors.*

116. CATTELL, R. B. Concepts and methods in the measurement of group syntality. *Psychol. Rev.*, 1948, 55, 48–63. (*107*)

*The approach to the study of groups is discussed in terms of factor analysis and experience in personality research. Three kinds of variables are raised as foci of investigation: (a) syntality (analogous to personality); (b) internal structure; (c) population (or aggregate values). Problems to be considered in design of experiment are discussed.*

117. CATTELL, R. B. Determining syntality dimension as a basis for morale and leadership measurement. In H. Guetzkow (Ed.), *Groups, leadership and men: Research in human relations.* Pittsburgh: Carnegie Press, 1951. Pp. 16–27.

*The description of any group must attend to population (background and personality), structure, and syntality, and these categories should be defined by empirical (i.e., factorial) research. An experi-*

*ment in which 80 groups are factorized with respect to their performances and characteristics on some 150 observed variables is described, and techniques for measuring group synergy and the effectiveness of leaders are presented.*

118. CATTELL, R. B. New concepts for measuring leadership, in terms of group syntality. *Hum. Relat.*, 1951, 4, 161–184. (See # 115.)

*Group description and roles within the group are considered in terms of three classes of observation, those having to do with the population, the structure, and the syntality. Emphasis is placed on the use of group performance rather than internal interaction among the members for the identification of leadership.*

119. CATTELL, R. B. On the theory of group learning. *J. soc. Psychol.*, 1953, 37, 27–52.

*The concept of the group learning (as distinguished from learning in groups) is considered. Conditioning learning does not appear to be directly applicable, and dynamic learning appears a more relevant representation. Group learning is both in respect to means of operation and ends sought and the relation of these to reward.*

120. CATTELL, R. B., SAUNDERS, D. R., & STICE, G. F. The dimensions of syntality in small groups. *Hum. Relat.*, 1953, 6, 331–356. (*305*)

*A factor analysis of 80 groups on 93 variables indicated the existence of 15 factors, 14 of which are identified. The variables included personality, behavior, and various ratings, considered as group phenomena. Relationships found suggest the possibility of prediction of the "emergents" in a group, and also the discernment of characteristics which are related to the make-up (population) of the group as contrasted to its experience in process.*

121. CATTELL, R. B., & WISPE, L. G. The dimensions of syntality in small groups. *J. soc. Psychol.*, 1948, 28, 57–78.

*Pioneer demonstration of the factor analysis of groups. Sample of 21 groups showed appreciable factors of syntality such as: "group intelligence," morale, group integration, and group aggresiveness.*

122. CHAPPLE, E. D. Measuring human relations: An introduction to the study of interaction of individuals. *Genet. Psychol. Monogr.*, 1940, 22, 3–147.

*A method is described for the measurement of interaction in events and the analysis of hierarchies.*

123. CHAPPLE, E. D. The measurement of interpersonal behavior. *Trans. N.Y. Acad. Sci.*, 1942, 4, 222–233.

*A method for quantitative and automatic recording of observed interaction, which reveals differences that correlate with a psychologically normal-abnormal difference, is proposed.*

124. CHAPPLE, E. D. The standard interview as used in interaction chronograph investigations. *Hum. Organization*, 1953, 12, 23–32.

*Variations of the interviewer's behavior to create a sequence of behavioral situations are proposed to elicit characteristic personality and temperament traits.*

125. CHAPPLE, E. D., & LINDEMANN, E. Clinical implications of measurements on interaction rates in psychiatric interviews. *Appl. Anthrop.*, 1942, 1, 1–11.

*A series of interviews between an examiner and normal, psychoneurotic, and psychotic individuals were observed, and the amount and patterning of activity and inactivity were recorded on a chronographic device. Characteristic curves are found for the varying diagnoses as well as specific differences between the curves.*

126. CHITTENDEN, GERTRUDE E. An experimental study in measuring and modifying assertive behavior in young children. *Soc. Res. Child Develpm. Monogr.*, 1942, 7, No. 1.

*Domination, cooperation, and non-assertion are observed in pairs of children playing with one toy. After training ("helping" dolls to play better with one toy) there is a significant decrease in dominative behavior and an increase in cooperation.*

127. CHOWDHRY, KAMLA, & NEWCOMB, T. M. The relative abilities of leaders and non-leaders to estimate opinions of their own groups. *J. abnorm. soc. Psychol.*, 1952, 47, 51–57. (*235*)

*On familiar and relevant issues leaders of four college groups are superior to non-leaders and isolates in their ability to evaluate group opinion, on non-familiar issues there are no differences, and on intermediate issues there are no consistent results.*

128. CHRISTENSEN, H. T., & PHILBRICK, R. E. Family size as a factor in the marital adjustments of college couples. *Amer. sociol. Rev.*, 1952, 17, 306–312.

*A negative correlation is found between size of family and adjustment.*

129. CHRISTIE, L. S., LUCE, R. D., & MACY, J., JR. *Communications and learning in task oriented groups.* Cambridge, Mass.: Research Laboratory of Electronics, 1952.

*For some communication networks considerable changes in distributions of acts to complete a trial took place over trials, and this change was attributed to learning. In task situations where action and time are restricted, group and individual decision-latency data are theoretically related. Group errors are simply explicable in terms of a measure of noise.*

130. CLARK, R. A., & MCGUIRE, C. Sociographic analysis of sociometric valuations. *Child Develpm.*, 1952, 23, 129–140.

*The sociograph, which arranges subjects systematically by cliques and indicates cleavages in group structure, is proposed as a method of organizing and presenting sociometric data.*

131. COCH, L., & FRENCH, J. R. P., JR. Overcoming resistance to change. *Hum. Relat.*, 1948, 1, 512–532. (See #115.)

*Change in methods of work and ensuing piece rates (incentive system) may be introduced through use of group meetings in such a way that resistance to change and grievances may be minimized. Effective communication by management of the need for change and participation of workers in planning the changes are found crucial.*

132. Cocherell, D. L. A study of the play of children of pre-school age by an unobserved observer. *Genet. Psychol. Monogr.*, 1935, 17, 377–469.

*A systematic observational study of children in relation to various playthings and to companions.*

133. Coffey, H. S. Socio and psyche group process: Integrative concepts. *J. soc. Issues*, 1952, 8 (2), 65–74.

*The concepts of socio and psyche groups are suggested for differentiating types of therapy, group work, and adult education groups.*

134. Coffey, H. S., Freedman, M. B., Leary, T. F., & Ossorio, A. G. (Eds.), Community service and social research: Group psychotherapy in a church program. *J. soc. Issues*, 1950, 6 (1), 1–65.

*A systematic approach to group psychotherapy for mental health development is discussed.*

135. Cooley, C. H. Social Organization. New York: Scribner, 1909. (*15*)

*A classic general thesis with an early emphasis on the importance of the analysis of informal structure and the primary group.*

136. Coombs, A. W., & Taylor, C. The effect of the perception of mild degrees of threat on performance. *J. abnorm. soc. Psychol.*, 1952, 47, 420–424.

*Mild degrees of threat tend to increase amount of time required and errors in a coding problem. The content of some of the sentences coded and cautions of examiner were used as threat conditions.*

137. Cottrell, L. S., Jr. The analysis of situational fields in social psychology. *Amer. sociol. Rev.*, 1942, 7, 370–382. (57)

*A brief systematic formulation of theory concerning interpersonal relations, social action, and related concepts. Use is made of four illustrations.*

138. Cottrell, L. S., Jr., & Gallagher, Ruth. Developments in social psychology 1930–1940. *Sociometry Monogr.*, 1941, No. 1.

*Developments in social anthropology, psychiatry, studies of collective behavior, quantitative, and experimental method are reviewed.*

139. Coyle, Grace L. *Social process in organized groups.* New York: R. R. Smith, 1930.

*The theoretical analysis of the processes by which an organized group acts is arranged under the organized group in its social setting, the process of group formation, determination of membership, functions of leadership, communication, esprit de corps, collective thinking, and social functions.*

140. Coyle, Grace L. (Ed.) *Studies in group behavior.* New York: Harper, 1937.

*Case studies of five club groups.*

141. Criswell, Joan H. Sociometric methods of measuring group preferences. *Sociometry*, 1943, 6, 398–408.

*Methods of considering in-group and out-group choice tendencies are discussed.*

142. Crutchfield, R. S. Assessment of persons through a quasi group-interaction technique. *J. abnorm. soc. Psychol.*, 1951, 46, 577–588.

*A technique is presented for simulating group interaction for the subject (under conditions of limited communication) which may be standardized for all subjects. The Group Squares Test is a problem-solving situation adapted for this use, and relationship of personality tests to performance in the test is given.*

143. Cunningham, Ruth, et al. *Understanding group behavior of boys and girls.* New York: Teachers Coll., Columbia Univer., Bureau of Publications, 1951.

*A handbook on techniques of group investigation for use of teachers and group leaders is presented. Particular emphasis is given to schoolroom problems.*

144. Curran, C. A. *Personality factors in counseling.* New York: Grune & Stratton, 1945.

*Non-directive therapeutic interviews are analyzed using a category system for content analysis (negative emotion, positive emotion, insight and choice).*

145. Dahlke, H. O. Determinants of sociometric relations among children in the elementary school. *Sociometry*, 1953, 16, 327–338.

*In a sociometric study of grades 2 to 8 of an elementary school, sex status and personality adjustment are related to choice status, but social class structure of the community tends to occur within a class, and most groups are self-preferred in relation to children with semi-skilled worker and clerical parentage.*

146. Darley, J. G., Gross, N., & Martin, W. E. Studies of group behavior: The stability, change, and interrelations of psychometric and sociometric variables. *J. abnorm. soc. Psychol.*, 1951, 46, 565–576.

*The homogeneity of thirteen groups on personality and sociometric variables is examined; test and retests are compared. "Satisfaction" of girls with their dorm life is found to be related to stability of dorm population, high in-group choices and high mutual choices.*

147. Darley, J. G., Gross, N., & Martin, W. E. Studies in group behavior: Factors associated with the productivity of groups. *J. appl. Psychol.*, 1952, 36, 396–403.

*The efficiency of the house organization to carry out a task (produce a plan for improvement) correlates highest with the quality of the plan produced. Other factors considered do not appear to increase the prediction appreciably.*

148. Dashiell, J. F. An experimental analysis of some group effects. *J. abnorm. soc. Psychol.*, 1930, 25, 190–199.

*Subjects are given a set of multiplication problems in four situations; together, in competition, and under observation. Under observation subjects are faster but less accurate. Rivalry tends to facilitate work.*

149. DASHIELL, J. F., Experimental studies of the influence of social situations on the behavior of individual human adults. In C. Murchison (Ed.), *A handbook of social psychology*. Worcester, Mass.: Clark Univer. Press, 1935, 1097–1158.

*Literature is reviewed on the following effects on the individual's work: presence of spectators or auditors (speeds up but makes less accurate), co-workers (inconclusive), competition (inconclusive), social encouragement or discouragement (inconclusive), group discussion (inconclusive), majority and expert opinion.*

150. DAVIS, F. J. Conceptions of official leader roles in the Air Force. *Soc. Forces*, 1954, 32, 253–258.

*Some incongruence is found between the conceptions of official leader roles held by official leaders and those held by their followers, but success in predicting follower adjustment from congruence scores was limited.*

151. DAWE, HELEN C. The influence of the size of kindergarten group upon performance. *Child Develpm.*, 1934, 5, 295–303.

*Increasing of size of kindergarten group from 14 to 46 and increasing the distance of the child from its teacher lowers the percentage of participants in discussion and the average amount of remarks per child.*

152. DEUTSCH, M. An experimental study of the effects of cooperation and competition upon group process. *Hum. Relat.*, 1949, 2, 199–231. (See # 115.)

*Ten five man groups were reorganized into two units of five man groups each, matched on discussion productivity. One set of groups was motivated to compete as groups among themselves. For the second set, members were motivated to compete with each other within a group (not compete with all other persons). In the former (cooperative) groups, persons perceive themselves as more interdependent, allow more "substitutability for similarly intended actions," show more positive affect, less resistance, and more helpfulness to each other. In terms of group functioning the competitive groups showed less coordination of efforts, less subdivision of activities and diversity in contributions among members, less achievement pressure, less attentiveness to fellow members and comprehension of communication, less orientation and orderliness, less productivity per time unit, lower quality of product and discussions, less friendliness and less favorable evaluation of the group and its products, fewer group functions, lower perception of effects on others and lower incorporation of attitudes of generalized other, less productivity in a puzzle problem, but more productivity in the human relations problem and more individual functions. The author concludes that greater group or organizational productivity results from the cooperative interrelationships.*

153. DEUTSCH, M. A theory of cooperation and competition. *Hum. Relat.*, 1949, 2, 129–152.

*A review and development of theory with special reference to small groups.*

154. DEUTSCHBERGER, P. The *tele*-factor: Horizon and awareness. *Sociometry*, 1947, 10, 242–249.

*The ability to create and enter into mutual social relationships consists of a horizon in which awareness is great, a high level of choice expenditure exists, and perceptions of interrelations are accurate, and of an unstructured region with tentative choices to which reciprocation is mainly by chance.*

155. DITTMAN, A. T. The interpersonal process in psychotherapy: Development of a research method. *J. abnorm. soc. Psychol.*, 1952, 47, 236–244.

*In psychotherapeutic interviews the responses of the therapist and progressive or regressive movements of the patient are rated. Progressive movement is associated with high participation and deeper response by the therapist.*

155a. DURKHEIM, E. *Division of labor*. Glencoe, Ill.: Free Press, 1947. (*5*)

*An advanced society requires a division of labor which in turn produces solidarity because the division of labor creates a system of rights and duties which link men together in a lasting way.*

156. DYMOND, ROSALIND F. A scale for the measurement of empathic ability. *J. consult. Psychol.*, 1949, 13, 127–133. (*226*)

*An approach to the measurement of empathic ability (accuracy of perception) is presented. Data on reliability and validity are given.*

157. DYMOND, ROSALIND F., HUGHES, ANNE S., & RAABE, VIRGINIA L. Measurable changes in empathy with age. *J. consult. Psychol.*, 1952, 16, 202–206.

*Two empathy measures used (one projective and one quasi-sociometric) showed greater perceptive ability on the part of 11 than 7-year-old children. More popular children have better insight according to the sociometric test. Caution in interpretation is stressed since many variables are involved in the age differences, including communication ability.*

158. ELLIOTT, H. S. *The process of group thinking*. New York: Association Press, 1928.

*Group thinking in a discussion group is analyzed, and discussion procedures and methods are proposed.*

159. FARIS, R. E. L. Development of small-group research movement. In M. Sherif, & M. O. Wilson (Eds.), *Group relations at the crossroads*. New York: Harper, 1953. Pp. 155–184.

*Present-day research on the primary group is the center of concern in the study of personality and the most logical meeting place of sociology and social psychology.*

160. FAUNCE, D., & BEEGLE, J. A. Cleavages in a relatively homogeneous group of rural youth: An experiment in the use of sociometry in attaining and measuring integration. *Sociometry*, 1948, 11, 207–216.

*A sociometric study of a teen-age farmer's camp found group cleavages by age, sex, and county of origin, with sex and county (but not age) becoming less important as new acquaintances were formed at camp.*

161. FESSENDEN, S. A. An index of cohesiveness-morale based on the analysis of sociometric choice distribution. *Sociometry*, 1953, 16, 321–326.

*In a permissive group, the sociometric choice pattern will approach a curve approximating a normal distribution of personality characteristics. Analysis of sociometric choice patterns provides an index of cohesiveness-morale of a group.*

162. FESTINGER, L. The role of group belongingness in a voting situation. *Hum. Relat.*, 1947, 1, 154–180.

*In the election of a leader in small experimental groups of Catholic and Jewish girls, Catholics tend to (change) vote for Catholics when religion is identified. However, both types of girls tend to favor their own religious group. Jews are more accurately guessed in identification. Jewish girls appear more conscious of the religious question.*

163. FESTINGER, L. The analysis of sociograms using matrix algebra. *Hum. Relat.*, 1949, 2, 153–158.

*Matrix algebra is discussed as a method of analyzing sociometric data. Operations can reveal the number of a given type of connection.*

164. FESTINGER, L. Informal social communication. *Psychol. Rev.*, 1950, 57, 271–292. (See # 115.)

*A review of some experiments on communication process with emphasis on the conceptualization of the sources of pressure to communicate.*

165. FESTINGER, L. Laboratory experiments: The role of group belongingness. In J. G. Miller (Ed.). *Experiments in social process.* New York: McGraw-Hill, 1950. Pp. 31–46.

*Laboratory experiments do not influence real life situations but can test generalizations. The author's experiment in group belongingness in a voting situation is summarized.*

166. FESTINGER, L. Architecture and group membership. *J. soc. Issues*, 1951, 7 (2), 152–163. (See # 115.)

*The studies of a Veteran's housing project at MIT by Festinger, Schacter, and Back, and of a government housing project for shipyard workers by Festinger and Kelley, are reviewed to illustrate how knowledge of group membership and group life can contribute to the field of housing.*

167. FESTINGER, L. Informal communications in small groups. In H. Guetzkow (Ed.), *Groups, leadership and men: Research in human relations.* Pittsburgh: Carnegie Press, 1951. Pp. 28–43.

*Research is reviewed dealing with social pressures in informal groups, the exertion of influence through social communication, the determinants of the direction of influence and rejection for nonconformity, and the amount of change accomplished by the influence process.*

168. Festinger, L. An analysis of compliant behavior. In M. Sherif & M. O. Wilson (Eds.), *Group relations at the crossroads.* New York: Harper, 1953. Pp. 232–256.

*A theoretical distinction is made between public compliance or conformity* without *private acceptance which will occur if the person in question is restrained from leaving the situation and if there is a threat of punishment for noncompliance and public compliance* with *private acceptance which will occur if the person desires to remain in the existing relationship with those attempting to influence him. Experimental evidence which bears on this distinction is presented.*

169. Festinger, L. Laboratory experiments. In L. Festinger, & D. Katz, *Research methods in the behavioral sciences.* New York: Dryden Press, 1953. Pp. 136–172.

*Choice of subjects, expectations and cognitive structure provided them, type of activities and subjects' attitude all depend on the variables studied. Pre-experimental instruction, false reporting, use of paid participants, and restriction of behavior are ways to control and manipulate variables.*

170. Festinger, L. Theory of social comparison processes. *Hum. Relat.*, 1954, 7, 117–140. (*163*)

*Social influence processes and some kinds of competitive behavior are theoretically classed as manifestations of the same process, the drive for self evaluation (which is of necessity based on comparisons with other persons). Differences are caused by the unidirectional upward push in ability and the lack of such push in opinion evaluation.*

171. Festinger, L., Gerard, H. B., Hymovitch, B., Kelley, H. H., & Raven, B. The influence process in the presence of extreme deviates. *Hum. Relat.*, 1952, 5, 327–346.

*Deviates in groups show greater readiness to change their opinions and less confidence than conformers. Deviates show less tendency to influence others, but more tendency to redefine boundaries to exclude those with extremely divergent opinions than do conformers. In high cohesive groups members communicate more than in low cohesive groups, and, in the former, deviates who change opinion communicate less than those who do not, while in the latter there is a difference marking each group. Deviates in high cohesive groups reveal stronger pressures to uniformity than those in low cohesive groups, but this relationship does not hold for conformers. Effects of conditions of "experts present" and "no experts," and "no correct answer" and "correct answer," are also given.*

172. Festinger, L., & Katz, D. *Research methods in the behavioral sciences.* New York: Dryden Press, 1953.

*A collection of articles on methodology of social psychological research covering research settings, sampling procedures, data collection and analysis, and application of findings.*

173. Festinger, L., Pepitone, A., & Newcomb, T. Some consequences of de-individuation in a group. *J. abnorm. soc. Psychol.*, 1952, 47, 382–389. *(290)*

*When members do not pay attention to each other as individuals (de-individuation), there is a reduction of inner restraint and an increase in satisfaction with the group.*

174. Festinger, L., Schachter, S., & Back, K. *Social pressures in informal groups: A study of human factors in housing.* New York: Harper, 1950. (See #115.)

*In a homogeneous housing project for married veteran college students, the pattern and number of passive contacts depends on physical and functional distance. Such contacts determine friendships and group membership. Cohesiveness of a psychological group is an important determinant of the number of deviants and how effectively a group norm can be maintained. Isolation is both a cause and an effect of deviation.*

175. Festinger, L., & Thibaut, J. Interpersonal communication in small groups. *J. abnorm. soc. Psychol.*, 1951, 46, 92–99.

*Communication is directed differentially to persons who take extreme positions in the group, and this is emphasized when there is high pressure for conformity (uniformity of response) or when the group is perceived as homogeneous. Pressure toward uniformity and perception of the group as homogeneous are accompanied by greater change toward conformity.*

176. Festinger, L., Torrey, Jane, & Willerman, B. Self-evaluation as a function of attraction to the group. *Hum. Relat.*, 1954, 7, 161–174.

*Although the experimental manipulation of group attractiveness is not effective, individual members who are attracted to the group feel adequate when they do well and inadequate when they do not.*

177. Fiedler, F. E. Assumed similarity measures as predictors of team effectiveness in surveying. *Univer. of Ill., Coll. of Educ., Tech. Rep.*, 1953, No. 6, Contract N6ori-07135. Pp. 1–20.

*Persons chosen as most preferred co-workers in accurate student surveying teams tend to perceive little similarity between themselves and those they reject as co-workers, and perceive a relatively great difference between those that they prefer and those they reject as co-workers.*

178. Fiedler, F. E. Assumed similarity measures as predictors of team effectiveness. *J. abnorm. soc Psychol.*, 1954, 49, 381–388. *(252)*

*Previous studies of basketball and surveying teams by the author are summarized. Effective teams choose as their preferred co-worker a player who perceives his preferred and rejected co-workers as differing, and perceives little similarity between himself and his co-workers.*

179. FIEDLER, F. E., HARTMANN, W., & RUDIN, S. A. The relationship of interpersonal perception to effectiveness in basketball teams. *Univer. of Illinois, Coll. of Educ., Tech. Rep.*, 1952, No. 3, Contract N6ori-07135.

*Members of winning basketball teams choose as their preferred co-worker a player who perceives relatively little similarity between himself and his co-workers, and also perceives his preferred and rejected co-workers as differing.*

180. FIEDLER, F. E., WARRINGTON, W. G., & BLAISDELL, F. J. Unconscious attitudes as correlates of sociometric choice in social group. *J. abnorm. soc. Psychol.*, 1952, 47, 790–796.

*Fraternity men (26) were found to perceive group members they liked best as more similar to themselves than group members they liked least.*

181. FINDLEY, W. G. A statistical index of participation in discussion. *J. educ. Psychol.*, 1948, 39, 47–51.

*An index of participation is presented. Its maximum is when all group members contribute equally and its minimum is when two members monopolize the discussion.*

182. FISCHER, P. H. An analysis of the primary group. *Sociometry*, 1953, 16, 272–276.

*Frequency of contact and hours of contact per week of members of group are best predictors of group intimacy, according to results of questionnaire given to 75 college students. Increase of number of primary group affiliations does not significantly lessen contact per group. As size of group increases, the frequency of its occurrence decreases.*

183. FLANDERS, N. A. Personal-social anxiety as a factor in experimental learning situations. *J. educ. Res.*, 1951, 45, 100–110.

*Teacher-supporting group climate creates student hostility (withdrawal, apathy, aggressiveness), while student-supportive climate elicits problem orientation and decreased anxiety from students.*

184. FLEISHMAN, E. A. The leadership role of the foreman in industry. *Engng. Expt. Sta. News*, Ohio State Univer., 1952, 24, 27–35.

*Study of a training program for foremen in "consideration," showed that the school pre-post tests indicate more consideration, while in actual practice the foreman had less consideration.*

185. FORSYTH, ELAINE, & KATZ, L. A matrix approach to the analysis of sociometric data: Preliminary report. *Sociometry*, 1946, 9, 340–347.

*The analysis of sociometric data in a matrix through the arrangement of rows and columns is proposed. This has become one of the more usable semi-analytic techniques of sociometric analysis of structure.*

186. FOULKES, S. H. Group therapy: A short survey and orientation with particular reference to group analysis. *Brit. J. Med. Psychol.*, 1950, 25, 199–205.

*A review indicating the variety of methods in group therapy.*

187. Fouriezos, N. T., Hutt, M. L., & Guetzkow, H. Measurement of self-oriented needs in discussion groups. *J. abnorm. soc. Psychol.*, 1950, 45, 682–690. (See #115.)

*A rating system for the self-oriented needs of dependency, dominance, aggression, and catharsis is described. The self-oriented needs of participants in discussion groups are found to be related to process but negatively correlated wtih satisfaction.*

188. Frank, J. D. Experimental studies of personal pressure and resistance: I. Experimental production of resistance. *J. gen. Psychol.*, 1944, 30, 23–64.

*When an activity is presented to subjects as though it were implied in previous agreement, there is little resistance, but when challenged in advance to do or not do the activity (with the implication that they will be coerced) strong resistance develops. If the subjects are already in the activity when the challenge is made the response is mixed.*

189. Frank, J. D., Margolin, J., Nash, Helen T., Stone, A. R., Varon, E., & Ascher, E. Two behavior patterns in therapeutic groups and their apparent motivation. *Hum. Relat.*, 1952, 5, 289–317.

*Two behavior patterns identified in the early stages of therapy groups are described: (a) help-rejecting—complainer, (b) doctor's assistant.*

190. Freedman, M. B., Leary, T. F., Ossorio, A. B., & Coffey, H. S. The interpersonal dimension of personality. *J. Pers.*, 1951, 20, 143–161.

*Data of the total personality must deal with three levels: Public (interaction), conscious (perception of self and others), and private (symbols and projective). A category system is presented (16 complementary items in a circular continuum) for the interaction behavior, and corresponding categories for the conscious and private level are indicated. Reliability between raters with these categories appears satisfactory. The possibility of using the same variables for the classification of normals and deviants is presented.*

191. French, J. R. P., Jr. The disruption and cohesion of groups. *J. abnorm. soc. Psychol.*, 1941, 36, 361–377. (See #115.)

*Comparing eight (previously) organized groups (six-man) with eight unorganized groups, the former were found to show more social freedom, we-feeling, motivation, interdependence, frustration, interpersonal aggression, and equality of participation. Disruptive forces associated with group frustration (induced) are seen to be (a) competing paths to the same goal, (b) differing goals, and (c) factors not related to the goal such as status rivalry, personality incompatibility, etc.*

192. French, J. R. P., Jr. Organized and unorganized groups under fear and frustration. *Univer. of Iowa Stud. Child Welf.*, 1944, 20, No. 409, 231–308.

*Group identification and the stronger power field of the organized groups resulted in more frustration, aggression, motivation, equal par-*

*ticipation, and interdependence than was found in the socially restrained, unacquainted groups under a frustrating puzzle condition and an experimentally-produced fire.*

193. French, J. R. P., Jr. Field experiments: Changing group productivity. In J. G. Miller (Ed.), *Experiments in social process: A symposium on social psychology*. New York: McGraw-Hill, 1950. Pp. 79–96.

*A review of field experiments studying group productivity.*

194. French, J. R. P., Jr. Group productivity. In H. Guetzkow, *Groups, leadership and men: Research in human relations.* Pittsburgh: Carnegie Press, 1951. Pp. 44–45.

*The determinants of group productivity are process (amount of contribution and participation), structure (cohesiveness and prestige), personality, environment (such as the structure of the task), and cognitive structure (goal orientation and perception of abilities).*

195. Furfey, P. H. Some factors influencing the selection of boys' chums. *J. appl. Psychol.*, 1927, 11, 47–51.

*Friendship pairs are found to involve association either in the neighborhood or in class, and chums tend to be similar in age, size, intelligence, and maturity.*

196. Gage, N. L., & Exline, R. L. Social perception and effectiveness in discussion groups. *Hum. Relat.*, 1953, 6, 381–396.

*In four discussion groups (15–22 members), an individual's accuracy in predicting (a) group opinion, (b) satisfaction, (c) ratings of productivity, was not found to be correlated with effectiveness. Similarity of individual and group opinion was not correlated with productivity.*

197. Gates, Georgina S. The effect of an audience upon performance. *J. abnorm. soc. Psychol.*, 1924, 18, 334–342.

*In the tests used, mere presence of one or many spectators appears to have only a slight, if any, effect on the performance of the individual. Better performers may be more disrupted by an audience.*

198. Gekoski, N. Predicting Group Productivity. *Personnel Psychol.*, 1952, 5, 281–292. Also in Group characteristics and industrial productivity. *Engng. Exp. Station News*, Ohio State Univer., 1952, 24, 39–42.

*High productivity of groups is associated with a difference in age between supervisor and average of the group, similarity of ages of members, cross training for jobs, and a supervisor who structures the interactions of members of the group.*

199. Gerard, H. B. The effect of different dimensions of disagreement on the communication process in small groups. *Hum. Relat.*, 1953, 6, 249–271.

*In discussion groups, minority members needed more support than did majority members. Pressure toward uniformity was greater in homogeneous groups, and heterogeneous groups showed pressure to agree with experts. These pressures, in both cases, were greater under high pressure to uniformity. There was a greater tendency toward group sub-division in heterogeneous groups.*

200. Gibb, C. A. The principles and traits of leadership. *J. abnorm. soc. Psychol.*, 1947, 42, 267–284. (*87*)

*A review of the literature suggests that leadership is not a quality but arises in group interaction in a problem situation and is determined by the goal of the group. However, in the Army, men with certain general characteristics tend to be chosen as leaders more often.*

201. Gibb, C. A. The sociometry of leadership in temporary groups. *Sociometry*, 1950, 13, 226–243. (*526*)

*In temporary groups of men sociotelic and psychotelic choices are found to overlap, and sociotele structures are more inclusive than psychotele structures. Neither type of choice has a high correlation with leadership. (Sociotelic-relationship is dependent upon a socio or collective criterion; psychotelic on a private criterion.)*

202. Gibb, C. A. An experimental approach to the study of leadership. *Occup. Psychol.*, 1951, 25, 233–248.

*A comprehensive report of an experiment utilizing data of personal characteristics of members (psychometric), interrelationships of members (sociometric), physical setting, and the group behavior. Groups are seen to vary in degree of leadership, and this is linked to the structure and orderliness of the group. Autocratic leadership is associated with greater efficiency but democratic leadership is part of the pattern recognizable as high morale.*

203. Gilchrist, J. C. The formation of social groups under conditions of success and failure. *J. abnorm. soc. Psychol.*, 1952, 47, 174–187.

*Successes (persons) tend to be chosen by successes and failures. Subsequent failure by successes does not elicit realignment of choices.*

204. Goldman-Eisler, Frieda. The measurement of time sequences in conversational behavior. *Brit. J. Psychol.*, (*Gen. Section*), 1951, 42, 355–362.

*Records made of conversations indicated that of four classes of behavior, short silences, short actions, long silences, and long actions, the long silences are the most characteristic (reliable) indices of an individual's conversational activity.*

205. Goodacre, D. M., The use of a sociometric test as a predictor of combat unit effectiveness. *Sociometry*, 1951, 14, 148–152.

*Sociometric scores (positive expansiveness) for combat groups are found related to performance on a field problem.*

206. Goodacre, D. M. Group characteristics of good and poor performing combat units. *Sociometry*, 1953, 16, 168–178.

*Poor and good performing groups (13 squads each) were compared. Men in good performance groups socialized together more after hours, took unauthorized initiative during the problem more often, reported fewer disagreements on how the leader ran the problem, more satisfaction with their status and more pride in their squad.*

207. Goodenough, Florence L., & Anderson, J. E. *Experimental Child Study.* New York: Century, 1931.

*A manual for child study with some emphasis on the techniques of observing children alone and in social settings.*

208. Gorlow, L., Hoch, E. L., & Telschow, E. F. *The nature of nondirective group psychotherapy.* New York: Teach. Coll., Columbia Univer., 1952.

*A review of the literature, followed by reports of investigation into the processes in therapy. Interpretation of the processes focuses on the roles of therapist and participants.*

209. Gouldner, A. W. (Ed.), *Studies in leadership.* New York: Harper, 1950.

*A collection of articles on types of leaders, (formal, informal, authoritarian, or democratic), group settings of leadership, and the ethics and technics of leadership.*

210. Green, Elise H. Friendships and quarrels among pre-school children. *Child Develpm.*, 1933, 4, 237–252.

*Girls reach peak number of friendships and begin decline earlier, reach high point of quarrelsomeness earlier, and have a smaller ratio of quarrels to friendships, than do boys. As children grow older, they tend to decrease the number of different companions that they have, and to increase the frequency of companionship with a few, specific children. Quarreling correlates with friendships, and seems part of friendly intercourse at the nursery school level.*

211. Green, Elise H. Group play and quarreling among pre-school children. *Child Develpm.*, 1933, 4, 302–307.

*From an observational study of nursery school pupils, it was found that the amount of group play and size of the group increase with age, that three-year-old children are the most quarrelsome of the pre-kindergarten children, and that dramatic play elicits the most social cooperation while sand play brings out the most quarrelsome behavior.*

212. Green, G. H. Insight and group adjustment. *J. abnorm. soc. Psychol.*, 1948, 43, 49–61.

*Rating of self and group on a five-point scale of leadership is used to measure an individual's ability to estimate his own position as seen by the group. Over-estimation of own position may be a cause of failure to adjust to the group and an indication of neurosis.*

213. Green, N. E. Verbal intelligence and effectiveness of participation in group discussion. *J. educ. Psychol.*, 1950, 41, 440–445.

*ROTC students in discussion groups of 9–10 members are rated on their effectiveness in discussion and scored on a vocabulary test. The most effective participators have higher vocabulary scores.*

214. Greenberg, Pearl J. Competition in children: An experimental study. *Amer. J. Psychol.*, 1932, 44, 221–248.

*Children aged 2 to 7 years, observed in pairs for evidences of competition (considered as a desire to excel), show that competition develops gradually and is not found in all children of a given age. Competition, a function of ability to understand the idea of excelling and to handle problems, as well as of personality, appears first at age four.*

215. Greer, F. L., Galanter, E. H., & Nordlie, P. G. Interpersonal knowledge and individual and group effectiveness. *J. abnorm. soc. Psychol.*, 1954, 49, 411–414.

*Appointed leaders, popular individuals, and members of effective groups have greater knowledge of group preference hierarchy of members in their groups.*

216. Grinker, R. R., & Spiegel, J. P. *Men under stress.* Philadelphia: Blakiston, 1945.

*An analysis of the psychological mechanisms used by men to deal with stress situations such as combat, and a description of neurosis appearing in soldiers overseas or in veterans, are presented.*

217. Gross, E. Some functional consequences of primary controls in formal work organizations. *Amer. sociol. Rev.*, 1953, 18, 368–373.

*Informal clique groups provide controls supplanting inadequate institutional controls, and thus enable fulfillment of formed purpose. Cliques which cross speciality lines, due to coincidence of leisure periods, reduce conflict. Primary control devices are employed to discover desirable characteristics in personnel, or try to develop them if they are absent.*

218. Gross, E. Primary functions of the small group. *Amer. J. Sociol.*, 1954, 60, 24–30.

*Highly cohesive groups tend to be satisfied with the Air Force and its goals in general, but dissatisfied with their location and work.*

219. Gross, N., & Martin, W. E. On group cohesiveness. *Amer. J. Sociol.*, 1952, 57, 546–554. Schachter, S. Comment. 554–562. Gross, N., & Martin, W. E. Rejoinder. 562–564.

*Some small group studies of cohesiveness are found to be deficient because they do not measure dimensions nominally defined; different aspects of cohesiveness are not highly correlated; and negative cases are not explained.*

220. Gross, N., Martin, W. E., & Darley, J. G. Studies of group behavior: Leadership structures in small organized groups. *J. abnorm. soc. Psychol.*, 1953, 48, 429–432.

*Strongly and weakly supported "formal" leaders are used as criteria for classification of 13 groups. In the strongly supported groups more productivity, active participation, and interest in the group task were found (7 variables), but the differences were not significant.*

221. Grosser, D., Polansky, N., & Lippitt, R. A laboratory study of behavioral contagion. *Hum. Relat.*, 1951, 4, 115–142. Also in Dorothea F. Sullivan (Ed.), *Readings in group work.* New York: Association Press, 1952. Pp. 284–317.

*In a situation of strong need to act in addition to strong social restraints against acting, impulsive initiation of acts by paid collaborators served to overcome restraints and even determine specific activity direction of the child-subject.*

222. GUETZKOW, H. (Ed.) *Groups, leadership and men: Research in human relations.* Pittsburgh: Carnegie Press, 1951.

*The papers in this collection are divided into three areas: group behavior, leadership, and individual behavior.*

223. GURNEE, H. Maze learning in the collective situation. *J. Psychol.*, 1937, 3, 437–443.

*Group maze learning is definitely superior to average individual learning probably because of a scattering of individual errors. The most efficient groups are those composed of all, or nearly all, of one sex.*

224. GURNEE, H. A comparison of collective and individual judgments of facts. *J. exp. Psychol.*, 1937, 21, 106–112.

*Group judgments by vote of acclamation are more frequently correct than the average member's judgment, and equal the judgment of the best member.*

225. GURVITCH, G. Microsociology and sociometry. *Sociometry*, 1949, 12, 1–31.

*Moreno's work is contrasted and compared with the contribution and conceptualization of the author.*

226. GYR, J. Analysis of committee member behavior in four cultures. *Hum. Relat.*, 1951, 4, 193–202.

*Interviews with delegates at a conference tentatively indicate cultural differences in committee procedure.*

227. HAGMAN, ELIZABETH P. The companionships of preschool children. *Univer. Iowa Stud. Child Welf.*, 1933, 7, No. 4 (New ser. No. 255).

*Choice of companion in a nursery school group is related to previous non-school association and not to chronological or mental age, weight, height, or frequency of opportunity in school. From an experimental situation in which the subjects were asked to name those they liked best, the results showed some but not a very certain relation to the actually observed frequency of companionship.*

228. HAIMAN, F. S. *Group leadership and democratic action.* Boston: Houghton Mifflin, 1951.

*The literature on democratic leadership is summarized in text form.*

229. HALPIN, A. W. The leadership behavior and combat performance of airplane commanders. *J. abnorm. soc. Psychol.*, 1954, 49, 19–22.

*Ratings by the superior officers of airplane commanders are correlated negatively with the latter's consideration score (friendship, mutual trust, etc. with the crew) and positively with their initiating structure score (organization and definition of relationship with the crew). The correlation between these factors and crew satisfaction with their commander showed an opposite trend.*

230. HANFMANN, EUGENIA P. Social structure of a group of kindergarten children. *Amer. J. Orthopsychiat.*, 1935, 5, 407–410.

*Ten children are observed in pairs in a play situation to establish a "pecking order." Patterns of dominance are discussed.*

231. HARDEE, MELVENE D., & BERNAUER, MARGARET. A method of evaluating group discussion. *Occupations*, 1948, 27, 90–94.

*Counselor self-ratings (on effectiveness of technique) tend to be lower than student's ratings of them, with only slight agreement between them on rating the best or weakest techniques.*

232. HARDY, M. C. Social recognition at the elementary school age. *J. soc. Psychol.*, 1937, 8, 365–384.

*Social recognition (sociometric popularity) is associated with superiority of intelligence, health, adjustment, physical achievement, and rating of one's home.*

233. HARE, A. P. A study of interaction and consensus in different sized groups. *Amer. sociol. Rev.*, 1952, 17, 261–267. (See # 115.)

*Groups of 5 and 12 persons indicate that in the smaller group the leader has more influence, although skill differences are not important. In the larger groups skill appears as a more important factor since it correlates with amount of consensus change. Members of the larger groups have less opportunity to speak and are less satisfied with the discussion.*

234. HARE, A. P. Small group discussions with participatory and supervisory leadership. *J. abnorm. soc. Psychol.*, 1953, 48, 273–275 (556)

*Boy leaders given instructions for participatory leadership are more effective in increasing the amount of agreement in a group than boys given instructions for supervisory leadership. The participatory leaders also have more influence on the group.*

235. HARE, A. P., & HARE, RACHEL T. Family friendship within the community. *Sociometry*, 1948, 11, 329–334.

*From interviews with 70 families in a student veteran community a positive correlation is found between the number of family friends and the length of residence, number of children, and amount of social activity. The husband initiates most of the family friendships.*

236. HARROCKS, J. E., & BUKER, MAE E. A study of the friendship fluctuations of pre-adolescents. *J. genet. Psychol.*, 1951, 78, 131–144.

*Sociometric tests of pre-adolescent school children over a period of time show correlation between greater stability in friendship and increasing chronological age and grade. (Continuation of: Harrocks, J. E., & Thompson, G. G. A study of the friendship fluctuations of rural boys and girls.* J. genet. Psychol., 1946, 69, 189–198.)

237. HARROCKS, J. E., & THOMPSON, G. G. A study of the friendship fluctuations of rural boys and girls. *J. genet. Psychol.*, 1946, 69, 189–198.

*Children from 11 to 17 years of age demonstrate similar stability in friendships from pre-adolescence to adolescence, but during adolescence stabilization is in direct correlation to age.*

238. HARTLEY, RUTH E., FRANK, L. K., & GOLDENSON, R. M. *Understanding children's play*. New York: Columbia Univer. Press, 1952.

*Dramatic play releases tensions of the child, leads to understanding problems, and to the emotional re-education of children in classrooms. Other types of play are also sensitive indicators of the development of the child's personality.*

239. HARVEY, O. J. An experimental approach to the study of status reactions in informal groups. *Amer. sociol. Rev.*, 1953, 18, 357–367.

*Using dart-throwing as the task, high status in a group was found associated with overestimating one's performance. A high (social) status group tends to overrate the performance of members. The correlation between a person's status in a group and overestimation was higher among the low (social) status groups.*

240. HAYS, D. G., & BUSH, R. R. A study of group action. *Amer. sociol. Rev.*, 1954, 19, 693–701.

*Two mathematical models for interaction of three man groups are compared; a voting model which considers the majority opinion, and a "group actor model" which treats the group as an individual. Results of an experiment of group prediction do not allow the authors to reject either model.*

241. HAYTHORN, W. The influence of individual members on the characteristics of small groups. *J. abnorm. soc. Psychol.*, 1953, 48, 276–284. (*330*)

*NORC students (16) were organized into 20 four-man groups in such a way that no two persons were paired more than once. Each group worked on a reasoning, a mechanical assembly, and a discussion task. Personality data (Cattell factor test) and sociometric data were collected. Group members and two independent observers rated characteristics of their groups. It is found that individual members significantly affect the characteristics of small groups. Effective group functioning was found to be facilitated by cooperativeness, efficiency, and insight, while behavior that reduced cohesiveness and friendliness was generally indentified as "striving for individual prominence." Personality characteristics of maturity and "accepting" facilitated, while suspiciousness and nonaccepting depressed smooth functioning.*

242. HEINICKE, C., & BALES, R. F. Developmental trends in the structure of small groups. *Sociometry*, 1953, 16, 7–38.

*Developmental trends over four sessions of initially leaderless groups are presented. Status consensus (sociometric) is used to dichotomize the groups. Groups initially high in status consensus show a decrease and then an increase in the consensus, while low groups show irregular pattern. All groups appear to go through a period of social emotional conflict (during the determination of the structure), but for the high consensus groups it is more focused in time and in terms of the status of persons involved. After the "crisis" or social emotional conflict, usually associated with the second session, high status persons in the high status consensus groups initiate less and less overt interaction in certain categories highly associated with status. High status consensus groups are more satisfied with the groups' solutions of the problems, and are more " efficient."*

243. HEISE, G. A., & MILLER, G. A. Problem solving by small groups using various communication nets. *J. abnorm. soc. Psychol.*, 1951, 46, 327–336. (*353*)

*The three-man group is observed under* five *communication net conditions,* three *conditions of noise interference, and with* three *types of problems. The problems requiring intercommunication of members were found to be best solved in the organization where intercommunication could be facilitated, and these problems were also most subject to interference by noise.*

244. HEMPHILL, J. K. Situational factors in leadership. *Ohio State Univer. Educ. Res. Monogr.*, 1949, No. 32.

*A system of 15 group dimensions was developed to describe characteristics of the group (pertaining to group as a whole were size, homogeneity, flexibility, stability, permeability, polarization, autonomy, intimacy, and control; and pertaining to respondent's relation with the group were position, potency, participation, hedonic tone, and dependence). Leadership adequacy was related to ratings of morale and effectiveness of group, and acceptance of the leader as an individual. Leaders exhibit behavior indicative of ability to advance the group's purpose and competence in administration, to inspire greater activity, and to free themselves from self-interest. There is an interrelation between hedonic tone, viscidity, leadership adequacy, and leader's behavior.*

245. HEMPHILL, J. K. Relations between the size of the group and the behavior of "superior" leaders. *J. soc. Psychol.*, 1950, 32, 11–22.

*From respondents' descriptions of groups it is found that in larger groups (31 or more members) the demands on the role of the leader are more numerous and exacting, but that there is greater tolerance for leader-centered direction.*

246. HEMPHILL, J. K., & WESTIE, C. M. The measurement of group dimensions. *J. Psychol.*, 1950, 29, 325–342.

*A set of sixteen scales for the description of groups, with reliability data, is presented.*

247. HENRY, J. Family structure and the transmission of neurotic behavior. *Amer. J. Orthopsychiat.*, 1951, 21, 800–818.

*A category system is described to identify a rigid pathogenic interaction pattern (neurosis) transmitted through family interaction.*

248. HENRY, W. E. & GUETZKOW, H. Group projection sketches for the study of small groups. *J. soc. Psychol.*, 1951, 33, 77–102.

*A projective test for use with groups (rather than individuals in groups) is presented. No data on reliability or validity of the method are given.*

249. HERBERT, ELEONORE, L., & TRIST, E. L. The institution of an absent leader by a students' discussion group. *Hum. Relat.*, 1953, 6, 215–248.

*The method of interpretative group discussion (proposed and used by Bion) is applied to a training group of teachers. Group demands and basic assumptions of dependency and flight-fight were revealed in the topics of discussion. The absentees, who had chosen flight, formed a sub-group, with one member as leader, and thus served as a rival reference group to the aims and leadership of the discussion group.*

250. HERBST, P. G. The measurement of family relationships. *Hum. Relat.*, 1952, 5, 3–35.

*A Lewinian analysis of family topological and behavioral relationships (with associated tension) made from interviews with children. Adjoining regions, as determined by participation, were found to have similar interaction patterns, and autonomic, autocratic, and syncratic types of family structure were associated with different levels of tension.*

251. HERBST, P. G. Analysis and measurement of a situation: The child in the family. *Hum. Relat.*, 1953, 6, 113–140.

*Nine basic types of situation structure which may exist for a person are defined in terms of the constellation of forces which may operate within the field of the person. Coalitions are formed when a subset of persons act as a single source of pressure. Optimum adjustment occurs when any one situation structure may be adopted if, at the moment, it leads toward or maintains a state of dynamic equilibrium.*

252. HEYNS, R. W., & ZANDER, A. F. Observation of group behavior. In L. Festinger, & D. Katz, *Research methods in the behavorial sciences.* New York: Dryden Press, 1953. Pp. 381–417.

*Category systems and rating scales as observation instruments are discussed. Category systems differ in the dimensions of exhaustiveness, inference, number of dimensions, and discrete vs. continuous categories. Rating scales are devices to define dimensions clearly, and ideally, the data provided should be comparable to that obtained by a category system with continuous categories.*

253. HILGARD, E. R., SAIT, E. M., & MARGARET, G. ANN. Level of aspiration as affected by relative standing in an experimental social group. *J. exp. Psychol.*, 1940, 27, 411–421.

*In groups sized 3 to 6, using a task of subtractions, subjects made private estimates of their future performance. The actual performance was made public (time as the criterion). The tendency of the estimates of future performance was in the direction of bringing the performance in line with the group mean, irrespective of whether the position of the person was determined by the difficulty of the subtractions, or whether, with equally difficult material, fast and slow workers were considered.*

254. HILL, R. Review of current research on marriage and the family. *Amer. sociol. Rev.*, 1951, 16, 694–701.

*Theoretical approaches are systematized and special foci of research, including the small group concept, are considered.*

255. HITES, R. W., & CAMPBELL, D. T. A test of the ability of fraternity leaders to estimate group opinion. *J. soc. Psychol.*, 1950, 32, 95–100.

*Leaders (elected and appointed) are found not to differ from nonleaders in the ability to judge the opinion of the group.*

256. Hoffman, P. J., Festinger, L., & Lawrence, D. Tendencies toward group comparability in competitive bargaining. *Hum. Relat.*, 1954, 7, 141–159.

*In an experiment on competitive bargaining in which the three members competed for points but had to form a coalition of two in order to earn points, the member with a large initial advantage in points had fewer opportunities to form coalitions and had to pay a relatively higher price to do so. This was more pronounced in a high task-importance group and in a group where members all regarded each other as comparable in ability.*

257. Hollingshead, A. B. *Elmtown's youth.* New York: John Wiley, 1949.

*Observed behavior of adolescents is related to the positions that their families occupy in the social structure of the community. Clique membership is primarily composed of students in the same school class, and the same prestige class or adjacent ones. Most of the dating is within the same prestige class, with the exception occurring between adjacent classes. Class V's (lowest) are differentiated more definitely in their own stratum than are any other class members.*

258. Homans, G. C. The Western Electric Researches. In Nat. Res. Council, *Fatigue of workers: Its relation to industrial production.* New York: Reinhold, 1941. (See # 507.)

*A comparison of the Relay Assembly Test Room and the Bank Wiring Observation Room experiments.*

259. Homans, G. C. The Western Electric researches. In S. D. Hoslett (Ed.), *Human factors in management.* Parkville, Mo.: Park Coll. Press, 1946. Pp. 152–185.

*In a review of the Western Electric researches, it is concluded that the rates of change allowed by the social organization of a small group of employees must be equal to the rate of change possible in the technical organization or the result will be blind resistance to change.*

260. Homans, G. C. A conceptual scheme for the study of social organization. *Amer. sociol. Rev.*, 1947, 12, 13–26.

*Theoretical analysis centering around the concepts of operation, sentiment, and interaction (as elements), primary and secondary, mutual dependence and equilibrium.*

261. Homans, G. C. Status among clerical workers. *Hum. Organization*, 1953, 12, 5–10.

*In the office of a department store, the informal group structure rates one job as higher in status than the other, while the management rates both as equal in pay. This, plus assigning women from the "higher" job to fill in at the other task when needed, creates dissatisfaction among the workers.*

262. Homans, G. C. *The human group.* New York: Harcourt, Brace, 1950.

*A system for the analysis of social interaction is presented in context of recent research of "informal" factors and small groups.*

263. Horowitz, M. W., & Perlmutter, H. V. The concept of the social group. *J. soc. Psychol.*, 1953, 37, 69–95.

*Past and present views on the reality of the group are reviewed. The authors conclude that a psychology of groups is possible.*

264. Horowitz, M. W., Lyons, J., & Perlmutter, H. V. Induction of forces in discussion groups. *Hum. Relat.*, 1951, 4, 57–76.

*Persons are seen as causal units in relation to their acts and the value of the person determines the value of the act. Actual behavior could not be predicted from the questionnaire data collected.*

265. Horwitz, M. The conceptual status of group dynamics. *Rev. educ. Res.*, 1953, 23, 309–328.

*Three systems (individual, group, institution) are presented in a matrix designed to handle problem solving behavior. Variables within or among systems are interdependent (given variation may affect variables in same or other cells of matrix).*

266. Horwitz, M. The recall of interrupted group tasks: An experimental study of individual motivation in relation to group goals. *Hum. Relat.*, 1954, 7, 3–38. (See # 115.)

*When tasks of the "group" are interrupted or not interrupted, then completed or not completed, it is found that group members recall tasks best when they are interrupted not completed. Generally, tension is associated with recall.*

267. Horwitz, M., & Cartwright, D. A projective method for the diagnosis of group properties. *Hum. Relat.*, 1953, 6, 397–410.

*Group properties derived from the analysis of a group's discussion of an ambiguous picture are correlated with independent measures, and intravariable relationships followed theoretical prediction, e.g., the hypothesis that group distractability should be inversely related to degree of membership orientation is supported by a negative correlation.*

268. Horwitz, M., Exline, R. V., & Lee, F. J. *Motivational effects of alterative decision-making processes in groups.* Urbana, Ill.: Bureau of Educ. Res., Univer. of Ill., 1953.

*Psychological oversatiation in five man groups working on a repetitive task varied under five group treatments. Satiation is lowest for a group of friends who received information about performance and are told strong agreement exists in the way the group sets goals and highest for strangers who do not set goals.*

269. Horwitz, M., & Lee, F. G. Effects of decision making by group members on recall of finished and unfinished tasks. *J. abnorm. soc. Psychol.*, 1954, 49, 201–210.

*In an experimental group, given the goal of voting in agreement with announced majority decisions, there was a tendency to recall unfinished tasks (i.e., disagreement with the group).*

270. Hubbard, Ruth M. A method of studying spontaneous group formation. In Dorothy S. Thomas (Ed.), *Some new techniques for studying social behavior*. New York: Teach. Coll., Columbia Univer., 1929. Pp. 76–85.

*A rating form is proposed for use of observers of spontaneous group formation in a nursery school. Some highly tentative findings are presented to illustrate data obtained by this method.*

271. Hunt, J. McV., & Solomon, R. L. The stability and some correlates of group-status in a summer camp group of young boys. *Amer. J. Psychol.*, 1942, 55, 33–45.

*Previous experience in camp, athletic ability, generosity, physical attractiveness, and lack of egocentricity are significantly correlated with group-status. Correlation between group-status and behavioral traits increases with length of time in camp.*

272. Hurlock, Elizabeth B. The use of group rivalry as an incentive. *J. abnorm. soc. Psychol.*, 1927, 22, 278–290.

*Group competition raises the performance of members. Girls and younger ages are slightly favored, and the influence of rivalry was generally increasingly more effective throughout the experiment. Incentive is more effective with persons of initially inferior scores.*

273. Hurwitz, J. I., Zander, A. F., & Hymovitch, B. Some effects of power on the relations among group members. In D. Cartwright & A. F. Zander (Eds.), *Group dynamics: Research and theory*. Evanston, Ill.: Row, Peterson, 1953, 483–492.

*High status (perceived power to influence) persons tend to be liked more than low status persons by both high and low status persons. Low status persons like others more than high status persons. Low status persons make and receive fewer communications. Low status persons perceive high status persons as liking them differentially more than low status persons (distortion). The amount of participation of low status persons is overrated.*

274. Husband, R. W. Cooperative versus solitary problem solution. *J. soc. Psychol.*, 1940, 11, 405–409.

*In code and jigsaw tests, pairs of subjects used less time than did those alone, and close friends took less time than did strangers.*

275. Jackson, J. M. The effect of changing the leadership of small work groups. *Hum. Relat.*, 1953, 6, 25–44.

*Foremen receive approximately the same rating on skill when transferred from one work group to another, if approximately the same skills are required in both groups.*

276. Jackson, W. M. Interaction in a college fraternity. *Appl. Anthrop.*, 1944, 3, 16–21.

*A case study of leadership and communication patterns in a college fraternity house finds that only actions originated by the president of the group achieved satisfactory group action.*

277. Jacobs, J. H. The application of sociometry to industry. *Sociometry*, 1945, 8, 181–198.

*Sociometric tests provide a measure of employee morale, for use by industry.*

278. James, J. Some elements in a theory of small groups. *Res. Stud., State Coll. Wash.*, 1950, 18, 144–152.

*A brief review and consideration of theory.*

279. James, J. A preliminary study of the size determinant in small group interaction. *Amer. sociol. Rev.*, 1951, 16, 474–477.

*Groups in interaction tend to be small, i.e., of two persons. Active groups may tend to be smaller than non-active groups.*

280. James, J. Clique organization in a small industrial plant. *Res. Stud., State Coll. Wash.*, 1951, 19, 125–130.

*Sociometric data were obtained for 444 persons (93%) of a small plant. Cliques were found to be formed of persons who were near each other functionally, spatially, and of the same sex. Women formed more cliques than men.*

281. Jansen, L. T. Measuring family solidarity. *Amer. sociol. Rev.*, 1952, 17, 727–733.

*A scale of family solidarity in eight types of interaction is proposed to predict marital adjustment and joint activity.*

282. Jenkins, D. H. Feedback and group self-evaluation. *J. soc. Issues*, 1948, 4 (2), 50–60.

*Effective discussion requires attention to the mechanics of operation, such as awareness of direction and goal, rate of progress, and use of ability for self-improvement. A group productivity observer and self-evaluation periods will serve to elicit and use these data.*

283. Jenkins, D. H., & Lippitt, R. *Interpersonal perceptions of teachers, students, and parents.* Washington, D. C.: National Education Association, 1951.

*Analysis of interview and questionnaire data of children, their teachers, and parents, reveals three themes which appear in more than one of the between-group relationships: teachers are most interested in friendliness in all of the relationships; power and control are paramount in both the teacher-student and parent-child relations; and the adults have a common interest in social and extra-curricular activities with the children. These commonalities are largely unperceived by the subjects.*

284. Jenness, A. Social influences in the change of opinion. *J. abnorm. soc. Psychol.*, 1932, 27, 29–34.

*Early research on the effect of group discussion on change of opinion is summarized.*

285. Jenness, A. The role of discussion in changing opinion regarding a matter of fact. *J. abnorm. soc. Psychol.*, 1932, 27, 279–296.

*Estimation of the number of beans in a bottle before and after discussion in a small group (2 to 4 members) does not show an improve-*

*ment in the accuracy of the average individual judgment after the discussion. The subjects are aware of differences in judgments. However, most of the individuals increase their accuracy. When subjects did not become aware of differences in judgment the same results were not found. Under both conditions the average change in opinion is greater for women than for men.*

286. JENNINGS, HELEN H. Structure of leadership—development and sphere of influence. *Sociometry*, 1937, 1, 99–143.

*Changes in the structure of leadership in cottages of girls are determined over a period of 2½ years. More isolates appear than leaders although some individuals hold both positions at different times. Leaders have large spheres of influence and more acquaintances.*

287. JENNINGS, HELEN H. Individual differences in the social atom. *Sociometry*, 1941, 4, 269–277. (*266*)

*Leaders and isolates differ not only in the degree to which they are chosen, but also in their patterns of choice and rejection of and by others.*

288. JENNINGS, HELEN H. Experimental evidence on the social atom at two time points. *Sociometry*, 1942, 5, 135–145.

*A new method for studying the extent of consistency exhibited by the social atom of the same individual at different periods results in the conclusion that the pattern does not vary randomly over time. The extent to which an individual reacts to other persons and the extent to which others react to him on a sociometric test remains relatively constant between different criteria although the gross amount of reaction varies.*

289. JENNINGS, HELEN H. Leadership and sociometric choice. *Sociometry*, 1947, 10, 32–49.

*A sociometric study of a community of 400 individuals (see* Leadership and isolation *for a complete report of this research). Leaders are found to be highly chosen and the implications of the data for a theory of leadership and the difference between the socio- and psychegroup is discussed.*

290. JENNINGS, HELEN H. Sociometric differentiation of the psychegroup and the sociogroup. *Sociometry*, 1947, 10, 71–79.

*In a further analysis of data for* Leadership and isolation, *the sociogroup (work group) is compared with the psychegroup (friendship group).*

291. JENNINGS, HELEN H. *Leadership and isolation.* New York: Longmans, Green, 1950 (2nd Edition). (See #31 & #115.)

*A classic study of social structure and personality using the sociometric approach. Techniques and assumptions are presented systematically.*

292. JENNINGS, HELEN H. Sociometric grouping in relation to child development. In Caroline Tryon (Ed.), *Fostering mental health in our schools.*

Washington, D.C.: Ass. for supervision and Curriculum Development, Nat. Educ. Ass., 1950.

*A review of findings in sociometric research on the operation of groups. Emphasis on the implications for the classroom situation.*

293. JENNINGS, HELEN H. Sociometric structure in personality and group formation. In M. Sherif & M. O. Wilson (Eds.), *Group relations at the crossroads.* New York: Harper, 1953. Pp. 332–365.

*Sociometric-sociodramatic investigation indicates that the individual's choice behavior facilitates expression, stimulates spontaneity and creativity, and is the very process of personality formation.*

294. JERSILD, A. T., & FITE, MARY D. The influence of nursery school experience on children's social adjustments. *Child Develpm. Monogr.*, 1939, No. 25.

*Children who had previously attended nursery school showed twice as many social contacts and twice as much participation as do new children during first weeks of school, but by spring the two groups were equal.*

295. JOEL, W., & SHAPIRO, D. A genotypical approach to the analysis of personal interaction. *J. Psychol.*, 1949, 28, 9–17.

*A category system based on the reactions of warmth, hostility, and flight is proposed for use with therapy and projective tests. No reliability or validity data are given.*

296. JONES, F. D., & PETERS, H. N. An experimental evaluation of group psychotherapy. *J. abnorm. soc. Psychol.*, 1952, 47, 345–353.

*Examination of patients with and without psychodramatic group psychotherapy indicates some significant effects on test scores by the therapy. Of the measures used in examining changes, the objective tests appear more reliable than the projective tests.*

297. KAHN, R. L., & KATZ, D. Leadership practices in relation to productivity and morale. In D. Cartwright & A. F. Zander (Eds.), *Group dynamics: Research and theory.* Evanston, Ill.: Row, Peterson, 1953.

*Review of research in the industrial setting indicates four variables which are associated with productivity: (a) supervisor's ability to play a differentiated role, (b) the degree of delegation of authority or closeness of supervision, (c) the quality of supportiveness by employees, and (d) amount of group cohesiveness (morale).*

298. KAPLAN, A., SKOGSTAD, A. L., & GIRSHICK, M. A. The prediction of social and technological events. *Publ. Opin. Quart.*, 1950, 14, 93–110.

*Predictions of future events made by the group are more likely to be right than those of individuals working alone.*

299. KATZ, D. Social psychology and group processes. *Annu. Rev. Psychol.*, 1951, 2, 137–172.

*The 1949–1950 literature on perceptual selection, suggestion, leadership, conference interaction process, group dynamics, action research, intergroup tension, group conflicts and morale, social structure, propa-*

*ganda, opinion and attitude research, is reviewed, and a 101-item bibliography is included.*

300. KEET, C. D. Two verbal techniques in a miniature counseling situation. *Psychol. Monogr.*, 1948, 62, No. 294.

*Two therapeutic techniques: the purely permissive, non-directive, and the permissive in combination with interpretive were compared by means of an experimental disturbance created by finding a disturbing word that the subject would fail to recall in a learning test. It was found that the combined use of expressive and interpretive methods proved consistently superior to the purely expressive in aiding the subject to react correctly, by recalling the forgotten word in a second learning situation.*

301. KELLER, J. B. Comment on "Channels of communications in small groups." *Amer. sociol. Rev.*, 1951, 16, 842–843. (See #28.)

*It is suggested that the matrix of interaction can be accounted for by the product of a matrix of initiating strength and one of receiving strength.*

302. KELLEY, H. H. Communication in experimentally created hierarchies. *Hum. Relat.*, 1951, 4, 39–56. (See #115.)

*In a study of status (desirable task assignment) and mobility (potential for upward or downward movement) it is found that more irrelevant communication is given by persons in the low status position and that potential for upward mobility decreases unattractiveness of low position and potential for downward mobility increases unattractiveness of high position. Persons in high position tend to indicate confusion and dissatisfaction less in their communications.*

303. KELLEY, H. H., & SHAPIRO, M. M. An experiment on conformity to group norms where conformity is detrimental to group achievement. *Amer. sociol. Rev.*, 1954, 19, 667–677.

*Subjects rated as acceptable and not acceptable in fictitious groups did not differ in their conformity to group norms. Subjects rated as acceptable who placed a higher valuation on group membership tended to deviate more than those not acceptable.*

304. KELLEY, H. H., & VOLKHART, E. H. The resistance to change of group-anchored attitudes. *Amer. sociol. Rev.*, 1952, 17, 453–465.

*In an attempt to change expressed attitudes in the direction of non-conformity to group norms, more change in opinion is expressed under "public" conditions than under "private." Under the private condition the influence of the communication is inversely related to how highly a boy values his membership.*

305. KELMAN, H. C. Effects of success and failure on "suggestibility" in the autokinetic situation. *J. abnorm. soc. Psychol.*, 1950, 45, 267–285.

*Suggestibility is found least in the presence of success, most in failure. Ascendancy, self confidence, and nervous tenseness are found related to suggestibility.*

306. Kephart, W. M. A quantitative analysis of intragroup relationships. *Amer. J. sociol.*, 1950, 60, 544–549.

*Formulas are presented for the calculation of various combinations of subgroupings.*

307. Killian, L. M. The significance of multiple-group membership in disaster. *Amer. J. Sociol.*, 1952, 57, 309–314. (See #115.)

*Community disasters accentuate ordinarily latent conflicts between multiple loyalties to primary and secondary groups. Loyalty to primary groups is usually most demanding, but such factors as training or strength of responsibilities may change this predisposition.*

308. Kinney, Elva E. A study of peer group social acceptability at the fifth grade level in a public school. *J. educ. Res.*, 1953, 47, 57–64.

*A study of fifth grade children using three groupings (entire grade, ability groups, and informal flexible groups) found that social acceptance of isolates may be increased with use of informal groups. This grouping also seemed to create more cohesion.*

309. Kirkpatrick, C., & Hobart, C. Disagreement, disagreement estimate, and non-empathetic imputations for intimacy groups varying from favorite date to married. *Amer. sociol. Rev.*, 1954, 19, 10–19.

*Accuracy of prediction of other person's responses is found to be above chance, with a differential accuracy between the dating stage and married stage. No consistent sex differences are found. The limited evidence indicates that selection of partners rather than influence of association may be the factor involved.*

310. Klein, A., & Keill, N. The experiencing of group psychotherapy. *Sociatry*, 1953, 5, 205–221.

*The dynamics of a therapy group (over a sequence of sessions) is studied by interpretation of the sentence completion of the members.*

311. Klubeck, S., & Bass, B. M. Differential effects of training on persons of different leadership status. *Hum. Relat.*, 1954, 7, 59–72.

*Leadership status changed after training, subject to individual differences, and persons of higher initial status profited most.*

312. Klugman, S. F. Cooperative versus individual efficiency in problem-solving. *J. educ. Psychol.*, 1944, 35, 91–100.

*Children working in pairs and individually are compared in terms of the number of correct arithmetic problems and time to complete the task. Pairs of children solve more problems than individuals, but take longer. Subgroups by grade, race, sex, age, and ability, all showed better performance of the pairs over individuals, both in terms of raw scores and time scores, but not all the differences were significant.*

313. Kotkov, B. A bibliography for the student of group therapy. *J. clin. Psychol.*, 1950, 6, 77–91.

*An eclectic bibliography of 579 items, overlapping in part the small group research area.*

314. Kozman, Hilda C. *Group process in physical education.* New York: Harpers, 1951.

*An applied study of group methods which contains a review of the literature.*

315. Krech, D., & Crutchfield, R. S. *Theory and problems of social psychology.* New York: McGraw-Hill, 1948.

*Basic psychological principles, as explanations of human behavior in a social context, are outlined and used to analyze social processes (beliefs and attitudes, structure and function of social groups, group morale and leadership).*

316. Landis, M. H., & Burtt, H. E. A study of conversations. *J. comp. Psychol.*, 1924, 4, 81–89.

*Eavesdropping on 500 conversations indicates that men talk most of business and money, and women talk mostly of men and clothes.*

317. Lanzetta, J. T., Haefner, D., Langham, P., & Axelrod, H. Some effects of situational threat on group behavior. *J. abnorm. soc. Psychol.*, 1954, 49, 445–453.

*In an experiment, locus of threat (whether external or internal to the group) and target of threat (directed to group or to individual member) did not reveal significant variation in effects of threat. However, threat vs. absence of threat, affected behavior negatively in three areas: interpersonal relations, utilization of group members' resources, and effectiveness of the group.*

318. Lasswell, H. D. Person, personality, group, culture. *Psychiatry*, 1939, 2, 533–561.

*Clarification of these four basic terms of interpersonal relations.*

319. Leavitt, H. J. Some effects of certain communication patterns on group performance. *J. abnorm. soc. Psychol.*, 1951, 46, 38–50.

*In controlled communication experiments in five man groups in a problem-solving situation, it was found that a wheel organization allowed the fastest single trial. The circle pattern used the largest number of messages. More errors are made in the circle and the chain than in the Y or wheel pattern of organization. In the general sequence from circle to chain to Y to wheel, the circle extreme has associated with it activity, lack of leadership, least organization and direction, but enjoyment by the members. The wheel at the other extreme shows opposite characteristics. Centrality (as measured in terms of the imposed structure is found to be an important concept). Persons who are central tend to be more satisfied, and satisfaction increases in time, while the opposite is true of persons in peripheral positions. Centrality determines behavior by limiting independence of action. Activity, accuracy, satisfaction, and leadership are thus determined (in a statistical sense), and recognizability of the pattern is also associated with centrality.*

320. Leavitt, H. J., & Mueller, R. A. H. Some effects of feedback on communication. *Hum. Relat.*, 1951, 4, 401–410. (*414*)

*Feedback increases accuracy of information transmitted, as well as confidence of receiver and sender. Feedback takes time, but with experience the amount of time decreases. A sender and receiver can improve without feedback experience, but free feedback will improve subsequent communication without feedback appreciably. Sender experience appears to be more important to communication than receiver's. An initial reaction of hostility appears to accompany the no-feedback condition.*

321. LEEMAN, C. P. Patterns of sociometric choice in small groups: A mathematical model and related experimentation. *Sociometry*, 1952, 15, 220–243.

*A baseline mathematical model for choice behavior, utilizing a concept of encounters between persons, is presented. The model is related to experimentation actually carried out, but with three persons only. The model is prohibitive for groups of larger size. The utility of this and other baseline models is indicated.*

322. LEMANN, T. B., & SOLOMON, R. L. Group characteristics as revealed in sociometric patterns and personality ratings. *Sociometry*, 1952, 15, 7–90.

*A comprehensive report of study of three girls' dorms, emphasizing sociometric indices of personality and rating scales. On a criterion of cohesiveness, the houses were ranked in the same order as the amount of insight (or accuracy of perception among members). Insight, however, was not significantly related to "social adjustment." Rejected persons tended to be the most "noticeable."*

323. LEUBA, C. J. A preliminary experiment to quantify an incentive and its effects. *J. abnorm. soc. Psychol.*, 1930, 25, 275–288.

*With a material incentive (candy), work greatly increased in speed, absolute differences between individual performances increased, and relative differences decreased.*

324. LEUBA, C. J. An experimental study of rivalry in young children. *J. comp. Psychol.*, 1933, 16, 367–378.

*When children aged two to six years, putting pegs in a board either alone or in pairs, are observed, it is found that the five-year-olds are the youngest in which rivalry reponses are dominant, and output is increased substantially in pairs.*

325. LEVINE, J., & BUTLER, J. Lecture vs. group decision in changing behavior. *J. appl. Psychol.*, 1952, 36, 29–33. (See #115.)

*Although both lecture and group decision changed ratings of supervisor, only in the latter was a "bias" favoring high-skill positions corrected.*

326. LEWIN, K. Frontiers in group dynamics: Concept, method and reality in social science: social equilibria and social change. *Hum. Relat.*, 1947, 1, 5–41. (*95*)

*A brief presentation of the method of analysis based on topology, using life space diagrams, etc. Data are presented from previous studies to illustrate the analysis of social interaction and the development of stable compatible systems.*

327. Lewin, K. Frontiers in group dynamics: 2. Channels of group life; social planning and action research. *Hum. Relat.*, 1947, 1, 143–153.

*A continuation. Data are presented in interpretation of the importance of sociological research to the field of planning and the resolution of conflict situations.*

328. Lewin, K. *Resolving social conflicts: Selected papers on group dynamics.* New York: Harper, 1948.

*This collection of articles covers three main areas of applied psychology in social settings; cultural change of autocratic Germany, conflicts in primary groups such as the family and in industry, and intergroup conflicts and group belongingness with reference in general to minority groups and in particular to the Jews.*

329. Lewin, K., *Field theory in social science.* New York: Harper, 1951.

*A collection of articles in which field theory is defined as a method of analyzing causal relations and of creating constructs; and this approach is applied to the problems of learning, regression, psychological ecology, and group dynamics.*

330. Lewin, K., & Lippitt, R. An experimental approach to the study of autocracy and democracy: A preliminary note. *Sociometry*, 1938, 1, 292–300. (*516*)

*The classic experiment contrasting the effects of authoritarian and democratic leadership on two children's groups is briefly described. The democratic group has less tension and more cooperation, objectivity, constructiveness, we-feeling, and stability of structure.*

331. Lewin, K., Lippitt, R., & White, R. K. Patterns of aggressive behavior in experimentally created "social climates." *J. soc. Psychol.*, 1939, 10, 271–299. (See #209.)

*Aggressive acts are more closely associated with autocratic leadership groups than democratic groups.*

332. Lewis, Helen B. An experimental study of the role of the ego in work: I. The role of the ego in cooperative work. *J. exp. Psychol.*, 1944, 34, 113–126.

*Use of recall of tasks to determine subject's attitude toward task finds that recall of interrupted tasks (partner-completed) is equal in frequency to recall of self-completed tasks in a cooperative work relationship.*

333. Lewis, Helen B., & Franklin, M. An experimental study of the role of the ego in work: II. The significance of task orientation in work. *J. exp. Psychol.*, 1944, 34, 195–215.

*Task orientation of subject favors recall of interrupted tasks (partner-completed), while the egooriented subject tends to recall completed tasks.*

334. LINDEMAN, E. C. *Social discovery.* New York: Republic, 1924.

*Methodology of the social sciences prior to 1924 is reviewed and improvements are proposed for the concept of group conflict and observer ratings of groups.*

335. LINDZEY, G. (Ed.) *Handbook of social psychology.* Cambridge, Mass.: Addison-Wesley, 1954.

*A collection of comprehensive review articles in selected fields, several of which are of direct relevance to the study of small groups; e.g., systematic observational techniques, sociometric measurement, etc.*

336. LINDZEY, G., & BORGATTA, E. F. Sociometric measurements. In G. Lindzey. *Handbook of social psychology.* Cambridge, Mass.: Addison-Wesley, 1954.

*A comprehensive review of sociometric techniques and findings.*

337. LINDZEY, G., & RIECKEN, H. W. Inducing frustration in adult subjects. *J. consult. Psychol.*, 1951, 15, 18–23.

*Frustrating adults by blockage of socially important motives (group expectation) is more successful than physical need-blocking (hunger).*

338. LINTON, H. B. Autokinetic judgment as a measure of influence. *J. abnorm. soc. Psychol.*, 1954, 49, 464–466.

*Data from experiments using autokinetic judgments as a measure of suggestibility actually are a function of two factors—the variability of actual perception of the movement, and the judgment of it. Since only the latter is subject to change a measure of statistical significance and a dichotomized sample are suggested to evaluate just the latter effect.*

339. LIPPITT, R. Field theory and experiment in social psychology: Autocratic and democratic group atmospheres. *Amer. J. Sociol.*, 1939, 45, 26–49.

*An experimental play group of five children led by an adult autocratic leader is compared with a similar group led by a democratic leader. Observations of the two groups indicate more leader direction in the autocratic group, less group goal involvement, and less freedom of locomotion. Two individuals shifted from one group to the other change their behavior patterns to conform with the new group.*

340. LIPPITT, R. An experimental study of the effect of democratic and authoritarian group atmospheres. *Univer. of Iowa Stud. in Child Welf.*, 1940, 16, 43–195. (See #31.)

*In a classic laboratory research experiment the author creates two children's clubs, one led by authoritarian and the other by democratic methods. The authoritarian group showed tendencies toward individual jobs, competition for status, hostility, and disintegration, while the democratic group showed group goals, "we-centeredness," lack of tension, spontaneous stability, and more creative and constructive work.*

341. LIPPITT, R. *Training in community relations: A research exploration toward new group skills.* New York: Harper, 1949.

*A report on a workshop for community leaders of interractial, intercultural, and intergroup programs discusses the methods used in recruiting and training these people. The learning situation is analyzed and its effectiveness is assessed and attributed to specific factors (cohesiveness of study group, role history of members, expectations of their community group).*

342. Lippitt, R., Polansky, N., & Rosen, S. The dynamics of power: A field study of social influence in groups of children. *Hum. Relat.*, 1952, 5, 37–64. (See # 115.)

*In a replication study with children, the following generalizations were found to be stable: The group member is more subject to the influence of a person with high power and will tend to imitate him. The high power person is likely to be approached by more non-directive techniques and with greater deference and is more likely to initiate and to be directive and successful in terms of influence, but to personally resist direct influence. High power children tend to be those with physical prowess who are liked. It was also found that perception of own power is related to rated power, and to the associated pattern of behavior. Social activity is found related to power, but non-social activity, experience in camp, and intelligence are not found related to the rated power.*

343. Lippitt, Rosemary. Popularity among preschool children. *Child Develpm.*, 1941, 12, 305–332.

*Three groups of preschool children, ranging in size from nine to twenty-one, were given a battery of tests, "sociometric" ratings, and observers' ratings (by teachers and experimenters) of the attractiveness of their personality and social behavior. Child and teacher estimates were found to be based on different criteria, with teachers using social behavior and social activity as criteria, while children are most sensitive to cooperation and adaptation to the situation.*

344. Loomis, C. P. Informal groupings in a Spanish-American village. *Sociometry*, 1941, 4, 36–51.

*Informal and kinship structure of a village is illustrated by patterns of visiting and work exchange.*

345. Loomis, C. P., Baker, W. B., & Proctor, C. The size of the family as related to social success of children. *Sociometry*, 1949, 12, 313–320.

*Little or no relationship is found between frequency of choice or rejection of a student and the number of his siblings.*

346. Loomis, C. P., & Pepinsky, H. B. Sociometry, 1937–1947: Theory and methods. *Sociometry*, 1948, 11, 262–283.

*Review of literature and trends.*

347. Luce, R. D., & Perry, A. D. A method of matrix analysis of group structure. *Psychometrika*, 1949, 14, 95–116.

*Two concepts (n-chain and clique), with simple relationships to certain matrices, are proposed for use in determining group structures and are applied in order to analyze some examples.*

348. Luchins, A. S. Social influences on perception of complex drawings. *J. soc. Psychol.*, 1945, 21, 257–273.

*A child's interpretation of a drawing was affected by the interpretation of a rehearsed subject only if the objective material was ambiguous and thus presented possibilities for conforming to the latter's description.*

349. Luchins, A. S. Group structures in group psychotherapy. *J. clin. Psychol.*, 1947, 3, 269–273.

*Development of group structure during group psychotherapy programs progressed from a mere assemblage of patients to a participating audience, to an interacting group.*

350. Lundberg, G. A. Some problems of group classification and measurement. *Amer. sociol. Rev.*, 1940, 5, 351–360.

*The possibility of classification and measurement is proposed on the basis of (then) newly developed methods of analysis.*

351. Maas, H. S. Personal and group factors in leaders' social perception. *J. abnorm. soc. Psychol.*, 1950, 45, 54–63.

*Twenty-two leaders (20-year-olds) of youth (adolescent) groups were found to modify their perception of the members' behavior as follows: Leaders who tended to project blame, who led open (informal) groups and leaders who tended to introject blame, who led closed (clearly structured) groups, showed desirable changes in perception (increased causal inferences). Reverse type of placement resulted in some undesirable changes.*

352. Maas, H. S., Varon, Edith, & Rosenthal, D. A technique for studying the social behavior of schizophrenics. *J. abnorm. soc. Psychol.*, 1951, 46, 119–123.

*A method for observing behavior is presented. The categories used are: Motor Activity (directed walking, pacing, other), Responses to External Stimuli (reading, other), Verbal Relating (to self, to staff, to female observer, to male observer), and Non-Verbal Relating. The method shows that the subjects have more outwardly purposeful activities and more verbal relationships with other people after a series of group therapy sessions.*

353. McBurney, J. H., & Hance, K. G. *The principles and methods of discussion.* New York: Harper, 1939.

*This is a text for discussion leaders.*

354. McCandless, B. R. Changing relationships between dominance and social acceptability during group democratization. *Amer. J. Orthopsychiat.*, 1942, 12, 529–535.

*Dominance, as a correlate of popularity, decreases as a group of boys are changed from autocracy to democracy.*

355. McCurdy, H. G., & Eber, H. W. Democratic versus authoritarian: A further investigation of group problem-solving. *J. Pers.*, 1953, 22, 258–269.

*Three man groups (six each) were structured under authoritarian and democratic instructions, composed of authoritarian and democratic subjects, to work in a three man problem solving situation. Democratic organization is not found superior to the authoritarian (directive), and in fact, there is a suggestion that performance of "authoritarians" in a democratic setup is depressed. Authoritarian organization leads to faster termination of the problem.*

356. McCurdy, H. G., & Lambert, W. E. The efficiency of small human groups in the solution of problems requiring genuine co-operation. *J. Pers.*, 1952, 20, 478–494.

*In solving a learning problem, individuals make fewer errors than groups of three. No difference in efficiency is found between groups in which free communication is allowed and those in which an appointed leader makes all decisions.*

357. McKeachie, W. J. Individual conformity to attitudes of classroom groups. *J. abnorm. soc. Psychol.*, 1954, 49, 282–289.

*Attitude changes are correlated with changes of group norms. Conformity between individuals' attitude and their perception of the group norm is less in group-centered classes, though members' liking for the group is more than in leader-centered classes. Group decision produces more conformity between individuals' attitude and objective group norm, but less between attitude and perceived group norm.*

358. Macy, J., Jr., Christie, L. S., & Luce, R. D. Coding noise in a task-oriented group. *J. abnorm. soc. Psychol.*, 1953, 48, 401–409.

*Task-oriented five man groups, required to communicate descriptions of colored marbles, make errors predictable by amount of ambiguities in coding-decoding process. Redundant coding is used to reduce error.*

359. Maier, N. R. F. The quality of group decisions as influenced by the discussion leader. *Hum. Relat.*, 1950, 3, 155–174.

*Skilled leaders with ideas obtain higher quality of problem-solving (and are more accepted) than less skilled leaders. Differences in quality of problem-solving for groups and individuals are found.*

360. Maier, N. R. F. An experimental test of the effect of training on discussion leadership. *Hum. Relat.*, 1953, 6, 161–173.

*Groups composed of persons having eight hours of training in making group decisions made more successful decisions (changes or partial changes) than groups having no such training. Trained leaders are concluded to be more effective than untrained leaders.*

361. Maier, N. R. F., & Solem, A. R. The contribution of a discussion leader to the quality of group thinking: The effective use of minority opinions. *Hum. Relat.*, 1952, 5, 277–288. (See #115.)

*In small groups (four and five persons) solving an arithmetic problem, it is found that if a discussion leader is used there is a greater shift to correct answers than if a non-participating observer is present, although both show marked and significant shifts.*

362. MALLER, J. B. Cooperation and competition: An experimental study in motivation. *Teach. Coll., Columbia Univer. Contrib. Educ.*, 1929, No. 384.

*A comprehensive investigation of individual as against group motivation on performance. Some sex differences are manifest. In general, cooperation appears to correlate to socialized behavior, mental age, intelligence, school deportment, moral knowledge, resistance to suggestibility, neurotic index, honesty and inhibition. Cooperation is negatively correlated to speed of work, variability of performance, health, and other physical indices.*

363. MALLER, J. B. Size of family and personality of offspring. *J. soc. Psychol.*, 1931, 2, 3–27.

*Size of family correlates negatively with intelligence, moral knowledge, cultural background, and honesty, and positively with degree of persistence at task. Child with one sibling rates higher than only child on above personality factors.*

364. MANDELBAUM, D. G. *Soldier groups and Negro soldiers.* Berkeley: Univer. of Calif. Press, 1952.

*The primary groups, in the formal structure of the armed forces, function when there is a breakdown in the ideal behavior outlined by the formal organization. They enhance feelings of security, reduce fear, and provide motivation. The success of ending segregation may be attributed to the fact that Negroes then become co-members of primary groups with the white soldiers and thus gain common loyalties.*

365. MARGOLIN, J. B. The use of an interaction matrix to validate patterns of group behavior. *Hum. Relat.*, 1952, 5, 407–416.

*Observations in a therapy group confirm two patterns of behavior previously identified by clinical analysis: (a) the help-rejecting-complainer, who is concerned with his own affairs, perceived as needing advice and as self-derogatory; (b) doctor's assistant who is concerned with others and is not offered advice.*

366. MARQUIS, D. G., GUETZKOW, H., & HEYNS, R. W. A social psychological study of the decision-making conference. In H. Guetzkow (Ed.), *Groups, leadership, and men: Research in human relations.* Pittsburgh: Carnegie Press, 1951. Pp. 55–67.

*In conferences self-oriented need behavior lowers satisfaction and productivity while raising residual disagreement. Satisfaction increases with cohesiveness and procedural structuring. Productivity increases with the urgency of the problem and the power of the group to deal with the problem.*

367. MARTIN, W. E., DARLEY, J. G., & GROSS, N. Studies of group behavior: II. Methodological problems in the study of interrelationships of group members. *Educ. psychol. Measmt.*, 1952, 12, 533–553.

*Using several sociometric criteria, groups are compared on mutuality and cohesiveness, and no simple relationship is found. Cohesiveness is associated with ingroup choices.*

368. Martin, W. E., Gross, N., & Darley, J. G. Studies of group behavior: Leaders, followers, and isolates in small organized groups. *J. abnorm. soc. Psychol.*, 1952, 47, 838–842.

*Leaders, followers, and isolates, sociometrically defined, are compared. Leaders were found superior in identification with middle class attitudes and self appraisal of motor skills. Informal leadership was associated with lower socio-economic status; being both a formal and informal leader was associated with confidence. Few distinguishing features of leaders were found by the trait approach.*

369. May, M. A., & Doob, L. W. Competition and cooperation. *Soc. Sci. Res. Council Bull.*, 1937, No. 25.

*A theory relating cooperation and competition to personality and culture is presented, and the literature is reviewed.*

370. Mayo, E. *The human problems of an industrial civilization.* New York: Macmillan, 1933.

*In this discussion of the classic Hawthorne Western Electric experiments the author shows how the problem was shifted from the physical environment to the social atmosphere or morale, as a cause of monotony, fatigue, or low production.*

371. Mead, G. H. *Mind, self, and society from the standpoint of a social behaviorist.* Chicago: Univer. of Chicago Press, 1950. (20)

*The individual, influencing the other, may also take the role of the other and so re-influence himself. Thus in social control the individual assumes the attitudes of the group so that the experience and behavior of it is directly presented to him in his own experience.*

372. Mengert, Ida G. A preliminary study of the reactions of two-year-old children to each other when paired in a semi-controlled situation. *J. genet. Psychol.*, 1931, 39, 393–398.

*Quantitative scores for friendliness of two-year-old children observed in pairs are higher than those for unfriendliness.*

373. Merrill, Barbara. A measurement of mother-child interaction. *J. abnorm. soc. Psychol.*, 1946, 41, 37–49.

*In a controlled study, mothers who are motivated to have their child perform "well" demonstrate more directing, interfering, criticizing, and structuring-a-change-in-activity types of behavior.*

374. Meyers, C. E. The effect of conflicting authority on the child. *Univer. of Iowa Stud. in Child Welf.*, 1944, 20, 31–98.

*In an experimental playground, two adults agreeing on a negative command produced the most inhibited activity in children, while commands giving opposing directions resulted in greater increases in unconstructive activity and oscillating behavior. Opposing commands phrased positively resulted in most disobedience, and all negative commands resulted in more nervous behavior.*

375. Miller, D. C. An experiment in the measurement of social interaction in group discussion. *Amer. sociol. Rev.*, 1939, 4, 341–351.

*A category system for analyzing interaction is proposed. Observation of a group is reported and descriptively interpreted. Participation is examined in terms of intelligence and personality factors.*

376. Miller, J. G. (Ed.) *Experiments in social process.* New York: McGraw-Hill, 1950.

*Representative samples of recent work in social psychology which could provide insight into human behavior in present day problems. Group behavior, committee operation, effective leadership, and the influence upon social activity of an individual's religion or race are discussed with a strong emphasis on methodology.*

377. Mills, T. M. Power relations in three-person groups. *Amer. sociol. Rev.*, 1953, 18, 351–357. (See # 115.)

*Power relations in ad hoc three man groups are found classifiable as transient patterns and terminal to which others tend. The solidary pattern (manifest support in a two man coalition above median) and conflicting pattern (support below median) are terminal. The terminal* structure, *i.e., temporally stable, is the solidary or coalition pattern.*

378. Mills, T. M. The coalition pattern in three person groups. *Amer. sociol. Rev.*, 1954, 19, 657–667.

*In a three man group, an individual's behavior in the group (as an isolate) is the same whether or not he held a different previous position within the group. A shift from coalition member to isolate does not appear to affect sociometric choice.*

379. Mintz, A. Non-adaptive group behavior. *J. abnorm. soc. Psychol.*, 1951, 46, 150–159.

*Competition spurred by individual rewards appears to foster "jamming" in a way not present when groups operate under cooperation instructions.*

380. Moldawsky, S. An empirical validation of a rigidity scale against a criterion of rigidity in an interpersonal situation. *Sociometry*, 1951, 14, 153–174.

*A role playing situation is used for observer judgments of rigidity. Two conditions, one anxiety-inducing and one neutral, were used, but under neither condition is the role playing behavior correlated to the paper and pencil test. Persons with experience in the task, selling, showed less rigidity.*

381. Moore, O. K., & Anderson, S. B. Search behavior in individual and group problem solving. *Amer. sociol. Rev.*, 1954, 19, 702–714.

*Three man groups are no more effective than individuals in solving problems in symbolic logic.*

382. Moreno, J. L. Foundations of sociometry, and introduction. *Sociometry*, 1941, 4, 15–35.

*Central concepts of sociometry such as tele, social atom, and psychosocial networks are discussed, and generalizations from previous sociometric studies are summarized. The relation between sociometry and the reconstruction of human society on a scientific basis is stressed.*

383. Moreno, J. L. Sociometry and the cultural order. *Sociometry*, 1943, 6, 299–344.

*The history, hypotheses, tests and procedures of sociometry, and its relation to group psychotherapy and psychodrama are reviewed. The unique emphasis in sociometric methodology, such as the centering of interest on only two-way, activated relationships, is discussed.*

384. Moreno, J. L. (Ed.) *Group Psychotherapy.* Beacon, New York: Beacon House, 1945.

*A collection of early essays on method of group psychotherapy.*

385. Moreno, J. L. Contributions of sociometry to research methodology in sociology. *Amer. sociol. Rev.*, 1947, 12, 287–292. (*99*)

*A concise review of "sociometric" contributions in the substantive and methodological areas, including the law of social gravitation or mobility, the sociogenetic law, the sociodynamic law, reality test, social atom, and tele.*

386. Moreno, J. L. *The theatre of spontaneity.* Beacon, New York: Beacon House, 1947.

*This translation of a 1923 German edition illustrates an early use of interaction diagrams.*

387. Moreno, J. L. *Sociometry, experimental method and the science of society.* Beacon, New York: Beacon House, 1951.

*A collection of Moreno's articles, some with relevance to small group analysis.*

388. Moreno, J. L. *Who shall survive?* (Rev. Ed.) Beacon, New York: Beacon House, 1953. (See # 507.)

*A revision of the classic printed in 1934. Materials have been added, some new and some reprints.*

389. Moreno, J. L., & Jennings, Helen H. Statistics of social configurations. *Sociometry*, 1938, 1, 342–374.

*Chance distributions and actual distributions of choices are compared and are found to be different.*

390. Moreno, J. L., & Jennings, Helen H. Sociometric methods of grouping and regrouping: With reference to authoritative and democratic methods of grouping. *Sociometry*, 1944, 7, 397–414.

*When sociometric tests provide guides for seating arrangements in a training school for girls, mutual reciprocation of first choices increases and number of isolates decreases.*

391. Moreno, J. L., Jennings, Helen H., & Sargent, J. Time as a qualitative index to interpersonal relations. *Sociometry*, 1940, 3, 62–80.

*The amount of time that group members spend or would like to spend with each other is proposed as an index of attraction to supplement the sociometric test.*

392. Motz, Annabelle B. The role conception inventory: A tool for research in social psychology. *Amer. sociol. Rev.*, 1952, 17, 465–471.

*Two types of role conceptions (traditional and companionate) are identified among married college students. The roles incorporate six behavior areas (housework, employment, financial support, child care, community participation, and schooling).*

393. Mukerji, N. P. An investigation of ability in work in groups and in isolation. *Brit. J. Psychol.*, 1940, 30, 352–356.

*Groups exceed individuals in work ability. Boys appear to improve more than girls, but girls have higher ability.*

394. Murphy, G., Murphy, Lois B., & Newcomb, T. M. *Experimental social psychology.* New York: Harper, 1937.

*A comprehensive review of the experimental research in social psychology. A considerable portion of the book is devoted to early research in what is now the small group area.*

395. Murphy, Lois B. *Social behavior and child personality: An exploratory study of some roots of sympathy.* New York: Columbia Univer., 1937.

*Responses of individual children to each other indicate that personality needs and physical and social aspects of environment determine sympathy.*

396. Murphy, Lois B., & Murphy, G. The influence of social situations upon the behavior of children. In C. Murchison (Ed.), *A handbook of social psychology.* Worcester, Mass.: Clark Univer. Press, 1935. Pp. 1034–1096.

*Traits must be seen as aspects of whole organisms in whole situations. Behavior may appear inconsistent because of a change of needs and interests, or different overt expressions of the same motive. Responses in a social situation exist only in the relation between child and social environment, and not in either one alone.*

397. Newcomb, T. M. Role behaviors in the study of individual personality and of groups. *J. Pers.*, 1950, 18, 273–289.

*Role behaviors represent the best unit of observation from which to draw conclusions about individual personality and about the group since perception and change in personality are very closely associated with persistence and change in roles. The nature of a group changes or persists according to changes or persistence in its role system.*

398. Newcomb, T. M. An approach to the study of communicative acts. *Psychol. Rev.*, 1953, 60, 393–404. (*149*)

*Communicative acts are focal to the study of "interaction." Group properties may be predetermined by conditions and consequences of communicative acts. An assumption of the analysis defines the part played by communication among humans as enabling two or more persons to maintain simultaneous orientation to each other as communicators and toward objects of communication. Propositions derived or consistent with the assumption are presented and discussed, with reference to available research findings.*

399. Newcomb, T. M. Social psychology and group processes. *Annu. Rev. Psychol.*, 1953, 4, 183–214.

*Literature is reviewed under the following categories: attitudes as related to individual psychological variables or processes or as related to group membership variables, processes of interaction and communication, and methodological contributions.*

400. Newstetter, W. I. An experiment in the defining and measuring of group adjustment. *Amer. sociol. Rev.*, 1937, 2, 230–236.

*Cordiality is not strongly related to status, but receipt of cordiality is.*

401. Norfleet, Bobbie. Interpersonal relations and group productivity. *J. soc. Issues*, 1948, 4 (2), 66–69.

*Over a period of three weeks, five training groups developed common agreement on the most productive members, but not on choice of leisure-time partners. In two of the groups a high productivity rating was associated with a high interaction rate.*

402. Northway, Mary L. *A primer of sociometry*. Toronto, Canada: Univer. of Toronto Press, 1952.

*Sociometric studies, particularly Canadian products, are reviewed.*

403. Ort, R. S. A study of role-conflicts as related to happiness in marriage. *J. abnorm. soc. Psychol.*, 1950, 45, 691–699.

*The number of role-conflicts in marriage is related to self-happiness ratings. Females report less conflicts and rate selves higher on happiness.*

404. O.S.S. Assessment Staff. *Assessment of men.* New York: Rinehart, 1948.

*To reveal personalities and in an attempt to predict future behavior, candidates for the O.S.S. were assessed by means of standard intelligence and personality tests, projective tests, situational tests of leadership and stress, and sociometric studies.*

405. Parten, Mildred B. Social participation among preschool children. *J. abnorm. soc. Psychol.*, 1932, 27, 243–269.

*Social participation of nursery school children was observed by a time sampling procedure (one minute per child per hour) using objective and interpretive ratings. High reliability of the observation procedure is reported. Social participation is found to correlate with age groups and Intelligence Quotient.*

406. Parten, Mildred B. Leadership among preschool children. *J. abnorm. soc. Psychol.*, 1933, 27, 430–440.

*Previously reported materials on social participation are extended with leadership scores. The scores are found reliable and correlate with teacher ratings. Two types of leaders are discerned, "artful" ones and "bullies." Following behavior, reciprocal directing, and directing increase with age.*

407. Parten, Mildred B. Social play among preschool children. *J. abnorm. soc. Psychol.*, 1933, 28, 136–147. (See #31.)

*Size of group in which children participate increases with age, but most interaction is in groups of two. Most small groups (two) are of the same sex (65%), and friends more often are the same sex and age. Character of play and toys changes with age.*

408. Partridge, E. D. Leadership among adolescent boys. *Teach. Coll., Columbia Univer. Contrib. Educ.*, 1934, No. 608.

*Leaders excel in intelligence, athletic ability, scout rank, and tenure, and are older.*

409. Pellegrin, R. J. The achievement of high status and leadership in the small group. *Soc. Forces*, 1953, 32, 10–16.

*Four basic elements—interaction, activities, statuses, and norms—are universal elements of groups and may be used as analytical elements in a conceptual scheme for the study of intragroup status achievement and leadership.*

410. Pepinsky, H. B., Siegel, L., & Van Atta, E. L. The criterion in counseling: A group participation scale. *J. abnorm. soc. Psychol.*, 1952, 47, 415–419.

*A scale is devised of effectiveness of participation which distributes the population with high agreement on the part of choosers.*

411. Pepitone, A. Motivational effects in social perception. *Hum. Relat.*, 1950, 3, 57–76.

*Boys with different liking for basketball (high or low motivation) were confronted by a three man board, role playing three specific situations. Boys were found (judged) to distort perception in a beneficial direction for their goal. Greater distortion is indicated in the face of greater hostility, and greater motivation (or interest) appears to be related to more realistic perception.*

412. Perkins, H. V., Jr. The effects of climate and curriculum on group learning. *J. educ. Res.*, 1950, 44, 269–286.

*Group-centered teacher training groups learn more, show warmer and more objective attitude to children, and more insight than do those groups which are leader-centered.*

413. Perkins, H. V., Jr. Climate influences group learning. *J. educ. Res.*, 1951, 45, 1–3.

*A summary of previous research by the author.*

414. Perlmutter, H. V. Group memory of meaningful material. *J. Psychol.*, 1953, 35, 361–370.

*No significant differences in memory are found between three and two person groups and individuals.*

415. Perlmutter, H. V., & DeMontmollin, Germaine. Group learning of nonsense syllables. *J. abnorm. soc. Psychol.*, 1952, 47, 762–769. (*194*)

*Two-syllable nonsense words were presented to three man groups (23) and to the individual members for learning. Group experience with the task improved individual performance, but individual experience with the task did not improve group performance. The authors conclude that group life can contribute to individual learning of the same kind of task later, but there was no control for prior individual experience. Groups are found superior to individuals. For individuals who have had experience with the task in groups, the best individuals will perform as well as the group. The conditional superiority of the group is discussed.*

416. Pessin, J. The comparative effects of social and mechanical stimulation on memorizing. *Amer. J. Psychol.*, 1933, 45, 263–270.

*Learning is usually found to be more efficient under relatively quiet conditions than under conditions of mechanical (buzzer, flashing light) or social (spectator) stimulation, but retention of nonsense syllables learned under mechanical and social conditions is better than of those learned in relatively quiet conditions.*

417. Pessin, J., & Husband, R. W. Effects of social stimulation on human maze learning. *J. abnorm. soc. Psychol.*, 1933, 28, 148–154.

*Silent observers are not found to have any significant effect on the efficiency of an individual's maze learning, but may have some effect on the variability of performance.*

418. Peters, H. N., & Jones, F. D. Evaluation of group psychotherapy by means of performance tests. *J. consult. Psychol.*, 1951, 15, 363–367.

*Schizophrenics are tested on Porteus maze and mirror tracing before and after group psychotherapy. Marked improvement in score indicates that the tests are sensitive to the improvement in social adjustment which follows group therapy.*

420. Philips, E. L., Shenker, Shirley, & Revitz, Paula. The assimilation of the new child into the group. *Psychiatry*, 1951, 14, 319–325.

*Six seven-year-old girls are introduced as strangers to four three girl play groups. In the process of assimilation the movement is found to be from the new girl to the nucleus group. The newcomer's ability to influence the group increases from session to session, but is less than that of the nucleus members.*

419. Philp, Alice J. Strangers and friends as competitors and cooperators. *J. genet. Psychol.*, 1940, 57, 249–258.

*Pairing kindergarten children with strangers and with friends as competitors and cooperators affects only the quality of the response to the task. (Stranger pair is quiet, friendship pair noisy and excited.)*

421. Plank, R. An analysis of a group therapy experiment. *Hum. Organization*, 1951, 10, 5–21, 26–36.

*During non-directive sessions with veterans, the most frequently discussed topics were doubts about the treatment, treatment of others, parents, movies, and books. Some members develop social contacts and interact outside of the group, while others use the group as a target for hostility.*

422. Polansky, N. A., Lippitt, R., & Redl, F. An investigation of behavioral contagion in groups. *Hum. Relat.*, 1950, 3, 319–348.

*Groups of disturbed children were observed in terms of contagion and direct attempts to influence. The influence of a person in the group is related to his prestige and his perception of his position. Individuals with high prestige make more attempts at directly influenc-*

*ing others, and also are initiators of contagion. They resist attempts at direct influence, but are more subject to contagion than persons with low prestige. Attempts to influence behavior directly and contagion can be reliably discerned.*

423. POLANSKY, N., LIPPITT, R., & REDL, F. The use of near-sociometric data in research on group treatment processes. *Sociometry*, 1950, 13, 39–62.

*Choices on a near-sociometric test (like best to be with around camp) for small groups of boys and girls in summer camps have little correspondence with observed behavior. Liking is positively associated with helpfulness, negatively with reducing status. Prestige factors are better indices of an individual's influence on the group than popularity scores.*

424. PORTER, E. H., JR. The development and evaluation of a measure of counseling interview procedures. *Educ. psychol. Measmt.*, 1943, 3, 105–126, 215–238.

*A set of categories for the analysis of interviews (counseling), which are reliable, are described. Validity is inferred from correspondence to judges and face validity of development of procedure. The method is suggested as useful for discerning the consistency of a counselor, and similarities and differences among counselors (within and among different persuasions) are measurable.*

425. POTASHIN, REVA. A sociometric study of children's friendships. *Sociometry*, 1946, 9, 48–70.

*Sociometric friendship pairs and one-sided pairs are studied. Persons who have a mutual choice relationship, i.e., choose and are chosen, are more often chosen than those in the one-sided relationships, i.e., choose and are not chosen in return.*

426. PRECKER, J. A. The automorphic process in the attribution of values. *J. Pers.*, 1953, 21, 356–363.

*Students are found to project their values on their chosen faculty advisors.*

427. PRESTON, M. G. Note on the reliability and the validity of the group judgment. *J. exp. Psychol.*, 1938, 22, 462–471.

*Greater accuracy of group judgment as previously measured by coefficient of correlation is due to statistical rather than to psychological factors.*

428. PRESTON, M. G., & HEINTZ, R. K. Effects of participatory versus supervisory leadership on group judgment. *J. abnorm. soc. Psychol.*, 1949, 44, 345–355. (See #115.)

*Participatory leadership results in more group conformity than supervisory leadership. In the participatory groups the shift is more permanent, and members and leaders find the participation interesting and enjoyable.*

429. PROCTOR, C. H., & LOOMIS, C. P. Analysis of sociometric data. In Marie Jahoda, M. Deutsch, & S. E. Cook (Eds.), *Research methods in social*

*relations: With especial reference to prejudice.* New York: Dryden, 1951. Pp. 561–585.

*Four types of analyses—graphic, index, statistical, and matrix—are presented for use in studying sociometric data.*

430. Puffer, J. A. Boys' gangs. *Pedag. Sem.*, 1905, 12, 175–212.

*The characteristics of boys' gangs (nationality composition, activities, leader choice method) are presented, as they were reported by boys in a reform school.*

431. Puffer, J. A. *The boy and his gang.* Boston: Houghton Mifflin, 1912.

*An early treatment of the organization, activities, psychology, impulses, virtues, and importance of the boy's gang.*

432. Queen, S. A. Social interaction in the interview: An experiment. *Soc. Forces*, 1928, 6, 545–558.

*No verbal or non-verbal act in social worker-client interaction is greatly significant in itself, but in context non-verbal behavior may create social climate for client, or give a clue to the case worker.*

433. Rapaport, A. Mathematical theory of motivation interactions of two individuals. *Bull. Math. Biophys.*, 1947, 9, 17–28, 41–61.

*The behavior of two individuals, consisting of effort which results in output, is considered to be determined by a satisfaction function which depends on remuneration and on the effort extended. Assuming that each individual will act to maximize his satisfaction function, conditions of equilibrium are mathematically deduced as well as in the inverse problem where the form of behavior is given and the satisfaction function deduced.*

434. Rasmussen, G., & Zander, A. Group membership and self-evaluation. *Hum. Relat.*, 1954, 7, 239–251.

*An individual's level of aspiration conforms to the standards attributed to the group when he is a member and is attracted to it; hence he rates self a failure when he does not conform. Such nonconformity leads to a discrepancy between real and ideal levels of performance.*

435. Reckless, W. C. Case studies built around observations of individual foster-children in the playroom of a receiving home. *Amer. sociol. Soc. Papers*, 1930, 24, 170–173.

*Observation of children in a free play situation is found to reveal more of a child's situational personality and suitability for adoption than are background data or interviews.*

436. Redl, F. Group emotion and leadership. *Psychiatry*, 1942, 5, 573–596. Also in Dorothea F. Sullivan (Ed.), *Readings in group work.* New York: Association Press, 1952. Pp. 318–356. (*71*)

*Ten types of group formation, conceptually distinguished by the role played by the central person, may be grouped into three categories: central person as identification object, as object of drives, or as an ego support. The discussion includes a critique of Freud's* Group psychology and the analysis of the ego *and is designed to supplement this work.*

437. Redl, F. Group psychological elements in discipline problems. *Amer. J. Orthopsychiat.*, 1943, 13, 77–81.

*All problems of discipline require some group psychological analysis and handling.*

438. Redl, F. Resistance in therapy groups. *Hum. Relat.*, 1948, 1, 307–313.

*Group resistance to change occurs in many forms in therapy groups.*

439. Rice, A. K. The use of unrecognized cultural mechanisms in an expanding machine shop. *Hum. Relat.*, 1951, 4, 143–160.

*Increase of numbers caused group of workers to attempt to find adaptive cultural mechanism. Using Bion's basic assumption theory, the author shows the group going from flight-fight to dependency and back to flight-fight.*

440. Richardson, Helen M. Studies of mental resemblance between husbands and wives and between friends. *Psychol. Bull.*, 1939, 36, 104–120.

*The literature on resemblance between pairs of friends is reviewed. Friends generally are found to be similar in intelligence and temperament.*

441. Riddle, Ethel M. Aggressive behavior in a small social group. *Arch. Psychol.*, 1925, 12, No. 78. (*35*)

*Psychological changes and social behavior were observed in six subjects in a poker game. The desire to beat an opponent was found to be related to the cards held and to the size of the bet. Subjects were more likely to notice bluffing when the stakes were high and to try to bluff the stronger players. A hierarchy of bluffers develops in the group. (This is probably the first experiment of this character reported in the literature.)*

442. Riecken, H. W. Some problems of consensus development. *Rural Sociol.*, 1952, 17, 245–252.

*In a review of several studies of emotional problems in groups, "boundary conditions" of conduct are found to affect the achievement of consensus.*

443. Roberts, B. H., & Strodtbeck, F. L. Interaction process differences between groups of paranoid schizophrenic and depressed patients. *Int. J. Group Psychother.*, 1953, 3, 29–41.

*Bales' Interaction Process Analysis is used to record interaction in a group of paranoid schizophrenic patients and in a group of depressed patients. Depressed patients have a higher ratio of positive acts and a higher per cent of acts to participants other than the leader, while they have a lower rate of acts per minute.*

444. Roberts, J. M. *Three Navaho households: A comparative study in small group culture.* Cambridge, Mass.: Peabody Museum of American Archeology and Ethnology, 1951.

*A survey of 38 categories (technology, food, living routines, etc.), in reference to three Navaho households of similar environmental, social, and cultural background, shows a substantial array of differences which serve to distinguish the households as individual small group cultures. The specific study of a single habit pattern (sheep butchering) and the inventories of material possessions show further intergroup variance distinguishing each small group as an independent culture.*

445. Rock, M. L., & Hay, E. N. Investigation of the use of tests as a predictor of leadership and group effectiveness in a job evaluation situation. *J. soc. Psychol.*, 1953, 38, 109–119.

*Interaction, TAT, and sociometric tests after pre-selection by pencil and paper tests, personal history, and work experience, are used to differentiate leaders from other members of a committee. The committee has a higher level of activity under the predicted leaders than when led by a predicted non-leader, and greater participation is shown by individuals when they are in their predicted roles.*

446. Roethlisberger, F. J., & Dickson, W. J. *Management and the worker.* Cambridge, Mass.: Harvard Univer. Press, 1939.

*A comprehensive presentation of the Western Electric studies.*

447. Roff, M. A study of combat leadership in the Air Force by means of a rating scale: Group differences. *J. Psychol.*, 1950, 30, 229–239.

*Superior's ratings of subordinates, or vice versa, on basis of the characteristics of effective combat leadership show little difference on matters relating to combat or flying proficiency, but superior's ratings are higher on those factors important in inter-personal relations. Ease of maintaining ground discipline was the most discriminating factor between very good or very poor leaders.*

448. Rohrer, J. H., & Sherif, M. *Social psychology at the crossroads: The University of Oklahoma lectures in social psychology.* New York: Harper, 1951.

*A transcript of a discussion of social psychology at the University of Oklahoma is divided into six sections: integrating individual and social approaches, biological factors and human behavior, interaction in the cultural setting, basic psychological functions, group structures and individual roles, and human behavior in the social psychological frame of reference.*

449. Roseborough, Mary E. Experimental studies of small groups. *Psychol. Bull.*, 1953, 50, 275–303.

*The literature is reviewed under five major headings: (a) comparisons of groups and individuals; (b) manipulated social structure variables; (c) values of the group; (d) situational variables; and (e) personality variables affecting group behavior.*

450. Rosenthal, D., & Cofer, C. N. The effect on group performance of an indifferent and neglectful attitude shown by one group member. *J. exp. Psychol.*, 1948, 38, 568–577.

*Non-participative behavior of indifference and neglect of one member of an experimental dart-throwing group produced a significant decrease in the group's belief in goal attainability and in the belief in the cooperation of the members. There was a decrease in the ease of setting a group level of aspiration.*

451. ROWLAND, H. Friendship patterns in a mental hospital. *Psychiatry*, 1939, 2, 363–373.

*Social life and friendship patterns are used to reveal the structure, social processes, and nature of the hospital community.*

452. RUBENSTEIN, A. H. Problems in the measurement of interpersonal communication in an ongoing situation. *Sociometry*, 1953, 16, 78–100.

*Problems in the field are discussed and compared to those of the laboratory.*

453. RUESCH, J., BLOCK, J., & BENNETT, LILLIAN. The assessment of communication: I. A method for the analysis of social interaction. *J. Psychol.*, 1953, 35, 59–80.

*Cards bearing statements relating to impressions that people have as a result of communication can be sorted into a continuum by a respondent as a method of assessing social relations.*

454. RUESCH, J., & PRESTWOOD, A. R. Interaction processes and personal codification. *J. Pers.*, 1950, 18, 391–430.

*Structural concepts (individual consideration of social situation vs. his views of self, others, in group and out of group) are used to explain interaction processes in psychotherapy.*

455. SAKODA, J. M. Factor analysis of OSS situational tests. *J. abnorm. soc. Psychol.*, 1952, 47, 843–852.

*Published correlations in* Assessment of Men *are factored. Each of four traits—effective intelligence, social relations, energy and initiative, and leadership—is analyzed in terms of the interrelationships of ratings in different situations. At least two types of situations clustered, "active" and "verbal," there being replication in the four analyses. Factor analysis of ratings on 10 traits tended to group the traits as abilities, interests and motivations, and social adjustment. The importance of situational factors in designation of the traits is emphasized, i.e., "active" intelligence and "verbal" intelligence.*

456. SALUSKY, A. S. Collective behavior of children at a preschool age. *J. soc. Psychol.*, 1930, 1, 367–378.

*Children's behavior toward group is determined by exogenous and endogenous stimuli in short term spontaneous groups. Duration and size of group are determined by past social experience of the individual, and its behavior is determined by environment and the stimulus of the experience.*

457. SANDERSON, D. Group description. *Soc. Forces*, 1938, 16, 309–319.

*The author illustrates a five point category system (identity, composition, inter-group relations, intra-group relations, structure and mechanism) with a description of the group structure of a Boy Scout troop.*

458. SANFORD, F. H. *Authoritarianism and leadership*. Philadelphia: Institute for research in human relations, 1950. (See #507.)

*Authoritarian-Equalitarian scale finds two distinct syndromes of attitudes toward leaders and leadership. Authoritarians accept status-laden, strongly directive leadership; show a material dependency and a demand for adherence to in-group values; and relate to a leader as a person rather than as a social function.*

459. Schachter, S. Deviation, rejection, and communication. *J. abnorm. soc. Psychol.*, 1951, 46, 190–207. (See #115.)

*Deviates are more rejected than persons who hold modal or tend to hold modal positions. If a relevant issue is involved, the rejection will be more emphatic. High cohesiveness is also associated with more pronounced rejection. Generally, communication to a deviate increases throughout a session, but an inflection and decline occurs if the group is a high cohesive one on a relevant issue. Relatively little communication is addressed to persons in modal positions.*

460. Schachter, S., Ellertson, N., McBride, Dorothy, & Gregory, Doris. An experimental study of cohesiveness and productivity. *Hum. Relat.*, 1951, 4, 229–238. (See #115.)

*In a study in which cohesiveness (instructions suggesting congeniality as basis of choice) and induction (pressure to work faster or slower by others in group) were controlled, after task completion the "cohesive" groups showed greater liking for each other. During the task positive induction is marked, i.e., higher productivity is shown. In negative induction, lower productivity is shown, but more so in the high cohesive than the low cohesive group.*

461. Schachter, S., & Hall, R. Group-derived restraints and audience persuasion. *Hum. Relat.*, 1952, 5, 397–406.

*In recruiting subjects for a psychology experiment, more students volunteer if group restraints are low. When restraints are high, more who volunteer actually appear.*

462. Scheidlinger, S. *Psychoanalysis and group behavior: A study in Freudian group psychology*. New York: Norton, 1952. (See #115.)

*Various emotional processes (identification, object-ties, relative loss of personal identity, growth-promotion) operative in group formation and interaction, are discussed along with the role of the leader as symbolic of the parental image. These Freudian propositions are evaluated in relation to social group work, education, and group psychotherapy.*

463. Schein, E. H. The effect of reward on adult imitative behavior. *J. abnorm. soc. Psychol.*, 1954, 49, 389–395.

*A significant number of subjects learned to imitate a model when such behavior was rewarded, but individual differences were large. Individual behavior was inconsistent from one item to the next, and the level of imitation was not high in an absolute sense. This imitative response was generalized to a similar but new, unrewarded situation.*

464. Schonbar, Rosalea A. The interaction of observer-pairs in judging visual extent and movement: The formation of social norms in "structured" situations. *Arch. Psychol.*, 1945, No. 299.

*Sherif's findings on group norm formation are confirmed using a less ambiguous, more objective stimulus (line length rather than autoki-*

*netic light). Norms are formed even when the stimulus offers a large number of cues to guide judgment objectively.*

465. Scodel, A., & Mussen, P. Social perceptions of authoritarians and non-authoritarians. *J. abnorm. soc. Psychol.*, 1953, 48, 181–184.

*While neither high nor low authoritarians perceived each other at their respective levels on this variable after a (two person) 20 minute general discussion, the low authoritarians perceived the high significantly above themselves. MMPI variables were also examined. Control of high with high, and low with low, is not a part of this experiment.*

466. Seeman, M. Role conflict and ambivalence in leadership. *Amer. sociol. Rev.*, 1953, 18, 373–380.

*Role conflict (incompatible behavioral expectations) is seen to have four dimensions: status, authority, institutional, and means-ends. Role conflicts are stated to be of three types: (a) Within the criterion group there is agreement that behaviors are difficult to mutually satisfy. (b) Within the criterion group there is disagreement regarding role definition. (c) Between criterion groups there is disagreement regarding the nature of a given role.*

467. Shartle, C. L. Ohio State leadership studies. *Engng. Exp. Station News*, Ohio State Univer., 1952, 24, 16–21.

*A review of the purposes and results of the Ohio studies.*

468. Shaw, Marjorie E. A comparison of individuals and small groups in the rational solution of complex problems. *Amer. J. Psychol.*, 1932, 44, 491–504.

*Groups have a greater proportion of correct solutions. This appears to be true because in a group incorrect solutions will be rejected and errors can be checked, while an individual person may not carry out these aspects. This rejection of incorrect solutions in the groups appears to be the role of a person not proposing the solution. Participation is not uniform in the groups. The average person reaches an erroneous solution in quicker time than the average group, indicating attenuation of accepting a wrong solution in the group.*

469. Sherif, M. *The psychology of social norms.* New York: Harper, 1936. (See #507.)

*An early text having emphasis on the importance of attitude and perception on behavior.*

470. Sherif, M. A study of some social factors in perception. *Arch. Psychol.*, 1935, 27, No. 187.

*Socially determined differential responses to identical stimuli are due to differing subjective norms (frame of reference). In an autokinetic experiment, subject creates own objective range and reference point if alone, and a group will establish a group reference point and range which will persist in the individual members, when they face the same stimulus alone later. Persons with an individual norm when put in a group will converge, but not as quickly as persons starting within group situation. Prestige suggestions act as reference point in formation of norms for the individual.*

471. SHERIF, M. *An outline of social psychology*. New York: Harper, 1948.

*Perception, as a function of group membership, can be studied to obtain a basis for an analysis of group life. Using a review of literature as a basis, the author theorizes about motives, groups and norms (effect of reference groups and the formation of group norms), individuals and social change, and individual differences in social reactions.*

472. SHERIF, M. A preliminary experimental study of inter-group relations. In J. H. Rohrer, & M. Sherif (Eds.), *Social psychology at the crossroads: The University of Oklahoma lectures in social psychology*. New York: Harper, 1951. Pp. 388–424. (See #447.)

*This is a condensation of* Groups in harmony and tension. *Experimentally induced inter-group tensions are observed to develop methods of studying judgmental, perceptual, learning, and motivational processes in an experimentally produced group setting.*

473. SHERIF, M., & CANTRIL, H. *The psychology of ego-involvements*. New York: John Wiley, 1947.

*The development of ego-involvement and component ego attitudes rests on identification with reference and membership groups. Gangs are the result of various sorts of deprivation and lack of social identification and, once formed, provide security within their unique set of norms and status relationships.*

474. SHERIF, M., & HARVEY, O. J. A study in ego functioning: Elimination of stable anchorages in individual and group situations. *Sociometry*, 1952, 15, 272–305.

*Using judgment in the autokinetic situation, individuals and pairs of individuals were examined for fluctuation in judgments under three conditions of uncertainty (anxiety?). It was found that the greater the uncertainty, the more individuals fluctuate in their judgments, and the more uncertain the situation, the more does the group interaction (pairs of persons) reduce the range of fluctuation.*

475. SHERIF, M., & SHERIF, CAROLYN W. *Groups in harmony and tension*. New York: Harper, 1953.

*Experimentally induced inter-group tensions are observed to develop methods of studying judgmental, perceptual, learning, and motivational processes in an experimentally produced group setting.*

476. SHILS, E. A. *The present situation in American sociology*. Glencoe, Ill.: The Free Press, 1948.

*An overview of literature in American sociology of the past half century, including the small group area.*

477. SHILS, E. A. Primary groups in the American army. In R. K. Merton, & P. F. Lazarsfeld, *Continuities in social research: Studies in the scope and method of "The American soldier"*. Glencoe, Ill.: Free Press, 1950. Pp. 16–39.

*Findings in* The American soldier *relevant to primary group theory were: primary group solidarity functions in the corporate body to strengthen the motivation for the fulfillment of substantive prescrip-*

*tions and commands issued by the official agents; the primary group sets and emphasizes group standards of behavior, and it supports and sustains the individual. Evidence on primary group assimilation and individual needs in relation to the establishment of primary groups is discussed.*

478. Shils, E. A. The study of the primary group. In D. Lerner, & H. D. Laswell (Eds.), *The policy sciences.* Stanford, Calif.: Stanford Univer. Press, 1951. Pp. 44–69.

*A review of the literature focussing on the primary group, showing stages of growth, results, and implications for further development.*

479. Simmel, G. The number of members as determining the sociological form of the group. *Amer. J. Sociol.*, 1902–03, 8, 1–46, 158–196.

*A theoretical discussion of the importance of group size in determining the value of group life. The dyad and triad are discussed in detail.*

480. Simon, H. A. A formal theory of interaction of social groups. *Amer. sociol. Rev.*, 1952, 17, 202–211. (*132*)

*A mathematical model based on four variables and three postulates is presented. The relationship of the model to Homan's* The human group *is indicated, and the utility of the model in interpreting problems of stability and equilibrium in interaction is demonstrated. Further uses of the model are noted.*

481. Simon, H. A. Comments on the theory of organizations. *Amer. pol. sci. Rev.*, 1952, 46, 1130–1139.

*The major problem areas of research in the theory of organizations include: decision making, power, rational and non-rational behavior, the social context, stability and change, and specialization and division of labor.*

482. Simpson, R. H. A study of those who influence and of those who are influenced in discussion. *Teach. Coll., Columbia Univer. Contrib. Educ.*, 1938, No. 748.

*Those with most immediate and persisting group influence in discussion were least likely to be influenced themselves, had more scholastic ability, and were more desired as personal friends by classmates. No significant relationships were found between either type of influence and standard mental or personality tests.*

483. Sims, V. M. The relative influence of two types of motivation on improvement. *J. educ. Psychol.*, 1928, 19, 480–484.

*With tasks of rate of reading and rate of substituting, individual motivation (surpass self and paired competitor) is superior to group motivation (group surpass group). The latter is only slightly better than no motivation (try to improve).*

483a. Slater, P. E. Role differentiation in small groups. *Amer. sociol. Rev.*, 1955, 20. (*498*)

*An analysis of sociometric ratings and interaction reveals two distinguishable role types, the task specialist and the social-emotional specialist. Degree of specialization is negatively related to amount of group consensus on the status of its members and positively related to personal rigidity.*

484. Slavson, S. R. *Creative group education.* New York: Association Press, 1938.

*Author discusses the benefits of group participation for the individual's personality development, and the nature and problems of the group and classroom leadership. There is special emphasis on the skill of the leader in creating an educative atmosphere.*

485. Slavson, S. R. (Ed.) *The practice of group therapy.* New York: Int. Univer. Press, 1947.

*Several group therapy approaches are discussed in relation to special settings and types of patients.*

486. Smith, M. A method of analyzing the interaction of children. *J. juv. Res.*, 1933, 17, 78–88.

*Using Reckless' method of recording and analyzing data collected to reveal patterns in the social behavior of young children, the data for a single case are given and interpreted in terms of averages of other group members.*

487. Smucker, O. Near-sociometric analysis as a basis for guidance. *Sociometry*, 1949, 12, 326–340.

*The possibility of using sociometric indices of peer acceptance for guidance programs in a college is discussed.*

488. Snyder, W. U. An investigation of the nature of non-directive psychotherapy. *J. gen. Psychol.*, 1945, 33, 193–223.

*Content analysis of 48 therapeutic interviews indicates that the objectives of the non-directive therapy in terms of conduct of sessions were in fact being achieved. Sequence changes in the desired directions are found.*

489. Sorokin, P. A., Tanquist, Mamie, Partin, Mildred, & Zimmerman, Mrs. C. C. An experimental study of efficiency of work under various specified conditions. *Amer. J. Sociol.*, 1930, 35, 765–782.

*Pairs of children working for individual rewards are found to be more efficient than when working for group rewards, and more efficient on manual tasks than in competition.*

490. South, E. B. Some psychological aspects of committee work. *J. appl. Psychol.*, 1927, 11, 437–464.

*One-sex committees are more efficient than mixed; the females are quicker and more accurate in the personal and interesting tasks while the males are superior on more abstract Multiple Choice Problems; and a definite time limit on a task improves committee efficiency.*

491. Steinzor, B. The development and evaluation of a measure of social interaction. *Hum. Relat.*, 1949, 2, 103–121.

*A category system is described for the measurement of intent, purpose, and direction of verbal interaction in a small group. Inter-judge reliability is given.*

492. Steinzor, B. The development and evaluation of a measure of social interaction: Part II. *Hum. Relat.*, 1949, 2, 319–347.

*Five types of discussion groups are analyzed using a category system based on the intents and purposes underlying verbal interaction. Some evidence of the validity of the method is presented.*

493. Steinzor, B. The spatial factor in face to face discussion groups. *J. abnorm. soc. Psychol.*, 1950, 45, 552–555. (*348*)

*In groups in a circular seating arrangement, it is found that the greater the distance between persons, the more likely is one to follow the other in discussion.*

494. Stendler, Celia, Damrin, Dora, & Haines, Aleyne C. Studies in cooperation and competition: I. The effects of working for group and individual rewards on the social climate of children's groups. *J. genet. Psychol.*, 1951, 79, 173–197.

*Second grade children in groups of eight show more positive interaction when working for a group prize than when working for individual prizes.*

495. Stephan, F. F. The relative rate of communication between members of small groups. *Amer. sociol. Rev.*, 1952, 17, 482–486.

*A geometric progression fits data for relative rate of communication between members in discussion groups.*

496. Stephan, F. F., & Mishler, E. G. The distribution of participation in small groups: An exponential approximation. *Amer. sociol. Rev.*, 1952, 17, 598–608. (*367*)

*The distribution of participation among the members of small groups is shown to follow a simple exponential model. Size of group is found related to the distribution. Groups* composed *of high participators and low participators fit the model, but the high participator groups were found to be more homogeneous in activity level. Groups with active and passive leaders also fit the model.*

497. Stogdill, R. M. Personal factors associated with leadership: A survey of the literature. *J. Psychol.*, 1948, 25, 35–71.

*A bibliography of 124 items on leadership is indexed under 8 methodological headings and 29 variables. Leadership is found to be not just a combination of traits but a working relationship among group members.*

498. Stogdill, R. M. Leadership, membership and organization. *Psychol. Bull.*, 1950, 47, 1–14. (See #115.)

*Problems of definition and analysis are considered.*

499. Strodtbeck, F. L. Husband-wife interaction over revealed differences. *Amer. sociol. Rev.*, 1951, 16, 468–473. (*464*)

*Revealed differences in judgments between husbands and wives examined in four cultural contexts indicated that amount of activity, and power as defined in the culture, were related to the way the differences were settled.*

500. Strodtbeck, F. L. The family as a three-person group. *Amer. sociol. Rev.*, 1954, 19, 23–29. (*473*)

*Research reported by Mills with ad hoc groups is repeated using families. Regularities in the distribution of support reported by Mills are not substantiated, nor the tendency for solidary high participators (coalition) to dominate decision-making. Decision-making is found to be associated with high participation, and Mills' finding on the stability of participation rank in the coalition is confirmed.*

501. Strodtbeck, F. L., & Hare, A. P. Bibliography of small group research: (From 1900 through 1953). *Sociometry*, 1954, 17, 107–178.

*A comprehensive bibliography of small group research.*

502. Sullivan, H. S. Psychiatry: Introduction to the study of interpersonal relations. *Psychiatry*, 1938, 1, 121–134.

*The individual's perceptions of himself and of the person with whom he is interacting are viewed as the creation of "illusory" persons. Interaction is seen as occurring between the currently perceived "I" and "you."*

503. Swanson, G. E. The development of an instrument for rating child-parent relationships. *Soc. Forces*, 1950, 29, 84–90.

*An instrument to rate childhood frustration stemming from family relationships is described. Its reliability is estimated.*

504. Swanson, G. E. Some problems of laboratory experiments with small populations. *Amer. sociol. Rev.*, 1951, 16, 349–358.

*The applications of laboratory approaches to sociological problems are explored.*

505. Swanson, G. E. Some effects of member object-relationships on small groups. *Hum. Relat.*, 1951, 4, 355–380.

*Clinical judgments of individual object-relationships (Blacky test) correlate with participation, being liked, and influence.*

506. Swanson, G. E. A preliminary laboratory study of the acting crowd. *Amer. sociol. Rev.*, 1953, 5, 522–533.

*The crowd is studied by focussing on the relevant qualities in the small (3 person) group. Acquaintance with the task and co-workers on the task is associated with: lack of suggestibility, low volume of communication, communication directed to one person rather than two, high expression of self-oriented needs, low fixity of role behavior, good task performance, more satisfaction with co-workers.*

507. Swanson, G. E., Newcomb, T. M., & Hartley, E. L. (Eds.) *Readings in social psychology*. (Rev. Ed.) New York: Holt, 1952.

*A selected set of readings in the general area, a number of which are pertinent to the small group area.*

508. Symonds, P. M. Role playing as a diagnostic procedure in the selection of leaders. *Sociatry*, 1947, 1, 43–50.

*Role play as used in the OSS assessment program is discussed. Situations are classified by type of social relationship involved, and the qualities of personality which each situation is designed to test are outlined.*

509. TAGIURI, R. Relational analysis: An extension of sociometric method with emphasis upon sociometric perception. *Sociometry*, 1952, 15, 91–104. (*246*)

*Diadic relationships involving sociometric choice and perception are detailed. A study is reported indicating that cleavage, sociometrically defined, is accompanied by a cleavage in the expectation of choices. "Well-adjusted" students were found to be different from "maladjusted" ones in terms of popularity, expansiveness, and perception of expansiveness of others.*

510. TALLAND, G. A. The assessment of group opinion by leaders, and their influence on its formation. *J. abnorm. soc. Psychol.*, 1954, 89, 431–434.

*The leader's individual opinion more nearly represents group opinion after discussion than before discussion since the leader influences the opinion.*

511. TALLAND, G. A. Task and interaction process: Some characteristics of therapeutic group discussion. *J. abnorm. soc. Psychol.*, 1955, 50, 105–109. (*457*)

*Analysis of therapy groups with the Bales interaction process categories does not reveal the phases in problem-solving nor a tendency to establish equilibrium in successive cycles.*

512. TALLAND, G. A., & CLARK, D. H. Evaluation of topics in therapy group discussion. *J. clin. Psychol.*, 1954, 10, 131–137.

*When subjects in small therapy groups rate the value of topics discussed, little differentiation is made between subjects of value to individuals or the group. Topics which cause disturbance and those which can be discussed only in the permissive therapeutic group are judged of greatest importance.*

513. TAYLOR, D. W., & FAUST, W. L. Twenty questions: Efficiency in problem solving as a function of size of group. *J. exp. Psychol.*, 1952, 44, 360–368. (*208*)

*The game of twenty questions used as a test of problem-solving on individuals and groups of two and four. Group performance excels that of individuals in terms of the number of questions, number of failures, and time per problem, but groups of four were not superior to groups of two except in terms of number of failures to reach solution. In terms of man-minutes needed per problem, performance of individuals excels that of groups, and groups of two excel groups of four. Individuals improve as rapidly, practicing alone, as do members of groups practicing as groups.*

514. TAYLOR, F. W. *The principles of scientific management*. New York: Harper, 1911.

*Steel workers do more when "apart" than "together" in a classic example of an experimental design in a natural setting.*

515. TAYLOR, J. H., THOMPSON, C. E., & SPASSOFF, D. The effect of conditions of work and various suggested attitudes on production and reported feelings of tiredness and boredness. *J. appl. Psychol.*, 1937, 21, 431–450.

*There is an inverse relationship between amount of work and tiredness or boredom. Rewards facilitate work without affecting reported boredom, while inter-group talking or laughter partially inhibits boredom. Solitary workers produce more than do groups, but are equally bored.*

516. TERMAN, L. M. A preliminary study of the psychology and pedagogy of leadership. *Pedag. Sem.*, 1904, 11, 413–451. (*24*)

*An early comprehensive research on the factors of leadership. Stability and visibility of leadership are reported. Qualities of leadership are examined in terms of questionnaire responses.*

517. THELEN, H. A. Engineering research in curriculum building. *J. educ. Res.*, 1948, 41, 579–596. (See #52.)

*Group processes, group structure, and productivity are described as three distinguishing characteristics of social groups, and research findings are organized into a theory based upon interrelations among the three characteristics.*

518. THELEN, H. A. Group dynamics in instruction: Principle of least group size. *Sch. Rev.*, 1949, 57, 139–148.

*The hypothesis is presented that: the size of group should be the smallest group in which it is possible to have represented all the socialization and achievement skills required for the task.*

519. THELEN, H. A. Educational dynamics: Theory and research. *J. soc. Issues*, 1950, 6 (2).

*The author's theory of human dynamics states that satisfaction of needs from group membership creates the degree of group loyalty and internalization of group values. Methods for developing hypotheses and techniques for collecting data on group interaction are outlined in the two concluding chapters.*

520. THELEN, H. A. *Dynamics of groups at work.* Chicago: Univer. of Chicago Press, 1954.

*Practical suggestions for organizer, leader, and member of group are given in the following areas: citizen action, education, faculty self-training, administration and management, human relations, and public meetings. Concepts such as needs of group members and leadership development are presented as background for the above.*

521. THELEN, H. A., & WHITHALL, J. Three frames of reference: The description of climate. *Hum. Relat.*, 1949, 2, 159–176.

*Teacher-centered and learner-centered emotional climates, created by experimental teachers, were measured by observers' ratings, self-involved observers using two blocs of illustrative behavior as norms, and pupils' pushing of buttons on an audience reaction machine. Gross agreement is found between the three techniques although they differ as to depth and number of aspects presented.*

522. THEODORSON, G. A. Elements in the progressive development of small groups. *Soc. Forces*, 1953, 31, 311–320.

*Eight groups (15–22 members) were observed over 15 sessions, and reports of non-participating students at each session were analyzed. A summary description of the changes in the groups discerned from the reports is given.*

523. THIBAUT, J. W. An experimental study of the cohesiveness of underprivileged groups. *Hum. Relat.*, 1950, 3, 251–278. (See #115.)

*Using sets of groups matched for cohesiveness, changes of cohesiveness within the group are observed under frustration. Cohesiveness of groups at least persists or improves for unsuccessful low status and consistently high status groups.*

524. THIBAUT, J. W., & COULES, J. The role of communication in the reduction of interpersonal hostility. *J. abnorm. soc. Psychol.*, 1952, 47, 770–777.

*It is found in a controlled communication experiment, that after an act of hostility, subjects permitted to communicate back to the instigator immediately after the act showed more post-experimental friendliness to the instigator than those not permitted to communicate. Newcomb's autistic hostility hypothesis is discussed, and it is generally concordant to the findings: the communicating persons show less loss of friendliness, and initially hostile subjects show less change than friendlier subjects.*

525. THOMAS, DOROTHY S. (Ed.) *Some new techniques for studying social behavior.* New York: Teach. Coll., Columbia Univer., 1929. Also in *Child Develpm. Monogr.*, 1929, No. 1.

*A collection of studies presenting a method for objectively recording and analyzing the social and emotional responses of the pre-school child.*

526. THOMAS, DOROTHY S. A symposium on the observability of social phenomena with respect to statistical analysis. I. An attempt to develop precise measurements in the social behavior field. *Sociologus*, 1932, 8, 436–456. II. *Sociologus*, 1933, 9, 1–24.

*Attempts to develop reliable methods of statistically recording observational data, by using categories and by reducing observational biases are discussed in theory and as they have been applied in actual studies. There are critiques of the article by F. Stuart Chapin, James W. Woodard, Stuart A. Rice, E. B. Wilson, and Mortimer J. Adler.*

527. THOMAS, DOROTHY S., LOOMIS, ALICE M., & ARRINGTON, RUTH E. *Observational studies of social behavior: Volume 1-Social Behavior Patterns.* New Haven: Inst. of Hum. Rela., Yale Univer., 1933.

*An observational technique based on time sampling, in which acts are classified as social, material, and self is used with nursery school, kindergarten, trade school, and industrial groups. Reliability and validity of the method is discussed in detail.*

528. THOMAS, W. I., & THOMAS, DOROTHY S. *The child in America: Behavior problems and programs.* New York: Knopf, 1928.

*An intensive consideration and review of findings and methods of studying the child.*

529. Thompson, W. R., & Nishimura, Rhoda. Some determinants of friendship. *J. Pers.*, 1952, 20, 305–314.

*Individuals tend to view their friends (pairs) as they view their "ideal," and friends tend to have the same "ideal" in common.*

530. Thorndike, R. L. On what type of task will a group do well? *J. abnorm. soc. Psychol.*, 1938, 33, 409–413.

*Group superiority in mental work is greater in materials permitting a greater range of response, but high complexity appears to limit effectiveness of group work.*

531. Thorndike, R. L. The effect of discussion upon the correctness of group decisions, when the factor of majority influence is allowed for. *J. soc. Psychol.*, 1938, 9, 343–362.

*Majority vote is slightly more correct than that of average member, and discussion slightly increases percentage of correct decisions. Individuals who are right will hold their position more strongly than those who are wrong.*

532. Thrasher, F. *The gang.* Chicago: Univer. of Chicago Press, 1927. (*38*)

*Characteristics of gangs are described in statistical terms and in case histories.*

533. Timmons, W. M. Decisions and attitudes as outcomes of the discussion of a social problem. *Teach. Coll., Columbia Univer. Contrib. Educ.*, 1939, No. 777.

*High school students who both studied the facts on a controversial question and held discussions approximated the decisions of experts more closely than those who merely studied the facts. There were no significant differences between the groups in more generalized attitudes after the experimental treatment.*

534. Timmons, W. M. Can the product superiority of discussors be attributed to averaging or majority influences? *J. soc. Psychol.*, 1942, 15, 23–32.

*Discussants score significantly higher than non-discussants when the influences of averaging and the majority factor are allowed for, either separately or in combination.*

535. Toeman, Zerka. Role analysis and audience structure: With special emphasis on problems of military adjustment. *Sociometry*, 1944, 7, 205–221. Also in *Psychodrama Monogr.*, 1945, No. 12.

*A detailed role analysis of a military psychodramatic production is presented together with an analysis of the vote structure of three audiences.*

536. Torrance, E. P. Crew performance in a test situation as a predictor of field and combat performance. HFORL Report No. 33, ARDC. Bolling A.F.B., Washington 25, D.C., 1953.

*Aircraft crews (71) were ordered in terms of: not getting to combat, effectiveness ratings of superiors, and actual success in missions. While effective combat crews were not different from less effective or dropout crews in problem-solving scores, manner of team performance, and perception of group interaction, they were better in use of manpower, completeness of participation, coordination, control, and flexibility. In perceiving a story (projective test) the effective groups tended to see more successful outcomes, remaining with the group, orderliness, and productivity. In another story the effective groups perceived more discord, less harmony, more association on a friendship basis, and a higher degree of hedonistic pleasure. The classification of crews was by follow-up. Ratings were collected earlier in a performance test stage in training.*

537. Torrance, E. P. Methods of conducting critiques of group problem-solving performance. *J. appl. Psychol.*, 1953, 37, 394–398. (*560*)

*Crews who have critiques which are structured, more frequently show improvement in a subsequent problem-solving situation than those in less structured critiques. The crews receiving the unstructured non-authoritarian and self-critique do not perform significantly better than control crews receiving no critique (in a subsequent problem-solving situation).*

538. Torrance, E. P. Perception of group functioning as a predictor of group performance. *Res. Stud., Wash. State Coll.*, 1953, 21, 262–265.

*Crews rated "good" by instructors perceive (in projective sketches) more satisfactory outcomes, less leaving the group, more orderly functioning and productivity, more interpersonal harmony, and fewer status differences.*

539. Torrance, E. P. Some consequences of power differences on decision making in permanent and temporary three-man groups. *Res. Stud., Wash. State Coll.*, 1954, 22, 130–140. (*482*)

*In permanent and temporary three-man plane crews, individuals with high status have the most influence on group decision, although the tendency is somewhat less in the temporary crews.*

540. Torrance, E. P. The behavior of small groups under the stress of conditions of "survival." *Amer. sociol. Rev.*, 1954, 19, 751–755.

*Plane crews survive when an unstructured situation is clarified, communication resumed, and a goal established.*

541. Travers, R. M. W. A study in judging the opinions of groups. *Arch. Psychol.*, 1941, 47, No. 266.

*Errors of individual judgment of group opinion in college classes are large. However, the average tends to be a fairly good estimate of group opinion. Ability to judge group opinion is not differentiated by sex or general ability, but is related (over situations) to personality adjustment and minority position. (Projection is noted.)*

542. Travers, R. M. W. A study of the ability to judge group-knowledge. *Amer. J. Psychol.*, 1943, 56, 54–65.

*Individual estimates of percentages of members with given information are unreliable, and mean estimates tend to be more reliable. An individual's prediction is correlated to his own knowledge, but accuracy appears to be a more general characteristic. No significant relationship is found between intelligence and accuracy, but certain measures of personality are significantly related to accuracy.*

543. TRAVERS, R. M. W. The general ability to judge group-knowledge. *Amer. J. Psychol.*, 1943, 57, 95–99.

*Students in two classes were more accurate in estimating the proportion of their classmates knowing the meaning of a number of words than in estimating that of the adult U.S. population. Ability to judge is not found to be related to intelligence but may be related to personality adjustment.*

544. TRIPLETT, N. The dynamogenic factors in pace-making and competition. *Amer. J. Psychol.*, 1898, 9, 507–533.

*One of the earliest examples of the use of a laboratory setting in the study of "together and apart" factors.*

545. TROW, W. C., ZANDER, A. E., MORSE, W. C., & JENKINS, D. H. Psychology of group behavior: The class as a group. *J. educ. Psychol.*, 1950, 41, 322–338.

*Conclusions from the study of group dynamics are considered in terms of the problems of the teacher and the classroom.*

546. TURNER, C. E., Test room studies in employee effectiveness. *Amer. J. publ. Hlth.*, 1933, 23, 577–584. (*44*)

*Telephone relay assemblers were selected and segregated in a test room in order to discover optimal working conditions. In spite of any adverse experimental variation in the physical conditions, production and satisfaction increased steadily indicating the general importance of mental attitudes and friendly supervision.*

547. TUTHILL, C. E. A postulational system on social interaction. *J. Psychol.*, 1950, 29, 355–377.

*A theoretical framework is proposed based on concepts of ego-status and reciprocity in interaction.*

548. UPDEGRAFF, RUTH, & HERBST, EDITHE K. An experimental study of the social behavior stimulated in young children by certain play materials. *J. genet. Psychol.*, 1933, 42, 372–390.

*Two-year-old children watch each other more and accept suggestion more when playing with clay than when playing with blocks. Clay elicits more imitation and sociable, cooperative behavior.*

549. VAN DUSEN, A. C. Measuring leadership ability. *Personnel Psychol.*, 1948, 1, 67–79.

*Nominating technique is used to identify leaders and non-leaders. Characteristics of leaders are interest and knowledge of main group activity, cooperativeness, adaptability, and honesty.*

550. VAN ZELST, R. H. An interpersonal relations technique for industry. *Personnel*, 1952, 29, 68–76.

*The sociometric test is described and some industrial uses suggested. The literature on sociometric studies in industry is reviewed.*

551. VON WIESE, L., & BECKER, H. *Systematic sociology: On the basis of the Beziehungslehre and Gebildelehre.* New York: John Wiley, 1932.

*Sociology is defined as a distinct science and is systematized in method. Inter-human action patterns and communications, and plurality patterns or group communications are analyzed. The author for purposes of analysis divides groups into small and large groups (small groups are defined in terms of Simmel's dyad-triad, and larger groups are those with five or more members).*

552. VREELAND, F. M. Social relations in the college fraternity. *Sociometry,* 1942, 5, 151–162.

*Choices in college fraternities are found to favor one's own class and the upperclassmen.*

553. WASHBURN, RUTH W. A scheme for grading the reactions of children in a new social situation. *J. genet. Psychol.,* 1932, 40, 84–99.

*Observed behavior of children in a new situation is characteristic of them as known from other situations, and the passage of time does not alter the type of reaction.*

554. WATSON, G. B. Do groups think more efficiently than individuals? *J. abnorm. soc. Psychol.,* 1928, 23, 328–336.

*The group (thinking) product is better than the average of members or of the best member. The larger the group, the better the quality of the product (within the range 3–10).*

555. WESCHLER, I. R., TANNENBAUM, R., & TALBOT, E. A new management tool: The multi-relational sociometric survey. *Personnel,* 1952, 29, 85–94.

*In a sociometric test subjects are asked to identify others with whom they are supposed to deal, actually do deal, would like to deal, and would like less to deal in specific activities. Indices based on the responses are derived, and some uses of the instrument in the study of formal organizations are suggested.*

556. WHEELER, D., & JORDAN, H. Change of individual opinion to accord with group opinion. *J. abnorm. soc. Psychol.,* 1929, 24, 203–206.

*Opinions disagreeing with group tend to be inhibited when group opinion is made known, and the number of those agreeing with group is increased.*

557. WHITEHEAD, T. N. *The industrial worker.* Cambridge: Harvard Press, 1938.

*An intensive observational study of a small group—the relay test room.*

558. WHITTEMORE, I. C. The influence of competition on performance: An experimental study. *J. abnorm. soc. Psychol.,* 1924, 19, 236–253.

*In the competitive situations subjects produced more work, but of poorer quality. Slowest subjects improve most.*

559. WHYTE, W. F. *Street corner society: The social structure of an Italian slum.* Chicago: Univer. of Chicago Press, 1943. (See #209.)

*An observational study of a community with particular emphasis given to the informal groups or "clubs" which form strata in the social structure.*

560. Whyte, W. F. The social structure of the restaurant. *Amer. J. Sociol.*, 1949, 54, 302–310.

*Restaurant organizations are described.*

561. Whyte, W. F. Observational field-work methods. In Marie Jahoda, M. Deutsch, & S. W. Cook (Eds.), *Research methods in social relations: With especial reference to prejudice.* New York: Dryden, 1951. Pp. 493–513.

*Principles, outlined for use in community participant observation, concern relations with people in the community, amount of participation, units of observation, method of recording and organizing data, reliability and validity, and training of observers.*

562. Whyte, W. F. Small groups and large organizations. In J. H. Rohrer, & M. Sherif, *Social psychology at the crossroads: The University of Oklahoma lectures in social psychology.* New York: Harper, 1951. Pp. 297–312.

*Leadership as initiation of action should be studied by observation of overt behavior of the group as a sequence of events in time. The small group should be studied in relation to the larger organizations in which they are found.*

563. Whyte, W. F. Leadership and group participation. *Bull. 24, New York State Sch. of Indus. and Labor Rela.*, Cornell Univer., 1953.

*Principles of group dynamics are explored in terms of the author's experience at the Bethel workshop and with published materials.*

564. Willerman, B., & Swanson, L. An ecological determinant of differential amounts of sociometric choices within college sororities. *Sociometry*, 1952, 15, 326–329.

*When some members of an organization live within the organization confines and others outside it, those living together tend to choose each other more frequently than those living apart choose each other. Between the two groups there is no asymmetry in choices.*

565. Williams, Ruth M., & Mattson, Marion L. The effect of social groupings upon the language of pre-school children. *Child Develpm.*, 1942, 13, 233–245.

*When size of group of pre-school children is varied from one to three (plus experimenter), most talking occurs in groups of two, number of words per sentence remains fairly constant, and only one of six children talks when completely alone.*

566. Williamson, E. C. Allport's experiments in "social facilitation." *Psychol. Monogr.*, 1926, 35, No. 163, 138–143.

*The author presents a serious challenge to the appropriateness of treatment and interpretation of Allport's social facilitation experiments.*

567. WILSON, L. Sociography of groups. In G. Gurvitch, & W. E. Moore (Eds.), *Twentieth century sociology*. New York: Philosophical Library, 1945. Pp. 139–171.

*An overview of literature of the twentieth century dealing with sociography (groups as basic objects of classification) to reveal trends and define the present status of the field. A schema for classification and identification of groups is presented.*

568. WIRTH, L. Social interaction: The problem of the individual and the group. *Amer. J. Sociol.*, 1939, 44, 965–979.

*In a symposium on "The relation between the individual and the group," in* Amer. J. Sociol., 1939, 44, *a trend is noted toward the recognition of the significance of social interaction as the basic process in the formation of both human nature and the social order.*

569. WISPE, L. G. Evaluating section teaching methods in the introductory course. *J. educ. Res.*, 1951, 45, 161–186.

*Students participate more in permissive class sections, which they find interesting and enjoyable, but prefer directive classes for exam preparation.*

570. WISPE, L. G. Teaching methods research. *Amer. Psychologist*, 1953, 8, 147–150.

*Problems of conceptualization of hypotheses to be tested in comparing lecture-centered and discussion-centered groups are considered.*

571. WITHALL, J. The development of a technique for the measurement of social-emotional climate in classrooms. *J. exp. Educ.*, 1949, 17, 347–361.

*A category system is presented, primarily oriented toward distinguishing learner-oriented from teacher-oriented statements. Seven categories are used: (a) learner-supportive statements, (b) acceptant and clarifying statements, (c) problem-structuring statements, (d) neutral statements, (e) directive or hortative statements, (f) reproving or deprecating remarks, and (g) teacher self-supporting remarks. Evidence of the reliability and validity of a climate index is given.*

572. WITHALL, J. The development of the climate index. *J. educ. Res.*, 1951, 45, 93–100.

*An index categorizing teacher statements (learner-supporting, accepting or clarifying, problem-structuring, neutral, directive, disapproving, or teacher-supportive) is presented as a tool to assess social-emotional climate in the learning situation.*

573. WITTENBERG, R. M., & BERG, JANICE. The stranger in the group. *Amer. J. Orthopsychiat.*, 1952, 22, 89–97.

*The personality and role of a negro girl in a white scout troop is described in a case study.*

574. WOLFF, K. H. *The sociology of Georg Simmel.* Glencoe, Ill.: The Free Press, 1950. (*9*)

*Simmel's major work is collected in this volume. Part II on quantitative aspects of the group is relevant for small group theory, especially the discussion of the dyad and triad.*

575. Wrightstone, J. W. An instrument for measuring group discussion and planning. *J. educ. Res.*, 1934, 27, 641–650.

*A check sheet for describing group discussions is presented.*

576. Wrightstone, J. W. Measuring the social climate of a classroom. *J. educ. Res.*, 1951, 44, 341–351.

*A teacher-pupil rapport scale for describing the social climate of a classroom is described. Data on reliability and validity are given.*

577. Zander, A. F. The WP club: An objective case study of a group. *Hum. Relat.*, 1948, 1, 321–332.

*The use of an observer rating sheet is illustrated by a case study of a girls' club.*

578. Zander, A. F. Systematic observation of small face-to-face groups. In Marie Jahoda, M. Deutsch, & S. W. Cook (Eds.), *Research methods in social relations: With especial reference to prejudice.* New York: Dryden, 1951. Pp. 515–538.

*The problems of developing an observation instrument, reliability, and observer training are discussed.*

579. Zeleny, L. D. Characteristics of group leaders. *Sociol. & soc. Res.*, 1939, 24, 140–149.

*Leadership status in classroom discussion groups, as rated by participants, is positively related to group participation, knowledge, intelligence and likeableness. Also, participation, self-confidence, and prestige are the traits which distinguish leaders from non-leaders most clearly on a rating scale of leadership traits scored by participants.*

580. Zeleny, L. D. Sociometry of morale. *Amer. sociol. Rev.*, 1939, 4, 799–808.

*The "shared feeling of like" (degree of expansiveness of group) is proposed as an index of morale. Social adjustment is defined as the degree of reciprocated acceptance (choices). Reliability and validity data are presented.*

581. Zeleny, L. D. Experimental appraisal of a group learning plan. *J. educ. Res.*, 1940, 34, 37–42.

*Students favor five man discussion groups over traditional teaching methods although differences in knowledge gained and attitudes changed are slight.*

582. Zeleny, L. D. Measurement of social status. *Amer. J. Sociol.*, 1940, 45, 576–582.

*A mathematical expression of a social status ratio and score is developed, using degree of acceptance of a person by his associates in a group as a definition of social status.*

583. Zeleny, L. D. Measurement of sociation. *Amer. sociol. Rev.*, 1941, 6, 173–188.

*Measures of sociation, status, and adjustment based on the sociometric test are proposed.*

584. ZNANIECKI, F. Social groups as products of participating individuals. *Amer. J. Sociol.*, 1939, 44, 799–812.

*Human groups are combinations of social roles, rather than of biological entities. They must be viewed in terms of status and functions of members, as well as in terms of their existence as social entities in themselves.*

# *Index for Bibliography*

ALL ITEMS *in the annotated bibliography are listed in the following cross index under one or more of the categories. The numbers in italic type refer to articles which are reprinted in this volume. The page number of each article reprinted in this volume is given at the end of the reference in the bibliography.*

*The index is divided into five major parts: Review of literature, Theory, Methodological and statistical problems, Measurement techniques, and Variables. Sub-headings under Measurement techniques and Variables are listed alphabetically.*

A NOTE ON THE

# *Type*

IN WHICH THIS BOOK IS SET

THE TEXT *of this book was set on the Linotype in* JANSON, *a recutting made direct from type cast from matrices made by Anton Janson. Whether or not Janson was of Dutch ancestry is not known, but it is known that he purchased a foundry and was a practicing type-founder in Leipzig during the years 1660 to 1687. Janson's first specimen sheet was issued in 1675. His successor issued a specimen sheet showing all of the Janson types in 1689. His original matrices are now in the possession of the Stempel foundry, Frankfurt am Main.*

*His type is an excellent example of the influential and sturdy Dutch types that prevailed in England prior to the development by William Caslon of his own incomparable designs, which he evolved from these Dutch faces. The Dutch in their turn had been influenced by Garamond in France. The general tone of Janson, however, is darker than Garamond and has a sturdiness and substance quite different from its predecessors. It is a highly legible type, and its individual letters have a pleasing variety of design. Its heavy and light strokes make it sharp and clear, and the full-page effect is characterful and harmonious.*